THE Canadian Polity

A COMPARATIVE INTRODUCTION

Sixth Edition

Ronald G. Landes
Saint Mary's University

Prentice
Hall

Toronto

National Library of Canada Cataloguing in Publication Data

Landes, Ronald G., 1945–
    The Canadian polity : a comparative introduction

6th ed.
Includes bibliographical references and indexes.
ISBN 0-13-091417-7

1. Canada — Politics and government. I. Title.

JL65 1983.L36 2002   320.971   C2001-902201-8

ISBN 0-13-091417-7

Vice-President, Editorial Director: Michael Young
Acquisitions Editor: Andrew Wellner
Executive Marketing Manager: Christine Cozens
Developmental Editor: Martina van de Velde
Production Editor: John Housez / Joe Zingrone
Copy Editor: John Housez
Production Manager: Wendy Moran
Page Layout: Hermia Chung
Photo Research: Susan Wallace-Cox
Art Director: Julia Hall
Cover Design: Alex Li
Cover Images: Parliament Building in Ottawa—Kevin Miller/Stone; White House in
        Washington D.C. and Big Ben in London—Corel Photo Library

1 2 3 4 5   05 04 03 02

Printed and bound in Canada.

*To my wife, Peggy, and
our adult children, Megan and Donny.*

Brief Contents

Contents

LIST OF TABLES AND FIGURES

PREFACE TO THE SIXTH EDITION

For a student beginning the study of politics, the continuing evolution of both political institutions and political processes in all polities might not be readily apparent. However, for a political scientist seeking to keep abreast of such developments, the pace of change seems, at times, daunting. New leaders, new parties, and new problems mandate revised descriptions and reassessments of both institutions and processes. A specific polity is a moving target; the Canadian polity is no exception.

ORGANIZATION

The assumption of this textbook is that the study of the politics of one's own country should be an exciting experience, for politics and government determine not only our present condition, but our future survival as well. To that end, we have sought to provide an interesting examination of how the Canadian political system operates. We begin with an overview of the nature of government and politics (Part One), proceed to a consideration of basic political institutions (Part Two), and then present an analysis of political processes and political behaviour (Part Three). In Part Four, we focus on the problems that arise when comparing democratic polities by making a "democratic audit" of our three basic polities (Canada, Britain, and the United States) and by analyzing the impact of technology on the future of liberal-democracy.

In considering such topics, we seek to introduce the student to three main areas of investigation: first, the nature of political analysis; second, the fundamentals of Canadian government; and third, the study of comparative government. These three goals are intertwined throughout the text and should be borne in mind by students as they read the various chapters.

FEATURES

Quotations
Each chapter opens with one or more quotations that express the chapter's main theme. Upon completion of each unit, the student should return to these opening ideas and think about them.

Chapter Previews
Each chapter has a brief, point-form chapter preview, which the student should read before beginning the actual analysis in each chapter.

Margin Inserts
Each chapter contains a number of margin inserts, such as quotations or interesting facts. These margin inserts are designed to illustrate the theoretical material in the text itself.

Chapter Summaries and Concept Files

Each chapter has a summary and a concept file as a way of emphasizing the key points and theoretical ideas contained in each chapter.

Recommended Readings

At the end of each chapter, there is a list of recommended readings. These items include several of the most important historical works on each topic, along with more current publications. Except in a few cases, these works should be accessible in most university libraries and should prove intellectually rewarding for the beginning student.

Footnotes

A footnote style different from the one you may be used to is employed throughout the text. Instead of footnote numbers with references at the bottom of the page or at the end of the chapter or book, relevant bibliographical information is included in the body of the text itself. The first item refers to the author's last name, the second to the year of publication of the work cited, and the third to the page number, if the reference is to a particular passage. This format does not break the reader's train of thought, but allows the reader to see immediately whose work is being quoted. Full reference information for each item cited appears in the bibliography at the end of the book. For major historical works, the original date of publication is given in the text, with dates for both the original and later editions included in the bibliography.

Politics on the Net

This exciting feature gives students a list of useful websites relating to each chapter. The sites have been researched and tested for quality and relevance.

SUPPLEMENTS

Instructor's Resource Manual with Test Item File

The Instructor's Resource Manual with Test Item File provides classroom lectures for each chapter in addition to a Test Item File containing items in multiple-choice, short answer, and essay formats. Questions are identified by degree of difficulty and the answers to all questions are page referenced to the text.

NEW TO THE SIXTH EDITION

The enthusiastic reception of the first five editions of *The Canadian Polity*, by both students and instructors, has been most gratifying. Many have taken the time and effort to offer suggestions for this new edition, and many of their ideas have been incorporated. In response to both reviewers' and users' suggestions, some restructuring of the text has been done in this edition. While the basic structure of the text remains in place, the following major changes have been made.

Throughout, we have updated both the examples and analysis, while trying to make the coverage of recent political events as current as possible. For example, the recent national election campaigns in Canada (2000), the United States (2000), and Britain (2001) have been incorporated into the new edition.

The recommended reading lists have been updated, but reduced in length. Margin inserts have been updated, but reduced in number, while a number of new political cartoons have been added as well. Chapter previews and chapter summaries have been expanded. The "Politics on the Net" sections at the end of each chapter have been expanded and annotated.

Specific major changes include the following revisions. In **Chapter One** (The Nature of Government and Politics), two new governmental characteristics have been added: first, that government is democratized; and second, that government is globalized. In relation to political ideologies, a new subsection, "a feminist view of politics," has been added. Under basic concepts of political analysis, a new subsection, "political violence," has been added.

In **Chapter Two** (Constitutional Government), in relation to Britain, the development of devolution and a pattern of "quasi-federalism" are analyzed. A major new subsection has been added on the Canadian Constitution entitled "Nonfederal Constitutional Patterns," which discusses the creation of Nunavut and a growing pattern of aboriginal governance. In addition, for Canada, "Extra-Constitutional Reforms" have been included regarding the 1996 Regional Veto Act, the 1998 *Quebec Secession Reference*, and the 2000 Clarity Act.

In **Chapter Three** (The Executive Branch of Government), the election victories of George W. Bush, Jean Chrétien, and Tony Blair have been included.

In **Chapter Four** (The Legislative Branch of Government), the most significant change has been made with respect to the House of Lords in Britain: a new subsection entitled "The evolving Lords: 1999 onward" has been added to the analysis.

In **Chapter Five** (The Judicial Branch of Government), the following major changes have been included in our analysis: the growing impact of the Canadian Charter of Rights and Freedoms and the Supreme Court on Canadian politics; the basis for the development of judicial review in Britain; and the impact of the 2000 presidential election on future Supreme Court appointments in the United States.

In relation to political culture in **Chapter Six** (Political Culture and Political Socialization), the growing Americanization of Canadian politics is examined, as well as the continuing problems with the pattern of consociational politics. The latest voting and turnout figures from the recent election campaigns are included in **Chapter Seven** (The Electoral Process) and **Chapter Eight** (Electoral Systems). The growing use of nonplurality electoral formulas in Britain and the debacle in the state of Florida regarding the electoral college in the 2000 U.S. presidential race are both included in the analysis.

In **Chapter Nine** (Political Parties), the discussion of the Canadian party system includes the following developments: Jean Chrétien's third consecutive majority government; the demise of the Reform Party and the creation of the Canadian Alliance; and the increasing use of universal membership vote (UMV) systems for selecting party leaders. In Britain, the changing method of Tory leadership selection is explained, as well as the impact of the 2001 general election.

The discussion of interest groups in **Chapter Ten** now includes an update of the "gag law" controversy in Canada and the growing impact of interest groups as a result of the Charter.

Finally, a new Part Four (**Chapter Eleven**) has been added to this edition. This chapter (Liberal-Democracy in the 21st Century) makes a brief "democratic audit" of all three systems (Canada, Britain, and the United States) and then looks at the impact of technology on the future democratic process in a section entitled "Politics.com."

Any suggestions or comments concerning this text would be most appreciated by the author, especially those that might be incorporated into future editions. Please send your views to the Political Science Department, Saint Mary's University, Halifax, Nova Scotia, Canada, B3H 3C3, or by e-mail to **ron_landes@hotmail.com**.

—Ronald G. Landes
Saint Mary's University

ACKNOWLEDGMENTS

In writing this textbook the author quickly realized how much he depended on others. Over the years, numerous teachers, students, and researchers have contributed in their own way to *The Canadian Polity*. Their help is hereby gratefully acknowledged.

Others have also been essential in the development of the previous five editions of this work. Saint Mary's University aided in a number of ways, in particular, by granting a sabbatical leave in 1979–1980, during which time this book began to take shape. A special note of thanks for all those involved in the reviewing, assessment, and production of the first five editions! For this edition, a special thanks to my "golfing buddies," who dragged me out of my office and onto the links, thereby protecting some small piece of my sanity: Bob Cordy, Bill Cordy, Emmett Austin, and George Diamond. Of course, I should also note that this edition might have been completed much earlier if they had not spent so much time in the woods looking for lost balls.

For the fifth and sixth editions, Ms. Colleen Devereaux of the Saint Mary's University Political Science Department displayed uncommon patience and word processing wizardry as she somehow managed to produce revised manuscripts in record time; to her much credit should be given. Finally, I also wish to thank the following reviewers for their helpful and informed comments on the current edition: Robert Boardman, Dalhousie University; David Docherty, Wilfrid Laurier University; Jonathan Malloy, Carleton University; Chaldeans Mensah, Grant MacEwan Community College; Steve Patten, York University; Elizabeth Smythe, Concordia University College of Alberta; and Lucy Znotins, Lambton College.

The current edition was under the capable guidance of the following people at Pearson Education Canada: Andrew Wellner, acquisitions editor; Martina van de Velde, developmental editor; Joe Zingrone, production editor; John Housez, copy editor; and Wendy Moran, production manager.

Finally, recognition must be given to my loving family, without whose cooperation this project would not have been possible. Somehow, my family has managed to endure not only me, but all six editions of this book — and to them it is, once again, lovingly dedicated.

PART 1

Comparing Canadian Politics

To compare is a natural way of thinking. Nothing is more natural than to study people, ideas, or institutions in relation to other people, ideas, or institutions. We gain knowledge through reference. (Dogan and Pelassy, 1984: 1)

For the Greeks and the Romans, as for us, all political science was in a sense comparative politics. Political science has its beginning when an observer notes that another people is not governed as we are. Why? (W.J.M. Mackenzie, quoted in Rose, 1991: 446)

The Nature of Government and Politics

What was the most dynamic activity of the 20th century? The answer is government. At the beginning of the century, the governments of today's high-income countries were already powerful. But what they were was nothing to what they were about to become. The 20th century was the era of the democratic Leviathan. (Wolf, 2000: C15)

To put it in simplest terms, politics defines what people want; government decides what they get. For democracy to work, government must respond to politics. (Shogan, 1982: 5)

Politics consists in a ceaseless and bitter argument about who has the power to do what to whom, at what price, for how long and with what chance of redress ....(Lapham, 1995: 191)

CHAPTER PREVIEW

- Government is concerned with the organization of power, while politics focusses on the ways in which power is exercised. Both government and politics must deal with political conflict, including political violence, and political consensus.

- All governments share certain characteristics: government is ubiquitous, multiple, necessary, varied, democratized, and globalized. Political systems are increasingly interdependent both in terms of their political structures and political practices.

- Different types of government organize and exercise power in different ways. Basic classifications of governmental types include liberal-democratic versus totalitarian systems, federal versus unitary systems, and presidential versus parliamentary systems.

- Political analysis is the attempt to explain the various types of governmental structures and distributions of political power.

- Political ideologies are an important explanatory variable in the analysis of political structures and political processes. Different political ideologies (conservatism, liberalism, Marxism, democratic socialism, feminism) help to produce different political structures and political processes.

- Key concepts in political analysis include political power and influence, political resources, political authority, and political violence.

- Basic principles of political analysis focus on the difference between political theory and political practice, the importance of political customs and political conventions, the impact of time and political change on the political process, the differences between legal and political decisions, and the relationship between political structures and political functions.

- A comparative approach to political analysis helps us to understand both the variety of the world's polities and the uniqueness of the Canadian political experiment.

In Canada, as in no other modern democratic system, the politics of our constitution are the constitution of our politics. Constitutional reform is our never-ending treadmill, the leitmotif of the political process. Three times in a dozen years (1980–1992) constitutional initiatives have threatened to rend the Canadian polity asunder: the Canada Act from 1980 to 1982; the Meech Lake Accord from 1987 to its defeat in 1990; and the Charlottetown Accord from 1990 until its rejection in the October 26, 1992 referendum. The narrow defeat of the separation option in the Quebec provincial referendum in 1995, the Supreme Court's ruling on the legality of Quebec independence in its 1998 *Quebec Secession Reference*, the passage by the federal government of the Clarity Act in June of 2000, and the continuing threat of a third provincial independence referendum in Quebec ensure that constitutional debates will continue to be placed high on the Canadian political agenda.

If anything is evident from these constitutional reform battles, it is that Canadian government and politics are not as uninteresting as they are rumoured to be. Moreover, a fundamental assumption of the analysis in this book is that Canadian government and politics can be best understood and appreciated in a comparative context. The problems encountered by the Canadian system are not necessarily unique, and in most cases they are not at all unique. Many countries face problems of regionalism, secessionist threats, new political parties, and constitutional change. Not only do comparisons with other countries teach us about other political systems, but they provide us with a basis for assessing the strengths and weaknesses, and advantages and disadvantages, of the Canadian political experiment. After outlining the nature of government and politics, we will consider why a comparative approach is a fundamental tool in the analysis and understanding of the Canadian polity.

THE NATURE OF GOVERNMENT

In beginning our comparative analysis of the Canadian **polity** or **political system**, we will first consider the nature of government. Much of what political science knows about the nature of government that is worth knowing can be summarized by six key characteristics: government is ubiquitous, multiple, necessary, varied, democratized, and globalized.

GOVERNMENTAL CHARACTERISTICS

Characteristic number one: government is ubiquitous

Government is ubiquitous (i.e., everywhere present) in both geographical and practical terms. Territorially the world is divided among governmental units called nation-states (189 members in the United Nations by 2001). Virtually all earthly domain is claimed by these nation-states — there is literally no place on earth (except, perhaps, Antarctica) that one can go to get away from governing authority. If people emigrate from one country to another, they do not rid themselves of government, but, in the modern era, merely exchange one governing authority for another. Attempts to create utopias of one kind or another may seek to do away with government, but, in the modern era, they do so on territory claimed by the government of a nation-state and are usually allowed to exist only as long as they present no immediate threat to existing political institutions. Even the possible escape to outer space appears to be unlikely without the monetary and technological support of an existing government.

Government is also ubiquitous in practical terms: little of what we do in life is free from government control and regulation. The taxes we pay, the conditions of our workplaces, the nature of the products we buy, our medical treatment, the procedures of birth, marriage, and death are all regulated by government. On a larger scale, governments decide questions of war, peace, and environmental protection, the consequences of which determine whether we live or die, as individuals and as a planet.

Although government is ubiquitous, it is difficult to define. This difficulty stems from the fact that government is a summary concept that organizes our perception of reality: we usually see the manifestations or results of government (e.g., taxes, laws), not government itself. One can physically see governmental buildings (such as the Parliament building in Ottawa), governmental personnel (cabinet officers, civil servants such as deputy ministers), and governmental processes (passage of a piece of legislation through Parliament, a federal-provincial

First Ministers' Conference). Yet there is no single place where one can go to see the government in total: government resides in many places. However, the varied perceptions of governing activity are likely to contain a common theme: we propose to define this common theme of **government** as *the institutional organization of political power within a given territory.*

Characteristic number two: government is multiple

A second characteristic of government is that it is multiple: each citizen is subject to a number of governments and governmental units. Some people perceive government as a cohesive organization, united in its goals, coherent in its programs, and consistent in the implementation of its policies. It is typical in political analysis to find phrases such as "the government decided."

Deeper investigation, however, suggests an alternative view: government is a plural, rather than a singular, phenomenon. For example, all people in Canada are subject to at least two levels of government: the federal government in Ottawa and the government of the province in which they reside. Both levels have the power to tax and to otherwise regulate our behaviour. All citizens also confront local governments. Some citizens in the major metropolitan areas are faced with an additional layer of government and other citizens are subject to various regional governmental units. Both metropolitan and regional governments interpose an additional layer of government between the local and provincial units of organization. An extreme example of the multiplicity of governments can be found in the array of governing authorities that control our nation's capital. At least eight governments (the federal government in Ottawa, the Ontario provincial government, the National Capital Commission, the regional municipality of Ottawa-Carleton, the City of Ottawa, and the municipal, regional, and provincial administrations that govern Hull in Quebec) all exert various sorts of jurisdiction over aspects of our nation's capital.

The complexity of government is further enhanced by the fact that each governmental level (federal, provincial) is composed of numerous governmental units. The term governmental units refers to such institutions and political structures as the executive, legislative, and judicial branches of government, as well as to various government departments and agencies. For example, there is a federal cabinet as well as 10 provincial cabinets, and a national Parliament as well as 10 legislative assemblies at the provincial level. The multiplication of governmental units within each governmental level has developed to such an extent that it would be difficult to make an accurate count of them at all levels of government. Thus, it is not surprising to find that one writer has insisted that "governments are like bees, birds, fish, cattle, or wolves; they come in swarms, flocks, schools, herds, or packs, but never alone" (Schattschneider, 1969: 12).

The number of governments imposed on the citizen by the state varies among political systems. In unitary political systems, such as those of Britain and France, the central government in the national capital governs, while local governmental structures are used primarily as a means for administering policies determined by that central government. A **unitary political system** is one in which *the central or national government has been granted all governmental power.* In contrast, a

federal political system *divides governmental power between a central government and several subordinate governments, with each level having formal political authority over the same territory and people.* Canada, as a federal political structure, interposes an intermediate level of government (i.e., the provincial level) between the central government and the citizen, while local government is also more independent in Canada than it is in either Britain or France. Thus, the Canadian citizen deals with more governments than do citizens in unitary political systems.

The multiplication of governments has proceeded the furthest in the United States. As a federal political system, the United States has 50 state governments (compared to 10 provincial governments in Canada), in addition to the national government in Washington. However, it is at the local level where the multiplication of government occurs most dramatically: if one counts all units with the power to tax (federal, state, and local governments, as well as school districts and special districts), there are today 85 000 governmental units in the United States, a reduction from the 155 000 such units that existed in the early 1940s.

Recognizing the multiplicity of governments helps us to understand how governments actually operate. If governments are multiple, then it stands to reason that each governmental level or unit may have its own goals or purposes. As a result, governmental actions often appear contradictory or lacking in consistency for the rather simple reason that they are contradictory and inconsistent. Understanding the multiplicity of governing authorities allows us to see why such a pattern develops: different government levels and units with varying goals rarely act with unanimity in the making of public policy. For example, the Canadian federal political system, which divides political authority between a central government and various provincial governments, encourages conflict over major policy decisions (e.g., social policy, equalization grants, tax policy). The same type of conflict and contradictory policy occurs between governmental units within the same level of government. Only through recognizing the multiplicity of governmental levels and units, and the political conflict that results from their possible contradictory policy objectives, can we understand the nature of the political process.

Characteristic number three: government is necessary

The fact that government is ubiquitous and multiple creates the impression that government is also necessary: governments exist because of the functions they perform, that is, because of what they do for society.

Governments carry out many different tasks or jobs; that is, they have many consequences for and effects on society. Governments are the institutional means for controlling and regulating conflict within society. Any society is composed of many individuals, groups, classes, parties, interest groups, and regions, each of which typically desires a competitive advantage over the others. In Canada, with 31 million people, 10 provinces, many regions, and at least several social classes, to name only a few of the more obvious divisions in Canadian society, some mechanism is required to ensure social order. Government is just such a structure.

Conflict develops in society primarily because of one fundamental fact of life: scarcity. Whether it is scarcity of wealth (gold, money, standard of living), natural resources (oil, natural gas, food), or status, the result is the same: conflict over who will control and benefit from the limited but highly valued goods and services. Given the scarcity of resources and the ensuing conflict over their distribution, government becomes the means for resolving these conflicts by certain agreed-upon rules of the political process.

Political systems attempt to channel and transform conflict (including violence, coercion, and force) into peaceful competitive pursuits. For example, in liberal-democratic political systems, election campaigns between competing political parties are one way of arriving at decisions about the goals and purposes of the government. Elections determine which party will control the government and thus, as a consequence, who will decide the allocation of scarce resources. Government budgets, for example, specify which groups, regions, or individuals receive the benefits of government, and which sectors of society bear the costs of these allocative decisions.

> *An anecdote about the nature of politics:* "My profession is the most important," the physician asserts. "The Lord created Eve from Adam's rib; it was a surgical procedure; we physicians were there at creation." "No, no," the engineer responds. "Take one step back. The Lord created the universe from chaos. It was the greatest engineering feat in history. My profession was there at the creation." "Fair enough," the politician replies, "But who do you think created the chaos?" (anonymous, quoted in Dallek, 1996: xii)

A second cause of social conflict is diversity. Linguistic, ethnic, economic, regional, and religious differences may all become linked to political concerns. In Canada, such socio-political cleavages have an important impact on the structure, operation, and future of the political system. Likewise, differences in values, that is, what people want and expect from government, may lead to conflict. In liberal-democratic political systems, governments seek to harmonize these divergent interests, not to eliminate them.

In most political systems, these two causes of conflict reinforce each other. For example, minority groups based on religious, regional, or ethnic differences are usually the same groups that receive the least in terms of the society's allocation of scarce resources. The combination of scarcity and diversity produces difficult challenges to any polity. In Canada, it is just such a pattern that continually challenges the wisdom of our leaders, if not the very existence of our political system.

In viewing government as the institutional means for the settlement of conflict resulting from both scarcity and diversity, we have emphasized the negative side of government: its role in mediating, reducing, and avoiding conflict. However, government can also be creative, or at least attempt to be. Government's second major function is positive in the sense of being purposive, of wanting to achieve certain desired goals. For example, Liberal leader John Turner's crusade against free trade in the 1988 election, what he called the "fight of my life," was, from his point of view, a way of preserving Canada's political and cultural independence.

Governments seek to be creative mechanisms when they promote our health and welfare (e.g., medical care, dental care, consumer and environmental protection); when they attempt to alleviate the negative economic results of a capitalistic system (e.g., unemployment insurance, retraining programs, disability and pension plans); when they promote widespread educational opportunity through financial aid to education and vocational training programs; and when they seek to develop a sense of national unity (e.g., the adoption of "O Canada" as the official national anthem in time for the 1980 Dominion Day celebration).

The utilization of government as both a regulator of conflict and creator of values helps to explain the previously cited characteristics of government. The ubiquitous and multiple nature of government stems, in part, from its attempt to regulate an ever-increasing number of policy areas in an ever-expanding political sphere. The use of government as a creative mechanism also leads to political conflict. Given the value differences among individuals, groups, or regions, it is not surprising that many political battles concern the goals and future direction of public policy.

Characteristic number four: government is varied

To utilize government in both its regulative and creative capacities, numerous types of governmental structures have been devised; in other words, government is varied. In some ways, of course, each government is unique: no two governments are identical in all respects. However, it would be an impossible task to describe in detail the historical and present array of governments if we assumed the absolute uniqueness of each political system. Instead, one of the significant tasks of political science and comparative political analysis is to look for patterns of similarities and differences among political systems so that various typologies or classifications of governments can be developed.

Although political science has produced a prolific number of classifications, we should keep in mind that there is no right or wrong way of classifying governmental types. Classifications should be developed and used with a specific goal in mind, which thus allows for the selection of the appropriate criteria on which the typology is to be constructed. Since we are primarily concerned with comparing the political systems of Canada, the United States, and Britain, we have chosen for consideration several typologies that highlight these systems' similarities and differences. In order to show the Canadian, American, and British pattern within the world context, we begin with a general classification of governments. The first typology emphasizes the similarities among the Canadian, American, and British forms of government. The second and third typologies to be discussed, namely the distinctions between federal and unitary and between presidential and parliamentary forms of government, focus on the differences in governmental structure among these three liberal-democratic political systems.

Classification Number One: Governmental Types   After surveying the historical development of governmental types, British political scientist Bernard Crick (1973: 69–73) concluded that three basic forms could be identified: autocratic, republican, and totalitarian.

> **Autocracy** . . . is the form of government which attempts to solve the basic problem of the adjustment of order to diversity by the authoritative enforcement of one of the diverse interests (whether seen as material or moral — almost always, in fact, both) as an officially sponsored and static ideology.

> **Republican government** . . . is the attempt to solve the basic problem of the adjustment to diversity by conciliating different interests by letting them share in government or in the competitive choosing of the government.

> **Totalitarian government** . . . is the attempt to solve the basic problem of the adjustment of order to diversity by creating a completely new society such that conflict would no longer arise: it attempts to do this by means of guidance and enforcement of a revolutionary ideology which claims to be scientific, thus comprehensive and necessary, both for knowledge and allegiance.

The advantage of Crick's classification is that the form of government (i.e., autocratic, republican, or totalitarian) is related to the functions of government (i.e., how government performs its regulative and creative tasks in reconciling diversity with political order). An autocratic system imposes one divergent interest over all others; a republican system conciliates competing interests; and a totalitarian system creates a new political society in which competing interests have been eliminated. Examples of autocratic governments would include the monarchies in Europe through the 18th century, Czarist Russia, and Iran under both the Pahlavi dynasty and the Ayatollah Khomeini and his successors; republican governments would include the current liberal-democratic systems of Europe and North America, along with Israel and Japan; and totalitarian governments would be exemplified by Nazi Germany and Soviet Russia under Stalin and his successors through the mid-1980s.

Because Crick's definition of republican government is unique (in that he does not make a distinction between republican and democratic government), and even though the term republican has been utilized for several centuries within the field of comparative politics, in recent times the concept of liberal-democracy has become more commonly used. In order to avoid any possible confusion, we will employ the term liberal-democracy — or just simply democracy — to refer to the type of government classified as republican by Crick. A **liberal-democratic system** *"is one in which public policies are made, on a majority basis, by representatives subject to effective popular control at periodic elections which are conducted on the principle of political equality and under conditions of political freedom"* (Mayo, 1960: 70; see also Ware, 1992).

The construction of any typology forces political analysts to specify the criteria which they feel are the most significant for investigating the similarities and differences among political systems. A classification scheme also produces an either/or decision by the political scientist; for example, Crick's classification results in the placement of any specific government in one of three possible categories. As a result, few political scientists would disagree that the Soviet Union under Stalin belonged in the totalitarian category. By contrast, under Nikita Khrushchev's leadership, the extent of state control and political repression in the Soviet Union receded, however modestly, while crackdowns on political dissent under Leonid Brezhnev and his immediate successors indicated a return to a more Stalinist approach by the leadership in Moscow. Such internal changes led some observers to claim that the Soviet Union no longer exemplified the characteristics of totalitarian government. However, if one considers all of its governmental characteristics, the Soviet Union clearly belonged in the totalitarian category, both in the past and through the leadership of Konstantin Chernenko, who died in 1985.

The rise to power of Mikhail Gorbachev and his dramatic reforms in the late 1980s, based on the ideas of *glasnost* (openness) and *perestroika* (restructuring), moved the Soviet Union away from some of the harsher characteristics of totalitarian government and toward the democratic model. With the demise of the Soviet Union on Christmas Day in 1991, this classification problem was solved — the Soviet Union no longer existed. However, a new and more difficult classification problem immediately emerged: Into what category should Russia and the new states of the former Soviet Union be placed? Certainly we could say that at least Russia, given its attempted economic and political reforms under Boris Yeltsin and Vladimir Putin during the past decade, should be considered as a more democratic country than in the past.

In addition to forcing either/or decisions on the political analyst, a second problem associated with the use of classifications is the assumption that a specific government exhibits all the characteristics of a particular category. For example, with respect to the control of property, the Soviet Union, as a pure totalitarian government, would never have allowed the existence of private property. In actual fact, however, private property was allowed to exist; at times it was even encouraged by the Soviet leadership, particularly with respect to private agricultural plots. Thus, no specific government necessarily exhibits, in all respects, every single characteristic of a particular classification scheme.

A good way of perceiving governmental types, therefore, is to see the classification as a continuum, with a specific government showing more or less of a particular characteristic. Such a procedure is especially useful when comparing governments within a particular category. For example, if we compare Canada, the United States, and Britain in terms of political participation with respect to the percentage of voting turnout in their national elections in 2000 (Canada and the United States) and 2001 (Britain), we would rank Canada first (61 percent in 2000), Britain a close second (58 percent in 2001), and the United States third (54 percent in 2000). However, if we use criteria other than voting turnout — such as the number of opportunities for political participation offered the average citizen in each country — a very different ordering of these three countries emerges. The United States, given the number of political offices filled through elections, the frequency of elections, the openness of the political recruitment process through the use of direct primaries, and the opportunities for utilizing the recall, initiative, and referendum techniques at the state and local levels, would be classified as the most participatory. Canada, which gives the average citizen the right to vote in national, provincial, and municipal elections as well as the occasional referendum, and also allows for limited participation in the leadership selection process through the national party leadership convention, would rank second in terms of opportunities for political participation. In such a comparison Britain would rank third, because of its closed recruitment process, the traditional selection by the two major parties of the party leader by the party caucus, and the use of only national and local election campaigns. These examples demonstrate an important aspect of comparative political analysis: the conclusions reached in any comparison depend to a large extent on the specific aspect of the political process that is being considered.

Finally, with respect to classifications we should remember that since political systems change through time, so does their placement in any typology. For example, Germany moved from autocracy in the 19th century to a democratic form of government during the Weimar Republic in the 1920s, to a totalitarian variety under Hitler and the Nazis, and back to a democratic form in West Germany and a totalitarian version in East Germany from the Second World War to 1989. The reunification of Germany (October 3, 1990) brought that country into the democratic category once again. Similarly, any particular government changes through time even within the same category. For example, Canada, Britain, and the United States are all more participatory today than they were 50 years ago. This problem of political change emphasizes an additional consideration in comparative political analysis: the conclusions reached depend on the historical period of the comparisons.

In addition to classifications that compare governments in total, more limited typologies, which focus on a particular aspect, may also prove useful, especially for comparing governments within a specific category. Two such limited typologies will be considered: first, the distinction between federal and unitary forms of government, and second, the differences between presidential and parliamentary governmental structures.

Classification Number Two: Federal vs. Unitary Systems   The classification of governments into federal or unitary systems is based on the structure of the central or national government and the resulting way in which political power is shared with the constituent political units (i.e., provinces in Canada, states in the United States). A **federal** form of government is constructed on *the principle of the division of powers between levels of government*: in other words, in Canada, governmental power is shared between the national government in Ottawa and the 10 provincial governments, while in the United States governmental power is divided between the national government in Washington and the 50 state governments. The organization of the political units in a federal nation-state is on a geographical basis (i.e., provinces or states) and represents an attempt to incorporate diversity (economic, cultural, linguistic, ethnic, regional) within an overall unifying framework. In such a system, each level of government can act directly on the citizen (e.g., taxation) and also independently exercise certain powers, which are usually specified in the country's constitution. Generally, some responsibilities are shared between the levels of government. As a result, federalism creates a structure of government as well as a process of governing.

After the initial design of a federal system, the continuing distribution and sharing of powers becomes a primary political issue. When jurisdictional disputes arise in a federal system, the judiciary is often called upon to act as an arbitrator of the precise role of each level of government. In other words, we can say that the essence of a federal system is the division of power between a national government and various constituent units. Political systems which are federal in structure include Canada, the United States, Australia, and Germany. Belgium, in an attempt to provide regional autonomy for its Flemish- and French-speaking regions, adopted a series of constitutional amendments that turned it from a unitary into a federal form of government in 1993.

A **unitary government** consists of *a single level of government, that is, a national or central government, with some power delegated to local government units*; in other words, in contrast to a federal structure, the second level of government (provinces or states) is missing. More importantly, the central government monopolizes political power and determines which power it will allow the local government to use. For example, while British Prime Minister Margaret Thatcher found it difficult politically to control the spending of the local authorities, the national government was perfectly within its constitutional powers to abolish a local authority, which it did to the Greater London Council on April 1, 1986. However, less than two years after taking power in the 1997 election, the Labour party under Tony Blair, which was, returning to office for the first time in 18 years, quickly moved to reinstate a modified version of the Greater London Council, now called the Greater London Authority. Local government does not exercise power independently of the central government; in addition, the powers, structure, and boundaries of the local units can be changed by the central government acting on its own initiative. What a unitary government grants, it may also take away. Examples of traditional unitary systems include Great Britain, Sweden, and France.

A third alternative, although rarely tried in the 20th century, is a **confederal** structure. In such a system *the constituent units create the national or central government, which then governs only with the consent of the constituent units.* The central government's authority is not independent; it acts on behalf of its creators. Such a system was tried in the United States after the American Revolution with the Articles of Confederation. Its failure led to the adoption of a federal system under the present American Constitution. In Canada, some proponents of provincial rights come close to advocating a confederal form of government under a revised Canadian Constitution. Many of the reforms proposed in the rejected Charlottetown Accord in 1992, such as provincial control over the exercise of the federal government's declaratory power, would have added an element of confederalism to our political process. However, even though Canada is called a confederation, what was intended and created by the Constitution Act of 1867 was a federal political structure, and a highly centralized one at that.

Classification Number Three: Presidential vs. Parliamentary Systems Our third classification, that of presidential or parliamentary systems, focusses on the structure of the executive (single or dual) and its relation (separation or fusion of powers) to the legislature within a single governmental level (Verney, 1979; McMenemy, 1999: 212). A **parliamentary system** has a split executive: that is, a head of state or **formal executive** with relatively limited political power (e.g., the British monarch; in Canada, at the federal level the governor general, and in the provinces the lieutenant governors) and a **political executive**, which is the repository of extensive political power (e.g., the British and Canadian prime ministers, the premiers of the 10 Canadian provinces). The formal executive performs primarily symbolic and ceremonial functions, while the political executive exercises effective political power.

A second characteristic of a parliamentary system is the executive's relation to the legislature: a parliamentary system is based on the principle of the **fusion of executive and legislative power**. Whichever party has a majority of seats in the legislature also controls the executive branch; in other words, the same group of political leaders operates both the executive and legislative institutions of government.

This fusion of executive and legislative power is accomplished through the cabinet, described in the British context by Walter Bagehot (1867: 68) as "a hyphen which joins, a buckle which fastens, the legislative part of the State to the executive part of the State." In turn, the cabinet is collectively responsible to the legislature for its actions and retains office only so long as it receives majority support in the legislature.

A third characteristic of parliamentary government is that a maximum time limit, usually five years, is set for how long a government can stay in office without returning to the people through an election to renew its mandate. Within this maximum time limit, however, elections are held at varying intervals. For example, in the last half-century federal elections in Canada occurred in 1957, 1958, 1962, 1963, 1965, 1968, 1972, 1974, 1979, 1980, 1984, 1988, 1993, 1997, and 2000. The timing of elections is generally within the powers of the political executive to decide.

An interesting variation of this parliamentary pattern of varying election calls inside a maximum time period in office has been proposed in British Columbia. Provincial Liberal leader Gordon Campbell announced in March of 2001 that, if elected in the May provincial election, the Liberals would adopt a system of fixed, four-year terms, except when a government was defeated on either a money bill or a confidence motion. Thus, the leeway of the political executive in making an election call would be severely constrained under such a proposal. The Liberals even went so far as to announce the date of the next election: May 17, 2005.

In contrast, each of these three characteristics of executive structure, executive-legislative relations, and the calling of elections operates differently in a presidential system (Lijphart, 1992: 2–5). First, a **presidential system** operates with a unified or single executive. In the United States, the president performs both the formal and political executive functions of government. Second, the relationship between the executive and legislature in a presidential system is based on the principle of the **separation of powers** (i.e., *that each branch of government operates independently from the others*). This separation of powers principle is maintained through a series of **checks and balances**, which are *the specific constitutional powers granted to each branch to control, in some respects, the operation of the other branches of government*. For example, in the American system the legislature may pass a law, but the president may in turn veto it. A countercheck is given to the legislature in that it may override a presidential veto by a two-thirds vote in both the House of Representatives and the Senate. Third, a presidential system is characterized by elections at set intervals: there is no leeway as to when an election will be held, because the dates are mandated by law. An American presidential election is held in November every four years: such elections are automatic and will be held in 2004, 2008, and 2012. The executive in the American presidential system has no power to determine when to seek a renewal of the mandate to govern. These various characteristics of parliamentary and presidential governments are summarized in Table 1.1.

In beginning our discussion of the presidential/parliamentary distinction, we indicated that these forms operated within a particular level of government. However, the presidential/parliamentary classification can be joined with the federal/unitary distinction to produce a combined classification of governmental

Table 1.1   Parliamentary and Presidential Governments

CHARACTERISTIC	STRUCTURE OF GOVERNMENT	
	Parliamentary	*Presidential*
1. structure of the executive	*dual:* both a formal and a political executive	*singular:* formal and political executive combined in a single office
2. executive-legislative relationship	*fusion of powers:* achieved primarily through the cabinet and based on the principle of collective responsibility	*separation of powers:* based on independent branches of government, maintained by a system of checks and balances; no collective responsibility of the executive to the legislature
3. elections	*maximum time period* fixed, with varying election periods within the maximum determined primarily by the political executive	*set time period* for elections, with the political executive playing no role in determining when elections will be called

forms. In Table 1.2, we present such a typology for various democratic governments. (A combination classification for other types of government could also be developed: for example, the Soviet Union, until Gorbachev, was a totalitarian government which had in theory a federal political structure, but in practice a unitary system of government.) Canada is parliamentary and federal in structure, Britain is parliamentary and unitary, the United States is presidential and federal, and France is presidential and unitary. All of these designations are clear-cut except perhaps in the case of France, which is usually labeled "quasi-presidential." The Fifth French Republic combines both parliamentary and presidential patterns, but since the presidential aspects tend to dominate, it is classified in the presidential category.

Our consideration of three basic classifications of government (autocratic, democratic, totalitarian; federal, unitary; presidential, parliamentary) demonstrates the useful nature of typologies in political analysis. Beginning with a criterion

Table 1.2   A Combined Classification of Democratic Governments

EXECUTIVE-LEGISLATIVE RELATIONSHIP	LEVELS OF GOVERNMENT	
	Federal	*Unitary*
Parliamentary	Canada	Britain
Presidential	United States	France

that appears to be an important point for comparing political systems (e.g., the structure of the executive-legislative relationship), a typology groups various systems in terms of their similarities within categories (e.g., all federal states share certain characteristics) and differences between categories (e.g., democratic governments vary from totalitarian governments in many ways). Thus, the classification of governments is a shorthand or summary method for describing their organizational structure and operating principles. For example, Canada's government is democratic, federal, and parliamentary in nature; Britain is democratic, unitary, and parliamentary; while the United States is democratic, federal, and presidential. To make such a description summarizes in three words a wealth of pertinent information concerning the operation and structure of these political systems. Therefore, classification is not merely an idle academic exercise — it is a particularly useful starting point for understanding both the nature of government and the nature of politics.

Characteristic number five: government is democratized

While our fourth characteristic of government emphasized the differences between types of political systems, our fifth and sixth characteristics focus on emerging similarities among the world's political units. Increasingly, the world's polities are adapting similar democratic political practices at the same time that they are becoming more interdependent with each other; that is, they are becoming both democratized and globalized.

As the great ideological struggles of the 20th century wound down during the 1990s, it appeared that liberal-democracy, whether by design or by default, was triumphant. While remnants of past ideological battles and types of government would continue to exist — as in China, Cuba, and much of the developing areas of the world — democracy flourished and expanded in the 1990s and into the new millennium. We define this development as **democratization**: *the spread and adoption of democratic structures and practices, that is, the process by which formerly nondemocratic polities become democratic in fact*. Undergoing a process of democratization is not the same thing as being a democratic polity. A successful democratization process will lead to a democratic system, while its failure may lead to new authoritarian or totalitarian regimes (Rose, 2001).

The extent and rapidity of the democratization process can be seen in the following figures (Dahl, 1998: 8). At the beginning of the 20th century, only six countries were democracies — a number which increased to 25 in 1950 and 37 in 1980. Then, between 1980 and 1990 the number of democracies doubled to 65 (out of 192 countries), as the Soviet Union disintegrated and Eastern Europe moved toward democratic practices. However, this study defined democracy in very generous terms — a more restrictive definition of actual working liberal-democracies might be half that number, with the other half in a "democratizing" category. By any measure, at least two-thirds of the world's polities remain in the nondemocratic category. The process of democratization still has considerable room for expansion in the 21st century (Piano and Puddington, 2001).

... despite the apparent development and spread of liberal democratic state forms in the world in the 1980s and 1990s, the possibilities for genuine and effective democratic governance are actually declining (Cerny, 1999: 1).

The impact of the process of democratization can be seen in a variety of contexts. Nondemocratic states, for example, which have no intention of becoming liberal-democracies, adopt democratic forms, such as elections, to increase their legitimacy. Political regimes which are undergoing a process of democratization adopt democratic forms before they seriously begin to acquire democratic content (i.e., Russia in the 1990s). Even long-established democracies face new pressures of democratization with respect to citizen participation and public consultation. New technologies, such as the Internet, may have profound implications for the future of the democratic process. Finally, the impact of globalization raises new challenges for the democratic polity.

> . . . the fact that representative democracy *per se* is not at risk does not imply that all is well with our political systems. Indeed, most of our fellow citizens believe that all is *not* well. Due regard for their views, as well as a prudent concern for the future, suggests that we should explore the sources of this democratic discontent (Pharr, Putnam, and Dalton, 2000: 23).

Characteristic number six: government is globalized

In a multitude of ways, the world has become smaller, and its states more interdependent. Communication facilities and capabilities, such as the Internet, along with such factors as the development of a global economy, have all produced an increasing integration and similarity of political, social, and economic processes. This pattern of **globalization**, that is, *the interdependence of political units, such as nation-states, in terms of their economies, their societies, and their political practices* has had both positive and negative influences on the modern polity (Waltz, 1999; Barber, 2000).

Globalization of the world's economy has helped to internationalize both political structures and political practices. A good example of this would be the increasing homogenization of democratic electoral practices seen in election campaigns around the world. Moreover, the current economic globalization, based on the success of the market economy of Western capitalism, has helped to spread the ideal of liberal-democracy around the world. With globalization and democratization has come increased economic prosperity, at least in the industrialized areas of the international economy. Democracy has become a key export of the international capitalist economy.

Unfortunately, such a development has potential negative effects on both the process of democratization and the operation of existing democratic polities (Cerny, 1999). Globalization of democratic ideas and formats is relatively easy; globalization of democratic substance is much more difficult. Moreover, globalization has increasingly transferred political authority to international bodies, such as the United Nations, the World Trade Organization (WTO), and the International Monetary Fund (IMF). Thus, democratically elected governments may lose their decision-making powers to such bodies, making a state's democratic process a moot point. Similarly, international corporations, through various free trade and other such agreements, may ignore or overrule the results of the democratic process. Finally, the Internet will likely have negative, as well as positive, effects on future democratic polities (see Chapter 11).

> At present, the encompassing practices of globalization have created an ironic and radical asymmetry: we have managed to globalize markets in goods, labour, currencies and information without globalizing the civic and democratic institutions . . . (Barber, 2000: 275).

THE NATURE OF POLITICS

Like it or not, politics is a fact of human existence. One can detest it, ignore it, or attempt to change it, but the pervasiveness of politics remains. Human behaviour occurs in the context of political communities organized in modern times on the basis of nation-states. As with birth itself, initial membership in a political system gives one little freedom of choice — it is a nonvoluntary option. We are automatically members of a political system at birth and are subject to the consequences of such membership throughout our lives. If government is ubiquitous, then politics is more so, for government constitutes only a portion of the broader process of politics. If government is the institutional organization of political power, **politics** can be defined as *the exercise of power and influence on matters that affect the community.*

While pervasive, politics is not found in every facet of human existence, although many actions have potential political implications. Matters which may be considered private and nonpolitical for the ordinary citizen can quickly generate potent political ramifications for a politician. For example, one's personal sexual behaviour and sexual preferences, including events that may have happened long before the individual entered the political arena, can have an impact on one's later political power and influence. While it may be true, as Pierre Trudeau said in 1967 (Gwyn, 1980: 64), that in a liberal-democratic society "the state has no business in the bedrooms of the nation," the converse does not seem to be true: the people often demand to know about the sexual behaviour and preferences of their leaders. American Democratic president Bill Clinton faced a series of allegations regarding his sexual behaviour, for which he was impeached but not convicted in 1999.

> Genuine politics — politics worthy of the name, and the only politics I am willing to devote myself to — is simply a matter of serving those around us: serving the community, and serving those who will come after us (Havel, 1992: 64).

If politics is the exercise of power and influence on matters that affect the community, then **political analysis** is *the attempt to explain why a specific pattern of power and influence emerges, how power is gained and lost, and why certain political events occur.* Thus, what we call political analysis is simply one approach used in answering that basic question of all the sciences, both natural and social: why? Political analysis is the exercise of imposing conceptual order on an apparently incoherent political process.

The political analyst assumes that things rarely happen by chance in politics. Even those events which appear at first glance to be part of a mysterious process are, upon closer inspection, understandable and explainable in the light of certain regularities of human behaviour. For example, although it may be difficult to explain why a particular individual voted for a specific candidate in a single election campaign, the political analyst can make general explanations of Canadian voting behaviour based on socio-economic factors such as class, occupation, region, religion, and ethnicity. One of the tasks of the political analyst is to search for such general patterns as a foundation for explaining what has happened.

In asserting that political life is founded on certain regularities of behaviour, such that we can describe and explain political events, we are not at the same time assuming that the political process is predestined to develop in a particular manner. One of the fascinating aspects of politics is the continuing occurrence of the unexpected, which reveals a fundamental point about the nature of politics: that is, the human basis of the polity. As a result, politics itself is an art, a way of organizing varieties of individual uniqueness into patterns of collective purpose.

Having lived in a political system for a number of years, most people, if they were asked to define what politics is all about, would likely respond with several basic ideas, which might include some of the following concepts: conflict, power, government, influence, the state, violence, decisions, patronage, laws, and corruption. Some people would see politics in a very favourable light; others might view it as a "dirty business." Some would perceive politics as involving almost all areas of social and economic life, while others would want to restrict the political sphere to rather narrow limits.

One would quickly realize that not only do definitions diverge widely among individuals, they also differ extensively in various historical periods and between types of political systems. For example, people within a democratic system conceive of the political sphere in much different terms than those who live in an autocratic or totalitarian system. Although individuals and societies may differ in their definitions of politics, a common theme is a concern with order, or the lack thereof:

> I had learned the first real lesson of politics, government and history: governments are instituted among men in the first instance, and accepted by men gratefully, to protect them from random violence and killing . . . . They offered protection. Many other lessons in politics and government were to follow over the years, but none more important than that (White, 1978: 101).

The reason for the emphasis in various definitions of politics on the theme of order, which can be labelled as the **godfather function of politics**, can only be appreciated in the context of how the political sphere initially developed as a distinct part of society in the Western world.

Early history was prepolitical; that is, the political system was not yet differentiated from other social systems. What we would now interpret as political power and influence were part of an integrated whole — human beings were a part of nature, not distinct from it. Speculative thought based on myth, rather than the rational and scientific approach of modern times, prevailed. However, such initial speculative thought served a function similar to that of later political thought: it sought to underpin "the chaos of experience" so that it might "reveal the features of a structure — order, coherence, and meaning" (Frankfort et al., 1949: 11).

The development of a political sphere was a long and complex process, which involved the basic step of separating human beings from nature. Nature became an inanimate object to be understood, manipulated, and controlled. Divorcing humans from nature meant that they had to find a rationale for this separate organization — nature could no longer be depended on to provide it. As a result of this redefinition, which began during the 6th and 5th centuries B.C. in Greece, political thought replaced speculative thought and thus assumed the function of providing order, coherence, and meaning. The task of the political philosopher was to "fashion a political cosmos out of political chaos" (Wolin, 1960: 8).

If the function of political thought is to develop a pattern from political chaos, then it is not surprising to find that most definitions of politics focus on the concept of order. Given this perspective, we can now expand our initial definition of politics to the following statement: **politics** is *the exercise of power and influence concerning the establishment, maintenance, and breakdown of order in the community.* The different types of political systems (autocratic, democratic, or totalitarian) establish different kinds of political institutions, with differing relationships between those institutions, in attempting to achieve order in the political community. One way of categorizing these numerous approaches to politics is to group them on the basis of whether or not they provide a normative or an empirical definition of the political sphere.

A comparison of normative and empirical interpretations reveals one basic difference: a **normative definition** is concerned with *what ought to be,* while an **empirical definition** is concerned with *what is.* A normative statement cannot be disproved, while an empirical statement may be. A normative statement is neither true nor false, while an empirical statement may be either. A normative conception of politics develops a desired or a preferred pattern of political organization, while an empirical approach is based on existing political reality. The perspective of this book is heavily cast in light of the second alternative; that is, an empirical assessment of the Canadian polity.

An example may help to explain the difference between the empirical and normative approaches. The statement that "All men are equal" may reflect a normative judgment that all men should be equal; as an empirical observation the assertion is simply false. The empiricist would ask, "Equal according to which characteristics: sex, height, weight, intelligence, educational training, or social class?" Does equality refer to **equality of condition** (i.e., *money, economic rewards*) or to **equality of opportunity** (i.e., *the right to become unequal by earning more money or completing more education than other people*)? Thus, the statement that "All men are equal" may be proposed or accepted as a normative view of how society should be structured; as an empirical statement it must be rejected. No political system, ancient or modern, of whatever type, has ever produced equality of social, economic, or political condition. No existing polity seems destined to change this historical assessment.

> In the unspoken assumptions that underlie everyday discourse, we are an elitist society because nothing else is logical. In the exchange of lies and euphemisms that constitutes the surface of polite discourse, we are egalitarian, because nothing else is diplomatic (Henry, 1994: 31).

IDEOLOGICAL DEFINITIONS OF POLITICS

Another important way of categorizing the multitude of possible definitions of politics is on an ideological basis. The politics of the 20th century, both domestic and international, was a battle of ideologies struggling for supremacy (Conquest, 1999). An **ideology** itself can be defined as *"a set of ideas held by a number of people:*

it spells out what is valued and what is not; what must be maintained and what must be changed; it shapes accordingly the attitudes of those who share it" (Macridis, 1980: 6). Different political ideologies project various conceptions of people's political experience: "As collections of ideas informed by political perspectives they are, or they provide, ways of looking at the world, and interpreting specific issues: ideologies play like often-wandering searchlights on events" (Duncan, 1987: 650).

To begin our discussion, we will analyze three basic ideological definitions of politics: conservative, liberal, and radical (Marxism). While no existing ideology is "pure," that is, unaffected by other ideologies or pragmatic considerations, these three form the basis, both theoretically and historically, for the development of other ideological alternatives. One such hybrid, democratic socialism, will also be presented. Finally, we will analyze a relatively new entrant into the ideological field, namely, feminism. These five ideologies have had the greatest impact on the three countries that form the basis of our comparative approach.

> It is a mistake to underestimate the power of ignorance in human affairs. It is, however, a still greater mistake to underestimate the power of principle. Political conflict is as deeply rooted in a commitment to values as in a failure to understand them (Sniderman et al., 1996: 257).

Our initial ideological definitions of politics — conservative, liberal, and radical (Marxism) — correspond to status quo, reformist, and revolutionary approaches. A **conservative** or status quo definition of politics is *one that defends and rationalizes "the existing economic, social, and political order"*; a radical or **revolutionary** view, such as Marxism, *advocates "far-reaching changes in the existing social, economic, and political order"*; a **reformist** perspective, exemplified by liberal theorists, falls somewhere between these two extremes by *favouring gradual or modest change in the existing system* (Macridis, 1980: 9). These three political ideologies and their views of politics differ most significantly with respect to the idea of political change: for a conservative, change is always suspect, if not downright detrimental; for a revolutionary, change, including the use of violence, is mandatory and often a desired state of affairs; for a liberal, incremental change (slow, modest change) is preferred: change if necessary, but not necessarily change. The more hybrid ideology of **democratic socialism** seeks *fundamental change in the social, economic, and political order, but through democratic means.* Change will be implemented, not by revolution, but by the ballot box. The final ideology of **feminism** offers a different perspective on the political process by focussing on the role of women as participants in and agents of political reform.

A conservative view of politics

Our example of a conservative view of politics will be from the writings of the late Professor Michael Oakeshott of the London School of Economics and Political Science. Oakeshott (1962: 168) is explicitly conservative, defining the conservative view as "a propensity to use and enjoy what is available rather than to wish for or to look for something else; to delight in what is present rather than what was or what may be." Thus, a conservative favours tradition over innovation: the imperfections of the present are preferable to the unknown possibilities of the future.

As a conservative, Oakeshott is opposed to many elements of modern political thought, which he labels as Rationalism. Rather than emerging from a people's tradition and accumulated experience, Rationalism, which he equates with modern political ideologies, attempts to structure the polity on the basis of preconceived principles. Oakeshott's (1962: 112) view of conservatism and his resulting critique of Rationalism is linked specifically to his definition of politics and political activity: "Politics I take to be the activity of attending to the general arrangements of a set of people whom chance or choice have brought together." Politics is not the pursuit of dreams or goals, but, instead, is a tradition of behaviour.

We have classified Oakeshott's view of politics as conservative because he prefers what exists to what might be: people are not only imperfect, but, quite likely, not perfectible. Politics and government are limited and specific types of activity that should not be confused with, or replaced by, rationalist thought. These themes are well expressed in the following metaphor:

> In political activity, then, men sail a boundless and bottomless sea; there is neither harbour for shelter nor floor for anchorage, neither starting place nor appointed destination. The enterprise is to keep afloat on an even keel; the sea is both friend and enemy; and the seamanship consists in using the resources of a traditional manner of behaviour in order to make a friend of every hostile occasion (Oakeshott, 1962: 127).

A liberal view of politics

If a conservative views politics as a tradition of behaviour, a **liberal** definition focusses instead on the individual's rights and responsibilities. A liberal philosophy argues for both the existence and expansion of basic human rights, such as the right to vote, and for the limitation of the state's role in interfering with these rights. Thus, liberalism has traditionally argued for limited government, with constitutional protection for fundamental political and civil liberties. The political system must be structured or organized in a manner that maximizes the rights and freedoms of the individual: the state exists to serve and to protect the individual. An interesting variation of what we would classify as a liberal view of politics can be found in British political scientist Bernard Crick's famous essay, *In Defence of Politics.*

Politics is defined by Crick (1964: 21) as the "activity by which differing interests within a given unit of rule are conciliated by giving them a share in power in proportion to their importance to the welfare and survival of the whole community." This perspective sees "politics as conciliation," as a process for accommodating diversity within the political order. The unique aspect of Crick's analysis is that he argues that the acceptance of diversity is the basis of politics, and since the value of diversity is only accepted in free societies, then politics can only occur in such a context. For Crick (1964: 18, 20), "politics are the public actions of free men," and the "unique character of political activity lies, quite literally, in its publicity."

Several important implications flow from this particular definition of politics. First, politics is not a universal phenomenon that occurs in all societies. For example, politics and its corresponding pattern of governance, which is labelled political rule, does not exist in totalitarian systems. Since totalitarian governments seek to eliminate diversity, they also at the same time eradicate politics. Second, Crick's definition takes a narrow view of politics. Basic arenas of social interaction, such as art, education, and beliefs are not inherently political: the attempt to make them so results in the demise of politics. Third, politics is anti-ideological — politics cannot exist where one ideology becomes dominant and eliminates all of its competitors. The diversity of political ideologies helps to sustain political rule, while the dominance of a single political ideology results in the demise of politics. Fourth, politics is a valued activity because the conciliation of divergent interests is a better alternative than the use of violence and coercion in the making and implementation of public decisions. Finally, Crick explicitly rejects both the conservative and revolutionary approaches to politics.

Crick's analysis of politics as a worthwhile endeavour contrasts sharply with the negative view of politics and politicians currently dominant in many Western political systems. For Crick, politics is not only a virtuous activity, but the essence of freedom itself.

> Politics, then, is civilizing. It rescues mankind from the morbid dilemmas in which the state is always seen as a ship threatened by a hostile environment of cruel seas, and enables us, instead, to see the state as a city settled on the firm and fertile ground of mother earth. It can offer us no guarantees against storms encroaching from the sea, but it can offer us something worth defending in times of emergency and amid threats of disaster (Crick, 1964: 140).

A revolutionary view of politics

An example of our third ideological definition of politics is a revolutionary conception, namely, the **Marxist** view of the political sphere. Marx perceived politics in an extremely negative light: politics was a mechanism for the exploitation of people by people, the means by which the dominant class ruled over other classes. Since politics represented class domination, in the final stage of history, when class conflict was eliminated, politics would also disappear — there would be a "withering away of the state." In order to understand this perspective, a few essential aspects of Marxism must be discussed.

Three basic themes of Marxism can be identified: first, history operates through a recognizable series of economic laws, what is called dialectical materialism; second, history moves through various stages of development, culminating in a communist society; and third, the moving force of history is the class struggle or class conflict. Underlying these themes is a basic assumption that relates political development and organization to the economic sphere: for Marx, economics largely determines and controls politics.

> Ideas that claimed to transcend all problems, but were defective or delusive, devastated minds, and movements, and whole countries, and looked like plausible contenders for world supremacy. In fact, humanity has been savaged and trampled by rogue ideologies (Conquest, 1999: xi).

History evolves as people's relationship to the means of production shifts. The various stages of history (feudalism, capitalism, socialism) reflect differences in the basis and ownership of the means of production. For example, under capitalism, the capitalist class or bourgeoisie, operating under the principle of private property, owns the means of production, while under communism, the proletariat or working class acquires such control. The dominant class in each historical period is the class that owns the productive capacity of society.

As a result, the political system is one means of institutionalizing and perpetuating the dominance of the ruling class. Thus, at the base of all societal relationships lies economic reality (i.e., ownership of the means of production), which can be labelled the economic base or substructure; all else, including politics, art, law, and religion, are elements of the superstructure. If, for Marx, "politics is superstructure," then it is not surprising that he had a negative view of politics and felt that it would be and should be eliminated in the final stage of history.

Since the class structure at any given historical moment represents a pattern of domination by the ruling class and a pattern of subordination for those excluded from the ownership of productive forces, the classes of society find themselves in an antagonistic and possibly violent relationship with each other. This adversarial pattern is magnified as the substructure of economic relationships changes from one type of economic system of production to another (e.g., from a feudal pattern of production based on the landed aristocracy to a capitalist mode of production based on commerce and manufacturing). At some historical juncture the class struggle will reach a boiling point of frustration, the exploited class will rise up and in a revolution overthrow the previously dominant class, and a new pattern of dominance and subordination, based on a new series of economic relationships, will emerge. In the final stage of history, this class struggle will abate, because in a communist society, classes, and the dominance-subordination syndrome, will have disappeared.

The Marxist view of politics stands in sharp contrast to both the conservative and liberal definitions with respect to two essential aspects: the nature of political change and the relationship between the economic and political sectors of society. Given the nature of class conflict, the antagonistic relationship between social classes, and the use of the political system by the dominant class to ensure the continuation of the existing system of exploitation, political change can only be achieved through revolution. Revolution is a tidal wave of political change that crashes onto the shore of mother earth, sweeping it clean, and thus creating the conditions for the restructuring and rebuilding of economic and political relationships. This emphasis on revolutionary change in Marxism is diametrically opposed to the conservative's view of "politics as tradition" and the liberal's perspective of "politics as conciliation."

> The emphasis on political and economic modernization in the twentieth century produced so many ideological excuses for the abuse of power by governments that most of us forgot that tyranny, rather than diminishing, was actually as common as ever, and far more abusive than in the past (Chirot, 1994: 1).

A second distinctive aspect of Marxism is its view of the relationship between economics and politics, with the former controlling the latter. The causal arrow runs from the economic structure to the political structure. By contrast, conservative and liberal theories reverse the Marxist pattern of causation; that is, politics determines economic relationships. In Marxism, economics is the substructure and politics the superstructure, while in conservative and liberal views, politics is the substructure and economics the superstructure.

A democratic socialist view of politics

The reason we have classified democratic socialism as a hybrid ideology is apparent in the name itself: "socialism" is the noun which emphasizes economic equality, while "democratic" is the adjective which describes the political means for achieving such a goal. Democratic socialism excludes the revolutionary technique advocated by Marxism and replaces it with a reformed political process, which is an outgrowth of liberalism's emphasis on political rights and liberties. Economics prevails over or dominates politics, but the political process will be used to transform, peacefully, the distribution, control, and use of private property. Socialism will be achieved by evolution, not revolution.

Democratic socialists share with Marxists several key assumptions: first, the economic basis of society; second, the importance of economic equality as a goal; third, the need to prevent capitalists from controlling the economic system; and fourth, a utopian vision of an ideal society. Where democratic socialists and revolutionary socialists disagree is on the means for achieving their goal of equality. Democratic socialists are committed to political and civil liberties and to the existing constitutional system; revolutionary socialists are not. Democratic socialists want to revolutionize society by reforming it; revolutionary socialists want a revolution.

The alternative of democratic socialism developed in the European context in the late 19th and early 20th centuries. A leading exponent was a German, Eduard Bernstein, whose book, *Evolutionary Socialism,* was first published in 1899. In it, Bernstein provided a definitive critique of Marxism and argued for democratic socialism as an alternative. A parallel development occurred in England, with the establishment of the Fabian Society in 1888. Among its members were Sidney and Beatrice Webb, George Bernard Shaw, and H.G. Wells. The Fabians argued that socialism could be achieved by democratic means through a gradual transformation of society.

In the political systems of Britain, Canada, and the United States, democratic socialism has had a far greater impact than revolutionary socialism. While revolutionary socialists have retained their ideological purity, they have had little impact on the game of power. In contrast, by accepting the legitimacy of the democratic and constitutional regime, democratic socialists have had a major impact on the political systems in Britain and Canada. In Britain, democratic socialists helped to found and develop the Labour party, one of the two main party rivals. In Canada, the New Democratic Party, while never winning power federally, has been responsible for much progressive social legislation and has been a major participant in the provincial political arena. In the United States, democratic socialists have been absorbed, for the most part, into the Democratic party, leaving the official socialist parties as the ineffectual repositories of revolutionary socialism.

A feminist view of politics

One of the most significant changes in the operation, as well as the analysis, of political life in the last decades of the 20th century has been the emergence of women as participants in the political processes of the modern polity — especially in liberal-democratic systems. Much of the impetus for such a change came from women themselves, through litigation, interest group activity, electoral politics, and the women's movement. Such an array of activity and political reform was based on a new philosophy or ideology of politics that can be described by the term feminism. While recognizing that there are many different versions of feminist theory, we can generally define **feminism** as *an approach to politics and political analysis that recognizes the unequal position of women in social, economic, and political life and seeks to change it.*

Examples of political discrimination against women are not hard to find. Even in the much-vaunted Athenian democracy in Greece, women were excluded from political participation, as well as citizenship. When Aristotle called "man a political animal," he was not using the term in a generic sense. Women only received the right to vote in liberal-democracies two decades into the 20th century; in Quebec and France, it was nearly mid-century before the right to vote was granted. In Canada, in the famous "Persons case" in the 1920s, the Supreme Court ruled in 1928 that under the 1867 British North America (BNA) Act women were not "persons" and, therefore, could not be appointed to the Senate. Although this ruling was overturned by the Judicial Committee of the Privy Council in 1930, this case has long symbolized the subordinate role of women in Canadian politics. Internationally the pattern of discrimination is much the same. The first female prime minister in the world was Sirimavo Bandaranaike of Ceylon (now known as Sri Lanka), elected in 1960.

Recognition of and desire to change such an overt pattern of discrimination against women in political life is the basis of the feminist perspective. A starting point for all feminist analysis is the rejection of **patriarchy**, defined as a *"political system characterized by institutionalized male dominance, in which men are dominant in all state institutions and favoured by the balance of power in other important social institutions"* (Vickers, 1997: 13). Feminism seeks to account for the development of this pattern of male domination, to describe its current operation, to explain how and why it should be altered, and to bring about the needed political reforms. As such, feminism seeks not only to change our understanding of how political processes operate, but to actually change the way those political processes will operate in the future. Moreover, feminism argues that the way we analyze the polity must be altered as well, whether we are investigating international relations (Keeble and Smith, 1999), interest group activity (Dobrowolsky, 2000), or public policy (Mazur, 1999). What Francis Fukuyama (1999: 36) said of international relations is also true of domestic politics: once one views it "through the lens of sex and biology, it never looks the same again." From a feminist perspective, the way a polity would operate under female leadership would differ dramatically from the traditional patriarchal polity.

The above consideration of five ideologically based views of politics (conservative, liberal, revolutionary, social democratic, and feminist) should amply demonstrate the array and complexity of such definitions. While numerous other perspectives are possible, these five illustrate that definitions of politics vary with respect to their images of politics (whether it is a positive or negative activity; whether it is gender-based), to the scope of politics (conservative and liberal approaches define politics more narrowly than Marxism or democratic socialism), to the type of political change allowed or desired (a conservative defends the existing order; a liberal favours change on an incremental basis; a revolutionary argues for radical change in the existing order; a democratic socialist argues for radical change by democratic means), and finally, to the relationship between the economic and political spheres (liberals and conservatives assert the dominance of politics over economics, while Marxists and democratic socialists argue the contrary position). Whatever their nature, however, all such ideological definitions of politics deal with the crucial problem of establishing order for the political community, which means that they must deal with the key concepts of power and influence.

BASIC CONCEPTS OF POLITICAL ANALYSIS

Power and influence

If politics is the exercise of power and influence concerning the establishment, maintenance, and breakdown of order in the community, then power and influence are two essential concepts that must be defined as precisely as possible. Power and influence share several attributes. First, both concepts deal exclusively with human behaviour and human relationships. If a dog chased a cat up a tree, we would not say that the cat had been influenced by the dog (scared perhaps, but not influenced). However, if one person's behaviour is modified or changed as a result of another person's behaviour, then we can speak of influence or power.

Not only are these important concepts particular to humanity, but more significantly they can result only from a relationship or pattern of behaviour. In other words, for power or influence to exist, there must be a relationship involving interaction between two or more people. If there is no such interaction, there is no relationship, and hence influence or power cannot be exercised. For example, if after attending a political rally and listening to a speech by a political candidate, a person decides to vote for that candidate, then we can say that the candidate has influenced how that person would vote. However, if another person attended the same rally and listened to the same candidate, but had already decided to vote for the candidate, then no influence was exercised. Although power and influence are based on human relationships between two or more people, such interaction need not be direct or on a face-to-face basis. A voter may watch a political advertisement on television for a particular candidate and decide to vote on that basis. In such a case, the interaction or relationship is indirect, but influence has still been exercised.

In emphasizing that power and influence are evident in the pattern of human interactions, we are also implying a second common attribute of both concepts, namely, the idea of causation. We cannot directly observe power and influence, but we can assess their presence in light of events. For example, we can say voters were influenced by a candidate if, after a rally, they vote differently than they would have otherwise. Likewise, politicians are judged to be powerful or not on the basis of their ability to influence or direct people's actions. A prime minister is seen as more powerful and influential than an ordinary citizen because a prime minister can make cabinet appointments, can participate in the legislative process, and can change the direction of public policy. In other words, power and influence are not directly observable, but the results of power and influence are.

In saying that power and influence deal with causal relationships, we are also asserting that they are exercised before the change of behaviour is observed. For Factor A to cause Event B, it must occur prior to Event B: causation is thus antecedent to its behavioural result. In our previous illustration, a speech by a candidate was deemed to have influenced the behaviour of the voter because it occurred before the voter had decided how to vote; in the other example, the candidate's speech did not influence the individual's voting intention because it was presented after the voter had already made a decision on how to vote.

A third characteristic of power and influence is that they may be specifically political. Power and influence are political when they affect the operation of the wider community or society, which thus distinguishes political power and influence from other forms, such as religious influence or economic power. For example, a minister who changes an atheist into a regular churchgoer may have exercised religious influence, but few would say the minister had also exercised political influence. However, if a preacher delivers a sermon on the evils of capital punishment to a congregation which includes a politician, and that politician, because of that sermon, introduces a bill to outlaw capital punishment, then the preacher has exercised political influence. In this example, political influence has not been exercised simply because the person affected was a politician, but because the bill to abolish capital punishment is an action that affects the decision-making structure and concerns of society. For similar reasons, patterns of influence and power within the family are not normally considered political in form. Given these considerations, we can say that political power and influence are concepts that describe human relationships that are causal in nature and public in their import.

Although political power and influence share several attributes, these concepts describe somewhat different aspects of human interaction. Generally speaking, influence is the broader term, with power seen as a specific type of influence. People exercise **influence** when they *change another person's attitudes or behaviour.* Individuals have been influenced when their attitudes or behaviour have been modified from what they would otherwise have been. In our previous example, a candidate influenced a voter as a result of a speech because the voter's later behaviour was modified. **Power**, likewise, *represents a change in a person's behaviour, but for a different reason: namely, the use of sanctions.* For example, if a candidate says to an elector, vote for me or you will lose your job, and the elector votes for the candidate because of the promised sanction, then the candidate has exercised power over the elector. Sanctions are usually more effective as threats than as actual behaviour. People over whom power is being exercised must, however, believe that the threat will be subsequently carried out if their behaviour is not modified.

Political resources

Having delineated the basic meaning of influence and power, our next concern is with what makes an individual or group influential. People are influential to the extent that they both control political resources and are willing to exercise the control necessary to translate potential influence into actual influence. Although political resources may vary from one political system to another and from one historical period to the next, the following definition should adequately illustrate the nature of **political resources**:

> A political resource is a means by which one person can influence the behaviour of other persons. Political resources therefore include money, information, food, the threat of force, jobs, friendship, social standing, the right to make laws, votes, as well as a great variety of other things (Dahl, 1984: 31).

The transformation of political resources into political influence is at least a two-stage process: first, a person must have control of resources, either directly, such as by being personally wealthy, or indirectly, such as by having wealthy political supporters; second, a person must have the willingness and ability to translate control of resources into actual influence. For example, wealth does not, in and of itself, generate political influence. A few people are able to translate wealth into power and influence, as the political success of Pierre Trudeau in Canada and John F. Kennedy in the United States demonstrates. But many wealthy individuals abstain from political activity or involvement.

Other individuals may try to convert wealth into power and influence, but may lack the necessary skills and expertise to effect the transformation successfully. An illustration of this point would be the 1992 and 1996 American presidential campaigns of Ross Perot. Even though he won 19 and 8 percent of the popular vote, respectively, Ross Perot received no votes in the electoral college in either campaign, even in 1992 after spending $73 million of his own money. Similarly, Steve Forbes, in contesting for the Republican presidential nomination in 1996 and 2000, spent approximately $70 million of his own money — in both cases he was quickly eliminated from the process. Wealth in no way guarantees political success, although it certainly can facilitate one's climb up the political opportunity structure. Thus, combined with political skills, political resources such as wealth and time are the tools needed for obtaining political influence.

Political authority

Given the fact that in all political systems the control of political resources is unequally distributed and that various political actors differ in their willingness and ability to translate their potential for influence into actual influence, all political systems end up with some people and groups having more influence and power than others. If political influence is unequally allocated, the question becomes one of explaining why people accept such a pattern. A differential distribution of influence is permissible as long as it is seen as legitimate, and as long as it is accepted by the people as a justifiable, if not a preferred, state of affairs. *When an individual's influence is perceived as legitimate,* it is usually referred to as **authority**.

Numerous ways of legitimating influence have been used historically, including racial, religious, and ethnic bases. Perhaps the best known classification of the means for legitimating influence is Max Weber's typology of traditional, legal-rational, and charismatic modes of authority (Gerth and Mills, 1958: 294–301).

The **traditional basis of authority** is a justification of influence which claims that the simple fact that things have been done a certain way in the past is reason enough that they should be continued in the same manner in the future. An example of a traditional basis of authority is the existence of a monarch as head of state, typified by the Queen in Britain and Canada.

> Tradition means giving votes to the most obscure of all classes — our ancestors. It is the democracy of the dead. Tradition refuses to submit to the small and arrogant oligarchy of those who merely happen to be walking around (G.K. Chesterton, quoted in Lapham, 1995: 151).

In contrast, the **legal-rational basis of authority** asserts that a distribution of influence is accepted because certain procedures or "rules of the game" have been followed in acquiring it. For example, if a political party in a parliamentary system wins an election by gaining a majority of seats in the legislature, it is accepted as the legitimate government with the right to run the country until the next election campaign. In a legal-rational system of authority, individuals do not necessarily like the result, in that they may have voted for a different party in the election. However, the results of the election are accepted as granting legitimacy to the winning party because certain well-established procedures were followed. One accepts the authority of a Jean Chrétien or a Kim Campbell because he or she occupies the office of Prime Minister of Canada. Authority resides with the office (i.e., prime minister, premier, mayor, president, senator) and not with the individual who happens to occupy that office at any particular time.

Weber's third basis of authority is what he labelled charisma or "gift of grace." **Charismatic authority** refers to rule over people in which *"the governed submit because of their belief in the extraordinary quality of the specific person"* (Gerth and Mills, 1958: 295). The individual leader is seen as being more than human, of having powers and capabilities well beyond those of most mortals. Historical examples would likely include Christ, Hitler, and Gandhi.

Unfortunately, the concept of charisma has become less useful in political analysis in recent decades since it has become overused, particularly in journalism.

> Charisma without substance is a dangerous thing (1986 comment by future Canadian prime minister Kim Campbell).

Popularity, in terms of winning elections, is often equated with charisma; in political analysis, the two are not necessarily synonymous. Jean Chrétien did not become a charismatic figure just because he won three consecutive majority election victories (1993, 1997, and 2000). Typically, democratic political systems such as those of Canada, the United States, and Britain are more often characterized by leaders who lack, rather than exemplify, charismatic qualities.

While political systems vary in the emphasis given to each method of legitimating authority, these three bases are usually present, in differing degrees, in any particular political system. As a general comparison, legal-rational authority predominates as the basic mode of legitimation in Canada, Britain, and the United States; charismatic authority is only rarely present; traditional authority is primarily used to reinforce legal-rational authority, especially in Britain and Canada.

For example, although the prime minister of Canada prepares the Speech from the Throne, it is read and presented by the governor general. Similarly, although the governor general may have no alternative but to ask the leader of the party with a majority of seats in the legislature to form a government, no government is formed until the governor general so acts. Even though such actions are symbolic, they nevertheless reinforce the legitimacy of those who have acquired political influence on a legal-rational basis. An important form of traditional authority in Canada, which is often overlooked, is the role that custom and convention play in the operation of the political system (e.g., that a member of the Canadian cabinet is expected to also be a member of the House of Commons). Many key aspects of Canadian politics are based on "the practice," that is, on tradition. As a result, traditional authority is a significant, if secondary, base of political influence.

Even in the United States, where legal-rational authority prevails, there are elements of traditional authority. For example, the 160-year dominance of the Republican and Democratic parties has established a "tradition" against new parties or third parties in presidential election campaigns, illustrated by John Anderson's dismal failure in the 1980 contest, Ross Perot's lack of electoral college votes in both 1992 and 1996, and Ralph Nader's unsuccessful campaigns for the Green Party in 1996 and 2000. Traditional authority is probably the strongest, among our three countries of comparison, in Britain, best typified perhaps by the longstanding deference toward political authority and political institutions such as the monarchy, even if it has become somewhat attenuated by the 21st century. Custom and convention play a significant role in the operation of the British political system, because Britain lacks a comprehensive, written constitution, preferring instead to rely on traditional modes of behaviour. As these examples illustrate, each political system is a mixture or combination of the various bases of authority, and the strength of the differing bases of legitimation changes from one political system to the next.

If political systems seek to legitimate their distribution of influence through traditional, legal-rational, or charismatic means, then one can properly ask that basic question of political analysis: why? The answer is relatively straightforward: "Authority is a highly efficient form of influence. It is not only more reliable and durable than naked coercion, but it also enables a ruler to govern with a minimum of political resources" (Dahl, 1984: 54). No political system which rested on the sole use of sanctions and coercion to maintain a particular pattern of influence could long endure. People are taught to obey, to accept the legitimacy of particular political institutions and political processes, thus making coercion unnecessary: the "vast majority of men have the habit of law-abidingness" (MacIver, 1965: 58).

When a particular distribution of influence loses its legitimacy, assuming it was accepted as legitimate in the first place, and when a new distribution of influence is sought, then coercion and violence may become important aspects of the political process. Both those who wish to continue the existing arrangements and those seeking a new pattern of influence may turn to coercion and violence to accomplish their ends. Events in South Africa and the former Soviet Union in the 1990s offer excellent illustrations of such a pattern. No political system is immune from such a development: "In politics we are always living on volcanic soil. We must be prepared for abrupt convulsions and eruptions" (Cassirer, 1946: 280).

Political violence

While all kinds of political systems must continually face the possibility of the occurrence of political violence in their domestic politics, democratic and totalitarian polities differ in their use and control of coercion. Democratic political systems seek to eliminate political violence from their normal political processes, while authoritarian and totalitarian systems often use political violence as a means of state control (Sederberg, 1994: 11–35).

Examples of political violence are not hard to find: assassinations of political leaders like John F. Kennedy, Robert Kennedy, Martin Luther King, Jr., Yitzhak Rabin, and Indira Gandhi; terrorist acts against individuals or governmental representatives, including bombings such as of the World Trade Center in New York (in 1993 and its later destruction on September 11, 2001) or the killing of diplomatic personnel; and excessive use of government force, ranging from the abuse of police powers to the use of pepper spray to quell demonstrations against government policies. Given these examples of political violence, we can define **political violence** as *violence related to government and politics whose aim is to alter the pattern and results of the political process by non-legitimate means.*

> Governments have practiced political terror for thousands of years. Although its use varies with a given regime's capacity and willingness to employ it, it is safe to assume that any system and any people may experience political terror (Dallin and Breslauer, 1970: 9).

From a comparative perspective, the use of political violence in democratic systems is rare, although it does occur more often than many people realize. While it may appear both harmless and humorous, the attack (a cream pie in the face) on August 16, 2000 on Prime Minister Jean Chrétien is an example of the use of political violence. In Canada, the willingness of the FLQ in the late 1960s to use violence (bombings, kidnappings, and murder) to overthrow the existing political system led to the October Crisis of 1970 and to the use of coercion by the government (the War Measures Act) to stop the apprehended insurrection. When Deputy Premier of Quebec Pierre Laporte was kidnapped and murdered, the government responded by imposing the War Measures Act, suspending political and civil liberties, and arresting hundreds of suspected FLQ supporters and throwing them in jail. Ominously, the death of Pierre Trudeau on September 28, 2000 and the approaching 30-year anniversary of the 1970 October Crisis saw a pattern of renewed violence in Quebec. A terrorist group calling itself the Brigade d'Autodéfense du Francais claimed responsibility in early October 2000 for bombing three Montreal Second Cup coffee shops, presumably because of their English-only business name. Later in October, Rhéal Mathieu, who had served a seven-year prison sentence for his part in the FLQ's terrorist campaign in the 1960s and 1970s, was charged with the fire bombings. Threats were also received concerning possible attacks on former prime minister Pierre Trudeau's grave. Similarly, Britain's continuing problems in dealing with the conflict in Northern Ireland show that no system can entirely avoid the use of political violence. For example, the IRA claimed responsibility for bombing the hotel in Brighton, England where the Conservatives were holding their annual meeting in October 1984. Prime Minister Margaret Thatcher, as well as most of her cabinet, narrowly missed being killed.

In democratic systems, the use of political violence is considered to be outside the parameters of political legitimacy, while such is not the case in authoritarian and totalitarian systems. An obvious use of political violence is that of Nazi Germany and the Holocaust, especially the role of the concentration camps (Sofsky, 1999). Currently, the crackdown by the Communist Chinese government against religious dissidents, such as the Falun Gong sect, is an example of state-directed political violence. Moreover, in March of 2001 Amnesty International reported that during the 1990s China had executed over 18 000 prisoners, including political prisoners and dissidents. The use of political terror in communist political systems, such as the Soviet Union, to gain, maintain, and exercise power has been well documented (Dallin and Breslauer, 1970; Courtois et al., 1999).

> Lenin was literate. Stalin was literate, so was Hitler. As for Mao Zedong, he even wrote verse. What all these men had in common, though, was that their hit list was longer than their reading list (Joseph Brodsky, Nobel laureate).

The basic cause of political violence is an individual's or group's rejection of a political regime's structure, personnel, or policy, such that they refuse to accept the regime's political legitimacy and can thus justify the use of extreme measures to facilitate the process of political change (Sederberg, 1994). Justifications for political violence may be based on a political ideology, such as Marxism-Leninism, on a racial or religious perspective, such as the Nazi attack on and attempt to eliminate Jews, or on a nationalist base, which may lead secessionist movements, such as the Basques in Spain, to adopt a policy of violence (von der Mehden, 1973: 7–16). Whatever the cause, all political systems must be ready to confront and to control the use of political violence. Thus, political violence is an important, even if often unrecognized, aspect of the political process.

> What should by now be clear is that while assassination has generally failed to *direct* political change into predetermined channels, it has repeatedly demonstrated the capacity for affecting, often in the most drastic fashion, situations which, in the absence of lethal violence, might conceivably have developed very differently (Ford, 1985: 381).

BASIC PRINCIPLES OF POLITICAL ANALYSIS

The concepts of political influence, power, authority, and resources are the basic building blocks of political analysis. However, they only provide a starting place, not our final destination. In using these basic concepts, we must also be familiar with a number of more general items, what we have called basic principles of political analysis. Each of these five basic principles focusses on how we study and analyze political phenomena.

Principle one: political theory versus political practice

In the sphere of politics, considerable distance separates the practices or reality of the political process from the way that process was designed to operate. The political analyst is particularly concerned with the discrepancy between intent and practice.

A classic example of the difference between theory and practice concerns the respective roles of the governor general and prime minister in the Canadian system. While the Constitution Act of 1867 contains an extensive description of the duties of the governor general, no mention is made of the prime minister. However, no political analyst would seriously argue, as a result, that the governor general is more influential and powerful than the prime minister. To assume that the governor general's role is the same as that described in the 1867 Constitution Act would give one a totally fallacious perspective of the political influence of Canada's formal executive (Dawson, 1970: 59).

An analogous argument could be made about the respective powers of the monarch and prime minister in British politics: the monarch reigns, the prime minister governs. What has happened is that the political executive in both Canada and Britain has followed "the technique of the hermit crab, the crustacean that destroys a mollusk in order to set up housekeeping in its shell. The outer appearance is scarcely altered but the interior is completely changed" (Duverger, 1974: 51–52). In other words, the governor general has retained some of the trappings of power in the Canadian system, while the prime minister has acquired its substance.

Any political system provides numerous instances of the differences between theory and practice. In the United States, for example, the Vietnam War created a major constitutional debate over which branch of government (executive or legislative) had the right to commit American power and prestige to a foreign conflict. Although the United States Constitution is explicit in granting Congress the power to "declare war" (Article I, Section 8), in practice the president, as Commander in Chief of the armed forces, can commit troops or take other actions to involve the United States in a war. In passing the War Powers Resolution in 1973, Congress attempted to reconcile this conflict by asserting its own power to limit a president's authority to send troops abroad. However, as a result of a 1983 American Supreme Court decision, the legislative prerogative to declare war in current circumstances is largely a formality.

Similar examples of the differences between theory and practice are evident in other countries as well. In theory, the former Soviet Union was a federal political structure; in practice, it was more unitary than federal. What these examples show is the importance in political analysis of recognizing the difference between how a political system was theoretically designed to operate and how it works in fact. The political analyst usually begins with a consideration of intent and concludes with a focus on actual political practice.

Principle two: political custom and convention

The emphasis on actual political practices brings us to our second principle of political analysis, which stresses the role of custom in any political system. In many respects, this principle is an outgrowth of Oakeshott's argument that politics in any country represents a "tradition of behaviour." Some of that tradition may be embodied in law; much of it, however, reposes in the custom of the polity. **Political custom** and convention fill in the interstices of the political structure, turning abstract principles into working institutions. For example, if a constitution provides a structural skeleton for the political system, custom and convention flesh out the body politic.

In Canada, the role of custom and convention is particularly significant. Many of the most important aspects of the Canadian Constitution are not written down. For example, the notion of responsible government, that a government must have the support and confidence of the House of Commons in order to remain in power, is based on political tradition, not law. The need for a cabinet minister either to have a seat in the House of Commons or to be appointed to the Senate is similarly undefined. Custom requires ministers to seek a seat at the earliest reasonable opportunity, but if they lose in the first election bid, they can remain in the cabinet and try again later. The composition of the cabinet is likewise based on custom. The working of the representation principle, that all provinces and major groups, whenever possible, be given cabinet portfolios, which has been the basis of cabinet selection since John A. Macdonald, has become a "rigid convention" of the Canadian political process (Matheson, 1976: 27).

Custom and convention may even modify those aspects of the political process which have been defined in law. For example, the legal right of the federal government to disallow any piece of provincial legislation within one year of its passage has been greatly restricted in actual practice. The last time a provincial act was disallowed was 1943. The federal government, because of the convention of only considering disallowance if the provincial legislation usurps federal jurisdiction or powers, has allowed its legal power to fall into disuse. The legal basis for disallowance remains; the political will to exercise it has been circumscribed by custom.

In some cases, a specific custom or convention may be recognized as so important that it is later incorporated into law. For example, until 1940 in the United States no individual had ever served for more than two terms as president of the United States. However, when Democrat Franklin D. Roosevelt broke this tradition with his four presidential victories (1932, 1936, 1940, and 1944), the Republicans, when they won control of Congress, secured the Twenty-Second Amendment to the American Constitution, which limited all future presidents to two terms. Thus did a 150-year-old custom become law in 1951.

Although custom and convention fill in the details of a political structure, too heavy a reliance on tradition can create some difficult political conflicts. If everyone, or at least all major political actors, is agreed on what the convention is and how it operates, few problems arise. However, when there are differing interpretations of a political custom, controversy may result. A good example of this point is the Canadian Constitutional Crisis of 1968: a Liberal government, defeated on a tax measure, refused to resign, claiming that its defeat did not constitute a motion of non-confidence. So much for the convention that a defeat of a government's money bill constitutes a defeat of the government itself.

Custom and convention pervade all aspects of the political process, as the polity accommodates itself to its political environment. Custom and convention, then, flesh out the workings of the body politic. In particular, custom and convention are adaptive mechanisms for reconciling the political structure to evolving circumstances. As such, they point to the importance of our third principle of political analysis — namely, the significance of political change.

Principle three: time and political change

Time is probably the most overlooked element in political analysis. More often than not political analysis has ignored the historical dimension, concentrating instead on the problems of the present. However, "without knowledge of the details and patterns of the past, a student of politics is like a man without a memory" (McNaught, 1983: 89). The political patterns of the present are the children and grandchildren of the political battles of the past. One cannot adequately understand the present polity without some understanding of how we got here.

Every major issue facing the Canadian system has been influenced by how that issue was dealt with previously. For example, the desire by the Mulroney government in 1984 to move toward freer trade with the United States reflected past historical battles. Previously, the support of free trade, then known as reciprocity, had led to the defeat of governments in general elections (e.g., the Liberals in the 1911 federal election). Thus, the Conservatives in 1984–1985 initially spoke neither of reciprocity nor of free trade, but instead chose the term freer trade, hoping to rid themselves of some of the historical legacies of the other concepts. Likewise, Canadian-American relations must be seen in an historical context, otherwise more current problems may appear to be unintelligible. Similarly, the way particular political institutions, such as Parliament, have evolved can only be appreciated in their historical context.

Time, then, is the context of history, which provides the setting for the drama of politics. Time is also involved in the process of political change for the simple reason that birth is highly correlated with death: no political leader can last forever (not even those, like Mackenzie King, with extensive contacts in the spirit world). For example, the tension during the 1990s between Prime Minister Jean Chrétien and his Minister of Finance, Paul Martin, Jr., is a case in point. The longer the prime minister stayed as leader of the Liberal party, especially in seeking a third electoral mandate, the more difficult it would be for Paul Martin, Jr., because of his advancing age, to become his successor.

> The important thing in politics is timing — and the greatest thing in timing is luck (Pierre Elliott Trudeau, 1988).

Time is also a direct influence on the polity because many basic political events are conditioned by when they occur. For example, the timing of a budget, a cabinet shuffle, or an election call can have an important bearing on the distribution of influence in a political system. While our analysis will centre on present political practices in Canada, Britain, and the United States, we will attempt to show how these current patterns have evolved historically.

Principle four: legal versus political decisions

Our fourth principle of political analysis focusses on the differences between a legal decision or action and a political decision or action. We use "legal" in the sense of pertaining to the law: a **legal decision** is *one based on the law and constitution, or one that is assumed to be consistent with the law*, even though it may not be specifically dealt with in a particular statute. A **political decision** is *one based on considerations of influence and power*. While we would expect that political decisions would also be legal ones, especially in democratic systems, such a congruence need not be the case. The legitimacy of government is certainly enhanced when legal and political decisions mesh, and undercut when they do not.

The difference between a legal and a political decision is well illustrated by the federal government's reaction to the introduction of Bill 101 by the Parti Québécois (PQ) and its passage by the National Assembly after the PQ's 1976 provincial election victory. There was no doubt that certain aspects of Bill 101, which moved Quebec toward being a unilingual province, infringed on the language rights guaranteed by the British North America Act of 1867 (now the Constitution Act of 1867). In particular, Section 133 of the Constitution, which gave protection to both the English and French languages in the Quebec provincial legislature and the federal and provincial courts in Quebec, was explicitly disregarded by Bill 101, as subsequent court rulings made clear. Why then did the Quebec government pass the legislation in the first place and why did the federal government, in response, not disallow such a measure? The answer to both questions should be obvious: the provincial and federal governments were making political, not legal, decisions.

Having won their first provincial victory on a "nationalist" program designed to protect the French language and culture in Quebec, the Parti Québécois had little to lose and much to gain by being seen as the only political party with the will to take strong action to protect French interests in the province. With 80 percent of the population French-speaking, being in favour of the linguistic rights for that sector could only be politically rewarding, particularly in light of the party's 41 percent popular vote in the recent provincial election. An emotive issue like language rights was being used to appeal to those members of the public who had not voted for the party in 1976. Moreover, vigorous action in promotion of the French language undercut the political base of the opposition parties, particularly the Liberals, who were labelled by the government as the party defending English interests in Quebec. No party could survive such an image, since it would be impossible to win power in any future election on the basis of the English sector alone. Thus, certain provisions of Bill 101 were known in advance to be contrary to Section 133 of the British North America Act — a fact that did nothing to deter the provincial government's passage of the legislation. The possibility of Bill 101 being disallowed by the federal government was also a political plus for the Parti Québécois: such a move by Ottawa could then be seen as further proof that the French culture would survive only through independence.

The federal government's response to Bill 101 was political, rather than legal, in form. Even though Prime Minister Trudeau repeatedly condemned the legislation, Ottawa decided not to use its power of disallowance against Bill 101, because of the political repercussions such an action might precipitate in Quebec. The federal Liberals took a legal hands-off attitude, while at the same time encouraging private groups and individuals to challenge the legislation in the courts. It must also be remembered that the Liberal party was in a majority position in the national legislature in 1976, making it most unlikely that their stance on this issue could bring about their defeat. Furthermore, the Liberal party's dominance in national politics resided in their Quebec stronghold. No federal party based in Quebec could use the power of disallowance against their "home" province on a piece of legislation designed to protect the French language and culture in Quebec. Hence, for political reasons, the federal Liberal party did not invoke the disallowance power against Bill 101: legally it could have done so, but the political judgment was contrary, and it prevailed.

Many events in the political process can be understood only if the distinction between legal and political actions is kept in mind. For example, the formal executive in Canada, the governor general, has the legal basis for refusing a request coming from the prime minister for a dissolution of Parliament. Politically, however, such an action by the governor general is unlikely, except in the most extreme circumstances. Such an argument could be made about other aspects of the formal executive's role in Canada as well: as one writer asserted, the governor general is "a legal survivor who has contrived to remain a political necessity" (Dawson, 1970: 143).

While the governor general's role illustrates the pattern of having a legal basis for decisions, even though such action is rarely taken for political reasons, governments also find that political decisions are made without having a legal foundation for them. For example, considerable evidence presented to the McDonald Royal Commission on RCMP Activities showed that political actions which had been taken during the 1970s had been clearly illegal. The most notorious situation involved the burning down of a barn in Quebec so that a group of political radicals could not hold their meeting. One wonders whether the old Forum arena in Montreal might also have been torched if the radicals had decided to meet at a hockey game. Other actions were also clearly illegal, but seen as politically necessary, as when the computer tapes containing the membership files of the Parti Québécois were stolen, copied, and then returned.

If too many such examples come to light, they might undercut the legitimacy of the government. As a result, governments may make legal those decisions they consider to be politically necessary. The federal government's move in the mid-1970s to provide a legal basis for wiretapping is a case in point. Similarly, in response to the RCMP wrongdoings revealed before the McDonald Royal Commission in the late 1970s, both major parties, when in office, took the view that the way to handle the situation was to make whatever the RCMP was doing legal in the future.

Even if political actions are challenged in court and ruled illegal, the government can always call the legislature into session and, in most cases, pass what is known as retroactive legislation. **Retroactive legislation** can be defined as *legislation that changes the law as it was in a previous time period*. Such legislation may change the law so that previously illegal actions are declared legal after they have occurred — a convenient weapon in the arsenal of government power. A citizen may also find that a previously legal action can be declared illegal by the government, with penalties imposed retroactively. For example, with the imposition of the War Measures Act in 1970, it became a crime, retroactively, to have ever been a member of the FLQ, even though being an FLQ member in the 1960s was not illegal (Stewart, 1971: 59)! Such examples demonstrate the importance of our fourth principle of political analysis.

Principle five: political structures and political functions

Our final principle of political analysis looks at the difference between political structures and political functions. A **political structure**, such as the House of Commons or the cabinet, is composed of *a set of political roles or expected patterns of behaviour.* No matter which party or individual happens to fill these roles, certain behavioural patterns can be discerned. For example, the House of Commons will be presided over by the Speaker or deputy Speaker, the government will sit on the Speaker's right-hand side and the opposition on his or her left, and legislation will be passed after proceeding through First, Second, and Third Readings. In other words, the House of Commons is a structure composed of regular and recurrent patterns of action. Political analysis usually begins with a look at political structures, presenting a description of the framework or institutional context of the political process.

Political functions refer to *the consequences or results of the various political structures: the jobs or tasks the structures perform for the political system.* To describe the structure of the Canadian cabinet, a political analyst would discuss its size, how its members are selected, how it arrives at decisions, and how it is internally composed of various cabinet committees. In describing the function of the Canadian cabinet, the political analyst would look at its effects on the political process in terms of a policy-making function (i.e., it is the primary policy-making institution) and possibly a representation-symbolic function (i.e., it represents the various groups in the Canadian parliamentary system).

Any political structure can perform one or more political functions, and any political function can be carried out by one or more political structures. A structure such as a political party provides several functions, including the recruitment of candidates to run for office, the organization of the electorate around certain policies and programs, and, if it wins the election, the provision of people to occupy the top political positions in the country. An example of a function being performed by several structures would be the policy-making function, exercised by the cabinet, the Prime Minister's Office, and the civil service. Thus, in political analysis we must distinguish between structures and functions and deal with both topics in examining any particular political system.

The above five principles of political analysis, as well as the basic concepts, will serve as our guide in investigating the political process in Canada, Britain, and the United States. These principles and concepts reflect a combination of the various ways through which we study political phenomena, as well as providing the basis for our comparative political analysis of these three democratic polities.

A COMPARATIVE PERSPECTIVE ON CANADIAN GOVERNMENT

In analyzing the nature of government and politics, we have suggested the need for viewing any particular political system from a comparative perspective. Such a view implies that there is something distinctive about both the subfield of comparative politics and its method of analysis. At its most basic level, comparative politics is focussed, obviously, on politics in two or more countries. Comparative politics analyzes political phenomena in several countries as a way of describing and explaining the nature of the political process. Hence, **comparative political analysis** refers to *the method used in making such comparative descriptions and explanations.*

The importance of bringing just such a comparative focus to the study of Canadian government can be justified on several grounds. First, people's political experience, both historical and contemporary, has produced an array of possible political systems. Only a comparative approach can begin to introduce students to this diversity of political institutions and processes. Second, in learning about other political systems, students can overcome the parochialism of their own limited political experience. Few people directly experience different forms of government. Knowledge of alternative political arrangements can thus broaden one's intellectual perspective. Third, the increasingly complex interdependence of nations means that it has become impossible to isolate domestic from foreign politics. Other political systems directly affect the internal politics of Canada. For example, it would be extremely difficult to make a precise demarcation between domestic and foreign politics when analyzing the Canada – U.S. Free Trade Agreement or the North American Free Trade Agreement (NAFTA) between Canada, the United States, and Mexico.

In addition to recognizing the diversity of political experience, overcoming the parochialism of a single system focus, and emphasizing the interdependence of political systems, a comparative approach to politics seeks to develop generalizations or hypotheses that explain the similarities and differences among political systems. It is this search for similarities and differences between political systems, and an explanation of such patterns, which has been described as the "highest objective of comparative analysis" (Scarrow, 1969: 8). However, before explanations can be developed, one must start with description, that is, a knowledge of what exists. After an understanding of the workings of several particular political systems has been developed, the student can then begin to focus on the explanation of important patterns of political phenomena.

The reasons for utilizing a comparative approach in studying any particular political system are as applicable to Canada as to any other country. For example, the decade of the 1970s saw the beginning of a much-needed focus among Canadian political scientists on an analysis of our own political system. However, as a consequence, an older tradition has been downplayed, if not entirely forgotten: that is, the explicit, comparative analysis of Canadian politics (Bryce, 1921; Corry, 1947; Brady, 1947). A comparative perspective is an aid, not a hindrance or substitute, for understanding the Canadian political experiment. Similarly, the interdependence of the modern world has particularly affected Canada. It is often forgotten that Canada is the only country in the world that bordered on both superpowers during the Cold War. Likewise, Canada's economic interdependence with other countries, particularly with the United States, is extensive.

A comparative approach is also useful because Canada's polity embodies an interesting combination of political principles. For example, in 1867 Canada was the first political system to counterpose federal and parliamentary institutions within a single government. As a result, Canada provides an interesting case study for comparing these principles with other possible variations. To date, however, the Canadian political system has often been neglected within the field of comparative politics.

Although we have argued for the need to compare Canada with other political systems, we have not yet justified the selection of countries to be used in our comparative analysis. While other political systems may be utilized on specific points, most comparisons will centre on Britain and the United States. Our choice is based on both historical and theoretical criteria. Historically, Britain and the United States have exercised the greatest impact on the evolution, development, and structure of the Canadian polity. In fact, Canada is often viewed as a mix of the political principles and practices of these two countries. Until World War II, Britain was the dominant influence on Canada, a position since relinquished to the United States in both domestic and foreign affairs. Both political systems have been important influences on Canadian politics.

> In the development of its political institutions Canada has been, placed as it is between the United States and Britain, more like the ham in the sandwich than the link between the two. Our political structure and processes are based on the examples of both other countries (Franks, 1983: 201).

SUMMARY

1. The nature of government can be described by six attributes: government is ubiquitous, multiple, necessary, varied, democratized, and globalized. Each of these characteristics points to a significant element of government in the modern era.

2. Classifications of different types of government can focus on broad comparisons — such as the typology of autocratic, democratic, and totalitarian systems — or on a more limited criterion — such as the differences between federal and unitary or presidential and parliamentary systems.

3. The Canadian polity is democratic, federal, and parliamentary. Britain is democratic, unitary, and parliamentary. The United States is democratic, federal, and presidential. Such classifications are an important tool in comparing the various institutions and processes of a polity.

4. Politics can be defined as the exercise of power and influence on matters that affect the community, while political analysis is the attempt to explain why a specific pattern of power and influence emerges, how power is gained and lost, and why certain political events occur.

5. Politics can be defined in numerous ways, with normative approaches stressing "what ought to be" and empirical ones focussing on "what is." Politics can also be defined in ideological terms, with a conservative definition seeing "politics as tradition," a liberal one viewing "politics as conciliation," a revolutionary perspective, such as Marxism, perceiving "politics as superstructure," and democratic socialism seeing politics as radical reform through the democratic process. Feminism stresses the role of women in the political process and argues that traditional political science fails to understand a female perspective with respect to power and influence.

6. Political power and influence are concepts that describe human relationships that are causal in nature and public in their import. People exercise influence when they change other people's attitudes or behaviour, and they exercise power when such changes are accomplished by the use of sanctions, real or apprehended. Authority is legitimate influence and can be based on tradition, charisma, or legal-rational norms. Political violence occurs when there is a breakdown in the existing pattern of political authority.

7. In analyzing politics, five principles should be kept in mind: first, the difference between political theory and political practice; second, the importance of political custom and convention; third, the historical dimension and political change; fourth, the difference between legal and political decisions; and fifth, the difference between political structures and political functions.

8. Comparative political analysis, which is based on a consideration of politics in two or more countries, helps to overcome the parochialism of only dealing with one's own country, while at the same time it aids in a recognition of the strengths and weaknesses of various kinds of political institutions and political systems.

CONCEPT FILE

authority
autocratic government
charismatic authority
checks and balances
comparative political analysis
confederal government
conservative ideology
democracy
democratic socialism
democratization
empirical definition of politics
equality of condition
equality of opportunity

federal government
federalism
feminism
formal executive
fusion of powers
globalization
godfather function of politics
government
ideology
influence
legal decision
legal-rational authority
liberal-democracy

liberal ideology
Marxist ideology
normative definition of politics
parliamentary system
patriarchy
political analysis
political authority
political customs
political decision
political executive
political function
political resource
political structure
political system

political violence
politics
polity
power
presidential system
republican government
reformist ideology
retroactive legislation
revolutionary ideology
separation of powers
traditional authority
totalitarian government
unitary government

RECOMMENDED READINGS

The Nature of Government

BARBER, BENJAMIN R. (2000) "Can Democracy Survive Globalization?" *Government and Opposition*, Volume 35, Number 3, pp. 275–301.

CERNY, PHILIP G. (1999) "Globalization and the Erosion of Democracy," *European Journal of Political Research*, Volume 36, Number 1, pp. 1–26.

CHIROT, DANIEL (1994) *Modern Tyrants: The Power and Prevalence of Evil in Our Age.* Princeton, New Jersey: Princeton University Press.

COURTOIS, STÉPHANE et al. (1999) *The Black Book of Communism: Crimes, Terror, Repression.* Cambridge, Mass.: Harvard University Press, translated by Jonathan Murphy and Mark Kramer.

CRICK, BERNARD (1973) *Basic Forms of Government: A Sketch and a Model.* London: Macmillan Press.

—— (1993) *In Defence of Politics. 4th ed.* Chicago: University of Chicago Press.

FINER, S.E. (1997) *The History of Government. 3 vols.* Oxford: Oxford University Press.

HALBERSTAM, MICHAEL (2000) *Totalitarianism and the Modern Conception of Politics.* New Haven, Conn.: Yale University Press.

KAPLAN, ROBERT D. (1997) "Was Democracy Just a Moment?" *The Atlantic Monthly*, Volume 280, Number 6, pp. 55–80.

LIJPHART, AREND, ed. (1992) *Parliamentary versus Presidential Government.* Oxford: Oxford University Press.

LINZ, JUAN J. (2000) *Totalitarian and Authoritarian Regimes.* Boulder, Colorado: Lynne Rienner Publishers.

MACPHERSON, C.B. (1977) *The Life and Times of Liberal Democracy.* Oxford: Oxford University Press.

PHARR, SUSAN J. et al. (2000) "Trouble in Advanced Democracies? A Quarter-Century of Declining Confidence," *The Journal of Democracy*, Volume 11, Number 2, pp. 5–25.

PIANO, AILI and ARCH PUDDINGTON (2001) "The 2000 Freedom House Survey: Gains Offset Losses," *The Journal of Democracy*, Volume 12, Number 1, pp. 87–92.

SMITH, DAVID E. (1999) *The Republican Option in Canada, Past and Present.* Toronto: University of Toronto Press.

WALTZ, KENNETH N. (1999) "Globalization and Governance," *PS: Political Science and Politics*, Volume 32, Number 4, pp. 693–700.

ZILLER, JACQUES (2001) "European Models of Government: Towards a Patchwork with Missing Pieces," *Parliamentary Affairs*, Volume 54, Number 1, pp. 102–119.

The Nature of Politics

BARKER, ERNEST, ed. (1962) *The Politics of Aristotle.* New York: Oxford University Press.

CONQUEST, ROBERT (1999) *Reflections on a Ravaged Century.* London: John Murray.

DAHL, ROBERT A. (1998) *On Democracy.* New Haven: Yale University Press.

DE JOUVENEL, BERTRAND (1962) *On Power: Its Nature and the History of Its Growth.* Boston: Beacon Press.

FUKUYAMA, FRANCIS (2000) "The March of Equality," *The Journal of Democracy*, Volume 11, Number 1, pp. 11–17.

FURET, FRANCOIS (1999) *The Passing of an Illusion: The Idea of Communism in the Twentieth Century,* trans. Deborah Furet. Chicago: University of Chicago Press.

INGERSOLL, DAVID E. et al. (2001) *The Philosophic Roots of Modern Ideology: Liberalism, Communism, Fascism, Islamism.* 3rd ed. Upper Saddle River, New Jersey: Prentice Hall.

MERRIAM, CHARLES E. (1964) *Political Power.* New York: Collier Books.

SUSSER, BERNARD (1995) *Political Ideology in the Modern World.* Boston: Allyn and Bacon.

WALKER, IGNACIO (1991) "Democratic Socialism in Comparative Perspective," *Comparative Politics*, Volume 23, Number 4, pp. 439–458.

Comparative Political Analysis

BECKWITH, KAREN (2000) "Beyond Compare? Women's Movements in Comparative Perspective," *European Journal of Political Research*, Volume 37, Number 4, pp. 431–468.

BLONDEL, JEAN (1999) "Then and Now: Comparative Politics," *Political Studies*, Volume 47, Number 1, pp. 152–160.

CHEHABI, H.E. (2001) "The Political Regime of the Islamic Republic of Iran in Comparative Perspective," *Government and Opposition*, Volume 36, Number 1, pp. 48–70.

DOGAN, MATTEI and DOMINIQUE PELASSY (1990) *How to Compare Nations: Strategies in Comparative Politics.* 2nd ed. Chatham, N.J.: Chatham House Publishers.

ECKSTEIN, HARRY (1998) "Unfinished Business: Reflections on the Scope of Comparative Politics," *Comparative Political Studies*, Volume 31, Number 4, pp. 505–533.

ELGIE, ROBERT (1999) "The Increasingly Difficult Art of Comparative European Politics," *European Journal of Political Research*, Volume 35, Number 4, pp. 465–482.

FUKUYAMA, FRANCIS (1998) "Women and the Evolution of World Politics," *Foreign Affairs*, Volume 77, Number 5, pp. 24–40.

NORRIS, PIPPA (1997) "Towards a More Cosmopolitan Political Science?" *European Journal of Political Research*, Volume 31, Numbers 1–2, pp. 17–34.

ROBERTS, GEOFFREY K. (1972) *What Is Comparative Politics?* London: Macmillan.

—— (1997) "Comparative Politics Matters, " *European Journal of Political Science*, Volume 31, Numbers 1–2, pp. 99–107.

VICKERS, JILL (1997) *Reinventing Political Science: A Feminist Approach.* Halifax, Nova Scotia: Fernwood Publishing.

WILSON, GRAHAM K. (1998) *Only in America? The Politics of the United States in Comparative Perspective.* Chatham, New Jersey: Chatham House Publishers.

POLITICS ON THE NET

GENERAL: Basic entry points for key governmental websites for our three countries of comparison can be located as follows: (1) **Canada: *www.canada.gc.ca.*** — go to the "About Government" listing and then to "Government at a Glance," (2) **Britain: *www.open.gov.uk*** — go to specific government sites and departments, and (3) **United States: *www.governmentguide.com*** — go to "Officials and Agencies" and then select "Find Government Agencies."

The official websites for the **Canadian Political Science Association** (***www.uottawa.ca/associations/cpsa-acsp***) and the **American Political Science Association** (***www.apsanet.org***) offer excellent linkages to various sites for political science research. In the CPSA website, go to "Electronic Resources of Interest to Political Scientists"; see especially the "National Library of Canada" link, which allows you to find Canadian information arranged according to subject (***www.nlc-bnc.ca/caninfo/ecaninfo.htm***).

Political science resource sites can be found in several locations. "Political Science: A Net Station" (***www.library.ubc.ca/poli***) has basic Canadian websites and excellent linkages for other countries. "Political Resources on the Net," which is organized on a country-by-country basis, can be found at ***www.politicalresources.net***, while another useful site, especially for Britain, is ***www.politicsdirect.com***. A good general access point is the search engine Yahoo (***dir.yahoo.com/government/index.html***). See also the political science resource site at Hunter College: ***maxweber.hunter.cuny.edu/polsc/link.html***, which has excellent links to other political science resource sites.

NATURE OF GOVERNMENT AND POLITICS: The CIA's "World Factbook 2000," which contains basic information on each country, can be found at ***www.odci.gov/cia/publications/factbook/index.html.*** Also useful is the official website of the United Nations (***www.un.org***).

For **political ideologies** and information on various political philosophers, see the following sites: ***www.library.ubc.ca/poli/theory.html*** and ***www.unet.brandeis.edu/~teuber/polphil.html.*** For sites on **feminism** and the role of women in politics and society consult the following home pages: (1) CAWP: Center for American Women and Politics (***www.rci.rutgers.edu/~cawp/Connected.html***), (2) "Feminism and Women's Studies" (***english-www.hss.cmu.edu/feminism.html***), and (3) for a general site with good linkages consult ***www.feminist.com.*** For studies of **political violence and terrorism**, locate the site for the Centre for the Study of Terrorism and Political Violence at the University of St. Andrews in Scotland: ***www.st-and.ac.uk/academic/intrel.***

PART 2

The Political Structure of the Canadian Polity

Source: The Canadian Press

Institutions are living things, and they do not easily yield their secrets to the printed word. Predominately, that is not because they are in themselves mysterious. It is rather because they change with changes in the environment within which they operate, and partly because they differ, from one moment to the other, in terms of the men who operate them. (Laski, 1940: 1)

Institutions are like fortresses. They must be well-designed and properly manned. (Popper, quoted in Johnson, 1983: 91)

I am not an advocate for frequent changes in laws and constitutions, but laws and institutions must go hand in hand with the progress of the human mind. As that becomes more developed, more enlightened, as new discoveries are made, new truths discovered and manners and opinions change, with the change of circumstances, institutions must advance also to keep pace with the times. (Thomas Jefferson, 1816)

Constitutional Government

For a Constitution does not merely provide the means of settling present disputes, it is a legal garment that reveals the values that we hold. It is a document expressing that decent respect which the present owes the past; it is, at the same time, a document addressed to future generations. (Berger, 1982: xiv)

Every constitutional question concerns the allocation and exercise of governmental power. No constitutional question, therefore, fails to be "political." (Black, 1963: 1)

. . . the most ancient, the most persistent, and the most lasting of the essentials of true constitutionalism still remains what it has been almost from the beginning, the limitation of government by law. (McIlwain, 1947: 22)

CHAPTER PREVIEW

- Systems of constitutional government provide a means of effectively controlling and limiting the power of the political elite.
- Constitutions typically include four elements: a preamble, an organizational chart, an amending clause, and a bill of rights.
- The Canadian, American, and British systems all produce constitutional government, but they use different techniques in producing these outcomes.
- Canada is a constitutional polity based on federalism and various constitutional customs and conventions. Canada has moved from a highly centralized to a highly decentralized federal system.
- In relation to its northern territories and Aboriginal communities, Canada contains some elements of a unitary system.
- Britain's centralized unitary system of constitutional government has been significantly altered by the process of devolution in relation to Scotland, Wales, and Northern Ireland.
- The American pattern of constitutionalism focusses on limiting power through a series of mechanisms: federalism, separation of powers, checks and balances, and a bill of rights. The American system has evolved into a highly centralized federal system.

Somewhere in the world today there is bound to be a busy group of constitution writers scribbling out their design for either a new or a reformed political system. For example, in Ottawa in April of 2000, the Bloc Québécois announced plans to begin working on a constitution for a future sovereign Quebec. Although we live in an era of constitution-making, we do not, at the same time, exist in an age of constitutional government. Constitutionalism is an unrealized ideal for the vast majority of nation-states in the international system, while in others it is no longer even a goal to be sought. Nonetheless, political systems continue to produce constitutions, even when they may not be operative for any great length of time, because constitutions render important political functions.

Constitutions structure the polity by establishing the boundaries of political action; that is, they outline the basic rules of the political game. For example, when a new political system is being established, such as after a revolution, the first task to be faced is the form the desired polity will be given. Constitutional design, therefore, is an act of political creation, an attempt to translate political principles into actual institutions of government.

The daily workings of the political process take place within these rules of the game, with constitutional matters usually becoming salient only during times of crisis. For example, the federal government's imposition of the War Measures Act in Canada during the October Crisis of 1970 sent concerned members of the public and constitutional scholars scurrying to the textbooks to brush up on the Act's provisions, since the last time it had been imposed was in 1939.

By establishing some of the key rules of the political game, constitutions not only structure power, but they do so in a way that helps some groups gain power and influence, while limiting the political significance of others. The rules of the political system are never neutral in their effects, although their legitimacy is certainly enhanced when they are so perceived by the public. Constitutional rules protect the interests of the people who write them and determine the kinds of issues and concerns likely to be dealt with in the political process. As James Mill put it in 1824, the "favorite opinions of people in power are the opinions which favor their own power." Although all kinds of systems typically utilize constitutions as a way of outlining the key features of the political regime, only in a small group of political systems does having a constitution also mean having a constitutional form of government.

CONSTITUTIONAL GOVERNMENT

In the current international system, there is not a strong correlation between having a piece of paper called a constitution and actually running the polity on constitutional principles. A constitution may aid in the creation of a constitutional government, but it certainly does not guarantee it. Almost all countries have constitutions, but few embody the principle of constitutionalism. A **constitutional government** is *one wherein the constitution effectively limits the power of the political* *elite.* Thus, in a constitutional polity the "constitution organizes, but also restrains" (Friedrich, 1968: 133).

The key idea of constitutional government is the effective restraint of power, not simply whether such theoretical limitations are specified in a constitutional document. Although constitutions in the former Soviet Union (e.g., the Stalinist Constitution of 1936 and the revised Constitution or fundamental law of 1977) granted each Union Republic the "right freely to secede from the USSR," no such right existed in fact, as illustrated by the denial of nationalist aspirations in the Baltic republics. While other examples could be cited, the Soviet Union's use of a constitution illustrates that constitutional government is ultimately dependent on political restraints and political forces, not constitutional niceties.

A constitutional format does not lead inexorably to constitutional substance. Constitutionalism is dependent on appropriate belief and behaviour patterns to buttress an initial constitutional structure. Such a pattern of constitutional forms, reinforced by appropriate beliefs and political activity, is found in democratic systems, while autocratic and totalitarian polities may have constitutions, but not systems of constitutional government.

> Political liberty is a difficult food to digest. It is only extremely robust constitutions that can take it (de Tocqueville, quoted in Commager, 1984: 71).

CONSTITUTIONAL ELEMENTS

Particularly in those countries with constitutional government, the constitution usually contains four basic elements: a preamble, an organizational chart, an amending clause, and a bill of rights (Duchacek, 1973: 25–38). The preamble serves as a political manifesto, setting out the goals and priorities of the polity. Most manifestoes are nationalistic in outlook and emotional in content, a summary statement of political idealism. Once the broad goals are defined, the rest of the constitution usually outlines the basic structures of government.

Constitutions provide an organizational chart or "power map" of the polity. In so doing, the constitution delineates whether the political institutions are to be federal or unitary, presidential or parliamentary in nature. For example, if a federal structure is created, then the constitution attempts to specify which level of government can exercise which political functions, which tasks are exclusive to a single level, and which functions can be performed by both levels.

Since political goals and functions change over time, constitutions may also incorporate a procedure for their own future revision, that is, an amending clause. Amending clauses are often made difficult to use, on the assumption that the "supreme law of the land" should not be routinely changed or manipulated. An amending clause attempts to specify who is involved, the nature and kinds of amendments allowed, and the procedures to be utilized.

Finally, constitutions may contain a **bill of rights**, based on the assumption that individuals need extra protection from their own government, as well as from the actions of their fellow citizens. Certain liberties, such as freedom of speech and freedom of assembly, are so fundamental to a democratic polity that they must be made immune from attack, no matter what the size of the government's majority or the state of public opinion. Unfortunately, it is often forgotten that popularity has nothing necessarily to do with constitutionality. In fact, it is when what is constitutional is also unpopular that the real mettle of constitutional government becomes apparent.

If constitutions outline the ingredients of the political structure and the basic rules of the political game, then they are inherently political by their very nature, for they help to determine the distribution of influence and power in the polity. The notion of constitutional impartiality is a myth, because constitutions are political documents with significant political consequences. Although constitutions are often valued as somehow being "above mere politics," such a belief has to be interpreted as a means of legitimating the constitution, rather than a description of its role in the political process.

Constitutions are political mechanisms of considerable import because they deal "with the hard core of all politics, namely who leads whom, with what intent, for what purpose, by what means, and with what restraints" (Duchacek, 1973: 9). Constitutions are also political in the sense that they may become symbols of national unity or disunity. In many countries, especially in those which have thrown off a colonial power, a constitution is an initial symbol of sovereignty and of political independence in the international arena. Constitution-making is, therefore, an ingredient of nation-building, of creating a national identity where none may have existed before.

> Constitutional politics consists in deciding how decisions are to be made. A constitution represents a form of metapolitics, summarizing agreements on how agreements are to be reached and enforced. The exceptional politics of constitutions thus bound the normal politics of public policy (Sniderman et al., 1996: 159).

Reforming a constitution or writing a new one is a reflection of a changing distribution of influence and power. For example, with the formal demise of the Soviet Union on December 25, 1991, Russia and the other republics faced the daunting task of constitutional creation. However, because the process of constitutional reform is often difficult, political practices may simply evolve. Thus, there is often a considerable discrepancy between the political process envisaged in the constitution and the realities of current practice. Political systems modify constitutional intent through such devices as judicial interpretation, custom and convention, and changing public beliefs. As a result, a constitution must be interpreted not only with respect to its initial design, but also in light of its adaptation to present circumstances.

THE CANADIAN CONSTITUTION

While the Canadian polity is an example of constitutional government, the nature and specifics of that constitutional system are complex. Much of its intricacy stems from the difficulty of delineating exactly what is included in Canada's Constitution. For example, while the Constitution Act of 1867 (formerly the

British North America Act of 1867) is certainly the basic constitutional document, it is not the only one. Other documents of constitutional consequence would include the Bill of Rights, the War Measures Act and the 1988 Emergencies Act, the Statute of Westminster, the Supreme Court Act, and the various acts which have added new provinces since 1867. If the rejected 1987 Meech Lake and 1992 Charlottetown Accords had been ratified, they would have also become important parts of Canada's constitutional system. The failure of the Meech Lake and Charlottetown Accords led the federal government to take several actions that are of considerable constitutional significance: the 1996 Regional Veto Act, the Supreme Court's 1998 *Quebec Secession Reference*, and the Clarity Act, which was passed in June of 2000. Thus, while Canada is usually classified as having a written constitution (i.e., the Constitution Act of 1867), it has more than one written constitutional document.

Canada has had, in fact, a series of Constitution Acts. The major revisions to the initial act are entitled Constitution Acts as well. For example, the Constitution Act Number Two of 1949 empowered the federal government to amend its own structure and operation without resort to the British Parliament. Thus, the Canadian constitutional system includes all Constitution Acts from 1867 to the present (minus those that have been repealed, such as the Constitution Act Number Two of 1949), plus the various constitutional documents, such as the 1988 Emergencies Act. The latest addition to this series of Constitution Acts, the Constitution Act of 1982, has brought the amending power to Canada from Britain, as well as adding the Canadian Charter of Rights and Freedoms, which applies to both the federal and provincial governments.

> Of all constitutions based on a parliamentary framework, Canada's Constitution surely offers the richest mine of materials for the political scientist and the constitution maker. It teaches a number of lessons about the mechanics of constitution making and it raises questions about almost every major problem of constitutional government . . . (Marshall, 1988: 156).

The complexity of constitutional government is further enhanced by the importance of custom and convention in the Canadian context. Some of the most essential aspects of the polity are nowhere written down. For example, the two key ingredients of the political process, the prime minister and the cabinet, are not mentioned in the Constitution Act of 1867. The principle of the collective responsibility of the cabinet to the House of Commons, the assumption that a cabinet minister will hold a seat in the Commons, the relationship between the formal and political executives, and the practice that a defeat on a major piece of government legislation is also a defeat of the government are all examples of crucial customs of parliamentary government that are constitutional in import but unspecified in law. Thus, when we speak of constitutional government in Canada, we include such constitutional practices, in addition to the series of constitutional documents.

The Constitution Act of 1867 created a political structure based on the principles of parliamentary sovereignty and federalism. As set forth in the preamble, the provinces of Canada, Nova Scotia, and New Brunswick desired to be "federally united" in a new political structure, "with a Constitution similar in Principle to that of the United Kingdom." The "similar in principle" phrase, in effect, designated a parliamentary structure for Canada; at the same time, it enshrined an important role for custom and convention in the Canadian polity. Unfortunately, the principles of parliamentary sovereignty and federalism are potentially contradictory in operation, especially in a decentralized federal system. However, the highly centralized federation outlined in 1867 did not bring the potential discrepancies between federalism and parliamentary sovereignty immediately into the open.

The initial structure of power provided for in the Constitution Act of 1867 strongly favoured the federal government over the provinces. This highly cen-

> Canada: Administered under the third oldest constitution in the world, which causes Canadians to insist that it has never worked and must be changed (Saul, 1995: 53).

tralized federalism, which seemed almost unitary in design, is well illustrated with respect to the following areas: the initial allocation of federal and provincial powers outlined, for the most part, in Sections 91 and 92; the residual power clause; the declaratory power; and the powers of disallowance and reservation.

THE FEDERAL DIVISION OF POWER

The principle of **federalism**, that is, *the division of powers between levels of government*, created two layers of government in Canada: the national or federal government in Ottawa and the various provincial governments. The allocation of powers to these respective levels could theoretically range from a highly centralized federal system (i.e., most of the power retained by Ottawa) to a highly decentralized one (i.e., most of the power retained by the constituent units or provinces), with numerous variations between them (see Figure 2.1). The intent of the Fathers of Confederation clearly placed Canada in the first category, as witnessed by the political functions assigned to each level.

In Section 91, the federal government was granted 29 classes of subjects, ranging from several minor functions (Section 9: Beacons, Buoys, Lighthouses, and Sable Island; Section 11: establishment and maintenance of Marine Hospitals) to

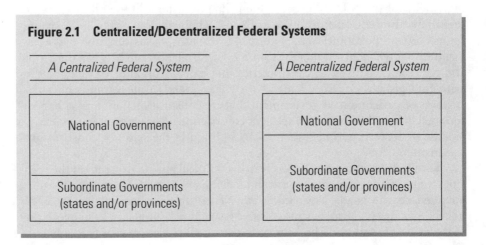

Figure 2.1   Centralized/Decentralized Federal Systems

A Centralized Federal System

National Government

Subordinate Governments
(states and/or provinces)

A Decentralized Federal System

National Government

Subordinate Governments
(states and/or provinces)

major ones (Section 2: Regulation of Trade and Commerce; Section 3: any Mode or System of Taxation; Section 7: Militia, Military and Naval Service, and Defence; Section 14: Currency and Coinage). It must be remembered that government itself in the mid-19th century was limited, but of the political functions performed at the time, the federal government received the vast majority. In addition to the powers already mentioned, the federal government was given control over the public debt and property, public credit, the postal service, navigation and shipping, banking, Aboriginal peoples and their lands, marriage and divorce, and criminal law.

In contrast, the remaining political functions allocated to the provinces were mostly minor ones, perhaps best stated in Section 92(16) as "Generally all Matters of a merely local or private Nature in the Province." Such powers included prisons in and for the province, the borrowing of money on the sole credit of the province, licences for the raising of provincial revenue, and the administration of justice in the province. While limited in their initial effect, several classes of subjects in Section 92 would later become significant, particularly the control of public lands, property and civil rights, and municipal institutions. Moreover, Section 92(7) laid the basis for provincial control over health and welfare, although such powers did not emerge as major ones until well into the 20th century.

Provincial control of municipal institutions in Section 92(8) means that the federal system created in 1867 was composed of two levels of government, not three as popularly perceived. The constitutional position of local government is subservient to the provincial level, and no relationship at all is established by the Constitution Act of 1867 between local government and the national government in Ottawa. For example, a provincial government can legally rearrange local government, setting up regional or metropolitan governments as it desires. A provincial government, acting through the provincial legislature, can cause two towns or cities to merge. For example, on April 21, 1997, the provincial government of Ontario, led by Tory Premier Mike Harris, amalgamated the various parts of metropolitan Toronto into a single government. A court challenge to this amalgamation was unsuccessful, because the province of Ontario was deemed to be operating within its constitutional powers. When in May of 2000 the City of Toronto voted to hold a referendum on making itself a "city-state" (i.e., withdrawing provincial control over Toronto), the provincial government dismissed the suggestion outright and said that it would proceed to pass legislation that would give the province a veto over future municipal referendums. Moreover, local governments are typically forced by their provinces to balance their budgets, a restriction which is obviously inapplicable to the provinces themselves.

The power of the provinces over local government is also seen with respect to the process of constitutional reform and federal-provincial agreements. Local government representatives may be included for political reasons as part of a province's delegation, but they have no legal right to participate or even to have their views presented. Several times in recent years the Canadian Federation of Municipalities has requested that all the municipalities be recognized as a separate level of government within a revised constitutional structure, and just as regularly have the provinces ignored their pleas.

While the provinces have demanded more power from the federal government, they have obstinately refused to give up any of their own power to local government. In an attempt to make an end run around provincial control of the municipalities, the federal government created the Ministry of State for Urban Affairs in 1971. However, the outcry from the provinces was such that this experiment was largely unsuccessful and the ministry was disbanded in 1978. The result is that when the federal government deals with the municipalities, it does so through their respective provincial governments. For example, as part of their 1993 campaign platform, the federal Liberals, in order to create jobs, promised to spend approximately $6 billion ($2 billion each by the federal, provincial, and municipal governments) on an infrastructure program (e.g., roads, sewers, municipal services). After assuming office the Liberal government negotiated the terms of these agreements with the provincial governments, without direct municipal participation. Each province determined how its funds would be spent and which municipalities would be entitled to participate in the program.

In addition to the powers already mentioned with respect to Sections 91 and 92, another important one is the area of taxation. The federal level was given the superior taxing power in Section 91(3), since it could raise "Money by any Mode or System of Taxation," while the provinces were limited by Section 92(2) to "Direct Taxation within the Province in order to the raising of a Revenue for Provincial Purposes." The consequence of this inequity has meant that throughout Canadian history the federal level has more easily raised revenue than have the provinces. As a result, the provinces have legally given up a portion of their power by agreeing to an amendment to the Constitution Act of 1867 that has allowed the federal government to pay for a social program that is technically within an area of provincial jurisdiction. For example, the 1940 amendment added Section 91(2a) to the list of federal powers, giving Ottawa the legal basis for providing unemployment insurance. The superiority of the federal taxing power is one reason why the initial expansion of government in Canada was an expansion of the national government.

The allocation of powers and functions between the two levels of government in Sections 91 and 92 was predicated on the assumption that the tasks of government could be neatly delineated and given to one or the other level. This pattern of federalism has often been labelled as **classical federalism** (Smiley, 1976: 54). For example, if the provinces were given control of municipal institutions, then the federal government was excluded from that area of activity. Similarly, federal jurisdiction over defence, the money supply, and the post office meant lack of provincial participation in such concerns. Thus, by and large, Sections 91 and 92 delineate areas of **exclusive jurisdiction**. Another example can be found in Section 93, which gives the provinces control over education, although the federal government was granted the task of protecting religious minority educational rights. Thus, even from the beginning in some areas, exclusive control was limited by exceptions to exclusivity.

A second type of jurisdiction is also apparent in federal constitutions, namely, the idea of **shared** or **concurrent jurisdiction**. In these areas of activity both levels of government may legislate: for example, in Section 95, both the national and provincial governments may regulate with respect to agriculture and immigration. Since both levels may legislate in these areas, there is a need for negotiation and co-operation between the federal and provincial governments. For example, in February of 1978 the federal government and Quebec signed an agreement over what powers Quebec was to exercise with respect to immigration. In particular, Quebec was given the power to define the type of immigrant it desired to reside in the province. The ideal candidate was seen as married, French-speaking, with several children under the age of 12, and predisposed to living and participating within a francophone society. The shared jurisdiction over immigration between Ottawa and Quebec City was further refined in February of 1991, when a new agreement was signed. Most importantly, this change significantly increased Quebec's powers to control the selection of immigrants for that province. In 1997, the federal government also negotiated a devolution of power in the immigration area to the provinces of Ontario, British Columbia, and Alberta.

If both levels can legislate in areas of concurrent jurisdiction, then a means must be established for deciding questions of precedence when federal and provincial laws conflict. Such a provision in a federal constitution is known as the **supremacy clause**. In Canada, supremacy in areas of concurrent jurisdiction, such as agriculture and immigration, is given to the Parliament of Canada. However, the supremacy clause does not apply to the division of powers in Sections 91 and 92, because that allocation was seen as exclusive in nature and hence no supremacy clause was logically needed.

Once matters of exclusive and concurrent jurisdiction are designated, the drafters of a federal constitution face an additional problem: which level of government is given control over the present or future activities of government not explicitly dealt with in the allocation of the exclusive and concurrent powers? Not everything can be specified in the constitution, so a **residual power clause** is included, which allocates those powers not dealt with to one or the other level of government. Typically, the residual power clause is given to that level of government that the constitution writers want to be paramount. In Canada, the residual power was granted to the federal government in the opening sentence of Section 91, which empowers Parliament to make laws for the "Peace, Order, and Good Government of Canada" (or, as a student once put it, "Peace, Order, and Good Times").

The residual power or **POGG clause** is a potentially sweeping grant of power to the national government. It takes little mental agility to be able to justify any government action under it, for what Peace, Order, and Good Government means is defined by the federal government itself. For example, the POGG clause served as the justification for the federal government to pass and use the War Measures Act. In addition, the residual power clause was the cornerstone for legitimating the imposition of wage-and-price controls in 1975. A 1976 court challenge to the anti-inflation program was rejected by the Supreme Court on the grounds that, if the federal government perceived an economic emergency, then such a situation existed in fact and could thus be dealt with under the residual power clause. While such powers are not invoked frequently, the POGG clause is an important reserve power retained by the federal government that allows it to become involved within areas of provincial jurisdiction.

In addition to the centralized allocation of governmental responsibilities and the residual power clause, a third aspect that sought to buttress the federal government's dominance over the provinces in 1867 was the declaratory power given to the national government. The **declaratory power** contained in Section 92(10)(c) allows the federal government to usurp provincial powers if the federal Parliament asserts that such an action is "for the general Advantage of Canada or for the Advantage of Two or more of the Provinces."

Significant is the placement of the declaratory power phrase in the 1867 Constitution Act: within the list of powers given the provinces in Section 92 is a means by which any of them may be taken over by the federal government acting on its own initiative. It is difficult to conceive of a power or activity that could not be justified or rationalized as to the benefit of at least two provinces. Interestingly, Canada is the only federal system in the world with such a power given to the national government. This declaratory power has been used 472 times to bring such diverse works as atomic energy and grain elevators under federal jurisdiction (Romanow, Whyte, and Leeson, 1984: 47–48).

Although the declaratory power has been rarely used in recent decades, it is not a dead issue in Canadian politics. In the defeated Charlottetown Accord in 1992, the federal government was prepared to sacrifice its declaratory power, which could thenceforth only have been used with provincial consent. The practical result of that proposed change would have been a virtual provincial veto of the declaratory power — it would never have been used in the future. The potential use of the declaratory power remains as a possible bargaining chip for the federal government. Currently, the declaratory power remains in place. The federal government last used the declaratory power in 1961.

A fourth set of techniques outlined in the Constitution Act of 1867 through which the federal government could exert control over the provincial units concerns the national government's powers of disallowance and reservation. Although they differ in the details of their application, the effect of disallowance and reservation is to give the federal government a potential veto power over the provincial legislature (Mallory, 1954: 169).

Disallowance is the procedure by which the federal government rules a provincial law null and void within one year of its passage. In other words, a provincial legislature passes a law, it receives royal assent from the lieutenant-governor, and it is enforced as a provincial law until the federal government decides otherwise. Provincial laws are sent to the federal Minister of Justice and, if he or she recommends, within one year from the date of receiving a copy of the legislation from the province, that the bill be rejected, then an order-in-council (i.e., a decision of the cabinet) is so issued.

The grounds for disallowance need to be neither explained nor specific: they can be as vague as claiming that the provincial law runs counter to "sound principles of legislation." Under disallowance the federal government can observe the implementation of a law before it decides whether or not to veto it. The last time the disallowance power was used was 1943. In total, slightly over 110 acts since Confederation have been disallowed.

Reservation is a procedure by which a provincial law is not applicable until the federal government reviews it. **Reservation** means that the bill has passed the provincial legislature, has been sent to the lieutenant-governor for royal assent, but the lieutenant-governor reserves the bill by neither granting assent nor refusing it. Such a bill is then sent to the federal government for a decision, wherein the governor-in-council (i.e., the cabinet) may or may not decide to allow the bill to become law.

In the case of reservation, a provincial bill, in effect, is held in abeyance until the federal government has a chance to consider it. Over 70 bills have been reserved since 1867, with about a dozen eventually allowed to become law. The last time reservation was used was in Saskatchewan in 1961. Thus, the national government's powers of disallowance and reservation placed the provinces in 1867 in a situation of colonial subordination to the federal government, just as the federal government itself was so positioned with respect to Britain. Interestingly, in the rejected Charlottetown Accord the federal government's powers of disallowance and reservation would have been revoked.

Given the original distribution of powers between the national and provincial governments, the granting of both the residual and declaratory powers to the federal level, and the national government's right to disallow or reserve provincial legislation, the intent of the Fathers of Confederation was clearly to establish a highly **centralized federal system**. The primary functions of government in 1867 went to the federal government, with those designated for provincial control able to be usurped by the national government acting on its own initiative. For such reasons, the Constitution Act of 1867 has been classified as containing important **quasi-unitary** attributes (Smiley, 1980: 22–27).

Umpiring the federal system

Although the Fathers of Confederation felt that the allocation of powers in the new federal structure was clear-cut, a federal political system inherently produces disputes and conflicts between the various levels of government over their respective powers. One way of settling such disputes is through a process of judicial review. On a general level, **judicial review** is *the right of the courts to make judgments respecting the constitutionality of executive and legislative actions.*

In Canada, a restricted view of such a process has traditionally been used to settle jurisdictional disputes between the federal and provincial governments. In such a federal polity, the courts may be used in a pattern of **limited judicial review**, *whereby they rule on which level of government can exercise what powers.* In that sense, then, the courts are used as the referees of federalism: their task is not to stop the game by declaring an action unconstitutional, but to decide which team (the federal or provincial government) has control of the ball so that the game can continue. For example, in September of 1997 the Supreme Court ruled that the federal government had the power to enact environmental legislation because it came within the federal government's exclusive powers to legislate with respect to criminal law.

The practice of limited judicial review has meant that, as long as the federal and provincial governments legislate within their powers as allocated in the 1867 Constitution Act, the courts will take a hands-off attitude toward the content of such legislation. By implication, such an approach favours the national government, since the courts are interpreting a document that created a highly centralized federal system.

The use in pre-Charter Canada of a pattern of limited, rather than full, judicial review is a reflection of the principle of parliamentary sovereignty. If the courts were to exercise full judicial review, the result would be that a supposedly supreme legislature was subject to the interpretations of an outside body. However, the pattern of limited judicial review initiated in 1867 is consistent with a federal and parliamentary system, because the courts are merely interpreting which legislature has the right to exercise supremacy with respect to which powers.

NONFEDERAL CONSTITUTIONAL PATTERNS

While the 1867 Constitution Act set up a highly centralized federal political system, other nonfederal political relationships were also created and continue to exist down to the present. For example, we have already pointed out that the power map between provinces and their municipal units is a unitary relationship. Moreover, units of government other than provinces were either maintained or created, leading to the establishment of three territorial governments: the Yukon, the Northwest Territories, and Nunavut. The relationship between Ottawa and these territories is basically a unitary pattern, not a federal one. Finally, the longstanding role of the federal government with respect to Canada's Aboriginal communities is a unitary (some would say dictatorial) relationship that is quickly changing into a more complex pattern, because of an emerging pattern of Aboriginal self-government (i.e., a relationship that is neither federal nor unitary).

At the time of Confederation in 1867, most of the land that is now part of Canada was not included in the constitutional settlement; only the former United Canadas (Ontario and Quebec) and New Brunswick and Nova Scotia were included. Prince Edward Island remained separate, as did the colony of Newfoundland and the vast land mass in what is now Western Canada (New Caledonia, which became part of British Columbia; the British-controlled North-Western Territory; and Rupert's Land, held by the Hudson's Bay Company). Section 146 of the 1867 Constitution Act provided for the admission of the colonies or new provinces to Confederation, along with Ottawa gaining control of Rupert's Land and the North-Western Territory. The transfer of political authority over the North-Western Territory and Rupert's Land was made by British order-in-council in 1870. Thus, Ottawa assumed a unilateral relationship with these new jurisdictions, which it had inherited from the British Crown. As new provinces were created and admitted to Confederation (Manitoba in 1870, British Columbia in 1871, and Alberta and Saskatchewan both in 1905), or as former colonies became provinces (Prince Edward Island in 1873 and Newfoundland in 1949), they entered into a federal, rather than a unitary, relationship with the Dominion government in Ottawa.

The remaining land mass contained in the Northwest Territories continued in a unitary political relationship with Ottawa. This pattern is well illustrated by the fact that Ottawa was given the power under Section 146 of the 1867 Constitution Act to determine if and when new provinces were to be admitted to Confederation, as well as the terms for such changes. Moreover, Ottawa retained near absolute control of the Northwest Territories, even when agreeing to its division to create the Yukon territory in 1898 and then to further divide the remaining Northwest Territories to create Nunavut in 1999.

For all of the territories, the unitary relationship with Ottawa is exemplified by the facts that they do not have provincial status and that they are administered by a federally appointed commissioner (a position similar to that of an appointed lieutenant-governor at the provincial level). The federal Department of Indian and Northern Affairs exercises a supervisory control position with respect to natural resources, economic and social development, and the Aboriginal communities. Moreover, the three territories are overwhelmingly dependent on Ottawa financially. The new territory of Nunavut will receive about 90 percent of its funds from Ottawa, as compared to the most dependent province (Newfoundland), which currently receives about 43 percent of its budget from the federal level.

Creating Nunavut: Canada's newest territory came into existence on April 1, 1999. It was created by carving off the Eastern Arctic from the Northwest Territories. Twice the size of Ontario, Nunavut is 2 000 kilometres wide and 1 800 kilometres deep, with a population of 25 000 — 85 percent of whom are Inuit. Following years of negotiations, the federal and territorial governments and the Inuit finally agreed in principle to the proposed division in 1990. This change was approved by a referendum in both the Northwest Territories and among the Inuit in 1992. Following that process, it was agreed that the new territory of Nunavut (which means "Our land") would begin on April 1, 1999. The first elections for the new government were held on February 15, 1999: the people of Nunavut selected 19 independent MLAs, from among whom the MLAs themselves would elect a premier and cabinet. Such a nonpartisan and consensus style of government reflects the traditions of the new territory, the first political unit in Canada to be predominantly governed by members of the an Aboriginal community.

Aboriginal Governance: The political relationship between the Aboriginal communities and the Crown is an extremely complex one and also one that is rapidly evolving into new patterns. Originally the Aboriginal communities had a direct and unitary relationship with the British Crown, symbolized by the Royal Proclamation of 1763. With the Confederation Settlement of 1867, this relationship between the British Crown and the Aboriginal communities was transferred to Ottawa. For example, in Section 91 (24) of the 1867 Constitution Act, the federal government is given exclusive jurisdiction with respect to "Indians, and Lands reserved for Indians." Thus, the provinces historically have had no direct constitutional relationship with the Aboriginal communities, a pattern that remains largely in place.

Acting on this power, the federal government passed the Indian Act in 1876, which gave Ottawa total control over the affairs of the Aboriginal communities, including the aim of assimilating Aboriginals into the larger community. Every aspect of Aboriginal life was controlled by Ottawa, including even the definition of who was a member of the Aboriginal communities in terms of Ottawa's distinction between status and non-status Indians. Although this relationship remains largely in place between Ottawa and the Aboriginal communities, it began to change in the 1970s, with an increasing emphasis by Ottawa on dealing with such matters as land claims.

A significant sign of a changing pattern, as well as an impetus for future change, occurred in 1982 with the adoption of the Canadian Charter of Rights and Freedoms. Section 35 of the Charter states that "the existing aboriginal and treaty rights of the aboriginal peoples of Canada are hereby recognized and affirmed." From the viewpoint of the Aboriginal communities, such a statement implied a recognition of their long-held position that the treaties with the British government and Ottawa were "government to government" or "nation to nation," rather than part of the unitary and subservient pattern of Canadian politics. For example, in a series of cases, based on the Charter, the Supreme Court of Canada has ruled that the Aboriginal communities retain their rights granted by treaty in areas of jurisdiction such as hunting and fishing and forestry. However, while ruling that the Aboriginal communities retained such rights, the Supreme Court also said that the federal government retained the right to regulate such areas. Thus, conflict quickly developed over what rights the Aboriginal communities had in fact, leading to physical confrontations and violence in the Maritime provinces in 1999 and the summer of 2000.

Increasingly, the Aboriginal communities have taken the position in the past two decades that through land claims and treaties a pattern of Aboriginal self-government must be created in Canada. In other words, in dealing with the federal, provincial, and territorial governments, the Aboriginal communities will interact with those units on a government-to-government basis, creating a "third order of government" in Canada which is neither federal nor unitary in its relations with the other political structures. Considerable confusion has already developed over matters of political authority — a pattern that will greatly increase in the years ahead. Regardless of their exact outcome, questions of Aboriginal governance have not only moved to near the top of the political agenda, but they have also introduced new nonfederal constitutional patterns into the structure of the Canadian polity. Canada now incorporates federal, unitary, and government-to-government political relationships within its various constitutional patterns.

CONSTITUTIONAL ADDITIONS

In addition to the matters dealt with in the 1867 Constitution Act, both federal and nonfederal, three major enactments since then have grafted important elements onto the initial constitutional structure: the War Measures Act from 1914 to 1988 and its replacement, the 1988 Emergencies Act; the Bill of Rights in 1960; and the Constitution Act of 1982. It is important to look at each of these modifications and refinements in the Canadian pattern of constitutional government.

The War Measures Act

Although highly centralized in design, the Constitution Act of 1867 did not specifically deal with the means by which the federal government could act to meet either domestic or international crises. For 50 years it was assumed that the federal government's residual and declaratory powers were sufficient to counter any such threats. However, by the early 20th century the growing pattern of decentralization and the judicial restriction of the POGG clause, in conjunction with a world crisis, prompted the federal government to give itself emergency powers. Passed in 1914 as a federal statute, the War Measures Act set up a system of **constitutional dictatorship** under the direction of the prime minister and cabinet.

In effect, the federal government could rule by decree, usurping not only Parliament's powers, but those of the provinces as well. Moreover, penalties for failure to observe the new regulations could be imposed, with a fine of $5 000 and/or five years in jail for each offence. A person could also be detained for a maximum period of 21 days, without being charged for a specific violation. Such regulations could also be made retroactive: in the 1970 October Crisis it became illegal to ever have been a member of the FLQ! Under the War Measures Act, basic civil and political liberties could be suspended on the grounds that such actions were necessary to preserve the body politic. For example, at the height of the 1970 crisis, Prime Minister Trudeau was asked by a reporter how far he would go in suspending basic liberties in order to defeat the FLQ. The prime minister's response was blunt and vintage Trudeau: "Just watch me!"

The bringing into force of the War Measures Act was accomplished by a proclamation of the governor-in-council (i.e., the prime minister and cabinet) that there existed a situation of "war, invasion, or insurrection, real or apprehended." Of interest is the phrase "real or apprehended," which meant that if the federal government perceived a crisis involving war, invasion, or insurrection, then a crisis existed. No evidence to support such a view needed to be presented.

Once the Act was in place, it was a prerogative of the federal government to decide how long it remained — there was no legal time limit on its application. The War Measures Act could last several months, as in 1970, or several years, as during the Second World War, from 1939 to 1945. The government could also relax the extent of its control, once the immediate crisis had passed, but not to the position of returning to its normal powers. In this situation, it could impose a Public Order Temporary Measures Act, which limited some of its own arbitrary authority. This procedure was used in both the 1970 crisis, when a Public Order Temporary Measures Act was in place from December 1970 to April 1971, and after World War II from 1945 to 1954. The decisions about whether to use this procedure, the extent of the powers retained by the federal government, and the length of the application of a Public Order Act were all taken by the federal government itself.

Although there was no legal restriction on how often such emergency powers could have been used, for political reasons they were not likely to be resorted to too often. Since its passage, the War Measures Act was utilized on three occasions: during both world wars and the October Crisis in 1970. Even though it was a federal statute like any other law, the War Measures Act was a constitutional document with respect to both its content and its consequences for the political system.

The 1988 Emergencies Act

The rather extreme power given to the federal government under the War Measures Act led to suggestions for its reform or replacement. After the 1970 October Crisis, the Trudeau government promised new emergency powers legislation, but none was ever passed. In January of 1985, Defence Minister Robert Coates indicated that the Mulroney government would be bringing forward new legislation to replace the War Measures Act. After several delays, the federal government finally introduced its replacement for the War Measures Act in June of 1987, with royal assent granted on July 21, 1988.

The 1988 Emergencies Act defines four broad classes of emergencies. Unlike the draconian War Measures Act, which, from 1914 to 1988 was either imposed in total or not at all, the Emergencies Act allows for a graduated response to different types of crises:

1. *Public welfare emergencies*: floods, accidents, pollution, or diseases. Under this provision, authorities can requisition property, order the evacuation of areas, or restrict travel.

2. *Public order emergencies*: threats to Canada's security that are so serious that they cannot be handled by a province. The October Crisis of 1970 would now fall into this category.

3. *International emergencies*: acts of violence which threaten Canada or its allies. Under this provision, the government can prevent citizens from leaving the country, seize property, and authorize searches and seizures without warrants.

4. *War emergencies*: a war or imminent conflict for Canada or one of its allies that is so "serious as to be a national emergency." Powers under this provision are similar to those of the original War Measures Act.

In addition to defining different types of crises and possible responses, the Emergencies Act allows for compensation to individuals who may be harmed by its application, allows a review by Parliament of its necessity, and is subject to the limitations of both the Bill of Rights and the Canadian Charter of Rights and Freedoms. As such, the Emergencies Act is a much-needed improvement upon the War Measures Act.

The 1960 Bill of Rights

While the War Measures Act and its replacement both dealt with threats to the Canadian constitutional structure, a further area of revision concerns the protection of individual rights in the Canadian polity. The second major addition to Canada's constitutional structure came in 1960, with the passage of the Bill of Rights, although most of its provisions have now been superseded by the Canadian Charter of Rights and Freedoms contained in the 1982 Constitution Act. It is well to remember, however, that the Bill of Rights is still operative, even after the adoption of the new Charter of Rights. For example, in July of 1988, the Bill of Rights, not the Charter of Rights, was the basis for a ruling by the Federal Court of Canada against the Immigration Department.

The basic assumption of a bill of rights or charter of rights is that the people need protection from their government, a view that challenges a core belief of parliamentary government. Historically, Parliament has been seen as the guarantor of people's freedoms, but a bill of rights asserts, in effect, that Parliament is not only incapable of continuing to protect the public, but also that the public needs a means of defence against its protector.

A bill of rights is designed to establish a series of civil and political liberties that no government can ignore or abuse. One way such protection is enhanced is to place the bill of rights explicitly in the constitution, a process known as **entrenchment**. Since constitutions are usually made to be difficult to change, having a bill of rights entrenched means it is less likely to be done away with or changed by the government of the day. An effective bill of rights stands, therefore, as a limit on parliamentary supremacy.

The adoption of the Canadian Bill of Rights nearly 100 years after Confederation was a reflection of Parliament's belief that no such rights were needed as a protection against itself. However, public pressure and opinion was such that Parliament finally acquiesced and passed the legislation that created a potential check on its own power. The Bill of Rights was a normal piece of federal legislation that was not entrenched in the Constitution Act of 1867. The Bill of Rights also reflected the impact of federalism, because it applied only to the federal level of government. However, by the mid-1970s, all provinces had enacted some type of "human rights" legislation, although most of these bills were not as comprehensive as their federal counterpart.

The result of its lack of entrenchment and its applicability to only the federal level left the constitutional position of the Bill of Rights open to question. These concerns were reflected in the fact that it was nine years before the Supreme Court, in the *Drybones* decision of 1969, used the Bill of Rights to invalidate a section of federal law. However, in later decisions in the mid-1970s, the Supreme Court backed off from the full implications of such a stand and seemed reluctant to consider the Bill of Rights as a basis for challenging the legislative or executive actions of the federal government. It turned out that this decision was the only time the Supreme Court used the Bill of Rights to rule a law invalid between 1960 and 1982 (i.e., until the adoption of the Canadian Charter of Rights and Freedoms).

The provisions of the Bill of Rights were fairly typical in content, in that they protected a series of civil and political liberties. Unfortunately, these protections were not as effective as they appeared to be, because they could be bypassed by the federal government, using the **notwithstanding clause**. By inserting the phrase "notwithstanding the Canadian Bill of Rights," any act of Parliament could be made immune from the application of these basic freedoms. Fundamental freedoms were simply not as fundamental as the principle of parliamentary supremacy.

A second limitation concerned the relationship between the Bill of Rights and the War Measures Act, with the latter taking precedence over the former. In times of crisis, when protection of basic civil and political liberties was most needed, fundamental human rights were held in abeyance. For example, the Bill of Rights in Part Two, Section 6(5), with reference to the War Measures Act, asserts that any action taken under the emergency powers provision "shall be deemed not to be an abrogation, abridgement or infringement of any right or freedom recognized by the Canadian Bill of Rights."

Although the War Measures Act took precedence over the Bill of Rights, nevertheless the Bill of Rights did modify the procedure for imposing emergency powers. After 1960, any use of the War Measures Act had to be accompanied by a notice to Parliament that a crisis existed. If Parliament was sitting, notification had to be done "forthwith," that is, without undue delay. In a situation where Parliament was not in session when the emergency was declared, it had to be informed within the first 15 days of its next sitting. Within 10 days of Parliament's notification, any 10 members in either House could have forced a debate on the proclamation of the War Measures Act. If, at the conclusion of this debate, both Houses of Parliament resolved "that the proclamation be revoked, it shall cease to have effect." However, the government, if it felt it necessary because of a continuing crisis or because of a new one, could have legally invoked the War Measures Act a second time.

The lack of entrenchment, its application to only the federal level of government, the ability of the federal government to bypass it, and its inapplicability with respect to the imposition of the War Measures Act were some of the major deficiencies of the Bill of Rights that led to a search for a more comprehensive and effective document. The result, in part, was the adoption of the Canada Act, including its most important section — the Canadian Charter of Rights and Freedoms. Once passed, this act was known as the Constitution Act of 1982, the third major addition to Canada's constitutional structure since 1867.

The 1982 Constitution Act

Following the preamble, which humbly requests the Queen to act, on our behalf, one last time by laying before the British Parliament the Canada Act of 1982, the **Canadian Charter of Rights and Freedoms** is specified (Table 2.1). The Charter begins with its own mini-preamble, affirming that "Canada is founded upon principles that recognize the supremacy of God and the rule of law," which is followed by a series of political, legal, and language rights in Sections 1 through 34. Approximately one-half of the Canada Act is devoted to these basic civil and political liberties. However, perhaps prophetic in its long-range implications for the Charter is Section 1 (the **reasonable limits clause**), which limits these rights and freedoms before they are even recognized: "the rights and freedoms set out in it subject only to such reasonable limits prescribed by law as can be demonstrably justified in a free and democratic society." In other words, the basic rights protected by the Charter can be limited by law, as long as that limitation is demonstrably justified in a free and democratic society.

Sections 2 through 5 protect some of the basic civil and political liberties, such as the freedoms of speech, assembly, religion, and voting. Section 6 represents a new addition to the traditional list of human freedoms, in that mobility rights

CHAPTER 2: *Constitutional Government* **69**

Table 2.1   Basic Provisions of the 1982 Canada Act

Section	Content
Preamble	Request to the Queen to submit the Patriation Resolution to the British Parliament for passage.

Constitution Act
Part One: Charter of Rights and Freedoms

Section	Content
Section 1	General guarantee of rights and freedoms
Section 2	Fundamental Freedoms (religion, speech, etc.)
Sections 3–5	Democratic Rights (voting, yearly sitting of Parliament)
Section 6	Mobility Rights (rights of citizens to enter and leave country, to move between provinces)
Sections 7–14	Legal Rights (protection against unreasonable search and seizure, right to counsel, etc.)
Section 15	Equality Rights (protection against discrimination on the basis of race, national or ethnic origin, colour, religion, sex, age, or mental or physical disability)
Sections 16–22	Official Languages (protection of bilingualism in the federal government and New Brunswick)
Section 23	Minority Language Educational Rights (where numbers warrant, education to be provided for from public funds in language first learned by the child)
Section 24	Enforcement (right to appeal to the courts if rights in the Charter are violated)
Sections 25–31	General (protection of Aboriginal rights and equality of males and females, Charter to be interpreted so as to protect multicultural heritage of Canada

Section	Content
Sections 32–34	Application of Charter (applies to both federal and provincial governments, but an opting out or notwithstanding clause is included)

Part Two: Rights of Aboriginal People

Existing Aboriginal and treaty rights of Aboriginal peoples recognized and affirmed

Part Three: Equalization and Regional Disparities

Both levels commit themselves to promote the well-being of Canadians, to further economic development, to provide essential public services, and to maintain equalization payments.

Part Four: Constitutional Conference

Required meeting of all first ministers within one year of the passage of this Act

Part Five: Amending Procedure

Details of procedure specified, with several different types of formulas used, depending on which sections of the Constitution are to be amended

Part Six: Amendment to the BNA Act of 1867

Protection of provincial powers over natural resources reaffirmed by adding Section 92A to the BNA Act of 1867

Part Seven: General

Housekeeping provisions: Constitution of Canada declared to be the supreme law of the land; all BNA Acts are now to be renamed as the Constitution Acts; English and French versions of the Constitution Act are equally authoritative.

are explicitly recognized for the first time in Canada. At the insistence of the federal government, mobility rights were included in an attempt to prevent the "balkanization" of the polity, so that the provinces could not continue to pass legislation designed to hinder inter-provincial migration. The necessity of including mobility rights in the Charter reflects the strength of regionalism, as well as an attempt to limit it in the years ahead. However, some restrictions on mobility rights are allowed, if a province's rate of employment is below that of the national average.

The legal rights of Canadian citizens contained in Sections 7 through 14 begin with the "right to life, liberty, and security of person and the right not to be deprived thereof except in accordance with the principles of fundamental justice." However, such "principles of fundamental justice" are left undefined, so that the judiciary will be required to specify their nature through the decisions they are called upon to make in the course of constitutional litigation. The series of legal rights protected include the right to be free against unreasonable searches or seizures, arbitrary detention and imprisonment, or any cruel and unusual treatment or punishment. One's right to counsel, reasonable bail (not to be denied "without just cause"), and trial ("within a reasonable time") are also specified. Protection against self-incrimination, except in perjury cases, and against being tried a second time for an alleged crime after an initial acquittal are also contained in the section on legal rights. These provisions are basic ones for protecting the individual against the possible abuses of state power.

The equality rights contained in Section 15 guarantee that "every individual is equal before and under the law and has the right to equal protection and equal benefit of the law without discrimination and, in particular, without discrimination based on race, national or ethnic origin, colour, religion, sex, age or mental or physical disability." Most of these rights were included in the 1960 Bill of Rights, although the Charter has added protection on the grounds of ethnic origin, age, and mental or physical disability. However, government programs designed to overcome the effects of previous discrimination (i.e., affirmative action programs) are allowed. Unlike most provisions of the Canada Act, which became effective as soon as the new Constitution was formally proclaimed, the array of equality rights specified in Section 15 of the Charter could not be applied for three years (April 17, 1982 to April 17, 1985) from the date of the Constitution Act's proclamation (Section 32, Subsection 2). Since many of these rights fell within the areas of traditional provincial jurisdiction, the provinces wanted time to accommodate their existing legislation to those new provisions.

Protection of Canada's two official languages is contained in Sections 16 through 22, which basically entrench in the Constitution the existing language rights as previously specified in the federal government's Official Languages Act and New Brunswick's version of that Act. Entrenchment enhances the extent of language protection, since constitutional provision for it is less immune to future change than are legislative statutes. The official languages are recognized with respect to the procedures of the courts, legislatures, and bureaucracy, although in the latter case only where numbers warrant. Quebec is not included in these provisions, but language protection continues in that province under Section 133 of the British North America (BNA) Act of 1867 (now the Constitution Act of 1867). However, language protection in Quebec is not extended under this provision to an individual's dealings with the bureaucracy — only language use in the courts and the legislature is specified for Quebec in the 1867 Act. Thus, the combination of the Constitution Acts of 1867 and 1982 guarantees language protection in dealings with the federal government and the provinces of New Brunswick and Quebec.

Language protection is extended to the educational system by Section 23 of the Charter. Citizens of Canada have the right to education in their mother tongue, where numbers warrant, and to have such instruction paid for out of public funds. The background of this aspect of the Charter is complex, raising the whole issue of minority rights and language use throughout Canadian history. Its inclusion, at the insistence of the federal government, was a reaction to the politicization of the language issue in Quebec during the 1960s and 1970s and the passage in 1977 of Bill 101 by the Quebec National Assembly. Section 23 attempts, in effect, to correct, even if somewhat belatedly, an oversight in the original BNA Act.

The enforcement of the Charter of Rights is allocated to the judiciary by Section 24. Anyone who feels that their fundamental rights and freedoms have been infringed or denied "may apply to a court of competent jurisdiction to obtain such remedy as the court considers appropriate and just in the circumstances." This explicit recognition of the potential role of the courts in protecting fundamental rights increases the potential for a more activist judiciary in Canada, if citizens are willing to challenge possible violations of the Charter by bringing them to the attention of the judicial branch.

Sections 25 through 31 of the Charter, labelled General, are a miscellaneous group of provisions not easily accommodated in the previous sections. Section 25 guarantees Aboriginal rights, including those that might accrue by means of future land claims settlements. Section 28 specifically recognizes the equality of "male and female persons." These two provisions, at first glance, appear to duplicate the bar against discrimination on the basis of sex and national or ethnic origin contained under Section 15 on equality rights. However, Section 15 did not take effect until three years after the Charter was proclaimed (i.e., April 17, 1985) and, more importantly, unlike Section 15, the protections of Sections 25 and 28 cannot be overridden using Section 33 of the Charter. Thus, these two provisions were applied immediately between 1982 and 1985 and cannot be taken away by legislative fiat at some future point. Also contained within the miscellaneous category is an extension of the Charter to the Yukon and Northwest Territories (Section 30), a proviso that the Charter "shall be interpreted in a manner consistent with the preservation and enhancement of the multicultural heritage of Canadians" (Section 26), an assertion that "nothing in this Charter extends the legislative powers of any body or authority" (Section 31), and, in case some rights may have been overlooked, a claim that lack of inclusion of any such rights in the Charter cannot be taken to mean that they do not exist (Section 26).

The final major section of the Charter of Rights concerns its application. Section 32 specifically enforces the Charter on both the federal and provincial levels of government, as well as on the Yukon and Northwest Territories, although the equality rights of Section 15 are delayed for three years. Most significant is Section 33, the **override clause**, which allows either the federal or provincial governments to bypass any rights specified in Section 2 or Sections 7 to 15 of the Charter of Rights. Thus, Section 33 continues the practice of placing the principle of parliamentary supremacy over the application of fundamental freedoms, whether these freedoms are entrenched in the Constitution or not. The use of the override or notwithstanding clause is limited to five years, although it may be re-enacted repeatedly in a series of five-year terms. There is no apparent means by which an override action by either the federal or provincial legislatures can be legally challenged by the citizen. The recourse to a misuse of this power must be defeat of the government at the next election, rather than through a process of constitutional litigation.

Parts Two through Four of the Canada Act are relatively brief and straight-forward. The "existing aboriginal and treaty rights" are "recognized and affirmed" in Part Two, along with a definition of the concept of "aboriginal peoples of Canada" (i.e., Indian, Inuit, and Métis). Part Three reflects the impact on the Canadian polity of regionalism, in that the federal and provincial governments commit themselves, very generally, to the reduction of regional disparities through equalization payments to the provinces. No formula for determining equaliza-tion grants or funding levels is included, thereby protecting the flexibility of the gov-ernments involved in negotiating these matters. Quite likely, the federal and provincial governments will continue to have different views of what constitutes "sufficient revenues" to the provinces. Part Three was a major concession by the federal government to the poorer provinces in order to try to win their grudging acceptance of the constitutional reform package.

Part Four required that the prime minister convene a Conference of First Ministers within one year of the proclamation of the Constitution Act. Part Four also mandates that matters affecting Canada's Aboriginal peoples must be con-sidered by this conference, that representatives from these groups must be invited to attend so as to participate in the discussions of these matters, and that elected representatives of the Yukon and Northwest Territories will also be in attendance to discuss any matters that directly affect them. For the first time, there is a legal requirement that someone other than the federal and provincial political execu-tives be involved in the process of constitutional negotiation.

A crucial addition to Canada's constitutional structure is Part Five of the Canada Act, which specifies amending clauses for future constitutional reform efforts. Thus, a major flaw of the BNA Act of 1867 has finally been corrected. However, the amendment of the Constitution Act is complex; in fact, five differ-ent procedures are prescribed. For example, within certain limits, the existing right of the provinces to determine their own structure and operation, as well as the power of the federal government to do likewise, is recognized in Sections 45 and 44, respectively. A third variation concerns an amendment that affects at least two provinces, but not all (Section 43). In this situation, a proclamation by the governor general is required, after "resolutions of the Senate and House of Commons and of the legislative assembly of each province to which the amendment applies." The fourth amending procedure (Section 41) differs from the third in that the unanimous consent of all provinces must be obtained with respect to any amend-ments to the offices of the formal executive (Queen, governor general, lieutenant-governor), the composition of the Supreme Court, the use of the English or French languages within a province, and the right of a province to have at least the same number of members in the House of Commons as it has senators.

The most general amending procedure, and the fifth possible alternative, is contained in **Section 38**, which is now the heart of the amending process in Canada. Under this technique, known as the **7/50 rule**, an amendment is proclaimed by the governor general when authorized by "resolutions of the Senate and House of Commons" and by "resolutions of the legislative assemblies of at least two-thirds of the provinces that have, in the aggregate, according to the then latest general census, at least 50 percent of the population of all the provinces." However, even if it is passed under these conditions, the remaining provinces may opt out of any such amendment. If the amendment opted out of transfers powers in the education or cultural fields to Ottawa, then the provinces are entitled to financial compensation. These amending procedures, particularly Section 38, represent a major change in the nature of constitutional reform in Canada, transforming a process based on convention into one based on constitutional prescription.

An important alteration of the Senate's role in the amending process is contained in Section 47, which gives the upper chamber a **suspensive veto** (i.e., *the ability to delay legislation*), of 180 days with respect to all amending procedures except those relating to either the provincial or federal levels changing their own structure and operation. If a resolution authorizing an amendment is passed by the House, but is not passed within 180 sitting days of Parliament by the Senate, then the House can pass the resolution a second time, at which point the amending procedure moves ahead. Because the Senate can be effectively bypassed, if necessary, what Section 47 does is to give ultimate control of the basic amending processes to the House of Commons. The Senate can even be gotten around with respect to amendments that change both the powers of and method of selecting members of the upper House.

Part Six of the Canada Act amended the original British North America Act of 1867 by adding a definition of, and additional protection for, provincial control over natural resources (Section 92A). The newly emerging wealth of Alberta, Saskatchewan, and British Columbia and the hoped-for wealth of the Atlantic provinces is based on the natural resource sector, one which these provinces fear the federal government covets. Thus, part of the trade-off for the Charter of Rights wanted by the federal government was enhancement of provincial control over the natural resource sector.

The final part of the Canada Act (Part Seven, Sections 52 through 60) is another catch-all series of provisions: how the Canada Act can be cited, the fact that the English and French versions are considered equally authoritative, and that the Constitution of Canada is the "supreme law of Canada."

Our survey of the major provisions of the Canada Act might lead one to conclude that what appears simple at first glance is, in fact, an extremely complex constitutional document with many significant implications for the future direction of the polity. While it is a consolidation of a number of existing constitutional provisions, the 1982 Canada Act, by itself, is not a comprehensive constitutional document — elements of the 1867 BNA Act and the 1960 Bill of Rights remain as significant ingredients of the total constitutional context in Canada. A considerable portion of the 1982 Canada Act is simply a repetition of existing constitutional enactments. For example, much of the Canadian Charter of Rights and Freedoms was already contained in the 1960 Bill of Rights.

However, a number of new elements have been added, including the mobility rights and minority language educational rights in the Charter, the entrenchment of fundamental freedoms in the Constitution, and the Charter's applicability to both levels of government. Outside of the Charter, the Canada Act has also added protection of Aboriginal rights, enhanced provincial control over the natural resource sector, and provided a series of constitutionally designated amending procedures. The major provisions of the Canada Act each represent the result of political accommodations between the federal and provincial governments in the struggle for influence and power in the future Canadian polity.

UNSUCCESSFUL CONSTITUTIONAL REFORMS

Given the difficult battle to patriate the Constitution and to add a Charter of Rights to the Canadian constitutional system, as well as the political repercussions of the 1980–1982 period, it might seem likely to expect a generation to pass before such issues were raised again. However, in Canada constitutional reform is a never-ending process. The consequences of the patriation of the Constitution in 1982 were two further attempts at constitutional renewal in the late 1980s (the Meech Lake Accord) and early 1990s (the Charlottetown Accord and the referendum in October of 1992). While it is important to remember that both packages of constitutional changes failed, their content and the repercussions of their failures have set the parameters for later constitutional debates and reforms. We have, therefore, included a brief analysis of both the Meech Lake and Charlottetown Accords.

> Canada: The most decentralized country in existence, which causes Canadians to complain constantly about the power of the central government (Saul, 1995: 53).

The Meech Lake Accord

The popular term, the **Meech Lake Accord** — named after the place where the original agreement was negotiated — is technically incorrect. Instead, the proper term is the Constitution Amendment, 1987. In fact, the Meech Lake Accord consists of three documents: first, the original agreement in principle of April 1987 (the 1987 Constitutional Accord); second, the Resolution presented to Parliament to authorize the agreement; and third, the actual constitutional changes needed to implement the 1987 Constitutional Accord (the Constitution Amendment, 1987). Thus, the 1987 constitutional negotiations did not produce a new Canadian constitution; instead, they produced a series of proposed amendments to the Constitution Act, 1867 and the Constitution Act, 1982.

After the 1987 Constitutional Accord and the Constitution Amendment, 1987 were agreed to in June, the ratification process was allowed three years (until June 23, 1990 — three years from the date of the first legislature to approve the Accord). The initial response to the Meech Lake Accord was quite favourable. However, as provincial governments and leaders were changed (Manitoba, New Brunswick,

Newfoundland) and as the deadline drew near, considerable opposition to the proposal developed. The last few months (January to June, 1990) of the ratification process were extremely contentious, with the Meech Lake Accord failing to receive provincial approval in Manitoba and Newfoundland.

The primary constitutional problem facing Canadian politics in the mid-1980s was how to draw Quebec back into the constitutional family. Because it was the only province not to agree to the 1982 Canada Act, most politicians felt it essential, as soon as possible, to have Quebec become a full partner in the federal polity. Although not a top priority on the political agenda between 1982 and 1987, this problem of Quebec led to another round of constitutional negotiations which culminated in the 1987 Constitutional Accord — much to everyone's surprise.

> English Canada will only yield — and even this is not assured — if there is a knife at its throat (Léon Dion, father of federal Minister of Intergovernmental Affairs, Stéphane Dion, quoted in Simpson, 1993: 312).

Over half of the 1987 Constitution Amendment consists of proposed revisions to the Constitution Act, 1867. First, Quebec was recognized as constituting "a **distinct society**," and Canada was recognized as a bicultural society composed of French-speaking and English-speaking citizens, both inside and outside of Quebec. The "distinct society" clause was seen as crucial by Premier Bourassa to Quebec's future participation in, and support for, the federal system. However, critics of the Meech Lake Accord saw the "distinct society" clause as providing recognition of a special status for the province of Quebec.

The second major change to the 1867 Constitution Act concerned the method of selecting senators. The traditional method, selection by the prime minister, would have been replaced by a process which gave the provinces a significant role in choosing members of the upper House of the national legislature. When a Senate vacancy occurred, the government of the province (i.e., premier) in which that vacancy existed would have submitted a list of names to the Queen's Privy Council for Canada (i.e., prime minister) of those who might be summoned to the Senate. The prime minister would have selected the nominee from that list.

In many ways, this proposed procedure merely specified in law what had happened in practice for many years. However, by formalizing the process and the provinces' role in it, this revision would have forced the prime minister to relinquish some of his or her power in this area. Contrary to popular impression, the provinces would not have appointed members to the Senate under the Meech Lake Accord, but would only have recommended the names from which the prime minister would have chosen. There was nothing to force a prime minister to act. If the prime minister was not happy with the list of names submitted, he or she could have refused to appoint anyone, leaving the Senate seat vacant until a suitable name had been put forward by the province.

In an attempt to speed up the process of Senate reform, the province of Alberta, which wanted the Senate to be an elected body, used an election to determine their first list of Senate nominees. Six candidates vied for the position, with Stan Waters, representing the newly formed regional protest party — the Reform Party — easily winning over his rivals. On October 20, 1987, Alberta

Premier Don Getty submitted his list of nominees to Prime Minister Mulroney. Even though at this point the Meech Lake Accord had not been formally ratified, the Prime Minister had agreed to follow its provisions regarding Senate appointments. Athough selected under its auspices, Stan Waters was, in fact, opposed to the Meech Lake Accord, calling it a "seriously flawed document." However, Prime Minister Mulroney did not immediately act to appoint Stan Waters to the Senate, although he later did.

A third area of constitutional reform that would have been made by the Meech Lake Accord related to the judiciary. The Supreme Court of Canada, along with its composition and structure, would have been entrenched in the Constitution. For example, the Supreme Court was specified as consisting of nine justices (a Chief Justice of Canada and eight other judges), with three of these justices admitted from the bar of Quebec. A significant modification was made in the selection of Supreme Court judges. As with Senate appointments, the Queen's Privy Council of Canada — for all practical purposes the prime minister — would have chosen the judges from lists of names provided by the provinces.

In addition to these amendments to the 1867 Constitution Act, other changes would also have been made by the Meech Lake Accord to the 1982 Constitution Act. Sections 40–42 of the 1982 Constitution Act, for example, were to be modified, extending the range of areas for which provinces would receive financial compensation and over which each province would have a veto (since unanimous consent would have been required). For instance, unanimous consent would have been needed for any changes to "the powers of the Senate and the method of selecting Senators," "the Supreme Court of Canada," and "the establishment of new provinces." Previously these areas of reform only required the support of two-thirds of the provinces with 50 percent of the nation's population. Thus, each province would have had a veto over crucial areas of potential constitutional reform.

If these changes to the 1867 and 1982 Constitution Acts had been made, the Meech Lake Accord would have altered the direction of Canadian federalism. In contrast to Pierre Trudeau's vision of Canada and the centralizing tendencies of his rule and the 1982 Canada Act, the rejected Meech Lake Accord, by enhancing the role and power of the provinces, would have created a decentralizing pattern in the federal polity.

Within months of the death of the Meech Lake Accord (June 1990), the issue of constitutional renewal once again resurfaced. From November 1990 — with the appointment of the Citizens' Forum on Canada's Future (the Spicer Commission) — to February 1992 — with the report of the Special Joint Parliamentary Committee on a Renewed Canada (the Beaudoin-Dobbie Committee) — the Canadian polity, once again, became consumed with constitutional matters. The result of this two-year public consultation process was the emergence of at least a partial consensus on several key reform issues — enough at least to proceed to formal talks between the federal and provincial governments.

The Charlottetown Accord

Without Quebec in attendance, the first federal-provincial meeting to discuss constitutional matters since the death of the Meech Lake Accord was held in

March of 1992. With the negotiations making some progress, the federal government introduced enabling legislation in May of 1992 for a national referendum. By August, the first ministers reached a "draft consensus" at their Charlottetown meeting. On September 9, Parliament was recalled, with a referendum on the **Charlottetown Accord** scheduled for October 26, 1992. The referendum, it should be remembered, was only advisory and not required by the existing process of constitutional amendment.

The results of the referendum on the Charlottetown Accord were clear: an overwhelming national NO! Across the country nearly 55 percent of those voting rejected the Accord, with 45 percent in its favour. On a provincial basis the following provinces were opposed: Nova Scotia, Quebec, Manitoba, Saskatchewan, Alberta, and British Columbia. Ontario voted in favour, but just barely: 49.8 percent "yes" to 49.6 percent "no."

In contrast to the Meech Lake fiasco, where the political leaders' support had been divided, the Charlottetown Accord was strongly supported by all three major federal parties and the premiers in all of the provinces. Thus, the rejection of the Charlottetown Accord was not simply a rejection of a specific constitutional proposal, it was more fundamentally an explicit rejection and repudiation of Canada's political elite by the ordinary citizen.

Although defeated, the provisions of the Charlottetown Accord will continue to reverberate through the Canadian political process for many years to come. As with the Meech Lake Accord, the major thrust of the Charlottetown Accord would have been a further decentralization of power from the federal to the provincial governments. Such a pattern of potential decentralization can be seen in the major provisions of the Charlottetown Accord.

One of the great difficulties of the whole process of the Charlottetown Accord was that many of its provisions were vague and nonspecific. For example, the legal text of the draft consensus was not released until the referendum campaign was half-over (October 9, 1992) and then these provisions were subject to further review and clarification. In addition, over two-dozen key provisions were simply either general statements of broad principles or agreements to negotiate the specific details at a later date. Those provisions of the Charlottetown Accord that were detailed clearly represented a potentially fundamental alteration of the Canadian political process, at both an institutional and political level.

1. A "Canada Clause" stating the fundamental values of Canada was included, along with the recognition of Quebec's distinctiveness.

2. The social and economic union bases of Canada would be recognized, including specific social policy objectives (health care, education, social services) and economic policy objectives (reducing internal trade barriers, guaranteeing the federal government's role in equalization and regional development).

3. Recognition of the inherent right of self-government for Canada's Aboriginal peoples, including a constitutional role in future constitutional processes and guaranteed representation in federal institutions.

4.   Restrictions on the use of the federal spending power in areas of provincial jurisdiction, with financial compensation to any province not participating in any new national shared-cost programs.

5.   Recognition and increased role of the provinces in policy areas such as immigration, telecommunications, regional development, forestry, mining, and urban affairs.

6.   The amending formula would be changed to increase the number of areas in which unanimity would be required for future constitutional reform efforts, including the Senate, the House of Commons, and the Supreme Court.

7.   The provinces would be given an explicit role in the nomination of Supreme Court justices and a First Ministers' Conference would be required annually.

8.   The Senate would become an elected body, with a reduction from 104 seats to 62: six for each province and one from each territory. Aboriginal representation would be in addition to the number of 62. Senate elections would be held in conjunction with those for the House of Commons. Each province would determine its own method of Senate selection, with Quebec electing its senators by the Quebec National Assembly. (Several provinces, such as British Columbia and Nova Scotia, indicated that they would require half of their Senate seats to be guaranteed to women.) The Senate would have a 30-day "suspensive veto" with respect to revenue and expenditure bills. The Senate would not become a confidence chamber.

9.   In order to compensate those larger provinces that would lose seats in the Senate, their representation would be increased in the House of Commons. The size of the Commons would go from 295 to 337 seats after 1996. Regardless of population, Quebec would be guaranteed 25 percent of the seats in the House of Commons.

10. The federal government's powers of disallowance and reservation would be eliminated. The federal government's declaratory power would be restricted in the future, because the province or provinces affected would have to agree to its exercise.

Even though both the Meech Lake and Charlottetown Accords ultimately failed, they both have already had a profound impact on the future of Canadian politics by their effect on future reform efforts. Both Accords sought to revise the pattern of Canadian federalism by decentralizing power to the provinces.

Megaconstitutional politics and beyond

Both the Meech Lake and Charlottetown Accords attempted to bring about massive and wholesale change to the Canadian political structure, an approach that has been labelled **megaconstitutional politics** (Russell, 1993: 75). Such an approach deals not only with matters of political structure but, more specifically, goes to the core of the definition of the political community, typically resulting in a highly emotional and symbolic confrontation of the contending political forces. The point of contention in both the Meech Lake and Charlottetown Accords was the federal structure.

The **distinct society clause** in the Meech Lake Accord served as the lightning rod for the debate about Quebec. On a practical (*de facto*) basis, Quebec has been a distinct society since the beginning of Confederation and it has grown more distinct in recent decades. Quebec was given powers in 1867 that no other province had and has acquired others since that time, including the following: seats in the House of Commons are allocated to all provinces based on the number assigned to Quebec; the province is guaranteed three of the nine positions on the Canadian Supreme Court; it has its own legal system based on the civil law tradition; it has its own language and culture; it has its own tax and pension systems; and it has its own immigration policy. These points illustrate that Quebec is a distinct society; to argue otherwise is to ignore much of the Canadian historical experience!

Why then did the distinct society clause proposed in the Meech Lake Accord cause such a controversy? The simple answer is this: to recognize Quebec as a distinct society based on custom and convention is one thing, but it is quite another to explicitly recognize this by constitutional guarantees (i.e., a *de jure* recognition). Many in English Canada could not grant Quebec specific constitutional recognition on this point. A distinct society recognition for Quebec meant **special status** for Quebec and an acknowledgment of a pattern of official inequality among the provinces. A recognition of special status for Quebec would have produced a new type of federal system in Canada, what has been called asymmetrical federalism (McMenemy, 1994: 12).

Asymmetrical federalism is *a system in which the subordinate units in the federal system are not equal.* (Such a pattern can occur in either a centralized or decentralized federal system.) In Figure 2.2, we present a diagram of a pattern of asymmetrical federalism as projected by the Meech Lake Accord. While all provinces would have gained some power, Quebec would have been the clear winner. In an attempt to overcome this impasse, the Charlottetown Accord basically gave all the provinces the same powers as Quebec, which would have meant a massive decentralization of the current federal system (see Figure 2.3). The Charlottetown Accord would have given the provinces more power than the federal government and would have attempted to provide equality among the subordinate units (i.e., a special status solution for each province). Thus, we could characterize such a federal system as **decentralized symmetrical federalism**.

The defeat of the Meech Lake and Charlottetown Accords and the Liberal victory in the 1993 federal election led to a temporary respite from the megaconstitutional battles. Constitutional reform was not on the political

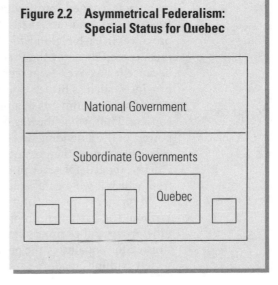

Figure 2.2   Asymmetrical Federalism: Special Status for Quebec

National Government

Subordinate Governments

Quebec

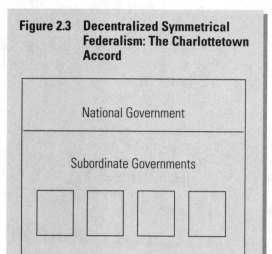

Figure 2.3   Decentralized Symmetrical Federalism: The Charlottetown Accord

National Government

Subordinate Governments

agenda as a priority and it appeared that new megaconstitutional reforms were very unlikely. However, the respite from constitutional politics did not last. The separatist government in Quebec called an independence referendum for the end of October 1995. While technically not an explicit vote for separation, its practical effects would have been a move toward Quebec independence. The referendum was narrowly defeated by less than 1 percent of the popular vote (49.4 percent for the YES side; 50.6 percent for the NO side). A handful of votes prevented the demise of the 128-year-old Canadian political system!

EXTRA-CONSTITUTIONAL REFORMS

Following the defeat of the separatist option, the federal government proceeded in 1995 to try and placate Quebec, but without going through a process of megaconstitutional politics that was likely to fail. Two actions were immediately taken: first, the federal Parliament passed a resolution recognizing Quebec as a distinct society; and second, the federal government decided to give Quebec and all the other provinces as well a veto over future constitutional amendments. Basically, what the federal government did in the 1996 **Regional Veto Act** was to unilaterally change some of the amending formulas (especially Section 38) provided for in the 1982 Constitution Act. The federal government agreed "to lend" its amending power to the provinces in the following way: before the federal government would agree to an amendment, the provinces would have to have given their prior approval. The country is divided into five regions: Ontario, Quebec, British Columbia, the Prairies, and Atlantic Canada. For the Prairies and Atlantic Canada, at least two provinces in each region with at least 50 percent of the population of that region must agree. Thus, for the Prairie region, Alberta has, in fact, been given a veto, because it has over 50 percent of the regional population. Moreover, several provinces, such as British Columbia, now require approval by the people of constitutional amendments in a provincial referendum prior to granting provincial consent. Thus, while the Regional Veto Act does significantly enhance provincial powers in the amending process, it also means that formal constitutional change is less likely now than at any time in recent decades. In an attempt to placate Quebec, the federal government has put itself into a constitutional straightjacket from which it will be difficult to extricate itself.

A further extra-constitutional reform was undertaken in September of 1997. Without the participation or agreement of Quebec Premier Lucien Bouchard, nine provincial premiers agreed to the **Calgary Declaration**. This statement stressed the equality of the provinces, as well as the "unique character of Quebec society within Canada."

However, such actions by the federal government and the provinces failed to satisfy the demands of Lucien Bouchard and separatist supporters in Quebec. With the threat of another referendum on the horizon and with the Quebec government claiming that only Quebec would decide that province's future in the federal system, the federal government requested the Supreme Court to issue an advisory or reference decision on the legality of Quebec separating from Canada. The Supreme Court issued its decision in August of 1998 in the ***Quebec Secession Reference***. The ruling was that Quebec did not have the right to unilaterally separate from Canada under either Canadian or international law. However, the Supreme Court went on to say that if "a clear majority vote in Quebec on a clear question in favour of secession" occurred, then the rest of Canada would have to recognize the legitimacy of such a request.

There then ensued a battle between Quebec and Ottawa over who would define and decide what was meant by "a clear question" and "a clear majority." Rejecting Quebec's claims to be the final voice in such matters, Ottawa moved to declare its role in such a process. The federal government's **Clarity Act**, which was passed in June of 2000, gives the national government, and particularly the House of Commons, the right to determine the clarity of the referendum question, as well as the result obtained. The Clarity Act also spells out areas of concern that would have to be negotiated with Quebec before an amendment would be made to the Constitution allowing Quebec to secede from the federal union. Whether intended or not, the *Quebec Secession Reference* and the Clarity Act have now specified the process by which the Canadian polity can be destroyed. Quebec's response was to pass Bill 99 in December of 2000, which reasserted Quebec's claim that the province can separate in defiance of Canadian law and the actions of the Canadian Parliament.

In contrast to this recent pattern of passing resolutions in the present to deal with potential future conflicts, most of Canadian history has seen, instead, a pattern of constitutional evolution based on custom and convention used as a way of adapting a fairly rigid constitutional structure to developing political realities.

THE EVOLVING CONSTITUTIONAL MILIEU

As in most countries, the intended constitutional structure may not be reflected in actual constitutional practice. The present Canadian Constitution operates very differently than the initial design would seem to indicate, a reflection, perhaps, of the view that a "constitution that did not change would, by definition, be nominal and not normative — an exercise in logic and not in life" (McWhinney, 1979: 9). Before analyzing the major causes for its evolution, we must first begin with a description of how Canada's constitutional system has developed since the Confederation agreement. The general pattern of change can be summarized as follows: Canada has moved from the highly centralized political structure of 1867 to one of the most **decentralized federal systems** in the world. However, within this broad trend there have been alternating periods of centralization and decentralization.

Canada was a centralized polity during both world wars, when the political system was run under the emergency powers legislation. Moreover, it is often forgotten that for 15 years, from 1939 to 1954, the polity was overwhelmingly Ottawa-directed. From this highly centralized system of the mid-1950s emerged a new round of provincial demands for greater autonomy, best symbolized by the Quiet Revolution in Quebec in the early 1960s. By the 1970s, the provinces had gained a rough equality of power with the federal government, reflected in the Alberta-Ottawa battles over energy-pricing.

This growing trend of decentralization was a prime motivation for Pierre Trudeau's entry into federal politics. One of the tenets of Trudeau's political philosophy was that the decentralization of the early 1960s had gone too far and too fast and, as leader of the Liberal party and prime minister, he tried to reverse that pattern. Changes sought by Pierre Trudeau in the early 1980s with respect to limiting Ottawa's financial role in areas of provincial jurisdiction, refusing to allow a further decline in Ottawa's constitutional powers in relation to the provinces (especially concerning Quebec), and passing the 1982 Constitution Act have all reflected a reassertion of the national government's role in the Canadian federal system. The basic equality of power established between the two levels of government by the early 1980s meant that neither level could govern effectively, for any extended period, without the co-operation of the other.

While the formal attempt to decentralize powers back to the provincial units in the Meech Lake and Charlottetown Accords failed, there has nevertheless been an enhancement of provincial powers. Through both financial and other agreements, Ottawa has turned back power in some areas to the provinces, symbolized by the regional veto given the provinces by the federal government in 1996. As the same time, especially with respect to Quebec, the federal government has reasserted its power, symbolized by the *Quebec Secession Reference* and the Clarity Act. Moreover, Ottawa has exercised its financial muscle — given its huge budget surpluses — in areas such as health care. Thus, the start of the new century saw the federal government in a more ascendant position over the provinces than was true a decade earlier.

The causes of constitutional evolution

While the reasons for the change to a decentralized political system are complex, five interdependent causes seem to be important. First, the provinces quickly became dissatisfied with the highly centralized structure created in 1867 and began, by the last decade of the 19th century, to demand greater powers. A federal system tends to make politicians in both levels of government believe that their level should be pre-eminent. Thus, the actual powers of each level of government in the federal system are always in a constant state of change.

A second cause of decentralization should perhaps be seen as a corollary of the first: as the provinces gained power, several of the key powers of the federal government became restricted. The legal basis for the exercise of these powers remained, but the federal government's political will to use them did not. Three important powers would fall into this category, namely, the declaratory power, disallowance, and reservation.

Based on custom and convention, these powers of the federal government had become largely inoperative by the 1940s. For example, the declaratory power was last exercised in 1961 on a relatively minor matter, disallowance last occurred in 1943, and the power of reservation was last exercised by a lieutenant-governor in 1961. However, these dates tend to hide the fact that the pattern had already been well established. For example, while reservation occurred in 1961, it did so without the direction of the federal government, which then quickly moved to allow that piece of legislation to become law. Thus, the powers of disallowance, reservation, and declaration remain legally available to the federal government, but their exercise has been severely restricted by custom and convention. The use of these powers is still possible in a crisis situation, but their exercise is dependent on a political judgment by the federal government that it can get away with their implementation.

The third and the most important reason for enhanced provincial powers was a series of judicial decisions which began in the 1880s and continued into the early decades of the 20th century. Until the establishment of the Supreme Court of Canada in 1949 as the final court of appeal for Canadian cases, the highest court of appeal was the **Judicial Committee of the British Privy Council (JCPC)**. Composed mainly of members of the British House of Lords, the JCPC rendered a series of decisions that had the effect of restricting federal powers and enhancing those of the provinces. For example, the broad grant of power to the federal government in the residual power clause was interpreted restrictively; that is, it was seen as only applying under special circumstances. In contrast, some of the powers of the provincial units, such as their control of property and civil rights, were generously applied by the JCPC. The result of such judicial decisions was to reinforce the evolving pattern of decentralization characteristic of the Canadian federal system in the 20th century.

A fourth contributing factor is the effect of the changing nature of society on the respective powers of the federal and provincial governments. Some of the activities granted the provinces in 1867, which were minor governmental functions in the 19th century, have since become major ones. For example, while the provinces obtained exclusive control of education in Section 93, few people received any schooling, despite the existence of a public school system. The acceptance of the notion of universal, public education through the high school years caused a massive expansion of this provincial government responsibility. A similar pattern has occurred with respect to the health and welfare functions. The result has been that provincial governments now spend about one-half of their entire budgets on these three concerns. Thus, minor provincial powers in 1867 have become major ones, and with that change has come more influence for the provincial units in the federal system.

A final reason for Canada's decentralized federalism is, perhaps, an outgrowth of the first four causes, that is, the emergence of a pattern of **province-building**. This concept stresses the development and significant role of the provincial governments in the federal structure (Hockin, 1976: 31). The growth of the provincial governments with respect to their size and areas of responsibility is both a cause and consequence of the enhanced power of the Canadian provinces. The trend in recent decades for the provinces to establish their own departments of intergovernmental affairs or, at least, to have a provincial minister given responsibility for handling relations with the national government is an indication of this change.

The evolution of the Canadian system from a pattern of centralized to decentralized federalism has occurred, for the most part, as the result of custom and convention rather than formal constitutional amendment. The lack of an explicit amending clause in the 1867 Constitution Act made the amending procedure difficult to use. In order to adapt to a changing environment, the Canadian polity simply altered the way it operated, without formally changing the rules of the game. This pattern is one basic reason why custom and convention play such a significant role in the Canadian political experience. Although explicit amending formulas are now included in the 1982 Constitution Act, as modified in 1996, and were utilized in the failed reform efforts of the 1980s and 1990s, it is still important to understand the amending dilemma that confronted the political system from 1867 to 1982.

Constitutional amendment 1867–1982

Two factors seem to account for the initial absence of an amending clause in the original Constitution: first, because Canada was a colony, there was no need for a specific amending procedure since any changes would be made by the British Parliament; and second, the allocation of powers was seen as comprehensive by the Fathers of Confederation and, thus, no changes appeared to be needed in the immediate future (Stevenson, 1979: 207–208). Such an optimistic view appears shortsighted in retrospect. The lack of a specific amending procedure created two obstacles that had to be overcome whenever a change in the Constitution was proposed: agreement had to be reached on the amendment procedure and on the content of the reform. However, questions of process and substance could not be easily divorced.

Before delving further into these intricacies we must first qualify our assertion that Canada lacked an amending formula. In fact, between 1867 and 1982 three different ways of formally changing the constitutional structure existed (Mallory, 1971: 375–378). First, from the very beginning, the provinces have been empowered to change their own structure and operation. The 1867 Constitution Act sets forth the structure of government for the four initial provinces, with the stipulation that such institutions would exist "until the provinces otherwise provide." For example, acting on this amending power, the provinces of Quebec (1968), Nova Scotia (1928), and New Brunswick (1892) all abolished their upper chambers or legislative councils.

The second way of amending the Constitution was for the federal government to claim the same power for changing its own structure and operation as that given the provinces. The Constitution Act (Number Two) of 1949 formally established the federal government's legitimacy in this regard. For example, changes in the size of the House of Commons are made possible without a formal amendment, as long as the rules for the allocation of seats between the provinces specified in the 1867 Constitution Act (as amended) are not violated.

The real amending problem developed with respect to the third area, that is, the **safeguarded portions** of the Constitution Act of 1867 (i.e., federal and provincial powers in Sections 91 and 92; minority religious educational rights in Section 93; language protection in Section 133). These responsibilities could only be altered by an amendment passed through the British Parliament at the request of the Canadian government. Several facets of Britain's power to amend the Canadian Constitution must be kept in mind: first, no amendment was ever made except at the request of the Canadian government; second, no request from the Canadian government was ever refused; and third, the amending power remained in Britain because of the lack of an agreement within Canada itself on an amending formula. If points one and two, in particular, are kept in mind, then Canada has always had the *de facto* power to amend even the safeguarded portions of the Constitution, if agreement on the content of such an amendment could be achieved in Canada.

Disputes about the content of such amendments to the safeguarded portions invariably raised concerns about procedure as well. Such amendments usually resulted after the federal Parliament passed a resolution outlining the contents of the changes proposed to Britain for implementation. The key procedural problems occurred prior to this resolution: whether and when the provinces were to be consulted and, if consulted, what kind of consensus was to be required before the federal government could proceed. From a narrow legal point of view, the federal government could act unilaterally. However, the custom and convention soon developed that the provinces should be consulted, or, at least, those provinces that were directly affected by the proposed amendments. If consultation did not lead to agreement between the federal government and the provinces, then the federal government, on political grounds, would usually not proceed with the reforms. Thus, the content of the proposed amendment affected the procedure for its adoption, and both content and procedure limited the frequency of altering the Constitution from 1867 to 1982.

OPERATING THE FEDERAL SYSTEM

Difficulties of making formal amendments, a changing distribution of power between the federal and provincial levels, the impact of judicial decisions, and a changing political environment have all contributed to the complexity of the Canadian federal system. One result has been that both levels of government are involved in almost every major policy area. The exclusive powers of Sections 91 and 92 have, in many instances, become concurrent powers in practice. For example, the exclusive control of education given to the provinces has not prevented the federal government's extensive participation in university and vocational education programs: in the 1998 federal budget Finance Minister Paul Martin announced the creation of the Millennium Scholarship Foundation, with a ten-year endowment of $2.5 billion designed to create 100 000 scholarships with an average value of $3,000. Because of objections from provincial governments, especially Quebec, that this program interfered with a provincial area of jurisdiction, the money had to be sent through the provincial governments to the students, based on agreements negotiated by the Foundation with each provincial government.

Such complexity requires a constant process of negotiation between the two levels of government in order to keep the federal system functioning. This bargaining pattern between the elected and appointed officials of the two levels of government has been labelled **executive federalism** (Smiley, 1980: 92). The process of negotiations is best symbolized by the Conference of First Ministers, which usually meets once a year, or sometimes more often, to handle special concerns such as economic problems or constitutional reform. A good example of the work of the Conference of First Ministers occurred on September 11, 2000 in relation to health care funding. After years of federal financial cutbacks, followed by several years of negotiations between the federal government and the provinces, a unanimous agreement was announced by Canada's first ministers regarding federal funding for health care. Over a five-year period, federal funding would increase by over $23 billion. Attended by the prime minister and the 10 premiers, plus a retinue of other elected and appointed officials, these conferences resemble meetings between heads of state. This pattern is a reflection, perhaps, of the current powers of the provincial units, as well as the fact that the first such conference, held in 1927, was organized along the lines of the Imperial Conference (an international meeting of nation-states in the British Commonwealth).

In addition to the First Ministers' Conference, the premiers, themselves, hold an annual meeting to discuss their common concerns. For example, at their August 1989 meeting the provincial premiers unanimously rejected as unacceptable the proposed new 9 percent federal sales tax. (Although the Goods and Services Tax or GST was eventually adopted by the federal government, the rate was lowered to 7 percent, partly as a result of such provincial opposition.) As well, the Western premiers meet annually, and the Maritime premiers quarterly. Bilateral talks between two premiers are common, and Alberta and British Columbia even held a joint cabinet meeting in the summer of 1981. More important, perhaps, are the almost daily contacts and discussions behind the scenes by various interprovincial and federal provincial committees. Such constant contact, interaction, and bargaining have been important mechanisms for adapting an inflexible written constitution to a changing environment.

Financing federalism

One of the key areas in the Canadian federal system is finance, probably the most complex aspect of federal-provincial relations. The basic conflict in the area of **fiscal federalism** stems from the fact that each level of government wants credit for beneficial programs, yet at the same time it seeks to get the other level to pay the expenses.

Provincial reliance on federal largesse is well illustrated by the equalization grants the poorer provinces receive from Ottawa, which mushroomed from $136 million in 1958 to $2.5 billion by the mid-1970s. By the end of the 1991–1992 fiscal year, **equalization payments** were more than $8.3 billion. By the mid-1980s, as much as 45 to 55 percent of some provincial budgets were federal dollars. Total federal transfers to the provinces (including equalization payments as well as specific purpose transfers for such items as medicare and education) reached $18.5 billion in 1984–1985. By the 1989–1990 fiscal year, total federal transfers to the provinces were $24 billion. By 1992, if all types of **transfer payments** from Ottawa to the provincial governments are included, the cost to the federal treasury was about $40 billion.

Because the provinces spend the money, they receive credit for such programs as health, education, and medical care, while the federal government pays the bills. By limiting its rate of growth in these areas, the federal government not only appears to be holding its expenditures in line, but also forces the provinces to assume more of the financial costs of these popular programs. Although the Mulroney Conservatives promised better federal-provincial relations during the 1984 campaign, by the end of their first year in office they too — like the Trudeau Liberals before them — found the provinces opposed to any reductions in their transfer payments from the federal government. In September 1985, Finance Minister Michael Wilson announced that the cutbacks in EPF (established program financing) funding would begin a year earlier than previously indicated (i.e., the increase would be only 5 percent, not the anticipated 7 percent). Between 1982 and 1994, the federal government unilaterally altered (i.e., reduced) the EPF formula six times. These reductions in the rate of growth of transfer payments saved the federal government $9 billion by 1994.

Such conflicts regarding federal-provincial financial arrangements as that over EPF are inherent in the Canadian federal system, regardless of who is prime minister or which parties are in power. A similar battle in relation to fiscal federalism began in 1990 concerning federal funding for the Canada Assistance Plan (CAP). Begun in 1967 on a 50-50 cost-shared basis, CAP allowed Ottawa to get involved in paying for provincial social welfare programs. However, in its 1990 budget the federal government unilaterally announced that it was imposing a ceiling of 5 percent on its CAP payments to the wealthy provinces of Alberta, British Columbia, and Ontario. The provinces challenged the federal government's action in the judicial system, but lost before the Supreme Court (August 1991). By placing a cap on the funding for CAP, the federal government would save approximately $2 billion between 1990 and 1995.

In the 1980s and 1990s, the major battles over fiscal federalism centred on offloading between the federal and provincial governments. **Offloading** is cutting federal spending (and by implication the federal deficit) by reducing the amount of federal transfer payments to the provinces. As a result, the provinces are forced to cut services, raise taxes, or increase their debt — singly or in combination. Offloading results, at least in theory, in the provinces bearing the financial and political costs of the federal government's spending reductions.

However, a look at the pattern of federal transfer payments (equalization, EPF, and CAP) presents a somewhat different picture. What the federal government has done has been to reduce the rate of growth in transfer payments such as EPF and CAP, while the actual amount of money transferred to the provinces has increased substantially. For example, in 1984–1985 total federal transfers to the provinces stood at $25 billion, a figure which had increased to $40 billion a decade later. However, between 1995 and the fiscal year 2000–2001 the total amount of federal transfers remained steady at approximately $40 billion — a sure sign of the success of the federal government's offloading strategy. Moreover, it was clear by the end of the 1990s that the money saved by the federal government was being used to fund new high-profile spending initiatives by Ottawa in areas such as health and education, thus bypassing the provincial governments.

The continuing decades-old battle over financing federalism led the federal government to a major policy innovation that was announced in 1995. Previous programs, such as EPF and CAP, would be eliminated and replaced by the **Canada Health and Social Transfer (CHST)**. The program began (perhaps symbolically) on April 1, 1996. A single transfer payment would be made by the federal government to each province; in return, the provinces would gain control of how those funds would be spent. However, the drawback for the provinces was that the total CHST during its first two years of operation (1996–1998) would be cut by $7 billion and it would be up to the provinces to decide how to treat that shortfall. Critics derisively labelled the CHST as MOAT — the "mother of all transfers." The obvious result of the CHST was the continued downsizing of the federal government and a decentralization of power and finance to the provincial units.

Provincial complaints, as well as a burgeoning federal surplus, lead to a revision of the CHST in September of 2000. For fiscal year 2001–2002, the CHST would be increased by $2.8 billion, with a total increase of over $21 billion by fiscal year 2005–2006. In addition, beginning in April 2002 an automatic escalator clause of four percent would be applied to the CHST. Additional funding on health care, for such items as new equipment, was funded at $2.3 billion. Thus, after years of cutbacks, primarily at the expense of the provinces, the federal government began to restore some of the funding for social programs paid for by the CHST.

Our survey of the constitutional structure of the Canadian polity has emphasized that there is considerably more to it than simply the Constitution Act of 1867. Beginning with a highly centralized federal structure, the Canadian political system has evolved into a decentralized one, characterized by an intermingling of federal-provincial responsibilities and finance. This pattern reflects the needs of a changing society, as well as the impact of judicial decisions and evolving public beliefs about the role of the federal and provincial levels. Moreover, major additions to the initial constitutional structure, including the 1988 Emergencies Act and 1982 Constitution Act, have been effected. This combination of reforms has filled in some of the interstices of constitutional government, so that Canada has not only a series of written constitutional documents, but significant constitutional customs and conventions as well, both of which combine to produce a particular version of constitutional government.

THE BRITISH CONSTITUTION

In describing the British system one is faced with a problem: the British pattern of constitutional government is not outlined in a written constitution. Instead, as former prime minister Harold Wilson (1977: 208) put it, the British Constitution is "based on seven hundred years of mainly pragmatic experience." As a result, constitutional principles are significantly embodied in the customs and conventions of the political process, although disagreements do exist over some of the specific ingredients of British constitutionalism (Verney, 1976: 37–38).

Although Britain is characteristically classified as lacking a written constitution, such a view must be modified, because Britain does have a series of written constitutional documents. Such constitutional statutes would include the following: the Magna Carta (1215), the Petition of Rights (1628), the Habeas Corpus Act (1701), the Parliament Acts of 1911 and 1949, the Government of Ireland Act (1920), and the Representation of the People Acts (1948 and 1949). Also of constitutional import are the Reform Acts (1832, 1867, 1884), the Statute of Westminster (1931), the emergency powers legislation (1914, 1939), the Peerage Act (1963), and the 1972 European Communities Act.

More recently, the Labour party, after its 1997 election victory, proceeded with a series of significant constitutional reforms (Blackburn and Plant, 1999). These new constitutional statutes would include the following: the Scotland Act (1998), the Government of Wales Act (1998), the Northern Ireland Act (1998), the House of Lords Act (1999), and the Greater London Authority Act (1999). Each of these constitutional documents helps to delineate the workings and structure of major segments of the British constitutional system. However, what is missing in Britain is a single, written, and comprehensive constitutional statement.

> For the British Constitution is essentially a political constitution, one whose operation depends upon the strength of political factors and whose interpretation depends upon the will of its political leaders (Bogdanor, 1988: 71).

The most important characteristic of the British state is that it is **unitary**, meaning that there is *one sovereign government in London which is granted political authority by Parliament*. Subordinate governments, such as local and regional authorities, may exist, but they do so at the pleasure of the central government. What a central government grants, such as local government, it can also take away.

Thus, while British government remains a unitary state, it has devolved power to local and regional authorities. **Devolution** can be defined as *the delegation of political authority by a central government to subordinate units of government*. In 1998 and 1999, constitutional reforms moved Britain away from the strict definition of a unitary state to a pattern that has been called **quasi-federalism** (Hazell and Sinclair, 1999: 177). Significant grants of political authority have been given to Scotland, Wales, Northern Ireland, regional governments, and the City of London.

Britain thus began the new millennium as a modified or hybrid unitary state, somewhere between a unitary structure and a federal form of government. It is important to remember that devolution in a unitary state is not the same thing as creating a federal political system, as in Canada. The reason for this assessment is simple: what a central government grants in a unitary state can be rescinded by a later parliament without the agreement of the subordinate units of government — an action that could not take place in a federal political system.

In addition to its series of constitutional documents, and its traditional unitary form of government, the third significant element of constitutionalism in

Britain is custom and convention. Tradition, for example, established the relationship between the various governmental institutions that is indicated in the concept of the dual executive. The evolution of power from the formal to the political executive and the present pattern of their interaction is unspecified in any constitutional document. Similarly, notions of the collective responsibility of the government to the House of Commons, as well as the evolution of a system of party discipline and party government, both reflect custom rather than law. The lack of any comprehensive constitution has made the role of custom and convention even more significant in British politics than in the Canadian system.

A fourth aspect of constitutionalism concerns the role of the courts and the common law in Britain. Although the judiciary interprets the law in Britain, it in no sense takes an activist role in challenging Parliament's authority to define the law. Moreover, the concept of the **common law**, that is, the *law based on custom and convention*, has been an important ingredient of constitutionalism by establishing basic civil and political liberties, such as freedom of speech. Britain, for example, does not have a specific bill of rights to protect individual freedoms: instead, the Bill of Rights of 1689 established parliamentary control over the monarch. These ideas concerning judicial decisions and the common law are perhaps best summarized by the concept of the **rule of law** (Coxall and Robins, 1994: 91–92).

The various traditional elements of British constitutionalism (i.e., the series of constitutional documents, a unitary structure, customs and conventions, and the rule of law) are reflected in the major institutions and principles of government. Of paramount importance is the principle of parliamentary sovereignty, which is theoretically unlimited in Britain. The law is what Parliament says it is and there is no legal basis for challenging its authority, since Britain has never traditionally accepted the American principle of full judicial review or the need for a bill of rights to protect human liberties. Second, the structure of the polity is unitary in form, and, thus, the national government does not share power with other political units. Local government exists at the prerogative of the national government — it is not a separate level of government with independent authority. The acceptance of the idea of devolution in 1998–1999 has only begun to change the traditional unitary structure of the British polity. Third, Britain is a constitutional monarchy; that is, the Queen reigns, but the political executive, working through Parliament, governs. A monarchical form does not produce monarchical power, with the modern British monarch fulfilling primarily the symbolic and ceremonial tasks of the state. Fourth, cabinet government, centred around its collective responsibility to the House of Commons, has been combined with party discipline and unity to produce a pattern of governance classified as party government. **Party government** is the motor of the modern British parliamentary system, the key technique for the fusion of executive and legislative powers. Finally, explicit protection of civil and political liberties is neither traditionally provided nor thought to be needed, since Parliament itself will seek to guarantee their existence.

The above five factors of traditional British constitutional practice have created a political system strongly centralized in both theory and practice. From a legal point of view, there is very little that the government of the day could not achieve, including doing away with basic civil and political liberties. For example, in the fall of 1988, in an attempt to combat the continuing problem of IRA terrorist activities, the Thatcher government introduced legislation taking away the centuries-old right in British jurisprudence of a suspect (in Northern Ireland) to remain silent. However, the customs and conventions of the polity usually limit the potential abuse of such a system of concentrated power, even if they do not eliminate such a possibility altogether. A political system of concentrated power is not inconsistent with constitutional government, as long as that power is constrained in use and effectively circumscribed by the customs and conventions of the polity.

The major advantage of the British constitutional system is its traditional flexibility in reacting to changing public beliefs and circumstances. Since the basic constitutional documents are simply acts of Parliament like any other, they can be readily modified or replaced. For example, in two years (1998–1999) the Blair government introduced a series of far-reaching constitutional reforms — the most significant alterations to the British constitution in over a century (Hazell et al., 2000: 242–261). These changes included the process of devolution to Scotland, Wales, Northern Ireland, and the City of London, as well as a major restructuring of the House of Lords and an expanded recognition of the authority of the European Parliament over British legislation. Thus, there is no need for a specific amending procedure or a long, drawn-out debate about the content of the reforms, as there is in Canada. Moreover, since so much of British constitutionalism is dependent on custom and convention, its flexibility is further enhanced because the practices of politics are modified in the daily workings of the political institutions and processes of government. A final advantage of a British-style system is its ability to act, to get its legislative program passed, and to meet both domestic and international crises. Concentration of power has never been seen as automatically deleterious to constitutional government but, often in the modern era, as a prerequisite for its continuation. In contrast, the philosophical assumptions of constitutional government in the United States are based on the desire to limit any such concentrations of political authority:

> Lord Acton's famous phrase that "power tends to corrupt and absolute power corrupts absolutely," while that of an Englishman, has nevertheless found greater acceptance in the United States than in Great Britain itself (Mitchell, 1970: 109).

THE AMERICAN CONSTITUTION

The nature of constitutional government in the United States has to be understood in the context of the American Revolution and its consequences. First, by achieving independence through the force of arms, the colonial leaders were confronted with the need to specify in a written, comprehensive document the structure of a new system of government. However, their initial attempt in the Articles of Confederation failed, which led ultimately to the present American Constitution. Second, the revolutionary context resulted in a revised philosophy of democratic government, which, in contrast to the British pattern of concentrated authority, emphasized the need to limit government. The Fathers of the American Constitution "did not believe in man, but they did believe in the power of a good political constitution to control him" (Hofstadter, 1948: 3). Finally, popular sovereignty was the ideal: power was to flow from the people to the government. This outlook was summarized best in the words of the Declaration of Independence, which asserts that humans are "endowed by their Creator with certain unalienable rights, that among these are life, liberty, and the pursuit of happiness," and that to secure such rights, "governments are instituted among men, deriving their just powers from the consent of the governed." This view contrasts sharply with the British-based, conservative Canadian view of government's role as the provider of "peace, order and good government," and reflects an important difference in the constitutional perspectives of these two political systems.

The essence of American constitutionalism is the view that the people must be protected from government. To achieve limited government, any undue concentration of political authority must be prevented. Such a philosophy of democratic government was explicitly argued in *The Federalist Papers,* a series of newspaper editorials written to convince the people of the need to adopt the new system of government. The best summary of the American political philosophy remains *Federalist Paper Number 51,* written by James Madison, who is often referred to as the Father of the American Constitution.

> But the great security against a gradual concentration of the several powers in the same department consists in giving to those who administer each department the necessary constitutional means and personal motives to resist encroachments of the others. The provision for defence must in this, as in all other cases, be made commensurate to the danger of attack. Ambition must be made to counteract ambition. The interest of the man must be connected with the constitutional rights of the place. It may be a reflection on human nature that such devices should be necessary to control the abuses of government. But what is government itself but the greatest of all reflections on human nature? If men were angels, no government would be necessary. If angels were to govern men, neither external nor internal controls on government would be necessary. In framing a government which is to be administered by men over men, the great difficulty lies in this: you must first enable the government to control the governed; and in the next place oblige it to control itself. A dependence on the people is, no doubt, the primary control on the government; but experience has taught mankind the necessity of auxiliary precautions.

In addition to being the closest thing to poetry in the conversation of political analysts, this quotation stresses the need to limit government through the use of certain "auxiliary precautions," that is, those principles of government upon which the American system is founded. These auxiliary precautions are fourfold: separation of powers, checks and balances, federalism, and a bill of rights. The heart of American constitutionalism is reflected in the way the political structures embody these four principles, all of which seek to fragment and restrain the use and concentration of influence and power by the political elites.

SEPARATION OF POWERS

The adoption and implementation of the separation of powers doctrine represents one of the unique contributions of American politics to the art of democratic government. **Separation of powers** refers to *the establishment of several branches of government (executive, legislative, and judicial), the allocation of governmental powers among these three branches, and a pattern of political and constitutional independence of each branch of government from the other.* The separation of powers principle is a reflection of the view that "ambition must be made to counteract ambition." Each branch of government is inherently in conflict with the others, as it jealously guards its own prerogatives and seeks to carry out the tasks assigned to it (Jones, 1995). Moreover, each branch must have the co-operation of the others in order to carry out these activities. Such co-operation among branches is essential in order for the American system to work, while such a pattern is made difficult by the structure of government so created. By fragmenting power among the several branches, co-operation among all three institutions was made improbable. In that sense, the American polity was created to prevent government activity — a goal that has, more often than not, been admirably achieved (Knight, 1989).

The political and constitutional independence of the three branches of government is explicitly provided for in the Constitution. For example, the officers in each institution are kept distinct, since no individual can serve in two branches of government at the same time. Thus, a separation of powers doctrine is implemented, in part, by a separation of personnel, in sharp contrast to the fusion of powers in the Canadian and British parliamentary systems. A further means of creating political independence for each branch is to have the executive, legislature, and judiciary responsive to varying political constituencies. Thus, the president and vice-president have a national constituency, members of the Senate a statewide electorate, members in the House of Representatives a locally-based constituency, and judicial appointees a combination of such bases, depending on which court an individual serves. Moreover, members of each branch remain in office for differing time periods: the president serves a four-year term, with the possibility of being re-elected once; senators are chosen for a six-year period, with one-third elected every two years; all representatives are voted on every two years; and judicial appointees generally serve for life. With each branch of government composed of different personnel, responsive to different constituencies, and staying in office for different time periods, individuals' outlooks and political interests rarely coalesce. The result is the prevention of any undue concentration of political power.

> "If you are ever again taking an exam on American government," the professor scolded his students, "and come up against a question you can't figure out, for heaven's sake just put down 'separation of powers.' It explains roughly half of everything that happens" (Ladd, 1986: 3).

> There are two fundamental arguments for a constitutional system of separate institutions sharing powers: it helps preserve liberty and it slows the pace of political change. These arguments are as valid today as they were in 1787 (Wilson: 1987: 49).

CHECKS AND BALANCES

In order to guarantee the continuation of the separation of powers principle once the political structure began operating, the second auxiliary precaution — namely, a series of checks and balances — was included in the Constitution. In other words, **checks and balances** are *the constitutionally specified mechanisms and powers designed to preserve the political independence of each branch of government.* For example, **executive privilege**, the right of the executive branch not to turn over information to either the legislature or judiciary, is a major means for protecting its independence. Such a procedure is also a key defence against legislative supremacy, that is, the development of a parliamentary-style system.

Numerous other such checks and balances could be cited. For example, Supreme Court appointments are recommended by the executive, but must be approved by the Senate. A treaty negotiated and signed by the president must be approved by a two-thirds vote in the Senate before becoming law. Any piece of legislation must be approved by both the executive and legislative branches of government, except when the legislature overrides a presidential veto. Even when approval by both branches is gained, the Supreme Court may rule such legislation null and void.

The result of the separation of powers principle and the series of checks and balances has been to create a governmental system "of separated institutions sharing power," and a pattern of "mutually dependent relationships" (Neustadt, 1980: 26, 28). In such a system every branch of government is given a certain portion of executive, legislative, and judicial power. For example, while the executive branch exercises most of the executive authority, both the legislature and judiciary are also given executive powers. The same argument holds true for the other branches. Thus, each "department is given a voice in the business of the others, and each is made dependent on the co-operation of the others in order to accomplish its own business" (Peltason, 1997: 24).

The ultimate example of the impact of both the separation of powers and checks and balances in recent American politics came in late 1995, in the political stalemate over the budget between Democratic president Bill Clinton and the Republican majorities in both legislative houses. Because Congress and the president could not agree to a compromise on the various appropriation measures, the government literally ran out of money and consequently shut down — for six days in November and a further twenty-one days in December and January (Hill, 2000). A pattern of mutual dependence means that neither the president nor Congress can govern without the co-operation of the other; it is likely that James Madison was smiling in his grave.

> It was too much to expect that vice could be checked by virtue; the Fathers relied instead upon checking vice with vice (Hofstadter, 1948: 7).

FEDERALISM

The third major restriction on the concentration of power is the principle of **federalism**, previously defined as *the division of powers between levels of government.*

The division of powers and the separation of powers are principles that are not interchangeable in political analysis. In the American system, each level of government (i.e., national and state) is structured internally on the separation of powers principle. For example, the national government is composed of three branches of government, as are each of the 50 state governments. Thus, a federal structure is consistent with either a presidential system based on the separation of powers principle or a parliamentary system founded on a fusion of powers doctrine.

Although both Canada and the United States are federal political systems, the federal principle was adopted for very different reasons in each country. Canadian federalism was a means primarily of handling ethnic diversity, while American federalism was designed to fragment and mitigate the concentration of political power. To enhance that fragmentation, the American federal system was initially decentralized. Although for generally similar reasons as in Canada, the evolution of American federalism runs counter to the Canadian experience: beginning with a largely decentralized federal structure, American federalism has become highly centralized, especially during the past 70 years.

The American Constitution allocated a series of explicit powers to the national government in Article I, Section 8, which included the right to collect taxes, provide for the common defence and general welfare, coin money, declare war, establish post offices, regulate commerce, and borrow money. Such functions are referred to as **enumerated powers**, with the national government also given the **implied powers** that might be needed to carry out the enumerated ones. Of interest is the fact that, after the list of powers given to the federal government, there followed a list of powers denied to Congress (Section 9) and a list of powers denied to the states (Section 10). No specific allocation of powers was made to the states, because it was assumed that all powers not specifically granted the national government were retained by the states. A specific **residual power clause** was later added as the Tenth Amendment, to confirm the reserve power of the several states. However, within those powers granted to the national government, its laws would be supreme over those of the states (Article VI).

Local government was not recognized as a separate level, but was assumed to be under the powers retained by the states. Although local government was, therefore, in a unitary relationship with its respective state, over the years the municipalities have gained a good measure of independence. Despite considerable objections from the states, the national government has been able to deal directly with local governments, thus bypassing the intermediate state level. Such a development runs counter to the Canadian experience.

The American Constitution initially did not contain any provisions for emergency powers for the national government, nor have any such powers been added by the amendment process. However, the implied powers of the national government, with respect to defence and the general warfare functions, have been a sufficient basis for strong governmental action, when required. In addition, the prerogative powers of the president, especially those growing out of his role as Commander in Chief, combined with special emergency powers granted to him by Congress, have been sufficient to meet any crisis situation. As a result, the

United States has no specific counterpart to the Canadian War Measures Act, or its successor, the 1988 Emergencies Act.

Finally, the American Constitution, unlike the Canadian, contained a specific amending clause (Article V). Two ways of proposing amendments and two methods for ratifying such changes were outlined, thus producing four possible amending procedures. The usual method has been for an amendment to be proposed by a two-thirds vote in both Houses of Congress, followed by ratification by three-fourths of the state legislatures. Neither the president at the national level nor the governors at the state level have any veto power with respect to the amendment resolutions. However, such procedures are difficult to use, with the result that in over 210 years, with over 11 000 proposed amendments, only 27 formal amendments have been made to the American Constitution.

An extremely unusual example of the amendment process concerns the most recent one — the Twenty-Seventh Amendment passed in 1992. First proposed by James Madison in 1789 in the very first Congress, the Twenty-Seventh Amendment requires that no pay raise to the Senate or House can be given effect until after the next election for the House of Representatives. Thus, legislators must face the people before they can inflate their own salaries. While the modern practice since 1919 is for Congress to set a specific time limitation on the amendment process (usually seven years), no such limit was imposed in 1789, thus leading to a 203-year amendment process.

Although the initial federal structure was decentralized, currently the United States is an example of a strongly centralized federal system. Changes in society, governmental functions, and court interpretations have all contributed to such a pattern. For example, decisions of the American Supreme Court enhanced the powers of the national government with respect to three key areas: trade and commerce, taxation, and the war power (Burns et al., 2000: 57–67). Remember that in Canada, court decisions restricted the powers of the national government.

Another cause of a centralized federalism in the United States can be seen in the responses to both domestic and international crises. Until the 1930s, American government remained decentralized, but in order to respond to the Great Depression, the national government assumed many of the previous functions of the state and local units with respect to welfare, unemployment, and economic development. As in Canada, for example, the superior taxing power of the American national government eventually led to its participation in matters originally under state and local control. Through a series of financial mechanisms, such as the program of revenue-sharing, the American federal government has become extensively involved in financing of state and local government.

In addition, the Second World War and the emergence of the United States as a superpower in international affairs have greatly expanded the powers of the American presidency and, by implication, those of the national government. Such changes, more often than not, have been based on developing beliefs and conventions, rather than on explicit constitutional amendments. Finally, social changes, such as the civil rights movement of the 1960s, the urban crisis of the 1970s, and problems of societal disintegration in the 1980s and 1990s, have drawn governments, especially the national government, into new areas of activity. For these reasons, the national government has become the dominant level in the American federal system.

BILL OF RIGHTS

The final auxiliary precaution, a bill of rights, was not included in the original Constitution. However, in order to gain public support for its ratification, the backers of the Constitution promised that a bill of rights would be a priority of the new government. Thus, the first 10 amendments to the Constitution were adopted in 1791 and they comprise the American **Bill of Rights**.

Protections are given to basic civil and political liberties, including freedom of speech, religion, and assembly. Citizens are guarded against unreasonable searches and seizures by the government, granted the right of reasonable bail and the due process of law, prevented from self-incrimination, and guaranteed a trial by jury in common law cases. Although it was entrenched, the American Bill of Rights only applied initially to the national government. Beginning in the 1920s and continuing through the 1960s, a series of court decisions effectively "national-ized" the Bill of Rights, making it applicable to the states as well as to the federal government. This development was accomplished by judicial interpretation rather than by formal constitutional amendment.

The four auxiliary precautions of the separation of powers, checks and balances, federalism, and a bill of rights are the centrepieces of American constitutional practice. Based on the assumption of the inherently evil nature of political power, all four principles were designed to prevent its accumulation in the polity. Concentration of power, and by implication its misuse, was made improbable by dividing political power between two levels of government (federalism); by splitting power within each level into executive, legislative, and judicial arenas (separation of powers); by structuring each department of government so that it would jealously guard its own powers and prerogatives (checks and balances); and by limiting the powers of any government through a series of civil and political liberties (a bill of rights). According to the American perspective, the way to create constitutional government is to structure a government of limited and circumscribed powers.

> Under the U.S. constitution, there is no master of the American political universe, nor will there ever be (Canadian Ambassador to the United States, Allan Gotlieb, 1989: A6).

COMPARING CONSTITUTIONS

The most significant element in any political analysis of constitutions is determining whether or not they effectively restrain governmental power, that is, whether they produce, in fact, a pattern of constitutional government. Distinctions such as those between **written** and **unwritten constitutions** are secondary to questions of constitutionalism. However, to classify a polity as a constitutional government, one has to go beyond the literal constitution to consider such things as whether or not a political system allows political dissent and political opposition. If a pattern of constitutional government does exist, then the way in which it is produced in different political systems becomes a significant basis for comparing political systems.

The structure of government itself may contribute to a system of constitutionalism. For example, some constitutional polities are presidential in format, while others are parliamentary. A presidential system, based on a separation of powers doctrine, seeks to constrain executive authority, while a parliamentary system concentrates power through the fusion of the executive and legislative branches of government. Some political systems are unitary in structure, while others are federal. If a polity is federal, then questions of how many levels of government have been created and their respective powers become significant. In analyzing federal systems, an important consideration is not only the initial distribution of powers outlined in the constitution, but the way in which those powers may have changed in practice. If there have been changes, then one must investigate how they have occurred and how the initial allocation of powers has been modified. The causes for the evolution and development of the pattern of power in a federal system are complex, but usually include a changing environment, the impact of judicial decisions, and modified public beliefs about the proper political role of each level of government.

Changes in constitutional systems may be accomplished by a formal amending process, but, more often than not, are produced by the evolving customs and conventions of the polity. These customs and conventions have a significant bearing on the existence and operation of constitutional government. The nature of these conventions, their strength, and the result of any non-observance of them are all significant indicators for comparing the varieties of constitutional government.

A final point for the comparison of constitutions concerns their protection of civil and political liberties. A political analyst must consider what human freedoms are protected and how. The typical pattern in the modern era is to have some sort of bill of rights, which can be either entrenched in the constitution or passed in its own right. In federal systems a key question is the application of such guarantees to each level of government: do human rights exist in relation to one or both levels of government? Moreover, in times of crisis, can a bill of rights be bypassed through the application of emergency powers and, if so, how long do such actions hold human freedom in limbo?

Three main areas, therefore, form the basis for any comparative analysis of constitutions: first, whether a constitution has helped to produce a constitutional government in practice; second, the kind of political structure that is outlined in the constitution (e.g., presidential or parliamentary, federal or unitary); and third, the mechanism, if any, that is used to protect basic human freedoms.

SUMMARY

1. A constitution is a political mechanism that structures the institutions of government; it is a power map of the polity. However, no such outline of the basic rules of the political game is ever neutral in its effects: constitution writers defend their own interests above all others. A country's constitution usually includes not only a written part, but significant political customs and conventions as well.

2. Having a piece of paper called a constitution and having a system of constitutional government are not necessarily synonymous developments. Few constitutions produce constitutional government, that is, a polity that places effective limits on the powers and actions of its rulers.

3. The Canadian Constitution includes not only the Constitution Act of 1867, but a series of constitutional documents as well. Moreover, political customs and conventions are significant elements in Canada's federal and parliamentary constitutional matrix. Beginning with a highly centralized federal structure, Canada has evolved to a decentralized federal pattern. Three major additions to the constitutional pattern have been made since Confederation: the War Measures Act and its successor, the 1988 Emergencies Act; the 1960 Bill of Rights; and the Constitution Act of 1982, which includes the Canadian Charter of Rights and Freedoms.

4. Given the difficulties of using formal constitutional amendments, as well as the failure of the Meech Lake and Charlottetown Accords, the Canadian federal government has acted on its own to meet the perceived secessionist threat from Quebec. Three major federal actions are of considerable constitutional significance: the Regional Veto Act, the Supreme Court's *Quebec Secession Reference*, and the Clarity Act.

5. In addition to its basic federal structure, Canada has also had elements of a unitary structure with respect to the Yukon and Northwest Territories (including the recent creation of Nunavut) and its traditional relationship with its various Aboriginal communities.

6. The British Constitution is unwritten in the sense of having a comprehensive constitutional statement. However, Britain does have a series of constitutional documents, plus an array of political customs and conventions, all of which produce a pattern of constitutionalism. Although political power is concentrated as a result of the government's unitary and parliamentary structure, it is restricted in use, thus producing a unique example of constitutional government.

7. Britain, in the past few years, has witnessed significant constitutional changes with respect to the House of Lords and to its unitary structure. Devolution of power to Scotland, Wales, Northern Ireland, and the City of London has produced an increasingly quasi-federal structure in Britain.

8.   American constitutionalism is predicated on the view of the evil nature of political power and the need to restrict its concentration in the polity. Four basic techniques are used to achieve such a result: separation of powers, checks and balances, federalism, and protection for civil and political liberties. Probably the unique contribution of the American example to the art of constitutional government is the principle of the separation of powers and its implementation through the various checks and balances. From the American perspective, the way to create constitutional government is to fragment and decentralize political power.

CONCEPT FILE

amending formula
asymmetrical federalism
auxiliary precautions
bill of rights (general)
Bill of Rights (Canada)
Bill of Rights (United States)
Calgary Declaration
Canada Health and Social Transfer (CHST)
centralized federal system
Charlottetown Accord
Charter of Rights and Freedoms (Canada)
checks and balances
Clarity Act (2000)
classical federalism
concurrent (shared) jurisdiction
Constitution Act (1982)
constitutional dictatorship
constitutional government
decentralized federal system
decentralized symmetrical federalism
declaratory power
devolution
disallowance
distinct society
distinct society clause
Emergencies Act (1988)
entrenchment
enumerated powers
equalization payments

exclusive jurisdiction
executive federalism
executive privilege
federalism
fiscal federalism
implied powers
Judicial Committee of the Privy Council (JCPC)
judicial review
limited judicial review
Meech Lake Accord
megaconstitutional politics
notwithstanding clause
offloading
override clause (Section 33)
party government
POGG (Peace, Order, and Good Government of Canada) clause
province-building
Quebec Secession Reference (1998)
quasi-federalism
quasi-unitary
reasonable limits clause
Regional Veto Act (1996)
reservation
residual power clause
rule of law
safeguarded portions (Constitution Act 1867)
Section 38 (7/50 rule)
separation of powers

special status
supremacy clause
suspensive veto
symmetrical federalism

transfer payments
unwritten constitution
War Measures Act
written constitution

RECOMMENDED READINGS

Constitutional Government

ANDERSON, GAVIN W., ed. (1999) *Rights and Democracy: Essays in UK – Canadian Constitutionalism.* London: Blackstone Press.

FRIEDRICH, CARL J. (1968) *Constitutional Government and Democracy: Theory and Practice in Europe and America.* 4th ed. Waltham, Mass.: Blaisdell Publishing Co.

GIBBONS, ROGER (2000) "Federalism in a Digital World," *Canadian Journal of Political Science,* Volume 33, Number 4, pp. 667–689.

GORDON, SCOTT (2000) *Controlling the State: Constitutionalism from Ancient Athens to Today.* Cambridge, Mass.: Harvard University Press.

IGNATIEFF, MICHAEL (2000) *The Rights Revolution.* Toronto: Anansi.

JONES, DAVID S. and T.K.K. IYER (1989) "The Nature of Political Conventions in a Written Constitutional Order: A Comparative Perspective," *Governance,* Volume 2, Number 4, pp. 405–424.

MARSHALL, GEOFFREY (1971) *Constitutional Theory.* Oxford: Oxford University Press.

ORDESHOOK, PETER C. and OLGA SHVETSOVA (1997) "Federalism and Constitutional Design," *Journal of Democracy,* Volume 8, Number 1, pp. 27–42.

REHNQUIST, WILLIAM H. (2000) *All the Laws but One: Civil Liberties in Wartime.* New York: Vintage, Random House.

ROBINSON, DONALD L. (1992) "The Comparative Study of Constitutions: Suggestions for Organizing the Inquiry," *PS: Political Science and Politics,* Volume 25, Number 2, pp. 272–280.

ROSSITER, CLINTON (1963) *Constitutional Dictatorship: Crisis Government in the Modern Democracies.* New York: Harcourt, Brace and World.

WATTS, RONALD L. (1999) *Comparing Federal Systems.* 2nd ed. Kingston, Ontario: Institute of Intergovernmental Relations, Queen's University.

YOUNG, ROBERT A. (1994) "How Do Peaceful Secessions Happen?" *Canadian Journal of Political Science,* Volume 27, Number 4, pp. 747–771.

The Canadian Constitution

CAIRNS, ALAN C. (1991) *Disruptions: Constitutional Struggles, from the Charter to Meech Lake.* Toronto: McClelland and Stewart.

—— (1992) *Charter Versus Federalism: The Dilemmas of Constitutional Reform.* Montreal: McGill-Queen's University Press.

DOBROWOLSKY, ALEXANDRA (2000) *The Politics of Pragmatism: Women, Representation, and Constitutionalism in Canada.* Don Mills, Ontario: Oxford University Press Canada.

FURSTON, BERNARD W. and EUGENE MEEHAN (1998) *Canada's Constitutional Law in a Nutshell.* 2nd ed. Toronto: Carswell.

HEARD, ANDREW (1991) *Canadian Constitutional Conventions: The Marriage of Law and Politics.* Toronto: Oxford University Press.

HEARD, ANDREW and TIM SWARTZ (1997) "The Regional Veto Formula and Its Effects on Canada's Constitutional Amendment Process," *Canadian Journal of Political Science,* Volume 30, Number 2, pp. 339–356.

HOGG, PETER W. (2000) *Constitutional Law of Canada: 2000 Student Edition.* Toronto: Carswell.

MENDELSOHN, MATTHEW (2000) "Public Brokerage: Constitutional Reform and the Accommodation of Mass Publics," *Canadian Journal of Political Science,* Volume 33, Number 2, pp. 245–272.

MONAHAN, PATRICK J. (1997) *Constitutional Law.* Concord, Ontario: Irwin Law.

RUSSELL, PETER H. (1994) *Constitutional Odyssey: Can Canadians Be a Sovereign People?* 2nd ed. Toronto: University of Toronto Press.

RYNARD, PAUL (2000) " 'Welcome In, But Check Your Rights at the Door': The James Bay and Nisga'a Agreements in Canada," *Canadian Journal of Political Science,* Volume 33, Number 2, pp. 211–243.

SCHNEIDERMAN, DAVID, ed. (1999) *The Quebec Decision: Perspectives on the Supreme Court Ruling on Secession.* Toronto: James Lorimer and Company.

SNIDERMAN, PAUL M. et al. (1996) *The Clash of Rights: Liberty, Equality, and Legitimacy in Pluralist Democracy.* New Haven, Conn.: Yale University Press.

TARNOPOLSKY, WALTER SURMA (1975) *The Canadian Bill of Rights.* 2nd rev. ed. Toronto: McClelland and Stewart.

TRUDEAU, PIERRE ELLIOTT (1968) *Federalism and the French Canadians.* Toronto: Macmillan of Canada.

VICKERS, JILL (1993) "The Canadian Women's Movement and a Changing Constitutional Order," *International Journal of Canadian Studies,* Volumes 7–8, pp. 261–284.

WHITTINGTON, MICHAEL S. (2000) "Aboriginal Self-government in Canada," pp. 105–125 in Michael Whittington and Glen Williams, eds., *Canadian Politics in the 21st Century.* 5th ed. Scarborough, Ontario: Nelson, Thomson Learning.

The British Constitution

BAGEHOT, WALTER (1867, 1963) *The English Constitution.* London: Collins, The Fontana Library.

BLACKBURN, ROBERT and RAYMOND PLANT, eds. (1999) *Constitutional Reform: The Labour Government's Constitutional Reform Agenda.* London: Longman.

HAZEL, ROBERT et al. (2000) "The British Constitution in 1998–99: The Continuing Revolution," *Parliamentary Affairs,* Volume 53, Number 2, pp. 242–261.

HOOPER, DAVID (1987) *Official Secrets: The Use and Abuse of the Act.* London: Secker and Warburg.

JOWELL, J. and D. OLIVER, eds. (2000) *The Changing Constitution.* 4th ed. Oxford: Oxford University Press.

LAFFIN, MARTIN (2000) "Constitutional Design: A Framework for Analysis," *Parliamentary Affairs,* Volume 53, Number 3, pp. 532–541.

MARSHALL, GEOFFREY (1984) *Constitutional Conventions: The Rules and Forms of Political Accountability.* Oxford: Oxford University Press.

STARMER, KEIR and STUART WEIN (1997) "Strong Government and Weak Liberties: An Overview of Political Freedom in the UK," *The Political Quarterly*, Volume 68, Number 2, pp. 135–142.

The American Constitution

BERGER, RAOUL (1973) *Impeachment: The Constitutional Problems.* New York: Bantam Books.

HAMILTON, ALEXANDER, JAMES MADISON and JOHN JAY (1788) *The Federalist Papers.*

HAMMONS, CHRISTOPHER W. (1999) "Was James Madison Wrong? Rethinking the American Preference for Short, Framework-Oriented Constitutions," *American Political Science Review*, Volume 93, Number 4, pp. 837–849.

HANDLIN, OSCAR (1993) "The Bill of Rights in Its Context," *The American Scholar*, Volume 62, Number 2, pp. 177–186.

HILL, ALFRED (2000) "Opinion: The Shutdowns and the Constitution," *Political Science Quarterly*, Volume 115, Number 2, pp. 273–282.

KERSCH, KEN I. (1997) "Full Faith and Credit for Same-Sex Marriages?" *Political Science Quarterly*, Volume 112, Number 1, pp. 117–136.

KNIGHT, BARBARA B. (1989) *Separation of Powers in the American Political System.* Virginia: George Mason University Press.

PELTASON, J.W. (1997) *Corwin and Peltason's Understanding the Constitution.* 14th ed. Orlando, Florida: Harcourt Brace and Company.

TARR, G. ALAN (2000) *Understanding State Constitutions.* Princeton, New Jersey: Princeton University Press.

WILSON, JAMES Q. (1987) "Does the Separation of Powers Still Work?" *The Public Interest*, Number 86, pp. 36–52.

ZVESPER, JOHN (1999) "The Separation of Powers in American Politics: Why We Fail to Accentuate the Positive," *Government and Opposition*, Volume 34, Number 1, pp. 3–23.

POLITICS ON THE NET

CONSTITUTIONS AND FEDERALISM: A number of websites provide collections of **world constitutions** and various constitutional documents. See, for example, the following: *www.cc.ukans.edu/carrie/docs/docs_con.html* or *www.chanrobles.com/worldconstitutions.htm*. A particularly useful site for both constitutions and **federalism** is the recently formed organization called The Forum of Federations: *www.forumoffederations.org*. The Forum, founded in part by Canada, "seeks to strengthen democratic governance by promoting dialogue on and understanding of the values, practices, principles, and possibilities of federalism." For constitutions and related documents from around the world (organized by country), go to the "Constitution Finder" website located at *confinder.richmond.edu*. For links to s ecessionist, independence, and nationalist movements around the world, see *www.wavefront.com/~homelands*.

CANADA: The federal **Department of Intergovernmental Affairs**, located in the Privy Council Office, can be accessed at ***www.pco-bcp.gc.ca/aia***. See, in particular, the "Distribution of Power and Functions in Federal Systems" (search for this document under "Quick Search"). In this document, go to the "Conclusion," especially Appendix B: "Distribution of Power and Functions in Federal Systems: A Comparative Overview." This site also has excellent links to other relevant web pages. The home page of the **Canadian Intergovernmental Conference Secretariat** can be seen at ***www.scics.gc.ca***. This site has links with the federal government, provinces, and territories, along with their respective Departments of Intergovernmental Affairs. Information on the role of the **municipalities** in the Canadian federal system can be accessed at the website of the Federation of Canadian Municipalities: ***www.fcm.ca***. For information on the history and creation of **Nunavut**, see ***www.gov.nu.ca***.

BRITAIN: For a summary of the **British constitution**, go to "United Kingdom — 'Constitution'" at the following website: ***www.uni-wuerzburg.de/law/uk00000_.html***. For British constitutional documents (the Magna Carta, the Petition of Rights, the Bill of Rights), go to the "Constitution Finder" website (as mentioned above) and click on United Kingdom. For websites relating to **local government** in Britain, go to ***www.open.gov.uk*** and then go to the section called "Home Office – Constitutional Issues." The work of the constitutional reform group called **Charter 88**, which seeks "a modern and fair democracy" in Britain, including a written constitution, can be located at ***www.charter88.org.uk***. Information on the process and impact of **devolution** can be found at the "Dev Web guide to UK Devolution," located at ***www.geocities.com/Athens/Ithaca/1562/dev***.

UNITED STATES: Basic information on the **American constitution**, including documents relating to American constitutional history, can be found at the website of the National Constitution Center at ***www.constitutioncenter.org***.

The Federalist Papers can be located online at ***www.law.emory.edu/FEDERAL***. For information on the **American states**, see the website for The Council of State Governments at ***www.statesnews.org***. For **local government**, see the U.S. Conference of Mayors homepage at ***www.usmayors.org***. For issues dealing with the **Bill of Rights** and civil and political liberties consult the website of the American Civil Liberties Union at ***www.aclu.org*** and the Freedom Forum at ***www.freedomforum.org***.

The Executive Branch of Government

For political theorists, conceptions of the ideal polity presuppose that certain types of leaders are optimal, if one is to maximize fairness, democracy, political stability, or government efficiency . . . . Who rules does indeed make a difference. (Bunce, 1981: 3, 256)

If one reduces politics to its bare bones, to what is most visible to most citizens, it is the national political leaders, both at home and abroad, that remain once everything else has been erased; they are the most universal, the most recognized, the most talked about elements of political life. (Blondel, 1987: 1)

Many modern countries govern without democracy, but none govern without bureaucracy. (Sutherland, 1993: 81)

CHAPTER PREVIEW

- All forms of modern government are controlled by their executive branches because executives dominate the public process by setting the political agenda and implementing its decisions.

- A parliamentary executive is divided between a formal executive (Queen, governor general) and a political executive (prime minister, cabinet). In the modern era, political executives govern while formal executives reign.

- In a presidential executive such as in the United States, the formal and political executive functions are fused in a single role, which explains why the American president has come to dominate the political process.

- Bureaucracies are hierarchically organized institutions that are designed, at least in theory, to be politically neutral mechanisms, but which, in fact, play key political and administrative roles.

- The prime minister in Canada and Britain dominates the political process, while the American president is constrained by the various checks and balances and public opinion.

- Cabinets are significant and powerful institutions in Canada and Britain, but the American cabinet is a minor player in the political process.

The centrepiece of all forms of modern government — autocratic, democratic, or totalitarian — is the executive branch. The growth of government in the past century has been both a cause and consequence of executive dominance. A combination of several factors has made the executive branch the engine of the political process, not the least of which has been the willingness of the political executives to provide leadership for the polity and to adapt themselves to a changing environment. Paralleling the growth of executive-centred government has been the phenomenal rise of the bureaucracy, the primary mechanism for implementing executive decisions. The growth of government and of the bureaucracy has been coeval: as governments have assumed more powers and functions, so has the bureaucracy in administering the public's business.

THE NATURE OF EXECUTIVE POWER

The frequent assertion of many analyses of the rise of executive government in the modern era is that executive power is a new trend. Unfortunately, the historical accuracy of such a conclusion is suspect, for few governments have ever been anything but executive-centred. The rise of executive government in the 20th century was a reassertion of the executive's traditional role, which was only temporarily lost to the legislature in democratic polities and never lost in autocratic and totalitarian systems. However, the reappearance of executive power has been accompanied by a change in the executor of that leadership in parliamentary systems from the formal to the political executive. The historical development of executive power has been from the king, to the king in Parliament, to the prime minister in Parliament, to the bureaucracy.

PARLIAMENTARY EXECUTIVES

The characteristics of a **parliamentary executive** include its dual structure (i.e., both a formal and a political executive), its relationship with the legislature, which is based on the fusion of powers principle, and its term in office, which is variable within a maximum time limit. The **formal executive** is *the monarchical element,* *such as the Queen or governor general, that performs primarily symbolic and cere-monial functions for the polity.* While an organizational chart of the executive branch would place the formal executive at its pinnacle, such a positioning represents the facade rather than the reality of political influence and power.

The **political executive** includes *the prime minister, cabinet, and bureaucracy — the real locus of influence in modern parliamentary systems.* Theoretically subservient to the formal executive, the political executive in fact controls the monarchical element. The formal executive reigns but does not govern, while the political executive governs but does not reign. This symbiotic relationship has always been an unequal one, with the formal executive initially controlling the political executive, while the reverse of this pattern is true in the reassertion of executive power in the modern age.

> A constitutional monarch protects democracy from the results of the bends at the heights of political power (MacKinnon, 1973: 61).

An interesting example of the power relationship between the formal and political executives in a modern parliamentary system occurred in Belgium in 1990. Because as a matter of personal conscience he could not sign a bill legalizing abortion, the formal executive, King Baudouin, was suspended as head of state at his own request. Prime Minister Wilfried Martens then signed the legislation, recalled the legislature, and restored the king to his throne.

The connection between the political executive and the legislature in a parliamentary system is based on two principles: collective responsibility and ministerial responsibility. The concept of **collective responsibility** emphasizes *the group basis of parliamentary government: as a team, the* **cabinet***, that is, the government of the day, is sustained or defeated in Parliament.* Individual government ministers cannot be rejected by a vote in Parliament. Moreover, unity of purpose is a necessary outgrowth of collective responsibility: the cabinet sings a common song, although some of its members may not always be in tune. Public disagreement with cabinet policy by a minister is rare. Typically, a cabinet minister who openly disagrees with government policy resigns, as did Lucien Bouchard in 1990 over disagreements with Prime Minister Mulroney concerning his open support for the principle of Quebec sovereignty. While initially developed as a means of legislative control over the executive, the combination of party discipline with collective responsibility has produced, in practice, executive control of the legislature.

In contrast to collective responsibility, the principle of **ministerial responsibility** emphasizes *the individual responsibility of each cabinet member to Parliament.* Individual ministers are responsible to the cabinet and the Commons for the conduct of their department, including its finances, programs, and policies. Ministers must explain to the House any wrongdoing of officials under their jurisdiction, as well as justify to the public the direction of their department's major public policy decisions. Ministerial responsibility does not necessarily mean that ministers are personally responsible for wrongdoings in their department, but it does mean they must answer questions and provide explanations to

> One of Parkinson's Laws holds that the ideal government cabinet contains just five members. One of them knows the law, one knows finance, one knows foreign policy, and one knows defense. The fifth member, the one who has failed to master any of these subjects, usually becomes the Prime Minister (Roberts, 1986: 22).

Parliament. They are also responsible for correcting present abuses and for trying to prevent their reoccurrence. Failure to guide their departments adequately or to live up to their party's or the public's expectations may lead to ministerial resignations. In modern parliamentary systems the practice of ministerial responsibility is in decline and can be circumvented (e.g., ministers can refuse to take responsibility for wrongdoings in their department), while that of collective responsibility remains largely, if not totally, in place.

PRESIDENTIAL EXECUTIVES

A **presidential executive** is *characterized by the singular office of president, which combines the formal and political executive roles of a parliamentary system; by its relationship with the legislature, which is based on the separation of powers principle; and by its election periods, which are fixed by law.* Because it has been rarely imitated, the American system remains the primary example of a presidential structure. As both the ceremonial and political leader, the American president has become the symbol of the nation. What has been created in the American presidential system is an executive office with the potential for leadership which, when combined with political skill and ambition, can make it the prime mover in the political process.

One of the most important distinctions between presidential and parliamentary government concerns the means of selecting the political executive. In a parliamentary system, the leader of the majority party is asked to form a government by the monarch. The prime minister is thus not technically elected by either the whole country (but is elected to the Commons from a single constituency, as is any other MP) or by Parliament. For example, in the 1993 federal election, Jean Chrétien was selected by the voters in the Quebec riding of Saint-Maurice to be their MP; he was then asked by the governor general to form a government. In contrast, presidential systems are based on a national constituency, which may select the president directly through popular election or indirectly through some sort of electoral college mechanism.

> There is no foreign institution with which, in any basic sense, it can be compared, because, basically, there is no comparable foreign institution. The president of the United States is both more and less than a king; he is, also, both more and less than a prime minister (Laski, 1940: 11).

This more direct relationship with the mass public, due in part to the increasing role of the media, has been an important reason for the enhancement of American presidential leadership in both domestic and international affairs. The dominance of the presidential office over the other political institutions is the basis for the idea of the **imperial presidency**, that is, *a dominant office that directs the course of events in the political process.* Transferring this idea to a parliamentary context has resulted in the concept of **prime ministerial government**, that is, *when one individual, the prime minister, becomes the key actor in the parliamentary system.* In such a system cabinet government is superseded: the prime minister is no longer *primus inter pares* (first among equals) for the simple reason that he has no equals. As former British Prime Minister Winston Churchill (1949: 14) put it: "In any sphere of action there can be no comparison between the positions of number one and numbers two, three and four." *The growth of prime ministerial power in parliamentary systems* has often been labelled as the **presidentializing of parliamentary government**.

EXECUTIVE BRANCH FUNCTIONS

Whether of the presidential or parliamentary variety, the functions of the executive branch of government are similar in most political systems. There are three basic executive functions: leadership, policy-making, and the implementation of public policy.

The leadership role focusses on the executive as the initiator of public policy, the branch of government given the responsibility for providing overall direction for the polity. In many cases, the leadership role of the executive branch is not constitutionally prescribed, but is based on custom and convention. A combination of circumstances, including the increasingly complex nature of both domestic society and the international system and the political will of the executive to exercise its powers, has contributed to the leadership dominance of the executive branch of government. If the executive does not lead, then stalemate and confusion may characterize the polity. Neither constitutional prescription nor political custom can force or guarantee executive direction. However, one result is apparent: if the executive fails to lead, no other political institution appears, on a continuing basis, to be either adequately equipped or politically willing to assume the leadership function.

Executive direction is provided through the development of public policy. A **policy** is *"an explicit set of preferences and plans drawn up in order to make the outcomes of a series of future decisions more nearly predictable and consistent"* (Deutsch, 1968: 77). A **public policy** is *a set of such preferences that has consequences for the community*. Public policies would include examples such as a government's budget, taxation rules, or specific content areas such as economic development, immigration, culture, education, and foreign affairs. For example, a budget can "be characterized as a series of goals with price tags attached" (Wildavsky, quoted in Bunce, 1981: 39).

The initiation, development, and passage of public policy differ among political systems. The traditional makers of public policy in a parliamentary system have been the cabinet and the civil service, while prime ministerial government has shifted such power to appointed advisors. In a presidential system, the cabinet is rarely the centre of policy decisions; while individual cabinet members may play a significant role, the key decision-making power lies with the president and his advisors. On occasion, the legislature may assume the initiative for policy formulation. More often than not, the legislature's role is to legitimate the policy decisions of the executive branch of government. Once a policy has been decided, the third function of the executive is to implement its provisions. The application and enforcement of public policy is the designated task of the bureaucracy, that portion of the executive branch referred to as the civil service. A brief look at the functions and characteristics of the bureaucracy will help us understand its significant role in the modern political process.

The nature of the bureaucracy

In addition to the factors that have contributed to the general growth of executive power, several others have enhanced bureaucratic powers. Some legislation is general in its provisions, leaving it up to the civil servants to fill in the details of how a policy will work in practice. The way a policy or law is implemented and applied may be more significant than the generalized wording as approved by the legislature. In this sense, applying a general law to specific cases gives the bureaucracy the power to make policy. Moreover, the bureaucratic role has been magnified by the expertise of its members. Knowledge and information are important political resources that the bureaucracy has often skillfully utilized to increase its own significance in the decision-making process. Modern government would quickly become inoperative without its bureaucratic component (or so the bureaucrats would like us to believe).

A **bureaucracy** is *a hierarchically structured organization, which implements public policy on the basis of impartially applied rules.* Composed of appointed officials or civil servants who have been trained in the art of public administration, the bureaucracy is the major point of contact between the individual and the political regime. In theory, the bureaucracy is designed to be free of political interference, applying set procedures to specific cases.

A common and, at the same time, an incorrect view of the role of the bureaucracy is that it simply implements public policy decided by other institutions; in other words, that politics and administration are divorced in theory and in practice. From this perspective, policy is decided by the executive, approved by the legislature, and implemented by the bureaucracy. Unfortunately, life is rarely so clear-cut and simple. In the modern era, politics and administration are intertwined like Siamese, not fraternal, twins.

Recognizing the interconnections between politics and administration helps us to define the functions of the bureaucracy. Two basic roles can be identified: first, a policy-making function; and second, an implementation function. In the first function, the bureaucracy is seen as a key player in the initiation, proposal, and development of public policy. In the second function, the bureaucracy implements that policy after it has been approved by the executive and legislature. The bureaucracy not only helps to make public policy, but administers that same policy as well. As a result, the potential for bureaucratic importance and power is self-evident. The significant power and role of the bureaucracy is recognized in the concept of the **administrative state**, that is, *a political system in which the state and government dominate the political process through bureaucratic structures.* In that sense, all major polities, whatever their type, are now administrative states, with some systems more so than others.

In carrying out its policy-making and implementation functions, the bureaucracy has developed some particular characteristics. The most famous description of such traits is Max Weber's ideal-type of bureaucratic attributes (Gerth and Mills, 1958: 196–204; Presthus, 1962: 27–58). The major bureaucratic characteristics would include the following patterns. First, bureaucratic organizations are hierarchically structured on the basis of graded authority roles. Second, officials are assigned fixed responsibilities and act only on the basis of specific regulations. Third, the officials are trained for their tasks, thereby bringing expertise to the organization. Fourth, the officials are appointed, usually for long periods, and paid compensation from public funds. Fifth, being an official is a career, not a hobby, so that outside ties that might produce any conflicts of interest are discouraged, if not banned outright. Sixth, the organization of officials in a bureaucracy provides a rational method of administration based on specialization, efficiency, and equality.

These typical characteristics of the bureaucracy have traditionally meant the exclusion of civil servants from direct involvement in the political process. To become overtly political is to put one's job on the line. A wise civil servant traditionally refrains from open political involvement, especially that of a directly partisan nature.

However, the view of the bureaucracy as impartial and outside of direct political involvement is wrong. Despite civil service examinations and appointments supposedly on the basis of merit, the bureaucracy remains a major bastion of partisanship and political patronage. Civil service regulations can often be circumvented. A party in power for any length of time can fashion the bureaucracy in its own image. Moreover, upon assuming office, parties usually demand the right to restructure at least the very top of the bureaucracy, that segment that plays a significant role in the policy-making process (Michelman and Steeves, 1985).

The roles of the bureaucracy in implementing public policy and of the political executive in its initiation and development have made the executive branch of government the dominant force in the political process of autocratic, democratic, and totalitarian systems. The factors that have produced this pattern seem unlikely to recede in the decades ahead — if anything, these trends will become more pronounced. However, what is open to change is the evolving relationship between the various segments of the executive branch of government.

THE FORMAL EXECUTIVE IN CANADA

It would probably surprise many people to discover that executive authority is legally granted to the formal executive or head of state in the Canadian political system (Constitution Act of 1867, Section 9). More surprising still would be the discovery that executive authority is vested in the Queen of Canada and is exercised by her representatives (governor general and lieutenant-governors) on a daily basis, a situation that was not altered by the 1982 Constitution Act. The formal executive is surrounded and aided by a group of advisors known as the Queen's Privy Council for Canada (Section 11). Neither the prime minister nor the cabinet, the two key operative elements of the modern executive, are mentioned in the delineation of executive authority in the 1867 Constitution Act. On the surface, therefore, the formal executive would appear to be pre-eminent. Consideration of the appointment of the formal executive and of the structure of the Privy Council should quickly dispel such an interpretation.

SELECTING THE FORMAL EXECUTIVE

Since the day-to-day functions of the formal executive are performed by the governor general, that person will be treated as Canada's head of state in the ensuing analysis. Although the governor general was initially selected by the British monarch, since 1926 the Canadian prime minister has recommended to the Queen the individual desired by the Canadian government. While still technically appointed by the Queen, for all practical purposes such a procedure puts the appointment power in the hands of the Canadian political executive. Although it has never happened, it would also appear that the governor general could be removed on the advice of the prime minister to the Queen. Thus, while an organizational chart places the formal executive over the political executive, the appointment process demonstrates the contrary.

The governor general's term of office is five years, although extensions of several months to several years have been granted. Since 1952, Canadians have been appointed (Vincent Massey, Georges Vanier, Roland Michener, Jules Léger, Edward Schreyer, Jeanne Sauvé, Ramon Hnatyshyn, Romeo LeBlanc, Adrienne Clarkson). The appointment of Edward Schreyer as governor general in 1978 produced a number of "firsts," probably the most significant being his youth and his Western Canadian background. The selection of Jeanne Sauvé as the 23rd governor general in December of 1983 produced Canada's first female occupant of that post. The naming of Senator Romeo LeBlanc as governor general in 1994 was the first time an Acadian had been selected for that position. When Prime Minister Jean Chrétien selected Adrienne Clarkson as Canada's 26th governor general in 1999, Madame Clarkson became the second woman and the first member of a visible minority to occupy the viceregal position. Born in Hong Kong, Madame Clarkson fled to Canada as a refugee in 1941. A long-time Liberal and CBC Television host, Adrienne Clarkson was installed in office on October 7, 1999.

> "Once," said the Mock Turtle at last with a deep sigh, "I was a real turtle" (from *Alice in Wonderland*, quoted in Forsey, 1985: 55).

At the provincial level, the formal executive is appointed by the governor general, to whom the lieutenant-governors are responsible. This selection procedure puts the effective appointment power for the provincial formal executives in the hands of the federal political executive, since the prime minister recommends to the governor general who is to be appointed. Usually, the provincial political executives are consulted, at least informally, by their federal counterpart before any appointment is made. The term of office for the lieutenant-governors is five years, with their salaries determined and paid for by the federal government ($97,200 in 2000).

Lieutenant-governors have more often been selected on the basis of patronage and political considerations than has the governor general. For example,

Pauline McGibbon of Ontario was the country's first female lieutenant-governor in 1974, while her successor, John Aird, was a former Liberal senator and party fundraiser. In turn, Aird's replacement was former Conservative MP and federal cabinet minister Lincoln Alexander, the first black Canadian to hold the position of lieutenant-governor. Political factors have influenced the selection of various viceregal occupants in other provinces as well. In 1989, Prime Minister Mulroney appointed David See-Chai Lam as lieutenant-governor of British Columbia, the first Chinese-Canadian to fill a viceregal office. In 1993, Yvon Dumont was named by Prime Minister Mulroney to be the new lieutenant-governor in Manitoba — the first Métis leader to hold the Manitoba post and the second Aboriginal Canadian to serve in that capacity. Appointments by Prime Minister Chrétien during his first term in office included the following; in 1994, Margaret McCain, wife of billionaire Wallace McCain, as lieutenant-governor in New Brunswick; in 1996, Senator Jean-Louis Roux, outspoken federalist, as lieutenant-governor in Quebec; in 1997, Hilary Weston, former fashion model and wife of billionaire Galen Weston, as lieutenant-governor in Ontario, and Lise Thibault, activist for the disabled and former unsuccessful Liberal candidate (federally and provincially), as lieutenant-governor in Quebec. During his second term in office, Prime Minister Chrétien appointed the following viceregal selections: in 1997, Marilyn Trenholme Counsell, a 10-year Liberal member of the provincial legislature as lieutenant-governor in New Brunswick; in 1999, Lynda Haverstock, former Liberal provincial party leader, as lieutenant-governor in Saskatchewan; and in 2000, Myra Freeman, school teacher and Liberal party organizer, as lieutenant-governor in Nova Scotia. Myra Freeman is the first member of the Jewish community to be appointed as lieutenant-governor in Nova Scotia — she brought the total number of female viceroys to six by the beginning of 2001.

The Administrator of Canada

If for some reason formal executives are unable to perform their duties (e.g., illness, travel outside the country), the 1867 Constitution Act makes provision for their replacement (Sections 10 and 67). At the federal level the governor general can be replaced by a person appointed as the **Administrator of Canada**, who can exercise all of the formal executive's traditional powers and who serves until the governor general reassumes the duties of the position. In such a situation, the Chief Justice of the Canadian Supreme Court becomes the Administrator of Canada, as happened following Jules Léger's stroke in the mid-1970s and his temporary replacement by Chief Justice Bora Laskin. A similar procedure is followed for the replacement of a lieutenant-governor at the provincial level.

The Privy Council

The structure and workings of the **Privy Council** are a second clear indicator of the dominance of the political executive over the formal executive in Canada. The advisors to the governor general are selected by the prime minister and, in fact, advise the prime minister rather than the formal head of state. The operative or working part of the Privy Council is the cabinet. However, since the cabinet is not mentioned in the 1867 Constitution Act, to acquire the right to exercise executive authority its members are sworn into office as members of the Privy Council. Decisions of the cabinet are issued as decisions of the Privy Council (i.e., orders-in-council or minutes-in-council).

While individuals are federal cabinet members only for the duration of their postings as determined by the prime minister, they continue as members of the Privy Council for life. After the new Liberal cabinet of November 1993, total membership of the Privy Council was about 260 members (about 265 in 2000). Since Confederation, about 670 privy councillors have been appointed. The first case of a person resigning from the Privy Council occurred in 1987, when former federal Liberal cabinet minister Jacques Olivier did so in order to run in a municipal election in Quebec.

Although former cabinet ministers remain privy councillors for life, they do not retain the right to advise the current government of the day. Pierre Trudeau had no right to sit in on the cabinet discussions of any of his successors. The cabinet meets frequently, but the full Privy Council rarely does so — only three times between 1945 and 1970 and nine times between 1900 and 1970. A Privy Council meeting is usually held when the Queen visits or on other special occasions (e.g., to receive the announcement from the Queen concerning the marriage of Prince Charles and Lady Diana).

While most members of the Privy Council are there as the result of once being in the cabinet, other individuals may be appointed as well. In honour of the centennial celebration in 1967, the provincial premiers were named to the Privy Council. In honour of the 1982 Constitution Act, all premiers were invited to join, with only Quebec Premier René Lévesque turning down the appointment. In January of 1991, New Democratic Party leader Audrey McLaughlin was made a member of the Privy Council so she could be briefed regarding Canada's participation in the Persian Gulf War. The appointments of Prime Minister Mulroney in 1992 further expanded the diversity of the Privy Council's composition, with selections from various sectors of Canadian society: Alex Colville, John Polanyi, Antonine Maillet, Rita Joe, and Maurice Richard.

These considerations on the structure of the Privy Council emphasize that while the formal executive was granted executive authority, it is exercised in fact by the political executive. The formal executive retains the facade of power, while its substance has been co-opted by the prime minister and cabinet.

FUNCTIONS OF THE FORMAL EXECUTIVE

The functions of the formal executive reflect this pattern as well. Two basic roles can be identified: a symbolic-ceremonial one and a political one. Most of a governor general's daily tasks fall into the symbolic-ceremonial category, which includes such duties as attending state dinners, receiving ambassadors, and officially granting memberships in the Order of Canada. For example, during her five-and-a-half-year term of office (1984–1990), Jeanne Sauvé presented 1 921 medals, gave 427 speeches, and travelled 573 000 kilometres. According to a 1999 study by the Monarchist League of Canada, the constitutional monarchy costs Canadian taxpayers about $23 million a year, or approximately 74¢ for each person. This total includes the cost of the governor general and lieutenant-governors, visits to Canada by members of the Royal Family, and the office and programs of the federal vice-regal.

As a symbol of national unity, the office of Governor General has been used to stress the bilingual and diverse aspects of the Canadian nation. For example, the first four Canadian governors general were from Ontario and Quebec, with an alternation between those who claimed English or French as their mother tongue. The fifth Canadian governor general, Edward Schreyer, broke this tradition by being of non-French and non-British origin and by coming from Western Canada. The sixth Canadian governor general, Jeanne Sauvé, was born in Saskatchewan, while Ramon Hnatyshyn, the first governor general of Ukrainian descent, was not bilingual at the time of his appointment. Although often viewed as a unifying office, critics are apt to point out that, with its ties to the British Crown, the Canadian monarchy may be a symbol of subjugation for French Canadians. Moreover, more recent immigrant groups that are neither French nor English may feel no emotional ties to the Canadian Crown at all, although the appointment of Adrienne Clarkson as governor general in 1999 may begin to change such a perception. The suggestion by Prime Minister Chrétien in 1998 that it was perhaps time to open a public debate on the future of the monarchy in Canada was not met by widespread approval. A survey by the research firm POLLARA, published in December of 1998, found 48 percent of Canadians in favor, with 39 percent opposed. Abolition of the monarchy would require the unanimous consent of the provinces, with Prince Edward Island Premier Pat Binns asserting that he would veto any such change.

The role of the governors general in Canada: If you think you have a lot of authority vis-à-vis the government . . . [you] would be in line for some surprises. That's not our role. We're not elected, we don't have any authority. We have a moral authority, if I can say that. We can encourage things (Governor General Romeo LeBlanc, October 1, 1999).

In its symbolic-ceremonial tasks, the formal executive exemplifies what Walter Bagehot described as the dignified elements of the constitution: "The duties of the Queen, Governor General, and Lieutenant Governors include the decorative functions to facilitate the conduct of public business" (MacKinnon, 1976: 136). These ceremonial or decorative tasks may not always be appreciated by either the public or the government of the day. In Quebec, for example, the position and financing of the lieutenant-governor was diminished by the Parti Québécois government of René Lévesque. This behaviour showed the PQ's view of the office as a reflection of both British and federal government influence in the province. For example, during his six years in office between 1978 and 1983, Lieutenant-Governor Jean-Pierre Cote was basically ignored by the Lévesque government, with personal contact with the premier limited to half-a-dozen occasions in as many years. In 1984, the budget for the office was cut by 37 percent, 10 people were cut from the staff, and one limousine was done away with — actions designed to clearly indicate to the new Lieutenant-Governor Gilles Lamontagne (a former federal Liberal cabinet minister) the attitude of the PQ government toward the monarch's representative in Quebec. The pattern of diminishing the role of the lieutenant-governor in Quebec continued under the separatist government of Lucien Bouchard. For example, in November of 1996 it was announced that the lieutenant-governor's official residence would be sold, to be replaced with only a modest apartment for the federally-appointed formal executive in Quebec.

The battle over the position and role of the lieutenant-governor in Quebec received national attention in 1996. In September, Prime Minister Chrétien, without consulting the government in Quebec City, appointed Senator Jean-Louis Roux as Quebec's lieutenant-governor. An avowed federalist, the new lieutenant-governor indicated that he might not approve a bill proclaiming Quebec sovereignty. The separatist government of Lucien Bouchard went on the attack. When it was revealed that Roux, in 1942, had worn a swastika while participating in an anti-conscription demonstration, the PQ government demanded that Roux resign, which he did. Moreover, the PQ government demanded that the position of lieutenant-governor be abolished (unlikely, since it would require unanimous provincial consent as a constitutional amendment); if that was not possible, they suggested that future formal executives in Quebec be elected by the National Assembly. Rightfully ignoring such constitutional posturing, Prime MinisterChrétien named Lise Thibault as the new lieutenant-governor in December 1996. On assuming office in January 1997, Thibault indicated that she would sign an independence declaration, unless instructed by the federal government not to do so — thereby ending, at least temporarily, this controversy.

While the formal executive carries out a number of political tasks, most of these take place only under highly unusual circumstances. The key remaining political role of the formal executive is to select a prime minister or premier, thus ensuring that there is always a government in office. However, even in this function, the governor general's leeway is greatly circumscribed by various political customs.

Sir John A. Macdonald had been absent from his office for a few days when the Governor-General sent out a search party, in the person of his aide-de-camp, to find him. He was located in bed enjoying a sherry and reading a book. The aide-de-camp bluntly told him to sober up and get back to work. Macdonald demanded to know whether he spoke in an official or private capacity, and the aide asked: "What difference does that make?" Macdonald thundered: "Just this! If you're here in your official capacity, you can return to the Governor-General, give him my compliments, and tell him to go to hell. But if you're simply a private individual, you can go there yourself" (Dunn, 1989: 11).

If, after an election, an opposition party has obtained a majority of seats in the House of Commons, then the governor general has no choice but to ask the leader of that party to form a government. (This assumes, of course, that the current prime minister has resigned, since he or she can remain in office until being defeated in the House of Commons). Another party leader asked to form a government would surely be unable and, quite likely, unwilling to do so, since it would be an impossible undertaking to gain the confidence of the Commons. No party leader except Jean Chrétien could possibly have formed a government after the election of 1993. When he won re-election in 1997 and 2000, Jean Chrétien simply retained his position as prime minister, without having to be selected again by the governor general.

In a minority election result, the theoretical discretion of the formal executive is enhanced in choosing a prime minister, once a vacancy exists, but in practice such discretion is rarely maximized. Since minority governments in Canada have usually been close to an actual majority of seats or for other reasons have been relatively stable, the governor general's leeway in naming a prime minister is limited. For example, while a coalition of the Liberal, NDP, and Social Credit parties could have governed after the 1979 federal election, its stability in office would have been weak. Moreover, since the Conservatives had a 22-seat margin over the Liberals, custom required that they be given the first chance to govern, once Prime Minister Trudeau had resigned.

In a minority election result, the parties sometimes act on their own to limit the formal executive's potential discretion. For example, after the Liberal minority victory in 1972, Liberal leader and Prime Minister Pierre Trudeau called a press conference to announce that his government would unofficially have the backing of the New Democratic Party. Trudeau was immediately followed to the microphone by NDP leader David Lewis, who confirmed the "working majority" between their two parties. Although either the Conservatives or Liberals could have governed with NDP support, the Liberal-NDP arrangement precluded a Conservative government. Thus, after the 1972 election, Pierre Trudeau simply continued on as prime minister. During his career, Trudeau was appointed as prime minister (i.e., asked to form a government) only twice: in 1967 and in 1980.

In addition to majority or minority election results, other scenarios are conceivable that might increase the discretion of the formal executive in naming a prime minister. For example, if a prime minister were to suddenly die in office and if there was either no obvious successor or the governing party was divided on its choice, the governor general could name a prime minister until the governing party could hold a national party leadership convention or use some other mechanism to decide upon a new leader. However, it is unlikely that the governing party would not agree on a successor, thereby eliminating any discretion by the formal executive.

Another possible scenario would be a major political scandal involving the prime minister and key cabinet members. If those individuals resigned, the formal executive might be forced to ask another member of the cabinet or of the full House of Commons to form a new government. Such a case is possible, but not very probable; for all practical purposes, the formal executive has very minimal discretionary powers in naming the person who will become the prime minister.

The remaining political tasks of the formal executive are theoretically important and legally possible, but even more than with respect to selecting the prime minister, they rarely involve any real exercise of power. The various legislative tasks of the formal executive clearly demonstrate such a pattern. For example, while the governor general officially summons, prorogues, or dissolves Parliament, this is done on the initiative of the political executive. For example, in Manitoba in 1984, with the provincial legislature in the middle of a bell-ringing episode over the NDP government's legislation on French language guarantees, the government of Howard Pawley advised the lieutenant-governor to prorogue the House (Mackintosh, 1985: 60–66).

Similarly, the governor general delivers the Speech from the Throne to open Parliament but does not write it, even though phrases such as "my government will recommend" are liberally distributed throughout the address. The prime minister, in consultation with advisors and ministers, determines the content of the throne speech. The formal executive may be consulted or the broad outline of government policy may be discussed between the formal and the political executive, but there is no legal requirement for this. A formal executive does not have the right, based on custom and convention, to make changes or additions to the throne speech.

A second legislative task, which has become a formality, is the granting of assent. When a bill has passed both the Commons and the Senate, the assent procedure is held in the upper chamber. In some provinces, the entire work of a legislative session is presented in total to the formal executive for approval at the end of a session.

The formality of the assent procedure is illustrated by the fact that assent has never been refused a federal piece of legislation in Canada. The granting of assent by the formal executive is such a foregone conclusion that people rarely check to see if it has been carried out. For example, the passage of the language legislation (Bill 101) by the Quebec National Assembly in August 1977 only received assent in its French version. Lieutenant-Governor Hugues Lapointe apparently refused to sign the English version into law, a fact that was not revealed until January 1978. At that point, the lieutenant-governor was presented with another English copy of the law, which he signed in early February. The reason for Lapointe's refusal to sign the English version of Bill 101 the first time remains unexplained, but this incident illustrates the view that assent by the formal executive is assumed to be automatic. This example also reveals the irony that Bill 101, which was designed to make Quebec a unilingual French province, had to be passed in a bilingual format.

A final duty of the formal executive, which illustrates the difference between legal niceties and political reality, concerns the granting of dissolution when requested by the prime minister (Forsey, 1974). If the political executive has been defeated on a non-confidence motion or if it desires a new election without having suffered such a defeat, it must obtain a dissolution of Parliament from the governor general. If the government has a majority or if it is the only party capable of forming a "working majority" even though it has only a minority of seats, the governor general has no leeway for refusing a dissolution request. However, if another party could form a government, then legally the governor general might not grant a dissolution, but instead ask another party leader to form a government.

Such a situation did develop in the 1920s during the King-Byng Affair, when Governor General Lord Byng refused a dissolution request from Prime Minister Mackenzie King. Unfortunately for monarchists, this controversy ended up as an issue in the ensuing 1926 election campaign, with Mackenzie King vowing to prevent any future governor general from saying no to a dissolution request. When King won the election, he proceeded to undermine the power of the governor general, with the result that, since that time, the formal executive has, for all practical purposes, lost the ability to deny the political executive a dissolution of Parliament.

A more recent example came to light in December 1979, with the defeat of the Joe Clark government. After his Thursday night defeat, Prime Minister Clark met with Governor General Schreyer on Friday morning to ask for a dissolution of

Parliament. After nearly an hour's meeting, no dissolution was forthcoming; the governor general made the prime minister return to his office before he was given his requested dissolution (Simpson, 1980: 38). In a later interview, Governor General Schreyer maintained that he had the right to consider the dissolution request, without being simply a rubber stamp for the prime minister (Valpy, 1981: 10). However, such reflection lasted only an hour, demonstrating a more acute political judgment by Governor General Schreyer than by Lord Byng a half a century earlier. A political realist would seriously doubt whether the formal executive could have said no to Prime Minister Clark and gotten away with it. Governor General Schreyer was probably asserting his political independence in his recently acquired job, rather than attempting to enhance the formal executive's power in the Canadian polity of the 1980s. In contrast to the 1979 example, on October 22, 2000 Prime Minister Jean Chrétien visited Governor General Adrienne Clarkson at Rideau Hall and within minutes held a press conference to announce the dissolution of the 36th Parliament and the start of the 2000 federal election campaign.

In considering both the structure and functions of the formal executive in Canada, we have emphasized that the head of state embodies the facade, rather than the substance, of political influence and power. Most of the governor general's legal duties, such as opening Parliament or granting a dissolution, are exercised on the initiative of the political executive. Even those tasks in which some theoretical power remains, as in selecting a prime minister, are tightly circumscribed by custom and tradition. The formal executive's daily impact on the political system is thus modest, because the possible exercise of the position's potential powers becomes tenable only during the gravest of constitutional emergencies. Fortunately, such worst-case scenarios rarely develop, so that the potential influence of the formal executive is infrequently tested in the heat of political battle.

THE POLITICAL EXECUTIVE IN CANADA

In contrast to the office of the formal executive, that of the political executive occupies centre stage in the struggle for policy, power, and patronage. The public visibility of the formal and political executives reveals much about their relative influence in the Canadian political process. While the role of the formal executive is poorly understood or, for that matter, scarcely recognized, that of the political executive is the focus of public attention.

This dominant role of the political executive is primarily a consequence of custom and convention, rather than a result of legal prescription. The prime minister and cabinet are not mentioned in the 1867 Constitution Act, although the prime minister is named in other statutes. The evolution and development of the prime minister's tasks reflect an important mechanism of adaptation by the political system to a changing environment. Moreover, to a considerable extent the role of the prime minister depends on the individual who occupies that office. Given such a context, the prime minister has come to be the key political actor of

Prime Minister Jean Chrétien on prime ministerial power: I have very good ministers with me and I suspect that a few of them are dreaming of succeeding me eventually. And it's good. It's good. It's not a sin to have the desire to be Prime Minister. But they know they have to do their job. Because if they are too preoccupied with running in case I go, I will give them all the time they need to campaign — from the back bench (December 1997).

Canadian politics by combining political resources and skills with a political will so as to provide leadership on major questions of public policy. The pre-eminence of the prime minister is an outgrowth of the incumbent's relationship with the public, the formal executive, the party, and the cabinet.

With respect to the ordinary citizen, the prime minister is the most visible and salient symbol of political leadership in the country. Rarely will a prime minister escape or seek to escape the limelight — for visibility can be an important political resource of the office. It is not entirely coincidental that the growth of prime ministerial influence in the past few decades has occurred at the same time that television has become the essential political medium. The impact of television and its intimate relationship with the enhancement of the prime minister's role is clearly evident in recent election campaigns, which have become partisan-based media contests. Moreover, between election campaigns the prime minister can clearly dominate the other party leaders with respect to news coverage: when the prime minister speaks, people listen, even if not always attentively or reverently.

The second basis of prime ministerial pre-eminence is the relationship between the formal and political executives. Once the governor general has named a prime minister by asking that individual to form a government, the prime minister is the sole link between these two parts of the executive. As the head of the political executive, the prime minister alone deals with the governor general. For example, only the prime minister — not the cabinet, personal aides, opposition parties, or even Parliament as a whole — can request a dissolution of Parliament from the formal executive. Although others may be consulted, it is the prime minister who recommends to the governor general those individuals who are to be named to the Privy Council, Senate, and other governmental institutions. Since much of the formal executive's role is only carried out on the initiative of the political executive and since the prime minister determines when those powers will be exercised, the prime minister's indirect control over the formal executive also enhances the direct control over the other elements of the political executive, such as the cabinet.

A third element of prime ministerial influence reflects the political executive's role as a party leader: control of the party organization, when combined with the principle of party discipline within Parliament, gives the prime minister control of the legislative branch of government. Failure by the party leader to control the party makes it difficult to be elected prime minister, since the public probably perceives such an individual to be lacking in the necessary leadership qualities required by the job. Such a fate was that of Conservative leader Robert Stanfield. And those who gain the office of prime minister may lose it, at least in part, because of their difficulty in controlling their party caucus or organization (e.g., John Diefenbaker and Joe Clark). While the fusion of powers between the executive and legislature is imposed by the cabinet, it is embodied to an ever greater extent in the role of the prime minister.

The combination of these first three factors creates a fourth basis of prime ministerial leadership, namely, the prime minister's supremacy over the cabinet. Control over cabinet selection gives the prime minister or a premier the power to make or break the political careers of others. In December of 1992, for example, Premier Ralph Klein of Alberta, in constructing his first cabinet after winning the Tory leadership, eliminated all five of his cabinet colleagues who had supported his leadership rival Nancy Betkowski. Talent, in and of itself, is not necessarily enough for cabinet promotion — that talent must be recognized by the prime minister.

> Canadian prime ministers have in their hands all the important levers of power . . . Each of these levers of power taken separately is a formidable instrument in its own right, but when you add them all up and place them in the hands of one individual, they constitute an unassailable advantage (Savoie, 1999b: 653).

THE PRIME MINISTER AND THE CABINET

Once a person has gained a cabinet nomination, a further prime ministerial prerogative becomes significant. Remember that, after the pay increase of June 2001, elevation to the federal cabinet increases a backbencher's salary by about $63,000 per year. The prime minister not only determines the number of cabinet members and the structure of departmental responsibilities, but also the portfolios assigned to individual ministers. Federal cabinets under Pierre Trudeau were usually large — about 35 members in his later years. The first cabinet of Brian Mulroney set a size record for federal cabinets at 40 members; after his victory in 1988, his first new cabinet, at 39 (January 1989) was only slightly smaller. The leanest cabinet in recent years has been that of the new Tory cabinet in Nova Scotia in August of 1999, which had only 10 members. Perhaps more typical was the intermediate size of the British Columbia cabinet (March 2000) of 21, the Quebec cabinet (1998) of 26, or the Ontario cabinet (1995) of 19. If any trend is evident in recent years regarding cabinet size at both the federal and provincial levels, it is the attempt to reduce the number of cabinet ministers and the resulting number of government departments. However, the pressure to increase the size of the cabinet is inherent, given the representation function of this structure. For example, within five years of his first cabinet (1995) of 19, Premier Mike Harris of Ontario had increased its size to 25 (2000). Similarly, during Prime Minister Chrétien's first two terms in office from 1993 to 2000, the size of the federal cabinet increased from 23 to 28.

Once the question of size is determined, which itself sets limits on the allocation of departmental duties (and vice versa), then specific ministers for each department must be named. Political careers can be crushed or enhanced at this point, with probably even more devastating effect than with respect to cabinet elevation in the first place. It was difficult, in the 1970s and 1980s, to become a national political figure when one was made Minister of State for Fitness and Amateur Sport. However, a high-profile ministry, such as Justice, External Affairs, or Finance, need not be a political advantage. Much depends on what the individual makes of the assignment. For example, New Brunswick Liberal MP Andy Scott — who had been elevated to the cabinet in 1997 because his province needed a cabinet representative — resigned as Solicitor General (December 1998), because he had been overheard on an airplane discussing a case that he might have to be involved in later in his official position as a Minister of the Crown. For a minister in charge of the RCMP, federal prisons, and the Canadian Security Intelligence Service, "loose lips" are an unattractive personal characteristic.

Some portfolios are seen more as liabilities than as stepping-stones to higher political office. For many decades, the position of Minister of Finance has often been the suicide portfolio of Canadian politics, as the subsequent career patterns of former finance ministers Walter Gordon and Edgar Benson illustrate. Moreover, even though former finance minister John Turner ended up becoming prime minister, his stay in that portfolio led to his resignation from the Trudeau government and put off for nearly a decade his "race for the rose" and the leadership mantle of the Liberal party. Interestingly, Prime Minister Jean Chrétien's main rival (Paul Martin, Jr.) for the leadership of the Liberal party during the 1990 party convention was selected as the Minister of Finance in Chrétien's first cabinet (November 1993) and remained in that portfolio through the 2000 election campaign and beyond. Paul Martin's success as finance minister, particularly during a period of severe budget reductions, and his continuing popularity at the beginning of the Chrétien government's third term in office are rare exceptions for those serving in finance portfolios.

Once in the cabinet, a minister must also be concerned about **cabinet shuffles**, that is, *reallocations of ministerial responsibilities.* Since the status or prestige of each portfolio is well known, cabinet shuffles reveal who is on the "up" or "down" side of the political escalator, as well as the minister's current influence in Ottawa's political pecking order. Cabinet shuffles are a convenient means for the prime minister to help out ministers who are in political trouble in their current portfolios by moving them to a different posting.

Sometimes it appears that the prime minister does not want to salvage a minister in trouble. For example, Human Resources Minister Jane Stewart, seen by many as a potential successor to Jean Chrétien, suffered serious political damage as the alleged jobs grant scandal in Human Resources Development Canada (HRDC) became public (January 2000) shortly after she was made the minister. While the previous minister, Pierre Pettigrew, who had been shifted to the international trade portfolio, remained largely unscathed by the scandal, Jane Stewart faced the brunt of the allegations for most of 2000 — remaining in her position as Human Resources Minister through the 2000 election campaign.

The extent of a prime minister's influence over the cabinet is also clear from the way ministers depart from the inner sanctum of power. For those loyal allies who have retained the prime minister's support, leaving the cabinet is made easier by appointment to the Senate or some other government institution. For those who have alienated their leader, a return to the backbenches may be their only reward for past service. There are few instances in which a minister who has been demoted from the cabinet has ever returned to it. A rare exception was the situation of Liberal Herb Gray, who asked so many questions of his own government from the backbenches that, in order to silence him, then Prime Minister Trudeau brought him back into the cabinet. However, when ministers who are liked by the prime minister have been forced to leave the cabinet, the prime minister may resurrect their political careers by reappointing them. For example, Minister of National Defence and Veterans Affairs David Collenette resigned in October of 1996 over a letter he sent on behalf of one of his constituents to the Immigration Board. Seven months later Prime Minister Chrétien returned him to the cabinet as Minister of Transport (and as the top political minister for Metropolitan Toronto.) A prime minister has the ability to breathe life back into apparently dead political careers.

In addition to being ousted by the prime minister, cabinet members may leave of their own accord, although not necessarily willingly. Sometimes resignations reflect personal problems, as when the Alberta Solicitor General Graham Harle resigned (November, 1983) after being found by police in a government car with a prostitute. Another example would be that of Newfoundland's Minister of Fisheries, Jim Morgan, who resigned from the provincial cabinet in October 1984 after he was found guilty of illegal salmon fishing. Other resignations are the result of political problems. In British Columbia, Moe Sihota, the first Indo-Canadian elected to a Canadian legislature and the first Indo-Canadian cabinet minister, resigned from the provincial cabinet twice and was ejected a third time during his career (1986–2001).

Resignations can be a symbol of protest against the prime minister's policies, but they also demonstrate that the minister who has resigned is an outcast in the cabinet and the governing party. For example, in December of 1988, three anglophone members of Quebec Premier Bourassa's cabinet resigned in protest against the government's language policy. Even when ministers have quit the cabinet, they have no right to explain in detail why they resigned, unless the prime minister releases them from the oath of secrecy they take upon being sworn into the cabinet. Ministers who have resigned rarely remain in the public eye for long.

CABINET COMPOSITION

While it is a prime minister's prerogative to decide the size of the cabinet, its departmental structure, the frequency of cabinet shuffles, and the individuals to be named to this key decision-making body, some of the prime minister's leeway in these matters is circumscribed by political tradition. For example, each of the parties contains various ideological strands that insist on having representatives in the cabinet. Likewise, a prominent party figure with a significant base of support in the country usually cannot be overlooked in the process of cabinet construction. At times, dissidents within the party are promoted to the cabinet to silence them by their co-optation into the party and governmental hierarchy. Probably the most important restriction on cabinet composition, however, is the representation principle, a crucial convention of the Canadian political process.

The **representation principle** refers to *the practice of naming representatives of the various regions, provinces, and major social and economic interests of Canadian society to the cabinet* (Matheson, 1976: 22–46). This practice was instituted with respect to the composition of Canada's first federal cabinet by John A. Macdonald and has been followed ever since. The workings of the representation principle are embodied in a series of informal rules.

Where possible, each province should receive at least one cabinet appointment. However, having elected all Liberals in the 1988 contest, Prince Edward Island received no cabinet representation in the Tory Cabinet of January 1989. In those cases where a province has not elected anyone to the governing party's caucus, then a prime minister may appoint a senator from that province to the cabinet. It would run counter to political custom to use only senators from a province in the cabinet if the government had seats in the Commons from the same province. Minimal representation in Quebec for the Conservatives in the 1979 election and no representation in the Commons at all from British Columbia, Alberta, and Saskatchewan for the Liberals in the 1980 election forced both Joe Clark and Pierre Trudeau, respectively, to use several senators in putting together a cabinet. When Nova Scotia did not elect any Liberals in the 1997 election, it was represented in the cabinet for the next three-and-a-half years by a minister named from the Senate. Such a practice diminishes the extent that the winning party in the general election gains seats from each province. With the Liberals winning four seats in Nova Scotia in the 2000 election, one of the newly elected MPs, Robert Thibault (West Nova), became the province's cabinet representative. The massive Tory victory in 1984 and the solid win in 1988 allowed Brian Mulroney to choose only one member from the Senate (the Government's Senate Leader) for his cabinet — a return to the traditional pattern in this regard. The practice of including only one senator in the cabinet — that is, the government's house leader in the upper legislative chamber — was continued by Jean Chrétien during his three terms in office. The convention of one cabinet position for each province means that the prime minister's leeway in choosing that representative may be narrow, especially for the smaller provinces, when only one or two government members are elected to the Commons.

> Give me better wood and I'll make you a better cabinet (Canadian Prime Minister John A. Macdonald).

More than one seat in the cabinet is allocated for the larger provinces. Under Pierre Trudeau, Ontario and Quebec were typically granted about 10 seats each in a 30-seat cabinet, with British Columbia receiving from two to four positions. The exact number of such portfolios for each province varies from one government to the next, but the general pattern remains: Ontario and Quebec, which have a majority of the population and a majority of seats in the Commons, also receive a majority (from one-half to two-thirds) of the cabinet postings. In Brian Mulroney's first cabinet of 40 members, Ontario and Quebec received 22 positions (11 each), the four Western provinces got 13, and Atlantic Canada obtained five portfolios. After the second Tory electoral victory in 1988, the 39-member cabinet of January 1989 was regionally composed as follows: Central Canada 25 positions (13 from Quebec, 12 from Ontario); Western Canada 10 positions (British Columbia 4, Alberta 3, Manitoba 2, Saskatchewan 1); and Atlantic Canada 4 (New Brunswick 2, Nova Scotia 1, Newfoundland 1, PEI 0). In 1993, the smaller cabinets of both Kim Campbell (June) and Jean Chrétien (November) forced a specific reduction in the number of cabinet positions given to the larger provinces. For example, in the 1993 Chrétien cabinet, the initial regional breakdown of portfolios was as follows: Ontario 10; Quebec 5; the West 5 (including 2 for Alberta); PEI 0; all other provinces 1.

The number of posts for the more populous provinces are distributed throughout that province, a pattern of regionalism within regionalism. For example, Northern Ontario usually receives one cabinet post, as do the major metropolitan areas. Major cities like Toronto and Montreal have often had more cabinet positions each than the Atlantic provinces in total.

Once the regional allocation has been made, other factors such as race, ethnicity, sex, and religion are considered. For example, Quebec's cabinet representatives include French-speaking Catholics (a majority of posts) and English-speaking Protestants (usually several portfolios). However, in the last two decades religion has become a less significant factor in cabinet composition. On an ethnic basis, those of non-English or non-French origin have traditionally been under-represented, although since the Second World War other ethnic groups are receiving greater attention (e.g., John Diefenbaker appointed the first minister of Ukrainian descent). In recent decades, the federal cabinet has increasingly contained members of various ethnic and religious groups (Jewish, Italian, Asian, Aboriginal). Women are the most under-represented group in the cabinet, a reflection of the fact that traditionally few women have been candidates for office. The first woman appointed to the federal cabinet was Ellen Fairclough, selected as secretary of state by John Diefenbaker in 1957. In comparison to the "average Canadian," the cabinet, on factors such as age, sex, education, and occupation, is quite unrepresentative. In this regard, the representation principle refers primarily to provincial and regional concerns, rather than to ethnic and religious ones, and only coincidentally to such factors as sex, age, and occupation.

Whatever the reasons for their selection to the cabinet, once there, MPs are expected to speak for their province or region, irrespective of their specific portfolio. A Minister of External Affairs from Alberta is Alberta's cabinet representative. A Minister of Public Works from Ontario is expected to be a representative for Ontario in the cabinet's policy-making process. Ministers' portfolios may change, but their role as defenders of provincial interests does not.

Based again on custom, certain portfolios have come to be associated with particular provinces. For example, Public Works, which is a key patronage department because of the number of jobs and contracts that it controls, is usually given to a minister from the governing party's "home" province or provinces, although in Chrétien's 1993 cabinet it went to Nova Scotia. Responsibility for Agriculture is allocated to a minister from the West or perhaps rural Ontario, while Fisheries goes to a minister from the Atlantic Provinces (Brian Tobin) or British Columbia (Jack Davis, John Fraser). Finance is typically granted to an English-Canadian, usually from Ontario, who has strong ties with the business community. Jean Chrétien's brief stint as Minister of Finance in the mid-1970s was the first time a French-Canadian had ever served in that post. Responsibility for an agency such as ACOA (Atlantic Canada Opportunities Agency) goes to someone from that region (in 2001 it was Liberal MP Robert Thibault from

Nova Scotia), while the Minister for the Canadian Wheat Board comes from Western Canada (in 2000 it was Ralph Goodale from Saskatchewan). The prime minister may assume the role of a minister with departmental responsibilities, such as that of External Affairs. However, the custom in recent decades has been not to do so, a pattern continued by Trudeau, Clark, Turner, Mulroney, Campbell, and Chrétien. At the provincial level, premiers more often assign themselves a specific portfolio: Premier Grant Devine of Saskatchewan, who has a Ph.D. in the subject, became his own Minister of Agriculture in 1986, and Ontario Premier Bob Rae designated himself as Minister of Intergovernmental Affairs in 1990. These traditional assignments of particular portfolios to specific regions or interests is a reflection of the impact of the representation principle. Nothing legally prevents a Minister of Fisheries from coming from a Metropolitan Toronto constituency; however, the political absurdity of such a move renders it highly unlikely.

In addition to circumscribing the leeway of the prime minister in forming a cabinet, the representation principle has other significant effects on the political process. First, because it is designed to protect regional and provincial concerns, the cabinet has become the key decision-making body, as well as the primary defender of provincial interests, effectively usurping, in the process, the designated role of the Senate. Second, until the 1990s, the size of the cabinet kept increasing, as more and more sectors of society demanded representation. One internal cabinet result of this increase in size has been a specialization of function, which has resulted in turning over a considerable amount of the effective decision-making power to a series of cabinet committees. Third, the cabinet is not necessarily composed of the most talented individuals available, for the most talented rarely have had the foresight to be elected to the Commons on a regional basis. As Conservative Senator Jacques Flynn put it, in commenting on the Trudeau cabinet of 1981, in "a cabinet of pygmies, a midget can be king." Fourth, the cabinet, in its attempt to accommodate the various regions and interests, is not very efficient in its operation.

While the representation principle affects the allocation of the departmental portfolios, some cabinet members are also named as political ministers. **Political ministers**, sometimes referred to now as **regional ministers** (Bakvis, 1989), are *cabinet members who are given the additional party responsibilities of party organization and patronage for the governing party within their province*. These positions are allocated by the prime minister and reflect the political influence of the individual so named. To assess a minister's overall role in the cabinet, one needs to know his or her official responsibility and his or her party responsibility, if any. To be the political minister for a province is often more significant for one's political influence and power than are one's departmental responsibilities. For example, even though many expected Lucien Bouchard to be named as the political minister for Quebec after the 1988 election, Marcel Masse (Minister of Communications) was retained in that position in the cabinet shuffle of January 1989. For the larger provinces several political ministers may be named (e.g., one for Northern Ontario, one for Southern Ontario, one for Metropolitan Toronto), while only one is typically selected for the smaller provinces.

CABINET ORGANIZATION

Once the composition of the cabinet has been finalized, it is up to the prime minister to determine its uses and internal organization. Under the guidance of the prime minister, the cabinet determines its own structure and operation. The frequency of its meetings, the kinds of questions or issues it deals with, the decision-making procedure that it follows (i.e., majority vote or consensus) all emerge from the prime minister's intent, as well as from the evolving practice of the cabinet itself. Since the internal structure of the cabinet is undefined in law, its organization and role tend to reflect the prime minister's leadership qualities. Diefenbaker's demise as prime minister reflected the disintegration of his cabinet, while Trudeau's longevity was attributable, in part, to the restructuring of the cabinet decision-making process instituted on his becoming prime minister in 1968.

The Trudeau cabinet

The revisions made in the cabinet decision-making process by Trudeau reflected two fundamental assumptions: first, decision making needed to be more rational; and second, the cabinet, rather than the traditional bureaucracy, had to become the effective decision-making centre. Two major structural innovations of the cabinet corresponded to these two goals: first, the cabinet, in order to become more efficient in its handling of issues and problems, greatly revised its committee structure; and second, in order to gain independent advice, the cabinet developed its own bureaucracy, which resulted in a significant expansion of its support staff in the **Privy Council Office (PCO)**.

The use of cabinet committees reveals a specialization of function caused by the increasing size of the total cabinet and the complexity of modern legislation. Eight cabinet committees were set up, four dealing with broad policy areas and four others concerned with co-ordination of policy and purposes among the various departments and agencies. Each minister typically served on two committees. As an issue was brought to the cabinet by a minister, the bureaucracy, or public protest, it would be referred to the appropriate cabinet committee for detailed consideration. After studying the problem and deciding how to act, the cabinet committee would report back to the full cabinet. Except on highly controversial issues, the cabinet usually accepted the decision of the cabinet committee. For this reason, on many matters, real decision-making power had evolved to the cabinet committees acting in the name of the larger cabinet. Votes were rarely taken; instead, a consensus was sought, with the prime minister playing a critical role in its formation. Once the cabinet had settled on policy, it was communicated to the departments and bureaucracy for implementation.

The second major change instituted by Trudeau concerned the size and functions of the **Prime Minister's Office (PMO)** and the PCO, both of which were greatly enhanced. Together, the task of the PMO and PCO is to give the political executive advice and policy recommendations independent from that of the civil service. This counter-bureaucracy had the expertise and political clout to free the cabinet from its former dependence on the advice coming from the policy advisors at the departmental level. Some of the fiercest battles of the Trudeau years concerned the organization and the role of the PMO and PCO structures. With the backing of Prime Minister Trudeau, the PMO and PCO, and especially the latter, won a leading role in the policy-making process. Enhancement of the PMO and PCO and a revised cabinet committee structure were the major organizational changes implemented by Prime Minister Trudeau (1968–1979) in order to make the decision-making role of the political executive more rational and efficient. The same basic pattern was reasserted on his return to power during the 1980–1984 period.

The Clark cabinet

The flexibility of cabinet organization is illustrated by the fact that each new prime minister reorganizes it in some manner. The major innovation of the short-lived Clark government in 1979–1980 concerned the first formal use of an inner and outer cabinet in Canadian history. Based on the British practice of making a distinction between all departmental ministers (the ministry) and the major departmental ministers (the cabinet), the inner-outer cabinet model sought to overcome the problem of the excessive size of federal cabinets; at the same time, it rationalized and made more efficient the decision-making process.

From a cabinet of 29 members, 10 were chosen for the inner cabinet. Although decisions from the inner cabinet could be appealed to the full cabinet, this was rarely the case in the Clark government. Besides setting up a highly visible caste system within the cabinet, the major flaw of the inner-outer cabinet structure in the Canadian context was its rigidity and inability to implement the representation principle. For example, the initial Clark inner cabinet contained no representation from British Columbia, so John Fraser (MP for Vancouver South) was added, while an individual as prominent as David Crombie, former mayor of Toronto, was excluded (Simpson, 1980: 94–95). While all prime ministers have had an informal inner cabinet or "kitchen cabinet" composed of their most influential aides and ministers, to formally structure the cabinet along the same lines meant that the primary cabinet function of regional and provincial representation could not be sustained. An inner-outer cabinet structure can be justified by the need to make the decision-making process more efficient, but it failed in the Canadian context because it ignored the representation principle of cabinet composition.

The Turner cabinet

Although the government of John Turner may go down as simply an asterisk in Canadian political history, in the sense that it only lasted about three months before facing the second largest defeat in the country's electoral history, it produced some interesting variations on the cabinet structure of both of his nearest predecessors. Basically, the cabinet of John Turner rejected the patterns of decision making of Joe Clark and Pierre Trudeau.

First, Turner rejected Clark's formal inner-outer cabinet structure. Second, the size of the cabinet was reduced to 29, considerably smaller than the 36 or 37 members of the last years of Pierre Trudeau. Prime Minister Turner also indicated that the cabinet might be reduced further, if he won a mandate from the

people. Third, Trudeau's cabinet committee system was streamlined and simplified: Turner specifically sought to dismantle much of the bureaucracy which had
come to surround the process of cabinet decision making. Fourth, Turner desired
to increase the power of departmental ministers, a move which would have been
at the expense of both the PMO and PCO.

These alterations in the structure of the cabinet and its decision-making
process indicated that the new Liberal leader was rejecting many of the significant changes instituted during the 15-year reign of Pierre Trudeau. The Turner cabinet was reminiscent of that of previous Liberal leaders such as Lester Pearson.

The Mulroney cabinet

Their many years in opposition, during which they strongly criticized the Trudeau
pattern of cabinet decision making, combined with Clark's failure in instituting an
inner-outer cabinet structure, led the members of the Mulroney government to try
what they thought would be an innovative cabinet structure. The Mulroney Tories
instituted a system that, while reforming some of the minor aspects of the Trudeau
years, had more in common with them than most Conservatives would probably want to admit.

In their two terms in office, the Mulroney government and cabinet could be
characterized by one broad theme: an increasing centralization of power and influence in the position of the prime minister and his staff in the Prime Minister's
Office (PMO). This centralization proceeded further and faster under Brian
Mulroney than under Pierre Trudeau. The PMO became the locus of policy, patronage, and power. As a result, the Privy Council Office (PCO), which had become
the key player under Trudeau, suffered a decline in significance. One result of this
shifting balance between the PMO and PCO was a decline in the power of the
cabinet and of the traditional departments. Key policy decisions were made in
the PMO, not around the cabinet table. As a corollary of this new pattern, the
power of the civil service, particularly that of its senior mandarins, was reduced as
well. The charges of "presidentializing" the Canadian parliamentary system that
were made so often against Pierre Trudeau would be heard about Brian Mulroney
as well, particularly after the changes in the cabinet's structure announced with the
cabinet shuffle of January 1989.

The size of the cabinet remained large, dropping only marginally, from 40 to
39. The most significant changes occurred internally, shifting power away from the
full cabinet to several of its component parts. First, the growth in the importance
of the Priorities and Planning Committee (P&P) that was started under former
prime minister Pierre Trudeau was enhanced by the 1989 cabinet modifications of
Prime Minister Brian Mulroney. P&P, which increased in size to include the prime
minister and 18 ministers, became an unofficial inner cabinet consisting of the
key ministers in the most significant areas of public policy. The P&P committee was
made responsible for all new government spending.

The second cabinet change was the addition of a new cabinet committee
called the Operations Committee. Informally started in the spring of 1987, this new
committee was primarily concerned with short-term political planning. Composed
of the prime minister and eight key ministers, the Operations Committee served

as a kind of "executive committee" of P&P. Nothing went to P&P that did not first pass through the Operations Committee. Thus, an inner cabinet (the Operations Committee) within an inner cabinet (P&P) was created.

A third modification of the cabinet structure concerned its committees, which increased from 10 to 14. However, the membership on the policy committees was reduced, from a previous high of 25, down to between 7 and 12 members. Most importantly, the standing committees of cabinet no longer decided, or even really had a role in, allocating government expenditures.

Combined with the centralization of decision making in the hands of the prime minister and the PMO, what these 1989 cabinet changes signified was that the cabinet, as a whole, represented the facade, rather than the foundation, of political power in Canada in the 1990s.

The Campbell cabinet

After winning the leadership of the Conservative party and becoming the first female prime minister in Canadian history, Kim Campbell, as one means of distancing herself from the Mulroney years, slashed the size of the federal cabinet to 25 and imposed a major structural reorganization on the federal bureaucracy. Prime Minister Campbell had thus created the smallest federal cabinet in three decades.

In addition to its smaller size, several aspects of the Campbell cabinet of June 1993 are significant. First, because of the number of long-time cabinet ministers not expected to re-offer in the expected election or having already resigned, Prime Minister Campbell was able to include a large number of new individuals (eight) in her ministry. Second, the smaller cabinet increased the difficulty of meeting the principle of regional representation. Premier Bob Rae of Ontario was particularly unhappy that Ontario received only 8 of the 25 positions. Third, the representation for women actually declined under the country's first female leader — from seven in Mulroney's last cabinet to five (counting herself) with Campbell's first (and last) cabinet membership. Finally, by greatly reducing the size of the cabinet, Prime Minister Kim Campbell set a precedent for other prime ministers in the immediate future.

The Chrétien cabinet

While continuing the trend toward a smaller cabinet (23), the initial cabinet of Prime Minister Jean Chrétien (announced in November of 1993) maintained, but also modified, the principle of regional representation. Every province except Prince Edward Island received a cabinet portfolio, with the West also gaining the Senate's government leader. The largest provinces gained two-thirds of the assignments (Ontario 10 and Quebec 5), with Metropolitan Toronto receiving 5 (equal, in other words, to the West or Quebec and more than the Atlantic provinces). Most surprising was that British Columbia only received, as the country's third-largest province, one portfolio — indicating perhaps that regional representation reflected a province's numbers within the governing caucus rather than simply reflecting population totals. In addition to its regional composition, the initial Chrétien cabinet included four women (one less than Kim Campbell's cabinet), 12 lawyers, no non-whites, one senator, and seven holdovers from previous Liberal governments. At the end of Chrétien's second term in office, the regional breakdown of the Chrétien cabinet was as follows: Ontario (12), Quebec (7), British Columbia (2), and 1 from each of the other provinces. In October of 2000, women were represented by 7 members of cabinet (out of 28) and 9 members of the ministry (out of 37).

In terms of structure, while it maintained the basic pattern of reorganization created by Kim Campbell, the Chrétien cabinet also adopted a modified version of the British pattern of cabinet structure, by making a distinction between the key cabinet portfolios (23) and eight secretaries of state to be included in the larger ministry. In some ways reminiscent of Joe Clark's inner-and-outer cabinet structure, the secretaries of state were made members of the Privy Council, but their salaries would only be 75 percent of a full minister's pay. The secretaries of state were not, therefore, part of the official cabinet, although they were available to attend specific meetings in relation to their specific areas of expertise. As a result of this cabinet structure, critics were quick to argue that the actual cabinet size was 31, not 23. In the major cabinet shuffle of January 1996, Prime Minister Chrétien increased slightly the size of the cabinet to 25 and the number of secretaries of state to 9, bringing the total ministry to 34. By October of 2000, prior to the election call, the size of the cabinet had increased to 28, with an additional 9 secretaries of state, bringing the total ministry to 37. Finally, in contrast to the Mulroney and Trudeau years, the number of cabinet committees was greatly reduced to just four, although ad hoc committees were occasionally created.

While the initial changes made to the cabinet and its committee structure by the prime minister in his first term (1993–1997) appeared to increase the power of the cabinet and its ministers and return to Ottawa a decision-making style reminiscent of Lester Pearson in the 1960s, by the end of his second term (1997–2000), Prime Minister Chrétien was increasingly being described as arrogant for having centralized all key decision-making powers in the PMO. This trend to a concentration of power in the hands of the prime minister and a small circle of advisors has been increasingly true of all recent political executives who have been in office for any length of time (Trudeau, Mulroney, Chrétien). As one recent study concluded, the prime minister is no longer *primus inter pares* (first among equals), because all that is left is *"primus:* there is no longer any *inter* or *pares"* (Savoie, 1999a: 71). Such a trend, given the continuing basis of prime ministerial pre-eminence, seems destined to remain in place in the years ahead.

Conclusion on cabinet structure

Our brief look at the cabinet structures and decision-making patterns of the governments of Prime Ministers Trudeau, Clark, Turner, Mulroney, Campbell, and Chrétien seems to support the conclusion that "all cabinet systems are designed by prime ministers to suit their own personal styles and the particular circumstances of the time" (Clark, 1985: 191). Since the modern cabinet started with the Trudeau era, it has served as the basis for our analysis of later developments. Each cabinet, no matter how briefly in power, sets a pattern that is either accepted or rejected according to the outlook of each new government.

Whatever its internal structure and operation, the key political functions of the cabinet are the initiation, development, and implementation of public policy under the direction of the prime minister. If the prime minister and cabinet fail to lead, there is little that can be done, except elect a new prime minister at the next election. Matters such as the representation principle are significant because they help to determine the quality of that leadership and the content and effectiveness of public policy.

The complex nature of the executive branch of government in Canada reflects, in part, its political role as the core or centre of the political system. The basic features of the executive branch are outlined in Figure 3.1, although this figure would have to be adapted to apply specifically to any particular cabinet. For example, the use of parliamentary secretaries by the Chrétien government could be illustrated by having them placed outside of the cabinet box in Figure 3.1, but attached to it by a dotted line. However, the general pattern of development must be kept in mind: through constitutional evolution and political tradition, the formal executive has become a bit player in the drama of Canadian politics, while the political executive, especially the prime minister and the cabinet, have assumed the leading role.

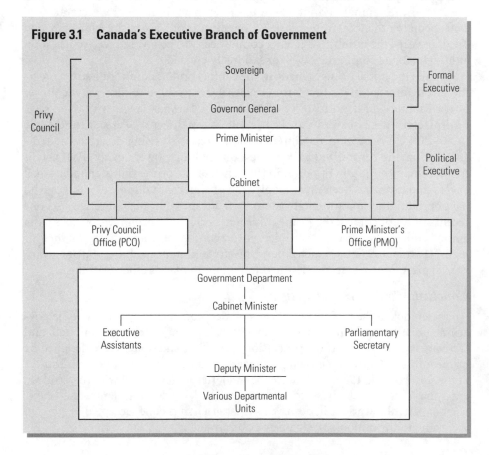

Figure 3.1   Canada's Executive Branch of Government

THE CANADIAN BUREAUCRACY

The important role of the bureaucracy as a key component of Canada's political executive can be seen in the way in which decisions are made regarding public policy. Canada is a polity that minimizes the role of political ideology in the decision-making process. Instead, public priorities are dependent on political considerations of party, personnel, and patronage.

In addition to its nonideological nature, several other aspects of the decision-making process characterize the nature of public policy in Canada. First, most policy is **incremental** in design, implementation, and effect; that is, *change is slow, modest, and usually inefficient.* Incrementalism means building on existing policy and practices, rather than starting over in a wholesale fashion. For example, tax reform in Canada involves tinkering with the existing structure, such as raising the tax on some items, lowering it on others, or adding or deleting specific tax loopholes. A pattern of incremental decision making reflects not only general bureaucratic tendencies, but certain elements of Canada's political culture (e.g., deference, elitism, and conservatism). A second characteristic of decision making concerns the particular role of cabinet ministers as **generalists**, rather than as specialists. One of the assumptions of cabinet government, one that is probably incorrect, is that *a minister can adequately direct and control any department, irrespective of the content of that department's responsibilities.* Cabinet shuffles specifically reflect such a view, since a minister can be in charge of Finance one day and External Affairs the next. If one is a competent administrator, then supposedly one can administer any department.

Canadian cabinets are overwhelmingly composed of generalists — there are few specialists in the inner sanctum of power. In fact, sometimes competence in a particular policy area keeps a minister from being named to the most relevant cabinet post. Eric Kierans, with extensive business and financial expertise, became Postmaster General in Trudeau's first cabinet, instead of receiving a portfolio that dealt with economic matters. Similarly, David Anderson from British Columbia, well known as a supporter and participant in the environmental movement, was named as Minister of National Revenue in the Chrétien cabinet of 1993, rather than receiving the Environment portfolio to which he was later appointed. Incremental public policy developed and administered by generalists is the context of the bureaucratic function and a most important source of the power of the civil service in the Canadian political process.

The theoretical or designed role of the bureaucracy is to implement the decisions regarding public policy that have been made by the political executive and authorized by the legislature. However, direction concerning the course of public policy may be vague, so that the act of implementation puts the bureaucracy in a policy-making role. To apply general policy to specific situations is neither easy nor neutral; it necessitates a decision-making function for the civil service.

Considerable bureaucratic influence flows from its role as the interpreter of the meaning of the general law, or what is called delegated power. For example, **delegated legislative power** means that *the legislature has passed a bill that authorizes the executive and bureaucracy to flesh out the details of the bill's general* *provisions.* A classic illustration of this pattern is demonstrated by the wage-and-price control legislation (Bill C-73), which passed the House of Commons on December 3, 1975. Section 3 of the Anti-Inflation Act provided the authority for detailed specification by the civil service of how the wage-and-price restraint plan would work: "The Governor in Council may from time to time cause to be published and made known guidelines for the guidance of all Canadians in restraining profit margins, prices, dividends and compensation." The initial bureaucratic guidelines (many more were to follow later), known as the Anti-Inflation Act Regulations, were 60 pages long — four times the size of Bill C-73 itself!

A second basis of bureaucratic influence is the reputed expertise of the civil service with respect to the nature and content of public policy and of the government regulations based thereon. For example, there are probably very few politicians or civil servants in the entire country who can explain in detail the provisions of Canada's equalization formula. Moreover, because civil servants have long tenure in office (generally they can be removed only for "cause"), they have become significant participants in the decision-making process. Cabinet ministers come and go, while the bureaucracy remains in place. In British Columbia, between 1996 and 2001, 109 cabinet appointments were made, including nine Ministers of Labour. A recent study of provincial ministerial career patterns (White, 1998) found that provincial ministers have less previous parliamentary experience than in earlier decades, that they do not remain in cabinet for as long a period of time, and that they are more frequently shuffled between portfolios, thereby increasing the power of the bureaucracy. In a spirit of derision, bureaucrats may refer to their cabinet bosses as "our political masters." Often in Canadian history, the so-called political masters have been controlled by their servants, and not always in a civil fashion.

The bureaucracy is intimately involved not only in the implementation of public policy, but also in its initiation and formulation. The structure of the departments of government reflects this pattern (see Figure 3.1). At the head of each department is a cabinet minister, surrounded by various aides and executive assistants who are directly responsible to him or her. The purpose of these ministerial assistants is to help the cabinet minister establish control over the bureaucracy.

Also included in this entourage are the **parliamentary secretaries**, who are *MPs assigned to help the cabinet minister.* Parliamentary secretaries are allocated to the major portfolios (Ministers of State usually receive no such help) on a regional basis according to the representation principle. Parliamentary secretaries are not members of the cabinet, but the position has been used as a training and testing ground to spot future cabinet material. These backbench MPs of the governing party often serve as stand-ins for the minister on speaking engagements and as "lightning rods" to attract any political flak away from the minister. The involvement of parliamentary secretaries in the decision-making process is usually very modest.

In terms of authority in, and direction over, a government department, the second in command to the cabinet minister is the deputy minister. As administrative head of a department, the deputy minister is responsible for the overall direction and day-to-day operation of the bureaucracy. A **deputy minister** is not an MP, but is, in effect, *the top civil servant assigned to each department.* Deputy ministers are appointed by the prime minister and are removable by the PM. But, as career public servants, such a change would cost them only power, not job security.

Deputy ministers are more directly involved in the political process than most civil servants and, therefore, occupy a rather distinctive position in the bureaucracy. As the "permanent" department head, the deputy minister fulfills not only an administrative role, but a political one as well (Hodgetts, 1985). Deputy ministers are usually important participants in the policy-making process. As a result, a shuffle of deputy ministers may be more significant as an indicator of changing government priorities than a shift of cabinet portfolios would be. Because a shuffle of deputy ministers is usually less frequent than one of cabinet ministers, and given their expertise and knowledge, deputy ministers often control the cabinet ministers who in theory direct the department. Some departments have been particularly affected by frequent cabinet shuffles. Under Pierre Trudeau, the Defence portfolio was changed eight times and that of National Revenue eleven times. In such a situation, deputy ministers often acquire and exercise power at the expense of their ministers. Arrayed beneath the deputy ministers are the component units of each government department, a structure that varies from one department to the next.

The important political role of the bureaucracy in the decision-making process means that, despite the civil service's supposed impartiality, all governments seek to control its composition and influence. A government that has been in power for any length of time can fashion the bureaucracy in its own political image. At the top of the bureaucracy (i.e., deputy minister level), the governing party has the prerogative to appoint and remove civil servants as it desires, while at the intermediate levels, civil service hiring guidelines are flexible enough to allow the government to shape its structures and hiring procedures.

The political nature and importance of the bureaucracy is clearly evident when an opposition party, especially one that has been out of office for a long time, wins an election and forms a government. At least some highly visible public servants lose their jobs, if for no other reason than as a symbol of the changing of the political guard — such an interpretation can account for the departure of Privy Council Clerk Michael Pitfield, Trudeau's long-time friend and confidant, shortly after the Clark government took office in 1979. Sometimes the leaving of imbedded allies of the former government can be a messy business. Such problems between a new government and the bureaucracy are common at the provincial level as well, where the bureaucratic turnover after an election is apparently more extensive. For example, after two years in power in Ontario, Conservative Premier Mike Harris had retained the services of only 9 of 25 deputy ministers that had served the previous NDP government. Similarly, after the 1996 election in Prince Edward Island, hundreds of seasonal workers complained that the new Tory government of Pat Binns had dismissed them for solely political reasons. By the end of 1997, the Tory government had agreed to pay $750 000 to 314 seasonal workers to settle the controversy.

Once the initial turnover of key positions in the civil service has been accomplished, the government has considerable leeway in establishing and extending its influence throughout the bureaucracy during its stay in office. Parties in opposition are usually in favour of rather drastic civil service reform. The concern of all governments to control the structure, operation, and composition of the civil service is a reflection of the political nature of the bureaucracy and its significant role in the policy-making process.

THE BRITISH EXECUTIVE

In broad outline, the structure and operation of the British executive parallels that of the Canadian. On a number of specific points, however, British and Canadian practices diverge with respect to both the formal and political executives.

The formal executive in Britain — what has been referred to as "the Rolls Royce of Monarchies" — is hereditary in terms of succession and constitutional with respect to its role in the polity. The slow evolution and public acceptance of the British monarchy, which traces its origins back 10 centuries, has traditionally placed it in a far more secure position than its Canadian counterpart. Popular support for the monarchy and Royal Family is traditionally extensive, although some members may be held in less than high regard. The legitimacy of the monarchy is rarely challenged and, when it is, the result is usually an overwhelmingly positive response from the public in defence of the formal executive.

Admittedly, some undermining of this traditional position emerged in the late 1980s and 1990s. While Queen Elizabeth herself continued to be held in high esteem, her children and the "lesser royals" were not. Much-publicized scandals centring on marital problems and inappropriate behaviour began to undercut the legitimacy of the monarchy. Some analysts saw the situation as the most serious challenge to the monarchy since the abdication of Edward VIII in 1936, while the crisis of confidence led anti-monarchists, such as Labour MP Tony Benn, to introduce legislation in the Parliament calling for the elimination of the monarchy. Such problems led Queen Elizabeth to describe 1992 as *annus horribilis*: "1992 is not a year on which I shall look back with undiluted pleasure." As well, concern over the increasing costs of the monarchy led the Queen to announce in February of 1993 that she would begin paying taxes as of April 6, 1993 — thereby ending a 56-year royal tax exemption.

One reason why the British monarchy has survived for centuries has been its ability to adapt to changing circumstances. The German origin of the current British Royal Family, for example, was successfully disguised, for obvious political reasons in 1917, when it changed its name from the "House of Saxe-Coburg-Gotha" to the "House of Windsor." The nadir of public support probably came in 1997 with the tragic death of Diana, Princess of Wales. Since then the Royal Family has begun to reinvent itself, once again. For example, it has sought to mingle more often with the general public and to pay attention to shifting patterns of public support by hiring, in 1998, a public-opinion polling firm. By the end of the 1990s, public support was on the rise again, especially for Prince Charles. However, members of Tony Blair's Labour government have suggested various reforms that would weaken the monarchy. Moreover, in July of 2000 the Labour government imposed a 10-year pay freeze on the Queen's salary and forced the monarchy to pay for more of its own costs.

Britain is also an example of a constitutional monarchy, where the head of state or monarch exercises his or her powers on the advice of the political executive. Historically, monarchs governed as they desired, with few limitations on their roles or powers, a situation sometimes classified as absolute monarchy. However, as Parliament and, much later, the political executive emerged to challenge the monarch, the latter became more and more a figurehead, serving primarily symbolic and ceremonial roles. Thus, the monarch was once dominant over the political executive in Britain.

Although the British monarch acts on the advice of the government, a procedure that strongly circumscribes his or her political role, some political functions remain. For example, as in Canada, the formal executive is not to become involved in partisan politics or to make statements of a political nature. However, participation by the Royal Family in the public debate occurred in June of 2000, with Prince Charles openly criticizing genetically modified foods in British supermarkets, and with his father, Prince Phillip, and his sister, Princess Anne, taking the opposing point of view. Given the legitimacy of the monarchy in Britain, the King or Queen has more leeway and thus more influence in such matters than the governor general in Canada.

On several occasions in the 20th century, the British monarch has been called upon to take an active role in naming a prime minister. For example, in 1957 there was no clear successor within the Conservative caucus to Prime Minister Anthony Eden. Two people were possible successors — Harold Macmillan and R.A. Butler — and after it was clear that the Conservative party could not quickly settle the question among themselves (a specific leadership election mechanism was not used until 1965), the Queen asked Macmillan to form a government, thus making him prime minister. A more complex situation occurred in 1931 when no party had a majority of seats in the House of Commons. The King took the initiative to bring the various party leaders together for consultation, but, rightly, he did not advocate which of them he preferred as prime minister. What these examples indicate is that the monarch infrequently acts on his or her own initiative and, on those rare occasions, proceeds in an impartial and nonpartisan manner. While in theory the monarch can dismiss ministers, or refuse assent to a piece of legislation, in practice a much more modest constitutional role has evolved for the formal executive in Britain: the "monarchy survives because it is politically weak" (Rose, 1982: 50).

The real power of the executive branch is granted to the occupant of Number 10 Downing Street, the British prime minister's official residence. The prime minister in Britain is pre-eminent with respect to public policy, party, and Parliament to an even greater degree than the Canadian prime minister. Since the traditional political structure is unitary and remains largely in place even with the beginnings of devolution, the prime minister does not share either power or the political limelight with the leaders of an intermediate level of government. Thus, the British prime minister's policy-making role is greater than in Canada, where it is limited by the federalization of responsibility between the national and provincial governments. Moreover, British parties have traditionally been highly centralized in structure and operation, as well as disciplined within Parliament itself. British party leaders, especially Conservative ones, have usually exerted strong control over their party's parliamentary wing. These considerations reveal that a British prime minister is not constrained by some of the typical limitations imposed on any prime minister in Canada.

Cabinet composition is also based on different premises in Britain than in Canada, because the rigid representation principle regarding regional and provincial interests does not apply. For example, the cabinets of Margaret Thatcher in the late 1980s witnessed few positions for MPs from Scotland because the Tories won few seats there in 1983 and 1987. Moreover, the major parties have usually received some Commons seats from all areas within Britain, so regionalism need not be the major factor for cabinet selection or promotion. Instead, ideology plays a significant role in a cabinet's composition, with all major factions traditionally included. Margaret Thatcher's emphasis on "ideological purity" in cabinet composition was, and still is, something of an exception in modern British politics. The cabinets of her successor, John Major, were more typical in this regard, in that they represented a wider array of political figures across the party's ideological spectrum. Tony Blair's first cabinet in 1997 included powerful party figures, such as Gordon Brown and John Prescott, that he simply could not exclude from his ministry.

The British cabinet is less of a "mirror image" of society than its Canadian counterpart. For example, John Major's first cabinet in 1990 contained no women. In contrast, Tony Blair's first cabinet in 1997 included 5 women (out of 22), which was increased to 7 in the July 1999 cabinet shuffle. The 1999 cabinet shuffle left the number of ministers at 22, but did alter the total ministry with 14 resignations, 14 lateral moves, and 13 new junior ministers. Included was Britain's first black female minister, Baroness Patricia Scotland, as parliamentary undersecretary in the Foreign Office. Following the June 2001 election, the cabinet size was increased to 23, which included the selection of 4 new female cabinet officers. In Britain, ministers may be appointed from either House of Parliament, although the vast majority are from the Commons. Members from the House of Lords are more frequently used in British cabinets than are senators in Canadian ones.

British Prime Minister Margaret Thatcher on the cabinet (1979): There are two ways of making a Cabinet. One way is to have in it people representing the different points of view within the party, within the broad philosophy. The other way is to have in it only the people who want to go in the direction which every instinct tells me we have to go: clearly, steadily, firmly, with resolution. As Prime Minister, I could not waste any time having internal arguments.

On the surface, the size of the British cabinet is small, averaging about 22 members in recent years. Since the representation principle has not been applied in cabinet composition, the size of this key decision-making body has been kept limited (22 out of 659 members in the British House). However, the importance of the cabinet can only be appreciated by distinguishing it from the ministry. In Canada, the cabinet and ministry have been traditionally identical (at least until the Chrétien cabinet of November 1993), while in Britain the cabinet is the smaller operative part of the ministry. A British ministry includes all cabinet officers, plus the parliamentary secretaries and parliamentary undersecretaries. The ministry may typically number over 100 members, while only the key portfolios are designated as cabinet ones. The positions included as part of the cabinet are based on tradition and on the desires of the prime minister with respect to how the government should be organized. Thus, the British cabinet is small, while the ministry is large. Appointments to the ministry often provide a means of recruitment and socialization for future cabinet appointees. In Britain, the ministry rarely, if ever, meets, while the cabinet does so on a regular basis. Decisions of the cabinet are based on a consensus approach, with only rare challenges to its authority emanating from the ministry, party caucus, or Parliament.

The power of the prime minister with respect to the cabinet has resulted in the thesis that the prime minister, not the cabinet, is the centre of influence and power in modern British politics. This thesis has been forcefully stated by former professor and Labour party minister Richard Crossman. Because a skillful prime minister can control the party, the Parliament, and the bureaucracy, the concept of cabinet government has become a myth: "the best description of the present system of control is that it is not Cabinet Government any more but Prime Ministerial Government" (Crossman, 1972: 29–30). In effect, then, the concept of collective responsibility has been replaced by prime ministerial responsibility to party and nation, bypassing or at least manipulating Parliament in the process. The facade of power has expanded from the formal executive to elements of the political executive as well: the cabinet reigns, the prime minister governs.

While the thesis of prime ministerial government is becoming a common one in assessments of British politics, it is premature to accept it uncritically. Much depends on the political skills and the political will of the occupant of Number 10 Downing Street. While the position of Prime Minister creates the potential for prime ministerial government, it does not guarantee it. Moreover, the cabinet, if pushed too far, can make life very unpleasant for the prime minister, even to the extent of forcing him or her to resign (e.g., the resignation in 1917 of Prime Minister Asquith). The unprecedented move by the Tory caucus to oust Margaret Thatcher as their leader and thus to end her 12-year reign as prime minister in November of 1990 is also an excellent example of this conclusion. Much of the dissatisfaction with Thatcher's leadership emanated from current or former members of her cabinet, with the final blow being the resignation of Deputy Prime Minister Sir Geoffrey Howe. The prime ministerial thesis ignores the constraints of custom and convention that have limited the prime minister's actual role in cabinet composition, direction, and control (Wilson, 1977). A prime minister must "carry his or her colleagues" with him or her on major policies and programs. To the extent that the prime ministerial thesis emphasizes the key role of the prime minister in modern British politics, it is correct; to the extent that it ignores the collegial nature of that leadership, it is wrong.

As our discussion shows, the nature of executive power in Britain is divided between a hereditary and constitutional monarch and an elected and temporary political executive. The formal executive retains primarily symbolic and ceremonial tasks, while the prime minister and cabinet have become the engine of the political process. Backing up the power of the prime minister and cabinet is the bureaucracy, a key aspect of executive dominance in the modern British polity.

THE BRITISH BUREAUCRACY

Descriptions of the British bureaucracy frequently use two terms, that of Whitehall and of the mandarins. Whitehall is, in fact, a street on which many of the major departments of the British government are located. As a result, **Whitehall** is used as a term to describe *the political executive and bureaucratic components of government.* (The prime minister lives at Number 10 Downing Street, a small avenue off Whitehall, with Parliament itself located at the end of Whitehall.) The senior officials and administrators of the approximately 20 main government departments are often call **mandarins**, after the Chinese term for *a high-ranking official.* The term mandarin would certainly include the top 1 000 people in the administrative class, individuals likely to play some significant role in the policy process.

The role of the bureaucracy has been a significant one in the policy-making process, because in Britain the relationship between the civil service and the government of the day has usually been an intimate one. It appears that the Canadian practice of bypassing the traditional bureaucracy by setting up a counter-bureaucracy around the office of the prime minister has not been a major development in British politics. Instead, a counter-bureaucratic structure has been created, which parallels the structure and political functions of the civil service. These organizations, estimated to total in the range of 6 700 in 1994 (5 500 of these with some executive powers), have been labelled **quangos** *(quasi-autonomous non-governmental organizations).* Since members of the quangos are appointed by the ministers, the positions are usually patronage-based because normal civil service hiring rules do not apply.

In Britain, the old adage that a minister proposes while a bureaucrat disposes no longer is entirely correct. The tradition of generalist ministers has certainly enhanced the power of the bureaucratic specialists. Moreover, some ministers may be temporary birds of passage of one or two years' duration, while members of the administrative class may spend decades, if not their entire adult lives, within the confines of a single department. For example, "between 1944 and 1967, there were nineteen Ministers of Education" (Norton, 1982: 84). Rapid turnover of ministers increases the potential of civil service influence. Moreover, the growth of government departments and services has rendered the day-to-day supervision of the civil service nearly impossible. In 2001, a ministry of about 100 people oversees a civil service of about 430 000, compared to a ministry of about 60 persons in charge of a civil service of 50 000 in 1900.

Rapid turnover of generalist ministers is exacerbated by the techniques the bureaucracy can use to frustrate the will of a new minister. These bureaucratic games have been analyzed by former labour minister Tony Benn (1982: 53–61). Techniques that enhance civil service power include secrecy, ministerial briefings, control of information, setting the broad framework of policy, expertise, patronage, and bargaining within Whitehall. The problem for the minister is to control his or her department without being controlled by it. The necessary balance is often a difficult one to achieve: the "effective Minister is the man who wins the support of his Department without becoming its cherished mascot" (Crossman, 1972: 65).

One of the long-held views of the British bureaucracy is its vaunted political neutrality — no matter which party or individual assumes office, the civil service will carry out its functions and specifically assigned tasks. A good example of this nonpartisan outlook occurs during an election campaign: the bureaucracy prepares a throne speech for each party based on the parties' platforms. As former prime minister Harold Wilson (1977: 60) put it, the "Civil Service is extremely agile and politically, almost cynically, dispassionate in reading the electoral portents."

The supposed neutrality of the civil service is surely tested when a switch occurs between Labour and Conservative governments. Because British parties are ideological and class-based, with specific party manifestoes, a change in party can lead to a major reorientation of government policy. Few would mistake former prime minister Margaret Thatcher's policies with those of her predecessor, James ("Sunny Jim") Callaghan, or her successor, John Major. Historically, the gaining of power by the Labour party after the Second World War and the rather enthusiastic implementation of its policy of nationalizing certain key industries by the civil service is often cited as a demonstration of Whitehall's nonpolitical stance to new governments. Moreover, when an opposition party gains power, few top-level bureaucrats lose their jobs — certainly far fewer on a percentage basis than in Canada or the United States.

Recruitment to the civil service has traditionally been narrowly conceived, with most recruits — certainly for the senior levels — coming from those who have attended Oxford or Cambridge. However, in terms of more general population characteristics, this has meant that the civil service was almost a distinct caste in British society. Reforms of the last several decades have opened up the recruitment basis for the civil service, thereby producing a more representative bureaucracy in Britain.

In addition to factors of expertise, education, and political neutrality, the civil service plays a significant policy-making role in the political process because of the structure of the political system. The parliamentary system, with its fusion of powers between the executive and legislature, has enhanced the power not only of the political executive, but of its handmaiden, the civil service, as well. Moreover, the traditional unitary nature of the institutional structure means that when something is decided as policy in Whitehall, it becomes policy without the need to negotiate compromises with other levels of government, as in Canada and the United States. While political leaders may come and go, and while parties may change course or direction over the specifics of the political agenda, the bureaucracy remains in place, exercising considerable influence in the political process.

THE AMERICAN EXECUTIVE

The Office of the President of the United States, often described as the most powerful elective office in any democratic system, has become the focal point of the American political process. This central leadership role of the president has clearly emerged in the past 70 years, a development based primarily on political convention rather than on any explicit constitutional enhancement of presidential powers.

As the national government became the key player in the American federal system, American presidents often seized the opportunity to exert their influence in both domestic and foreign affairs. In the process the presidency became the symbol of the American nation, embodying high principles of political virtue backed by popular support. American citizens believe "that no matter how the faith may be destroyed elsewhere, at one particular point — the Presidency — justice will be done beyond prejudice, beyond rancor, beyond the possibility of a fix" (White, 1976: 332). This democratization of the presidency allowed for the further growth of presidential power to such an extent that by the early 1970s the office was increasingly referred to as the **imperial presidency** (Schlesinger, 1974: 10).

> The Presidency is the focus for the most intense and persistent emotions in the American polity. The President is a symbolic leader, the one figure who draws together the people's hopes and fears for the political future. On top of all of his routine duties, he has to carry that off — or fail (Barber, 1985: 2).

The public reaction, however, to misuses of presidential power such as over Watergate and the Vietnam War provided for at least a temporary retrenchment of the imperial presidency. The inability of Republican President Gerald Ford (1974–1977) and Democrat Jimmy Carter (1977–1981) to provide successful leadership in either domestic or foreign affairs reflected the decline of presidential power in the 1970s. In contrast, Republican Ronald Reagan's landslide electoral victories in the 1980 and 1984 presidential contests allowed him to reassert the powers of the presidency. The mundane and status quo presidency of Republican George Bush (1989–1993) was certainly not imperial, while the two terms of his successor, Democrat Bill Clinton, cannot be so classified either. President Clinton faced a series of allegations concerning personal and political wrongdoings, especially with respect to his private sexual behaviour with Monica Lewinsky. While remaining personally popular throughout his second term, the presidency, as an institution, was certainly diminished in the public's perception (Pious, 1999). As only the second president in American history to be impeached (but not convicted and removed from office), Bill Clinton clearly tarnished the presidency in American politics. By the end of Clinton's second term, the imperial presidency of the 1960s had become the imperilled presidency of the 1990s (Neustadt, 2001: 3). The selection as president in 2000 of George W. Bush, widely regarded as an intellectual lightweight, will do little to change this perception. This ebb and flow of presidential power illustrates the ambivalent attitude most Americans feel about the presidency itself: they are "excited by its potential for good, yet fearful of the abuse of power" (Pious, 1979: 10).

The creation of the presidency provides for an understanding of such a paradox. The American presidency was designed to be a revised combination of the British formal and political executives of the mid-18th century; as Theodore Roosevelt described it, a position "almost that of a king and a prime minister rolled into one." Thus, the tasks or functions of an American president are extensive, because they include the symbolic and ceremonial duties of a formal executive and the political functions of a prime minister. This fusion of roles is an important basis of presidential power in the American system and illustrates why Duverger (1974: 52) classified the American president as a "democratic transplant of the king of England."

> Put simply, the president, elected directly and separately, is virtually secure from all possible removal . . . . The prime minister, however, lives far more dangerously in that he can be ousted from office at very short notice if he loses control of Parliament (Wilson, 1977: 206).

PRESIDENTIAL ROLES

The importance of the presidency in the American political process is clearly revealed in the various roles the president is called upon to play. First, the president is Head of State, that is, the symbolic and ceremonial leader of the nation. In this capacity the president carries out the duties of a formal executive in a parliamentary system. A considerable portion of a president's time is spent in greeting foreign leaders, attending social functions such as state dinners, or meeting representatives of various social and economic sectors of society.

An important ingredient of the president's role as Head of State is the ability to veto legislation, a power similar to the formal executive's granting of assent to a piece of legislation in a parliamentary system. However, unlike the assent procedure, which has become a formality in Canadian and British politics, the veto power is real, effective, and frequently utilized in American politics. Between 1789 and 2000, the presidential veto has been utilized 2 530 times. The extent of usage of the veto by recent presidents is as follows: Jimmy Carter, 31; Ronald Reagan, 78; George Bush, 46; and Bill Clinton, 37. A presidential veto usually acts to defeat a bill, although it is possible for Congress to override a presidential veto with a two-thirds vote in both the House of Representatives and the Senate. For example, in his two terms of office, President Ronald Reagan vetoed 78 items, but only 9 were overridden by Congress. During his one term in office, President George Bush vetoed 46 items, with only one successful override action against his veto. President Bill Clinton vetoed 18 items, with only 2 overridden. In total, from 1789 to 1999, only 106 vetoes have been overridden. Thus, unlike assent, which is automatic, in American politics presidential approval of a bill need not be: the monarchical element or royal prerogative remains an important weapon in the arsenal of presidential power.

The second major role of the president is that of Chief Executive, that is, the head of the government. This job is equivalent to the prime minister's role in a parliamentary system, sometimes referred to as the Chief of State's role. As the Chief Executive, the president plays the leading role in the domestic policy-making process and supervises the administration of all federal government departments and personnel.

The president, in his role as Chief Executive, is a significant actor, as well, in the legislative process, since most major bills are in fact proposed and drafted by presidential advisors. Although the president is not formally involved in passing legislation until the very end of the process (when a bill is either signed or vetoed), political tradition permits the president to take an active role by using the influence of the executive position to persuade the legislature to pass a given bill.

Once passed, it is the duty of the Chief Executive to see that the laws are implemented, or, as the Constitution puts it (Article II, Section 3), "he shall take Care that the laws be faithfully executed." The vast size of the executive structure creates advantages and disadvantages for any president, although typically more of the latter than the former. If a president can exert control over the executive branch, it can become an important resource for, and basis of, national leadership — if not, the executive structure will frustrate the incumbent's leadership potential.

A third significant job of the American president is the role of Chief Foreign Policy Maker. Subsumed under this heading are the president's tasks as Chief Diplomat and Commander in Chief of the armed forces. For example, in this diplomatic capacity the president sends and receives ambassadors, recognizes foreign governments, and negotiates treaties or executive agreements with other countries. In recent decades, presidents have taken on explicit diplomatic tasks. A good example of this diplomatic function was the November 1985 summit between President Reagan and Soviet leader Mikhail Gorbachev. Moreover, the direction and content of American foreign policy can be changed solely by the president, as Richard Nixon's rapprochement with Communist China in the early 1970s clearly demonstrates. During his second term of office (1997–2001), Bill Clinton, under attack for personal and political problems, focussed his attention on the international system in such areas as Iraq, Northern Ireland, and the Middle East.

Backing up the diplomatic role is the constitutionally designated position as Commander in Chief: the president can make war by committing American troops to battle. Once the armed forces have become involved, public opinion will rally round, making it most unlikely that Congress will challenge presidential authority. For example, no official declaration of war was ever made by the United States during its long involvement in the Vietnam conflict, nor was any such declaration made regarding the American participation in the Persian Gulf War as a result of Iraq's invasion of Kuwait. During his two terms in office, President Clinton committed either American troops or air power in the following international conflicts: Iraq, Somalia, Haiti, Bosnia, and Yugoslavia. The significance of the president's role as Chief Foreign Policy Maker has been a major factor in the expansion of presidential power since the Second World War. The emergence of the United States as a superpower in world affairs automatically thrusts any American president into a leadership position in the international arena, which reinforces the president's domestic pre-eminence as well.

A final role, and one that is often overlooked, is the president as party leader. Although the president is deemed to be a unifying symbol and national leader, an individual obtains that exalted position as head of a political party. Moreover, if the president wishes to be re-elected for a second term, and most do, then party support is likely to be an important ingredient in that campaign. Between elections the president may find it helpful to be nonpartisan, but the historical record clearly demonstrates that the most successful presidents have been the most partisan-based presidents. The reason for such a pattern is clear: party support and organization make the president's other roles easier to accomplish, whether it be in terms of passing legislation, having a treaty approved by the Senate, gaining congressional approval of appropriations to be used by the military in foreign affairs, or asserting control over the vast reaches of the federal bureaucracy. For example, President Clinton's role as party leader, especially with respect to party fundraising, is probably his most positive legacy for the Democratic party.

As the discussion of the role of the president as party leader indicated, the various tasks of the American presidency need not be harmonious. For example, a president often has to choose between foreign policy priorities and domestic ones — usually described as the choice between guns and butter. The success of any American president depends both on an ability to fulfill each role separately and on a political judgment of how to combine the multiple roles when they are in conflict. The defeat of George Bush in his try for a second presidential term in the 1992 election provides a good example of this point. In spite of his foreign policy success in the Persian Gulf War, George Bush was rejected in his re-election bid largely due to his unwillingness and inability to deal with the serious situation regarding the American domestic economy.

> Certainly, presidents are constrained by law, precedent, public sentiment, and competing institutional centers of political power and authority. Furthermore, no president fully controls his own or our destiny. Yet, between constraint and fate lies a vast arena of presidential discretion (Renshon, 2000: 42).

While the American presidency combines the typical roles of both the formal and political executives of a parliamentary system, it would be incorrect to conclude that the president of the United States is more powerful than a prime minister in Canada or Britain. Much of a president's power stems from the superpower position of the United States in the international arena. An American president may be the most powerful elected official with respect to world affairs, but in domestic affairs this is not the case, given the separation of powers principle. Since the executive does not control the legislature, no American president can guarantee the passage of a legislative program. In contrast, prime ministers, especially in majority government situations, usually have a success ratio of nearly 100 percent in passing their major policies. For this reason, we can conclude that a Canadian or British prime minister has considerably more power in domestic affairs than any American president. Prime ministers have even more power to control the foreign policy of their countries than do American presidents. For example, a prime minister can conclude a treaty with a foreign country and, unlike an American treaty, it does not need the approval of the legislature before it becomes binding. What makes the American presidency such an important political office is the role of the United States in world affairs, not the president's constitutionally prescribed duties in the domestic political process.

THE VICE-PRESIDENCY

The second significant element of the American executive is the position of vice-president of the United States. Elected in conjunction with the president, the vice-president has two main constitutionally defined roles. First, the vice-president, in the event of the death or disability of a president, becomes the new president.

For example, with the assassination of John F. Kennedy on November 22, 1963, Lyndon Baines Johnson immediately became president. In the event of a temporary disability, the vice-president becomes "acting president" under Section 3 of the Twenty-Fifth Amendment. The first time this provision was used occurred in July of 1985, when Ronald Reagan was hospitalized for a minor cancer operation. While the president was being operated on, George Bush served as "acting president" for eight hours. Moreover, holding the office gives a vice-president a head start over party rivals when seeking the presidency at a later date. Since the Second World War, former presidents Truman, Johnson, Nixon, Ford, and Bush had all served as vice-presidents before assuming the mantle of the American presidency.

The second designated task of the vice-president is to serve as President of the Senate, the upper house of the legislature. This position is one of very little influence or power and is primarily ceremonial in nature. However, on the rare occasion when there is a tie vote on the Senate floor, the vice-president can cast the deciding vote, as Vice-President Al Gore did on May 20, 1999, when he cast the tie-breaking vote on a bill to toughen restrictions on gun sales at gun shows and pawn shops.

> Professors don't raise students to become VPs. Better they should play piano in a house of ill-repute (Richard E. Neustadt, memo of October 6, 1992, reprinted in Jones, 2000: 131).

An even more interesting role for the vice-president of the United States occurred following the 2000 presidential election. Given the unprecedented tie in the American Senate between Republicans and Democrats (50 senators each), the vice-president, as President of the Senate, was expected to be in a position to cast a series of tie-breaking votes. However, this situation only lasted four months until Vermont Republican Senator James Jeffords left the GOP to sit as an independent in May of 2001. This defection gave the Democrats control of the Senate (50 to 49 with 1 independent) for the first time since 1994, thereby reducing the likelihood of tie-breaking votes by Republican Vice-President Dick Cheney.

Outside of these two tasks, the daily functions of the vice-president are determined by the president. Historically, once in office most vice-presidents have been ignored, although recent presidents have attempted to upgrade the vice-presidential role by allocating to it an effective part in the decision-making process. Walter Mondale was a very active vice-president for Jimmy Carter, as was George Bush for President Ronald Reagan. Vice-President Dan Quayle played a more modest decision-making role than either of his two predecessors, while President Bill Clinton elevated the status and functions of his vice-president, Al Gore, to new heights during their two terms in office. For example, Vice-President Gore was given the task of debating the North American Free Trade Agreement (NAFTA) with former independent presidential candidate Ross Perot on live national television (on *Larry King Live*) on November 9, 1993. Gore's successful defence of NAFTA was a crucial turning point in the free trade debate, eventually leading to NAFTA's passage by Congress. The significance of the vice-presidency expanded greatly in 2001, as President George W. Bush gave his vice-president, Dick Cheney, crucial roles in the new administration.

However, while the vice-president is only a heartbeat away from the presidency, this individual's day-to-day involvement in the direction of the executive branch has traditionally been minimal: "The Vice-President has only one serious thing to do: that is, to wait around for the President to die" (Arthur M. Schlesinger, Jr., quoted in O'Connor and Sabato, 1993: 229). The key player in American politics is the president; traditionally the vice-president rarely grabs the political limelight or has much influence in the American political process.

THE CABINET AND BUREAUCRACY

In addition to the presidency and vice-presidency, several other components of the executive branch are worthy of mention. First, surrounding the American leader is the Executive Office of the President, which includes a retinue of personal aides, policy advisors, bodies such as the Council of Economic Advisors, and technical support staff. The president's staff has assumed a major policy-making role in the political arena in the last 70 years. In American politics, an important political resource is proximity to the president, a fact that gives advisors an often critical role in the decision-making process. Any president's chief of staff is likely the second-most powerful person in Washington, D.C. Such an assessment would be valid for most individuals who have served as the president's chief of staff in the modern era. In Canada, the growth of the staff of the PMO and PCO parallels this American development and is one reason for the argument that the Canadian polity has become "presidentialized."

Unlike the various members of the White House staff, the American cabinet has almost no influence or even an accepted group role in policy-making. The cabinet is made up of about 20 individuals, including the president, vice-president, the heads of the executive departments (14 in 2001) and others — such as the CIA Director and the United Nations Ambassador. Technically, under the Constitution, a president is not required to even form a cabinet or to meet with it. Since there is no collective responsibility in a system based on the separation of powers principle and because its use and functions depend on the desires of the incumbent president, the American cabinet usually meets infrequently, carries little weight as a group in the policy-making process, and performs primarily administrative tasks.

Individual members of the cabinet may have considerable influence but, if they do, it is because of their relationship with the president and not because of their cabinet title. For example, Henry Kissinger's role as probably the most significant member of Richard Nixon's administration stemmed from his personal relationship with the president, not from his cabinet portfolio as secretary of state. A similar argument could be made about James Baker, the secretary of state (1989) for President George Bush, who was often described as the president's best friend. In recent decades, presidents' wives, such as Nancy Reagan or Hillary Clinton, often have been thought to carry more political clout than the typical cabinet officer. In the American context, elevation to the cabinet is not usually a political promotion or a stepping-stone to higher office (i.e., the presidency itself).

The public bureaucracy plays a vital role in policy-making, by serving as the support staff to the president and cabinet officers. Moreover, as in Canada, the bureaucracy may often be the initiator of new policy proposals. This potential impact of the civil service can be seen in terms of its size. By the year 2000, the U.S. federal government employed nearly 3 million civilian employees, with state and local governments adding another 16 million to the total. There are 14 cabinet-level departments (e.g., Education, Defense, Agriculture) headed by a cabinet member, under which are arrayed various agencies and subunits of government.

The problem of presidential and executive control of this vast bureaucracy is perhaps best exemplified by the fact that the president has the power to hire and fire slightly over 4 000 of the top bureaucratic positions. While this seems like a large number, it is not in comparison to the total size of the federal bureaucracy. Moreover, upon taking office only about half of that number can be immediately replaced (about 2 600 for President Clinton in 1993). Given that a new president only has about two months from election to inauguration day, even that lesser number of positions may be difficult to fill. For example, one reason that the Clinton administration got off to a rough start was that most of the Republican party appointees from 1980 to1992 that were still in government resigned rather than help with the transition process. As a result, many bureaucratic positions were vacant in the early months of the new Democratic administration. Such transition problems are particularly acute when there is a change in the party controlling the presidency. The delay in determining the winner of the 2000 presidential race meant that George W. Bush had only about half the usual time to put together his new administration. Even with that delay, the transition was far smoother in 2001 than it had been eight years earlier.

COMPARING EXECUTIVES

Of the various institutions of government, the executive branch was created first, remains the most complex, and has re-emerged as the core of modern government. The political process is executive-centred and controlled, even though the specific structures and contexts of the executive branch differ from one polity to the next.

The executive branch is the centre of modern government because it both makes and implements policy with the help of the civil service. Executives have the potential for leadership and typically the will and resources to turn that potential into action and decisions on major matters of public policy: "the nature of our political institutions in both the broad and narrow sense places them at the centre of political consciousness" (Young, 1978: 282). If executives do not lead, then it is most unlikely that any other branch or institution of government will do so — the polity will drift without a rudder. Of course, this should not be taken to mean that a political system will not drift, even with executive direction.

In seeking to provide leadership, the executive branch in democratic systems is typically structured along either parliamentary or presidential lines, with different functions for its component parts. A parliamentary executive is a dual one, with the formal executive performing primarily symbolic and ceremonial duties, while the political executive (prime minister, cabinet, and bureaucracy) governs. The fusion of powers in a parliamentary system guarantees the success of the government's program, at least in a majority situation. In contrast, the separation of powers principle of the American presidential system tends to limit the power of the executive branch, although it remains the centre of the political process in the United States.

In comparing executives, therefore, we must identify the location of executive power, on whose initiative or prerogative that power is exercised, and in what contexts. Such considerations would lead us to the following conclusions in comparing the parliamentary executives in Canada and Britain with each other and with the American presidential executive. While similar in broad power, the formal executive in Britain has more influence and plays a somewhat more active political role than its Canadian counterpart. Moreover, because the British political executive is not constrained by the factors of federalism or the representation principle of cabinet composition, prime ministerial government is a more correct description of British than of Canadian politics. In both systems, the cabinet is a crucial mechanism of executive power, second only to that of the prime minister.

In contrast to these two parliamentary systems, the American presidency finds itself constrained, particularly with respect to the legislature, given the separation of powers principle. Moreover, other factors such as a two-term limit, the need to gain legislative approval for treaties, and the public reaction to such fiascos as the Vietnam War have further limited presidential prerogatives in recent decades. In both domestic and foreign affairs — especially in the former — no American president ever approaches the power of a Canadian or British prime minister. Thus, the power of the American president stems, in large measure, from the role of the United States in world affairs, rather than from presidential power over the other branches of government.

Given this comparison, it should be obvious that the idea of presidentializing the Canadian parliamentary system would mean a considerable decrease in prime ministerial power. From a comparative perspective one would have to ask why any prime minister would want to be a president and thereby give up this grip on the polity. The expansion of the PMO and PCO has not caused prime ministerial preeminence, for the prime minister has always dominated Canadian politics. What the recent trends in the executive branch have done is to strengthen the prime minister's already firm grasp on, and leading role in, the Canadian polity, thereby helping to transform cabinet government into prime ministerial government.

SUMMARY

1. The executive branch is the engine of the modern political process, performing the tasks of leadership, policy-making, and policy implementation.

A parliamentary executive is dual, dividing the executive functions between a formal and a political executive. Founded on the fusion of powers concept, a parliamentary executive operates under the principles of both collective and ministerial responsibility. In contrast, a presidential executive is based on the separation of powers principle, with neither collective nor ministerial responsibility.

2. The public service or bureaucracy plays a key role in the initiation, development, and implementation of public policy. A bureaucracy is a hierarchically organized institution based on written rules and staffed by officials paid from public funds.

3. The formal executive (governor general) in Canada is an appointed, non-hereditary position of limited duration that performs primarily symbolic and ceremonial tasks for the polity. The most significant political function retained by the formal executive is to see that there is always a government in office. In practice, however, the governor general's choice of the prime minister is greatly limited by political traditions. Most of the formal executive's remaining powers are exercised on the initiative of the political executive. The formal executive represents the facade, rather than the substance of power.

4. The political executive dominates the Canadian political scene, a role based on custom rather than on the Constitution. The prime minister is pre-eminent within the political executive; this leading position is an outgrowth of the prime minister's relationship with the public, the formal executive, the party, and the cabinet. In spite of extensive powers over the structure, composition, and function of the cabinet, the prime minister is constrained by the workings of the representation principle. Public policy is under the direction of the prime minister and cabinet, although aided by the bureaucracy.

5. The formal executive in Britain is hereditary, a prime symbol of national unity, constitutional with respect to its powers, and, at times, an important participant in the political process. The centre of executive power is the British prime minister and the cabinet. In contrast to the Canadian political executive, the British prime minister is not circumscribed by the application of the representation principle, but political tradition does limit the full development of prime ministerial government.

6. The American president performs the combined duties associated with the dual executives in Canada and Britain. The president of the United States is Head of State, Chief Executive, Chief Foreign Policy Maker, and Party Leader. The ability to fulfill these various roles, and the conflicts between them, largely determines a president's success. The president plays a leading role in the initiation, development, and implementation of public policy. Vice-presidents have frequently been elevated to the presidency by death, assassination, resignation, or election. The traditional vice-presidency was an office of little influence in the normal workings of the polity, but changes in the last 25 years have enhanced the vice-presidential role in American politics.

CONCEPT FILE

administrative state
Administrator of Canada
bureaucracy
cabinet government
cabinet ministers: generalists
cabinet ministers: specialists
cabinet shuffle
collective responsibility
delegated power
deputy minister
formal executive
imperial presidency
incremental policy-making
mandarins
ministerial responsibility
ministry
parliamentary executive

parliamentary secretary
policy
political executive
political ministers
presidential executive
presidentializing parliamentary
   government
prime ministerial government
Prime Minister's Office (PMO)
Privy Council
Privy Council Office (PCO)
public policy
quangos
regional ministers
representation principle
Whitehall

RECOMMENDED READINGS

The Executive Branch

BLONDEL, JEAN (1987) *Political Leadership: Towards a General Analysis*. London: Sage.

CAMPBELL, COLIN (1998) *The U.S. Presidency in Crisis: A Comparative Perspective*. New York: Oxford University Press.

EDINGER, LEWIS J. (1990) "Approaches to the Comparative Analysis of Political Leadership," *The Review of Politics*, Volume 52, Number 4, pp. 509–523.

ELGIE, ROBERT (1997) "Models of Executive Politics: A Framework for the Study of Executive Power Relations in Parliamentary and Semi-presidential Regimes," *Political Studies*, Volume 45, Number 2, pp. 217–231.

GAFFNEY, JOHN (2001) "Imagined Relationships: Political Leadership in Contemporary Democracies," *Parliamentary Affairs*, Volume 54, Number 1, pp. 120–133.

GOODSELL, CHARLES T. (1993) *The Case for Bureaucracy*. 3rd ed. Chatham, New Jersey: Chatham House Publishers.

PAGE, EDWARD C. (1992) *Political Authority and Bureaucratic Power: A Comparative Analysis*. New York: Harvester Wheatsheaf.

PETERS, B. GUY (1989) *The Politics of Bureaucracy: A Comparative Perspective*. 3rd ed. New York: Longmans.

PUTNAM, ROBERT (1976) *The Comparative Study of Political Elites.* Englewood Cliffs, N.J.: Prentice-Hall.

ROSE, RICHARD (1991) "Prime Ministers in Parliamentary Democracies," *West European Politics*, Volume 14, Number 2, pp. 9–24.

WELLER, PATRICK (1985) *First Among Equals: Prime Ministers in Westminster Systems.* London: Allen and Unwin.

WILSON, JAMES Q. (1989) *Bureaucracy: What Government Agencies Do and Why They Do It.* New York: Basic Books.

The Canadian Executive

AVIO, KENNETH L. (1987) "The Quality of Mercy: Exercise of the Royal Prerogative in Canada," *Canadian Public Policy*, Volume 8, Number 3, pp. 366–379.

BAKVIS, HERMAN (1991) *Regional Ministers: Power and Influence in the Canadian Cabinet.* Toronto: University of Toronto Press.

CONRAD, MARGARET (1996) " 'Not a Feminist, but…': The Political Career of Ellen Louks Fairclough, Canada's First Female Federal Cabinet Minister," *Journal of Canadian Studies*, Volume 31, Number 2, pp. 5–28.

GRANATSTEIN, J.L. and NORMAN HILLMER (1999) *Prime Ministers: Ranking Canada's Leaders.* Toronto: HarperCollins.

OSBALDESTON, GORDON F. (1989) *Keeping Deputy Ministers Accountable.* Scarborough, Ontario: McGraw-Hill Ryerson.

ROBERTSON, GORDON (2001) *Memoirs of a Very Civil Servant: Mackenzie King to Pierre Trudeau.* Toronto: University of Toronto Press.

SAVOIE, DONALD J. (1999) *Governing from the Centre: The Concentration of Power in Canadian Politics.* Toronto: University of Toronto Press.

—— (1999) "The Rise of Court Government in Canada," *Canadian Journal of Political Science*, Volume 32, Number 4, pp. 635–664.

SMITH, DAVID E. (1995) *The Invisible Crown: The First Principle of Canadian Government.* Toronto: University of Toronto Press.

STUDLAR, DONLEY T. and GARY F. MONCRIEF (1997) "The Recruitment of Women Cabinet Ministers in the Canadian Provinces," *Governance*, Volume 10, Number 1, pp. 67–81.

WHITE, GRAHAM (1998) "Shorter Measures: The Changing Ministerial Career in Canada," *Canadian Public Administration*, Volume 41, Number 3, pp. 369–394.

The British Executive

BARKER, ANTHONY and GRAHAM K. WILSON (1997) "Whitehall's Disobedient Servants? Senior Officials Potential Resistance to Ministers in British Government Departments," *British Journal of Political Science,* Volume 27, Number 2, pp. 223–246.

BOGDANOR, VERNON (1997) *The Monarchy and the Constitution.* Oxford: Clarendon Press.

—— (1997) "Ministerial Accountability," *Parliamentary Affairs*, Volume 50, Number 1, pp. 71–83.

BURCH, MARTIN and IAN HOLLIDAY (1999) "The Prime Minister's and Cabinet Offices: An Executive Office in All but Name," *Parliamentary Affairs*, Volume 52, Number 1, pp. 32–45.

CAMPBELL, COLIN and GRAHAM K. WILSON (1995) *The End of Whitehall: Death of a Paradigm.* Oxford: Blackwell.

CROSSMAN, RICHARD H. (1972) *The Myths of Cabinet Government.* Cambridge, Mass.: Harvard University Press.

KAVANAGH, DENNIS and DAVID RICHARDS (2001) "Departmentalism and Joined-Up Government: Back to the Future?" *Parliamentary Affairs*, Volume 54, Number 1, pp. 1–18.

MORAN, MICHAEL (2001) "The Rise of the Regulatory State in Britain," *Parliamentary Affairs*, Volume 54, Number 1, pp. 19–34.

POLIDANO, CHARLES (1999) "The Bureaucrat Who Fell Under a Bus: Ministerial Responsibility, Executive Agencies and the Derek Lewis Affair in Britain," *Governance*, Volume 12, Number 2, pp. 201–229.

—— (2000) "The Bureaucrats Who Almost Fell Under a Bus: A Reassertion of Ministerial Responsibility?" *The Political Quarterly*, Volume 71, Number 2, pp. 177–183.

The American Executive

CEASER, JAMES W. (1979) *Presidential Selection: Theory and Development.* Princeton, N.J.: Princeton University Press.

DALLECK, ROBERT (1996) *Hail to the Chief: The Making and Unmaking of American Presidents.* New York: Hyperion.

FALLOWS, JAMES et al. (2001) "Bill Clinton and His Consequences," *The Atlantic Monthly*, Volume 287, Number 2, pp. 45–69.

GREENSTEIN, FRED I. (2000) *The Presidential Difference: Leadership Style from FDR to Clinton.* New York: The Free Press.

IVINS, MOLLY and LOU DUBOSE (2000) *Shrub: The Short but Happy Political Life of George W. Bush.* New York: Random House.

KERWIN, COMELIUS M. (1999) *Rulemaking: How Government Agencies Write Law and Make Policy.* 2nd ed. Washington, D.C.: CQ Press.

NELSON, MICHAEL, ed. (2000) *The Presidency and the Political System.* 6th ed. Washington, D.C.: CQ Press.

NEUSTADT, RICHARD E. (1990) *Presidential Power: The Politics of Leadership from Roosevelt to Reagan.* New York: The Free Press.

—— (2001) "The Weakening White House," *British Journal of Political Science*, Volume 31, Number 1, pp. 1–11.

PFIFFNER, JAMES P. (1998) *The Modern President.* New York: St. Martins.

PIOUS, RICHARD M. (2000) "The Paradox of Clinton Winning and the Presidency Losing," *Political Science Quarterly*, Volume 114, Number 4, pp. 569–593.

RENSHORN, STANLEY A. (2000) "After the Fall: The Clinton Presidency in Psychological Perspective," *Political Science Quarterly*, Volume 115, Number 1, pp. 41–65.

ROZELL, MARK J. and CLYDE WILCOX, eds. (1999) "Scandal and Government: Current and Future Implications of the Clinton Presidency," *PS: Political Science and Politics*, Volume 32, Number 3, pp. 534–553.

SCHIER, STEVEN, ed. (2000) *The Postmodern Presidency: Bill Clinton's Legacy in U.S. Politics.* Pittsburgh: University of Pittsburgh Press.

SCHLESINGER, ARTHUR M., JR. (1997) "Rating the Presidents: Washington to Clinton," *Political Science Quarterly*, Volume 112, Number 2, pp. 179–190.

SIGELMAN, LEE and PAUL J. WAHLBECK (1997) "The 'Veepstakes': Strategic Choice in Presidential Running Mate Selection," *American Political Science Review*, Volume 91, Number 4, pp. 855–864.

SPITZER, ROBERT J. (1997) "The Constitutionality of the Presidential Line-Item Veto," *Political Science Quarterly*, Volume 112, Number 2, pp. 261–283.

WILDAVSKY, AARON and NAOMI CAIDEN (1997) *The New Politics of the Budgetary Process.* 3rd ed. New York: Longman.

WILLIAMS, ROBERT (1999) "The Persecution of the Presidency? The Role of the Independent Counsel," *Parliamentary Affairs*, Volume 52, Number 2, pp. 291–305.

POLITICS ON THE NET

THE CANADIAN EXECUTIVE: For the **governor general of Canada** see the following website: *www.gg.ca*. This site has links to the formal executives in the Canadian provinces and to the British monarchy. The **Privy Council Office** can be found at: *www.pco-bcp.gc.ca*. The official website for the **prime minister of Canada** is located at *www.pm.gc.ca*.

THE BRITISH EXECUTIVE: The official website for **Queen Elizabeth II** is *www.royal.gov.uk*, while that of **Prince Charles** is *www.princeofwales.gov.uk*. For the **prime minister**, the official website is located at *www.number-10.gov.uk*, while the **cabinet office** can be found at *www.cabinet-office.gov.uk*. Information on **quangos** can be accessed at *www.cabinet-office.gov.uk/quango*.

THE AMERICAN EXECUTIVE: The basic website for the **American president** is *www.whitehouse.gov*, which has links to the other major American executive agencies.

The Legislative Branch of Government

In most nations, legislators do not legislate. Executives legislate. True, many legislators have a formal role in lawmaking and many continue to debate, review, delay, and legitimize policies. But when it comes to initiating and enacting policies that regulate public behavior and allocate scarce resources, few legislators have much independent authority. (Obler, 1981: 127)

Legislative assemblies have long been experiencing difficult days. Where totalitarian movements have been successful in gaining power, the independence and autonomy of legislatures have been diminished or lost altogether. Elsewhere, under democratic conditions, legislatures have declined in popular esteem, at times to the point of disrepute. (Keefe and Ogul, 1985: 3)

CHAPTER PREVIEW

- From an historical point of view, legislatures were the first political institutions to allow for the public's role in the political process.

- Most national legislatures are bicameral, that is, composed of two houses. The lower legislative houses are based on direct popular election, while upper houses are usually based on either an appointment or hereditary process. In bicameral legislatures, lower houses dominate the legislative process.

- While modern legislatures still pass bills into laws, parliamentary sovereignty is a myth. The real law-making function is controlled by the executive branch, especially in parliamentary systems. The American Congress is the only modern legislature which retains an effective policy-making function.

- The Canadian and British Parliaments serve both legitimation and representation functions, but rarely a policy-making one.

- Legislative chambers are presided over by a Speaker, determine their own rules and procedures, are broken down into committees — where the real work of the legislature takes place — and rarely challenge executive power.

To the ordinary citizen, the legislative branch of government is mysterious and confusing, a little-understood institution, a jumble of rules and procedures with passing relevance to one's daily concerns. Outside of the pageantry of an opening of Parliament, a particularly rancorous question period, or the controversy usually accompanying an increase in the members' salaries, few citizens pay much attention to their legislators. As a member of the French National Assembly put it, one reason for the public's indifference, perhaps, is that the legislature is a "theatre of illusions" (Servan-Schreiber, quoted in Smith, 1980: 152).

The most basic of these illusions, which we are taught from childhood, is that the legislature is sovereign, that it makes the laws. Historically, however, legislative dominance has been restricted to the last decades of the 19th and the early decades of the 20th century: the golden age of legislatures was one of limited duration. Declining decision-making power of legislative institutions has led some observers to question their continuing relevance. The decline of the law-making function, however, has not meant the imminent demise of the legislative branch of government: "while parliament may never have been the sovereign, basic entity described by theoreticians, while it is no longer the majestic law-giver of liberal-democracy, it is still irreplaceable and important" (Duverger, 1974: 150). The continuing legislative functions of legitimating executive actions and representing the public in the governing process remain important duties. While the notion of parliamentary sovereignty may indeed be a myth, so also is the view of legislative non-importance.

THE NATURE OF LEGISLATURES

The significance of legislatures is reflected in the fact that they were the first political institutions designed to give the public a role in the political process, even though initially that public was only a tiny fragment of the total population. Legislatures were developed as representative institutions in the struggle with the king. As the mass public became incorporated into the body politic, the legislature became the symbol of liberal-democracy. Reflective, perhaps, of the public's power through the legislature is the prominence given to it in the American Constitution: Article I deals with the legislature and is twice as long as Article II, which delineates executive power and structure.

The public's role in the political process through the legislature, however, is once removed: representative government is an example of indirect democracy. In **indirect democracy** or **representative democracy** *citizens, through the electoral process, select representatives who govern on their behalf on a day-to-day basis.* In an attempt to guarantee the public's role through the legislature, democratic systems constitutionally require a yearly meeting of the legislature. For example, in Nova Scotia in 1993, following the May 25 provincial election, the new Liberal government was required to hold a legislative session before July 2. In order to comply with the Constitution, the Liberal government convened the Nova Scotia House of Assembly on June 28 for 15 minutes, before adjourning the new session until September. The origin of legislative institutions suggests, therefore, two key questions for evaluating their current status: first, what is the nature of the legislative-executive relationship; and second, what are their roles as representative agencies in the political process?

PARLIAMENTARY SOVEREIGNTY

The importance of the legislature as the public's representative is embodied in the principle of **parliamentary supremacy** or **parliamentary sovereignty**, which asserts *the fundamental right of the legislature to make any law whatsoever.* As British political leader Benjamin Disraeli once phrased it, "we are governed not by logic but by Parliament." Those who defy parliamentary authority discover their mistake in short order: for example, Jean-Claude Parrot, head of the Canadian Union of Postal Workers, spent time in jail for his failure to heed Parliament's back-to-work legislation to end a postal strike in the late 1970s. Moreover, parliamentary sovereignty is the basis for what is known as **retroactive legislation**, that is, *legislation which is passed after-the-fact to change the previously existing law.* For example, the provincial government in Newfoundland passed an amendment to its Labor Standards Act in 1984 regarding the time required for giving workers notice of layoff and made the amendment retroactive to 1978, thereby saving employers $27 million in potential claims.

As developed in Britain, parliamentary supremacy includes four essential features: "There is no higher legislative authority; no court can declare Acts of Parliament to be invalid; there is no limit to Parliament's sphere of legislation; and no Parliament can legally bind its successor, or be bound by its predecessor" (Punnett, 1980: 173). In the Canadian context, however, parliamentary sovereignty is circumscribed by law by the political principles of federalism and judicial review.

An important mechanism for maintaining the supremacy of Parliament is **parliamentary privilege**, that is, *a series of rights given to the legislature and to nobody else in order to ensure that Parliament and its members are collectively and individually free of any outside control.* Historically, parliamentary privilege was an outgrowth of the early battles between king and Parliament for control of the political system, with the privileges preventing the detention or arrest of any member during a legislative session. The right of members to carry on the public's business was not to be interfered with. For example, in November 1985, three MPs (Sheila Copps, Ian Deans, and Lorne Nystrom) were served with subpoenas in connection with a trial in Hamilton, Ontario. However, because of parliamentary privilege, they did not have to respond while the House of Commons was sitting.

In addition, parliamentary privilege gives the legislature the power to determine its own procedure. For example, the use of legislative committees, rather than the full legislature, to consider bills is a decision for the legislature alone to make. As confirmed by a Supreme Court decision (January 1993), it is also a matter for the legislature itself to decide whether its proceedings will be televised or not and under what rules reporters and photographers will operate. The reach of parliamentary privilege even extends to the physical surroundings of Parliament. In June of 1990, the House of Commons decreed that no protester could stand closer than 50 metres from any entrance to Parliament. As a further example of parliamentary privilege, in May of 1990 Parliament amended the Parliament of Canada Act to require the RCMP to notify an MP in the event that an investigation was being started into how the MP was spending his or her parliamentary budget. The Board of Internal Economy would then have 30 days to decide whether the MP had violated the rules and whether or not the RCMP investigation could proceed.

Parliamentary privilege also enables the legislature to discipline its own members and to determine its own membership. A member may be expelled from a day's sitting or for longer periods of time, with the legislature having the ultimate right to prevent a duly elected candidate from taking his or her place (e.g., a seat may be declared vacant, with a new election called). For instance, historically two important examples come to mind: both Louis Riel and Fred Rose (the only Communist ever elected to the Canadian House of Commons) were prevented from sitting in Parliament. Such parliamentary privilege even extends to the legislature in presidential-style systems like that of the United States. For example, John F. Fitzgerald (known as "Honey Fitz"), the maternal grandfather of John F. Kennedy, was prevented from sitting in the United States House of Representatives in 1919 because of vote fraud in his electoral victory (Hersh, 1997: 35–36).

A rather extreme demonstration of the power of a legislature to discipline its own members occurred in British Columbia in 1983. The ideological division and extreme animosity between the Social Credit government of Bill Bennett and the NDP opposition led by former premier Dave Barrett reached its height in October as the government sought to force its economic restraint package through the provincial legislature. Charges of "lying" (definitely unparliamentary language) were bandied back and forth between the government and opposition. When the Speaker refused to accept a motion of adjournment, opposition Leader Dave Barrett challenged this decision and refused to withdraw his challenge. After 45 minutes, the Speaker ordered Barrett expelled and the sergeant-at-arms literally dumped him out of his chair and dragged him by his feet down the centre aisle and out of the chamber. Thus, Dave Barrett became the only member of the British Columbia Legislature ever to be physically removed from the House. As a result, the Speaker then banned Barrett from the rest of the legislative session.

In addition, parliamentary privilege guarantees the right to free speech to members of the legislature carrying out the public's business within Parliament itself. For example, an individual member cannot be sued for libel for remarks made in the legislature; however, if those same statements are repeated outside the legislature, libel suits are a possibility. While such rights can be abused, free speech is considered essential for the conduct of the public's business.

Another, often overlooked, example of parliamentary privilege is the right of the legislature to determine its own worth, that is, to set its members' salaries (and pensions). There is no legal limit on what legislators can decide to pay themselves, although there are some real political constraints, in particular, the fear of electoral reprisal. In February of 1989, for example, the United States House of Representatives voted against a 51 percent pay raise because of public outrage over the proposed salary hike. Moreover, the controversy eventually resulted in the adoption (May 1992) of the Twenty-Seventh Amendment to the American Constitution ("No law varying the compensation for the services of Senators or Representatives shall take effect until an election of Representatives shall have intervened"). In Canada in June of 1993, the Senate approved an increase of $6000 in senators' expense allowances; however, within days, public outrage forced the Canadian Senate to reverse its decision. The theory behind allowing the legislature to determine its own salary is the fear that if any outside body determined salary levels, then control of the legislature would be possible, since the legislators might be bribed by extravagant salaries or forced into submission by the reduction of their pay to minimal levels.

LEGISLATIVE STRUCTURE

Although legislatures developed as a means of public representation in the political process, the public's influence was not only indirect but further restrained by the original design of legislative institutions. The first legislatures were bicameral rather than unicameral in structure. A **bicameral legislature** is *composed of two parts*, a lower house (e.g., the House of Commons in Canada and Britain, the House of Representatives in the United States) and an upper house (e.g., the Senate in Canada, the House of Lords in Britain, and the Senate in the United States). The lower houses are designed to be the closest to the people — hence they are based on popular election with relatively frequent elections (every two years in the United States; within five years in Canada and Britain). The upper houses are designed to check the power of popular passion as contained in the lower house by allowing for a "sober, second thought" on all legislation.

In order to provide the political basis for resisting the lower house, the upper legislative chambers were insulated from mass pressure by having their members appointed for long terms (e.g., Canada) or by using an indirect method of selection (e.g., senators in the United States were initially chosen by the state legislatures). By contrast, in a **unicameral system**, where there is only *one legislative chamber*, there is no mechanism within the legislature itself for checking the decision it has taken. The national legislatures in Canada, Britain, and the United States are bicameral; all of the American state legislatures are bicameral except for Nebraska; and all of the Canadian provincial legislatures are now unicameral in structure.

A federal political structure and a bicameral national legislature work together in an interesting way: the upper house of the national legislature is used to give representation to the constituent units of the federal system. For example, Senate representation is based on the provinces in Canada and on the states in the American system. The diversity that encourages the adoption of federalism also promotes use of the upper legislative chamber as a means of guaranteeing representation in the national government of various regional, religious, cultural, and ethnic groups. Thus, bicameral legislative structures function both as safeguards against popular passion and as tools for representing various interests within the national government.

THE CANADIAN LEGISLATURE

By the time the Canadian Confederation was established in 1867, the role of the legislature had been well developed, with the basic principles of parliamentary supremacy and parliamentary privilege accepted as fundamental. However, in contrast to the British pattern, the adoption of federalism and the resulting use of the courts to settle jurisdictional disputes between the two levels of government limited the supremacy of the Canadian Parliament. The federal and provincial legislatures were supreme, but only within their own areas of competence. From the beginning, Canadian federalism has made parliamentary sovereignty something of an illusion.

Likewise, the notion of the legislature making the laws has been a mirage. While in the early years of Confederation governments had their legislation rejected in Parliament (Forsey, 1974: 123–138), defeating a piece of legislation is reactive, and not the same thing as writing legislation. Moreover, it is often forgotten that the so-called golden age of legislatures occurred at a time of extremely limited government: governments passed little legislation in few substantive areas in the late 19th century.

> The Canadian Parliament is a good source of examples for anyone who wants to demonstrate the decline of parliaments (Kornberg and Mishler, 1976: x).

The expansion of government in the 20th century is the fundamental reason why executives have become the key actors in the political process. Power between institutions, as with individuals, is relative: executives and legislatures both gained power in the 20th century, but executives did so at a much faster rate. Canadian legislatures currently deal with more topics in a greater number of areas in more detail than ever before; in that sense, legislators in the modern era have little in common with their 19th century counterparts. Moreover, although the national legislature in Canada is bicameral, the two parts have never been equal. The House of Commons has always been pre-eminent and has become more so in recent decades: from a broad historical perspective, rarely does the Canadian Senate awake from its institutional slumber to take an active, if fleeting, role in the political process.

THE HOUSE OF COMMONS

The institutional and physical structure of the House of Commons influences the way it performs its various political functions. After the 1991 census and redistribution of parliamentary seats based on it (implemented in January 1997), the size of the House of Commons was increased to 301 seats from its previous number of 295. Ontario gained four seats and British Columbia two, with further increases projected after each decennial census. Seats are allocated among the geographical units (provinces) primarily on the basis of population: the largest province, Ontario, has 103 seats, while the smallest province, Prince Edward Island, has 4.

Criteria other than population are also included in the seat allocation process (Sections 51 and 51A of the 1867 Constitution Act, as amended). For example, no province can have fewer seats in the House than members in the Senate, which means that the small provinces are overrepresented in the Commons. In order to protect the French-Canadian minority, Quebec is basically assigned a given number of seats and the other provincial seat allocations are then computed from that starting point. Thus, the membership structure of the House is territorially based around the provincial units, with population the main basis in assigning provincial seat totals.

The physical structure of the Commons is divided between government and opposition members, with the Speaker of the House presiding over both. The government sits on the Speaker's right and the opposition on his or her left, a seating arrangement with perhaps Biblical connotations. However, in Prince Edward Island and Newfoundland the seating arrangement is reversed, due apparently to the historical anomaly that the heater in the legislature was positioned on the opposite side. Perhaps this fact is indicative of the opposition's legislative power.

Each member is assigned a particular seat, with government and opposition members facing each other across the centre aisle, symbolic of the antagonistic and adversarial relationship between them. The prime minister and cabinet occupy the first two rows in the centre on the government side, with the official opposition leader and his or her shadow cabinet facing them. The **shadow cabinet** is *the official opposition's "proposed cabinet" if they were to win power, with its structure paralleling that of the government's cabinet.* Those *MPs not in the cabinet or shadow cabinet* fill in the remaining rows on each side of the aisle; hence, they are called **backbenchers**. If more than two parties are in opposition, the minor parties sit on the opposition benches farthest removed from the Speaker, with any independents on the far side of them.

The Speaker of the House

The most important position in the House of Commons is that of the Speaker. The Speaker was, until 1986, nominated by the prime minister but elected by the House; since then, the House of Commons has been directly electing the Speaker. As the presiding officer it is the Speaker's job to ensure the smooth and fair functioning of the lower House. In so doing, he or she recognizes those members who wish to participate in the debate, attempts to be impartial in the business of the House, and rules on disputed questions of procedure.

Decisions of the Speaker should be nonpartisan and fair to all participants: if they are not seen as impartial, then the ability of the legislature to carry out its political tasks becomes seriously impaired. The Speaker is expected to be bilingual; by tradition, the choice of Speaker alternates between members with English or

French as their mother tongue. A deputy Speaker, whose primary task is to re-place the Speaker when the Speaker is unable to carry out the job, is selected as well. For example, in May of 1993, when Commons Speaker John Fraser suffered a mild heart attack, he was replaced by Deputy Speaker Andrée Champagne. The deputy Speaker needs to be bilingual, although his or her mother tongue is usu-ally opposite to that of the Speaker.

The importance of the Speaker's role can be seen in the kinds of decisions he or she is called upon to make. For example, the Speaker decides who is recog-nized to talk, and if the Speaker chooses not "to see" a member, that member is ex-cluded from the debate. Failure to get Speaker John Bosley to recognize him led Tory MP Jack Shields to complain in 1986 that the only way to get on national television was to "moon the Speaker." The Speaker likewise rules on whether a member has exceeded the time limit for discussion and whether a member's par-liamentary privileges have been violated, and he or she resolves disputes about parliamentary procedure, ranging from motions of adjournment to those of clo-sure to acceptable amendments. In March of 2001, for example, the Deputy Speaker Bob Kilger rejected a joint opposition party motion for an emergency parlia-mentary debate concerning Prime Minister Jean Chrétien's business dealings in his Saint-Maurice riding. In a majority government situation, the Speaker must pay particular attention to ensure that the government does not trample on the rights of the opposition or of Parliament as a whole (Newman, 1973: 88).

A fascinating example of the Speaker's power occurred in February of 1996. After the 1993 election, the Bloc Québécois, with 54 seats, became the official op-position, much to the dismay of the Reform Party, which had gained 52 seats. With the loss of two seats, including that of the Bloc Québécois leader, Lucien

Source: Reprinted from *The Leader-Post* (Regina, Saskatchewan). By permission of the paper and Brian Gable.

Bouchard, who resigned in January of 1996, the Bloc Québécois and Reform Party each had 52 seats in the Commons. The Reform Party, in February of 1996, sought the Speaker's recognition of them as the official opposition. Speaker Gilbert Parent denied the request.

One aspect of the Speaker's role is to prevent the use of unparliamentary language. It is the Speaker's job to require members to withdraw unacceptable language and to avoid racist, sexist, and other discriminatory comments. For example, in February of 1999, Speaker Ken Kowalski of the Alberta Legislature issued a list of 239 words and phrases that could not be used in parliamentary debate. The list of objectionable phrases and words included idiot, scuzzball, scab, cowbell, bovine excrement, commie, and trained seal. In December of 1998, a Bloc Québécois MP, who called Prime Minister Chrétien a hypocrite, was ejected by the Speaker from the House of Commons.

The Speaker, in addition to handling matters relating to unparliamentary language, is also called upon to deal with incidents and allegations of unparliamentary behaviour. For example, in October of 1991, NDP MP Ian Waddell, in the heat of debate, grabbed at the ceremonial mace. The next day he was called to the bar of the Commons and publicly reprimanded by Speaker John Fraser — the first time that such an incident had occurred in the Canadian House of Commons. At the provincial level, in December of 1999, the House leader for the opposition Liberals (Paul Connolly) in Prince Edward Island was expelled after throwing papers at the Speaker and overturning his desk.

The Speaker is also faced at times with opposing the government of the day, as in the winter of 2001, when Speaker Peter Milliken reprimanded the government for allowing the Department of Justice to brief reporters about a piece of legislation before the matter had been introduced in the Commons. In the Ontario legislature in May of 2000, Speaker Gary Carr warned his party's leader, Premier Mike Harris, that he would be expelled if he continued to make negative comments about Liberal leader Dalton McGuinty.

An even more dramatic confrontation between the Speaker and government occurred in the Manitoba legislature in 1984. At the height of the debate on Franco-Manitoban rights, the Conservative opposition members walked out, producing a bell-ringing incident. The frustrated NDP premier, Howard Pawley, ordered the Speaker, James Walding, to call a vote on the matter, even if the opposition parties did not return to participate. Speaker Walding, however, refused to do so. Interestingly, he was widely criticized by his party and faced two challengers for his party's nomination in January 1986. Despite rhetoric to the contrary, even the NDP, at times, trespasses on the Speaker's supposed nonpartisanship. Although Walding won re-election in the 1986 provincial election, he was not reappointed as Speaker or named to the cabinet. On March 8, 1988, NDP backbencher James Walding voted with the opposition parties and brought down the minority NDP government of Howard Pawley.

The Speaker is called upon to supervise the running of the House of Commons itself, a not insignificant task, given that its yearly budget in 2001 was about $275 million dollars. For example, in December of 1998, Speaker Gilbert Parent ordered the removal of a beer-filled vending machine from the health club for members of the Commons.

In carrying out such tasks, the Speaker is expected to be nonpartisan, which, in many ways, is another illusion of the legislative system. Since the federal Speaker was, until 1986, nominated by the prime minister, but technically elected by the Commons, the position has always been a partisan one, even though the person chosen need not be a member of the government party. Most often the Speaker was a government party member who had been bypassed for the cabinet, as illustrated by the selection of John Bosley in 1984 after the Conservative election victory in September of that year.

Even when a government party member is not picked, the Speaker may still have been chosen on political grounds. For example, a common traditional practice of both federal and provincial minority administrations has been to appoint an opposition member as Speaker, thus reducing the opposition caucus by one vote and redressing slightly the government's chance of defeat in the legislature. This pattern was expanded in September of 1997 when Prime Minister Jean Chrétien, having won a reduced electoral majority, appointed Ian McClelland, a member of the Reform party, as deputy Speaker of the House. Although the Speaker votes only in the case of a tie, it would be most unlikely, based on convention, for him or her to vote against the government. Although a minority government may choose an opposition member as Speaker, the political nature of the position is clearly evident if that minority government gains a majority position. The opposition member Speaker is usually dumped in favour of a government backbencher.

In addition to the political considerations evident in the traditional selection process, the Speaker's role is also political in another sense; that is, the Speaker's rulings help to determine the influence of individual members and parties within the House, and, on occasion, in the country as a whole. Rulings on procedural disputes, on matters of privilege, and on question period influence individual and party standings in the eyes of the electorate, as illustrated in the famous Pipeline Debate in 1956 (Newman, 1973: 37–43). Thus, although the Speaker has been selected historically on partisan grounds and even though the Speaker's rulings have the potential to greatly affect individual and party influence both inside and outside of the legislature, one of the sustaining myths of parliamentary government is the Speaker's impartiality (Stewart, 1971: 147).

The traditional pattern of Speaker selection underwent a dramatic political reform in the federal House of Commons in 1986. Following the September 5th resignation of Speaker John Bosley, which was alleged to have been the result of political pressure from the Prime Minister's Office, the new Speaker-selection process was utilized for the first time. In a free vote on October 1, 1986, the House of Commons named Speaker John Fraser to replace John Bosley. The selection process took 11 hours and 11 secret ballots under the new rules. The significant aspect of this reform was that the House of Commons itself, and not the prime minister, determined its own presiding officer.

In the 1988 election, although he ran as a Conservative candidate, John Fraser attempted to run a largely nonpartisan election campaign. On December 12, 1988, he was re-elected as Speaker on the first ballot. With the retirement of John Fraser, who did not run in the 1993 federal election, it was necessary for the House of Commons to select a new Speaker, which they did on January 17, 1994. The election took six ballots (including a tie vote on the fifth ballot), with Gilbert Parent assuming the Speakership of the lower House. After the 1997 election, Speaker Parent faced a serious challenge to retain his job from three significant candidates. He was finally re-elected on the fourth ballot, but only after beating independent MP John Nunziata. With the 2000 election call, Speaker Parent announced his retirement. In January of 2001, the House of Commons selected Peter Milliken as their new Speaker. The procedure took six hours and five ballots to select the winner from among 11 initial candidates. By 2001, six provincial legislatures had also adopted the practice of electing their own presiding officer.

Party organization

The work of the House is facilitated by the political party organizations. Each party selects a House leader and party whips, who help to ensure an orderly flow of business. The party's House leader is usually different from the national party leader, so that the party leader is able to be absent from the Commons without disrupting the public's business. The House leader is chosen by the party leader, usually in consultation with the major figures in the party caucus. The government House leader is a cabinet-level position, with the person so selected sometimes being named in recent years as president of the Privy Council.

Party whips are *those members of the party caucus who are chosen to "whip," at least symbolically, the party members into cohesive groups in the legislature.* The job of the party whips is to make sure their caucus members know the party's stand on a given issue, know when the vote is taken, and have their members on the floor of the House to support the party's leadership. An extreme example of a party whip's job was apparent in the events leading to the Constitutional Crisis of 1968: as the division bells were kept ringing for over an hour, the Liberal whips searched the bars of Ottawa, bringing several members back to the party fold, but not enough were rounded up to prevent defeat (Stewart, 1971: 196–198). A similar incident occurred on March 29, 2001. With only 70 of 172 Liberal caucus members present, the opposition parties moved to adjourn: the motion carried by a count of 98 to 95, thus embarrassing the Liberal government. However, the usual business of the party whips is more mundane, since most members are more than willing to follow the decisions of the party leadership.

The importance of the political parties in organizing the work of the legislature is probably best demonstrated by the **principle of party discipline**, that is, *the parties work as cohesive groups* rather than as an array of disparate (a cynic might say desperate) individuals. Party discipline is so pervasive and accepted that it is rarely challenged; most party members never vote against their party during the course of their entire political life. Those members who do openly challenge party unity may find their party careers to be of short duration. For example, Liberal MP and former leadership candidate John Nunziata, who voted against the Liberal budget because of the party's failure to live up to its 1993 election promise to repeal the Goods and Services Tax (GST), was expelled from the Liberal caucus in April of 1996. Party discipline even extends to the party organization: in May of 2000, former Liberal MP and cabinet minister Doug Young was expelled from the Liberal party for buying a membership in the Canadian Alliance party. However, most members accept "the whip" or party discipline because they want to, and because they know that future party and governmental promotions are dependent on it. Party discipline, which became firmly established throughout the 20th century, is the key to understanding both party control and executive dominance of the legislative branch of government.

Party discipline is strongest in the governing party, where a break in party ranks might cost the party control of office. Opposition parties are somewhat more lenient in demanding party unity, because it makes little difference in their current position. For example, former Liberal leader and prime minister John Turner backed the Conservative government's position on the Persian Gulf War in January of 1991 rather than supporting his leader, Jean Chrétien. However, a tough stand on party unity was taken by NDP leader Alexa McDonough in June of 1999 when she reprimanded MP Svend Robinson for demanding the word "God" be removed from the preamble of the Constitution. MP Robinson was removed from the party's front benches in the Commons — and he responded by accusing his leader "of political stupidity." By October the dispute had been patched up, with Robinson returning to the NDP's front benches.

Committee structure

In addition to party organization in the house, the Commons is also structured into a series of small committees, where much of the intensive work of the legislative branch takes place. The use of legislative committees, however, is a modern development in Canada, with the standing-committee structure blossoming in the 1965 and 1968 parliamentary reforms. The late adoption of small legislative committees is a reflection of the principle of parliamentary supremacy; Parliament as a whole was very reluctant to give up any of its functions and powers. The reforms were finally adopted in the mid-1960s as a result of the pressures of time: Parliament was becoming so bogged down in the details of bills that little government legislation was being passed.

There are numerous kinds of legislative committees. The two most important types are the striking or selection committee and the standing committees. The **striking committee** is *the committee which decides on the membership of all the other committees in the legislature.* It meets in the first few days of a session and is composed of party representatives. In practice the striking committee accepts the committee assignments decided on by the parties themselves, rather than getting into the contentious practice of assigning individual members to specific committees. Each party caucus, in consultation with its party and House leaders, decides which of its members will sit on which committees. The party whips then take these committee assignments to the striking committee, which approves them. Such a process avoids the possibility that the government party could use its majority to assign the least able opposition members to the most important committees, thereby undercutting the effectiveness of the opposition in the legislature.

The second and most important committee type is the **standing committee**, that is, *those committees which give clause-by-clause consideration to each piece of legislation between its second and third readings.* It is at the standing committee stage where much of the real work of the legislature occurs, in that detailed consideration, sometimes including witnesses both for and against the legislation, is given.

The structure of the standing committees is roughly parallel to that of the executive departments, with each committee considering the legislation related to one or more departments. During the Mulroney years, for example, while the executive had a Department of Veterans Affairs and a Department of National Defence, the Commons had a single standing committee called National Defence and Veterans Affairs, which oversaw the legislation for both departments. Membership on each standing committee, given recent rule changes, is now set at a minimum of 10 and a maximum of 15; cabinet members are not assigned to them but a cabinet minister's parliamentary secretary may be; and the committees have the legal power to call witnesses, with testimony given under oath. Each committee selects a chair and vice-chair to preside over its meetings.

The composition of the standing committees, as well as of all other types, is party-based. The basic principle is that a party's strength in the full House is reflected within each committee. For example, if a party has 60 percent of the seats in the Commons, it will gain approximately 60 percent of the positions on each committee. Since the committees select their own chair and vice-chair, these positions are typically allocated to the governing party as well. Based on custom only, the **Public Accounts Committee**, which oversees government expenditures, is chaired by an opposition member. Not even that small token of influence has been granted the opposition in some provinces: in Nova Scotia, for example, during the 1970s, the Liberal Minister of Finance was also chair of the Public Accounts Committee, which produced a fairly blatant conflict of interest between his executive and legislative roles.

The party-basis of the standing committees means that party discipline ensures executive-dominance of the legislative process. In a majority government situation, the standing committees will often refuse to investigate matters that might be embarrassing to their own party. At the federal level, for example, former prime minister Pierre Trudeau always refused to allow his top aides, in particular Michael Pitfield, to testify before parliamentary committees. Only once in his career, on November 4, 1980, did Trudeau condescendingly appear before a Commons committee. A similar pattern of committee control was evident during the Chrétien years. In May of 2000, the Liberal chair of the House of Commons committee stopped the meeting that was hearing testimony from Human Resources Minister Jane Stewart regarding alleged financial problems in her department when the questions became hostile. In October of 2000, just days before a federal election was called, Liberal members did not show up at the committee meeting to hear the Auditor General's report regarding the Human Resources Development Canada (HRDC) scandal.

In a majority situation, the standing committees, given this party base, are not in a position to change government legislation against the wishes of the government. Even if they do revise a bill, such alterations can be reversed when the bill reappears at third reading before the full House. If a committee does object to a government bill, recalcitrant government committee members can always be removed and replaced. Moreover, committee assignments can be used to enforce party discipline. For example, Newfoundland MP George Baker "resigned" as chair of the committee looking into management problems in the fishery after the committee issued a highly critical report of its own government in September of 1998. Likewise, Ontario MP Albina Guarnieri was transferred from her position as chair of the Human Resources Committee after publicly criticizing Justice Minister Anne McLellan.

In a minority government, the influence of the committees is temporarily enhanced if the opposition parties can overcome their differences and work together to amend the government's legislation. For example, in 1973, the Conservative and New Democratic parties combined at the committee stage to amend the minority Liberal government's wiretap legislation. The opposition parties inserted a notice provision in the bill requiring the government to inform people that they had been under surveillance if, after 90 days, no wrongdoing had been discovered. When the bill came back to the full House, the government tried to have the notice amendment deleted, but was unsuccessful. However, even in a minority government situation, the opposition parties usually do not co-operate, since they are usually more opposed to each other than to the government of the day. Minority governments create the potential for increased standing committee influence in the legislative process, but they certainly do not guarantee it.

The passage of legislation

Having considered the institutional structure and context of the House, we can now proceed to a discussion of how legislation is passed. The rites of passage that turn a bill into a law are extremely complex: it may take a neophyte MP several sessions before even the basic intricacies are mastered. The fundamentals, however, centre around three topics: first, the different types of bills; second, the stages of legislation; and third, legislative procedures such as closure and question period.

Any member of Parliament can introduce legislation, but the kind of legislation proposed and its chance of passage varies depending on whether it is a government bill or a private member's bill. A **government bill** is *one that is part of the ruling party's legislative program, is introduced by a minister, and is backed by the full weight of the government party caucus.* Government bills are given priority and are usually passed, especially under majority governments.

Private members' bills are *those bills introduced by an MP that do not have government support.* They are most often introduced by opposition members, but may be introduced by a government backbencher as well. Private members' bills are given little time for consideration in the Commons, have been traditionally dealt with in the order in which they were introduced (which means that many are not even debated), and are almost never passed. A rare exception occurred in September of 1996 when, despite clear objections from key cabinet members, Liberal backbenchers managed to pass a private member's bill that outlawed the practice of negative billing used by cable companies. However, before the bill was completely through the legislative process in the House, it died on the order paper when the House was dissolved for the 1997 election. In 1998, all five parties in the Commons agreed to strengthen the possibility of passing private members' bills, with one result being the passage again of a private member's bill in 1999 to ban the practice of negative billing.

The most common use of private members' bills is to influence public opinion, with the intent of changing future government policy. Reform proposals have often appeared first as private members' bills, only to be co-opted as government bills in later Parliaments, as public support and acceptance of the individual ideas become apparent.

Although specific details may vary from one type of bill to the next, all legislation goes through six stages: first reading; second reading; committee stage; third reading; consideration by the other House; and royal assent. Even this six-stage process greatly simplifies the actual passage of a bill by Parliament. In most cases, first reading, third reading, and royal assent are mere formalities; the crucial steps are the second reading and committee stages.

At **first reading**, the bill is introduced into the legislature by indicating the title of the bill and perhaps giving a very brief statement about the bill's subject matter. The legislation at this point is not open to amendment or debate, although in extremely rare cases it may be rejected. For example, in an almost unprecedented move, the Conservatives in the Ontario legislature denied a member the right to introduce a bill at first reading in May 1981.

The initial debate on a bill takes place at **second reading**, which is known as "approval in principle." The bill cannot be amended, but must be accepted or rejected in total. Second reading usually involves the major debate on a bill, for once it has been "approved in principle" it becomes difficult, although not impossible, to defeat it at a later stage.

In contrast to steps one and two, the committee stage does not usually involve the full House, but only a part of it. In most instances, a bill is sent to one of the standing committees for detailed, clause-by-clause review. It is at this step that the bill can be amended for the first time, in addition to being debated. Witnesses, both pro and con, may be called to testify, and the process may take a number of weeks.

Once the committee is finished with a bill, it is sent back to the full House for **third reading**. It is possible for the committee to have made changes in the legislation, but the full House has the right to accept or reject such revisions when it receives the bill back from the committee. If approval in principle has been given to a bill at second reading, plus a detailed look at its contents has been made during the committee stage, then there is little work to be accomplished at third reading. Usually, by this time, it is a foregone conclusion that the bill will pass, although the opposition parties may debate a controversial bill at some length at third reading. Government defeats, however, can happen at this stage, as with the rejection of a tax bill that provoked the Constitutional Crisis of 1968.

Once the bill is passed by one of the Houses of the legislature, the same basic steps are repeated by the other House of Canada's bicameral legislature. Although either House may initially consider any bill — except for money bills, which have to originate in the Commons — the usual practice is for government legislation to be presented first to the Commons and then to the Senate. Although the Senate may traditionally make minor changes in a piece of legislation, for all intents and purposes its approval has been, in most eras, perfunctory. However, in a bicameral legislature, the bill as passed by both Houses must be identical, so that if the Senate amends legislation coming from the Commons, the revisions must be sent back to the lower House for its approval.

The sixth and final stage concerns approval by the formal executive through the royal assent procedure, which takes place in the Senate chamber. Royal assent has never been refused to a federal piece of legislation, and the bill usually becomes the law of the land as soon as royal assent has been granted. In some instances, a section of the bill or the entire bill itself may not become operative until it is proclaimed. For example, NAFTA (the North American Free Trade Agreement) was passed by the Conservative government of Brian Mulroney in 1993, but it was not proclaimed by the new Liberal government of Jean Chrétien until December 30 — to go into effect on January 1, 1994.

Given this process for the passage of legislation, it should not be surprising to discover that legislative approval is often a long-drawn-out affair consuming many weeks, months, or even years. If the opposition parties make full use of their rights to talk and debate, as well as to propose amendments, then the government may be delayed, but not defeated, in obtaining legislative enactment of its policy proposals. For example, in September of 2000, the Bloc Québécois, in an attempt to stop the Liberal government's revisions to the Young Offenders Act, proposed a record 3 133 amendments to the bill. In order to prevent future use of this tactic, the Liberal government, using closure, changed the rules of the House in February of 2001 to allow the Speaker to reject motions or amendments that are deemed to be "frivolous" or "vexatious."

Each step of the legislative process normally occurs on a different day, with several days required between some steps, as between the committee stage and third

Source: Reprinted from the *Ottawa Citizen* (June 25, 2000). By permission.

reading. If the opposition desires it, the legislative process can become very time-consuming. However, if the parties in the House are in agreement, a piece of legislation can literally breeze through. In June of 1998, the House of Commons voted itself a $13,000 pay increase after two hours of debate. However, the record for speedy action appears to be held by the provincial legislature in Newfoundland, which voted itself a 7 percent pay raise, without debate, in just 41 seconds in December 1998. There is nothing like self-interest to make short work of the legislative obstacle course.

Such consensus in the legislature is rare, however; typically, the parties confront each other over almost every piece of legislation. If the government has a majority mandate, there is usually no way that the opposition parties can stop the ruling party's legislative program from becoming law. If the opposition parties utilize their delaying tactics and if the government is adamant about the need for a particular measure, then the government can always force it through the legislature by invoking closure, or by using a somewhat less powerful version of closure known as "time allocation." For example, in April of 1997, in an attempt to stop the Ontario Conservative government from merging the various Toronto municipalities into one large mega-city, the opposition in the provincial legislature proposed over 11 000 amendments to the bill. As expected, the government moved to limit the debate. **Closure** is *the cutting off of debate by the government*, and it is a powerful tool for ensuring the passage of government legislation.

Historically, closure has been only occasionally used in the Canadian House, although the frequency of its usage has increased in recent years. For example, the Mulroney government, in February of 1990, moved closure to end the debate at the second reading of its controversial legislation to implement the Goods and Services Tax (GST). In its first six years of government, the Mulroney Tories utilized closure 27 times. In contrast, since it was first adopted, closure was used only 19 times from 1913 to 1984. Every major piece of legislation adopted by the Mulroney government between 1984 and 1990, except for the Meech Lake Accord, was passed with the use of closure or time allocation. In 1991, changes in the procedures of the House of Commons that make the use of closure easier were adopted by invoking closure! Between 1993 and 2001 the Chrétien governments invoked closure an unprecedented 70 times.

At the provincial level, closure has been more rarely used than at the federal level. For example, the use of closure in the Manitoba legislature in January 1984 was the first time it had been used since 1929. However, in British Columbia in the fall of 1983, the Social Credit government, in forcing its restraint package through the legislature, invoked closure extensively (20 times between September 19 and October 13, 1983). Previous to this brutal use of majority power, closure had only been invoked once (in 1957) in British Columbia's entire history (*The Globe and Mail*, October 14, 1983). The first use of closure in the history of Saskatchewan did not occur until August 1989.

The threat of closure is often sufficient to bring the opposition into line, unless the opposition is attempting to force the government to use closure, so it can then claim that the government is "abusing Parliament." Closure, combined with party discipline, ensures the passage of the government's legislation, especially in a majority context. Using closure, it would take approximately 10 sitting days of Parliament for any bill to become law. Thus, if a majority government is not successful in enacting a bill, it is for the quite simple reason that it does not really want it passed (e.g., the failure of freedom of information legislation throughout the late 1970s and early 1980s).

With this process of legislative approval, it is apparent that much of the work of the legislature involves disputes about procedure rather than about content or subject matter. The reason for a procedural emphasis is quite clear: with a government that has a majority mandate, the substance of legislation cannot be altered without that government's concurrence. Hence, if the opposition wants to delay a bill, it will try to tie it up in a series of procedural disputes and points of privilege. While such tactics may not defeat a government, they may embarrass it, as in December 1974, when the NDP pointed out to the Speaker that a quorum of MPs was not present to vote on a 47 percent increase in their own salaries.

In minority government situations, the opposition may be more successful, for the government may agree to substantive changes rather than risk defeat in the House. However, minority governments have rarely feared legislative rejection: several examples, such as Trudeau's defeat in 1974 or Clark's defeat in December 1979, probably indicate that the executive wanted to be brought down in each case so as to force an election. It would be hard to demonstrate in either situation that the legislature was exercising effective control over the executive.

Although the government is rarely defeated in the legislature, it is, nonetheless, kept from doing everything its little heart desires. Probably the best check against government pigheadedness, incompetence, or downright malfeasance is the oral question period in the Commons. **Oral question period** is *the process by which members of the legislature can ask the government questions that the government is required to respond to.* When the House is in session, the opposition members, or once in a while a brave government backbencher, can challenge the government over its past, present, or projected behaviour, for 40 minutes a day. Since the government ministers do not know what the questions will be, the opposition attempts to embarrass them over policy, patronage, or corruption.

Opposition, n. In politics the party that prevents the Government from running amuck by hamstringing it.

The King of Ghargaroo, who had been abroad to study the science of government, appointed one hundred of his fattest subjects as members of a parliament to make laws for the collection of revenue. Forty of these he named the Party of Opposition and had his Prime Minister carefully instruct them in their duty of opposing every royal measure. Nevertheless, the first one that was submitted passed unanimously. Greatly displeased, the King vetoed it, informing the Opposition that if they did that again, they would pay for their obstinacy with their heads. The entire forty promptly disemboweled themselves.

"What shall we do now?" the King asked. "Liberal institutions cannot be maintained without a party of Opposition."

"Splendor of the universe," replied the Prime Minister, "it is true these dogs of darkness have no longer their credentials, but all is not lost. Leave the matter to this worm of the dust."

So the Minister had the bodies of his Majesty's Opposition embalmed and stuffed with straw, put back into the seats of power and nailed there. Forty votes were recorded against every bill and the nation prospered. But one day a bill imposing a tax on warts was defeated — the members of the Government party had not been nailed to their seats! This so enraged the King that the Prime Minister was put to death, the parliament was dissolved with a battery of artillery, and government of the people, by the people, for the people perished from Ghargaroo (Bierce, 1911: 94).

While the opposition cannot force ministers to answer, their failure to do so, or their seeming unwillingness to do so, influences their own and their party's image among the electors. It is quickly apparent whether a minister has control over, or an understanding of, his or her department. Yet ministers with political savvy can answer a question without really being specific, thereby frustrating the opposition. Another possibility is to take the particular question "on notice," that is, to say that one does not have the answer on hand, but will, of course, search diligently for it and report back. On highly controversial matters, a court case may have started or a royal commission may have been appointed to look into the matter. In these situations, the minister refuses to answer the questions on the grounds that he or she does not want to prejudice the court case now underway, or refuses to respond since a royal commission is investigating the problem. In the late 1970s, anyone appointed to the position of solicitor general had to learn two things: first, the oath of office; and second, a statement indicating an inability to answer any questions about RCMP activities and wrongdoings because the McDonald Royal Commission was currently investigating the matter.

Such techniques of avoidance have done much to undercut the effectiveness of the question period, but it remains one of the few ways the legislature, and particularly the opposition, can bring the government to task. The fact that the question period is significant in its impact is demonstrated by the lengths to which governments sometimes go to try to undercut it. One technique of undermining the question period is evident in the practice of not allowing past ministers to answer questions, even if they are still members of the House. A new minister can feign ignorance of past events, and the former minister, sitting only a few feet away, is not forced to respond.

The most serious attack on question period occurred between 1968 and 1972, after former prime minister Trudeau's first election victory. Arguing that it was inefficient to have all ministers present every single day (an outside observer might assume that it was part of their job), Trudeau introduced the infamous **roster system**, whereby *only a given number of ministers would be present (say one-half) on any specific day*. Amazingly, a number of ministers who were to have been absent from question period would appear on the floor once the routine business of the House began. The roster system was rightly attacked by the press and opposition parties as a blatant attempt to muzzle question period. After the Liberals won only a minority government in 1972, the roster system was dropped at the insistence of the opposition members. Although it has not been formally reintroduced, many governments unofficially follow it: a common complaint of federal and provincial opposition members is the poor turnout of government ministers during question period.

An interesting development with respect to question period occurred in New Brunswick after the Liberals won all 58 seats in the 1987 provincial election. For three years there was no question period in the New Brunswick Legislature. However, in an unprecedented move in 1991, Premier Frank McKenna allowed the opposition parties to sit in the press gallery and to ask questions of the government as though they were elected opposition members. Fortunately, this unusual parliamentary invention was not needed for long: in the 1991 provincial election, the opposition parties gained 12 seats and, thus, question period returned to its more traditional format.

Functions of the House of Commons

It should be clear from our discussion of both the structure and procedure in the House of Commons that its role is heavily influenced by the nature of the executive-legislative relationship. In the Canadian parliamentary system, the fusion of executive and legislative power, based on party cohesion and cabinet direction, has meant that the notion of parliamentary supremacy is a myth. Parliament does not write the legislation, revise it to any great extent, or defeat the government's program. Control of the legislature by the executive has, however, produced a system wherein the government of the day has the capacity, if not always the will, to act decisively. Given such a pattern, these questions might rightfully be asked: Why is the concept of parliamentary supremacy maintained? If Parliament does not in any real sense make the laws, what functions does the legislature perform?

The principle of parliamentary sovereignty is retained because it is useful for the legislature in carrying out its two most important remaining and interdependent political functions of legitimation and representation. In approving executive decisions, the legislature legitimates the exercise of influence and power by the prime minister and cabinet; that is, it makes the government's actions acceptable to the public. Because it is a representative institution, the House of Commons can continue to serve as a repository of public authority, even if that authority is effectively exercised by the political executive. People may not like increases in their taxes, but if approved by Parliament, then they will most likely accept them. In many respects, Parliament is based on both traditional and legal-rational bases of authority. If the traditional basis is not sufficient, then the fact that the proper procedure has been followed can be used to justify obedience.

A good example of the legitimation function of the legislature can be seen with respect to a government's budget. Probably no piece of legislation is more fundamental than a budget, for it sets the priorities of the polity. The typical and traditional procedure in a budget's preparation, which is done in secret, is for the Minister of Finance, in consultation with the prime minister and perhaps several other cabinet ministers, to set the broad outlines of policy, which are then specified in detail by the bureaucracy. The budget is written and printed before the full cabinet sees it or before the government party caucus is informed of its content. It is then presented by the Minister of Finance in the Commons and becomes the subject of a special debate. Following the 1993 election, the new finance minister, Paul Martin, opened up the budgetary process, which included "public consultations" before the budget was finalized. However, clear government control of the budget process remains in place.

However, while the budget debate rarely changes the content of the document, it gives the opposition a chance to air public grievances about the decisions already taken. Such a procedure allows the legislature to legitimate decisions that have already been taken by the political executive. If any further evidence of this point is required, then the implementation of wage-and-price controls in the mid-1970s would provide it. Although Pierre Trudeau went on national television in early

October 1975 to announce the immediate imposition of wage-and-price controls, the bill authorizing such a move was not passed by Parliament until several months later. The extent to which Parliament can effectively legitimate such actions is based in part on the public's perception of it as a representative institution.

The House of Commons is representative in the obvious sense that the people, through the election process, select its members. However, the representative function usually comprises more than simply the process of selection, including in most cases the implication that once the members are chosen they will make known the concerns of their constituents and reflect the socio-economic attributes of the electorate. With respect to the latter point, it is clear that Canadian legislators have never been a mirror image of the general public. Lawyers have traditionally dominated the membership in the House (about 30 percent are now lawyers), but they currently rank third behind MPs with business or educational backgrounds. In 1988, 39 out of 295 MPs were women, with that number increasing to 60 (out of 301) after the 1997 election and to 62 (out of 301) in the 2000 election. However, minority women (i.e., other than French or English) and other social and ethnic groups are still poorly represented in Parliament (Black, 2000).

Legislators attempt to represent their constituents by their activities in the House, including the debates, committee hearings, and question period. Through such mechanisms, individual MPs, particularly opposition members, make their constituents' views known and publicize government wrongdoing or incompetence in handling the affairs of the nation. In that sense, then, the "essential day-to-day business of the Canadian House of Commons is not decision-making but representation" (Hockin, 1973: 361).

Although the current legislative functions of representation and legitimation are not as grand as the principle of parliamentary sovereignty, they are important tasks. The House of Commons has adapted to changing circumstances and thereby has maintained a significant place for itself in the political system. In the process, some of the initial patterns of Canadian politics have been altered, such as the lack of party unity in the Commons. Moreover, parliamentary privilege, which emerged historically in the battles between the king and Parliament, is now used to buttress the representational tasks of the legislators, guaranteeing their right to question the government, as well as to raise issues of concern to their constituents. The 20th century witnessed changes in the structure of the House (e.g., number of members and number of provinces) and in its procedures (e.g., closure, standing committees). Such changes reflect the evolution of the House of Commons from a law-making institution (if it ever truly was) to one concerned with the remaining functions of representation and legitimation.

> Reforms are for Oppositions. It is the business of governments to stay in office (Sir Wilfrid Laurier).

In adapting to its changing functions and environment, the House of Commons has often been seen as a focal point for political reform. Opposition parties favour reform, while governments typically become reluctant to consider major changes, especially after they have been in office for any length of time. As a result, reform is typically high on the political agenda when there has been a turnover in the governing party.

THE CANADIAN SENATE

Unfortunately for Senate admirers (one assumes there are a few, at least, outside of current, former, or prospective aspirants), the upper House of Canada's legislature has neither performed as expected nor adapted to the changing circumstances of the 21st century. As a result the Senate, although never the equal of the House of Commons, has witnessed a steady erosion of its legislative role. For example, one study of the Canadian Parliament uses the "terms parliament and House of Commons interchangeably," because of the minimal legislative power retained by the Senate (Kornberg and Mishler, 1976: 17–18). Technically, however, Parliament includes the Senate, the House of Commons, and the formal executive. While the imminent demise of the Senate is not apparent, neither is its permanent rejuvenation, even given its temporary resurgence around a limited number of issues, such as the GST, in recent years. After a brief look at the structure of the Senate, we will consider its current functions in the political process, particularly its relationship with the House of Commons.

Structure of the Senate

The basic institutional composition of the Senate is outlined in Sections 21–36 of the 1867 Constitution Act. In contrast to the Commons, which is directly elected, the Senate is an appointed body. Although formally chosen by the governor-in-council (i.e., the prime minister and cabinet), Senate selection, for all practical purposes, has become a prerogative of the prime minister, even though others may be consulted in the process.

Legal qualifications are fairly straightforward: an individual must be 30 years of age, a resident of the province for which he or she is appointed, a natural born or naturalized subject of the Queen, and have real property, over and above all debts, of $4,000. For Quebec senators the province is broken down into 24 districts, with the person appointed being either a resident of that district or meeting the property qualifications therein. Based on custom, Senate appointments are spread throughout a province, with senators being designated for particular areas. For example, legally all of Ontario's representatives could be appointed from Toronto, but such a pattern would be bad politics and, hence, has never happened. It is revealing that the monetary requirement of $4,000 has remained constant, despite inflation. A barrier to most people in 1867, the $4,000 figure now disqualifies relatively few people.

The allocation of Senate seats is based on the provinces and regions, with a current maximum total, if all the positions were filled, of 105 members: Quebec, 24; Ontario, 24; the Maritimes, 24 (Nova Scotia 10, New Brunswick 10, Prince Edward Island 4); the West, 24 (6 for each province); Newfoundland, 6; Yukon, 1; Northwest Territories, 1; and Nunavut, 1. The creation of Nunavut in 1999, with one Senate seat, increased the total size from 104 to 105. To break a deadlock between the House of Commons and the Senate, the BNA Act of 1867 (Section 26) gave the governor general the right to appoint either a group of four or a group of eight additional senators. This provision for additional senators had never been used until Brian Mulroney did so in 1990, in order to get the GST approved by the Senate.

Initially, senators held office for life, but any senator appointed from 1965 onward must retire at the age of 75. However, a number of quite elderly senators remained in the Red Chamber, despite the 1965 reform. For example, 87-year-old Senator Salter Hayden, the last surviving appointee of Mackenzie King, resigned from the Red Chamber in 1983, after serving for 43 years. In 1986, the oldest senator was Elsie Inman from Prince Edward Island; when she died that year at the age of 95, she had been a senator for 31 years. When 91-year-old Senator John M. Macdonald from Cape Breton, Nova Scotia (who had been appointed to the Senate in 1960 by Prime Minister John Diefenbaker) died in 1997, life appointments to the Senate ended as well — 32 years after the 1965 reform. A senator may be removed from office (Constitution Act of 1867, Section 31) for failing to attend two consecutive sessions, by ceasing to be a citizen, or by failing to meet the requirements of residency or financial solvency. A senator may also resign from office.

The selection process

The main criterion for Senate appointment is based on custom and convention: the upper House is selected on the basis of patronage or party service. The combination of patronage and being an appointed body in a democratic age has seriously eroded the legitimacy of the Senate and has helped to reduce its legislative powers to minimal levels. To classify a practice as one of **patronage** means that *the controlling factor in appointment is past party work and loyalty*, although that does not necessarily mean that people of talent will not be chosen. Because of patronage, the Senate has become a base for national party organization: the work is not too taxing or time-consuming and the pay is good and from public, not party, funds (Cameron, 1995). Those who raise the party finances and those who organize election campaigns are often made senators. Senator Keith Davey, often dubbed "the rainmaker" because of his influence in the Liberal party organization during the Trudeau years, is one example, as is Senator Lowell Murray for the Tories during the Mulroney years.

Patronage appointments have also created a severe party imbalance in the upper House, since one party (the Liberals) controlled national office for most of the time between 1921 and 1984. The Liberals, in the 1960s and 1970s, held a four-to-one ratio over the Conservatives in the upper chamber, with minor parties or independents usually excluded from service. The imbalance was becoming so acute in the late 1970s that then Prime Minister Trudeau adopted a policy of appointing Conservatives to fill vacancies caused by Conservative deaths or retirements. However, because of the appointments made by Joe Clark in 1979 and Brian Mulroney after 1984, the overwhelming Liberal dominance of the Senate was quickly reduced. When Brian Mulroney assumed office in 1984, he faced a three-to-one lead for the Liberals in the Senate: Liberals, 72; Conservatives, 22; independents, 4; and vacancies, 6. By the time he left office in 1993, Brian Mulroney had transformed the Senate into a bastion of Tory patronage: Conservatives, 58; Liberals, 41; and independents, 3. After the 1993 election and following a number of Senate resignations and retirements, plus a series of obvious patronage appointments by the new Chrétien government, the Liberals regained majority control of the upper House in 1997. At dissolution in October of 2000, the party balance stood as follows: Liberals, 57; Conservatives, 35; and independents, 6.

While the final selection is a prime ministerial prerogative, considerable jockeying and infighting occurs within the party organization over who should be called to the Senate. The interests of the provincial and national party organizations must be reconciled, as well as other competing interests (ethnic, religious, and racial). For example, in early 1986 the one vacant Senate seat in Ontario produced party infighting between the provincial and federal wings of the Conservative party as four candidates lobbied for support (Frank Miller, Norman Atkins, Hal Jackman, and John Bassett); eventually Norman Atkins was selected as a senator. It is not unknown for an individual to campaign extensively behind the scenes for a Senate appointment, as Sam Bronfman did in seeking to become the first Jewish member in the Red Chamber (Newman, 1979: 47–60).

A number of vacancies have traditionally been kept open until shortly before an election, in order to exact as much work or money as possible out of Senate aspirants. A good indicator of a forthcoming election, therefore, is a series of Senate appointments, as the governing party tries to use up all of its patronage powers before calling an election that might result in the loss of office. Few parties are willing to gamble that they will win. In contrast, the Liberals were so confident of victory in 1957 (they had, after all, been the government since 1935) that 16 positions were not utilized, which allowed the Conservatives a chance to appoint a large number of new senators after winning power. In 1993, Brian Mulroney, after announcing his upcoming retirement, filled all 15 remaining Senate vacancies. Among the appointments were key party workers (David Angus, chief fundraiser and head of the PC Canada Fund; David Tkachuk; Duncan Jessiman; Ron Ghitter), as well as personal friends (Fernand Roberge, former president and part owner of the Ritz-Carlton Hotel in Montreal). In contrast, Prime Minister Jean Chrétien left eight Senate vacancies unfilled at the start of the 2000 election.

Despite much criticism of the patronage nature of Senate appointments during the reign of Conservative Prime Minister Brian Mulroney, the pattern was continued by Liberal Prime Minister Jean Chrétien after the party's return to power in 1993. The following are a few examples of the continuing role of patronage in the Senate selection process: Robert Gauthier, former 22-year Liberal MP; John Bryden, Liberal party organizer in New Brunswick; Céline Hervieux-Payette, former cabinet minister from Montreal; Wilfred Moore, party fundraiser and organizer in Nova Scotia. The pattern continued after Jean Chrétien's re-election victory in 1997 with the following Senate appointments: in 1997, former Liberal premier of Prince Edward Island Catherine Callback, former New Brunswick Liberal MP Fernand Robichaud, and former Liberal MP and cabinet member from Quebec Serge Joyal; in 1998, Ontario Liberal organizer Isobel Finnerty; and in 1999, former Nova Scotia finance minister Bernie Boudreau.

Given the party basis of the appointment process, there are many political uses to which the Senate can be put. Before the adoption of a pension plan and the large salary increases of recent years for members of the House of Commons, the Senate was often utilized as a retirement pension for loyal MPs. Senate appointments have also been used to ease members out of the cabinet gracefully, without forcing a long-time minister to return to the backbenches (e.g., Paul Martin, Sr.'s appointment to the Senate).

The prime minister may also manipulate the Senate selection process to open up a safe seat in the House. What seems destined to become a classic example of this practice occurred in July 1981, when 45-year-old Peter Stollery, MP for the Spadina riding in Toronto, was appointed to the Senate to make room for Jim Coutts, who had been principal secretary to the prime minister for many years. The Spadina constituency, which was heavily populated with ethnic members who had strong ties to the Liberal party, was touted to be the "safest" Liberal seat outside of Quebec. Stollery, who had spent a decade as a Liberal backbencher and had never been selected for the cabinet, had no immediate prospects for such a development. With the pay increase of 1981, Stollery's Senate appointment, given his mandatory retirement age of 75, was worth over $1 million in salary alone. Unfortunately for Jim Coutts' electoral career path, which was rumoured to include a cabinet position as well as a try for the Liberal party leadership upon Trudeau's departure, the voters of Spadina rejected him in the August 17, 1981 by-election.

Senate appointments may also attempt to produce internal disunity within an opposition party, as revealed in Trudeau's appointment of Claude Wagner to the Senate, again as a prelude to the 1979 contest. Wagner had been Joe Clark's primary rival for the party leadership in 1976, losing by only a handful of votes on the fourth ballot. Moreover, Wagner was one of the few Conservative MPs from Quebec, around whom the party had hoped to rebuild. Although they had tried strenuously to beat him in the previous elections, the Liberals selected Wagner for the Senate because it would hurt the Tory rebuilding effort in Quebec, as well as producing disunity within the Conservative party organization there.

Such continuing machinations regarding Senate appointments explain why senators have "on the whole . . . turned in what must be considered an undistinguished performance" (Dawson, 1970: 283). Moreover, the patronage and party organization uses to which the Senate has been put have undercut its legislative role and its relationship with the House of Commons.

Functions of the Senate

The initial design of Canada's upper House reflected two main purposes: first, to serve as a check on the lower House and, second, to represent the provinces and regions within the national government. Neither function remains very viable currently.

The Senate has never been equal to the House. For example, all money bills must be introduced in the Commons first and the government is responsible for retaining legislative support there. While the Senate can theoretically defeat a bill, such a defeat would not bring the government down. The Canadian Senate is not a **confidence chamber**, that is, *a legislative chamber which has the political authority to defeat a government, thereby forcing a new election.* Thus, the power of the Senate in the bicameral federal legislature was designed to be inferior to that of the Commons in 1867 and has become more so since then.

A good indicator of the Senate's power is its typical work week. The average formal work week for the Senate is nine hours long, divided down among Tuesday evening, Wednesday afternoon, and Thursday afternoon. Even with such a schedule, the Senate can still run out of something to do. A legislative body that had any real power would meet more frequently. As Senator Heath McQuarrie (PEI) once put it, the "way the Senate keeps its power is by not using it." In 1987, for example, the Senate sat for only 91 days, but one-fifth of the membership attended less than one-half of these meetings. In 1999, the Senate sat for 77 days.

Considerable debate surrounds the extent of the Senate's current legislative role. In theory, the Senate retains the right to reject legislation coming from the Commons; in practice, it almost never happens nor, for that matter, is the issue of rejection frequently contemplated. An important distinction must be made between vetoing legislation in total or making significant amendments to it and the more limited approach of revising the work of the Commons. The Senate often revises legislation coming from the Commons by making many technical or housekeeping amendments to a piece of legislation. These revisions can be quite numerous on a complicated bill and are usually accepted by the Commons without any controversy. Moreover, the Senate can make major changes, but only if the Commons does not see them as a challenge to its own dominance in the legislative process. If the House perceives the Senate's actions as a challenge, then a major confrontation between the two Houses occurs, and the House of Commons carries the day.

An example of this took place in late 1973 and early 1974 over the Liberal minority government's wiretap legislation. As discussed earlier, the NDP and Conservative parties had combined forces at both the committee stage and in the House to insert a notice provision to persons under surveillance for 90 days. When the bill reached the upper House, the Liberal-dominated Senate removed the notice provision and sent the bill back to the Commons for approval. Justice Minister Otto Lang recommended to the Commons that the Senate revisions be accepted. In the House, the opposition Conservative and New Democratic parties were outraged, rightly perceiving that the Liberal minority in the House was attempting to use the Liberal majority in the Senate to circumvent the power of the Commons. Press and public reaction were scornful of the Senate, pointing to its patronage and nonelected base — in other words, questioning the legitimacy of its actions. John Diefenbaker, who had once gone so far as not to include any senators in his cabinet, declared that if the Senate wanted "a free-for-all, let's let them have it." Blunt talk of Senate abolition began to be heard. The Commons proceeded to reinsert the notice provision into the wiretap legislation and sent it back to the Senate, daring them, in effect, to have the guts to reject it or to revise it again. The second time the Senate acquiesced and the legislation was passed in the form preferred by the Commons.

The fact that these confrontations have been rare in recent decades is indicative of the dominance of the Commons over the Senate. Such battles are more likely, however, when the Commons and the Senate are controlled by different parties, thus giving the Senate-House confrontations a partisan basis (Newman, 1973: 295–321). Just such a situation developed in 1985, when a Liberal-dominated

Senate delayed the passage of a borrowing bill required by the new Mulroney government. Interestingly, the Commons had unanimously passed the bill, so that the Liberals in the Senate, including many new senators appointed by former prime minister Trudeau, were in opposition to their leader (John Turner) and their House colleagues. This battle, from which the Senate backed off, produced yet another round of Senate reform speculation. An analogous situation developed in 1988, when the Liberal-dominated Senate threatened, with the agreement of the Liberal opposition in the House of Commons, to stop the Conservative government's free trade legislation. Although it could not legally force the government to the polls, this Senate threat was certainly one factor in the government's decision to call an election. Temporary injections of geritol rarely save a dying patient, however.

A significant battle between the House of Commons and the Senate occurred in 1990 over the Tory bill regarding the new Goods and Services Tax. At the beginning of the battle, the Senate, controlled by the Liberals, was confronted by the large Tory majority in the House of Commons. By the end of the confrontation, the Tories had gained control of the upper House — by appointing the eight additional senators allowed under Section 26 of the 1867 Constitution Act — and had successfully forced through their controversial tax measure. The significant features of the GST battle were several: first, the Tories in the House successfully beat a Liberal-controlled and appointed Senate and its challenge to the elected Commons; second, during the process the Senate's legislative role was temporarily rejuvenated; third, by forcing a confrontation between the Commons and the Senate, thereby allowing the invocation of Section 26 of the 1867 Constitution Act, the Liberals lost control of the Senate; and fourth, the behaviour of the Senators during the GST debate was a further incentive for Senate reform and/or abolition.

Increased confrontations between the House and the Senate between 1984 and 1997 have been partisan-based. The large majority Tory governments of Brian Mulroney in 1984 and 1988 faced a Liberal majority in the Senate until the GST battle in 1990. With the Liberal victory in 1993, the Chrétien government in the House faced a hostile Tory majority in the Senate. Thus, this period of Senate rejuvenation is likely to prove temporary, since the Liberals (by 1997) had regained a majority in both parts of Canada's bicameral legislature.

While it rarely challenges the lower House directly, the Senate not only influences the Commons, but sometimes has been able to convince the lower House to accept revisions to its legislation. While most changes are minor, one investigation has argued that many of the so-called technical changes made by the Senate are in fact significant because they provide a means for business and corporate influence in the legislative process (Campbell, 1978: 10–19). It is in this role of a minor revising chamber that the Senate retains a modicum of influence in the Canadian legislative process.

The second intended function of the Senate in 1867 was to serve as an institution that would provide regional and provincial representation within the national government. The regional allocation of Senate seats prescribed in the 1867 Constitution Act was designed to guarantee such a result: thus, in a technical sense, the Senate continues to be based on regional and provincial interests. However, as a regional voice within the national government, particularly as an effective one, the role of the Senate has been disappointing.

From the time of Macdonald's first cabinet, in which he allocated portfolios on a provincial and regional basis, the lower House, through the cabinet, has usurped the Senate's role as the defender of provincial interests. Moreover, the inability of the Senate to defend provincial and regional interests is directly linked to its declining role in the legislative process: minimal legislative influence exacerbates the Senate's failure to be the defender of the provinces, even when it tries to undertake such a task. The patronage base of Senate selection has also meant that many members are not particularly concerned either with checking the work of the Commons or with being effective regional defenders. Few party warhorses at career's end are likely to be political activists, no matter what the intent of the body to which they have been appointed.

If the Canadian Senate does not serve as a restraint on the Commons or as an effective voice of regional and provincial concerns within the national government, what are its current functions? First and foremost, the upper House is a tool for party organization and development: declining legislative functions have been replaced by party tasks, especially for the governing party. Second, the Senate plays a minor revising role in the legislative process. Third, the Senate provides at least symbolic representation for the regions in the affairs of the national government, although the provinces seem less than satisfied with such a continuing role for the Senate.

Fourth, the Senate occasionally contributes to the political process over and above its minimal legislative tasks. Several senators have been active in investigating areas of social concern — Senator David Croll and his committee's look at poverty in Canada is an example. Other significant committee reports from the Senate have included a look at the Canadian Security and Intelligence Service, at human rights, and at the problem of delegated legislation. Such useful tasks, however, seem more dependent on the interests and concerns of an individual senator than a necessary outgrowth of the Senate's overall political role. Additionally, the Senate-sponsored hearings on Senate reform proposals in the late 1970s led to an advisory opinion from the Supreme Court of Canada in December 1979 that the federal government did not have the power unilaterally to alter the composition of the Senate. More recently, the Senate issued a significant report on euthanasia in 1995.

Fifth, the Senate is relatively infrequently called upon to provide regional representatives for the cabinet. Such a use of the Senate is a result, however, of inadequate provincial representation within the governing party in the House of Commons itself. For example, both Joe Clark in 1979 (for Quebec) and Pierre Trudeau in 1980 (for three Western provinces) made use of the Senate to bolster provincial representation in their cabinets. The appointment of Senator Robert de Cotret as Minister of Industry, Trade and Commerce by Joe Clark in 1979 marked the first time a major portfolio was given to a senator since 1935. In the 1997 election the Liberals won no seats in Nova Scotia, prompting the prime minister to appoint Nova Scotia Senator Alasdair Graham as that province's cabinet representative. Senator Graham was later replaced as Nova Scotia's representative when Bernie Boudreau was named to the Senate from Nova Scotia in 1999. However, once a party has gained seats in the House from a province, it would be contrary to custom to select senators rather than members of the House for ministerial positions. For example, after winning seats in all provinces in his landslide victory of 1984, Prime Minister Mulroney only included one senator (the government's Senate leader) in his initial cabinet. Given these reflections, the Senate's present role could be summarized as follows: an upper House with minor revising powers in the legislative process and a base for party organization and development, which rarely emerges as a significant actor in the political process.

Reforming the Senate

One thing is clear: the Senate seems to lack a large reservoir of public support. This was perhaps best exemplified by the demand for a **Triple-E Senate** (Elected, Equal, and Effective) as a crucial element of the constitutional negotiations leading to the Charlottetown Accord in 1990–1992. As a result, numerous reform proposals regarding the appointment and structure of the Canadian Senate have been advanced in recent years. One incentive for reform, in addition to the problems of patronage and minimal legislative duties, is simply cost. With the pay increases of recent years, the price tag of the Senate, for salaries alone, is about $8 million yearly. For many young recent appointees, who can serve 30 to 35 years before they reach mandatory retirement at age 75, these salary figures, along with projected increases over the years, will give them each a total guaranteed income of over $6 million. (It might also be kept in mind that senators are not prevented from holding other jobs. For example, Senator Edward Larson, Canada's top Teamster official, was reported to have received a union salary of $300,000 in 1984, in addition to his Senate salary. Similarly, after his appointment to the upper House, Senator Michael Pitfield served on the Boards of Directors of the following corporations: Power Corporation, Cadillac Fairview Corporation, Great-West Life Assurance, and Montreal Trustco.) Other costs include the parliamentary restaurant and library, printing, upkeep, pensions, and a host of ancillary services, which bring the direct Senate burden to many more millions a year (about $50 million). Rather than attempting to reduce its direct costs, the reform proposals have sought to enhance the Senate's role in the legislative process.

Reforms dealing with the age and patronage factors are generally modest in their contemplated changes to the Senate, while a greater legislative role would bring into question the current imbalance of power between the Commons and the Senate. The reform in 1965 requiring any senator appointed since that date to retire at the age of 75 led, over several decades, to a significant reduction in the average age of senators (of about 20 years) and to the elimination in 1997 of those serving for life. Nevertheless, an age problem remains. Now the problem is the trend toward appointing senators who are in middle age.

While youth may help to rejuvenate the Red Chamber, a person appointed at age 45 has a possible 30 years of service, with no performance review. For example, these senators, at the time of their appointment, had about three decades of possible service in the upper House: Peter Stollery, Anne Cools, Jerry Grafstein,

Michael Kirby, Lowell Murray, Michael Pitfield, Lorna Marsden, Gerald Comeau, Janis Johnson, and David Tkachuk. If the appointment of younger persons is the trend, then Senate appointments should be for a fixed term (e.g., 5 years or 10 years), with the possibility of one reappointment. Such a tenure might encourage senators to be active and would not create the problem of a member possibly not participating for several decades.

A new problem emerged in the 1990s with some of the appointments made by Prime Minister Chrétien. While some talented younger members were selected (for example, Jane Cordy from Nova Scotia became the youngest current senator at age 49 when appointed in June of 2000), a number of senators close to the mandatory retirement age of 75 were also named, such as Betty Kennedy in the spring of 2000. A short tenure in the Senate does not help the Senate as an institution, but it does allow the prime minister to make a greater number of appointments.

A second often-suggested reform is to make Senate selections from a wider range of people, and especially to include individuals for other than patronage considerations. While such appointments would create a Senate of greater diversity in its social and economic makeup, it is not apparent that such a change is in the self-interest of the major parties, particularly the governing party. For example, the first woman was only appointed to the Senate in 1930 (Cairine Wilson) and the first black person in 1984 (Anne Cools).

A third proposed change is to alter the dominance of the federal level in the selection process by giving the provinces control of half of the Senate seats. Such a change might at least prevent large imbalances in the upper House between the two major parties (Liberals and Conservatives) and would provide for some third-party representation (NDP, PQ) as well. Although this reform would alter the party balance, it would not change the patronage base of selection: half the appointees would be provincial patronage appointments instead of federal ones.

A final set of reforms aims at altering the Senate's role in the legislative process. For example, the Alberta government's proposal for a Triple-E Senate illustrates such a reform. So also does the reformed Senate structure contemplated in the now rejected Charlottetown Accord. Alternatively, the Senate may be renamed the House of the Provinces or the House of Confederation, a change that would coincide with the initial intent that the Senate would represent regional and provincial interests within the national government. However, to be effective, such a change would necessitate an increase in the Senate's current legislative powers. If the Senate cannot significantly alter legislation, it cannot protect provincial concerns. If senators are rarely included in the cabinet, how can they be effective defenders of provincial interests? Unfortunately, this question is not always asked by those making reform proposals.

Changes in the selection process, the age of those chosen, or the tenure of the appointment will do little to alter the current overall position of the Senate: it will fundamentally remain a minor revising body, patronage-based. Only in combination with additional powers will such changes do much to alter the Senate's political role in the current system. To grant the Senate more power would mean a reduction in the current status of the House and, by implication, the cabinet. Senate reform has been inhibited by the self-interest of other political institutions: the major stumbling block to a rejuvenation of the Senate is the House of Commons.

One proposal by Trudeau in 1978 would have given the Senate a suspensive veto power for six months. A **suspensive veto** is *the ability to delay legislation for a given period of time, rather than rejecting it outright.* In other words, the theoretical total veto would have been replaced by an actual veto of half a year. Many critics wrongly perceived this as a further reduction of the Senate's power. In fact, in our view, a six-month suspensive veto might mean an increase in the traditional power of the Senate, and as such would be unacceptable to the Commons. Another example of a change that would not be tolerated by the lower House would be the consistent use of senators in ministerial positions. However, such a reform would be necessary to make the Senate an effective defender of regional concerns, since the cabinet is the key decision-making body in the Canadian polity.

These examples indicate that the likelihood of Senate reform is related to the change such reforms would make in the overall balance of power between the two parts of Canada's bicameral legislature. The greater the proposed change in the Senate's role and powers, the greater will be the opposition to it coming from the Commons. The Senate thus finds itself between a rock and a hard place: even if it wanted to, which it probably does not, it could do little to reform itself. It is not in the political self-interest of the institutions that control its fate — the House of Commons and cabinet — to see a revived and effectively functioning Senate. For example, the 2000 Clarity Act eliminated any significant role for the Senate with regard to Quebec's separation from Canada in a future independence referendum. Any reform is likely to be illusory, leaving the basic role of the Senate intact, with its legitimacy further eroded in the years ahead.

THE LEGISLATURE IN GREAT BRITAIN

While the "mother of Parliaments" is a venerated institution, as most mothers are, and while the years have not been totally unkind to her, they have, nevertheless, taken their toll: the British "Parliament does not and cannot" govern (Bradshaw and Pring, 1972: 9). The basic trends regarding the role of legislatures in the political process, or the balance of power between the constituent parts of bicameral institutions, have not bypassed "this sceptered Isle." In the nation of its birth the principle of parliamentary supremacy has become a myth (Crossman, 1972). Because of the process of devolution, parliamentary sovereignty has become even more of a myth in the past few years. The creation of subnational parliaments in 1998 in Scotland, Wales, and Northern Ireland means that the British Parliament now shares power with other legislative institutions. However, at the national level, the House of Commons dominates the legislature, with the House of Lords generally continuing to recede in political significance. While in broad outline the British Parliament resembles its Canadian counterpart, both in structure and function, it differs on a number of important specific points.

THE HOUSE OF COMMONS

The predominant lower House is composed of 659 members elected in single-member plurality districts. Based on the latest redistribution, England has a total of 529 seats, with Scotland receiving 72, Wales 40, and Northern Ireland 18. Unlike the Canadian House, the physical structure of the British Commons is composed of benches that provide seats for only about 65 percent of its members. The result of such seating arrangements is an intimacy in the British House of Commons that is lacking in the Canadian and American legislatures, where there are individual desks or seats. Interestingly, when the Commons was destroyed by fire during the Second World War, no increase in the physical size or seating arrangement of the legislature was approved.

Internally, the Commons is under the direction of the Speaker of the House, who is expected to be nonpartisan. British Speakers are traditionally more independent than their Canadian counterparts in terms of both selection and tenure. For example, upon selection, the Speaker ends previous political connections and ceases to be a member of any political party. Upon retirement, custom prevents a former Speaker from taking up the partisan battle again. Thus, considerable controversy arose in early 1985 when former Speaker George Thomas, known as "Lord Tonypandy," published his autobiography, which was quite critical of many politicians still in the House of Commons. Once selected, the Speaker may run in the next general election as an independent and, if returned to the House, is usually re-elected to the Speaker's post. These conventions have made a British Speaker more independent, with greater status, than the more partisan-based Canadian office.

The more independent status of the British Speaker is clearly revealed by the details of the selection procedure. The Speaker's selection requires the approval, not only of the Commons, but of the Queen as well. Moreover, the British prime minister does not name the Speaker, even though he or she is likely to play a major role in the behind-the-scenes negotiations. In fact in 1983, in selecting the successor to George Thomas, the House of Commons chose Bernard Weatheril in part because he was known not to be the choice of Margaret Thatcher. In British politics, not even the "Iron Lady" had enough clout to force her choice of Speaker on a reluctant House of Commons. Following the Tories' fourth consecutive election victory in 1992, an interesting selection was made for Speaker of the House of Commons. By a vote of 372 to 238, Labour MP Betty Boothroyd was selected as the new Speaker. As the first woman elected as Speaker, Betty Boothroyd had broken a 700-year parliamentary tradition. She was also the first Speaker not chosen from the governing party since World War II. Following the 1997 election, Betty Boothroyd was once again selected to serve as Speaker of the House of Commons. In October of 2000, a new Speaker was selected, Michael Martin of the Labour party. In a contest with 11 other nominees, Martin was chosen, after a series of divisions (votes), by a vote of 370 to 8, becoming the first Catholic Speaker of the House of Commons since the Reformation.

> There are three golden rules for parliamentary speakers: stand up, speak up and shut up (J.W. Lowther, Speaker [1919], British House of Commons).

The committee structure in the British Commons is not as well developed as in Canada. The mother of Parliaments has been less than enthusiastic in delegating some of its authority to its constituent parts. The result has been the rather late and limited development of a standing committee system. The basic function of the standing committee is the detailed consideration of legislation between second and third readings, although these committees' structure and membership limit their power in this task.

As in Canada, the organization of the British House revolves around the political parties and, in particular, the principle of party discipline. The cohesive behaviour of the political parties within the legislature has long been cited as one of the hallmarks of the British party system. For example, in eight sessions since the Second World War, governments have successfully passed 100 percent of their legislative program, with the average success rate since 1945 standing at 97 percent (Rose, 1986: 90). Such results indicate that most members of Parliament willingly accept "the whip" and thus support their leader and party, both inside and outside the legislature. Interestingly, the whip received its name in typical British fashion from "the hunt": the concept "derives from the whippers-in of the hunting field who keep the hounds working as a pack and prevent them wandering" (Bradshaw and Pring, 1972: 30). Free votes, while relatively rare, still occur more frequently in Britain than in Canada. For example, in August of 2000, the British House of Commons held a free vote on the issue of whether or not to allow the cloning of human embryo cells for medical research.

The strength of party discipline is distinguished between **one-line, two-line,** and **three-line whips**, which *refer to the number of times an upcoming vote is underlined on the outline of the week's expected activities prepared for party members by the party whips.* The greater the number of underlinings, the greater is the expected loyalty of party members: rarely will a member vote against the party if a three-line whip has been called. For example, a three-line whip was called in the passage of the Canada Act through the British House of Commons. Because the national parties can play a direct role in the recruitment of candidates for office, party leaders may deny a straying member renomination in the next election.

Recent decades have provided examples of members increasingly defying their party whip, but the principle of party discipline remains as a basic operating rule of the British House (Coxall and Robins, 1994: 214–216). The example of a number of Conservatives voting against their government's budget in June 1981 is still rather exceptional in the House of Commons. So also is the unusual example in July of 1993 when the new government of John Major was defeated on the Maastricht Treaty by a vote of 324 to 316 in the Commons. More typical is the view of a member of Parliament as "a G.I. in a political army, whose rifle is his vote" (Crossman, 1972: 100).

The passage of legislation follows the usual pattern of three readings, with the committee stage occurring between the second and third readings. While the House of Lords repeats the process, for all practical purposes the legislative function resides with the House of Commons, which in turn is controlled by the political executive. The government determines the priorities to be dealt with by the Commons and can ensure the passage of its legislation through use of closure.

In contrast to the Canadian system, historically closure was frequently used. For example, between 1950 and 1970, closure was invoked 525 times in the British House (Bradshaw and Pring, 1972: 152), while in Canada closure was used only 7 times between 1913 and 1957 (Newman, 1973: 39). However, a reversal of this pattern has occurred in the past two decades; closure is infrequently used now in Britain, while it is becoming a common practice in the Canadian House.

More so than in Canada, the British political executive is not constrained by the legislature: the political process is executive-centred and executive-dominated. However, the British House of Commons is still involved in an important way in the representation and legitimation functions. It is representative not only in terms of its geographical constituencies, but also as a mechanism for registering individual and group concerns with the government of the day. Moreover, in its consideration of legislation and in its review and debate of a government's program, the House of Commons helps to legitimate executive actions. In other words, the British House of Commons "must be judged as a critical, not decision-taking, body and as a communications forum" (Ryle, 1994: 667). In this regard, the British and Canadian Houses of Commons reflect a distinct familial resemblance.

THE HOUSE OF LORDS

If there was one political institution in Britain that seemed immune to the winds of political reform it was the House of Lords. However, nearly 700 years of tradition was radically altered by the Labour Government in 1999 with the passage of the House of Lords Act, which has altered the size, composition, and role of Britain's upper legislative chamber. After looking at the traditional House of Lords, we will analyze the evolving pattern of Britain's second legislative chamber.

The traditional House of Lords

On a day-to-day basis, the upper House of the British Parliament typically plays a very minor legislative role. The dominance of the House of Commons has long been established in British politics, beginning with the Reform Act of 1832, consolidated by the Parliament Acts of 1911 and 1949, and enhanced by the 1999 House of Lords Act. In many respects, the traditional House of Lords was a monarchical, rather than a legislative institution, given its membership and overall role in the political process (Punnett, 1980: 279–291; Birch, 1983: 51–60). As one recent assessment of Britain's House of Lords concluded, it "remains an institution unscathed by democracy" (Shell, 1994: 721).

The composition of the traditional House of Lords was based on appointment, most of which was hereditary in nature. The total number was about 1 200 members, although most of these never actively participated in the legislative process; only about 400 members made an effort at regular participation in the business of the Lords. Approximately two-thirds of the Lords were **hereditary peers**: that is, *they either inherited their titles or they were given a peerage themselves as a reward for public service*. The remaining members were what are known as **life peers**, *those whose appointment to the upper House ends with their own death*.

For example, after being forced out as prime minister and leader of the Conservative party in 1990, Margaret Thatcher was given a lifetime peerage in 1992 — with the title Baroness Thatcher of Kesteven. Another example would be that of Elizabeth Smith, widow of Labour party leader John Smith, who was given a life peerage in 1994.

Selection to the Lords is a prime ministerial prerogative, although technically the appointments are made by the sovereign. The result, historically, was that the composition of the Lords reflected, in part, partisan control of the Commons. The Conservative party's dominance of British politics over the past century meant that the Lords was heavily weighted in favour of that party. Moreover, the preponderance of Conservative peers in the Lords reflected their traditional and appointive tie to the nobility. One reason for allowing life peers, beginning in 1958, was to correct this imbalance by giving the government greater flexibility in the appointment process. Most new peers in recent decades have been life peers and these members, as a group, are more active in the Lords than their hereditary counterparts. Since the prime minister has the right to create new peers, he or she can do so to break a deadlock between the Commons and the Lords: usually the threat of such action is enough to bring the upper House into line. Historically, the major confrontations between the Commons and the Lords occurred when the lower House was controlled by a party other than the Conservatives.

> In a nation that calls itself democratic, an unelected House of Lords is, of course, a splendid impertinence (Shenker, 1988: 34).

The hereditary and appointed composition of the House of Lords led some critics to refer to it as "a political geriatric unit" with few remaining significant functions in the political process: "a harmless political eunuch, possessing no power and little influence" (Hamilton, 1975: 9, 136). While such an assessment was perhaps extreme, most observers of the Lords agreed that in terms of legislation its major powers "have been reduced almost to nil" (Beer, 1973: 239). The traditional Lords did retain, however, a role as a revising and debating chamber, in addition to its ability to deal with the private members' bills and to consider certain kinds of legislation ahead of the Commons. In these respects the House of Lords relieved the Commons of some of its heavy workload. Perhaps the most revealing indicator of the remaining power of the House of Lords was its ability to veto legislation passed by the Commons, in particular the adoption and use of the **suspensive veto**.

As in most bicameral legislatures, either House traditionally shared the right to reject or veto legislation passed by the other chamber. The ability to veto measures passed by the Commons was first lost in 1911, when the Lords' total veto was replaced by a suspensive veto of two years' duration. For example, if the Lords rejected a bill and the Commons still wanted it, then the Commons could pass the legislation in three successive sessions (i.e., a minimum period of two years) and it would become law whether the Lords liked it or not.

The suspensive veto was further reduced from two years to 12 months in 1949. As might be suspected, the change to a suspensive veto and its decline to a period of one year were both opposed by the House of Lords. However, the Parliament Act of 1911 was passed after two general elections had been held on the issue and after the sovereign threatened, at the request of the government, to appoint enough new peers to the Lords to ensure the bill's passage. Rather than see their beloved chamber inundated by new and non-Conservative members, the Lords finally acquiesced and accepted the suspensive veto. The change in 1949 to reduce the suspensive veto to one year was passed after the Lords had delayed it for two years. More than anything else, the suspensive veto symbolized the declining role of the House of Lords in British politics. A rare use of the suspensive veto occurred in November 2000, when the Labour government of Tony Blair bypassed the Lords and sent a bill that lowered the age of consent for gay sex from 18 to 16 to the Queen for her approval.

While historically the Lords lost power in its battles with the Commons, in recent years, and particularly under the terms of office of Margaret Thatcher and John Major, it surprisingly reasserted its legislative role in relation to the government. For example, between 1979 and 1992, the House of Lords defeated the government 179 times on specific clauses and amendments. However, because the House of Lords is not a confidence chamber, such defeats did not cost the government its right to remain in power. Nevertheless, despite this evidence of at least a temporary renewed legislative interest of the Lords, the historical assessment that the House of Commons is the pre-eminent legislative chamber still remained true.

The evolving Lords: 1999 onward

Although the Labour party had long favoured reform of Britain's upper legislative chamber, its absence from power for nearly two decades (1979–1997) meant that its reform proposals were not taken seriously by most people. That view changed dramatically after the Labour party's large majority victory in the 1997 election. Although it had not been the top priority on the Labour party's agenda during the election campaign, reform of the House of Lords did fit into the government's goal of modernizing British political institutions and practices (Shell, 2000).

The reform process got seriously underway on November 24, 1998, with the Queen's speech to open the second session of the 1997 Parliament. The government indicated that it would "remove the right of hereditary peers to sit and vote in the House of Lords," and that this change would only be the start of the reform process. In January of 1999, the government issued its proposed reform in a White Paper, which clearly indicated that the House of Lords would not become a rival to the power of the House of Commons. In February of 1999, the House of Lords Bill was introduced in the House of Commons.

After much debate and jockeying for advantage, the parties agreed that the hereditary peers would be cut by 90 percent (from 751 to 75), not including the 15 hereditary peers then serving as deputy Speakers and the two positions of the Lord Great Chamberlain and the Earl Marshall — bringing the total of hereditary peers to 92. The regular 75 hereditary peers were then allocated among the parties, with the parties each determining which of their own members would remain in the Lords. On November 5, 1999, the new membership structure was implemented — 659 hereditary peers lost their legislative positions. However, hereditary peerages may still be granted and they will continue to pass from generation to generation — they will simply not be able to sit in the Lords unless selected as one of the 75 positions chosen by the parties.

Following this reform, by the 1999–2000 legislative session the membership of the House of Lords totalled 686: life peers (548), hereditary peers (90), peers appointed (2), and Bishops (26). Moreover, the number of life peers can continue to increase: in his first two years in office, Prime Minister Tory Blair appointed 170 peers, compared to Margaret Thatcher's total of just over 200 during 11 years in government.

While the first reform regarding the hereditary peers has been completed, further changes await the recommendations of a royal commission. The second round of political reform will consider a possible selection of the Lords through the electoral process and its future powers in the legislative process. Regardless of current and future changes, it appears clear that the House of Lords will remain subservient to the House of Commons.

THE AMERICAN LEGISLATURE

If any legislature in the world could be cited as an example that would belie the "decline of Parliament" thesis, it would be the American Congress. As a result of the separation of powers principle, which provides the potential for an assertive legislative branch, the continuing role of Congress in the law-making process runs counter to the trend in most countries (Loomis, 1996). Moreover, the American experience also differs with respect to the relationship between the two legislative chambers: the House of Representatives and the Senate were designed to be coequal in theory and, for the most part, they have remained so (Baker, 1995). In contrast to the Canadian Senate or the British House of Lords, the American upper House has successfully adapted to the demands of the democratic era. In so doing, the American Senate has preserved a vital role for itself in the political process. Since the House and Senate are coequal partners, we will consider them together with respect to three areas: legislative organization, procedures, and functions.

LEGISLATIVE ORGANIZATION

The physical structure of the Capitol places the House of Representatives and Senate at opposite ends, symbolizing, perhaps, their distinct roles, as well as their often adversarial relationship. However, unlike the seating arrangements in most British parliamentary systems, the parties in the American House and Senate do not face each other, but are instead arrayed in a semicircle around their presiding officers. This seating arrangement helps to mitigate antagonism between the parties within each House. Moreover, the concepts of government and opposition found in a parliamentary system would be hard to achieve in a polity based on the separation of powers, because the government — the party in control of the presidency and White House — is not necessarily the majority party within either legislative chamber.

> It could probably be shown by facts and figures that there is no distinctly American criminal class except Congress (Mark Twain).

Membership in both the House of Representatives and the Senate is based on direct, popular election, although the constitutional requirements for service and length of tenure vary in each. For the House of Representatives, an individual must be 25 years old, a citizen for seven years, and a resident of the state in which his or her legislative district is based. The term of office is two years, with the number of congressional districts allocated to each state based on population. For example, the House of Representatives has a total of 435 members, with the largest state, California, assigned 52 districts and the smallest states, such as Vermont and Wyoming, each receiving only 1.

For the Senate, a member must be 30 years old, a citizen for 9 years, and a resident of the state that he or she represents in the upper House. The allocation of Senate seats is on a geographical or territorial basis: each state, no matter its size, receives two Senate seats. Thus, with 50 states, the Senate is composed of 100 members. Initially senators were selected by their respective state legislatures: for example, the New York state legislature would select that state's representatives to the upper House of the national legislature in Washington. However, since the adoption in 1913 of the Seventeenth Amendment to the American Constitution, senators are popularly elected. This reform is a major reason why the Senate has remained an important element in the American governmental system. Senators serve a six-year term, with one-third of the membership elected every two years. For example, one-third of the Senate will be elected in 2002, one-third in 2004, and one-third in 2006; they will all serve a six-year tenure before facing re-election in 2008, 2010, and 2012, respectively.

Both the House and Senate generally organize themselves internally along similar lines. The House of Representatives is presided over by the Speaker of the House, who is chosen by the majority party. The person selected has usually been a senior member who has built up a power base within the legislature itself. The job of the Speaker of the House is not usually a stepping-stone to higher office in the American political system. In addition, each party elects a floor leader, whose function is similar to the Canadian House leader, as well as several party whips. The Speaker, majority and minority floor leaders, and party whips are responsible for organizing the day-to-day business and operation of the House of Representatives.

The Senate's structure varies slightly from this pattern: its presiding office is the president of the Senate, who is the vice-president of the United States. As Senate president, the vice-president is not an integral part of the legislature: the position is largely routine, with the incumbent casting a vote only in the case of a tie. A temporary change in the importance of the vice-president's role as president of the Senate occurred because of the results of the 2000 election. With the Senate initially evenly divided between Democrats and Republicans with 50 senators each, Vice-President Dick Cheney was expected to cast tie-breaking votes on a fairly regular basis. However, Republican Senator James Jeffords' decision in May 2001 to become an Independent — thus giving the Democrats majority control of the Senate — reduced the likelihood of tie-breaking votes being cast by the vice-president. In more usual circumstances, the vice-president does not preside, at which point the presiding officer of the Senate is the ***president pro tempore***, typically a junior member of the majority party. Effective power lies not with the office of the president of the Senate, but with the majority and minority leaders selected by each party. These positions are often ones of national prominence and can sometimes be used as springboards to national office. For example, Republican Bob Dole was able to use his position as majority leader in the Senate to help gain the Republican presidential nomination in 1996.

While the presiding officers and party leaders are influential positions within the legislature, their power is constrained by the nature of party discipline and the committee system. Although the leadership usually gets its way, it may be forced to compromise or even be defeated outright on a particular vote. The reason for this is that, while the political parties work as groups within the legislature, their degree of cohesion and unity is considerably lower than in a British parliamentary system.

The legislative parties are neither controlled nor directed by the executive, a reflection of the separation of powers doctrine. Moreover, the use of the primaries for political recruitment and the local power bases of both House and Senate members has meant that the party leadership has few resources or sanctions with which to ensure strong party cohesion. As a result, party discipline in the American legislative chambers rarely approaches 100 percent. Although party discipline is weaker than in Canada and Britain, it is still the most important factor in determining how individual members of Congress will cast their ballots. As a general rule, most congressmen vote with their party most of the time, meaning about 90 percent of the time in recent years.

The nature of party discipline in the American Congress was a key reason for the ability of Ronald Reagan to push his controversial programs through the legislature. During both of his terms of office (1981–1989), President Reagan forged a "conservative" coalition across party lines, allowing him to get around the numerical majority of Democrats in the House of Representatives. Even though in the first two years of his first term (1993–1994) President Clinton had a Democratic majority in both the House and Senate, he was unable to get major pieces of legislation, such as health care reform, passed. Republican legislative victories in the Congressional elections of 1994, 1996, and 1998, combined with the lack of any successful cross-party coalition building, resulted in President Clinton's legislative record being extremely weak for a two-term president. Because of an evenly divided Senate and only a very small majority in the House, George W. Bush found it necessary in the initial part of his presidency to seek to construct such cross-party coalitions. Such a pattern of cross-party coalitions became even more necessary following Senator James Jeffords' defection in May of 2001.

The second constraint on the party leadership is the committee system in each House. Unlike the committees in a parliamentary system, which are tightly controlled by the government, American committees have an independent power base, which results in considerable clout in the legislative process. While these committees have as their main function the detailed clause-by-clause analysis of a piece of legislation, there is little else about them that is similar to their Canadian counterparts. Significantly, American committees have the effective power to delay, to amend, or to defeat a bill outright. As such, they are a further example of the decentralization and fragmentation of power so typical of the American political process. Moreover, it is in the committees or "little legislatures" that most of the real work of Congress is accomplished.

Each chamber is divided into a series of standing committees: in the 106th Congress (1999–2000), there were a total of 16 in the Senate and 19 in the House, organized around substantive concerns such as agriculture, justice, and foreign affairs. Individual senators and members of Congress serve on several committees, move from one committee to another on a voluntary basis, and typically remain for many years on the same committees, thus building up considerable expertise in several policy areas. Party strength on the committees reflects the party's overall standing in each chamber, with the parties determining which of their members serve on the specific committees. In addition, each of the standing committees usually creates several subcommittees: in the 106th Congress, the 19 standing committees in the House of Representatives generated 86 subcommittees, and the 16 standing committees in the Senate created 68 subcommittees. Generally speaking, the standing committees in the House have more power than their Senate counterparts.

The committees are chaired by individuals who have traditionally been extremely powerful in the legislative process. Until the reforms of the mid-1970s, an individual committee chair could quite literally tie up the entire legislative process: today the chairs remain key actors in the House and the Senate. For example, Wilbur Mills, from a rural congressional district in Arkansas, for many years chaired the House Ways and Means Committee, one of the most important committees in the House of Representatives. During those years, the Democratic members on his committee served as that party's committee of selection, thus choosing all other committee assignments for the Democratic party. As a result, Wilbur Mills was the most influential and powerful member in the legislature. When he briefly entered the presidential race in 1971, one of his colleagues asked him, "Wilbur, why do you want to run for president and give up your grip on the country?" (Green, Fallows, and Zwick, 1972: 71). A few years later, Wilbur Mills was involved in a Washington sex scandal and lost his party and House positions.

The person who chairs the standing committee is usually determined by the seniority principle or, as critics have called it, the senility system. Based on custom, the **seniority principle** means that *the position of chair is usually given to the senior member of the majority party on each committee who has the longest continuous service.* The result of this practice is to reward members from safe districts, since it is necessary to win continuous re-election for many years in order to qualify to chair one of the key committees. Moreover, many of these districts have traditionally been rural in nature and based in the South. These powerful positions have often been filled, therefore, by elderly men from rural and mainly conservative constituencies, at a time when the American population was becoming young, urban, and based in the big-city states of the North. The South may have lost the Civil War, but for a century it controlled Congress and was able to prevent effective civil rights legislation from being passed until the mid-1960s. However, scandals such as those involving Wilbur Mills, as well as the autocratic power of many chairs, led to a revolt in the 1970s against this longstanding custom. For example, in 1975 the Democrats in the House of Representatives ousted three committee chairs. In 1995, under the direction of Speaker Newt Gingrich, the House Republicans selected three committee chairs who were not the most senior members on their committees, but who were more ideologically compatible with the new Republican majority. Reforms adopted in the mid-1970s have thus given members of the party caucuses more say in the choice of committee chairs and have curtailed some of the more blatant misuses of power. However, the seniority principle remains as the most important factor in selecting these individuals, whose powers are still considerable.

LEGISLATIVE PROCEDURES

A number of points should be kept in mind when trying to understand the passage of legislation in the American system. First, the already discussed rites of passage of a parliamentary system scarcely apply to the approval of a bill in a presidential-style process. Second, the American system was designed to make the enactment of legislation exceedingly difficult and it has succeeded admirably. Third, legislative politics are extremely complex because of both the coequal status of the House and Senate and the general fragmentation of power within each legislative chamber. Fourth, this decentralization of power has produced a series of **multiple veto points**, that is, *a series of checkpoints in the legislative process at which a single member or a small group of legislators can stop the passage of a particular bill.* These veto points and the access that they provide are a key reason for, and explanation of, the important role of lobbies in the American legislative process.

As a result, it is much easier to defeat a bill than it is to pass it. Simple majority support (more than 50 percent) in the full legislature is not enough to win: against determined opposition one must have overwhelming support (two-thirds of those present and voting). In such a system, reform legislation is not necessarily prevented from gaining approval, but the process for such legislation is difficult without strong public and congressional support. As an old adage on the American legislative process puts it, "those who care for the law and sausage should not watch either being made."

The passage of legislation can be broken down into four major stages: first, introduction of the bill in both Houses; second, committee action; third, consideration by the full House and Senate, sometimes called floor action; and finally, enactment into law upon presidential approval (Oleszek, 1995). Each stage involves a number of steps, with defeat of the bill possible at any single one. Except for money bills, legislation may be introduced in either House, although it is usually introduced simultaneously in both chambers. A bill must be passed by both Houses in an identical format before being sent on for presidential action.

Submission of a bill is normally routine, with only members having the right to introduce a piece of legislation. For example, the president cannot formally introduce a bill, but can and does get supporters to do so in both the House and Senate. Once introduced, a bill is sent to one of the standing committees.

It is at the committee stage that close scrutiny is given to a bill, the so-called clause-by-clause review. A committee may hold public hearings, ask for expert testimony, or have the committee's staff prepare reports on the expected consequences of the bill. Committees may allocate this responsibility to subcommittees, which then hold hearings and consider the bill as well. Once the full committee has reviewed the legislation, it votes either to send it on to the next stage or not. A committee can also "sit" on a piece of legislation; that is, it does not consider the bill and therefore it cannot proceed any further. This pattern is a fate that awaits most bills. Of the approximately 8 000 bills introduced during the 106th Congress, approximately 90 percent were killed at the committee or subcommittee stage.

From committee the bill moves on to stage three: discussion and debate by the full House and Senate. In most cases there remains the right to amend the legislation at this juncture. However, except on highly controversial bills, legislators usually accept the recommendation of the committee that has considered the bill in detail. To this point, then, the House and Senate have each considered the bill in committee and have each granted approval to it by their total membership.

Floor action is not complete, however, until the versions of the bill passed by the two chambers are identical. As the bill has proceeded through each chamber separately, it is quite likely that it has been revised and amended differently. If the versions passed by the full House and Senate are not identical, the bill is sent to the Joint Conference Committee to work out the differences. The Joint Conference Committee is composed of members from both the House and Senate committees that considered the bill at the initial committee stage. If a compromise is reached, the bill goes back to the full House and Senate for final approval, after which it is sent to the White House for presidential approval.

In the fourth stage, the president has traditionally had three options: to sign the bill; to let it sit for 10 days, after which it becomes law in any case; or to veto it and send it back to Congress. If both Houses pass the bill a second time with a two-thirds majority — what is called **overriding** a presidential veto, that is, *Congressional action to reverse a presidential veto* — the bill becomes law without the president's signature. For example, in March 1988, after a civil rights bill had been vetoed by President Ronald Reagan, the House of Representatives (292–133) and the Senate (73–24) overrode his veto. When the vetoed bill is returned to Congress, it goes back to the full House and Senate and does not have to go through the committee stage again. If Congress overrides a presidential veto, the bill is not sent back to the president for approval: the president cannot veto the bill the second time around. Beginning January 1, 1997, the president was given a fourth option with respect to legislation: the **line item veto**, that is, *the power to delete minor portions of a bill without having to veto the entire measure*. President Clinton aggressively used the line item veto 82 times in 1997–1998 before it was struck down as unconstitutional by the American Supreme Court. As this simplified outline should demonstrate, the passage of legislation is extremely complex and difficult in the American system. Moreover, at each juncture a bill can be defeated, while approval only comes after all the possible veto points have been successfully passed (Waldman, 1996).

Although legislative procedures in the House and Senate are very similar, there are several important differences that not only distinguish each chamber but demonstrate the extreme decentralization of power in the American Congress. For example, between the committee stage and floor action, the House of Representatives uses a special committee known as the **House Rules Committee**, through which most legislation must pass before reaching the full membership. This committee determines when a piece of legislation will be considered, how much debate will be allowed, and whether or not amendments to a bill can be made by the full House. If the Rules Committee refuses to pass "a rule" on a bill, then it has effectively defeated the legislation, because the bill cannot move forward without it.

A distinctive feature of the Senate is the **filibuster** (Binder and Smith, 1997), that is, *the right of unlimited debate by individual senators, who may talk for as long as they want on a piece of legislation.* This practice of unlimited debate can be used by an individual or small group of senators to bring the work of the upper House to a halt, thereby either preventing the passage of a bill or forcing the proponents of the legislation to compromise on specific points. Often the threat of a filibuster is sufficient to bring about such changes by the backers of a bill. One of the most successful uses of the filibuster was by former senator Wayne Morse of Oregon, who used to pin a fresh rose on his lapel and threaten to talk until it wilted. The record for giving the longest single speech in trying to stop a bill is held by Senator Strom Thurmond (now a Republican but then a Democrat). In 1957, in an attempt to stop a civil rights bill, Senator Thurmond spoke for 24 hours and 18 minutes.

A filibuster can be limited by the use of **cloture**, *a motion which cuts off debate and allows a vote on the bill.* However, a cloture vote is rarely won in the Senate, because most senators do not want to set a precedent for the device to be used against them at some future date. Moreover, until 1975, a cloture vote required a two-thirds majority of those present for passage; since then, a three-fifths vote of the elected membership (60 Senators) is needed. If a cloture motion is passed, then no more than 30 additional hours of debate may take place before a vote is required. As a result of this modification, filibusters have lost some of their power, but they still remain an important avenue for possible legislative obstruction.

LEGISLATIVE FUNCTIONS

While similar to other democratic legislatures in its representation and legitimation functions, the American Congress is unique in terms of its law-making tasks: "the constitutional separation of powers has preserved for Congress an independent role that distinguishes it from legislative bodies in most western democracies" (Oleszek, 1995: 219). Moreover, in carrying out its law-making functions, Congress is further distinctive because of the coequal status of its chambers, which means that the House of Representatives and the Senate each have the power to oppose the wishes of the other. As a result, the American legislature is a major participant in the political process, perhaps best symbolized by its independent power of the purse.

The basis of legislative significance is the principle of separation of powers, which creates the possibility of legislative independence from executive control. Although at times the American Congress was seen as an ineffective body controlled by a strong presidency (e.g., in the 1960s and early 1970s, there was the notion of an imperial presidency), the legislature reasserted its power in the late 1970s. More often than not, the American legislature can prevent executive action by vetoing, revising, or delaying a measure, although it is much less likely to take major policy initiatives on its own. A good example of legislative power was the series of federal government shutdowns in 1995 and 1996 (Williams and Jubb, 1996). Congress refused to submit to presidential direction, but was also unable to pass its own budget version, creating a political gridlock resulting from the separation of powers principle.

> Anyone who is unfamiliar with what Congress actually does and how it does it, with all its duties and all its occupations, with all its devices of management and resources of power, is very far from a knowledge of the constitutional system under which we live; and to everyone who knows these things that knowledge is very near (Wilson, 1885: 57).

The separation of powers doctrine forces a mutual dependence on the executive and legislative branches: the ability to withdraw co-operation is often the key to legislative power in the American political process. Moreover, if the executive does not co-operate with the legislature's priorities, then Congress may override a presidential veto to force a particular policy upon a reluctant executive. The basis for such a legislative role lies, of course, in the broad power allocated to Congress by Article I of the Constitution. While some of the specified tasks given to the Congress (e.g., the power to declare war) have been modified by events and custom, they remain the foundation for an assertive legislative branch.

COMPARING LEGISLATURES

While the structures, functions, and procedures of legislatures may vary widely among different types of political systems and historical periods, the view of these institutions as lawmakers is as widespread as it is illusory. Even in democratic systems, where there is the best chance for legislative importance, parliamentary supremacy is clearly a myth at the beginning of the 21st century. Only regarding the American system can one make a strong argument for legislative significance in the policy-making process. This conclusion reflects the basic differences between legislatures in parliamentary and presidential systems.

Central to an understanding of the role of the legislature in a parliamentary or presidential system is the nature of the relationship between the executive and legislative branches of government. The fusion of powers in a British parliamentary-style system between the executive and legislative institutions has reduced the legislature's role from one of policy-making to one of representation and legitimation. Parliament remains a symbol of authority, but effective decision-making power lies with the executive. By contrast, in the American presidential system, the separation of powers principle divorces executive and legislative institutions, thereby creating the potential for an assertive legislature. This potential, when combined with competent legislators and public support, can be translated into an effective policy-making role by the American Congress. Separate institutions sharing the power to pass bills give Congress a major bargaining chip with which to force compromises and concessions from the executive branch. Thus, the variation in executive-legislative relationships between parliamentary and presidential systems creates a somewhat different role for the legislature in each: in the American presidential system there is a policy-making function, in addition to the functions of representation and legitimation.

Presidential-parliamentary differences are also apparent with respect to the passage of legislation. In a parliamentary system the government (especially a majority one) clearly controls the ebb and flow of legislation, determining when it will be considered, whether it will be labeled a government bill or not, and whether closure or other techniques will be used. As long as party discipline holds, the legislative proposals of the government are assured of passage. By contrast, in the American presidential system, committees and committee chairs are independent bases of influence and power. An individual member of Congress can effectively bring the entire legislative process to a halt. Moreover, there is a series of multiple veto points, which makes it easy to defeat a bill.

A good example of the differences between parliamentary and presidential systems can be seen in the techniques of closure in the Canadian House of Commons and cloture in the American Senate. Closure is imposed by a majority vote and is applied against the opposition parties, while cloture requires a three-fifths vote and is applied against groups and individuals, not parties. In Canada, the use of closure is controlled by the government, while in the United States the imposition of cloture is not, thus symbolizing the difference between the fusion of powers and separation of powers doctrines.

In addition to the executive-legislative nexus, an important concern in analyzing bicameral legislatures is the relationship between the upper and lower chambers. The general pattern of the 20th century was a decline in the power and importance of the second chambers, again with the exception of the American Senate. What is often overlooked in assessing such a pattern is the fact that in most parliamentary systems the executive is responsible only to the lower House, which is one reason why upper chambers have receded in significance. Control of the legislature by the executive, or more precisely, by the political executive, is based on executive-dominance in the lower House. As a result, the second chambers have become increasingly superfluous in the legislative process. By contrast, the American Senate remains an integral part of the polity, a result due in no small measure to its coequal relationship with the House of Representatives within the legislature. And, unlike the Canadian Senate or the traditional British House of Lords, the American Senate has adapted, or been forced to adapt, to the demands of a democratic age (e.g., direct popular election).

While the upper Houses do not necessarily have to be popularly elected to survive, what they do need is a method of selection or appointment that is seen as legitimate by the public. Until such changes are accomplished, the Canadian Senate and the reformed British House of Lords will never have the potential for regaining a significant and continuing role in the legislative process. The initial legislative institutions were designed to give the public a voice in government and, although they rarely in fact make the laws, that first function remains a viable one for democratic legislatures in the decades ahead (Blondel, 1973: 135).

SUMMARY

1. While the concept of parliamentary sovereignty may be a myth, so is the view of legislative irrelevance. Legislatures in democratic systems serve both representation and legitimation functions, while in the United States a policy-making role has also been retained.

2. Structurally, legislatures may have either one (unicameral) or two (bicameral) chambers, with federal systems usually adopting a bicameral legislature so as to guarantee regional or cultural representation in the upper House. Typically, bicameral legislatures are now controlled by the lower House, which is selected by direct popular election. Upper Houses based on heredity or appointment have seen a major decline in their legislative role.

3. Canada's national legislature is bicameral, while all provincial legislatures are unicameral. Canada's lower legislative chamber, the House of Commons, is the confidence chamber and dominates the legislative process.

4. The Canadian House of Commons is structured primarily on the basis of representation by population and selected by direct popular election. The Commons is organized on the basis of party discipline and protected by the principle of parliamentary privilege. The Speaker of the House presides over the operation of the Commons and is now elected by the members themselves.

5. The Canadian Senate is an appointed body designed as a means for ensuring regional and provincial representation in the national government. Because of its appointed nature, the Senate is a patronage base for the major political parties — a pattern which undercuts its legitimacy and power in the political process.

6. The Canadian House of Commons has always been pre-eminent over the Canadian Senate — and has become more so in recent decades. Political reforms, such as a Triple-E Senate, are unlikely to happen.

7. Because of a strong pattern of party discipline, the executive dominates the Canadian Parliament; the principle of parliamentary sovereignty is a myth in the Canadian context.

8. In Britain's bicameral legislature, the traditional upper chamber or House of Lords was composed of appointed members who held office either as hereditary or life peers. The power of the House of Lords was greatly diminished in the 20th century, but it retained a suspensive veto over the lower House. The significant reforms of the House of Lords, beginning in 1999, have altered both its structure and its possible future role in the legislative process. The Commons is composed of members selected by direct popular election, is organized along party lines, and is the pre-eminent legislative chamber. However, even in the nation of its birth, parliamentary supremacy has become a myth.

9. Unlike its Canadian or British counterparts, the American legislature has retained for itself a significant role in the policy-making process, a result of the separation of powers principle. Again in contrast to the Canadian and British pattern, the American bicameral legislature was designed to be composed of two equal chambers and has, for the most part, remained so in practice. The House of Representatives and Senate are both chosen by direct popular election, with the House seats based on population and the Senate seats based on geography (e.g., the states). Passage of legislation in the American system is not only extremely complex, but difficult, given the multiplicity of veto points in the process. Influence and power are decentralized within each chamber, symbolized by the filibuster in the Senate and the traditional role of committee chairs in both Houses.

10. In understanding the role of legislatures, a key concern must be the nature of the executive-legislative nexus. In bicameral systems, an additional focus must be on the kind of relationship that exists between the two chambers. Does one chamber dominate or are the two houses roughly equivalent in power? While they are rarely law-making institutions, legislatures remain an important mechanism of communication between the governed and their governors.

CONCEPT FILE

backbencher
bicameral legislature
closure
cloture
confidence chamber
filibuster
first reading
government bill
hereditary peers
indirect democracy
life peers

line item veto
multiple veto points
oral question period
override motion
parliamentary privilege
parliamentary sovereignty
parliamentary supremacy
party whips
patronage
president pro tempore
principle of party discipline

private member's bill

Public Accounts Committee

representative democracy

retroactive legislation

roster system

Rules Committee

second reading

seniority principle

shadow cabinet

Speaker of the House

standing committee

striking committee

suspensive veto

third reading

Triple-E Senate

unicameral legislature

RECOMMENDED READINGS

Comparing Legislatures

HIBBING, JOHN R. and ELIZABETH THEISS-MORSE (1998) "Too Much of a Good Thing: More Representative is Not Necessarily Better," *PS: Political Science and Politics*, Volume 31, Number 1, pp. 28–31.

HUBER, JOHN D. (1996) "The Vote of Confidence in Parliamentary Democracies," *American Political Science Review*, Volume 90, Number 2, pp. 269–282.

LONGLEY, LAWRENCE D. and DAVID M. OLSON, eds. (1991) *Two into One: The Politics and Processes of National Legislative Cameral Change*. Boulder, Colorado: Westview Press.

MARSH, MICHAEL and PIPPA NORRIS (1997) "Political Representation in the European Parliament," *European Journal of Political Research*, Volume 32, Number 2, pp. 153–163.

PATTERSON, SAMUEL and ANTHONY MUGHAN, eds. (1999) *Senates: Bicameralism in the Contemporary World*. Columbus, Ohio: Ohio State University Press.

SAXONBERG, STEVEN (2000) "Women in East European Parliaments," *Journal of Democracy*, Volume 11, Number 2, pp. 145–158.

SHEPSLE, KENNETH A. (1988) "Representation and Governance: The Great Legislative Trade-off," *Political Science Quarterly*, Volume 103, Number 3, pp. 461–484.

WHEARE, K.C. (1963) *Legislatures*. London: Oxford University Press.

The Canadian Legislature

BLACK, JEROME (2000) "Entering the Political Elite in Canada: The Case of Minority Women as Parliamentary Candidates and MPs," *The Canadian Review of Sociology and Anthropology*, Volume 37, Number 2, pp. 143–166.

DOCHERTY, DAVID C. (1997) *Mr. Smith Goes to Ottawa: Life in the House of Commons*. Vancouver: UBC Press.

ERICKSON, LYNDA (1997) "Might More Women Make a Difference? Gender, Party and Ideology among Canada's Parliamentary Candidates," *Canadian Journal of Political Science*, Volume 30, Number 4, pp. 663–688.

FRANKS, C.E.S. (1987) *The Parliament of Canada*. Toronto: University of Toronto Press.

HAUSSMAN, MELISSA (2000) " 'What Does Gender Have to Do with Abortion Law?' Canada Women's Movement – Parliamentary Interactions on Reform Attempts, 1969–91," *International Journal of Canadian Studies*, Volume 21, pp. 127–151.

HOY, CLAIRE (1999) *Nice Work: The Continuing Scandal of Canada's Senate*. Toronto: McClelland and Stewart.

JOYAL, SERGE (2000) "The Senate That You Thought You Knew." Paper presented at the July 29, 2000 meeting of the Canadian Political Science Association.

LONGLEY, NEIL (1999) "Voting on Abortion in the House of Commons: A Test for Legislator Shirking," *Canadian Public Policy*, Volume 25, Number 4, pp. 503–521.

MAINGOT, J.P. JOSEPH (1997) *Parliamentary Privilege in Canada*. 2nd ed. Montreal: House of Commons and McGill-Queen's University Press.

MALLOY, JONATHAN (1996) "Reconciling Expectations and Reality in the House of Commons Committees: The Case of the 1989 GST Inquiry," *Canadian Public Administration*, Volume 39, Number 3, pp. 314–335.

SEIDLE, F. LESLIE and LOUIS MASSICOTTE, eds. (1999) *Taking Stock of 150 Years of Responsible Government in Canada*. Ottawa: Canadian Study of Parliament Group.

SMITH, JENNIFER (1999) "Democracy and the Canadian House of Commons at the Millennium," *Canadian Public Administration*, Volume 42, Number 4, pp. 398–421.

STUDLAR, DONLEY T. and RICHARD E. MATLAND (1996) "The Dynamics of Women's Representation in the Canadian Provinces: 1975–1994," *Canadian Journal of Political Science*, Volume 29, Number 2, pp. 269–293.

WEAVER, R. KENT (1997) "Improving Representation in the Canadian House of Commons," *Canadian Journal of Political Science*, Volume 30, Number 3, pp. 473–512.

The British Legislature

BROWN, ALICE (1998) "Building a Representative House in Scotland and the Role of Women in the Developmental Process," *PS: Political Science and Politics*, Volume 31, Number 1, pp. 17–20.

DOIG, ALAN (1998) " 'Cash for Questions': Parliament's Response to the Offence That Dare Not Speak Its Name," *Parliamentary Affairs*, Volume 51, Number 1, pp. 36–50.

DUNLEAVY, PATRICK et al. (1993) "Leaders, Politics and Institutional Change: The Decline of Prime Ministerial Accountability to the House of Commons, 1868–1990," *British Journal of Political Science*, Volume 23, Number 3, pp. 267–298.

JUDGE, DAVID (1999) *Representation: Theory and Practice in Britain*. London: Routledge.

MCALLISTER, LAURA (1999) "The Road to Cardiff Bay: The Process of Establishing the National Assembly for Wales," *Parliamentary Affairs*, Volume 52, Number 4, pp. 634-648.

MITCHELL, JAMES (1999) "The Creation of the Scottish Parliament: Journey without End," *Parliamentary Affairs*, Volume 52, Number 4, pp. 649–655.

NORRIS, PIPPA (1996) "Women Politicians: Transforming Westminster?" *Parliamentary Affairs*, Volume 49, Number 1, pp. 89–102.

SHELL, DAVID (2000) "Labour and the House of Lords: A Case Study in Constitutional Reform," *Parliamentary Affairs*, Volume 53, Number 2, pp. 290–310.

SMITH, DAVID E. (2000) "A House for the Future: Debating Second Chamber Reform in the United Kingdom," *Government and Opposition*, Volume 35, Number 3, pp. 325–344.

The American Legislature

BINDER, SARAH A. (1999) "The Dynamics of Legislative Gridlock, 1947–96," *American Political Science Review*, Volume 93, Number 3, pp. 519–533.

BINDER, SARAH A. and STEVEN S. SMITH (1997) *Politics or Principle? Filibustering in the United States Senate*. Washington, D.C.: Brookings Institution Press.

DEERING, CHRISTOPHER J. and STEVEN S. SMITH (1997) *Committees in Congress*. 3rd ed. Washington, D.C.: Congressional Quarterly Press.

DODD, LAWRENCE C. and BRUCE IAN OPPENHEIMER, eds. (1997) *Congress Reconsidered*. 6th ed. Washington, D.C.: Congressional Quarterly Press.

FISHER, LOUIS (1997) *Constitutional Conflicts Between Congress and the President*. 4th ed. rev. Lawrence, Kansas: University Press of Kansas.

GILL, LAVERNE MCCAIN (1997) *African American Women in Congress: Forming and Transforming History*. New Brunswick, New Jersey: Rutgers University Press.

HAMILTON, LEE (2000) "What I Wish Political Scientists Would Teach about Congress," *PS: Political Science and Politics*, Volume 33, Number 4, pp. 757–764.

KAPTOR, MARCY (1996) *Women of Congress*. Washington, D.C.: Congressional Quarterly Press.

KORN, JESSICA (1996) *The Power of Separation: American Constitutionalism and the Myth of the Legislative Veto*. Princeton, New Jersey: Princeton University Press.

LEE, FRANCIS E. and BRUCE I. OPPENHEIMER (1999) *Sizing Up the Senate: The Unequal Consequences of Equal Representation*. Chicago: University of Chicago Press.

LOOMIS, BURDETTE A. (1996) *The Contemporary Congress*. New York: St. Martin's Press.

LUBLIN, DAVID (1997) "The Election of African Americans and Latinos to the U.S. House of Representatives, 1972–1994," *American Politics Quarterly*, Volume 25, Number 3, pp. 269–286.

OLESZEK, WALTER J. (1995) *Congressional Procedures and the Policy Process*. 4th ed. Washington, D.C.: Congressional Quarterly Press.

THOMAS, SUE (1994) *How Women Legislate*. New York: Oxford University Press.

 # POLITICS ON THE NET

GENERAL: For links to parliamentary governments from around the world, see *www.polisci.umn.edu/information/parliaments/index.html*.

CANADA: The official website for the **Parliament of Canada** can be located at *www.parl.gc.ca*. This site has links to the web pages for the Senate and House of Commons and links to all of the provincial and territorial legislatures.

The website for the **Auditor General of Canada** can be accessed at *www.oag-bvg.gc.ca*.

BRITAIN: The official website for the **British Parliament** is located at *www.parliament.uk*. For the newly created subnational parliaments in Great Britain, consult the following: **Scotland** (*www.scottish.parliament.uk*); **Wales** (*www.assembly.wales.gov.uk*); **Northern Ireland** (*www.ni-assembly.gov.uk*).

UNITED STATES: The national legislature's official websites are as follows: the **House of Representatives** (*www.house.gov*) and the **Senate** (*www.senate.gov)*. The **Congressional Budget Office** is located at *www.cbo.gov*.

Several other sites offer valuable information on the American Congress: a basic site is *thomas.loc.gov*. The *Congressional Quarterly's* online service is located at *www.cq.com*, while the online version of the *Capitol Hill* newspaper can be accessed at *www.rollcall.com*. Other good sources on Congress include the following: *www.congress.org* and *www.c-span.org/questions*.

The Judicial Branch of Government

The duty of the court, as I envisage it, is to proceed in the discharge of its adjudicative function in a reasoned way from principled decision and established concepts. I do not for a moment doubt the power of the court to act creatively — it has done so on countless occasions; but manifestly one must ask — what are the limits of the judicial function? (Dickson, 1985: 213)

When justices interpret the constitution they speak for their community, not for themselves alone. The act of interpretation must be undertaken with full consciousness that it is, in a very real sense, the community's interpretation that is sought. (Brennan, 1987: 24)

CHAPTER PREVIEW

- The growth of judicial power in many democratic systems is helping to transform the ways in which political processes operate.

- While not as visible historically as the executive or legislative branches of government, the judicial branch is an increasingly significant political actor in modern polities.

- Even though most judges are selected in democratic systems on the basis of patronage, once appointed, judges are expected to operate independently from their political masters.

- The composition of the judicial branches is increasingly representative of the various groups and sectors of society.

- The principle of judicial review makes the judicial branch a potentially significant political actor.

- The Canadian judiciary has moved from a pattern of limited judicial review and judicial restraint to a pattern of political activism and full judicial review.

- The Canadian Charter of Rights and Freedoms has been the primary reason for the expansion of judicial power, along with Charter Canadians and the Court Party.

- While Britain has traditionally followed a pattern of no judicial review, recent political reforms, such as devolution, have moved even Britain into an era of expanding judicial power.

- Because of a pattern of full judicial review for two centuries, the American court system is the most powerful judiciary in the world.

In democratic systems the political process, and the public's perception of it, is dominated by the elected politicians of the executive and legislative branches of government. In most of these polities the third branch of government, the judiciary, rarely comes into public focus and, when it does so, its actions are little understood by the ordinary citizen. This traditional pattern of low political visibility is a reflection of the judiciary's typical **guardianship role** in the polity; its main task is *to protect the political system and the constitution from abuses of power.* The judiciary's legitimacy depends, in large measure, on the public's perception of its neutrality and nonpartisanship. To stay above mere politics necessitates that the court system abstain from active and direct involvement in the daily workings of the political process. However, low visibility does not necessarily preclude political power and influence. Despite the public's perception of their nonpolitical status, the courts are political institutions that render political judgments with, at least occasionally, far-reaching political consequences.

THE NATURE OF JUDICIAL POWER

As with many aspects of the political process, the often significant political role of the judiciary emerged from practice rather than from theory. Of the three branches of government, least attention is typically paid to the judiciary in most constitutions. Moreover, in the American system the principle of full judicial review was asserted by the judiciary itself, rather than being prescribed in the Constitution.

Although the court system was often viewed initially as a kind of disinterested referee of the political process (e.g., in federal systems, deciding which level of government could constitutionally exercise which powers), it was also conceived as a potential means for counteracting the effects of popular sentiment on the executive and legislature. In contrast to its conservative intent, however, the expansion of judicial power has coincided with the democratization of the political process. Paradoxically, an appointed branch of government in a democratic age has had the potential for increasing and protecting human rights against encroachments by the elected political institutions.

The court system's ability in Anglo-American democratic systems to counteract executive and legislative abuses of power reflects the principle of judicial independence. In broad terms, **judicial independence** means *the lack of political direction and control over the courts by any outside body*, including the executive and legislative branches of government. The fusion of powers between the executive and legislature in a parliamentary system does not extend to the judiciary, while the separation of powers principle in a presidential polity is a major reinforcement of judicial independence. Judicial independence is designed to prevent any person or institution from dictating to the courts the content of their rulings, a reflection of the view that the courts should be nonpolitical. Sometimes, however, certain groups seek to use extra-legal means to influence the court system (e.g., attempts by organized crime and others to intimidate or to bribe a judge or juror).

> Like it or not, the United States, in common with almost all nations in the Western tradition, is increasingly governed by judges (Bork, 2000: A18).

The independence of the judiciary in democratic systems is protected by giving the judges **legal immunity** from the consequences of their decisions; that is, *no legal action can be taken "against a judge for anything which he does or says in his judicial capacity in court"* (Mallory, 1971: 289). If judges, in carrying out their official duties, make an incorrect ruling, they cannot be sued as individuals. A redress of grievances can usually be sought, however, by suing the government. Technically speaking, an individual would sue the Crown, the embodiment of executive authority. Thus, the courts are protected by a legal immunity, as well as a political immunity, from outside intervention in their affairs. **Political immunity** means that *judges cannot be removed from office because of political considerations*. For example, in 1988, when a Nova Scotia Royal Commission (known as the Marshall Inquiry) sought to subpoena five appeal court justices to testify, the Chief Justice of Nova Scotia, Constance Glube, quashed the subpoenas on the grounds that they violated the independence of the judiciary.

Judicial independence is further enhanced by the nature of judicial tenure. Judges are either appointed for long terms of office or for life, although many systems have imposed a mandatory retirement age. Once appointed, a judge can be removed only for "cause," that is, some sort of improper behaviour (e.g., a criminal conviction). For example, in 1998 a Quebec judge, Richard Therrien, was removed from the provincial bench because it was discovered that he had concealed his criminal past from the government during the appointment process (he had been convicted of hiding FLQ terrorists during the 1970 October Crisis). However, removal for cause does not mean that people simply disagree with a judge's rulings. Such removal is often made difficult, so as to reduce any chance of government manipulation of judicial personnel. Moreover, salaries of judges cannot be individually tampered with, either up or down, thus preventing political pressure from being applied monetarily.

The principle of judicial independence has often been misinterpreted to mean that somehow the courts are above or outside of the political arena. Nothing could be further from the truth. The myth of judicial impartiality is an important basis for legitimating the political effects of court decisions, even as it provides an incorrect description of the role of the judiciary in the political process.

Courts are inherently political by reason of their composition, the content of their rulings, and the consequences of their decisions. For example, patronage has often been the leading criterion of court appointments in democratic systems, especially at the lower levels of the judicial structure. Even when explicit partisanship is not the prevailing basis of selection, the appointment of court members to reflect particular ideological views or to represent various interests of society (racial, regional, ethnic, linguistic) is often done for political considerations. The contents of judicial decisions are political because they involve the allocation of power and influence within the polity. For example, in a federal structure, court rulings have been a means of settling questions of jurisdiction between the levels of government.

Finally, the consequences of judicial decisions are political, for they may alter the existing distribution of power and influence or raise new issues, which must be handled by the other branches of government. For example, court decisions have had the political consequence of helping to alter the initial allocation of powers in both the Canadian and American federal systems. Thus, the principle of judicial independence does not exclude the court system from the political arena but, instead, creates the potential for its political involvement by keeping the judiciary free from executive or legislative tutelage.

An important means of such judicial participation in the political process is what is known as judicial review. Two basic types exist, which we have labelled as **full judicial review** *(interpretations of constitutionality)* and **limited judicial review** *(decisions regarding the allocation of powers in a federal polity)*. The concept of full judicial review includes the narrower idea of limited judicial review. For example, in the United States — which operates under full judicial review — the judiciary is still called upon to make decisions about which level of government can exercise what powers. During the late 1990s, the American Supreme Court made a series of decisions regarding the relationship between the national government and state governments (Greenhouse, 1999: 23). For example, for the first time since the New Deal era, in a case involving the right of the federal government to make school zones gun-free, the Supreme Court in 1995 limited the power of the federal government under the constitution's commerce clause. However, the more important task of the American judiciary regards rulings about whether or not any government can exercise certain powers (e.g., freedom of speech controversies). For example, in June of 2000 the American Supreme Court declared unconstitutional the saying of public school prayers before such events as high school football games, because they violated the constitutional principle of the separation of church and state.

The political consequences of full judicial review are potentially of far greater significance than those of limited judicial review. For example, a basic reason for the extensive political impact of the American judiciary stems from its application of full judicial review, while the historically more modest Canadian pattern of judicial review, until the impact of the Canadian Charter of Rights and Freedoms, is congruent with a limited judicial review process. In Britain, judicial review has not existed historically, since its application would be in direct opposition to the principle of parliamentary sovereignty. Only in the last few years, with the Human Rights Act of 1998 and the pattern of devolution, has a basis been provided for an evolving, but limited, pattern of judicial review in Britain. The greater the extent of judicial review, the greater the likelihood of the court system's involvement in politics, because court cases based on full judicial review often thrust the judiciary into a policy-making role.

Judicial review has been criticized as undemocratic, since it allows a small group of appointed officials to overturn the actions or legislation of elected ones. However, full judicial review has, at times, expanded civil and political liberties against the conservative interests that controlled the other two branches of government. A good illustration of this point is the civil rights rulings that began in the mid-1950s in the American system. However, the impact of full judicial review on the polity will depend, to a considerable extent, on the composition of the courts. The principle of judicial review supplies the legal basis for the assertion of judicial power. If such a pattern results, it depends, in large measure, on the individuals appointed to the judiciary.

Whether the judiciary operates under either full or limited judicial review, the interpretation of a constitution and its application in specific contexts is often a tricky business. Two broad approaches to constitutional interpretation can be identified: judicial restraint and judicial activism. In a pattern of **judicial restraint**, *the courts take a very narrow view of their own powers of interpretation.* In fact, the judges confine themselves to divining the literal and intended meaning of the initial constitution. This approach implies that it is not the role of the courts to adapt the law to changing circumstances, but to apply the law as it was written. If changes in the law are needed, then it is up to the executive and legislature to respond accordingly. In contrast, the second pattern, that of **judicial activism**, reflects *a willingness on the part of the judges to use their powers vigorously, to take a broad view of any powers delineated in the constitution and, if necessary, to adapt the law to changing circumstances*, especially if the other two branches are reluctant to do so.

> The popularity of judicial review as a constitutional institution is a post–World War II phenomenon, in Canada not less than in other countries (McWhinney, 1987: 63).

While patterns of judicial restraint or judicial activism depend, in part, on the individuals appointed to the courts, there is an important relationship between trends of judicial interpretation and the two basic kinds of judicial review. Full judicial review creates the potential for an activist judiciary, while limited judicial review makes more likely a pattern of judicial restraint. A pattern of judicial activism or restraint reflects a country's political culture and the prevailing attitudes about the proper role of the judiciary. Moreover, no judicial system is able to decide cases on its own initiative. Conflicts must be brought to the courts before the judicial branch can get involved. Like a car that only starts on a cold winter morning with the help of booster cables, the court system must be continually jump-started before it can render any decision.

The actual operation of the judiciary in Anglo-American democratic systems embodies several key features. First, in most instances, an individual is presumed innocent in criminal proceedings until proven guilty during the course of a judicial hearing. This assumption is a direct result of the principle of judicial independence: the judicial system, not the executive or legislature, decides the question of guilt or innocence. In contrast, totalitarian systems reverse this view, assuming that a person charged by the state is guilty until the individual proves otherwise. In such a system, the judicial structure is not independent, but is seen as a political extension of the state. The role of the courts in a totalitarian polity is to enforce the political decisions of the ruling party, with accusation of wrongdoing being tantamount to conviction. However, even in some democratic systems, such as France, which use the inquisitorial method, the individual is basically presumed to be guilty until the facts show otherwise (Abraham, 1985: 101).

The second tenet of a democratic judiciary concerns the process for arriving at decisions of guilt or innocence, that is, the **adversary** or **fight system of justice.** In this process *the court is an impartial arbitrator between the prosecution and the defence.* Both the prosecution, those trying to show that the individual is guilty, and the defence, those attempting to prove the individual's innocence, are given the opportunity to bring the facts of the case, as they see them, before the court. Then, the judge or jury acts as an impartial arbitrator, deciding guilt or innocence on the basis of the testimony presented. Assumptions of innocence and an adversary system of court procedure help to produce what is known as the **due process of law** in democratic polities, that is, *adherence to the proper procedures and constitutionally guaranteed rights.*

A final significant aspect of court procedure is the principle of *stare decisis*, or *the rule of precedent.* Once a court has ruled on a particular question or type of case, that ruling stands as a guide or precedent for similar cases in the future. Thus, the principle of *stare decisis* provides for some continuity of judicial interpretation, as well as limiting the number of cases the court system must handle. However, precedents may not be definitive, since they are often multiple, as well as contradictory. One can always argue that the facts of a particular case are different enough from previous similar cases as to require a further elaboration of the law. In addition, precedents change. Judicial rulings can be applied in new contexts or simply reversed, thereby creating a new precedent for further court decisions.

Once a court has issued a decision, the question of its implementation comes to the forefront. In democratic systems, the executive branch of government, either by constitutional prescription or custom, is typically required to enforce the decisions of the judiciary. Thus, a possible conflict of interest might arise when a judicial decision goes against the executive, for the executive is supposed to enforce such a decision against itself. These cases, however, are infrequent because of the prevalent belief in democratic systems that judicial decisions should be obeyed. Force is rarely needed to gain acquiescence with judicial intent.

The legitimacy of the judiciary, based on the belief of its impartiality, is usually sufficient so that court orders are self-enforcing. If they are not, a court can take several actions, in addition to notifying the executive of any nonobservance. For example, an **injunction** may be issued by the judiciary, *which may either command that some action be taken or order that certain actions be stopped.* Failure to comply with judicial decisions may also result in an individual or group being held in contempt of court, an offence that carries penalties meted out by the judiciary itself. Thus, the court system is not only lacking a self-starting mechanism, but it is given no direct means for implementing the decisions it has taken. As a result, the judiciary in most democratic systems has often been a reluctant participant in the political process.

THE CANADIAN JUDICIAL SYSTEM

In analyzing the nature of judicial power in any specific polity, four broad areas must be considered: the structure, composition, operation, and consequences of the court system. Comparing judiciaries on the basis of these criteria reveals more variation among Canada, Britain, and the United States than with respect to the other two branches of government.

JUDICIAL STRUCTURE

The structure of the Canadian judiciary is complex, with responsibilities and functions shared, or **federalized**, between the federal and provincial governments. Moreover, each province has the power to determine the organization of its own court system, thus producing considerable variation of detail. Overall, the Canadian court system is hierarchically structured and composed of three court levels: federal courts (Supreme Court and Federal Court of Canada); provincial courts (a provincial Supreme Court and superior, county, and district courts); and lesser provincial courts (such as family courts).

Responsibilities for the structure of the courts is federalized, that is, divided between the national and provincial governments, with the national government controlling the federal courts, the provinces in charge of the minor courts, and federal and provincial governments sharing jurisdiction over the intermediate level. For example, while the provinces determine the number and structure of the major provincial courts, the federal government was given the power of appointment, tenure, and salary of these same courts. In total, there are about 2 000 judges at all of the judicial levels in Canada, with about 1 000 judges appointed by the federal government. Thus, as an area of shared control, the intermediate court level can only function effectively on the basis of federal-provincial co-operation with regard to its structure.

Defining the law's content was also federalized, with the national government granted the right to determine the criminal code and procedure and the provinces allocated powers over civil procedure. Thus, an area such as the decriminalization of marijuana is a federal responsibility, while the "solemnization of marriage" is provincially determined.

The federalization of jurisdiction in defining criminal and civil law and of control over the intermediate court level has been incorporated, nevertheless, into an overall hierarchical court structure, now presided over by the Supreme Court of Canada. Athough it was first created in 1875 under the authority granted to the national Parliament (in Section 101 of the 1867 Constitution Act) to provide a "General Court of Appeal" for the Canadian system, the Supreme Court only became the highest court of appeal for constitutional cases in 1949. Before then, the ultimate court of appeal for Canadian cases resided in Britain with the **Judicial Committee of the Privy Council (JCPC)**. Moreover, even after its creation in 1875, many cases were never considered by the Supreme Court, since "it was possible for appeals to go directly from a court of appeal within a province to the Judicial Committee" (Cheffins and Tucker, 1976: 95).

The result of such a judicial structure was not only to make explicit the nature of Canada's colonial position, but to give the JCPC the role of being "the major interpreter of the Canadian constitution and the major expander of explicit views on the nature of Canadian federalism" (Stevenson, 1979: 55). Thus, Canada, like other Commonwealth countries, faced the anomaly of having judges trained in British law and its role in a unitary state trying to comprehend and interpret the nature of Canadian conditions and the evolving pattern of Canadian federalism.

While considerable controversy surrounds the overall impact of the JCPC on the Canadian polity, there is little question that its decisions at the end of the 19th century were an important contributing factor to the initial decentralizing trend within the federal system (McCormick, 2000: 6–11). Since any case that was before the courts at the time of the abolition of appeals in 1949 retained the right to appeal to the JCPC, a decade passed before the Supreme Court of Canada became, in fact, the final court of appeal in 1959. Canada was thus in a colonial-judicial relationship with Britain until the mid-20th century. With the Supreme Court's elevation to the position of the highest court of appeal, the composition, operation, and consequences of the Supreme Court became crucial for understanding the nature of judicial power in the Canadian context.

JUDICIAL COMPOSITION

There is strong reason to suspect that the composition of the Canadian judiciary is patronage-based, particularly at the lower levels of the court system. From this view it makes little difference which level of government has the appointment power: the party in office at either level rewards its own members more often than not. While judicial patronage is pervasive, it rarely becomes a matter of sustained public attention. Although opposition parties traditionally criticize such practices, they are usually quick to adopt them when they gain power.

Any listing of patronage-inspired judicial appointments would be lengthy. As an example, before leaving office in 1984, Prime Minister Trudeau made a rash of patronage appointments, including a number (five former MPs) to the bench. Three former Liberal cabinet ministers (Yvon Pinard, Mark MacGuigan, and Bud Cullen) were appointed to the Federal Court of Canada. In a report published in 1985, the Canadian Bar Association demanded that the appointment of judges be less political in the future, with Chief Justice Brian Dickson indicating that judges should be selected on the basis of ability, rather than partisanship. However, an immediate change in the basic patronage pattern of judicial appointments was not evident.

To overcome the image of a patronage-based selection process, a revised procedure was finally put into effect in January of 1989. All persons considered for a judgeship are now assessed by a provincial committee made up of "nonpartisan" members representing the Canadian Bar Association, the provincial law society, and the federal and provincial governments. This new process has reduced some of the most blatant examples of judicial patronage. Nonetheless, such patronage practices still exist. Roy McMurtry, former Conservative MLA and attorney general in Ontario, was appointed in 1991 as Associate Chief Justice of the Ontario Court of Justice by federal Justice Minister Kim Campbell. More recently (1999), former Liberal premier of Newfoundland Clyde Wells was appointed to that province's Court of Appeal and was later elevated to the position of Chief Justice. In addition, Premier Brian Tobin's aide Malcolm Rowe was appointed in 2000 to the Supreme Court of Newfoundland, even though he had little legal experience at the time. While such partisan abuses are infrequently associated with the Supreme Court of Canada itself, the selection of its members is still political in the sense of the ideological views the appointees bring to the Court. However, patronage remains a very significant, although declining, factor in the process of judicial selection (Russell, 1987: 114–115).

In addition to the patronage factor, other considerations influence court appointments. Since judges are selected from among members of the legal profession, the court members are typically unrepresentative of the total population in terms of such basic socio-political factors as race, ethnicity, education, and social class. For example, while the two charter groups of Canadian society are well represented, those of neither British nor French origin have traditionally received few judicial appointments. However, in recent decades the judiciary has become more representative of Canada's multicultural heritage, as illustrated at the Supreme Court level with the appointment in 1970 of the first Jewish member (Bora Laskin), the first Ukrainian-Canadian (John Sopinka) in 1988, and the first Italian-Canadian (Frank Iacobucci) in 1991. Particularly evident has been the lack of women in the Canadian judiciary. Perhaps that is not as surprising as it might seem, given the fact that in 1928 the Canadian Supreme Court, which was composed of all males, unanimously agreed that women were not "persons" as defined in the BNA Act of 1867 (Section 24) with regard to appointments to the Senate. Because traditionally few women have become lawyers or politicians, few have been appointed to the bench. However, a significant change in the representation of women in the judiciary has occurred in the past two decades in Canada, symbolized by the appointment of four women to the Supreme Court, including Canada's first female Chief Justice, Beverley McLachlin, in 1999. Thus, a trend toward more equitable judicial composition is evident over the last several decades.

To help ensure French-Canadian representation on the national courts, Quebec is guaranteed 3 positions on the Supreme Court and, since 1985, 8 of the 25 positions on the Federal Court, although no such guarantees exist for other groups. The main reason for Quebec's representation is to ensure that judges familiar with the civil law tradition of Quebec sit on cases that deal with such matters. Although some effort is made to distribute judicial appointments among the various socio-economic interests of society, the composition of the judiciary remains more immune to the democratic ethos than either the executive or legislature.

The tenure of judges in Canada is indeterminate, extending from their appointment to their mandatory retirement at age 75. Within this period judges are typically not subjected to any formal review or reappointment process. However, judges can be removed for "cause." For example, Section 98 of the 1867 Constitution Act empowers the federal government to remove any judge of the superior courts after an address by the governor general to both Houses of Parliament. The exercise of this legal power is rare, for a judge in trouble because of personal problems or alleged wrongdoing will usually resign before being removed from office.

Several such incidents have come to the public's attention in recent decades. A tragic case developed with British Columbia Supreme Court Judge Davie Fulton. A former federal Justice Minister and leader of the provincial Conservative party, Judge Fulton developed a serious drinking problem. After his second conviction for driving while intoxicated, Judge Fulton resigned from the court. In 1999, Quebec Superior Court Judge Robert Flahiff resigned from the bench after he was found guilty of laundering $1.7 million in drug money and sentenced to three years in jail. Such incidents, while rare, demonstrate that judges, like any other group, are human. On the whole, however, the quality of Canadian judicial personnel is good, despite the judiciary's patronage-base and sometimes human failings.

The Supreme Court of Canada is composed of nine justices, one of whom is named the Chief Justice and presides over and directs the work of the court (Table 5.1). In recent years, the workload of the Supreme Court has averaged about 100 appeals per year — from a high of 150 in 1993 to only 72 in 2000. The position of Canadian Chief Justice is one of considerable influence rather than one of power, although there is nothing that guarantees support from the other justices.

> Supreme Court of Canada justices have become our new philosopher-monarchs. These black-robed, secluded figures hand down solutions to society's problems from the Olympian detachment of the highest court in the land . . . . By the judges' own admission, politics and law are now inextricably linked and their fates joined (Hutchinson, 1987: A7).

The Supreme Court must contain three members from Quebec, with a quorum consisting of five of the nine justices (on any appeal from Quebec involving the civil code, two members of the quorum must be from that province). Those appointed must have considerable legal experience (i.e., 10 years of practice as a barrister) or be members of a provincial superior court. These requirements have usually prevented blatant patronage appointments to the highest court.

However, political considerations, such as regional representation, do intrude even at the Supreme Court level. By law, as mentioned above, three members of the Supreme Court must be from Quebec. Based on convention, Ontario is allocated a similar number of justices, with the Atlantic provinces receiving one and the West obtaining two (one from British Columbia and one from the Prairies). The political considerations of Supreme Court appointments can be seen in the 1997 appointment of New Brunswick Acadian Michel Bastarache to replace retiring New Brunswicker Justice Gerard LaForest. Because of the custom of rotating

Table 5.1   The Canadian Supreme Court 2002

Justices	Appointed by	Date	Province
Beverley McLachlin	Mulroney	1989	British Columbia
Chief Justice	Chrétien	1999	
Claire L'Heureux-Dube	Mulroney	1987	Quebec
Charles Gonthier	Mulroney	1989	Quebec
Frank Iacobucci	Mulroney	1990	Ontario
John C. Major	Mulroney	1992	Alberta
Michel Bastarache	Chrétien	1997	New Brunswick
W. Ian Binnie	Chrétien	1998	Ontario
Louise Arbour	Chrétien	1999	Ontario
Louis LeBel	Chrétien	2000	Quebec

appointments among the provinces in a region, such a move slighted the other Atlantic provinces, particularly Newfoundland, which in 50 years of Confederation has never received a Supreme Court appointment. Moreover, Bastarache had strong personal and political ties to Prime Minister Chrétien: he had been a colleague in the same law firm as the prime minister and a leading advocate, as national co-chair of the YES side, in the 1992 referendum on the Charlottetown Accord.

JUDICIAL OPERATION

In addition to the structure and composition of the judiciary, a third important attribute of the court system is its method of operation. The broad functioning of the judicial system in Canada, particularly from 1867 to 1982, can be described by the concepts of judicial independence, limited judicial review, and judicial restraint. With the adoption of the Canadian Charter of Rights and Freedoms in 1982, Canada now also operates under a pattern of full judicial review.

Although the principle of judicial independence has sometimes been violated, its acceptance has never been open to serious attack. The judiciary is designed to be free of executive or legislative control and when violations of such a principle become known, the political consequences can be severe. For example, in the famous Judges Affair in 1977, two federal cabinet ministers resigned or lost their portfolios because of reported interventions with a judge with respect to a contempt of court citation against one of their fellow cabinet officers. In January 1990, Fitness and Amateur Sport Minister Jean Charest resigned from the cabinet after phoning the office of a Quebec superior judge regarding the case of a coach who was seeking reinstatement to the Canadian team for the Commonwealth Games.

Judicial independence can also be challenged when a judge intervenes openly in current partisan controversy. Such a situation occurred when then Justice Thomas Berger of the British Columbia Supreme Court wrote a lengthy critique, published in *The Globe and Mail* on December 10, 1981, about the dropping of native rights from the patriation accord. Prime Minister Pierre Trudeau, who had appointed Berger to the judiciary, reacted bitterly to the critique, openly attacking Justice Berger for his views. In April 1982, a complaint against Justice Berger's intervention into the patriation controversy was brought before the Canadian Judicial Council.

> The rule of law, interpreted and applied by impartial judges, is the guarantee of everyone's rights and freedoms . . . . Judicial independence is, at its root, concerned with impartiality, in appearance and in fact. And these, of course, are elements essential to an effective judiciary (Canadian Supreme Court Chief Justice Antonio Lamer, 1994, quoted in Friedland, 1995: 1).

The **Canadian Judicial Council**, created in 1971, is composed of the 36 Chief Justices and Associate Chief Justices of the Canadian court system. Its purpose is to investigate complaints about judges (there were 177 complaints in 1999) and it may, if the facts warrant, recommend to the federal Minister of Justice an individual's removal from office. Since Confederation only five judges have been recommended for removal; however, those judges either resigned or died before Parliament took any action. Judicial councils have also been created at the provincial level. In the Berger case, the Council decided that his conduct had been indiscreet, but did not recommend removal from office. Justice Berger responded by saying that he would continue to speak out on minority rights in the future. However, quite likely as a result of this controversy, Berger resigned from the bench in 1983.

With the growth of judicial power in the last two decades, the Canadian Judicial Council has faced an increased workload, as have the various provincial judicial councils (Friedland, 1995: 90–113). In less than a decade, between 1986 and 1994, complaints filed with the Canadian Judicial Council increased from 44 to 164. While most of these are dismissed, if improper behaviour is found the Council's findings can be the start of the process to remove a judge for "cause." For example, Justice William Ian Binnie made an allegedly anti-gay comment after being nominated, but before being sworn in, as a member of the Canadian Supreme Court. An immediate complaint was made to the Canadian Judicial Council in March of 1998. Within 24 hours the Council had rejected the complaint.

The second operating principle of the Canadian judiciary is that of limited judicial review. This practice of delineating the respective powers of the federal and provincial governments is not directly contradictory to the principle of parliamentary sovereignty, since the judiciary determines only which level of government is supreme with respect to which powers. As already mentioned, such rulings can, however, have considerable impact on the balance of power between the two levels of government in a federal polity.

Examples of the exercise of limited judicial review would include the attempts by the provinces to deal with the problem of prostitution. These efforts were ruled unconstitutional because prostitution is a criminal matter that falls within the jurisdiction of the federal government. Thus, a Calgary bylaw was struck down by the Supreme Court in 1983, as was Nova Scotia's attempted use of an injunction in 1984 as a means of dealing with the prostitution matter. A further example of limited judicial review occurred in June of 1992, when the Supreme Court of Canada ruled that the Goods and Services Tax (GST) was constitutional and within the powers of the federal government to adopt and implement. Likewise, when the federal government passed the gun control law in 1995 (the Firearms Act), it was challenged by most of the provincial governments because they thought it violated provincial authority over property and civil rights. However, in June of 2000 the Supreme Court of Canada ruled that the Firearms Act is valid because it falls within the federal government's jurisdiction regarding criminal law. In another case, the Alberta provincial government sued the federal government in February of 2001 for $428 million in oil and gas revenues which it claimed that Ottawa had illegally collected. Such decisions are classified as examples of limited judicial review because they deal with the kinds of powers and functions that the federal and provincial governments may exercise.

The third operating principle of the Canadian courts is the traditional practice of judicial restraint, that is, the limited exercise of the limited powers given to them. In part, the pattern of restraint reflects the attitudes of the judges themselves (what could be called, perhaps, judicial self-restraint), as well as the overall constitutional position of the judiciary in Canada. Quite frankly, the other two branches of government, usually under some version or variation of the parliamentary supremacy doctrine, have typically sought to limit any expansion of judicial power. As a result, the umpire of the Canadian federal system has traditionally been called upon to make very few close calls at home plate.

A good example of the impact of limited judicial review and judicial self-restraint occurred during the internment and evacuation of Japanese Canadians during the Second World War. By the powers of the War Measures Act that was implemented through orders-in-council, the Canadian government, under Liberal Prime Minister Mackenzie King, attacked the fundamental liberties and rights of Japanese Canadians. Appeals to the Supreme Court of Canada and to the Judicial Committee of the Privy Council proved to be of no avail: "The issue was regarded as one for political judgment, in no way subject to the jurisdiction of the courts" (Berger, 1982: 118).

The fourth operating principle of the Canadian judiciary, that is, full judicial review, has only had a significant impact since the adoption of the Canadian Charter of Rights and Freedoms in 1982. Combined with a growing pattern of judicial activism on the part of the judges themselves, full judicial review has significantly transformed and expanded the power and consequences of the judicial branch in the current Canadian polity.

JUDICIAL CONSEQUENCES

Given the traditional patterns of limited judicial review and judicial restraint from 1867 to 1982, the political impact of the Canadian judiciary might be expected to be extremely modest. In fact, however, the Canadian courts have played a fairly significant political role, particularly considering the context within which they have traditionally operated. Such a conclusion is supported by a political analysis of the Supreme Court of Canada, a body that has not been immune to political controversies.

Since the Supreme Court is the final body to hear matters of federal-provincial conflict and because its members are appointed by the federal government, the provinces have always harboured the suspicion that the Supreme Court is biased in favour of the national government. This view is reinforced by the legal requirement that Supreme Court justices, after their appointments, must "reside in the national capital region" (Supreme Court of Canada Act, Section 8), thus supposedly helping to overcome any regional or provincial bias they may have had. Premier Peter Lougheed of Alberta put it bluntly in 1978 when he stated that it didn't matter where the Supreme Court justices were born, because after 20 years in Ottawa they all thought alike anyway.

However, a perusal of Supreme Court decisions from 1949 onward reveals a mixed pattern, with the Court sometimes ruling in favour of the provinces and sometimes in favour of the federal government. The decisions of the Laskin Court of the 1970s often upheld federal government powers, as in the wage-and-price control decision, but it also ruled in favour of the provinces (e.g., the December 1979 decision regarding Senate reform). Contrary to provincial perceptions, it would be difficult to make a strong case for inherent Ottawa bias in the decisions of the Supreme Court of Canada or to argue that judges are primarily appointed because they appear to be centralist or nationalist in their judicial outlook.

Instead of an explicit bias in favour of Ottawa, what seems more realistic as the cause of provincial concerns is the following pattern. The typically narrow or legalistic interpretation of the 1867 Constitution Act by judges operating under a pattern of judicial restraint and limited judicial review has been seen to support the national government because the 1867 Constitution Act itself remains, in theory, a highly centralized document, unreflective of the decentralized pattern of modern Canadian federalism. Perhaps revealing is a study of the Supreme Court undertaken by the Quebec government following the Parti Québécois victory in 1976. Released in 1978, the report claimed that there was no specific bias on the part of the Supreme Court simply because it was appointed by Ottawa. Any bias resulted instead from the Supreme Court's literal interpretation of a near-unitary document (*The Globe and Mail*, October 18, 1978).

Provincial suspicions remain, however, and help to determine some aspects of federal-provincial relations. For example, the provinces are reluctant to settle federal-provincial disputes in the courts if negotiations can possibly resolve the matter. Fear of federal bias has restricted the judicial alternative, as in the case of the Atlantic provinces' refusal in the 1970s to take questions of jurisdiction over offshore oil and natural gas to the Supreme Court for resolution. In the fall of 1981, federal Energy Minister Marc Lalonde openly dared Nova Scotia and Newfoundland to seek a court ruling, which they declined to do. However, failure to reach a negotiated settlement led the federal government to take the question of the ownership of resources off Newfoundland into the court system. In February 1983, the Supreme Court of Newfoundland ruled that Ottawa, not the province, owned offshore resources, a view that was later upheld by the Supreme Court of Canada in March of 1984. By refusing a negotiated settlement and forcing the federal government to turn to the judicial option, Premier Brian Peckford of Newfoundland initially lost it all; only later through political negotiations did Newfoundland recoup its jurisdictional loss. Interestingly, Nova Scotia, during this same time period, negotiated the issue with Ottawa. Thus, one reason for modest judicial involvement in political disputes has been a provincial fear of a federalist bias on the part of the Supreme Court of Canada.

In addition to the perceived centralist bias of the Supreme Court, a second important political element of judicial operation concerns the use of advisory or reference cases. An **advisory** or **reference case** is *one which is decided on by the court system on a possible constitutional issue or on a proposed piece of legislation.* Unlike some court systems where only actual cases are heard (i.e., the United States), the Supreme Court of Canada can be asked to rule on matters of legislation before a bill becomes law and is implemented. At the request of the governor-in-council (for all practical purposes, the prime minister and cabinet), the Supreme Court will issue an advisory opinion as to the constitutionality of a proposed course of action. Some of the most significant Supreme Court decisions of recent years fall into this category, including the rulings on the patriation proposal in 1981, Senate reform in 1979, and offshore jurisdiction in 1967.

What will likely be regarded in retrospect as the most important reference case in Canadian history occurred in 1998 in the *Quebec Secession Reference.* In response to Quebec's continuing claims regarding its right to unilaterally declare its separation from Canada, the federal government in 1996 asked the Supreme Court to answer three questions: (1) Can Quebec unilaterally secede from Canada? (2) Does international law give Quebec a right to secede from Canada? and (3) If there is a conflict between the answers to questions 1 and 2, which legal regime would apply to Canada? When the Supreme Court issued its decisions in August of 1998, it ruled that Quebec could not legally separate from Canada under either domestic or international law. However, the court then went further than expected and ruled that if perceived that there was a constitutional duty for the federal government and the provinces to negotiate with Quebec in the event that the citizens of Quebec decided in favour of the separatist option.

Although actual cases might lead to a challenge of an advisory opinion at a later date, the court is unlikely to change its opinion in the near future. An advisory opinion in its favour is an important political resource for either level of government. However, since the provinces cannot ask for advisory opinions from the Supreme Court, but instead must work their cases up through the hierarchical court system to the final court of appeal, the federal government has a decided advantage in this regard. Moreover, the federal government is unlikely to ask for such Supreme Court advice unless it feels that the court is likely to rule in its favour. If a negative advisory opinion results, the proposed legislation or government action can be modified to take account of the court's objections. If a positive decision is forthcoming for either level of government, then future court action will be unlikely, since the side which has lost will seek a negotiated settlement with the other level of government rather than risk a future anticipated loss before the Supreme Court.

A third political effect of judicial decisions has been to make the court system one element among many in Canadian political conflicts: "The court's declarations are often viewed as a factor in political bargaining, rather than as decisive statements" (McMenemy, 1980: 146). The determination to take a conflict or dispute into the court system is primarily a political, rather than a legal decision: "One of the most obvious consequences of judicial review is that political questions often come to the courts clothed as legal, constitutional questions" (Fletcher, 1977: 100).

A good example of this political use of the judiciary can be seen with respect to the powers of Quebec's Keable Commission in the late 1970s. Under the direction of Commissioner Jean Keable, the province of Quebec sought to investigate alleged RCMP wrongdoing in the province. To do so, the Keable Commission subpoenaed extensive information from the RCMP's secret files. As a federal body, the RCMP resisted, with the full backing of the Liberal government in Ottawa. The federal government proceeded to take the issue to the judiciary, arguing that no province had the right to investigate federal police matters, especially those which clearly fell under federal jurisdiction. Moreover, since criminal law was a federal responsibility, if the police

> The [Canadian Supreme] Court's abortion decisions can be understood as legal battles in a larger political war. Politics, not the Charter, brought these cases to the Court. The resulting judicial pronouncements provided the winners with new resources with which to return to the larger political struggle (Knopff and Morton, 1992: 291).

had broken any such laws it was a matter for federal prosecution and, thus, not of concern to the provinces. With the support of four other provinces, Quebec argued that since the administration of justice was a provincial concern, the province had a constitutional right to investigate even a federal police agency. The eventual outcome of this dispute was a court ruling that backed the federal position and effectively shut down the Keable Commission.

While it was shrouded in legal principles, what was really taking place was a political battle between the Parti Québécois government in Quebec and the federal Liberals in Ottawa, with each side seeking political support within the province. The clear intent of the provincial Keable Commission was to embarrass the federal government and to thus increase backing for the independence option, while the purpose of the federal government was to prevent such an investigation so as to protect its own political flank. However, not all judicial decisions are as definitive as the one on the Keable Commission — a court ruling may not settle these types of conflicts at all. The ruling of the Supreme Court on the Canada Act in September 1981 is a case in point: both the federal and provincial governments claimed victory, with the battle continuing until a politically negotiated resolution finally settled the matter.

Another aspect of the political consequences of court actions can be seen with respect to judicial protection of the broad areas of civil and political liberties. As with a constitution, so also with a bill of rights: the effectiveness of each depends more on their implementation than on their wording. Key to the maintenance of human freedoms is the willingness of the court system to use judicial power to make them effective in practice. A bill of rights or charter of rights depends, to a considerable extent, on the willingness of citizens to challenge arbitrary governmental actions and on the political will of the judiciary to prevent political abuses when it is given the opportunity to do so.

Unfortunately, the historical record of the Canadian courts in this area is not as encouraging as it could be. For example, the judiciary has typically backed the powers of the state and judges have resisted any effort to make them the agents of social change (McNaught, 1976: 160). Moreover, during the 1970s the Supreme Court made several significant decisions in relation to civil and political liberties. The judiciary ruled that illegally obtained evidence was admissible in court, with the only recourse left to the citizen being a suit against the individual police officer involved in the alleged wrongdoing. Of course, a person could be in jail a long time before such a suit was resolved. In a similar vein, the Supreme Court upheld the need to have a public permit for demonstrations in the city of Montreal, under the suspect view that such an assembly of citizens might lead to a breakdown of public order and safety. As a result, any group wishing to protest against local politicians, such as then Mayor Jean Drapeau, had to gain a permit from the city to do so. Needless to say, such permits were often difficult to obtain.

The historical pattern of limited judicial protection of limited rights began to change dramatically in 1982 with the adoption of the Canadian Charter of Rights and Freedoms. Because the Charter was entrenched in the Constitution, applied to both levels of government, and provided for the exercise of full judicial review, it quickly expanded the power of the judicial branch and provoked an ongoing debate about the proper role of judicial power in the Canadian polity.

The Charter and judicial power

While some political prognosticators predicted that the 1982 Constitution Act, especially the Canadian Charter of Rights and Freedoms, might have almost revolutionary consequences on the judicial process, others felt that it might end up having little effect, as did the Bill of Rights of 1960. Both views, given the events of the first two decades since the 1982 Charter, have turned out to be wrong. The most important long-term impact of the Canadian Charter of Rights and Freedoms is its impact on the power and political role of the judicial branch of government. Charter-based changes in the Canadian judiciary can be seen in the areas of judicial structure, judicial composition, and judicial review.

The most important impact of the Charter on the Canadian judicial structure has been to increase the number of both federal and provincial judges needed to handle the greater workload produced by the multitude of Charter cases and to deal with these cases within a reasonable period of time. More judges and more courts, of course, will produce more Charter politics in the future.

> Prior to the Charter's enactment in 1982, Canadian judges played a fairly restrained role in constitutional affairs . . . . The Charter changed all that. Now judges also determine whether a government, federal or provincial, has violated the rights of individual citizens (Bercuson and Cooper, 1997: D2).

At the very least, from the day of its proclamation on April 17, 1982 the Canadian Charter of Rights and Freedoms has had an important effect on the legal profession. It now seems to be almost obligatory for each case to have a Charter argument. As a result, there was an explosion of Charter-related cases after April 1982. In the Charter's first year, over 500 cases had arguments related to the Charter, with about 750 usages in its first three years of existence. However, these figures underestimate the total, since many lower court cases that include Charter arguments were then, and still are, not very visible. As a result, one estimate puts the probable number of Charter-related cases, in the first three years of its existence, at 1 500 (Russell, 1985: 369).

The volume of Charter cases has caused a certain element of confusion in the legal system, as the various provincial courts have given, at times, contradictory interpretations of the 1982 Constitution Act. Gradually, however, as the Supreme Court considers cases, a national pattern will emerge, since Supreme Court decisions are applicable in all of the provinces. Diversity of judicial interpretation will only last until the Supreme Court decides. Thus, it is apparent that the 1982 Constitution Act, and especially the Charter, will have a nationalizing, if not necessarily a unifying, impact on Canadian politics. For example, even though Quebec was not a party to the constitutional accord, the 1982 Canadian Charter of Rights and Freedoms and Supreme Court decisions based thereon still apply to that province.

In addition to its impact on the structure of the judiciary, the Charter is also having a significant effect on its composition. Because judicial appointments are made from those in the legal system and because, until recent decades, the legal profession has been male-dominated, the composition of the Canadian judiciary has never reflected the reality of Canadian society. As law schools and the legal profession opened their doors in recent years not only to women but also to various ethnic and racial minorities, the basis was laid for a more representative judiciary in the future.

The 1982 Charter provided a further impetus to such a development. One highly symbolic Supreme Court appointment was the selection on March 3, 1982 of Bertha Wilson as the first woman ever named to the apex of the Canadian judiciary. Justice Wilson has been followed to the Supreme Court by three further female justices: Claire L'Heureux-Dube (1987), Beverley McLachlin (1989), and Louise Arbour (1999). In addition, Madame Justice Beverley McLachlin began serving as Canada's first female Chief Justice of the Supreme Court in January 2000. Such appointments reflected the initial impact of the 1982 Charter, which protected the equality of men and women. How could an all-male Supreme Court maintain its legitimacy in deciding future cases involving matters of gender equality? Moreover, at the lower court levels representation of women is also gaining ground. By 1999, about 19 percent of the federal judicial appointments (from a total of about 1 000) were women, with the appointments of women in recent years reaching nearly 40 percent. In Alberta, the province's Court of Appeal had a majority of women (7 of 12) by 1999.

By the turn of the century, the composition of the judiciary was increasingly representative of the larger Canadian society. The impact of group claims on the judicial selection process was particularly noticeable at the lower court levels. For example, in January of 1994, federal Justice Minister Allan Rock selected two members of the Aboriginal community to serve as federal judges, thus increasing the number of Aboriginal federal judges to three. While it is

> If women lawyers and women judges through their differing perspectives on life can bring a new humanity to bear on the decision-making process, perhaps they will make a difference (Wilson, 1990: 10).

unlikely that the judiciary will ever be a "mirror-image" of the larger Canadian society, the representative nature of judicial appointments will continue to increase in the years ahead, due at least in part to the Charter. For example, in April of 1999 the provincial government of Quebec appointed the first black judge in that province's history.

The impact of the Charter with respect to the operation of the judiciary can be seen in terms of the kinds of cases that have been dealt with since its adoption in 1982. The vast array of cases so far have concerned the rights and privileges contained in the Charter and, of those, most have dealt with criminal cases. Given the volume of Charter-based cases, the following overview of several key cases is intended to give just a brief look at how the Charter can be used. In particular, these cases illustrate how some key political and civil liberties are protected and defined by the Charter, as well as suggesting the long-term political impact on the judicial branch of government.

Section 1 of the Charter (the **reasonable limits clause)** provides a general guarantee of rights and freedoms "set out in it subject only to such reasonable limits prescribed by law as can be demonstrably justified in a free and democratic society." In other words, rights and freedoms are fundamental, not absolute; they can be limited by the government, but only if such restrictions are "reasonable" and absolutely needed ("demonstrably justified"). Thus, governments that seek to restrict fundamental freedoms must be able to defend their actions to the judiciary.

> The gay community is a case study in how a stigmatized minority group can achieve dramatic political change without the support of vote-conscious politicians in the era of the Canadian Charter of Rights and Freedoms (Fine, 1992: A1).

The attempt to interpret the meaning of Section 1 was contained in a Supreme Court case in 1986 (*R. v. Oakes*). The so-called ***Oakes test*** has basically narrowed the latitude of governments wishing to invoke Section 1 as a means for limiting rights. Any violation of fundamental rights must be shown by the government to be justified by a "pressing and substantial" objective. Moreover, the means used to limit rights must be "proportional" to the ends sought. For example, censorship of films has been ruled to be acceptable as a reasonable limit, if the guidelines and criteria for such actions are clearly defined in law. However, the overall outcome of the *Oakes* test has been to minimize the willingness of governments to use Section 1 as a basis for restricting the existence and application of fundamental freedoms contained elsewhere in the Charter.

The democratic rights protected by Sections 3–5 of the Charter have produced relatively few court cases, although some are of particular relevance to the operation of Canadian elections. One extremely important area for the future impact of the Charter on the electoral process concerns the equality of population size of electoral constituencies (Knopff and Morton, 1992: 332–373; Courtney, Mackinnon, and Smith, 1992). Based on the voting rights guaranteed in Section 3 of the Charter, challenges were mounted against the existing provincial electoral redistributions in British Columbia (1989) and Saskatchewan (1991). The ultimate result was a Supreme Court decision on June 6, 1991, known as the ***Carter*** case, which fundamentally altered the nature of future provincial legislative electoral redistributions. While a rigid pattern of population equality was rejected by the

Supreme Court, electoral districts now had to be based on the "relative parity of voting power" to ensure the implementation of effective representation. The impact of the *Carter* case was to impose a redrawing of electoral constituencies for provincial legislatures across the country.

A series of legal rights are protected in Sections 7–14 of the Charter and have produced an avalanche of court challenges. Between 1982 and 1997, the Supreme Court ruled on 47 cases involving the legal rights contained in the Charter (Ostberg, 2000). In its initial impact, the Charter cases have dealt, to a large extent, with the question of procedural fairness in the Canadian justice system. For example, Section 8 of the Charter grants everyone the "right to be secure against unreasonable search or seizure." In a ruling in January of 1993, the Supreme Court determined that the power of Revenue Canada to gain search warrants to search homes and offices, including the wholesale seizure of documents, violated Section 8 of the Charter.

The right to a trial "within a reasonable time" has been the basis for having charges dismissed in several provinces. In Quebec, a Superior Court judge in November of 1983 quashed charges against seven current or former members of the RCMP who had been accused of stealing the PQ membership list back in 1973, because a decade (1973 to 1983) without a trial was deemed contrary to "within a reasonable time." In 1990, the Supreme Court of Canada, in the *Askov* ruling, decided that a period of six to eight months was a reasonable period of time in which to bring a defendant to trial. The impact of this decision was immediate and widespread: in Ontario alone between October 1990 and March 1992 about 50 000 criminal cases were dropped because of trial delays. In March of 1992, the Supreme Court, in a related judgment, indicated that the *Askov* ruling was only a guideline and that delays of longer than six to eight months did not automatically violate the Charter.

An interesting application of the Charter concerns Section 11, which states that a person has the right "to be presumed innocent unless proven guilty according to law." Under this protection, the so-called **reverse-onus clause** of the Narcotic Control Act (Section 8) was ruled unconstitutional by the Supreme Court of Canada (March 1986). Given that provision, a person accused of possessing a certain amount of drugs was assumed to be trafficking, unless he or she could prove otherwise. Previously, several provinces had already held that the "reverse-onus" provision was unacceptable under the Charter.

One of the most important cases considered to date by the Supreme Court of Canada concerns the testing of the cruise missile. The government of Pierre Trudeau agreed to let the American military carry out cruise missile tests over Canadian territory. However, a number of peace groups, led by Operation Dismantle, challenged the government's decision with respect to Section 7 of the Charter, which guarantees the "security of the person." Arguing that the cruise missile would increase the likelihood of nuclear war, thereby undercutting the security of the person, the peace groups challenged Ottawa's right to take such decisions, even in the areas of foreign policy and national defence. Ultimately, the Supreme Court of Canada rejected the view (May 1985) proposed by Operation Dismantle.

However, the significance of the cruise missile decision does not reside in whether or not the tests were allowed to go ahead, but in what the Supreme Court of Canada asserted was its right in making such a decision. The Supreme Court declared its prerogative to review cabinet decisions, a view which has potentially far-reaching implications for the scope of judicial review. The secrecy of cabinet decision making is no longer sacrosanct, since the judiciary can now review its results, including regulations and orders-in-council.

The "security of the person" provision of Section 7 also served as the basis for the Supreme Court's decision in January 1988 on the abortion question. The case concerned Dr. Henry Morgentaler and his associates, who had been convicted of performing abortions, contrary to section 251 of the federal Criminal Code. On appeal to the high court, Morgentaler argued that the abortion law violated the rights and security of the person of the pregnant woman. The Supreme Court agreed and declared Canada's abortion law to be unconstitutional, setting off another round of emotional political controversy on the issue.

This brief overview of some of the important court decisions based on the Charter reveals the significant current impact, as well as the potential future effect, of the principle of full judicial review in the Canadian context. Certainly the role of the courts as the umpires of the federal system and interpreters of the Charter has been greatly enhanced. Protection of individual rights and procedural fairness of the justice system have been promoted, although the courts have been more modest in their explicit challenges to legislative supremacy. The number of cases involving Charter issues since 1982 has been substantial.

The long-term impact of the Charter has been to alter some of the traditional institutional and political relationships (e.g., the political role of the judiciary). In particular, the potential for a more activist judiciary, based on full judicial review, has not only been put into place, but has also been put into practice. For example, between 1982 and 1998, the Supreme Court declared unconstitutional 58 statutes, with 31 at the federal level and 27 pieces of legislation at the provincial level. How far this pattern continues to develop will depend, to a great extent, on how the judiciary itself interprets key provisions of the Charter of Rights and Freedoms. As one initial assessment declared, "we have put a little more faith in the courts and a little less faith in the people" (Mallory, 1984: 8). A decade later, the assessment of the changing role of the Canadian judiciary was more emphatic: "Although the Court has deferred to legislative policy choices in specific instances, it has shown little restraint in building up its own powers of judicial review or in asserting its own preeminent authority over the development of Charter-related constitutional principles" (Manfredi, 1993: 212). By the year 2001, the debate was no longer about the potential growth of judicial power, but about its effects (Morton and Knopff, 2000). As the title of a recent book put it, the judiciary was "supreme at last" (McCormick, 2000), perhaps reflected in the decision by *Time* magazine to name the Supreme Court of Canada the "Newsmaker of the Year" in 1999.

> What is wrong with the Charter Revolution? Most obviously, it weakens the practice of democracy. It displaces the policy judgments of elected governments by those of unelected judges. The former can be removed and their decisions reversed; not so the latter (Morton, 2000: B3).

The significant and still expanding role of the Canadian judiciary is based not only on the Charter and a more representative and activist bench, but also on public support and interest group litigation. Those *Canadians who are advantaged by the Charter and who see the Charter as a weapon in the overall political process* have been labelled **Charter Canadians**. The defenders of the Charter and the power it grants to the judiciary have been called the **Court Party**, that is, *the academic and legal partisans who seek to enhance the future impact of the Charter through the judiciary* (Morton and Knopff, 2000: 24–32). The result of such developments has been the emergence of a public debate about the proper role of the courts in the Canadian political process (Morton, 2000: B3). Regardless of the outcome of that debate, it is clear that the judicial branch has not only gained power, but will continue to do so in the years ahead.

THE COURT SYSTEM IN BRITAIN

The most important fact about the British judiciary is its traditional lack of direct involvement in the political process (Le Sueur, 1996). The practice of judicial review as utilized in Canada and the United States is unknown in the historical British polity: "The British judiciary may influence the legislature's actions, but cannot ultimately check its power" (Rasmussen, 1993: 50). Parliamentary supremacy has rendered unacceptable any exercise of full judicial review concerning the constitutionality of government actions. As long as the government is exercising the powers granted to it, no court will intervene. If a person or group does not like the law, then the opportunity exists to change the law or to replace the lawmakers with new ones through the electoral mechanism.

In addition to the impact of parliamentary supremacy, the traditional unitary structure of the British political system has also eliminated the need for the exercise of a pattern of limited judicial review, as used historically in Canada. Since there is no division of powers between levels of government, there is obviously no logical or practical basis for delineating their respective powers. However, the significant constitutional reforms of the late 1990s, with respect to devolution and the creation of a quasi-federal state, have introduced changes which have begun to form a base for very limited judicial review in Britain. Now that Westminster shares power with other parliaments in Scotland, Wales, and Northern Ireland, disputes are bound to emerge over which government can exercise which powers. While the British Parliament can still ultimately change the political rules of the game if necessary, it now shares responsibilities with other governments — disagreements will inevitably arise. Some of the disagreements will be handled administratively: most government departments in Whitehall have created special devolution or constitutional units to deal with such matters (Hazell et al., 2000: 258). Constitutionally, a new court has been created within the Judicial Committee of the Privy Council to adjudicate the evolving devolution disputes (Hazell and Sinclair, 1999: 177). Thus, while the traditional role of the judiciary is still limited, its political role has begun to expand (Budge et al., 1998: 480–484), because of the impact of devolution (Laffin, 2000).

In addition to devolution, a second change has expanded the future of the court system in Britain, that is, the Human Rights Act of 1998, which incorporated (in October 2000) the **European Convention on Human Rights (ECHR**) (Hazell et al., 2000: 253–254). All legislation in Britain must now be certified by the government that it is in accord with the ECHR. If the government does not do so or if the government's certification is challenged, then it becomes possible for the judiciary to become involved — that is, the establishment of a pattern of judicial review.

Instead of settling such possible questions of constitutionality, British courts have been traditionally involved in interpreting executive or legislative actions in light of their statutory or legal basis (Oliver, 1989; Woodhouse, 1995: 405). For example, in September 2000 a British court was asked to rule on whether or not Siamese twins should be medically separated despite their parents' objections. Without an operation, both twins would most likely die; with the operation, one would most likely live. In such cases, if the executive or legislature has overstepped the authority granted to it (i.e., its statutory power), the judiciary may order a halt to such behaviour.

> ... the raw theory of parliamentary sovereignty, so often invoked as the rationale of judicial subordination, quickly crumbles at the edges when exposed to daylight . . . . In the British context . . . , judges do play a small but significant part in patrolling the boundaries of government (Drewry, 1992: 12, 25).

In a similar vein, if proper administrative procedures have not been followed, the courts may nullify government actions. For example, in October of 1992 the Conservative government of John Major unilaterally announced the immediate closing of 31 coal pits by British Coal. Because of the public outcry, this order was quickly modified, and it was then announced that only 10 pits would close, and that the fate of the other 21 would be reviewed. However, a ruling by the High Court (December 1992) overturned the government's decision to close the coal pits. In the opinion of the High Court, the government had acted "unlawfully and irrationally" because the miners had not been granted their required right of consultation in such matters. However, as long as government behaviour has a statutory basis, the courts will not become involved.

Even if executive or legislative actions are overturned, the government may simply pass retroactive legislation, giving itself authority for its previous behaviour and thus bypassing the court ruling. The consequence of a traditional pattern of neither limited nor full judicial review has kept the political role of Britain's third branch of government modest indeed (Drewry, 1992). As one author concluded: "Britain has parliamentary supremacy, the United States has judicial supremacy . . ." (Rasmussen, 1993: 132).

The organization of the judiciary in Britain is complex, divided down into both civil and criminal courts. Included in the civil court wing are the county courts and family courts, while at the bottom of the criminal court structure are the justices of the peace and the juvenile courts. Although there is no supreme court in Britain, appeals from the top civil and criminal courts may be sent to the House of Lords if they involve a matter of general public importance. Technically, the appeal is to Parliament, but the House of Lords has been given the specific judicial function of interpreting the laws of Parliament. However, the

Lords in general do not hear such appeals; they are only heard by the Lord Chancellor and the Law Lords (technically, the Lords of Appeal in Ordinary). The Lord Chancellor is a member of the government and thus changes when there is a government turnover. The Lord Chancellor and prime minister together share the responsibility for selecting members from the legal profession for judicial posts. The British court system operates under the principle of judicial independence; the judges are selected by the executive, and they may be removed for cause. For example, in 1983, a High Court judge, who had been caught smuggling whisky and cigarettes into Britain, was dismissed from office — the first British judge to be so treated in more than a century.

Given the traditional but changing pattern of no judicial review of government actions and neither a written constitution nor a specific charter of rights, the British polity continues to utilize a very different mechanism than either Canada or the United States to protect basic civil and political liberties. Instead of delineating citizens' rights in a bill of rights or a charter of rights, in Britain individuals are given all rights not denied them by law (Coxall and Robins, 1994: 316–319). Thus, British citizens enjoy such basic rights as freedom of speech and assembly, even though they have been traditionally unspecified in law.

THE AMERICAN JUDICIARY

In no other political system does the judicial branch of government play as significant or controversial a role as it does in the American system. The basic reason for such a pattern is the exercise of full judicial review by the American court system: "Judicial review is the authority of judges to interpret the Constitution and to refuse to enforce measures that, in their opinion, are in conflict with the Constitution . . ." (Peltason, 1997: 29). This tremendous power of full judicial review was not contained in Article III of the American Constitution, but developed from the initial assertion of judicial power by Chief Justice John Marshall in the famous case of **Marbury vs. Madison** in 1803. While the details of the case are complex, the result was the acceptance of the view that the courts are the official interpreters of constitutional matters in the American system. The political consequences of this development have been extremely significant, for they have made the court system in the United States more politically oriented and more powerful than the judiciary in any other democratic polity.

> The American ideal of democracy lives in constant tension with the American ideal of judicial review in the service of individual liberties. It is a tension that sometimes erupts in crisis (Bork, 1986: 5).

STRUCTURE AND COMPOSITION

The structure of the American court system is federalized in the extreme. Unlike the Canadian court system, which creates a hierarchical and unified structure of federal and provincial courts, the American court system has a complete set of both federal and state courts. Moreover, the large municipalities may have their own court system, thus further decentralizing the judicial structure. The jurisdiction of these court systems stems from the powers granted each level of government by the Constitution: federal courts hear cases involving the powers of the national government, while state courts generally consider all other matters. Some areas of jurisdiction may be shared, thus allowing the accused to be tried in either the state or federal courts, but not in both for the same wrongdoing. At the apex of the judiciary stands the American Supreme Court, which under Article III (Section 2) hears cases involving the national government or matters of dispute between citizens and governments in two or more states. Cases tried in the state courts can only be appealed from the state supreme courts to the national Supreme Court if they involve important matters of constitutional law under federal jurisdiction.

Composition of both the American federal and state court systems is patronage-based and politically motivated to an even greater extent than in Canada. For example, the creation of federal judgeships is a legislative prerogative, although the president nominates, with the advice and consent of the Senate, the individuals to fill the federal judicial positions. If Congress and the presidency are controlled by different parties, then a stalemate over new positions is likely. Moreover, if a presidential election is on the horizon, the majority party in Congress may wait to see if it is also able to win control of the executive branch, thus enhancing its patronage powers. For example, the Democratically controlled Congress refused to authorize any new judgeships for Republican President Gerald Ford (1974–1977), but was willing to create 152 new federal posts for his successor, Democratic President Jimmy Carter (1977–1981).

Once the judgeships have been established, the composition of the courts is further politically influenced because of the party basis of judicial selection. The overwhelming percentage of federal judicial appointments are from the same party as the president, with the average rate of partisan selection around 90 percent. For Ronald Reagan's two terms (1981–1989), 94 percent of the judges appointed were Republican; in total, he appointed 346 lifetime federal judges. During George Bush's one-term presidency (1989–1993), 89 percent of his judicial nominees were Republican. A similar percentage (88 percent) of partisan judicial appointments were made by Democratic President Bill Clinton during his two terms in office (1993–2001).

Since federal judicial appointments are held for life, judges often retire early or stay on the job, despite ill health, in an attempt to get a successor to their position modelled on their own image. Thus, a Democratic judge will seek to retire when a Democratic president is in office or will hold onto the judgeship in the hopes that the next president is a Democrat. For example, Supreme Court Justice William O. Douglas, a liberal-Democrat who had been appointed by Franklin D. Roosevelt, tried to stay on the bench, despite grave health problems, so as to let a Democrat appoint his successor. However, Justice Douglas was unsuccessful and resigned in 1975, thus allowing Republican President Gerald Ford to name John Paul Stevens to the Supreme Court. Similarly, Justice Thurgood Marshall, the first African-American to be appointed to the Supreme Court, failed in his efforts to outlast the Reagan-Bush era and resigned because of ill health in 1991. Justice Marshall's replacement, Clarence Thomas, was nominated by President George Bush in July of 1991, thereby replacing a liberal Democrat with a conservative Republican on the American Supreme Court.

Federal judicial appointments are highly political because of the practice of senatorial courtesy. Based on custom rather than on law, **senatorial courtesy** is *the right of a senator to reject a federal court nominee for a judicial posting in his or her state.* This customary veto power is especially strong when the senator has the same political affiliation as the president. Moreover, senatorial courtesy is a good example of the political interdependence created by the separation of powers principle: the executive recommends the nominee that the Senate accepts or rejects to fill a vacancy in the judicial structure. The practice of senatorial courtesy can be used to deny a judicial posting not just on partisan grounds, but on ideological and socio-political ones as well. Those of liberal or conservative persuasions tend to have an abiding affinity for their own kind; in patronage-inspired appointments, opposites repel.

While federal judges are appointed, many judicial posts are filled by election (nonpartisan) at the state and local levels. For example, in January of 1993, the former Minnesota Viking, pro football star Alan Page, became the first African-American to serve on the Minnesota Supreme Court, after winning the judicial election the previous November.

The most significant aspect of electing judges relates to its impact on the principle of judicial independence. Most court systems assume that an appointed judiciary will be insulated from political pressure. However, the various reform movements in American politics, such as Jacksonian democracy of the 1830s, viewed an appointed judiciary as a bastion of elite influence that had to be brought under public control. Electing judges would free the courts from elite manipulation and possible corruption, increasing their independence from big-business interests.

Judicial election was designed to enhance judicial independence from the special interest groups in society; at the same time, the judiciary was to be made more responsible to the people. If citizens do not like a judge's rulings, then they can try to beat that judge electorally the next time he or she seeks office. For example, in Ohio in July 1985 a judge ruled that an eight-year-old girl had consented to sexual acts. Outraged individuals and parent groups sought his resignation and started to work against his re-election plans. In California, senior judges face a periodic referendum in order to stay in office. In 1986, after nine years on the judiciary, the Chief Justice of the state Supreme Court, Rose Bird, was thrown out of office by a 2 to 1 vote, mainly because of her consistent rulings against capital punishment. However, in practice judicial election has rarely interfered with the principle of judicial independence.

For those judges who are appointed, removal from office can occur through two processes: death or impeachment. In the latter and, some would say, more difficult method, the legislature may remove a judge (or any other civil officer of the United States) for improper conduct. Impeachment, however, is not used to make the judiciary politically accountable for its decisions. Technically, impeachment means bringing charges of wrongdoing against an official before the House of Representatives. If the impeachment resolution passes, then the Senate sits as a court to hear evidence and to possibly convict the accused. If convicted by the Senate, individuals are removed from office, at which point they may be prosecuted as any other citizens would be. For example, in August of 1985 the House of Representatives voted 17 articles of impeachment against U.S. District Judge Alcee Hastings of Miami by a vote of 413 to 3. By 2001, a total of 15 federal judges had been impeached.

The structure and composition of the American Supreme Court can be described with respect to its size and method of appointment. The size of the Supreme Court is currently nine, a number determined by the legislature. There have been politically motivated attempts to change this number, the most famous being Franklin D. Roosevelt's court-packing plan of the late-1930s. In responding to the exigencies of the Great Depression, the federal government sought to lead in the revitalization of the American economy. However, a number of laws giving the national government the power to act were held to be unconstitutional by the Supreme Court. By enlarging the size of the Supreme Court, President Roosevelt felt that he could tip the balance of judicial opinion in his favour. The court-packing plan failed to gain approval, but shortly thereafter the Supreme Court started upholding the constitutionality of Roosevelt's key economic programs. The Supreme Court usually follows the election returns, even if somewhat belatedly.

In general, appointments to the Supreme Court are less blatantly partisan than those to the federal courts, although political considerations are not entirely removed (Table 5.2). Rather than partisanship, ideology is a leading criterion in nominations to the highest court, as are ethnic, racial, and other socio-political attributes. These factors are not legally required, but based on custom and convention. For example, the major religious groups often receive appointments, with an attempt made to select at least one Catholic and one Jewish justice. Justice Thurgood Marshall, appointed by President Lyndon Johnson in 1967, was the first African-American named to the Supreme Court, and President Reagan placed the first woman, Sandra Day O'Connor, on the Supreme Court in 1981.

During the 1984 presidential campaign, the nature of future Supreme Court appointments became an issue. Because several justices were ill and approaching possible retirement, the person winning the 1984 race might be able to appoint three to four justices to the Supreme Court. President Reagan favoured strict constructionists who conceived a narrow role for the courts. From Reagan's perspective, the judiciary should not "pre-empt legislative prerogatives or become vehicles for political action or social experimentation." The

Table 5.2 The American Supreme Court 2002		
Justices	*Appointed by*	*Year*
William H. Rehnquist	Nixon	1971
Chief Justice	Reagan	1986
John Paul Stevens	Ford	1975
Sandra Day O'Connor	Reagan	1981
Antonin Scalia	Reagan	1986
Anthony M. Kennedy	Reagan	1988
David H. Souter	Bush	1990
Clarence Thomas	Bush	1991
Ruth Bader Ginsburg	Clinton	1993
Stephen Breyer	Clinton	1994

contrary point of view was expressed by Justice William Brennan, who stated that so-called conservative or strict constructionists "have no familiarity with the historical record."

President Reagan's 1984 re-election meant that he was able to appoint two additional justices (Antonin Scalia in 1986 and Anthony M. Kennedy in 1987) to the Supreme Court, as well as elevating William Rehnquist to the position of Chief Justice in 1986. During the presidency of George Bush, two additional Supreme Court appointments were made (David H. Souter and Clarence Thomas). Thus, by 1994 eight of the nine Supreme Court justices, as well as the Chief Justice, had been selected by Republican presidents. The first Supreme Court nomination (1993) made by President Bill Clinton barely maintained a Democratic party presence on the Supreme Court. The appointment of Ruth Bader Ginsburg, who has been often described as a pioneering advocate of women's rights, was the first Supreme Court selection made by a Democratic president since 1967. Moreover, Justice Ginsburg became the second woman ever appointed to the Supreme Court, as well as the first Jewish member since 1969. In 1994, President Clinton made his second Supreme Court appointment, Stephen G. Breyer. Thus, the Republicans retained a majority on the Supreme Court through President Clinton's two terms in office. Given the age of Chief Justice Rehnquist and several other of the Republican nominees, the 2000 presidential election results may change the future partisan composition of the Supreme Court. However, given the 50/50 partisan split in the Senate after the 2000 contest followed by the defection of Republican Senator James Jeffords in May 2001, it is unlikely that George W. Bush will be able to nominate and get confirmed any strongly conservative judges for the Supreme Court. Consequently, the elderly judges may decide to stay on the Court until after the 2002 Congressional elections.

Although presidential nominees to the Supreme Court must receive Senate approval, the custom of senatorial courtesy does not apply. The Senate has traditionally approved the presidential recommendation, as long as the individual was deemed qualified. For example, President Nixon had two nominees rejected by the Senate, not because they were conservative and the Senate was liberal, but because they were deemed not to be among the best-qualified conservatives available. However, the Senate nomination battles over Supreme Court nominees Robert Bork (1987) and Clarence Thomas (1993) clearly showed an increasing politicization and polarization of the judicial selection process. By 2001, only 29 nominees for the Supreme Court (out of a grand total of 138 judges who had ever been nominated) had been rejected by the Senate. Once appointed, Supreme Court justices may be removed by impeachment and conviction, but no justice has ever been so treated and removed from office (one justice was impeached, but not convicted).

The political nature of American Supreme Court appointments is clearly demonstrated by the case of Clarence Thomas. Nominated by President George Bush to fill the vacancy created by the retirement of Justice Thurgood Marshall in 1991, Clarence Thomas would become the second African-American to serve on the Supreme Court. Denying that there was a guaranteed position for an African-American on the Court, President Bush maintained that Clarence Thomas was the "best man for the job." An African-American conservative Republican was being named to replace an icon of the liberal wing of the Democratic party, and the nomination of Clarence Thomas split the African-American community in terms of support. Major civil rights groups, for example, opposed his nomination. Interest groups, both pro and con, mobilized across the country.

Initially it looked like Clarence Thomas would be confirmed, although with substantial opposition in the Senate. However, during the weekend before the

> When Clarence Thomas's nomination was announced, the Republicans desperately wanted a black conservative in the post — and Patricia Ireland, president of the National Organization of Women declared, "We're going to bork him" (Moore, 1993: D5).

scheduled confirmation vote, the news media reported that law professor Anita Hill, one of Thomas's former colleagues, had accused Clarence Thomas of sexual harassment. In dramatic testimony carried live on national television, Professor Hill detailed her allegations, which were vehemently denied by the nominee. The controversy split the nation, although, at the time, public opinion favoured the Thomas nomination. Eventually, the Senate, in a close vote (52–48), approved the nomination of Clarence Thomas to the Supreme Court of the United States (Phelps and Winternitz, 1992; Chrisman and Allen, 1992).

The battles over Supreme Court appointments need to be understood in terms of their larger political contexts; such conflicts are both party-based and ideologically-based (Gimpel and Wolpert, 1995: 81). From the 1930s through the 1970s, the Supreme Court was typically dominated by Democratic appointments with liberal political outlooks. Republican presidents (Nixon, Reagan, Bush) tried to change both the party and ideological basis of the Supreme Court. When they attempted to do so, the liberal Democratic majority in the Senate tried to stop the Republican presidents by using the confirmation process as their weapon of choice. The partisan political climate forced President Clinton to adopt a different strategy. While recommending Democrats, President Clinton chose moderate or "centrist" candidates (i.e., Ruth Bader Ginsburg, Stephen G. Breyer), who would easily receive Senate confirmation. As a result, national political battles over Supreme Court nominees were absent during President Clinton's two terms in office.

OPERATION AND CONSEQUENCES

The operation of the American court system is based on the principles of judicial independence and *stare decisis*, with the Supreme Court standing as the highest court of appeal. Judicial independence is sometimes challenged, particularly when individuals or groups disagree with the content of court rulings. A movement may be undertaken to remove a particular judge, such as the attempt to impeach Chief Justice Earl Warren in the 1960s, or to overturn a court decision by passing new legislation to make a judicial interpretation inapplicable. The most blatant attempts in political memory to threaten judicial independence were evident in the Watergate episode, particularly the suggestion by the Nixon White House that they might ignore adverse court rulings, even those coming from the Supreme

Court itself. The second operating principle, that of ***stare decisis*** *(rule of precedent)*, helps to provide a degree of continuity in a judicial system with over 800 federal judges and about 10 000 members of the judiciary in total.

Several unique aspects of judicial operation are characteristic of the American court system. First, before a case can be taken to court the individual or group must be recognized as having **standing to sue**, that is, *a direct and immediate interest in a case.* In the American legal system, only those who are directly affected by a law or government action have the right to challenge it in court. Trumped up cases or those designed simply to allow judicial involvement do not have standing to sue and are rejected by the courts. The courts will only consider **justiciable disputes**, that is, *real cases that are capable of being settled by legal methods.* A second unique aspect relates to the nature of the cases presented: a law or government action can only be challenged after it has been implemented. The American judiciary does not give advisory or reference opinions on hypothetical cases. If the executive or legislature is unsure of the constitutionality of a proposed bill, the only thing they can do is to pass it into law and be prepared for possible judicial intervention at a later date. Third, the Supreme Court itself decides which cases it will hear from the approximately 7 500 presented to it annually for possible consideration. In recent years, only about 100 a year are selected and these are the cases the justices feel have broad public and constitutional significance.

The crucial element in the operation of the American judiciary is the previously explained principle of full judicial review, the basic reason for the often extensive political impact of court decisions. The pattern of full judicial review has given to the Supreme Court an inherent policy-making role, so that major areas of political conflict become matters for judicial, rather than executive or legislative, resolution. For example, in a dispute over racial equality in the city schools and the related issue of busing to achieve racial balance, the city of

> Scarcely any political question arises in the United States that is not resolved, sooner or later, into a judicial question (Alexis de Tocqueville, 1835).

Boston literally had its school system supervised for 11 years (1975–1985) by Federal Judge W. Arthur Garrity. Such day-to-day judicial policy-making is unique to the American system. In total, from 1798 to 2000, 159 federal pieces of legislation passed by Congress have been declared unconstitutional (out of a total of about 60 000 laws), as well as nearly 1 100 pieces of state legislation.

The exercise of full judicial review is particularly crucial in defence of the civil and political liberties established by the American Bill of Rights. Initially, the Bill of Rights applied only to the national government — no protection was given to the citizen from the state governments. This pattern began to change significantly in the 1920s, when the Supreme Court, in an exercise of judicial power perhaps only surpassed by the *Marbury v. Madison* decision of 1803, asserted the applicability of fundamental freedoms to all levels of government. This use of the power of judicial review had the effect of nationalizing the American Bill of Rights, thus providing the political basis for an even more activist Supreme Court in American politics in later decades.

The American judiciary, backed by the various checks and balances, operating under the principle of full judicial review, composed of judges often willing to exercise their potential for power, and repeatedly jump-started into action by a litigious citizenry, has played a significant and, at times, crucial part in the political process. This combination of factors has given the American Supreme Court a powerful and "often decisive role" in the polity, while at the same time making it the most "unique judicial body in the world" (Oddo, 1979: v). The definitive example of this point for many decades to come will be the Supreme Court's decisions in the Florida presidential vote count in November and December of 2000: the Republican members of the Supreme Court in effect selected Republican George W. Bush as president of the United States.

COMPARING JUDICIARIES

In considering the nature of the judicial branch of government in the democratic polities of Canada, Britain, and the United States, four factors have been analyzed as the bases of comparison: the structure, composition, operation, and consequences of the court systems. Such comparisons stress the role of the judiciary in the political process with respect to three areas: politics, patronage, and policy. Contrary to the legitimating myth of their non-involvement in the political arena, the judiciaries in democratic polities are intimately involved in political conflicts and the struggle for power and influence. The principle of judicial independence has not transformed the third branch of government into a political eunuch, impotent in its relationship with the executive and legislature.

The political nature of the judiciary is clearly evident with respect to the process of judicial selection: in most cases, the court system remains a bastion of political patronage in a democratic era. Judges are often created from among those individuals with past or present partisan ties. Such a criterion does not automatically produce either good or bad judges, for partisan affiliation is not necessarily a causal factor of judicial competence. Probably the most debilitating effect of a patronage-based selection process for judicial appointments is its impact on the legitimacy of judicial power in the eyes of the public. Since the effectiveness of a court ruling is heavily dependent on the public's acceptance of the judicial decision, any factor that undercuts the legitimacy of the judiciary should be a prime area for political reform.

Judges and their actions are also political because of the ideological views brought by them to the bench, beliefs which serve as an important factor in the process and content of judicial interpretation. Since judges typically serve long terms of office, these views may continue to have a political impact long after the politicians who appointed the judges have disappeared from the political landscape. Moreover, individual judicial temperament is also an ingredient in producing a pattern of judicial activism or judicial restraint. Some judges are willing to exercise their constitutional powers to the fullest, at times even expanding them, while other judges are content to take a narrow view of their own political role.

Finally, judges are political with respect to their constitutionally-defined roles, which can range from no judicial review, to limited judicial review, to full judicial review. The particular type of judicial review helps to create a specific style of judicial activism or judicial restraint: the greater the powers of judicial review, the greater is the potential for an activist judiciary. Whatever the type of judicial review, the court system is a political player that is sometimes given a bit part and on other occasions a leading role in the polity.

SUMMARY

1. The judicial branch of government is a significant political actor, especially in Anglo-American democratic polities. Basic operating principles of a democratic judiciary include the concept of judicial independence and the interpretive guideline of *stare decisis*.

2. The power of judicial review has expanded the power and political significance of the court system in most democratic polities. Configurations of judicial review can range from its traditional absence in Britain, to a limited judicial review process in Canada (1867–1982), to a full pattern of judicial review as in the United States. The type of constitutionally prescribed pattern of judicial review helps to create patterns of either judicial activism or judicial restraint.

3. The Canadian court system is patronage-based and hierarchically organized, even though responsibility for it is shared by the federal and provincial governments. Since 1949, the Supreme Court of Canada has become the highest appeals court, replacing the Judicial Committee of the Privy Council in Britain. Appointed by the federal government, the Supreme Court is sometimes viewed with suspicion by the provinces who are reluctant to take federal-provincial disputes into the court system. Operating historically under the principles of limited judicial review and judicial self-restraint, the judicial branch has nevertheless had significant political consequences for the Canadian polity. Judicial interpretations, for example, have been an important ingredient in the evolving pattern of federal-provincial power. However, with respect to judicial protection of civil and political liberties, the Canadian historical pattern leaves much to be desired.

4. The 1982 Canadian Charter of Rights and Freedoms has expanded the principle of full judicial review and produced, as a consequence, an increasingly activist judiciary. The Canadian Supreme Court is inexorably following the American pattern, as the effect of the Charter enhances the judiciary's relevance and power. Charter Canadians and the Court Party will expand the power of the judiciary even further in the years ahead.

5. Given the principle of parliamentary sovereignty, judicial review is unknown in the historical British context. While courts will rule on whether executive or legislative actions are within the statutory powers of these two branches of government, a redress of grievances in Britain must be politically, rather than judicially, obtained. However, with devolution and the European Convention on Human Rights, the bases have been provided for at least a pattern of limited judicial review in the British system.

6. The most powerful judiciary in any democratic system is the American judiciary, which is also the one most widely selected on the basis of patronage. The custom of senatorial courtesy gives the national legislature control of most federal court appointments, while at the state and local levels a majority of states now elect their judges. The structure of the American court system is federalized, with a complete set of both state and federal courts. The highest court of appeal is the United States Supreme Court, which has often played a significant political role, given the principle of full judicial review. As a consequence, the American judiciary is activist in outlook and intimately involved in the political process, often taking the lead in new areas of public concern, especially when the executive or legislature is reluctant to do so.

CONCEPT FILE

adversary (fight) system of justice
Canadian Judicial Council
Carter case
Charter Canadians
Court Party (Canada)
due process of law
European Convention on Human
    Rights (ECHR)
federalized judicial structure
full judicial review
guardianship role
injunction
judicial activism
Judicial Committee of the Privy
    Council (JCPC)

judicial independence
judicial restraint
judiciary's guardianship role
justiciable disputes
legal immunity
limited judicial review
Marbury vs. Madison (1803)
Oakes test
political immunity
reasonable limits clause
reference (advisory) cases
reverse-onus clause
senatorial courtesy
standing to sue
stare decisis (rule of precedent)

RECOMMENDED READINGS

The Nature of Judicial Power

ABRAHAM, HENRY J. (1998) *The Judicial Process: An Introductory Analysis of the Courts of the United States, England, and France.* 7th ed. Oxford: Oxford University Press.

ASZENSTAT, JANET (1997) "Reconciling Parliament and Rights: A.V. Dicey Reads the Canadian Charter of Rights and Freedoms," *Canadian Journal of Political Science,* Volume 30, Number 4, pp. 645–662.

CARDOZO, BENJAMIN (1921) *The Nature of the Judicial Process.* New Haven: Yale University Press.

EPP, CHARLES R. (1998) *The Rights Revolution: Lawyers, Activists, and Supreme Courts in Comparative Perspective.* Chicago: University of Chicago Press.

JACOB, HERBERT et al. (1996) *Courts, Law and Politics in Comparative Perspective.* New Haven, Conn.: Yale University Press.

HOLLAND, KENNETH, ed. (1991) *Judicial Activism in a Comparative Perspective.* New York: St. Martin's Press.

National Council of Welfare (2000) *Justice and the Poor.* Ottawa: Minister of Public Works and Government Services.

NELSON, WILLIAM E. (2000) *Marbury v. Madison: The Origins and Legacy of Judicial Review.* Lawrence, Kansas: University Press of Kansas.

WOLFE, CHRISTOPHER (1986) *The Rise of Modern Judicial Review.* New York: Basic Books.

The Canadian Judicial System

BOLDT, MENNO and J. ANTHONY LONG, eds. (1985) *The Quest for Justice: Aboriginal Peoples and Aboriginal Rights.* Toronto: University of Toronto Press.

FRIEDLAND, MARTIN L. (1995) *A Place Apart: Judicial Independence and Accountability in Canada.* Ottawa: Canadian Judicial Council.

HIEBERT, JANET (1996) *Limiting Rights: The Dilemma of Judicial Review.* Montreal: McGill-Queen's University Press.

MCCORMICK, PETER (2000) *Supreme at Last: The Evolution of the Supreme Court of Canada.* Toronto: James Lorimer and Company.

MORTON, F.L. and RAINER KNOPFF (2000) *The Charter Revolution and the Court Party.* Peterborough, Ontario: Broadview Press.

OSTBERG, C.L. (2000) "Charting New Territory? Fifteen Years of Search and Seizure Decisions by the Supreme Court of Canada, 1982–1997," *The American Review of Canadian Studies,* Volume 30, Number 1, pp. 35–54.

RUSSELL, PETER (1975) "The Political Role of the Supreme Court of Canada in its First Century," *Canadian Bar Review,* Volume 53, pp. 584–595.

SMITH, MIRRIAM (2000) "Political Activism, Litigation, and Public Policy: The Charter Revolution and Lesbian and Gay Rights in Canada, 1985–99," *International Journal of Canadian Studies,* Volume 21, pp. 81–109.

SNELL, JAMES G. and FREDERICK A. VAUGHAN (1985) *The Supreme Court of Canada: History of the Institution.* Toronto: University of Toronto Press.

The Court System in Britain

BLACKBURN, ROBERT (1999) *Towards a Constitutional Bill of Rights for the United Kingdom.* London: Pinter.

CRICK, BERNARD (1989) "The State of Our Civil Liberties," *The Political Quarterly*, Volume 60, Number 3, pp. 262–272.

DREWRY, GAVIN (1992) "Judicial Politics in Britain: Patrolling the Boundaries," *West European Politics*, Volume 15, Number 3, pp. 9–28.

EWING, K.D. and C.A. GEARTY (1990) *Freedom under Thatcher: Civil Liberties in Modern Britain.* Oxford: Clarendon Press.

FLINDERS, MATTHEW (2001) "Mechanisms of Judicial Accountability in British Central Government," *Parliamentary Affairs*, Volume 54, Number 1, pp. 54–71.

GRIFFITH, J.A.G. (1997) *The Politics of the Judiciary.* 5th ed. London: Fontana.

RIDLEY, F.F. (1984) "The Citizen against Authority: British Approaches to the Redress of Grievances," *Parliamentary Affairs*, Volume 37, Number 1, pp. 1–32.

STERETT, SUSAN (1994) "Judicial Review in Britain," *Comparative Political Studies*, Volume 26, Number 4, pp. 421–442.

STEVENS, R. (1993) *The Independence of the Judiciary.* Oxford: Oxford University Press.

WOODHOUSE, DIANA (1995) "Politicians and the Judiciary: A Changing Relationship," *Parliamentary Affairs*, Volume 48, Number 3, pp. 401–417.

The American Judiciary

ABRAHAM, HENRY J. (1996) *The Judiciary: The Supreme Court in the Governmental Process.* 10th ed. New York: Brown and Benchmark.

BAUM, LAWRENCE (1998) *The Supreme Court.* 6th ed. Washington, D.C.: CQ Press.

BOOT, MAX (1998) *Out of Order: Arrogance, Corruption, and Incompetence on the Bench.* New York: Basic Books.

LAZARUS, EDWARD (1998) *Closed Chambers: The First Eyewitness Account of the Epic Struggles inside the Supreme Court.* New York: Times Books.

MURPHY, WALTER E. (1986) "Who Shall Interpret? The Quest for the Ultimate Constitutional Interpreter," *The Review of Politics*, Volume 48, Number 3, pp. 401–423.

NAGEL, ROBERT F. (1994) *Judicial Power and American Character.* New York: Oxford University Press.

NEUBAUER, DAVID (1997) *Judicial Process: Law, Courts and Politics in the United States.* 2nd ed. Fort Worth, Texas: Harcourt Brace.

O'BRIEN, DAVID M. (2000) *Storm Center: The Supreme Court in American Politics.* 5th ed. New York: W.W. Norton and Company.

RYDEN, DAVID K., ed. (2000) *The U.S. Supreme Court and the Electoral Process.* Baltimore, Maryland: Georgetown University Press.

SCALIA, ANTONIN (1997) *A Matter of Interpretation: Federal Courts and the Law.* New Jersey: Princeton University Press.

SCHWARTZ, BERNARD (1995) *A History of the Supreme Court.* New York: Oxford University Press.

SIMON, JAMES F. (1996) *The Center Holds: The Power Struggle inside the Rehnquist Court.* New York: Touchstone, Simon and Schuster.

WOODWARD, BOB and SCOTT ARMSTRONG (1979) *The Brethren: Inside the Supreme Court.* New York: Simon and Schuster.

POLITICS ON THE NET

THE CANADIAN JUDICIARY: For the **Canadian Supreme Court**, go to *www.scc-csc.gc.ca*. This website contains information on the various justices and the background and operation of the Supreme Court. The **Federal Court of Canada**'s home page can be found at *www.fct-cf.gc.ca*, again with basic background information on structure and operation. The home pages for Canada's various courts can be found at *www.fja.gc.ca/en/index.html*, which is the site of the **Office of the Commissioner for Federal Judicial Affairs**. This site includes a detailed description of the federal judicial appointments process.

Basic information on the **Canadian Human Rights Commission** can be found at *www.chrc-ccdp.ca*. For the federal **Department of Justice**'s site see *canada.justice.gc.ca*. Information on the background, work, and decisions of the **Canadian Judicial Council** can be seen at its home page at *www.cjc-ccm.gc.ca*.

THE BRITISH JUDICIARY: For a good entry point in learning about the structure and work of the court system in Britain, go to *www.open.gov.uk* and then access "open.gov" and the "Topic index" provided. For Britain's highest court, select "**House of Lords –** Judicial Work and Judgments." This website includes a good description of the role of the House of Lords and its judicial functions, as well as access to its decisions in such recent actions as the *Pinochet* **case** (see its judgment for March 24, 1999). The role of the **Lord Chancellor** and his department can be studied at *www.open.gov.uk/lcd/ lcdhome.htm* and the **Court Service**, which provides administrative support for the Lord Chancellor, can be accessed at *www.courtservice.gov.uk*.

The British **Human Rights Act of 1998** can be found at *www.homeoffice.gov.uk/hract/hramenu.htm*. The work of the **Judicial Committee of the Privy Council** and its new role as the final court of appeal with respect to devolution issues can be located at *www.privy-council.org.uk/judicial-committee/index.htm*.

THE AMERICAN JUDICIARY: The **United States Supreme Court**'s official website is located at *www.supremecourtus.gov* and includes court opinions and orders, biographies of current justices, and basic information about the Supreme Court. For the home pages of the **federal judiciary**, go to *www.uscourts.gov*. An analysis of **FDR's court packing plan** can be found at *www.nara.gov/education/teaching/conissues/separat.html*. Supreme Court cases and opinions are referenced at *supct.law.cornell.edu/supct*. The **United States Department of Justice** has its website located at *www.usdoj.gov*.

PART 3 Political Processes and Political Behaviour

Source: The Canadian Press

The development of any institution . . . is a product of much more than rational thought. Accident, circumstance, the striving of politicians for political advantage, and technological and sociological change have all played an important role in shaping the evolution of the . . . system . . . . (Ceasar, 1979: 28)

It is not on political forms, it is on political forces that I dwell . . . . To really understand the character of social action, its modes of procedure must be studied in light of the character of those who apply them, and of the social and political conditions in which their wills are formed and manifested. (Ostrogorski, 1902)

The formal structures of government are only the scaffolding of power. They do not account for its human chemistry. (Smith, 1988: 42)

Political Culture and Political Socialization

National political communities do not simply exist "a priori" as objective realities. They must be invented. (Patten, 1999: 28)

National contexts greatly influence the practical significance of political universals. (Rose and Suleiman, 1981: preface)

Ultimately, we are governed by what we think . . . . Governing has much less to do with control of the bodies of people than it has with what is going on in their minds. (Schattschneider, 1969: 99)

The entire man is, so to speak, to be seen in the cradle of the child. (de Tocqueville, 1835)

CHAPTER PREVIEW

- Political beliefs form the content of a nation's political culture; they are examples of learned behaviour through the political socialization process.

- Each polity's political culture is unique, shaping both political structures and political functions.

- Political cultures differ with respect to their ideological content, to the role of the individual in the political process, and to their unity (integrated or fragmented).

- The Canadian political culture is characterized by the themes of elitism, regionalism, dualism, and continentalism. All four characteristics produce a fragmented political culture in Canada.

- The British political culture is traditionally seen as unified and consensual. However, growing social diversity, devolution of political power to Scotland and Wales, and major constitutional reforms to political institutions, such as the House of Lords, are transforming the British political tradition.

- The American political culture has always been integrated along nationalistic and patriotic lines. As with Britain and Canada, growing social diversity is altering the traditional American political landscape.

In the 2000 Canadian federal election, 12.8 million voters dutifully trudged to the polls to cast their ballots for their favourite (or the least objectionable) candidates and parties. Unless one makes the probably unwarranted assumption that such behaviour on the part of the Canadian voter is a reflection of inherited lemming-like traits, one is left with the basic question of all social scientific endeavour: why did this pattern occur? The answer appears deceptively simple: since human behaviour is learned, political behaviour is likewise the result of the learning process. Thus, the themes and values of a nation's political culture are learned. Each polity attaches a particular combination of meanings to its political structures and political practices (Jackman and Miller, 1996). An understanding of this subjective aspect of political action is necessary, for it provides the context within which the political system operates.

POLITICAL CULTURE: DEFINITION AND TYPES

As a concept that stresses the meaning of politics for the individual participants, as well as for the wider political community, **political culture** can be defined as *the attitudes and beliefs people have about the political system*: it is a "shorthand expression to denote the emotional and attitudinal environment within which the political system operates" (Kavanagh, 1972: 10). A political culture defines both the nature and scope of legitimate political activity and the individual's role in the polity. From the individual's perspective, his or her political self or political identity is a specific combination of the major themes of a country's political culture, while from the viewpoint of the political system, the political culture of a country is the total combination or mixture of political attitudes held by its members. A country's political culture reflects its history and shapes its future, while it influences the present operation of the polity.

Numerous ways of classifying political cultures have been developed. For our purposes, the most useful typologies are those that relate political culture to the role of the individual in the political process, focus on the degree of consensus in political values, or link political cultures to their ideological composition.

The role of the individual in the polity can be used as the basis for classifying political cultures as parochial, subject, or participant (Almond and Verba, 1965: 11–26). A **parochial political culture** is *one in which a specific political system has not developed and hence no particular political role has been assumed for the individual.*

In a sense, then, these systems are prepolitical. While no pure parochial cultures remain in the modern era, pockets of parochialism may exist within other systems. For example, a so-called national government in a capital city, headed by an autocrat, may have no relevance to isolated rural groups, which may remain either apolitical or parochial in outlook. In a **subject political culture**, the individual is aware of the specialized political structure, is affected by its decisions, such as paying taxes or serving in the army, and may accept the legitimacy of the system. The *role of the individual is a passive one, however, confined to obeying the decisions of the state.* A **participant political culture** is *one in which the person is given an explicit political role, with various opportunities provided for participation.*

All political cultures represent a mixture of parochial, subject, and participant orientations. For example, at the individual level, each person reflects a unique combination of political values as part of his or her political self, values that likely include subject ones (e.g., a willingness to obey laws), as well as participant ones (e.g., a desire to vote or to influence political leaders). At the system level, each political culture is mixed in the sense that different regions, classes, and ethnic groups may have varying conceptions of politics. Thus, one region might be classified as more participant or more subject in outlook than other regions in the same system. Generally speaking, democratic systems have participant political cultures, autocratic systems usually have a combination of subject and parochial values, and totalitarian systems stress subject orientations with participant values grafted on.

A second way of classifying political cultures is dependent on their degree of unity with respect to fundamental political values. On this basis, two types of political cultures can be identified, with many possible variations between these extremes. A **fragmented political culture** is *"one whose population lacks broad agreement upon the way in which political life should be conducted,"* while an **integrated political culture** has developed *a consensus about a core set of political beliefs* (Rosenbaum, 1975: 37–57).

> The sole function of a flag is to send a message . . . . In doing so, it forms the nation's premier graphic symbol, second in importance only to the nation's premier linguistic symbol — its name. Yet for nearly a century following Confederation Canadians lacked a national flag (Fraser, 1991: 64).

In a fragmented political culture, many people identify with governmental units other than the national government; patriotism and national identity are weak; distrust between the major socio-political groups is evident and often widespread; and the legitimacy of the existing political regime may be in question, as various sectors of the polity demand major changes in the social, economic, and political structure. Fragmentation may be based on such factors as race, religion, class, ethnicity, region, or language. When these various bases of fragmentation coalesce, conflict and violence may erupt, which further decreases the level of unity in the polity. Highly fragmented political cultures may spawn movements or parties that demand separation or independence from the larger political system. In contrast, an integrated political culture is characterized by identification with the national government; strong patriotic sentiments; a moderate to high level of social trust; acceptance of the existing social, political, and economic arrangements; and rare occurrences of open conflict and secessionist threats.

Fragmented political cultures are often associated with unstable political systems, for the bases of such fragmentation may be unresolvable through normal political processes. For example, questions of language, culture, and religion are often so intense that the political system may be torn asunder. Integrated political cultures have either dealt successfully with such issues in the past or they have managed to keep such issues from becoming focal points of contention. For example, the doctrine of the separation of church and state in Western society is one way of attempting to keep religious issues from becoming politicized. The fragmented or integrated nature of a country's political culture influences the way in which the political institutions are structured initially, as well as how they continue to function.

Our third way of analyzing political cultures focusses on their attitudinal and ideological composition: what are the specific beliefs that comprise their core elements? For example, such values as nationalism and social trust have often been seen as key elements of political culture. From a somewhat broader perspective, we might focus on a political culture's ideological mixture in terms of the major political ideas of the modern era: conservatism, liberalism, and socialism. The ideological approach to political culture emphasizes the content of beliefs, while the fragmented-integrated distinction focusses on the degree of consensus evident with respect to these fundamental political values.

> Even being a Canadian has become frightening. For more than a century, we were a blessedly bland people who did not bother to learn the words to our national anthem. Today, we are the Woody Allen of nations, a neurotic country caught up in a never-ending adolescent identity crisis (Josh Freed, quoted in Picard, 1995: A2).

Each of the three approaches to political culture suggests that a specific political culture will not only be complex, but also mixed, comprising a variety of values and beliefs not necessarily consistent with each other. What often happens is that *certain segments of a polity acquire a set of beliefs that distinguishes them from the dominant pattern*; we refer to such a pattern as a **political subculture**. These subcultures may be based on any of the major socioeconomic cleavages such as class, religion, race, and ethnicity, as well as on a particular ideology. *When such factors not only distinguish a group from the dominant pattern but also place the group in a specific geographical location*, then we refer to the subculture as a **regional political culture** (Landes, 1979). Some political cultures lack any subcultures, while others have many. Generally we would expect, for example, that integrated political cultures based on one dominant ideology would be unlikely to produce subcultures, while fragmented political cultures with a mixture of ideological beliefs might contain several distinctive subcultures.

THE CANADIAN POLITICAL CULTURE

The traditional pattern of core political beliefs in Canada can be summarized with respect to four major themes: elitism, regionalism, dualism, and continentalism. Each one has had a significant impact on the structure and operation of the political system. After analyzing these themes, we will discuss their interaction by taking a look at the nature and future of consociational politics in Canada.

CULTURAL THEMES

Theme number one: Elitism

Our first major theme is that of **elitism**, which can be defined as *a pattern of decision making in which "small groups of people . . . exercise considerable power"* (McMenemy, 1999: 95). While it is difficult to put an exact figure on the size of the elite, it is quite likely a very small group, based on any kind of percentage figure in comparison with the total population. For our purposes, an elite is a small group with both control over the crucial political resources and a willingness and ability to use such resources to determine the outcome of the decision-making process. Moreover, the elite is not a unified grouping but, as our definition indicates, is composed of a series of subgroupings. For example, democratic polities are usually seen as having a plurality of elites, which would, at least, include political, economic, and bureaucratic components. The exact nature of the Canadian elites — with respect to their structure, composition, and influence — is a controversial topic. However, observers agree on one conclusion: the various elites exercise considerable clout in the Canadian context (Panitch, 1981; Forcese, 1978; Presthus, 1973; Savoie, 2000).

Elitism is pervasive in the Canadian system, as is evident in the numerous actions by which governments can exempt themselves from the existing rules of the game. Even the 1960 Bill of Rights, for example, could have been bypassed if the government so wished, simply by the government declaring that a specific law was exempted from its protection (Bill of Rights, Part I, Section 2). The ability of the government to override certain protections in the Canadian Charter of Rights and Freedoms (Section 33) and to circumvent existing laws or to pass new regulations to protect itself from its own possible wrongdoings can only occur in a political system in which influence is centralized and accepted as legitimate by most people — in other words, in a polity characterized by elitism.

> In order that institutions may be stable and work harmoniously, there must be a power of resistance to the democratic element (George Etienne Cartier).

Consistent with an elitist pattern of control are deferential attitudes toward authority, limited means for citizen participation, and political structures that embody such values. Deferential views of authority can be seen in Canada's continuing ties to the monarchy and traditional forms of authority; after all, monarchical institutions are historically based on the assumption that a small group has a right to rule. It must also be remembered that the Fathers of Confederation were not fervent believers in democracy. Confederation itself was more of an attempt to stop democratic ideas from crossing the Canadian border than a means for the extension of the democratic ideal. The political system constructed in 1867 was federal, but it was a highly centralized structure in which few citizens participated. Indicative perhaps of what lay ahead were the methods used to create the new system: the "procedures restricted effective participation to a very small number of persons, and even symbolic participation by the voters was virtually excluded" (Stevenson, 1979: 45).

Although the polity has become democratized during the past century, as demonstrated best by the extension of the suffrage, few direct avenues for political participation are provided. Other than voting in federal, provincial, or local contests, most citizens rarely seek to influence their leaders between elections — an attitude and behaviour pattern encouraged by the political elite itself. Typical of the elite view of the public's participatory task is that expressed many times by former prime minister Pierre Trudeau: "[Trudeau] says that the role of the government is to govern, and the role of the public is to judge him on the quality of his performance when he chooses to call an election" (Stewart, 1971: 103). Such a description of the role of the public would seem to apply to Prime Minister Jean Chrétien also, as well as to premiers such as Lucien Bouchard and Mike Harris. Support for the practices of **direct democracy** (i.e., *citizens directly deciding public policy questions*), such as the initiative and recall, has traditionally been limited at the federal level of government, and in many provinces as well.

Such *a pattern of limited mass participation* has been classified as **quasi-participative politics** (Presthus, 1973: 38). A good example of quasi-participative politics can be seen in the rare use of the referendum: the public is only asked to decide on an issue when the elite chooses, but even when a referendum is held, the results do not legally bind a government to any specific policy. For example, in 1942 a national referendum was held over the conscription issue during the Second World War. The vote (80 percent in favour in the English-speaking provinces and 72 percent against in Quebec) only served, if it was necessary, to release Mackenzie King from his non-conscription promise. The next referendum in national politics was held 50 years later (October 26, 1992) on the Charlottetown Accord, which was overwhelmingly rejected by the public. A national referendum every half-century is unlikely to earn sustained praise from the advocates of direct democracy.

> Popular sovereignty receives here, as in every democracy, all the lip service it can desire. But it is not a self-assertive, obtrusive, gesticulative part of the national consciousness (Bryce, 1921: 42).

A number of historical developments have contributed to the traditional strength of elitist values in Canada. In addition to its continuing monarchical ties, Canada has never experienced a revolution, but instead has evolved slowly toward nationhood. The political culture of an evolutionary pattern of development is more conservative and traditional than a revolutionary society, perhaps best symbolized by the phrase in the 1867 Constitution Act that describes its purpose as "Peace, Order, and Good Government." Confederation was an act of counter-revolution, which sought to preserve the power of the elite. Moreover, such factors as the hierarchical class system (e.g., the Family Compacts); the nonegalitarian school system, dominated by the private schools such as Upper Canada College; religious groups, such as the Anglicans and Roman Catholics, which are hierarchically organized; and a weak sense of national identity have all helped to produce and to preserve elitist values in the Canadian context (Lipset, 1970: 1990). In particular, the government's parliamentary structure embodies and perpetuates elitism: "The effect of the British parliamentary system is to damp down the waves of public agitation" (Truman, 1971: 512).

Theme number two: Regionalism

The second major theme of the political culture is that of regionalism, a reflection of the fact that "nature and history have conspired to make geography central to the Canadian existence" (Schwartz, 1974: 1). Regionalism is both a cause and a consequence of the regional political cultures, producing different patterns of politics across the country (McCormick, 1989).

Regionalism is so pervasive that it is rarely overlooked; as such, it is a continuing political issue with respect to constitutional reform, as well as in relation to everyday political decisions (Savoie, 2000). Almost every major policy decision, whether it concerns employment insurance benefits, deficit reduction, military equipment and bases, or transfer payments, has differing consequences for the various regions of Canada. **Regionalism** refers to *the diversity of geographic factors and economic concerns that are politically important and are perceived as such by members of the political system.* However, it is sometimes difficult to specify precisely the nature of the regional units in the Canadian system. With few exceptions, most writers have assumed that the provinces, or some combination thereof, adequately delineate regional boundaries.

We should be aware, as well, that equating provinces and regions may lead us to neglect the extent of diversity within each provincial unit. The provinces themselves are not necessarily homogeneous in either socio-economic structure or in political attitudes. For example, considerable differences in quality of life and political values are evident between northern and southern Ontario, between northwestern and southeastern New Brunswick, between Cape Breton Island and mainland Nova Scotia, and between northeastern British Columbia and the crowded southern mainland. Such internal differences are true of every province, although they are minimal in the smallest province of Prince Edward Island.

The regional political cultures in Canada are, in effect, a series of political subcultures based around the territorially defined provincial units. These political subcultures reflect differences in the economic base of each region; their access to, and abundance of, natural resources; their rate of economic development and modernization; and the varying effects of urbanization and industrialization. The result of such factors has been to produce a series of regional economies. The various regions of Canada also differ with respect to their cultural, linguistic, and ethnic composition. English-French differences are important in Quebec, Ontario, and New Brunswick, but are less so in the remaining provinces. The idea of bilingualism in these three provinces may be popular and refers to the English and French languages. On the other hand, the two most useful languages to know in Cape Breton would be English and Gaelic, and in Saskatchewan, English and Ukrainian. The various regions also differ with respect to their religious composition and class structures.

The consequences of the regional economies and of the varying social and cultural makeup of each province have been the production of differences in political values and behaviour, that is, the creation of a series of regional political

It is imperative to take the initiative, to build firewalls around Alberta, to limit the extent to which an aggressive and hostile federal government can encroach upon legitimate provincial jurisdiction (Harper et al., 2001: A14).

cultures. Paralleling the variations in basic political orientations, the regional political cultures are also seen as composed of individuals with regional loyalties and identities. Regionalism implies a perceived commonality, that is, a regional consciousness among the individuals within each of the political units. In addition to being a major characteristic of the Canadian political culture, regionalism is also a valuable political resource, which the federal and provincial political elites seek to manipulate in order to enhance their own influence and power. For example, federal political leaders can argue that a strong central government in Ottawa is needed so that they can preserve national unity by overcoming the deleterious effects of regionalism. In contrast, provincial political leaders, in order to fulfill the regional aspirations of their constituents, may demand greater powers from the federal government. Conveniently, such a demand also helps to insulate the provincial political elites from their own people by focussing political discontent on the federal polity. These types of actions on the part of federal and provincial leaders suggest that the pattern of regionalism, once it became established in Canada, has been maintained perhaps more as a result of elite perceptions and behaviour than because of the attitudes held by the mass public (Gibbins, 1982: 188).

The presence of regionalism and the regional political cultures has significantly affected the structure, operation, and customs of the Canadian political system. For example, with respect to the political structure, Canada was made a federal system in order to preserve the various regions in existence at the time of Confederation. Explicit recognition of Canada's regional nature is reflected in the structure of the Senate, the House of Commons, and the Supreme Court of Canada, as well as in many other institutions of government. Moreover, the decision-making process, at both the federal and provincial levels, must continuously deal with the possible regional implications of any issue, whether it is one of constitutional reform, economic development, or social policy. Finally, the customs and conventions of the Canadian polity are rife with regional practices, perhaps best exemplified by the representation of the provinces within the federal cabinet.

Theme number three: Dualism

The third major theme of political culture is **dualism**, that is, *the impact of, and relationship between, Canada's major cultural groups (French and English)*, what Canadian historian Arthur Lower has called "Canada's tragic leitmotif." While Canada has become a multicultural society, especially since the Second World War, the political system has been slow to accommodate this change. Instead, the political structure reflects, and the major concern of domestic politics remains, the continuing problems between the two "charter groups." In addition, the pattern of dualism has combined with regionalism to produce Canada's most distinctive political subculture, in Quebec.

As the largest minority group in the political system, which has continually feared for its fate at the hands of the English-speaking majority, French Canada has developed several unique political values. First and foremost, French Canada,

which in recent decades has become increasingly concentrated within the province of Quebec, has used the
political process as a means of cultural defence. The key
concern of French Canada has always been the preservation of its language and culture. As a result, the relationship between Quebec and Ottawa and Quebec and
the other provinces, as well as the nature of politics
within Quebec itself, has focussed on the values of na-

> Whatever the future may hold for relations between the two nationalities that form present-day Canada, the reality of the one can never be expunged from the collective consciousness of the other (Monière, 1981: vii).

tionalism. It is not by chance that the provincial legislature in Quebec is named the
National Assembly. Indeed, during the nine years of Parti Québécois government
from 1976 to 1985, the Canadian flag was not displayed in Quebec's legislative
council room and it has never been displayed in the National Assembly itself.
Moreover, all parties in Quebec, whether at the federal or provincial levels, are
nationalist in orientation. It is ironic, perhaps, that within the provincial party
system there was not a serious "federalist" party competing between the 1950s
and the 1990s. When former Tory cabinet member and interim leader of the
Progressive Conservative Party of Canada, Jean Charest, resigned from the House
of Commons to return to Quebec to become provincial Liberal party leader, the
Liberal Party of Quebec became more "federalist" in outlook than it had been for
decades, which is one reason why it lost to the Parti Québécois in the 1998 provincial election. Typically, the party that represents Quebec in the national legislature in Ottawa is the one perceived to be the best defender of French-Canadian
interests in the federal system (e.g., the success in 1993 and 1997 of the Bloc
Québécois).

The necessity for cultural defence, combined with an agrarian society and
hierarchical church structure, helped to produce an adherence to the values of
centralized authority and elitism within the traditional political culture in Quebec
(McRoberts and Posgate, 1980). As a result, historically the political orientations
in French Canada have usually been classified as parochial and subject in nature,
at least in comparison to the more participant values of English Canada. A reflection of such beliefs, perhaps, was the late extension of the suffrage to women
in Quebec, about two decades later than in other provinces. The lack of participant
values was typified by French Canada's attitude toward democracy: "French
Canadians have not really believed in democracy for themselves . . ." (Trudeau,
1968: 103). Parliamentary democracy was foreign in origin and design and, instead of being used as a mechanism for the democratization of Quebec society, it
became a means for the defence of French-Canadian interests in the larger federal
system.

A third attribute of Quebec's traditional political values is revealed in attitudes toward the proper role of the state in the Quebec polity. Historically, the
role of the state has been limited in Quebec, with the scope of governmental activity and purpose narrowly conceived. This core value of "anti-statism" is illustrated
by the pattern of economic development under Quebec Premier Maurice Duplessis
(1935–1959): ". . . it was assumed that economic processes should remain in the
hands of private interests; the economic responsibility of the provincial government
was to facilitate the pursuit by private interests of their own objectives" (McRoberts

and Posgate, 1980: 61). What was true of the economy was applicable to other sectors as well, including the areas of both social and political reform. Quebec was a late entrant into the era of the expansive welfare state.

The characteristics of the traditional political culture in Quebec thus included a defence of the French language and culture and a resulting emphasis on nationalist values, acceptance of centralized authority and a pattern of elite decision making, and a negative view of the role of the state in the political process. Such attributes were dominant in Quebec until the 1950s, but beginning with the Quiet Revolution of the late 1950s and early 1960s, several of these core values were fundamentally altered. The **Quiet Revolution** refers to *the series of social, economic, and political changes in Quebec which transformed that province and its political culture into a "modern and nationalistic" political regime.* While the defence of the French-Canadian community remained fundamental, the method of survival was changed as a result of the Quiet Revolution.

Rather than defending the status quo, Quebec began demanding greater powers from the federal government so that the provincial unit could more adequately preserve French Canada's language and culture. Paralleling these new powers was a change in attitude toward the role of the state. Government acquired positive functions, with a corresponding increase in the scope and extent of state activity. Two prime examples are the creation of Hydro-Quebec in the early 1960s and the initial James Bay project in the 1970s.

Greater powers for defence led inexorably to an increased role for government in matters of social, economic, and political reform. Moreover, such changes modified the participatory elements of the political culture, moving Quebec into the forefront of democratic sentiments. For example, the use of the referendum in May 1980 is revealing in that the public was seen as a necessary source of legitimacy for any move toward the independence option, a view uncharacteristic of the previous elitist pattern of decision making. Legislation regarding the public funding of election campaigns and the control of how political parties finance themselves has helped to make Quebec a leader in democratic reforms. Thus, several of Quebec's traditional core political values have been modified, but constant throughout has been a concern for defending the language and culture of French Canada.

> We are Québécois. What that means first and foremost — and if need be, all that it means — is that we are attached to this one corner of the earth where we can be completely ourselves: this Quebec, the only place where we have the unmistakable feeling that "here we can be really at home" (Lévesque, 1968: 1).

Much of the continuing conflict between English and French Canada is reflected in concerns over language, perhaps best summarized in Richard Joy's (1972) **bilingual belt thesis**, which *argues that a bilingual zone around Quebec increasingly isolates an English unilingual population from a French one.* This buffer zone extends roughly from Sault Ste. Marie, Ontario, to Moncton, New Brunswick. While the Canada of the 19th century was a linguistic checkerboard of many languages, in the 20th century English and French became dominant. Moreover, these two pre-eminent languages have been increasingly separated on both a geographical and a practical basis. Over 90 percent of those claiming French as their mother tongue live within the territorial boundaries of the bilingual belt. In terms of language use, bilingualism is most often found among those with French as their initial language, although a very small and growing percentage of the total population is bilingual. The result of such a configuration is that, while Canada may be officially a bilingual country, it is overwhelmingly composed of unilingual citizens (Joy, 1972: 3–15). Interestingly, in the decades since Richard Joy's initial analysis these patterns have become more pronounced (Joy, 1992: 116–117).

A number of historical factors help to explain the development of such a pattern. Within the bilingual belt, the French language has been preserved because it is used in daily discourse, while outside of the belt it is dying the slow death of assimilation from disuse and from the preference for English in terms of the economic system. Moreover, those pockets of French culture in English Canada have lost more than the battle of language use: in recent decades, additional French-speaking immigration into those areas has dwindled to negligible levels, while young people who want to live in a French milieu are increasingly returning to Quebec. Inside Quebec the birth rate has changed from the highest in Canada to the lowest, while the large waves of non-English and non-French immigrants into Quebec have overwhelmingly chosen English as their new language. Moreover, French-Canadian emigration from Quebec has historically gone to the United States rather than to other areas of Canada. On the basis of these historical trends, Joy (1972: 135) concluded that "two languages of unequal strength cannot co-exist in intimate contact and that the weaker must, inevitably, disappear."

In an attempt to prevent such a development, both the federal government in Ottawa and the provincial governments in Quebec have passed legislation designed to protect the French language. At the federal level, the 1969 Official Languages Act declared both French and English to be the official languages of Canada, set up bilingual districts — where numbers warranted — so that citizens could deal with their federal government in the language of their choice, and sought to make the status of French equal to that of English throughout the country. The reaction of Quebec — one that was largely correct — was that the Official Languages Act was too little and too late, since, as the bilingual belt thesis argues, the French language outside of Quebec had already been lost.

Instead, the Quebec provincial governments of the past five decades, whether they have been formed by Liberal, Union Nationale, or Parti Québécois members, have all sought to use the powers of the provincial government to promote and defend the French language within Quebec itself. In that sense, the genesis of Bill 101, passed in 1977 by the Parti Québécois, is the relationship between English and French in the rest of the country: accepting the defeat of French outside of Quebec's borders, the party was determined to prevent such a pattern within Quebec itself. Generally, Bill 101 moved Quebec toward being, for all practical purposes, a unilingual French province, thereby seeking to emulate the pattern of English dominance in all the other provinces.

The reaction to Bill 101 inside Quebec was enthusiastic from the French-speaking segment, while English Canadians and recent immigrant groups were strongly opposed. Those individuals most upset, in fact, emigrated from Quebec, a trend which in the long run will help to further consolidate the growing unilingual nature of the province. For example, between 1976 and 1981 a total of 154 000 anglophones emigrated from Quebec to other parts of Canada, a total equal to about one-fifth of the English-speaking population remaining in that province (Joy, 1985: 94). Between 1991 and 1996, Quebec experienced a net loss of population (37 445), two-thirds of which were anglophones. Even the provincial Liberal election victory of Robert Bourassa in 1985 and his return to power, which initially softened some of the harsher aspects of Bill 101, did not change this overall trend. Moreover, Premier Bourassa's use of the notwithstanding clause (Section 33 of the Charter) and the Quebec Charter to overturn the Supreme Court decision in December of 1988 on two sections of Bill 101 served to further protect the dominance of the French language in Quebec. Not only did this action clearly rejuvenate the language issue, but it was also a key reason for the rejection of the Meech Lake Accord in 1990.

The 1991 Canadian census figures provided the bases for a continuing emphasis on language politics in Canada. For example, Quebec, which in 1951 had 30 percent of the total Canadian population, dropped to just under 25 percent of the total by 1991. A declining birth rate, as well as a failure to attract a proportionate share of francophone immigration, are two of the factors which have produced such a pattern. With the return of the Parti Québécois to power in Quebec City in the provincial election of 1994 and its re-election in 1998, the politics of language and culture returned to a priority position on Quebec's political agenda — perhaps best exemplified by the use of "language police" through the Office de la Langue Française. By 1997, the francophone segment of the Canadian population had dropped to 23.5 percent, with a further decline to 19 percent projected by 2050.

While dualism is perhaps best symbolized by current disputes over language, its impact is also clearly evident with respect to the structure and operation of the polity. For example, the federal principle was adopted as a means of guaranteeing the existence of both the English and French cultures, with the provinces given control of "those matters where the traditions of the English- and French-speaking communities of the former province of Canada differed significantly" (Smiley, 1980: 20). Moreover, within the federal government itself, English-French duality is indirectly recognized, as in the allocation of provincial seat totals in the House of Commons. The customs and conventions of Canadian politics also reflect the theme, exemplified by cabinet representation for Quebec as well as for francophone areas in New Brunswick and Northern Ontario and the typical alternation of French and English leaders within the Liberal party. Thus, through both institutional structures and political customs the theme of dualism has remained a (perhaps the) significant influence on the Canadian political process.

Theme number four: Continentalism

In contrast to the themes of elitism, regionalism, and dualism, which are based on internal realities and problems, our fourth theme of **continentalism** reflects the importance of external factors, namely, *the impact of the United States on Canadian politics.* American influence runs the gamut from basic principles of government, such as federalism, to political practices, such as the use of national party leadership conventions. In some cases we have imitated American practices, while in others we have resisted their encroachments. However, overall the impact of the United States on Canadian politics has been extensive.

One of the reasons, of course, for the movement toward Confederation in the 1860s was the fear of American expansionism and the attempt to prevent the absorption of the English colonies into the American orbit. While the results of the War of 1812 prevented a military conquest, Canada remained apprehensive about possible American intervention until the early decades of the 20th century. For example, until the 1920s Canada maintained a secret contingency plan of how to respond to an American invasion, even though such a threat had not been very likely for some time. The result has been an element of anti-Americanism among basic Canadian political values — as Frank Underhill once described us, Canadians are the "world's oldest and continuing anti-Americans." One consequence of the American impact has been a low sense of national identity, which in itself is defined in negative terms: we know what we are not (i.e., American), but we do not know what we are (i.e., the essential attributes of being a Canadian).

The desire to contain and possibly reduce American influence in Canada led to a growing movement of nationalism, particularly economic nationalism, during the 1960s and 1970s. For example, the preferential tax position for *Time* and *Reader's Digest* was removed, Canadian content regulations were established and implemented for the mass media, and the National Energy Program of 1980 sought to make the energy sector "Canadianized." In response to the impact of

Source: Malcolm Mayes, *The Edmonton Journal* (1999). By permission.

multinational corporations in Canada, a Foreign Investment Review Agency (FIRA) was established to screen all takeover bids; however, the subsequent success of takeover applications was high, usually in the neighbourhood of 80 percent or more. In foreign affairs, former prime minister Trudeau's policy review and his later actions during the 1970s and early 1980s were based on an attempt to reduce Canadian dependence on the American superpower and to give Canada a more independent position in the international arena.

However, partly as a reaction to the Trudeau years, the Conservative election victory of 1984 was based on the promise of improving Canadian-American relations. Brian Mulroney declared that Canada was "open for business" and he negotiated a "free trade" deal with the United States. Such a pro-American stance stood at odds with much of Canadian history and seemed likely to produce yet another swing of the political pendulum, with Canadian nationalism becoming, once again, a key political issue, as it temporarily did during the 1988 election. By the early 1990s, signs were growing of a renewed resentment of American influence in Canada (Hurtig, 1991; Bashevkin, 1991; Martin, 1993). For example, in 1993 Canadian Pacific, much to the dismay of Canadian nationalists, announced its new corporate logo — a combination of the Canadian and American flags. The new symbol was denounced on both sides of the border! However, by the mid-1990s anti-Americanism was in apparent decline, as Canadians seemed increasingly willing to accommodate themselves to their American neighbour (Granatstein, 1996). The close personal and political relationship between Jean Chrétien and Bill Clinton between 1993 and 2001 symbolized the continuing and growing integration of Canada with the United States, which was such that, by the end of 2000, some commentators were suggesting the adoption, by Canada, of the American dollar. The victory of George W. Bush in the American 2000 presidential race is likely to increase tensions between Canada and the United States, especially with respect to trade and defence issues.

Having discussed the four main themes of elitism, regionalism, dualism, and continentalism, we can now classify the Canadian pattern of core political beliefs in terms of the basic types of political culture. Overall, Canada has a fragmented political culture composed of a series of regional political orientations. The most distinctive political subculture is that of French Canada, which is increasingly centred in the province of Quebec. By comparison to most countries, Canada's political culture is participant, but the strength of elitism points to pockets of subject and parochial values that limit extensive participation in the political process. Moreover, the elements of regionalism, dualism, and continentalism have all contributed to a lack of national identity and unity, that is, to a pattern of attenuated nationalism. From an ideological perspective, liberalism has been dominant, although it must compete with both conservatism and socialism to retain such a position (Horowitz, 1968: 3–57). Canadian conservatism is unique in its collectivist emphasis and willingness to use the power of government for national objectives (e.g., John A. Macdonald's National Policy). Similarly, Canadian socialism is characterized by its British heritage and its belief in democratic socialism rather than Marxist socialism. This particular mixture of ideologies has helped to solidify the unique characteristics of the Canadian political culture.

CANADA AS A CONSOCIATIONAL DEMOCRACY

Given the ideological, regional, and cultural fragmentation of basic political values, the next concern might be with trying to explain how the overall system manages to stay together. The answer that has often been given is that Canada exemplifies a political system that can be classified as a **consociational democracy**, sometimes referred to as *a pattern of elite accommodation* (Presthus, 1973; McRae, 1974).

Based on the experience of how the smaller European democracies have been able to function successfully despite linguistic, cultural, and ethnic differences, the theory of consociational democracy indicates that a system's survival is heavily dependent on the intention and ability of the political elite to make it work. Effective decision-making power is given to the elite so that it can successfully accommodate and mediate between the various social, economic, and political interests. In addition, there is often the fear of an external threat, which reinforces the need of the elite to control the system. The policies adopted by the elite are pragmatic rather than ideological in scope, thus allowing for conciliation between the political subcultures. In such a system, the masses must be willing to delegate political authority to the elite, refrain from interference in the conciliation process, and accept the bargains struck by the political leadership. Mass participation is limited and is generally confined to voting in elections.

These characteristics of a typical consociational democracy are consistent with the four major themes of the traditional Canadian political culture. The elitist nature of the British parliamentary structure allows for the exercise of considerable power in the accommodation process, while the deferential attitudes toward authority make such a pattern legitimate. A limited degree of nationalism among the masses, along with a pattern of quasi-participation, restricts their ability to upset the bargains made by the elite. Fear of an external threat is symbolized by the American presence in Canada; that is, continentalism has historically been a major incentive to keep the present system going. The themes of regionalism and dualism reveal two of the fundamental policy areas that must be continually accommodated by the elite. Such conciliation is more effective when the elites themselves are representative of the various political subcultures.

The decline of consociationalism

Canada as a consociational democracy has been challenged in a number of areas in recent decades. For example, the future of this pattern of elite accommodation was obviously thrown into question as far back as the victories by the Parti Québécois in the Quebec provincial contests of 1976 and 1981. The assumption that the key actors of the political elite wanted to make the system work was no longer necessarily tenable. It is in the long-term interests of a separatist party to show that the existing system does not and cannot be made to work, thereby providing justification for independence. No amount of political reform or constitutional tinkering can accommodate or satisfy the national aspirations of the Parti Québécois. The defeat of the Parti Québécois in the 1985 provincial election and the return to power of Robert Bourassa brought back a bargaining style of leadership to

Quebec-Ottawa relations. However, the negative political reaction to the negotiations that produced the 1982 Canada Act, the rejection of the 1987 Meech Lake Accord, and the rejection of the 1992 Charlottetown Accord all indicate a decline in the public's acceptance of the results, as well as the process, of elite accommodation (Delacourt, 1993).

The question that needs to be asked at this point is as follows: what has produced the decline, if not the demise, of consociational politics in Canada? The total answer is complex, but certainly part of the answer is deceptively simple: the Canadian Charter of Rights and Freedoms. The Charter itself, of course, is a reflection of the changing nature of some of the key elements of the Canadian political culture. However, the Charter has also further accentuated such trends since it was adopted in 1982. Most significant has been the Charter's legitimation of the American principle of popular sovereignty, as opposed to the older British principle of parliamentary sovereignty. While popular sovereignty has been grafted on to the principle of parliamentary sovereignty, it has quickly taken root and flourished.

Nothing symbolizes this change more dramatically than the pattern of negotiation of the 1992 Charlottetown Accord by the political elites and the immediate and overwhelming rejection of the Accord by the public in the October 1992 referendum (Jeffrey, 1993). The Canadian constitutional amendment processes are a legal reflection of the longstanding pattern of elite accommodation based on parliamentary sovereignty. However, because of changing public expectations about the constitutional amendment process (i.e., that the public had the right to be involved), the political leadership felt compelled to hold a national referendum on the end product of their elite negotiations — which the public promptly rejected. What the defeat of the Charlottetown Accord demonstrates is that there is little, if any, room for the principle of popular sovereignty in a pattern of elite accommodation. The return to power of the Parti Québécois in the 1994 provincial election meant that, once again, a key actor was not committed to making the Canadian federal system work. Even more dramatic as a challenge to consociationalism was the October 1995 separatist referendum in Quebec, which came within less than 1 percent of victory. Clearly, as long as the Parti Québécois is in power in Quebec City (and it was re-elected in 1998), and as long as the Bloc Québécois is a significant player in the national legislature, hopes for a revitalized pattern of political accommodation appear remote.

Moreover, both the 1998 *Quebec Secession Reference* and the 2000 Clarity Act demonstrate less of a willingness on the part of the federal government to accommodate the needs of Quebec, and especially the Parti Québécois — an attitude returned in full measure by the PQ. Immediately following the strong Liberal majority victory in the November 27, 2000 national election, the PQ passed Bill 99 (against provincial Liberal party opposition) on December 7, 2000. In defiance of both the Supreme Court's ruling in 1998 and the Clarity Act, Bill 99 declares and asserts Quebec's right to unilaterally secede from the Canadian polity. It is doubtful that such an action will be interpreted as an example of elite accommodation. Furthermore, the resignation of Lucien Bouchard and his replacement by a more hardline separatist, Bernard Landry, in early 2001 will continue to undercut continuing attempts at elite accommodation. Referring to the Canadian flag as "bits of red rag," the new Quebec premier vowed to accomplish the PQ's goal of nationhood in the immediate future!

In addition to the decline of elitism and deference (Nevitte, 1996), other important developments have undercut the functioning of consociationalism. First, other regions and/or provinces besides Quebec have occasionally questioned their continuing role in the Canadian federal system — most notably Alberta and British Columbia. For example, in a December 8, 2000 editorial comment, Stephen Harper, president of the National Citizens' Coalition and former MP and founding member of the Reform party, argued for "separation, Alberta-style" (Harper, 2000: A18). In January of 2001, an even more ominous potential threat emerged with the formation of the Alberta Independence Party. Second, Canadian society, in terms of its ethnic and racial diversity, has changed dramatically in recent decades. The dominance of the French-English cleavage of dualism remains in place, but is increasingly challenged by the expanding pattern and impact of multiculturalism. Third, the recognition of Aboriginal rights has added other key actors to the constitutional reform process. Combined with expanding interest group claims, these developments have made a pattern of elite accommodation more difficult to achieve and implement.

While the basic patterns and structures of consociational politics remain in place in Canada, their legitimacy and operation will be increasingly challenged. The political and institutional structures of the Canadian polity encourage and, at times, require a consociational style of politics, while the evolving themes of the political culture, in particular multiculturalism and popular sovereignty, inhibit that same pattern.

> *Separatism — British Columbia style:* Canada has always been a matter of convenience . . . . This matters because — and I say this with no fear of contradiction — nothing but emotion (and inertia) today bind B.C. to Canada (Gibson, 2000: A14).

THE BRITISH POLITICAL CULTURE

Because Britain lacks a comprehensive written constitution, political custom and convention play a vital role in the political process. These conventions embody the core values of the British political culture, which include the importance of tradition, deferential attitudes toward political authority, and a consensus regarding key political norms and practices (Coxall and Robins, 1994: 51–60). In many respects, especially in its elitist and quasi-participative tendencies, the pattern of British political beliefs resembles the Canadian one.

The first characteristic of British political culture is the significance of **tradition**, a reflection of the evolutionary nature of the polity over the course of many centuries. The weight of history is heavy, as new beliefs and practices merge with existing ones (Rasmussen, 1993: 7–15). Two institutional survivors are the monarchy and the House of Lords. For example, while the substance of monarchical power is no longer exercised by the monarch, the institution remains in place:

"The British monarch is a powerful living symbol linking the British of today with a rich past and a royal future" (Roth and Wilson, 1980: 11). The role of tradition is emphasized by the symbols and ceremonies of the polity, what Walter Bagehot called the "theatrical show of society," such as the opening of Parliament or the pageantry of a royal marriage. One major result of the evolution of tradition has been to give a pragmatic thrust to British politics, which in most instances has taken precedence over ideological concerns.

The role of tradition is reinforced by the second characteristic of British political culture, namely, **deferential** attitudes toward political authority. Deference or respect for authority can be seen in the support of traditional political institutions, as well as in the acceptance of a class-based society and an elitist pattern of decision making. The "dignified" parts of the system — "those which excite and preserve the reverence of the population" (Bagehot, 1867: 61) — are a means of legitimating the power of the political elite to rule between elections. A further indicator of deferential beliefs is the acceptance of the "rule of law" and the notion that violence is not a legitimate means for achieving political goals.

This deferential nature of political values parallels the structure of the British polity. A system that has been traditionally unitary in form, based on the principle of parliamentary supremacy, and without a pattern of judicial review is inherently elitist in style and operation. Such a pattern may be democratic in form, but the overall result is a system "of government of the people, for the people, with, but not by, the people" (Amery, quoted in Beer, 1973: 140).

The third attribute of the British political culture is its **consensual** nature; that is, there is widespread agreement on political fundamentals (Heath et al., 1999). The rules of the political game have not been seriously challenged for several centuries: "Since the end of the seventeenth century, the British constitution and the government have been generally accepted" (Finer and Steed, 1978: 35). One reason why a political consensus has long dominated British politics is the ability of the political system to adapt to changing circumstances. No major group has been excluded outright from the political system, although several have "peacefully" forced their entry into the political game. Gradual adaptation rather than a politics of confrontation has successfully co-opted the major socio-economic interests into accepting the legitimacy of the political structure.

In addition to its adaptability, a second factor contributing to consensus has been the relatively homogeneous nature of British society. There have been few sharp cleavages, such as language or ethnicity, which might tear the political fabric asunder. Finally, the geographical compactness of Britain has helped to minimize the development of regional differences, which often characterize larger systems like Canada and the United States.

The traditional, deferential, and consensual characteristics of the British political culture all support the view that it is an integrated political culture, with a high sense of national identity and purpose. While generally participant in outlook, the deferential attitudes toward political authority reveal strong subject orientations as well. Few political subcultures can be identified and regionalism is minimal, with the major ideological differences revealed in the class-based structure of the polity.

While this interpretation of the British political culture is a fairly typical one, it can be challenged on several grounds (Rasmussen, 1993: 16–22; Coxall and Robins, 1994: 51–52). First, the characteristics apply better to England than to the United Kingdom (England, plus Wales, Scotland, and Northern Ireland). The inclusion of these areas greatly increases the diversity of core political values, reduces the homogeneity of the overall political culture, and recognizes the crucial factor of regionalism (Budge et al., 1998: 138–174). Second, while violence may have been excluded from the normal political process, it most certainly is an important ingredient in the internal politics of Northern Ireland, as well as in the conflict between that area and the British government in London. Third, the continuing pervasive nature of deference as a distinguishing characteristic of British values has been questioned (Kavanagh, 1980). Fourth, the social homogeneity of Great Britain has also changed, given the large increase in non-white immigration in the past several decades, as well as the continuation of nationalism in both Scotland and Wales. Fifth, the return to power of the Labour party in 1997 and its significant constitutional reforms have challenged and begun to change not only the role of tradition (e.g., the reform of the House of Lords), but also the longstanding unitary structure of the British polity (e.g., devolution of Scotland and Wales). Finally, class-based tensions can, at times, become magnified, symbolized for example by the Conservative government's confrontation with the coal miners in the early 1970s and the radicalization (e.g., leftward movement) of the Labour party in the early 1980s. While these developments may have begun to limit some of the traditional, deferential, and consensual aspects of the polity, by comparison to most systems, the British political culture remains a highly integrated one.

THE AMERICAN POLITICAL CULTURE

The core values of the American polity differ in certain key areas from the beliefs of both the Canadian and British political cultures. Overall, from a comparative perspective, the American pattern is an integrated one, although for different reasons than in Britain. Born out of a revolution, the United States was forced to define the nature of its core political values from the outset, in contrast to the evolution of political ideas in Canada and Britain. This delineation of goals was embodied in the writings of the English political theorist John Locke, as interpreted by the American founding fathers in such writings as *The Federalist Papers*.

Essentially the core political values embraced the doctrines of liberalism, which came to be seen as synonymous with the "American way of life." The dominance of liberalism was so pervasive that ideological diversity was discouraged, with the result that a consensus on political fundamentals quickly congealed. Symbolized by the Declaration of Independence and the American Constitution, this consensus has remained in place for over 200 years.

The manner in which diversity has been traditionally handled in the United States has served to reinforce this liberal pre-eminence. While the United States is

What joins the Americans one to another is not a common nationality, language, race, or ancestry (all of which testify to the burdens of the past), but rather their complicity in a shared work of the imagination (Lapham, 1992: 48).

socially complex and composed of immigrant groups from many lands (the 1990 American census needed 630 computer codes to cover the answers regarding ethnic origin or ancestry), the melting pot emphasis of the school system and of society has helped to produce a traditional unity of political outlook and sense of national identity that few other political cultures can match (Barrett, 1992). Due to such events as the Vietnam War, Watergate, the attempted impeachment of one president (Richard Nixon) and the actual impeachment of another (Bill Clinton), and the increasing diversity of its ethnic and racial mixture, the United States, at the start of the new century, is not as homogenous or integrated as it once was (Sinopoli and Gabrielson, 1999). For example, by the end of 2000 and for the first time since 1860, whites have become the minority in the state of California. However, in comparison to other countries, the American political culture is a highly integrated one.

The most significant regional political culture in American history has been the South. The last four decades, however, have witnessed its incorporation into the mainstream of American politics, best symbolized by the election of Jimmy Carter from Georgia as president in 1976 and reinforced by the victories of Bill Clinton of Arkansas in the 1992 and 1996 presidential elections (along with Vice-President Al Gore of Tennessee). While regionalism has declined, challenges to the consensual political culture remain (Erikson and Tedin, 2001: 170–207), particularly those based on race (Hacker, 1992; Schuman et al., 1997) and social class (Harrigan, 1993; Johnstone, 1999; Stonecash and Mariani, 2000).

To define the nature of the American political culture, therefore, is to describe the main tenets of liberalism, as they have been adapted in the American context (Mitchell, 1970: 105–121). First, Americans are inherently suspicious of political power and its uses, seeing it, at best, as a necessary evil that must be circumscribed in practice. If political power is evil, then the institutional organization of power, that is, government, is likely to be seen in a similar light. One result of such a view is a rather negative perception of politicians. Another consequence has been the desire to limit government's role and effectiveness, summarized in the view that "the government which governs least governs best." To minimize the possible abuse of power, government is structured in such a way as to make difficult its accumulation in any single institution or individual. Such an outlook is the basis for the separation of powers principle and a bill of rights as elements of the American Constitution.

Even though government was to be limited in both scope and purpose, the government that was created was to be controlled by the people. Lincoln's phrase that American government was a "government of the people, by the people, and for the people" symbolizes the importance of popular, not parliamentary, sovereignty in the United States. Participation was to be encouraged, with public officials elected rather than appointed and serving relatively short terms of office. State judges, county officials, and special tax districts of one kind or another are electorally based. The ballot is extensive in many states, often containing numerous tax proposals, constitutional amendments, and referendum questions. Thus, the belief in popular sovereignty led to the evolution of a political structure designed to promote public participation in, and control over, the elected political elite.

A third theme of American liberalism concerns the importance of individualism and its emphasis on the values of liberty and equality. Self-reliance is necessary in a system of limited government where liberty is defined typically as freedom from state intervention. Moreover, self-reliance or individualism parallels the American conception of equality as an "equality of opportunity" rather than an "equality of condition." An equality of opportunity philosophy puts the burden for one's own success, or lack thereof, on the individual. While liberty and equality are goals and are accepted by most Americans as admirable political values, their application in practice often leaves much to be desired, as the battle over civil rights illustrates.

A fourth theme of the American political culture can be called **political moralism**: "The moralistic fervor of many Americans has long been a source of both amusement and confusion to perceptive foreigners" (Mitchell, 1970: 118). One result of this moralistic outlook is that politicians, because they deal with power that is evil, must try to be better than ordinary citizens, to set an example of proper or exemplary behaviour. Corruption, dishonesty, or other lapses of morality can cost one political office, as illustrated by the Watergate scandal of the early 1970s with respect to Richard Nixon. More recently, questions about his "womanizing" effectively ended Gary Hart's bid for the 1988 Democratic presidential nomination. In 1992, Bill Clinton barely survived the presidential primary in New Hampshire after allegations that he had been involved in a long-term affair. A series of further allegations throughout his two terms of office, including his admitted wrongdoing in the Monica Lewinsky affair, led to his impeachment (but not his conviction) in 1999. Throughout the impeachment process, President Clinton's public ratings remained high and, in fact, increased. It seems that issues of political moralism have receded in significance in the American system (Bennett, 1998).

An emphasis on political morality has also led, through the course of American history, to alternating periods of political reform (e.g., John F. Kennedy's "New Frontier" and Lyndon Johnson's "Great Society") and political conservatism (e.g., the presidencies of Ronald Reagan and George Bush). Another outgrowth of political moralism in the United States is the typical and traditional American view of its own political system as not only unique, but superior to those of all other countries; as President Bill Clinton phrased it in his inaugural address in January of 1993: "Though we march to the music of our time, our mission is timeless."

These themes of the American political culture, an outgrowth of liberalism, have been challenged in recent decades by both foreign and domestic crises. They are goals of the polity that most people would agree with on a general level, but that become points of political conflict when applied in specific contexts or with regard to particular issues (Burns et al., 2000: 172–174). For example, equality is generally accepted as a goal, but busing (as a means to achieve equality of educational opportunity) or the protection of homosexuals in the American armed forces may not be deemed acceptable by everyone. The 1996 and 2000 elections witnessed attacks on minority rights, language rights, and affirmative action programs through the use of various ballot-initiatives. Whatever the outcome of such

issues, they illustrate that the homogeneity and consensus of the American political culture is not assured (Schlesinger, 1992; Erikson and Tedin, 2001: 153–155).
Such conflicts become frequent when the goals of a polity are seen as possibly
unattainable by major sectors of the political system (Dye, 1997: 32–44). However,
the dominance of liberalism remains largely intact; from a comparative perspective, the American pattern is a highly integrated and ideologically unified political
culture.

COMPARING POLITICAL CULTURES

In describing the major themes and patterns of the Canadian, British, and American
political cultures, we have focussed on three ways of comparing their core political values: the role of the individual in the political process (parochial, subject, or
participant political cultures); the degree of consensus on political fundamentals
(integrated or fragmented political cultures); and the ideological mix of political ideas (the content of the core political values). While other ways of classifying
political cultures could be considered, these three approaches all emphasize the influence of political beliefs on the structure and operation of the polity.

Source: CAM (Cameron Cardow), *The Ottawa Citizen* (1998). By permission.

With respect to the political structure, the core political values translate statutory requirements into working institutions of government. For example, while the 1867 Constitution Act details many of the considerations that must be taken into account in making Senate appointments, the most important factor, that of patronage, is based on beliefs and customs rather than law. In the American system, constitutional duties set the parameters of the presidential office, but the dominant place of the president in recent decades stems from public beliefs about the proper presidential role, not from constitutional prescriptions. In all three of the systems considered, support for the protection of civil and political liberties is more heavily dependent on popular and elite beliefs that these rights should be protected than on their specification in law. Thus do political beliefs transform legal structures into operating institutions of government.

A second manner in which beliefs influence the polity can be seen in the various functions of particular institutions and the way these change over time. When first created, a political structure might be designed with a specific task or function in mind. However, as beliefs change, so do the functions of particular institutions. For example, one of the initial functions of the Canadian Senate was to be the voice of provincial and regional concerns within the national government. However, from the time of John A. Macdonald's first government, the cabinet has performed this task. The initial delineation of Senate functions has not been changed, nor has such a task been assigned to the cabinet in law; however, the practice of Canadian politics has been so modified. Likewise, the evolution of the relationship between the formal and political executives in Canada primarily represents the changing public expectations about the proper role of each structure in the political system, rather than legally defined modifications. Thus, beliefs can alter the functions of various political institutions, while the political structures themselves remain in place.

If the core political values help to transform political structures into working institutions and if they help to modify the functions of these institutions over time, then political beliefs are an important mechanism for adapting the polity to changing circumstances. Beliefs are more readily transformed than are political structures. By modifying both the structures and functions of government, the core political values are an important mechanism of political change. Generally speaking, the beliefs and structures of the political system should reinforce each other. When they do not, then demands for political reform begin to be heard, with the aim being a reintegration of structures, functions, and beliefs.

THE POLITICAL SOCIALIZATION PROCESS

A nation's political culture is not inherited by the members of the polity. Instead, like other values and attitudes, political outlooks are a result of the learning process (Niemi and Junn, 1998). The *acquisition of political beliefs* leads us to a concern with their origins and development, that is, to a concern with the **political socialization**

process. The basic assumption of political socialization research is that the initial learning of political values and ideas in childhood and adolescence influences, to a greater or lesser extent, the later political values and behaviour of adults: "political ideas — like the consumption of cigarettes and hard liquor — do not suddenly begin with one's eighteenth birthday" (Niemi, 1973: 117).

Although political learning may begin in childhood, it is also important to remember that it is continuous throughout a person's life (Sears and Valentino, 1997). While many orientations and attitudes may be formed in childhood and adolescence, actual experience with and participation in politics as an adult may modify and change previously held ideas. In addition to being continuous and beginning early, the political socialization process, for most people, is also cumulative in nature: that is, the orientations acquired later in life are grafted onto and mixed with those adopted in childhood and adolescence. It is difficult to discard years of learning, political or otherwise, and to start over with a fresh set of beliefs (Erikson and Tedin, 2001: 139).

Different types of political systems utilize various techniques in attempting to control the learning of political values by the young. In democratic systems, the political socialization process is usually indirect and implicit. Few parents consciously seek to teach their offspring a particular set of political beliefs. Instead, children usually acquire values similar to those of their parents by observing the values parents exhibit in their own behaviour. Even when children are exposed to political content in the educational process, there is usually an attempt to avoid partisan debate (Frazer, 2000).

In contrast, both autocratic and totalitarian systems seek explicit control of the political socialization process by directly using state-controlled institutions, such as the school system and mass media, to forge a common set of political values among their citizens. How far this process had gone in the former Soviet Union was revealed in June 1988, when, as a result of the ongoing reform process, it was admitted that existing history textbooks were inaccurate and that history exams should thus be cancelled. In a similar vein, in the summer of 1991 the Chinese government banned politically incorrect T-shirts because they represented the obvious work of "antisocial elements." The T-shirts contained such revolutionary slogans as "Life Stinks" or "I'm fed up. Don't bug me." Whether state-directed or not, the various **agents of political socialization**, that is, *those social and political institutions (i.e., family, schools, peer groups, mass media) through which individuals acquire their political beliefs,* affect individuals in all political systems. For most individuals, political beliefs reflect a mixture of the influence of socialization agents and personal experiences with the political system.

While the specific mechanisms utilized in the political socialization process vary from one country to

Political Math — Cuban Style

Problem 1: There have been 3 000 lynchings in the United States in the last 20 years. What has been the average number of lynchings per year in that country?

Problem 2: A medicine which cost $4.75 before the Revolution can now be bought for $3.16. How much less do we pay for this product (Fagen, 1964: 68)?

Political socialization — totalitarian style: After the collapse of the Communist regime in East Germany, documents were discovered in 1990 that showed that parents who were convicted of espionage or had tried to defect to the West were stripped of their children because they were "unfit parents." Such children were then adopted by local Communist party members and denied any access to their biological parents.

the next, there are many similarities between political systems of each major type. After considering the political socialization process in Canada, we will briefly consider the nature of political learning in Britain and the United States.

POLITICAL SOCIALIZATION IN CANADA

Politics is not an especially salient focus of concern for the average citizen, a situation which reveals much about the nature of the political socialization process. For most Canadian youth, the learning of political orientations is indirect and implicit and perhaps based on the assumption that "politics, like sex, should be learned in the streets rather than the classroom" (White, Wagenberg, and Nelson, 1972: 193). However, the acquisition of political beliefs on a wide variety of topics begins early.

The learning of political information centres initially on political leaders rather than on political institutions (Landes, 1976; Burgess, 1997). By junior high school most children can correctly identify the prime minister, although provincial and local leaders are less well recognized. Identification of political executives (prime minister, premiers) far exceeds that of the formal executive positions (governor general, lieutenant-governors). However, understanding of the more complicated aspects of the political system, such as the job or role of these political leaders, reveals a minimum level of knowledge. For example, the Canadian Student Awareness Survey (Hurtig, 1975) found that 68 percent of high school seniors were unable to name the governor general, 61 percent were unable to name the BNA Act as (then) Canada's Constitution, and 70 percent had little or no idea what percentage of Canada's population was French Canadian. Similarly, a study of first-year history students at Glendon College (York University) in Toronto found little, if any, real understanding of Canadian history, especially knowledge of the Canada-Quebec debate (Burgess, 1997). Thus, the average Canadian adolescent would appear to have a rather low level of political knowledge. As one researcher phrased these findings, "I feel as though someone out there waged a war on knowledge, and I've been shell-shocked by the 'Ignorants.' Knowledge of Canadian geography is almost nonexistent, political awareness unbelievable, cultural knowledge abysmal" (Hurtig, 1975: 10). The recent debate about the role and relevance of Canadian history indicates that such an assessment still rings true in the new century (Granatstein, 1998).

Even though levels of political information are low, children and adolescents still develop an emotional tie to political leaders and the political system. The typical pattern is for the child to personalize the political system (i.e., to perceive politics in terms of leaders) and to develop supportive attitudes and positive feelings toward the polity. For example, a comparative study of English-Canadian and American school children, grades four through eight, found that the Canadian

> I don't read the newspapers. I don't watch the news. If something important happens, someone will tell me (Justin Trudeau, 2001).

child's affective (i.e., emotional) response to government in terms of benevolence, dependability, and leadership was greater than that of his or her American counterpart (Landes, 1977: 68).

Although the initial pattern of political affect is usually positive or supportive of the political regime, typically the level of political affect declines during the adolescent years and may even turn into feelings of alienation and cynicism. A particularly important affective tie is the child's early attachment to a specific political party. However, the development of party orientations among young people shows significant regional variations, with the West having the lowest and the Maritimes displaying the highest rate of partisan attachments (Gregg and Whittington, 1976: 78).

In addition to information, affect, and partisan ties, political socialization research has found that the major themes of Canada's political culture are reflected in the political learning process. By the adolescent years, for example, strong patterns of regional loyalties are evident. As Johnstone (1969: 22) concluded, "during the adolescent years Canadian young people become aware of the important sectional, regional, and provincial interests in Canadian life," so that the "adolescent years . . . could be characterized as the period of emergent sectionalism." Moreover, not surprisingly, a 1992 study of teenagers during the constitutional debate found that most were apathetic about the ongoing national unity debate (Picard, 1992). With respect to the dualism theme, a number of studies have discovered that English- and French-Canadian youth are taught different political values in the political socialization process (Lamy, 1975; Forbes, 1976). For example, an analysis of English- and French-Canadian history textbooks found that almost totally contradictory pictures of individuals and events were presented (Trudel and Jain, 1970). Such findings led one observer to conclude that "political socialization in Canada, then, seems to be for young French and English Canadians a process of socialization into discord . . ." (Lamy, 1975: 278).

Finally, the continentalism theme reveals the American impact on the learning of political values in Canada. For example, the American domination of the mass media has meant that many children are socialized to American rather than Canadian political values. Students often learn little of the Canadian political tradition, but much about American history and politics. As one student in the Canadian Student Awareness Survey concluded, "Never heard of them, so they must be Canadian" (Hurtig, 1975: 13). A study published in 1992 found an increasing preference among Canadian adolescents for all things American, including sports stars, music, and favourite politicians (McInnis, 1992). The American influence is so pervasive that the daughter of Heritage Minister Sheila Copps told her mother that she wanted to become an important politician and, therefore, wanted to grow up to be president of the United States (*The Globe and Mail*, January 15, 1997: A3). Combined with the early development of regional loyalties and English-French differences in political outlooks, the American penetration of the political learning process certainly exacerbates the poor development of a Canadian national identity.

An interesting example of how subtle American influences can be through the mass media was demonstrated by the way in which *Time* magazine (which is widely read in Canada) reported on the results of the 1984 general election. The cover of the September 17, 1984 issue pictured Brian Mulroney with the following caption: "Prime Minister-Elect." Of course, in a British parliamentary system the people do not elect the prime minister directly. A person becomes prime minister after he or she is successful in forming a government, after being asked to do so by the governor general. In other words, there is no such position in Canadian politics as "prime minister-elect," which is an interpretation based on the presidential-style system of American politics.

The content of the political socialization process is influenced by the nature of the socialization agents utilized. Although specific political orientations such as partisan attachments may be passed from parents to children, as a general pattern, "most Canadian families, however, are not consciously involved in politically socializing their members" (Kornberg, Smith, and Clarke, 1979: 228). The family's impact is most apparent in providing the child with certain circumstances of birth (e.g., a social class position, a place of residence in a particular region of the country) which may look nonpolitical to begin with, but which have important consequences for what the child eventually is taught and learns about his or her political environment. In addition, the influence of the family as an agent of political socialization depends in part on the homogeneity of the family unit. If the mother and father have the same political outlooks, then their effect on the child will be greater than if their political beliefs contradict each other. Finally, while the Canadian family remains an important agent in the political socialization process, it is increasingly in competition with the other intermediaries in the learning process.

The significance of schools as the second agent of socialization is suggested by the frequent battles over attempts to censor school textbooks and reading materials. For example, concerns about "political correctness" have become evident in the battles over school curricula. For instance, in 1991 the Toronto Board of Education recommended that certain long-time children's favourites such as *Mary Poppins* and *Doctor Dolittle* not be retained in elementary school libraries because of their alleged "racist and sexist biases." Censorship disputes are concerned with which community forces will control the content presented by the school as an agent of socialization: "some people fear that insidious professors or evil books may politically subvert the young" (Jaros, 1973: 113).

The role of Canadian schools as agents of political socialization can be summarized with respect to the following major points. First, since under the 1867 Constitution Act (Section 93) education is made an exclusive provincial jurisdiction, "political socialization via the schools is fragmented because of the ten different provincial systems" (Ogmundson, 1976: 18; Fraser, 1992). Second, as a public agent, the schools provide for most Canadians the only "exposure to formal political socialization by an instrument of the state . . ." (Kornberg, Smith, and Clarke, 1979: 228). Third, the extent of explicit political exposure through the schools is minimal, confined mainly to history and civics courses. Fourth, what little political content is presented is done so in nonpartisan terms, stressing a consensus version of Canada's political experience. Fifth, the result of the schools' efforts is an uninformed citizenry: "most high school graduates lack basic knowledge of Canadian political studies" (Symons, 1978: 50).

A third important element in the political socialization process in recent decades is the mass media, especially television. The potential impact of the mass media rests on two considerations: first, the nearly universal access most people have to newspapers, magazines, and television; and second, the ability of the mass media to bypass other intermediaries of socialization and to provide information directly to children and adolescents. Thus, it is not surprising to find that children and adolescents depend on television and the mass media for political news and for help in understanding political events. The mass media have also made young children aware of some of the harsher realities of political life, including wars, riots, revolutions, and assassinations. While these events usually occur in other countries, the fact that they are presented in the Canadian media means that such tragic events are helping to mold the political values and beliefs of our children.

Although other agents, such as peer groups or one's personal contacts with the political regime, may be significant shapers of political values, we will conclude our discussion of the political socialization process in Canada by emphasizing that the content of political learning is heavily influenced by the nature of the socializing agents. For example, the promotion and perpetuation of regional loyalties and French-English differences have been constitutionally facilitated by providing that education is an exclusive jurisdiction of the provincial governments. Likewise, the creation of a common national identity has been hindered not only by provincial control of education, but also by the dominance of the mass media. In addition, the indirect nature of political socialization through such agencies as the family and the minimal levels of political content presented to the child through the formal political socialization agent of the schools has meant the production of an uninformed citizenry. Any reform of this situation must contemplate major changes in both the content and the agents of political learning.

THE BRITISH AND AMERICAN PATTERNS

Since our general statements about the nature of the political socialization process in Canada apply to most democratic systems, we will focus here on only a few of the distinctive characteristics of learning in Britain and the United States.

With respect to the content of political socialization in Britain, two areas are significant: deferential attitudes toward political authority and the early acquisition of partisan identifications. As we indicated in the discussion of Britain's political culture, deference and a class-based social structure have long been cited as distinguishing attributes (Rasmussen, 1993: 44–58; Coxall and Robins, 1994: 60–62). While all political systems seek to instill respect for authority, the British system stands out among democratic ones in this regard, perhaps best reflected in the traditional popular support for the monarchy. Whether the scandals affecting the Royal Family in the 1990s will change this historical pattern on a long-term basis remains to be seen. While such a pattern of deference may be true of England, it is often forgotten that this view does not apply equally well to Great Britain, where sectors of the young may develop anti-English and nationalistic views (e.g., Northern Ireland, Scotland).

A second significant aspect of content in the political learning process concerns partisan identifications. While the saying that English children are born as "either a little Liberal or else a little Conservative" would have to be modified since the rise of the Labour and nationalist parties in British politics, it does emphasize the historical importance of learning a partisan attachment in the British context. Partisanship is acquired early and influences people's attitudes and behaviour in their adult years.

The transmission of partisan attachments from parents to children reveals the continuing importance of the family as an agent of socialization in Britain. Moreover, interest in politics and political activity is often the result of family influence. One fascinating study of British prime ministers has argued, for example, that "the long and meandering road that ends at 10 Downing Street begins its course in an unhappy home," with "the most eminent British political leaders . . . distinguished, to an exceptional degree, by childhood bereavement and personal isolation" (Berrington, 1974: 345). Thus, the family in Britain remains an important agent in the political socialization process, particularly with respect to political activity and leadership recruitment.

A second distinctive agent of political learning in Britain is the school system, especially the public schools, which are in fact private institutions. The educational system is class-based, with those receiving a university education, especially from the most prestigious schools, dominating the political process. Even the "Thatcherite revolution" of the 1980s has not altered the social, economic, and educational backgrounds of the British elite (*The Economist*, 1992). Such an educational system helps to reinforce the deferential attitudes and class basis of the British political culture.

In the American socialization process, two agencies have developed unique attributes (Burns et al., 2000: 257–259). First, the school system has traditionally been utilized as a means of developing a homogeneous political culture, as a key agency in achieving the American melting pot. The large waves of immigrants of the 19th and 20th centuries were to be molded into Americans — social differentiation was discouraged in the search for the common man and woman. The school system was a vital element of this process, teaching people a common language, history, and culture, often through specialized civics courses. Although the school system is probably not as influential today as it once was, it remains an important shaper of values, given the relatively high political content in many American schools.

A second significant agent in American political learning is the mass media (Kahan, 1999: 168–201). The early and widespread use of television in the United States, combined with a political process that encourages and demands coverage, has given the mass media an increasingly important role in the learning of political values. Wars, assassinations, elections, and state occasions, such as a presidential inauguration, receive extensive media exposure. Moreover, even children's programs on television have a high level of political content. The news media are consequently "a significant determinant of children's political attitudes and patterns of political participation" (Conway et al., 1981: 175).

With respect to the content of the political socialization process, the United States is highly nationalistic and patriotic, with an emphasis on the goodness of the American way of life and its values. National loyalty is traditionally inculcated early, through symbols such as the flag and through recitation of the Pledge of Allegiance. The national anthem is played to open sporting events — a practice which started with the outbreak of World War II. Extensive study of American history is compulsory, with historical figures such as Washington and Lincoln receiving almost saintly status. The uniqueness of the American political experiment is stressed, with an emphasis on the special nature of the land and its people. The typical interpretation of events stresses consensus, downplaying the differences that might separate any group from the mainstream of American political life. Thus, it is not surprising to find, as an example of censorship, that in 1987 a United States federal judge in Alabama banned 32 textbooks from the public schools because they "illegally promoted the religion of secular humanism." A second distinguishing attribute of the political socialization process in the United States is the dominant role of the president in a child's initial perception of politics. This dominance of the presidency is in part a reflection of the consensus image of American politics and the strong sense of nationalism, of which the presidency is a key symbol. While the dominant American political themes have been increasingly challenged in recent decades (Dye, 1997: 53–58), by most accounts they remain largely in place.

CONSEQUENCES OF POLITICAL SOCIALIZATION

Although each polity may have some unique characteristics with respect to the process of political learning, the goal of political socialization in all systems is to produce loyal citizens who accept the legitimacy of the existing political institutions. To accomplish such an objective, however, different kinds of systems place varying emphasis on, and control over, both the content and agencies of the political learning process. In democratic systems, political education is most often implicit and indirect, with little political content taught directly to the child. In totalitarian systems, the process is state-controlled, centralized, explicit, and direct, with a high level of political content contained in the school curriculum. Moreover, such systems place an emphasis on both adult and childhood political learning.

The result of the political socialization process for the individual is the learning and acceptance of the main elements of his or her country's political culture. From the perspective of the political system, political socialization processes are significant for their impact on the stability and continued existence of the political regime. All polities seek to influence, if not to control directly, both the agents and content of political education: "the stakes are simply too high for those in control not to attempt to influence who learns what, especially as that learning affects basic political values" (Dawson, Prewitt, and Dawson, 1977: 10).

SUMMARY

1. The political culture of a system refers to the attitudes and beliefs people hold about the polity and their role in it. Some political cultures have developed a consensus around key political values and hence are integrated, while others are internally divided along the lines of the basic socio-political cleavages and therefore are fragmented. Each political culture is a particular mix of ideological elements, illustrated by their various political values. Political cultures also differ with respect to the role of the individual in the political process (parochial, subject, or participant).

2. The Canadian political culture is characterized by the themes of elitism, regionalism, dualism, and continentalism. As a result, Canada has a fragmented political culture composed of an important series of political subcultures. The most distinctive of these regional political cultures is centred in Quebec, whose main political preoccupation is a defence of the French language and culture. Despite its fragmented nature, the Canadian system has traditionally managed to survive by operating a consociational style of political management. The constitutional battles of the 1980s and 1990s, as well as the changing nature of Canadian society, have thrown the consociational pattern into jeopardy.

3. The British political culture centres on the political values of tradition, deference, and consensus. The lack of a comprehensive written constitution enhances the importance of political beliefs and customs in the British context. Although increasingly challenged in recent decades, the British political culture is highly integrated in comparison to most political systems.

4. The overwhelming dominance of liberalism in the United States means that the American political culture is defined, for all practical purposes, in terms of its characteristics. Attributes of American liberalism include a negative view of political power and government, an emphasis on popular sovereignty, a stress on individualism, and a strong strain of political moralism. The political culture is an integrated one, although the application of the tenets of liberalism in specific contexts may lead to political conflict, as in the case of race.

5. Political beliefs are an important factor in comparing political systems because they shape both the structures and functions of government. Moreover, the influence of beliefs on both the structures and functions of the political system is a significant mechanism for adapting the polity to changed circumstances.

6. The learning of political beliefs through the political socialization process transmits the political culture from one generation to the next. In democratic systems, the political learning process is indirect and implicit, while in totalitarian systems it is direct, explicit, and state-controlled.

7. Although political learning begins early in Canada, by high school graduation very few individuals show very much interest in, or knowledge about, their political system. Initial contact with the political regime is personalized through identification with political leaders and political parties. As the child matures, the major values of Canada's political culture are acquired, especially the attitudes associated with regionalism and dualism. American influence is particularly evident with respect to two agents: the schools and the mass media. The creation of a common national identity in Canada has been inhibited by the fragmented and indirect nature of the political learning process.

8. While similar to Canada in their political socialization processes, both Britain and the United States show some unique traits. With respect to content, Britain stresses deferential attitudes toward political authority and early acquisition of partisan attachments, while the public schools are an important agent of political learning and recruitment. In the United States, the schools and the mass media are significant agents of socialization, with a traditional emphasis on a common national identity and national loyalty.

CONCEPT FILE

agents of political socialization
bilingual belt thesis
consensual political culture
consociational democracy
continentalism
deferential political culture
direct democracy
dualism
elitism
fragmented political culture
integrated political culture
parochial political culture

participant political culture
political culture
political moralism
political socialization process
political subculture
quasi-participative politics
Quiet Revolution (Quebec)
regionalism
regional political culture
subject political culture
tradition

RECOMMENDED READINGS

Political Culture

ALMOND, GABRIEL A. and SIDNEY VERBA (1965) *The Civic Culture: Political Attitudes and Democracy in Five Nations*. Boston: Little, Brown and Co.

COLOM-GONZALEZ, FRANCISCO (1996) "Dimensions of Citizenship: Canada in Comparative Perspective," *International Journal of Canadian Studies*, Volume 14, pp. 94–109.

FORBES, H.D. (1987) "Hartz-Horowitz at Twenty: Nationalism, Toryism and Socialism in Canada and the United States," *Canadian Journal of Political Science*, Volume 20, Number 2, pp. 287–315.

JACKMAN, ROBERT W. and ROBERT A. MILLER (1996) "A Renaissance of Political Culture?" *American Journal of Political Science*, Volume 40, Number 4, pp. 632–659.

HARTZ, LOUIS, ed. (1964) *The Founding of New Societies*. New York: Harcourt, Brace and World.

HENRY, WILLIAM A., III (1994) *In Defense of Elitism*. New York: Doubleday.

MERELMAN, RICHARD M. (1991) *Partial Visions: Culture and Politics in Britain, Canada, and the United States*. Madison, Wisconsin: The University of Wisconsin Press.

MORGAN, EDMUND S. (1988) *Inventing the People: The Rise of Popular Sovereignty in England and America*. New York: W.W. Norton and Company.

SEE, KATHERINE O'SULLIVAN (1986) *First World Nationalisms: Class and Ethnic Politics in Northern Ireland and Quebec*. Chicago: The University of Chicago Press.

Canadian Political Culture

AJZENSTAT, JANET and PETER J. SMITH, eds. (1995) *Canada's Origins: Liberal, Tory or Republican?* Montreal: McGill-Queen's University Press.

DION, LEON (1976) *Quebec: The Unfinished Revolution*. Montreal: McGill-Queen's University Press.

GRANATSTEIN, JACK (1996) *Yankee Go Home? Canadians and Anti-Americanism*. Toronto: HarperCollins.

HOROWITZ, GAD (1968) *Canadian Labour in Politics*. Toronto: University of Toronto Press.

HOWARD-HASSMEN, RHODA E. (1999) " 'Canadian' as an Ethnic Category: Implications for Multiculturalism and National Unity," *Canadian Public Policy*, Volume 25, Number 4, pp. 523–537.

MANCKE, ELIZABETH (1999) "Early Modern Imperial Governance and the Origins of Canadian Political Culture," *Canadian Journal of Political Science*, Volume 32, Number 1, pp. 3–20

MARTIN, LAWRENCE (1993) *Pledge of Allegiance: The Americanization of Canada in the Mulroney Years*. Toronto: McClelland and Stewart.

MCROBERTS, KENNETH (1997) *Misconceiving Canada: The Struggle for National Unity*. Toronto: Oxford University Press.

MONIERE, DENIS (1981) *Ideologies in Quebec: The Historical Development*. Toronto: University of Toronto Press.

PATTEN, STEVE (1999) "The Reform Party's Re-imagining of the Canadian Nation," *Journal of Canadian Studies*, Volume 34, Number 1, pp. 27–51.

PRESTHUS, ROBERT (1973) *Elite Accommodation in Canadian Politics*. Toronto: Macmillan of Canada.

RESNICK, PHILIP (2000) *The Politics of Resentment: British Columbia, Regionalism and the Canadian Identity*. Vancouver: University of British Columbia Press.

SAVOIE, DONALD J. (2000) "All Things Canadian Are Now Regional," *Journal of Canadian Studies*, Volume 35, Number 1. pp. 203–217.

SREBRNIK, HENRY (1998) "Vandals at the Garden's Gates? Political Reaction to the Maritime Union Proposal on Prince Edward Island," *The American Review of Canadian Studies*, Volume 28, Numbers 1–2, pp. 83–101.

STEVENSON, GARTH (1999) *Community Beseiged: The Anglophone Minority and the Politics of Quebec.* Kingston and Montreal: McGill-Queen's University Press.

VERNEY, DOUGLAS V. (1986) *Three Civilizations, Two Cultures, One State: Canada's Political Traditions.* Durham, North Carolina: Duke University Press.

British Political Culture

BAGEHOT, WALTER (1867, 1963) *The English Constitution.* London: Collins, The Fontana Library.

BROWN, ALICE et al. (1997) *Politics and Society in Scotland.* Edinburgh: Edinburgh University Press.

COOGAN, T.P. (1995) *TheTroubles: Ireland's Ordeal 1966–1995.* London: Hutchinson.

HASELER, STEPHEN (1990) "Britain's 'Ancien Regime'," *Parliamentary Affairs*, Volume 43, Number 4, pp. 415–425.

HEATH, ANTHONY et al. (1999) "British National Sentiment," *British Journal of Political Science*, Volume 29, Number 1, pp. 155–175.

MCGARRY, J. and B. O'LEARY (1995) *Explaining Northern Ireland.* Oxford: Blackwell.

ROSE, RICHARD (1982) *The Territorial Dimension in Government: Understanding the United Kingdom.* Chatham, N.J.: Chatham House Publishers.

American Political Culture

BENNETT, WILLIAM J. (1998) *The Death of Outrage: Bill Clinton and the Assault on American Ideals.* New York: The Free Press.

DE TOCQUEVILLE, ALEXIS (1835, 1945) *Democracy in America,* ed. Phillips Bradley. New York: Vintage Books.

HACKER, ANDREW (1993) *Two Nations: Black and White, Separate, Hostile, Unequal.* New York: Ballantine Books.

HARRIGAN, JOHN J. (1993) *Empty Dreams, Empty Pockets: Class and Bias in American Politics.* New York: Macmillan.

HARTZ, LOUIS (1955) *The Liberal Tradition in America.* New York: Harcourt Brace Jovanovich.

HOFSTADTER, RICHARD (1948) *The American Political Tradition.* New York: Vintage Books.

LAPHAM, LEWIS H. (1988) *Money and Class in America: Notes and Observations on Our Civil Religion.* New York: Weidenfeld and Nicolson.

LIPSET, SEYMOUR MARTIN (1996) *American Exceptionalism: A Double-Edged Sword.* New York: W.W. Norton and Company.

PARENTI, MICHAEL (1994) *Land of Idols: Political Mythology in America.* New York: St. Martins Press.

ROGIN, MICHAEL PAUL (1986) "The Countersubversive Tradition in American Politics," *Berkeley Journal of Sociology*, Volume 31, pp. 1–33.

ROSSITER, CLINTON (1963) *The Political Thought of the American Revolution.* New York: Harcourt, Brace and World.

SCHLESINGER, ARTHUR M., JR. (1992) *The Disuniting of America: Reflections on a Multicultural Society.* New York: W.W. Norton and Company.

SINOPOLI, RICHARD C. and TEENA GABRIELSON (1999) "Mirroring Modernity: America's Conflicting Identities," *Polity*, Volume 32, Number 1, pp. 67–92.

Political Socialization

BENNETT, STEPHEN E. (1997) "Why Young Americans Hate Politics, and What We Should Do About It," *PS: Political Science and Politics*, Volume 30, Number 1, pp. 47–53.

BRONFENBRENNER, URIE (1970) *Two Worlds of Childhood: U.S. and U.S.S.R.* New York: Simon and Schuster.

DAWSON, RICHARD E. et al. (1977) *Political Socialization.* 2nd ed. Boston: Little, Brown and Co.

FRAZER, ELIZABETH (2000) "Citizenship Education: Anti-political Culture and Political Education in Britain," *Political Studies*, Volume 48, Number 1, pp. 88–103.

GRANATSTEIN, J.L. (1998) *Who Killed Canadian History?* Toronto: HarperCollins.

HAHN, C.I. (1998) *Becoming Political: Comparative Perspectives on Citizenship Education.* Albany, New York: State University of New York Press.

LANDES, RONALD G. (1976) "The Use of Role Theory in Political Socialization Research: A Review, Critique, and Modest Proposal," *International Journal of Comparative Sociology*, Volume 17, Numbers 1–2, pp. 59–72.

—— (1977) "Political Socialization Among Youth: A Comparative Study of English-Canadian and American School Children," *International Journal of Comparative Sociology*, Volume 18, Numbers 1–2, pp. 63–80.

NIEMI, RICHARD G. and JANE JUNN (1998) *Civic Education: What Makes Students Learn.* New Haven: Yale University Press.

OSBORNE, KEN (2000) " 'Our History Syllabus Has Us Gasping': History in Canadian Schools — Past, Present, and Future," *The Canadian Historical Review*, Volume 81, Number 3, pp. 403–435.

PAMMETT, JON H. and MICHAEL S. WHITTINGTON, eds. (1976) *Foundations of Political Culture: Political Socialization in Canada.* Toronto: Macmillan.

POLITICS ON THE NET

POLITICAL CULTURE: For **symbols of Canada**, see *www.pch.gc.ca/ceremonial-symb/index.html*. For the **Dominion Institute**, a website for researchers and teachers of Canadian history, see *www.dominion.ca*. (results of the Institute's survey of the top ten defining moments of Canadian history are found here). For results of **public opinion polling** in the United States, see the website of the Gallup organization at *www.gallup.com*. For studies that analyze the content of **TV coverage of politics**, see the Annenberg Public Policy Center at *www.appcpenn.org*.

The Electoral Process

Every election is a contest between heritage and impulse, as the verities of the past compete with the risks of the future. (Newman, 1988: 29)

But the vote, and other markers of democratic citizenship, have fallen on hard times, criticized as too much of a bad thing. Votes don't matter, power does, and the vote only cajoles us into thinking we have power. Or, on the other hand, votes are too little of a good thing; they may matter, but they don't matter much. Democrats know better. (Elshtain, 1993: 116)

CHAPTER PREVIEW

- In the modern era, all types of political systems claim legitimacy on the basis of the election process. Only in democratic systems does the election process provide a competitive choice about who rules.

- Political recruitment — the selection of candidates to run for public office — is the first step in the election process. In most political systems, political recruitment is a closed process to the average voter.

- In democratic systems, most people only participate by voting. The key legal barriers to voting have been removed over the course of the 20th century. Other factors (social, political, and personal) still keep a large segment of the public from participating in the political process.

- Canada's political recruitment process is relatively closed, but becoming more open; its elections are now much shorter in length; its level of voter participation is now at an historic low.

- One of the most unique aspects of the American political process is the use of the direct primary to nominate candidates.

- Those individuals selected through the election process are not a mirror image of society. Certain groups are either advantaged or disadvantaged by the electoral process.

- Political participation, by individuals or by groups, is a powerful political resource in the struggle for political power.

The orchestrated cacophony of an election campaign is at once both the most visible and most vital ingredient of the public's role in the political process of democratic systems. Unfortunately, few voters understand either the mechanics or the consequences of the electoral process, both of which have a profound impact on the distribution of influence and power in the polity. The nature of the electoral process can be best understood in terms of its three component parts: first, how individuals are selected to run for public office (i.e., political recruitment); second, how the candidates so selected compete against each other for political power (i.e., elections); and third, how the average citizen becomes involved in deciding which candidate wins (i.e., voting).

THE NATURE OF THE ELECTORAL PROCESS

Elections became an important characteristic of all forms of government during the 20th century. However, there is considerable variation in the structure and functions of the electoral process in different types of political systems. In democratic systems, elections are competitive: that is, several candidates openly contest for power, with the winning party acquiring control of government through a peaceful and public transfer of power. In totalitarian systems, elections are noncompetitive: only one party runs a single candidate for each office. The real political battle is carried on in private among the political elites, with elections serving to ratify or legitimate the selection already made by the single party. In autocratic systems, elections may include several candidates or parties, but the result is never in doubt. The dominant party is assured of winning either through intimidation or electoral manipulation, exemplified by Cuba in 1998, when Fidel Castro won re-election with 7.6 million votes (out of 7.8 million eligible voters) in an election where only a single candidate of the Communist party contested for each office.

In democratic polities the basic function of elections is to select those individuals who will govern and direct the political process until the next campaign. By choosing the governors and forcing them to return to the people at regular intervals for a renewed mandate, the mass public indirectly influences the content and direction of public policy. The public's role in the electoral process is often misunderstood because the connection between the governors and governed is assumed to be immediate and direct — most often it is not.

Elections are a blunt instrument of popular control, because they are infrequent and party-based. Between elections, the selected elite has a relatively free hand in governing, although its members must always keep their eyes on levels of public support if they wish to retain office in the future. Governments are most responsive before an election campaign, usually providing new programs or promises of future improvements in public policy. After an election, governments may undertake unpopular measures (e.g., raising their own salaries, wage-and-price controls, tax increases to reduce the deficit), in the hope that their effects on the public will be forgotten or forgiven by the time a new mandate is sought. One reason why minority governments in Canada have typically been more responsive than many majority ones can be attributed, at least in part, to this electoral connection.

In the modern era, elections are party contests for power, not simply a series of individual battles in the various constituencies. Moreover, each party usually takes a stand on a series of issues, so that the electorate may have difficulty in determining which party to select. For example, if you think Party A is on the correct side of two issues, and Party B reflects your sentiments on two others, for which party do you cast your ballot?

> We cannot fool all of the people some of the time, or even some of the people all of the time — but if we can fool a majority of the people at election time, that's all the time we need (Charles McKenzie, Rhinoceros Party of Canada, September 1988).

Many people — quite likely a majority of voters — determine their choice of party on factors other than policy, including items such as religion, family ties, social class, personality, looks, and charisma. No wonder then that it is often an indirect impact that elections make on public policy. The electorate chooses its leaders, who in turn decide the content of the political agenda. Thus, voters rarely grant a specific mandate to any party with respect to the content of public policy, even though winning parties usually act as if their program has, in fact, received the public's benediction (Dahl, 1990; Ladd, 1993; Clarke et al., 1996; Flanigan and Zingale, 1998: 186–188).

While the broad purposes and structures of electoral politics are similar in parliamentary and presidential systems, they differ in several important characteristics. In a parliamentary context, election time periods are variable within a maximum tenure of office, typically five years. Election writs are issued after the formal executive grants a dissolution of Parliament, but the formal executive only acts on the initiative of the political executive. Individuals are eligible to vote if they meet minimum standards of age and citizenship and have their name included on the voters' list as a result of an enumeration process. Candidates for public office must qualify as voters and must also be nominated by a number of their fellow citizens, with most nominees running under a party label. The selection of candidates is carried out by the parties at the local or constituency level, usually without direct intervention from national party headquarters. In most cases, election campaigns are of short duration.

In a presidential system, elections are constant (e.g., every four years for the American presidency, every two years for the House of Representatives) and constitutionally prescribed: there is no leeway in the election call, since it is mandated by law. While historically the parties have exercised power over candidate selection in the United States, the introduction of the primary technique has undercut the role of parties in the nomination process. Moreover, citizens must take the initiative to have their names included on the list of eligible voters due to a registration, rather than an enumeration, procedure. Election campaigns may be very long: even though the formal American campaign extends from Labor Day to the first Tuesday in November in presidential elections, the informal campaign starts in January, and, in some cases, up to a year or more before that (i.e., nearly two years in total). Some would argue that, in fact, the 2004 presidential race started on election day in 2000; that is, an informal election period that is four years long. The different election procedures utilized in presidential and parliamentary systems help to determine the types of parties that will compete and the kinds of candidates nominated for public office.

Through the election campaign the public decides which set of party leaders will govern, while a second important election ingredient, and one prior to the election itself, is the nomination and selection of party candidates. Even though an individual may contest office as an independent, the nomination process is overwhelmingly a party matter, and will be so treated in the ensuing analysis. Parties are the prime agents in the **political recruitment process**, a concept that refers to *those "processes that select from among the several million socially favored and politically motivated citizens comprising the political stratum those several thousand who reach positions of significant national influence"* (Putnam, 1976: 46).

One factor, often overlooked, in getting people to run for office is what happens to them when they leave office. In rigid totalitarian systems, such as the Soviet Union under Stalin, loss of office often meant loss of life. For example, even though he begged for mercy, former KGB chief Lavrenti Beria was shot in 1953. In democratic systems, loss of office does not involve loss of life. Instead we pay our politicians to leave quietly and peacefully, by offering pensions as a reward for past service. For example, Canadian MPs who have served for six years start receiving their inflation-indexed pension at age 55; those who have not served six years receive severance pay of six months salary.

Sometimes other benefits are also available for retiring politicians. Upon René Lévesque's retirement, the Parti Québécois gave him thousands of dollars worth of airline tickets, presumably so he would be out of the country during the next provincial election campaign. Successful politicians also find that they are asked to serve as representatives on corporate Boards of Directors. However, if a party has become highly unpopular and suffers a devastating electoral defeat, most of its former members may find that few, if any, such appointments are available (i.e., the federal Liberals in 1984 and the federal Tories in 1993).

The political recruitment process is significant because, by determining who stands for office, it ultimately selects the makers of public policy. Moreover, it should not be overlooked that in many democratic polities nomination is tantamount to election, given the existence of safe seats for each party. A **safe seat** for a party is *a constituency in which that party has consistently won with large vote pluralities over the other parties.* Under normal circumstances, the party's candidate will win, no matter who that candidate happens to be. In these situations, the real electoral choice is made by the party at the constituency nomination meeting, not in the general election. During a normal election, that is, when one of the major parties retains office (e.g., Canada in 1988, 1997, and 2000), probably 50 to 60 percent of the seats in the House of Commons could be so classified — in Britain that figure is often as high as 65 to 75 percent. In American national legislative elections, incumbents won re-election 95 percent of the time between 1980 and 1990; in the 1998 congressional elections incumbents won 97 percent of the contests.

While theoretically it is possible for a considerable portion of the public to become involved in the process of political recruitment, either by becoming a candidate or by helping to nominate one, no known instance of such involvement has ever been observed. Instead, from among the many, few directly participate in the candidate selection process, with fewer still ever chosen to become official candidates. The recruitment process can be symbolized, perhaps, as a funnel, with the mouth of the funnel representing the electorate and the narrow end, those nominated and elected to public office. The further into the funnel one moves, the fewer are the people involved, but the greater is their power in the political recruitment process. *Those individuals who are directly involved in the choice of candidates* are often referred to as the **selectorate**, typically a small group in most democratic polities. The selectorate at the constituency level in parliamentary systems may range from several hundred to several thousand delegates in those ridings in which there is a battle for the nomination.

Since the nomination of candidates is *an internal party matter with limited mass participation*, the recruitment of candidates in a parliamentary system can be classified as a **closed political recruitment process**. In contrast, the American presidential system has an **open recruitment process**, that is, *the use of primaries to nominate party candidates, which allows for extensive public participation in the selection process*. Moreover, the primaries permit almost anyone a try at gaining the nomination, although in many cases it is the party-backed individual who wins.

The nature and operation of the recruitment process, therefore, reveal much about the political stratification of the polity, for the ability of the selectorate to control who leads ultimately determines the content of public policy. Moreover, those who recruit and are recruited are never a mirror image of society, but represent, instead, the political elite — what has been called the **law of increasing disproportion** (Putnam, 1976: 33). A paradox is thus created: representative government is often composed of individuals unrepresentative of some of the major sectors of the socio-political milieu. If this discrepancy becomes too great, the legitimacy of the polity itself might be called into question.

While a small segment of the public may be politically active in the political recruitment process, most citizens participate only intermittently in the electoral arena by casting a ballot in an election campaign. Given the impact and acceptance of the democratic ideal in the 20th century, people are encouraged to participate in the political process. Although many kinds of political activity are available to the individual, voting is the supreme act of participation for most citizens, especially those in democratic systems.

The rationale for voting can be viewed from the perspective of the overall political system or from that of the individual participant. In the democratic age, voting has become both a symbol of mass participation in the polity and a process for establishing the legitimacy of the political system. Participation through voting is a way of developing and enhancing a person's support for the political system: if one feels that one can influence political decisions by voting, one will be less likely to seek changes in the political structure. The legitimacy of the political system and the individual's corresponding support for it are important consequences of the voting process. From the individual's

> . . . in a modern mass democracy the ultimate political decisions concern not what the rulers shall do but who the rulers shall be. Determining who shall rule through periodic elections of public officials remains the sovereign people's weapon-of-last-resort for influencing what government does (Ranney, 1965: vii).

perspective, voting is also significant because, in democratic systems, it is the primary means by which he or she both selects those who govern and seeks to influence their behaviour.

Even though a person in a participant political culture may have adopted or learned the need to vote as a result of the political learning process, many other factors influence both the frequency and form of that involvement. On a general level, we can identify four major influences on voting participation: legal, social, political, and personal factors.

With respect to legal influences, the 20th century witnessed a gradual reduction of prohibitions to near minimum levels. However, it was not until 1984 that women were finally granted the right to vote in Liechtenstein, and 1989 in Jordan. In Kuwait in 1992, following the Persian Gulf War of 1991, women — as well as most men — were not entitled to vote in the first election to be held in that country in seven years, a pattern that was repeated in the 1996 Kuwaiti election. In 1999, the all-male parliament in Kuwait voted 32 to 30 to deny women the vote, but Kuwait's ruler issued a decree granting women the right to vote and run for office, beginning with the 2003 elections.

While not everyone can vote in liberal-democratic systems, restrictions are few and generally limited only by age (usually 18), residency (usually six months to one year), citizenship (usually limited to citizens only), and registration requirements. The latter factor is often overlooked, but the differences between the traditional enumeration process in a parliamentary system such as Canada and an individual registration procedure as in the United States affect the rate of voting turnout (Glass, Squire, and Wolfinger, 1985). In a rather strange example of the right to vote being universally extended, Yigal Amir, who assassinated former Israeli prime minister Yitzhak Rabin, was allowed to vote from his prison cell during the 1996 Israeli general election.

Other legal requirements sometimes influence the extent of voting as well. For example, in most democratic systems, voting is voluntary. Once people have met the requirements of age, residency, citizenship, and registration, they are entitled to vote, but may choose not to do so. However, some democratic systems have adopted **compulsory voting**, that is, *a voting system in which people are legally required to exercise their franchise in the electoral contest.* Among democratic countries, Australia is the most notable example, along with Belgium, Italy, and Costa Rica. The historically low voter turnout rate of 61 percent in the 2000 federal election in Canada prompted the chief electoral officer to suggest that Canada should perhaps begin to consider the idea of compulsory voting. In Australia, compulsory voting increased the rate of voter turnout by nearly 40 percent (Franklin, 1999: 206; Mackerras and McAllister, 1999), thus demonstrating the impact of legal rules on electoral participation.

Even if one meets all legal requirements, the remaining social, political, and personal factors may circumscribe an individual's political activity. Social characteristics include such things as a person's occupation, education, religion, social class, ethnicity, and region of residence. These factors are often classified as the basic socio-political cleavages that divide the political community. Membership in a particular ethnic, class, religious, linguistic, or regional group often has important political consequences. The various socio-political groups differentially participate in the political process and as a result wield different degrees of influence in the decision-making process. In a similar vein, political advantage accrues to particular ethnic, class, religious, linguistic, and regional groups in all societies. Rates of political participation are never neutral in their political consequences.

By political factors we mean the impact of leaders, policies, parties, and events on one's desire to participate. For example, a new leader may galvanize people into participating in the political system. If a particularly salient issue comes to the forefront during a campaign or if people perceive the outcome of the vote to be especially crucial, then participation increases. A political crisis or a referendum on a controversial issue may be the impetus for taking politics more seriously than in the past. Finally, identifying with a specific political party is often an incentive to increased participation. Such political factors suggest that the political process itself, in terms of its leaders, policies, and parties, has a significant bearing on citizen participation.

The personal characteristics of the individual citizen, which in most cases are psychological, are the final factor influencing political involvement. For example, a major incentive to participation are feelings of **political efficacy**, that is, *the belief or view that one is capable of influencing the political process.* Those persons with high levels of political efficacy participate at a much greater rate than those with low levels. By contrast, those individuals who are cynical, apathetic, or alienated tend to withdraw from active participation in the polity. Such personal characteristics are often developed before the individual becomes old enough to vote and, for the most part, demonstrate the results of the socialization process.

Source: CAM (Cameron Cardow), *The Ottawa Citizen.* By permission.

THE CANADIAN ELECTORAL PROCESS

While each particular polity will have unique electoral features of one kind or another, they all have to deal with the three component parts of the electoral process: political recruitment, elections, and voting. It is also important to remember that specific systems are typically updating and changing their procedures with respect to each of these three electoral components — the Canadian polity being no exception in this regard.

POLITICAL RECRUITMENT IN CANADA

Although parties have traditionally controlled both the recruitment and nomination of candidates for public office in Canada, the fiction was long maintained that those candidates were simply individuals rather than party representatives. For example, it was not until the 1972 federal election that a candidate's party affiliation was included on the ballot. As private organizations, the parties determine their own recruitment and selection procedures. The result, historically, has been for a pattern of elite control of the political recruitment process. An interesting variation on this theme occurred in Alberta in 1996, in the period leading to the 1997 provincial election. Those individuals seeking a Tory nomination to run with Premier Ralph Klein were required to pay up to $2,000 before they could enter the political recruitment process at the constituency level.

The legal qualifications to be a candidate are minimal. Generally speaking, any person qualified to vote — that is, any elector — has the right to stand for nomination and election to public office. Since the eligible electorate is currently about 20 million, the potential number of candidates is very large indeed. However, certain classes of people, such as those who have violated provisions of the Canada Elections Act in the previous campaign or government contractors, are excluded. For example, Paul Rose, convicted killer of Liberal cabinet minister Pierre Laporte during the 1970 October Crisis, was prevented from running as an NDP candidate in Quebec in the early 1990s, even though he had received a full pardon in 1980. Citizenship is a basic legal requirement for nomination, something which was overlooked by Peter Macdonald, leader of the Progressive Conservative Party of British Columbia, and which, as a result, prevented him from running in the 1991 provincial election.

A separation between the federal and provincial arenas is maintained in the recruitment process, since members of one level of government cannot be officially nominated or contest the election at the other level without resigning from their current office. For example, before former premier Brian Tobin re-entered national politics as an official Liberal candidate in the 2000 election, he resigned his seat in the Newfoundland House of Assembly.

In addition to being qualified as an elector, a second set of legal requirements must be met before an individual is officially nominated. Nomination papers, properly executed, must be filed before the date set for nominations to end.

Although some minor differences exist between federal and provincial requirements, the general pattern is that candidates must have their nomination papers signed by a number of qualified electors (100 in federal contests) in their electoral district. When the nomination papers are filed, a fee or deposit (federally it is $1,000) must be paid. This procedure was designed to prevent frivolous candidates from running for office, but in practice it does not appear to be a serious impediment to those with electoral ambitions: in the 1980s, about 1 600 individuals were officially nominated in federal elections. Given that 295 seats were being contested at the time in the House of Commons, this number averaged out to approximately five to six candidates for each constituency. With a number of new parties competing in the 1993 election, the total number of candidates nominated increased to a record high of 2 155 (1 680 men and 475 women) or an average of over seven per constituency. In 1997, the total number of candidates dropped to 1 672, but increased again in 2000 to 1 807 (an average of six per constituency). Only the Liberals nominated a complete slate of candidates (301) in the 2000 election. The other major parties attempted to do so, but had some of their nominees rejected by Elections Canada for failing to meet all of the nomination requirements: Canadian Alliance (4), NDP (3), and Conservatives (10). The Bloc Québécois had 75 candidates, all of them in Quebec. For the five main parties, of their 1 262 nominees only 242 or 19 percent were women. Finally, the nomination papers must contain a witnessed declaration by the candidate that he or she is willing to stand for election to public office.

To choose from a potential 20 million candidates approximately 1 800 who will actually contest for office in a federal election campaign reveals that the political recruitment funnel in Canada narrows quickly and precipitously. Between the potential and actual candidates stands the selectorate, the party activists who involve themselves in the nomination process. Most recruitment decisions are taken by the party elite before the nomination meetings are held, so that in many constituency contests only one individual is presented for consideration. While party rules allow for more than one name to be presented, so that the process appears to be competitive and democratic, a contested nomination is usually a sign that the political elite has either refused to coalesce around a single candidate or that, even when it has, some individual or group in the party fails to recognize the legitimacy of such backroom decisions. Thus, the vast majority of individuals who attend their party's constituency nomination meeting are not really given an effective voice in the political recruitment process: their task, instead, is to legitimate the choice of the party elite. The effective Canadian selectorate, therefore, might range all the way from one (e.g., the party leader) to several hundred or more, depending on the historical period, the competitiveness of the electoral district, and the extent of the political elite's control over the party organization. However, there were numerous examples of an increasingly competitive nomination process within the major parties during the last several federal election campaigns, especially in ridings where one party had a safe seat — making nomination the crucial step in the election process. For example, in 2000 in Calgary Northeast, the nomination for the Canadian Alliance party had five candidates and the membership list grew from 450 in 1997 to over 15 000 in the 2000 contest.

The traditional pattern of political recruitment has been for the party leader and a few key party organizers in each constituency to control the process. To this day, the leadership of the Quebec wing of the federal Liberal party, which has its own separate constitution, is allowed to reserve ridings for star candidates, thus obviating the need to even hold nomination meetings. Perhaps the longest lasting example of a party leader's control over the recruitment and nomination process at both the provincial and federal levels occurred in Newfoundland under Liberal Premier Joey Smallwood (1975: 186): "In Newfoundland, the leader of a political party exercised an authority that disappeared in mainland Canada long ago. It was the leader of the party who personally selected and appointed every individual candidate of the party in each election." Charges of elite control of the recruitment process in the federal Liberal party emerged in British Columbia in January of 1997 in the ridings of Burnaby-Douglas and Surrey Central, where apparent manipulation of the rules secured the nomination for the candidates perceived to be backed by the party establishment. Perhaps more significant still was the move by the federal Liberal party in August of 1996 to adopt rules that would allow some sitting MPs to be automatically renominated (i.e., not to have to win a constituency nomination meeting) for the then anticipated 1997 federal election.

Those involved in picking nominees often try to bring in some high profile candidates. For example, Ambassador Ken Taylor of Iranian hostage crisis fame was offered a safe seat for the 1984 contest by both the Liberals and Conservatives. However, Taylor turned down these offers to go into private business with Nabisco. In anticipation of the 1993 election, both the Liberal and Conservative parties openly courted Canadian Major-General Lewis MacKenzie as a possible candidate, after his impressive work for the United Nations in the former Yugoslavia in 1992. In anticipation of a 1997 federal election, in January Lewis MacKenzie announced he would seek the Tory nomination in the Ontario riding of Parry Sound-Muskoka, which he won in April. In the 2000 race, Prime Minister Jean Chrétien attempted to recruit some high-profile politicians (Frank McKenna, Roy Romanow, Brian Tobin), but only Brian Tobin agreed to run for the federal Liberals.

While the role of the party leader may be strong, the trend in recent decades is for increasing decentralization, with much of the control over political recruitment residing with the executive of the party's local constituency association. Although control is most often localized, party leaders may take the rare decision to disassociate themselves and their party from a particular candidate. In October of 1988, Prime Minister Mulroney announced that he would not sign the nomination papers of Sinclair Stevens, thus ending his candidacy for the Tories — even though he had won the York-Simcoe constituency nomination in July. In 1993, Prime Minister Kim Campbell refused to sign the nomination papers for several Tory MPs from Quebec who were facing various corruption charges.

An interesting case of nomination politics occurred in the NDP in British Columbia in 1994. After receiving the party nomination for the NDP in the provincial constituency of Matsqui, it was revealed that the candidate (Samuel Wagar) was a witch; he was a priest in the Covenant of the Goddess Church, which worshipped a pagan deity called The Horned God. Party officials promptly invalidated his nomination and called for a new nomination meeting; Mr. Wagar re-offered but was defeated at that meeting.

A leader may help to "parachute" a candidate into a local riding, but many such cases have been unsuccessful in Canadian politics. In **parachuting**, a local association may have no obvious candidate or they may desire one with more national stature, so that *the party leader may bring in an outsider to receive the nomination.* Because there is no legal residency requirement at the constituency level (i.e., a qualified elector may seek the nomination in any of the 301 ridings), such practices are possible. However, political tradition works strongly in favour of a local candidate, so that most candidates either live in the constituency they represent or close by. In contrast, at the party leadership level, parachuting has had a long history in Canada. On returning to politics, Jean Chrétien first gained a seat in New Brunswick, before returning to his home riding in Quebec. Other recent leaders have followed a similar route: Brian Mulroney (Nova Scotia, then Quebec); Joe Clark (Nova Scotia, then Alberta); Stockwell Day (Alberta [provincially], then British Columbia [federally]).

The local executive of a party's constituency organization attempts to maintain control of the recruitment process by several different methods. First, and most effectively, the local party elite must keep tabs on the sentiments within the constituency organization, so that they are aware of, and are able to defuse, possible challenges to their control of the recruitment process. Second, the party elite must decide, behind the scenes, on the candidate to be nominated and then ensure his or her success by coalition-building among the disaffected elements of the party organization. Third, if a contested nomination meeting is expected, then the rules of the game are often changed to limit last-minute memberships, to put an age requirement on those able to vote (e.g., 18), and to restrict access of the challengers to party membership lists.

A wise constituency executive never assumes that the obvious will happen — to do so may mean political failure. If the above caveats are not followed, then a constituency nomination meeting will become uncontrollable, as many outside, underage, and recently arrived party members vote for the party's candidate. For example, in the Trudeaumania of 1968, the Liberal association in the Davenport riding found that its membership "rose from 150 to 5 445 in a few weeks," with the outcome "determined by non-residents and ten-year-olds who, under the rules, could not be debarred from voting" (Beck, 1968: 401). A sudden surge in party membership at the constituency level prior to a nomination meeting indicates that the political elite's control is being challenged and that the nomination process will likely be a competitive one.

The recruitment and nomination process, as well as the nature of the selectorate, demonstrate the law of increasing disproportion. Nominees and elected representatives are not a mirror image of Canadian society, but are individuals from the better-off segments of society in terms of education, occupation, social class, and most other basic socio-economic attributes. The most glaring deficiency of the political recruitment process is the virtual exclusion of women. After the 1993 federal election, the number of women in the House of Commons rose to 53 (out of 295), up from 39 (out of 295) after the 1988 contest. In both the 1997 and 2000 federal elections, a total of 62 women were elected to the House of Commons. In fact, while women made up over 50 percent of the population, in the 20th century less than 1 percent of elected representatives in Canada at both the federal and provincial levels were women.

Many reasons can be advanced for the causes of this pattern, the most obvious of which is simply discrimination against females (Brodie and Chandler, 1995). In particular, male dominance and control over the party nomination process is an especially important explanation for why so few women ever get elected to the House of Commons. In an attempt to guarantee more women being nominated and elected, the defeated Charlottetown Accord would have allowed provinces (i.e., British Columbia, Nova Scotia) to require an equal number of constituencies for men and women. In a similar vein, in December of 1996 the commission designing the new territorial government for Nunavut (which began April 1, 1999) proposed the world's first gender-equal legislative assembly by requiring each constituency to elect both a male and a female representative — this plan, however, was not implemented.

Internal party changes in the selection of candidates for the 1993 federal election produced some interesting variations on the traditional patterns. For example, the New Democratic Party adopted the goal of a 50 percent quota of women candidates, while the Reform Party required potential candidates to fill out the "Reform Party's Candidate Questionnaire." The most dramatic change occurred within the Liberal party. Based on amendments to the Liberal party's constitution in 1992, the federal leader, Jean Chrétien, was empowered to bypass local constituency meetings and to directly nominate candidates in a selected number of ridings (14) across the country. The goal of such a procedure was to avoid highly divisive nomination battles at the local level, as well as to increase the number of women and minority candidates running under the Liberal party banner. In March of 1997, in seeking to meet the Liberal party goal of having 78 women run as candidates in the next election (i.e., 25 percent of the 301 constituencies in the House of Commons), Prime Minister Chrétien appointed four women as Liberal candidates (three in Ontario and one in British Columbia). The Liberal party did not repeat this procedure in the 2000 election campaign.

While the 1982 Canadian Charter of Rights and Freedoms has not been directly responsible for these changes in nomination politics — since political recruitment is an internal party matter not subject as yet to Charter jurisprudence — the Charter has indirectly influenced the candidate selection process. The concern of all of the major parties to increase their number of women and minority candidates — especially the authority granted to the Liberal leader in 1997 — is Charter-inspired. As such, these changes in the candidate selection process demonstrate the impact of the Charter on even the internal operations of the political parties — an influence that will expand in the future.

CANADIAN ELECTIONS

If the recruitment and nomination of political candidates departs from the democratic ideal, how can an election between candidates so selected be seen as contributing to the democratic nature of the larger political system? The key is in the choice between candidates and their respective parties. The overall system is democratic because it gives people a choice between competing candidates, not because those candidates have necessarily been selected in a democratic manner. The electoral battle in democratic polities allows the public to choose their governors at regular intervals — it rarely allocates to the ordinary citizen a role in selecting who those competitors will be. Between election campaigns, the individual is given few opportunities to influence the course of events. As former prime minister Pierre Trudeau said on several occasions during his long tenure in office, if the people do not like government policy, then they can kick out that government in the next election. Such a view implies, of course, that attempts by the public to control their governors between campaigns may not be seen as a particularly legitimate activity by the political elite.

In Canada, the life of any Parliament is limited to a maximum term of five years. Based on political tradition, majority governments usually return to the people after four years. Governments seek a new mandate when they perceive that the time is auspicious for success, which usually means, in the modern era, that the public opinion polls are in their favour. Minority governments may be forced into an election after only a short term in office if they suffer defeat in the legislature (e.g., the federal Conservatives in December 1979). However, most minority governments hold an election when they feel they can gain a majority (e.g., the federal Liberals in 1968 and 1974). Since the Second World War, minority governments have been of limited duration, not usually because of their lack of support in the legislature, but as a result of their desire to fashion a majority in a new election or because of their belief that, if an election were to be forced by the opposition, they would be re-elected.

The five-year maximum life of Parliament may be extended under special circumstances, if the decision for such an action is not opposed by more than one-third of the members of the House of Commons. Only once (during the First World War) was this extension provision utilized, so that over six years intervened between the federal elections of 1911 and 1917. Because extending the life of Parliament requires, in effect, a two-thirds vote in its favour and because the official opposition party (or opposition parties in total) normally has at least one-third of the seats in the Commons, it is politically improbable that a government could take such action simply to avoid an anticipated defeat at the polls.

The mechanics of the election process are relatively straightforward. Having requested and received a dissolution of Parliament from the formal executive, the prime minister and cabinet instruct the chief electoral officer to issue the election writs for each constituency. The election procedure in each riding is under the direction of the returning officer, whose job it is to prepare the voters' list, to make ready the necessary ballots, and to receive the nomination papers from those individuals who seek to be recognized as official candidates in the election. The tasks of the returning officer also include designating the various polling stations in each constituency (which may range from several dozen to upwards of 500), supervising the vote on election day, counting the ballots, and then declaring a particular candidate elected. Thus, the returning officer in each riding is responsible for the administration of the election in a fair and nonpartisan manner.

Of major significance for the citizen is the preparation of the voters' list. At the federal level through 1997, the list was prepared by an **enumeration process**, that is, *a door-to-door registration of urban voters after the election writs have been issued*. In rural areas until 1993, voters' lists were open, in that exclusion from them did not prevent a person from voting. The 1993 amendments to the Canada Elections Act standardized the enumeration process in both urban and rural polling divisions. In addition, in both rural and urban divisions, electors could be added to the voters' lists on polling day.

When enumerators were used at the federal level (note that some provinces still currently use an enumeration process), they were patronage positions. Two enumerators were traditionally required in urban ridings (one from each of the two parties that led in that constituency in the last election) and one in rural settings. Changes made in 1993 required two enumerators in each polling division. Given the number of individuals and households that had to be contacted in short order, there was considerable pressure on the enumerators to proceed as quickly as possible. The result was some inaccuracy in the voters' lists, since enumerators rarely inquired as to the citizenship, age, or residency of the individuals who happened to be at home when they knocked on the door. Contrary to correct procedure, enumerators often added to the list the names of individual family members who were not at home. It was thus possible to get one's name on the voters' list without meeting all of the legal requirements for voting. However, if your name was improperly registered on the voters' list, you were still not entitled to vote.

Although in recent elections the practice of having enumerators from both major parties prevented most corrupt practices, in the past, control of the enumeration process was used for partisan purposes. For example, what was known as the **graveyard vote** could be used to swing the results in closely contested ridings. If the government controlled the choice of enumerators, they could then *list dead people on the voters' list and have a party worker show up on election day to cast the ballot*. More than anything else, what probably prevented the use of such practices in recent decades is simply the size of the constituencies: so many names would have to be manipulated that it would be obvious to the parties contesting the election.

A related historical practice was to have the same person register more than once, using slightly different spellings of his or her name. Such techniques were widespread in Western Canada, particularly after the large waves of immigration from Eastern Europe in the 20th century. For example, in Manitoba the government often traded beer and favours in exchange for votes, a practice made possible because "undecipherable Slavic names made voters' lists elastic and impersonation unchallengeable" (Peterson, 1978: 66). While such practices largely disappeared after the 1970s, historically the voters' lists were reasonably accurate — the major deficiency seemed to be the number of individuals whose names appeared who did not meet all of the legal qualifications for voting.

The preparation of voters' lists was carried out each time a federal election was called. Thus, Canadian elections were based on what was known as a **temporary**

voters' list, because it was *used only for a single election before being discarded.* A rare exception to this practice occurred in 1980, with the unexpected defeat of the Clark government. The 1979 voters' lists were used in 1980 as well, with the normal enumeration period spent in revising and updating the records. Such a practice, however, did not serve as a precedent for the immediate introduction of a **permanent voters' list**, which would be *continued from one election to the next.* Before the 2000 election, a permanent voters' list was only used once at the federal level. Such a procedure was passed by Parliament in 1934 and used in the 1935 election but, because of complaints, the use of a permanent list was abolished in 1938. A slight movement toward a more permanent voters' list was made in 1993. The chief electoral officer was given the discretionary authority to decide that a new enumeration was unnecessary if an election was held within one year of polling day of a previous election or referendum. Thus, by holding the 1993 federal election on October 25 (one year less a day from the referendum of October 26, 1992), a new enumeration of voters was not required, which saved about $15 million.

A major change in the traditional Canadian enumeration process was approved by Parliament in 1996 and went into effect for any election held after April 23, 1997. Beginning April 10, 1997, the final door-to-door enumeration of voters in Canada took place in preparing a permanent voters' list, with the new computerized list completed on April 26 and the 1997 federal election called on April 27. Between elections, this permanent voters' list will be continuously updated using various government records. Thus, the 2000 federal election was the first one based on the new practice of a permanent voters' list. This move to a permanent voters' list will have two major effects: first, it will save about $30 million in each federal election and second, it will facilitate a significantly shorter election campaign.

The traditional use of a temporary voters' list had one major impact on the nature and organization of election campaigns in Canada, namely, to make them lengthy. Because the enumerators in urban areas until 1993 had to begin their canvass about seven weeks before the election date (45 days before polling day) and because it took some time to get enumerators appointed and trained, the duration of a federal campaign had to be nearly two months long (a minimum of 50 days). In the 1988 federal election, the thirty-third Parliament was dissolved on October 1, with the vote on November 21 and the election writs returned on December 12. The only practical way to significantly shorten the election period was to utilize a permanent voters' list. Instead of a seven- or eight-week contest, an election campaign might be held in four to six weeks. As indicated above, just such a change went into effect in 1997. As a result, the 2000 election campaign was only 35 days long (October 22 to November 27).

After each census, an automatic revision in the number and distribution of seats among the provinces is carried out. However, a time lag always exists, so that the 1984 federal election, for example, was based on constituencies drawn as a result of the 1971 census. The allocation of provincial seat totals was initially outlined by a series of rules specified in the 1867 Constitution Act (Section 51), with several modifications since that initial allocation. Although the rules are complex, seats in the House of Commons are primarily distributed on a population basis, with certain safeguards for Quebec and the smaller provinces. For example, Quebec is assigned a given number of seats, with the other provincial seat allocations determined from that base. The provincial distribution of these seats is indicated in Table 7.1. The 1993 election was based on the 1981 census figures, with the 1997 and 2000 elections based on the 1991 census results.

Several significant patterns are revealed by these data. First, the dominance of Ontario and Quebec is clear, since together they receive, on the basis of the 1991 census, 178 seats out of 301 or 59 percent of the total of all elected representatives to the national legislature. Second, although somewhat delayed in their impact, shifting population growth patterns are also apparent. For example, the four Atlantic provinces, while retaining the same number of seats in 1961, 1971, 1981, and 1991, are in fact losing representation, on a proportional basis, in the Commons (32 seats out of 264 in 1961; 32 seats out of 301 as a result of the 1991 figures). In contrast, the four Western provinces, most notably British Columbia and Alberta, are gaining seats. Third, Central Canada, especially Ontario, continues to gain seats as well. Although the West is gaining seats at a slightly faster rate than Central Canada, it will be many decades before the electoral dominance of Ontario and Quebec is seriously challenged. For example, the redistribution based on the 1991 census added four seats in Ontario and two seats in British Columbia, with no seats added in Alberta.

Table 7.1   Provincial Seats in the Canadian House of Commons

Province	Census			
	1961*	1971**	1981***	1991****
Ontario	88	95	99	103
Quebec	74	75	75	75
British Columbia	23	28	32	34
Alberta	19	21	26	26
Saskatchewan	13	14	14	14
Manitoba	13	14	14	14
Nova Scotia	11	11	11	11
New Brunswick	10	10	10	10
Newfoundland	7	7	7	7
Prince Edward Island	4	4	4	4
Northwest Territories	1	2	2	2
Yukon	1	1	1	1
Total	**264**	**282**	**295**	**301**

  * Results first applied in the 1968 election.
 ** Results first applied in the 1979 election.
*** Results first applied in the 1988 election.
**** Results first applied in the 1997 election.

A final distinction concerning the Canadian electoral process is the difference between a general election and a by-election. A **general election** results from *a dissolution of Parliament, so that all seats in the House of Commons are contested in a nationwide election*. A **by-election** is *an election in a single constituency to fill a vacancy that has developed between general elections*. A vacancy may occur as a result of a member's death or a member resigning from the legislature. When notified of a vacancy by the Speaker of the House, the prime minister, within six months, can select the date of the by-election. Although the prime minister must act within the six-month limit, the actual date of the by-election can be anytime in the future, up to the holding of the next general election. Thus, a prime minister can quickly call by-elections in those vacant constituencies the party feels confident of winning, and postpone, at least for a while, those in ridings the party is likely to lose.

The results of a by-election sometimes register the prevailing national political sentiment or shifts in it, or they can serve simply as a means of venting the electorate's anger against the government of the day. Consequently, opposition victories in by-elections do not accurately predict the results of the next general election. For example, the provincial Liberal party in Quebec won an impressive series of by-election victories after the general election of 1976, but ended up losing the provincial general election of 1981. However, after their 1981 loss, the Liberals once again won every by-election until the next general election, which they won in 1986.

The victorious party in the by-election often interprets the result as an indicator of political trends, while the losing party dismisses it as an aberrant result due to local or other special features not likely to be repeated in a general election. By-elections take on added significance if the government is in a minority position or if it has only a slim majority. In these situations, the loss of several by-elections might cost the government its right to remain in office.

THE CANADIAN VOTER

An important point of analysis regarding the electoral process concerns the problem of how many people participate in Canadian elections in comparison with the number of people who are eligible. Political activity was initially limited to white, adult males. Women were finally granted the suffrage in federal elections in 1918. Property qualifications were eliminated by the early decades of the 20th century. The age requirement for federal elections was reduced from 21 to 18 in 1970, with the age standard for participation in provincial elections now standing at either 18 or 19. In relation to the citizenship criterion, until 1970 Canadian citizens or British subjects residing in Canada could vote federally, but since 1975, only Canadian citizens are eligible. Landed immigrants cannot vote, which also means that they are excluded from political office, since to qualify as a candidate a person must be qualified as an elector. Residency requirements have traditionally been 12 months, with a person's residence defined as where he/she was living when the election was called. Because Quebec administered its own referendum in 1992 in conjunction with a national referendum in the remaining provinces, voters in Quebec had to meet the Quebec residency requirement of six months. As a result, approximately 20 000 Canadians living in Quebec were disenfranchised.

Legal discrimination has been virtually eliminated from voting criteria, although it was as late as 1950 that Inuit (then called Eskimos) were enfranchised and only in 1960 that discrimination against Aboriginals (then called Indians) was removed from the federal franchise. While such legal considerations as age, sex, citizenship, and residence have prevented otherwise eligible adults from voting throughout most of Canadian history, their elimination or reduction to minimal levels during the 20th century means that currently few individuals are legally disenfranchised. If an adult Canadian citizen does not vote, it is usually not the result of explicit legal barriers to political participation.

Source: MOU (Theodore Moudakis), *The Daily News*, Halifax, Nova Scotia. By permission.

The extent of voter participation is usually measured as the percentage of those individuals on the voters' list who in fact cast a ballot on election day. Over the past several decades in federal elections the rate of voter turnout has been about 75 percent, although in three consecutive elections (1958, 1962, 1963) it reached 79 percent. In 1997, the turnout rate was 67 percent, which dropped to 61 percent in 2000. In the October 1992 national referendum on the Charlottetown Accord, the turnout rate was 75 percent — with a provincial high of 83 percent in Quebec and a provincial low of 53 percent in Newfoundland. In provincial elections, voter turnout has exceeded the federal average in some provinces, such as Saskatchewan and Prince Edward Island, while in others, such as Alberta, it has been considerably lower. In an attempt to encourage participation in Western Canada, especially in British Columbia, voting hours in federal elections (as of April 1997) are now staggered, so that election results in Eastern Canada do not discourage voters in British Columbia from participating.

The high percentage of Canadians who vote means that most of the basic socio-political cleavages do not differentiate significant groupings in terms of rates of participation (Nevitte et al., 2000: 61–63). The variation in voting turnout among various groups has in most cases been small, leading one researcher to conclude that Canadians live in "a political melting-pot" which produces similar attitudes toward participation (Laponce, 1969: 178). For example, the social factors of ethnicity, religion, and gender traditionally produce few differences in rates of voter participation (Welch, 1975; Johnston et al., 1993). Even as pervasive an influence as regionalism seems to have little effect on political participation (Mishler, 1979: 58), although it may have some in certain contexts (Eagles, 1991). There is no apparent gender gap in terms of voter participation in Canada (Whittington and Van Loon, 1996: 427). In contrast, indicators of social class, such as occupation and education, are related to varying rates of participation: "It appears that Canadians who have a higher level of economic and social resources with which to participate in politics are more likely to do so" (Van Loon, 1970: 390; see also Whittington and Van Loon, 1996: 421–432). Although most of the basic socio-political cleavages have little impact on the rate of voting, their influence on the total electoral process is significant because of their strong association with partisan attachments, what we previously labelled the social basis of party support (Pammett, 1991; Bickerton, Gagnon, and Smith, 1999).

A further set of factors that influences participation is political in nature; we refer to the impact of parties, policies, and leaders. For example, an individual's attachment to a political party is a spur to activity, since parties are so intimately involved in the electoral process. A commitment to a party increases a citizen's interest, knowledge, and activity, while a lack of partisan beliefs is most often found among the inactive segment of the electorate (Johnston et al., 1993). Moreover, if the parties in a campaign are closely competitive, more voters will be drawn into the electoral process. For example, the election battles between Diefenbaker and Pearson in 1962 and 1963 had turnouts of 79 percent, while their respective contest in 1965 aroused less interest and a voter participation rate of 75 percent. Similarly, the 1980 election attracted half a million fewer voters than the election held only nine months earlier, in May 1979. Part of the reason for the lower turnout seems to have been the expected Liberal victory in 1980, given their 20-point lead in the public opinion polls when the election started. If the citizen views the results of an election as a foregone conclusion, then the incentive to vote is greatly diminished. Such a pattern was likely at work in the 2000 election: it was inconceivable that any party but the Liberals could form a government (either a majority or a minority one). Thus, voter turnout dropped to its lowest level (61 percent) in Canadian history.

With respect to policies, most people do not participate as a direct result of a single important issue. Rarely does an issue appear which by itself provokes an increase in political participation. A possible exception is the "independence option" in Quebec politics, which seems to have so polarized the political community that high rates of participation can occur, such as the 84 percent voter turnout in the 1980 provincial referendum. Even that high level of participation was surpassed in the 1995 Quebec referendum, which had an unprecedented turnout rate of 94 percent. More typically, issues are significant with respect to specific and usually small segments of the electorate, so that their impact on overall voting percentages is small or negligible.

A final example of a political factor that influences participation is the appeal of a particular leader. A new leader may attract people into the political arena by the strength of personality or the policies for which he or she stands. However, a strong personality may also offend many people, so that the overall impact on the extent of political activity is little changed. For example, while it is clear that

Trudeau brought many new people into the Liberal party ranks during the 1968 campaign, the percentage of those voting in 1968 (76 percent) was only 1 percentage point greater than in 1965 (75 percent).

Psychological attitudes toward politics, which we have classified as personal factors, have consistently been found to influence political participation. For example, individuals who have an interest in political matters, who have developed an adequate knowledge about their political system, or who have a feeling that a good citizen should be active in politics, have much higher rates of participation than those who do not exhibit such views (Van Loon, 1970: 394–396; Whittington and Van Loon, 1996). Similarly, those citizens who feel that they can influence the political system are most prone to political activism (Mishler, 1979: 76). These findings reflect the importance of perception in the world of politics: if people think they have a meaningful role in it, they are more likely to participate in the polity.

In examining the four factors that influence political participation (legal, social, political, and personal), we have discovered some items that usually have little impact (e.g., gender, legal requirements such as citizenship) and others with more specific political consequences (e.g., education, partisanship, efficacy, and interest). Voting participation in Canada is relatively high, but voter turnout tells us about the quantity of participation, not its quality. Recent assessments of the quality of participation have been somewhat pessimistic. Moreover, a comparative study finds Canada's ranking in terms of voter participation to be lower than many other democratic systems, with that ranking declining in recent years (Black, 1991).

THE BRITISH ELECTORAL PROCESS

The recruitment and nomination of candidates for the British House of Commons reflects several unique attributes. If the Canadian recruitment process is closed, then the British one is even more so. Candidate selection is a private, internal party matter, a practice which the major parties seem bent on retaining. A consequence of this tightly controlled recruitment process is that the British selectorate, under normal circumstances, is quite small. The selectorate's power, however, is extensive, because, in most elections, up to 75 percent of the seats in the House of Commons are safe ones.

The control of the national and local party elites over the recruitment process is clearly demonstrated by the traditional practice of **short listing**, that is, *the process by which the local party constituencies determine who is eligible to run for a party nomination.* When a constituency organization for a party is looking for a candidate, those who wish to have the nomination indicate their desire to the executive of the local organization. From this pool of possible candidates, which may be anywhere from a few people to many, a short list of the most desirable candidates is prepared. The short list typically contains up to half a dozen names and is prepared by a screening committee of local party officials. This screening committee may contain one- to two-dozen members and is often described "as the most critical single stage of the entire selection process" (Ranney, 1975: 42).

The short-listed individuals then appear before *a meeting of local party members*, usually several hundred, known as the **selection conference**, a meeting roughly similar to the constituency nomination meeting in Canada. After listening to a presentation by each potential candidate, the selection conference votes for one person, who becomes the party's candidate for public office. A final step involves the approval of the candidate by the national party organization. With rare exception, the procedure puts the control of the recruitment and nomination of candidates effectively in the hands of the party elite.

In addition to the closed nature of the recruitment process, several other characteristics of British practice are worthy of mention. Although similar to the Canadian tradition of not requiring candidates to be residents of the constituency in which they seek office, the British nonresidency rule has resulted in a considerable movement of possible candidates between constituencies from one election to the next, in contrast to the Canadian convention. In fact, there is a pecking order among constituencies for each party in terms of the likelihood of victory. Before gaining a nomination in a safe seat (safe seats are usually reserved for the party leaders and incumbent MPs), individuals will contest an election in a constituency in which they have almost no chance of winning. If a candidate makes a credible showing, he or she may be given the opportunity to run in a more winnable constituency in the next election — and so on, until gaining a seat in the Commons. Except as a result of an electoral redistribution, such movements by candidates between ridings are rare in Canadian politics.

A second distinctive aspect of the recruitment process in Britain is the early selection of candidates prior to an election call. All major parties select a considerable portion of their candidates well in advance of an expected general election, so that they are ready to do battle on short notice. This early selection of candidates is, in part, a reflection of the brief election campaigns in Britain: the parties cannot waste half of the official campaign simply getting their candidates chosen. In contrast, prior to the 1997 election, Canadian parties, especially the Liberals and Conservatives, traditionally selected most of their candidates for office after a dissolution of Parliament had been granted.

A third important attribute of the candidate selection process in Britain concerns the potential role of the national party leader and organization. In comparison to their Canadian counterparts, British parties are not only well organized, but also highly centralized. At least in theory, this centralization of party organization extends to the candidate selection process. For example, as outlined above, after being named as the party's nominee by the selection conference at the constituency level, the candidate must still be approved by the national party headquarters, a practice true of both the Labour and Conservative parties. Moreover, the national parties maintain lists of possible candidates that the local parties are expected to consult and use, whenever feasible. The national party offices may even recommend to a specific constituency particular candidates they wish to be considered.

The centralization of national party control over the candidate selection process, however, is more apparent than real. Most nominations are decided by the local parties without interference from the national organization. While the national party leadership can step into the process and reject a locally selected candidate, this rarely happens. It would be most accurate to see national party control as a reserve power that is rarely exercised. For example, in 1983 the Conservatives attempted to prevent right-wing elements from winning control over, and nominations in, the local constituencies by requiring that potential parliamentary candidates reveal whether or not they had ever been members of any other political organization. However, changes in the political recruitment process in the Labour party in 1997–1998 have greatly complicated the process of candidate selection, as well as enhancing the power of the national party organization (Shaw, 2001).

These characteristics of the British candidate selection process help to quickly narrow the political recruitment funnel (Norris and Lovenduski, 1993). For example, in 1997, from a population of approximately 59 million, about 45 million individuals were qualified as electors and thus, also, as potential candidates for public office. A record number of individuals (3 715) contested for public office in 1997, while fewer people ran for office (3 294) in 2001.

The closed nature of the candidate selection process, not surprisingly, has resulted in nominees for public office who are unrepresentative of the socio-economic characteristics of British society (Kavanagh, 1992; Norris, Geddes, and Lovenduski, 1992; Le Lohé, 1993; Saggar, 1997; Peake, 1997). Even more so than in Canada, the British political process is male-dominated, a statement that remains true despite Margaret Thatcher's success in becoming prime minister in 1979, 1983, and 1987. By 1997, the three major parties had selected 685 women candidates, compared to 341 in 1992. A record number of 120 women MPs were elected to the British House of Commons in the 1997 general election. However, on a percent basis, this record number (120 out of 659) still only represented 18 percent of the total (Lovenduski, 1997). In 2001, a total of 631 women stood for election to the House of Commons, with a total of 118 women selected as MPs.

Further, education from one of the elite public schools (comparable to the private schools of Canada) has traditionally characterized the candidates of both the Conservative and Labour parties, especially the former. In one study, the "Oxbridge" connection (university education from Oxford or Cambridge) was found to have been true of all prime ministers, 72 percent of all cabinet ministers, 37 percent of all Members of Parliament, but less than 1 percent of the total British population between 1955 and 1974 (Putnam, 1976: 35). While such a pattern has declined in recent decades, other socio-economic considerations reveal a similar pattern, so that one researcher concluded that "whatever else MPs may be representative of, it is not the social composition of their constituents, nor even the social composition of their own voting supporters" (Pulzer, 1972: 70). The class-based and deferential aspects of Britain's political culture are clearly revealed in the law of increasing disproportion, which characterizes the result of the candidate selection process (Norris and Lovenduski, 1993). Even the Labour party in the 1990s, despite representing the working class, had its parliamentary party overwhelmingly composed of members of the middle class and those with a university education (Budge et al., 1998: 384–385).

The mechanics of a British election resemble those of a Canadian one, with a few significant exceptions. The power to precipitate an election resides with the prime minister, who requests a dissolution of Parliament from the Queen. Because Britain has typically had majority governments since the Second World War, the prime minister has had considerable leeway in such matters. The only exception in the modern era would be the defeat of the Callaghan government on a non-confidence motion on March 28, 1979. Rather than giving the leader of the opposition party a chance to form a government, a dissolution of Parliament was sought and received by the Labour prime minister.

The length of the ensuing election campaign is revealing: only six weeks passed between the defeat of the Labour government in the Commons and the first meeting of the new Parliament under the victorious Conservative leader, Margaret Thatcher (Punnett, 1980: 33–34). The official campaign was even briefer: Parliament was dissolved on April 7, election notices were published on April 11, with the actual vote taking place on May 3, 1979. In 1992, the campaign was, once again, only four weeks long — from March 11 to April 9. However, in 1997 a longer campaign than normal was used: the election was announced on March 17, with the vote taken on May 1; this six-week campaign was the longest in the history of British elections. This extended campaign period was the result of the Tory government, trailing in most polls from 25 to 30 percent behind the Labour party, wanting a longer period to try and change their anticipated electoral defeat after 18 years in power. However, the typically short electoral battle reflects the impact of a permanent voters' list and the tradition in British politics of quickly resolving disputes about which party shall lead the country. In 2001, because the Labour party wanted a brief election campaign — given its huge lead in the polls — the campaign itself was only 25 days long (May 14 to June 7).

The nature of British parties has had an important impact on election campaigns. The ideologically distinct and class-based parties, which offer the voters a clear choice between their programs, give the British citizen a greater possibility of making a connection between his or her vote and public policy than is true in Canada. Moreover, the shortness of the campaign period means that the parties have little opportunity to change a person's voting intention. Even the 1992 election and the "unexpected" Tory victory, in which the Labour party appeared to hold a small lead in most public opinion polls, turns out, on inspection, to support such a conclusion (Newton, 1993: 130). Elections in Britain, more often than not, simply register public sentiment as it existed prior to the campaign (e.g., the 2001 election).

THE BRITISH VOTER

Throughout the 19th century, the right to participate in electoral politics was severely limited in Britain, although the series of Reform Acts (1832, 1867, 1884) did increase the percentage of male adults voting from roughly 5 to 30 percent.

Women were granted the right to vote in 1918, although there was a higher age qualification for women (30) than for men (21). Moreover, women were initially entitled to vote only if their husbands met the property qualifications then in existence. The age qualification for women was lowered to 21 in 1928, a legal restriction that stood for both men and women for 40 years until 1969, when adulthood was defined as 18. The extent of the franchise is no longer an area of controversy, since there are now only minimal legal restrictions on the franchise.

An interesting historical aspect of legal qualifications and voting in Britain concerns the use for certain groups of **plural voting**, that is, *where one individual was legally entitled to vote more than once*. For example, between 1918 and 1948, owners of a business could vote in both the constituency where their business was located and in the constituency where they lived, if separate constituencies were involved. As well, since the 14th century Britain had allowed a limited number of special university seats in the Commons. University graduates were entitled to two ballots: one for the university seats and one in their constituency of residence. Reforms adopted in 1948 abolished both types of plural voting, so that each elector is now entitled to only a single vote.

A further distinctive aspect of the legal qualifications in Britain concerns the electoral register (Halfacree, 1992). As in Canada, the government has assumed the responsibility for registering people to vote. However, instead of making up a new list when an election is called, Britain maintains a permanent voters' list, which is revised once a year in the fall and which indicates those eligible to vote as of October 10 of that year. This electoral register goes into effect the following February for a one-year period. For example, the 1997 general election was based on the electoral register of October 10, 1996. Most studies have suggested that the electoral register thus produced is quite accurate, with about 95 percent of those eligible to vote contained on the voters' list.

One legal qualification imposed on prospective voters in the 1992 election was the controversial poll tax (Winetrobe, 1992). The British **poll tax**, unlike the American poll tax after which it was named, was in fact *a replacement for local property taxes*. This tax, officially called a community charge, had to be paid before an individual was legally entitled to vote. Since the community charge hit especially hard at lower-income families — and expected supporters of the Labour party — its impact was to reduce the number of potential Labour voters. While some estimates have put the number disenfranchised by the poll tax at one million (Coomber, 1992: A7), others have discounted its significance for the election outcome (Butler and Kavanagh, 1992: 231–232). Since the Tories under John Major repealed the poll tax after the 1992 election (replacing it with a new tax), voters did not face this legal requirement in the 1997 election.

Minimal legal restrictions and a permanent voters' list have helped to produce high levels of voter turnout in British national elections (Denver and Hands, 1997). As a percentage of those included on the electoral register, the average turnout in general elections since 1945 is 75 percent. The highest level of voting occurred in 1950, with an 84 percent turnout, and the lowest rate was seen in 2001, with just under 60 percent participating. In 1997, the turnout rate had been 71 percent. On an average percentage basis, these figures indicate a slightly higher rate of participation in Britain than in Canada since the Second World War. However, such differences are very small and can probably be accounted for by the infrequency of British elections and the use of the permanent voters' list.

The impact of the various social, political, and personal factors on voter participation in Britain is comparable to that found in other democratic systems (Parry, Moyser, and Day, 1992; Sanders, 1993: 186–190; Geddes and Tonge, 1997; King et al., 1998). For example, the higher one's social class, occupation, education, and income, the greater is one's political involvement. Similarly, urban rather than rural residents, middle-aged rather than either very young or very old voters, and men rather than women demonstrate greater rates of voter turnout, although such differences may be small. As in Canada, the impact of these socio-political cleavages, the most important of which is social class in Britain, is mediated by an individual's party identification. Feelings of political efficacy, as well as having a partisan attachment, also increase the rate of political activity. Due to political factors, closely competitive or marginal seats have a higher turnout rate than safe seats. The nature of the party system contributes to voter participation as well: programmatic parties, one of which typically forms a majority government, should enhance the value of the individual's vote.

Since the legal requirements prevent few eligible voters from participating, the reasons for nonvoting must be found in a combination of the effects of the social, political, and personal factors. In most British elections since 1945, about 25 percent of the eligible voters did not participate (29 percent in 1997). However, in 2001 the rate of nonparticipation took a dramatic jump to 40 percent of the eligible electorate. While the causes of nonvoting at the individual level are complex, from the viewpoint of comparative analysis the total rate of abstention is revealing for what it demonstrates about the stability of the polity and the general attitudes toward political activity. The rate of nonvoting in Britain in this comparative perspective is relatively low: the same conclusion cannot necessarily be advanced with respect to political participation in the American system.

THE AMERICAN ELECTORAL PROCESS

Election campaigns are noisy, lengthy, expensive, and nearly continuous in the American polity. In the 2000 presidential election year, about 14 000 separate electoral contests took place in the United States. Moreover, the doctrines of individualism and popular sovereignty have been extended to the internal operations of the political parties themselves, so that a considerable portion of the public has the potential to become involved in the political recruitment process. Candidates for public office are nominated by an election method known as the direct primary — one of the most unique aspects of the American political arena. However, involvement in the process of candidate selection, as well as frequent elections, do not necessarily lead to effective control of public policy. The traditional non-ideological nature of the American political parties and the dominance of two competitive parties in the national party system have resulted in election campaigns that choose leaders, not the content of public policy.

In the American presidential system, elections are mandated by law, so that the executive has no control over when they are held. No matter what the state of the economy or world affairs happens to be, the election process continues. For example, the November 4, 1980 presidential election was held, much to the despair of the incumbent Carter administration, on the one-year anniversary of the seizing of the American diplomats by the revolutionary government in Iran, a timing that was less than auspicious for the Democratic party, which was seeking re-election. Similarly, President George Bush would likely have been re-elected in a landslide at the end of the Gulf War in the spring of 1991; instead he was defeated in the November 1992 presidential election.

Probably the most unusual, as well as the most significant, aspect of the American electoral process concerns the potential role of the ordinary citizen in the candidate selection procedures. Most candidates are now nominated through the use of direct primaries — a technique that remains uniquely American. A **direct primary** is *an election among party members that selects that party's candidates for the general election.*

The direct primary was developed to undercut boss rule and to give the ordinary citizen control over the nominees for political office. First adopted by the state of Wisconsin in 1903, the direct primary is the basic mechanism of political recruitment, although limited elements of older practices (e.g., conventions, caucuses) still remain. The thrust of the direct primary has been to democratize the candidate selection process, both in terms of the individuals who may seek office and in respect to the size of the selectorate. As a result, the American recruitment process, at least in theory, is the most open in the world. Presidential primaries, which are used in the selection of presidential candidates, are a special version of the direct primary technique.

While the direct primary provides the potential for the average citizen to become involved in the candidate selection process, it also means that a political party may not be able to control who runs under the party label. For example, in March 1987 in the Democratic primary in the state of Illinois, two candidates who were followers of Lyndon LaRouche won the Democratic nomination for statewide office. Mr. LaRouche, who has run three times for president, is an extreme right-wing ideologue who believes that the Queen of England is a drug pusher and that Henry Kissinger is a Communist agent. However, since they won the Democratic primary, his two candidates became the official Democratic nominees for the general election (although they ended up losing their bid for elective office). An analogous incident occurred in the Republican party in 1992 when David Duke, a former member of the Ku Klux Klan, sought to win (unsuccessfully) the governorship of Louisiana under the Republican party banner (Rose, 1992).

Election campaigns in the United States are, therefore, a two-step process: first, a series of primary elections to select the party nominees for each office; and second, a general election in which the various party candidates, so selected, compete with each other. Primary elections are an intra-party contest in which each party elects its candidates to compete against the other parties in the general election (the inter-party contest) (see Figure 7.1). Primary elections for all elective offices are normally held on the same day, usually at least several months before the general election. Many states have their primary election day in September, with the general election held in November.

The typical pattern of primaries is as follows: on primary election day, a voter who is registered as a Democrat will be given a ballot containing the names of all those seeking the Democratic nomination for each office. The candidate receiving the most votes in the Democratic primary for each office (i.e., a plurality system) becomes the officially recognized Democratic candidate in the ensuing general election. A similar procedure is followed for Republican voters on primary day. Thus, a primary election is best seen as an internal party election by party activists and supporters of their candidate, with the winning candidate then competing in the general election against the official candidates of the other parties. Although the intent of the direct primary was to give the general public or at least party members a role in the candidate selection process, its effect in practice has been far from that ideal. For example, the rate of participation in primaries is usually a small percentage of those eligible, ranging anywhere from 10 percent in some cases to upwards of 70 or 80 percent in others. The right to participate does not necessarily lead to actual participation.

At the candidate level, the law of increasing disproportion still operates: few ordinary citizens are likely to enter the battle for a party's nomination. Again, although the legal right is there, other factors work to limit a citizen from seeking and gaining nomination through the primary route. In particular, women and minority groups have not been beneficiaries of political recruitment through the primary process (Kaminer, 1992). Even in 1992, the so-called "year of the woman," only 4 of the 11 women senatorial candidates were elected, for a total of 6 women senators out of a total of 100 — a record high. By 1998, the total number

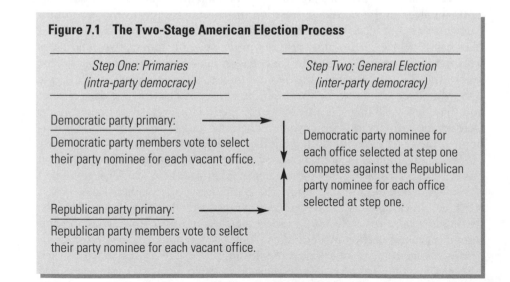

Figure 7.1   The Two-Stage American Election Process

| *Step One: Primaries* | *Step Two: General Election* |
| *(intra-party democracy)* | *(inter-party democracy)* |

Democratic party primary: ⟶

Democratic party members vote to select their party nominee for each vacant office.

Democratic party nominee for each office selected at step one competes against the Republican party nominee for each office selected at step one.

Republican party primary: ⟶

Republican party members vote to select their party nominee for each vacant office.

of women in Congress had increased to 67 (9 in the Senate and 58 in the House of Representatives). After the 2000 congressional elections, a total of 74 women were serving in the United States Congress (13 in the Senate and 61 in the House of Representatives).

An additional factor in this regard is a financial one: it may cost several hundred thousand dollars (often much more) to run a primary campaign for a major political office, even for a small district in the U.S. House of Representatives. For a Senate seat, millions of dollars are needed. For example, in New Jersey in 2000, Democrat Jon Corzine spent an estimated $60 million (most of it his own money) in winning first the Democratic primary ($5 million) and then the general election ($55 million) — his Republican opponent spent a combined total of only $6 million. Without public funding for nomination campaigns, few citizens can afford to attempt to gain their party's nomination, let alone pay for the costs of the general election if they happen to be successful at step one.

Even though the direct primary has enlarged the number of citizens who participate in the selectorate, the effectiveness of the public's involvement is open to challenge. The primary mechanism has introduced public competition into the candidate selection process by giving party members a chance to select which individual from the party's political elite will compete in the general election under the party label. Whether such a result, to an outside observer, is worth the cost and complex method of primary elections is not important, for it seems to be so to the American citizenry: "The American political tradition caps decisions made by popular vote with a resplendent halo of legitimacy" (Key, 1956: 133).

Although the American polity has enshrined the principle of popular sovereignty throughout its election process by electing more public officials in more elections on a more frequent basis than any other democratic polity in the world, neither the rate of political participation in voting nor the effectiveness of popular control over government has necessarily been improved (Rosenstone and Hansen, 1993: 211–227). The potential avenues for active political participation are widespread, but, in reality, the average citizen plays a more modest role. Thus, the study of political behaviour in the United States has revealed a fundamental paradox: while the opportunities for participation are multiple, the rate of political activity is much lower than in other democratic systems. This paradox is, in large part, the result of a unique combination of legal restrictions, which tend to disenfranchise a significant segment of potential voters (Teixeira, 1992; Flanigan and Zingale, 1998; 42–46).

THE AMERICAN VOTER

While the general historical trend has been for a removal of most legal restrictions on the right to vote, so that most adults over 18 are now enfranchised, the extension of the suffrage has produced bitter battles in the political arena. Some of these conflicts have been resolved through the process of constitutional amendment. If we discount the first 10 amendments, since they constitute the American Bill of Rights, of the remaining 17 amendments, 5 have been concerned with extensions of the suffrage: the Fifteenth Amendment (1870) prohibited discrimination in voting privileges based on race; the Nineteenth Amendment (1920) extended the right to vote to women; the Twenty-Third Amendment (1961) granted residents in the American Capital the franchise; the Twenty-Fourth Amendment (1964) prohibited the use of the poll tax; and the Twenty-Sixth Amendment (1971) lowered the age of participation to 18 in all elections. These constitutional amendments have been a significant factor in eliminating some of the gross injustices that prohibited significant segments of the population from voting.

Two legal restrictions, however, have remained as important factors in nonvoting even through the modern era: registration and residency requirements. Unlike the process of enumeration used in most democratic systems, the American voter is typically responsible for getting his or her name on the voters' list and for keeping it there. The individual must make the effort to register to vote by going to the proper government office, usually several weeks before the actual election. Moreover, states may remove a name from the electoral register if a person fails to vote in several consecutive elections.

While the emphasis on the individual's role in registering to vote is a reflection of the theme of individualism in American political culture, its impact on voter participation is significant, since a quarter or more of the population may disenfranchise themselves by failing to register. Because those not registered tend to come from groups which have traditionally supported the Democratic party, a priority for the Democratic party in the last three presidential elections was to get as many people registered to vote as possible.

Nonvoting, in short, is almost entirely concentrated among the unregistered . . . . In effect, restrictive registration procedures are the functional equivalents of earlier property and literacy qualifications (Piven and Cloward, 1988: 869).

Historically, registration procedures have been specifically used as a cover for racial discrimination, especially against African-Americans in the American South, through poll taxes and literacy tests (Kousser, 1974). The American **poll tax** was *a tax, usually only several dollars, which had to be paid before a person could cast a ballot*. Even though the amount was small, it effectively disenfranchised poor black and white people. **Literacy tests** (e.g., *ability to read, knowledge of the constitution*) could be rigorously applied against minority groups and not applied at all to majority group members.

The result of such practices was that a large segment of the potential electorate in the South could not vote until the end of the 1960s. Elimination of such discrimination began with the outlawing of the poll tax in 1964 and, more significantly, with the passage in 1965 of the Voting Rights Act, which allowed the federal government to send in people to register potential voters in the Southern states. The effects were dramatic: "in Mississippi, for example, the black registration rate jumped from 8.3 percent in 1965 to 67.6 percent in 1970, and the white rate from 57.9 percent to 92.2 percent" (Milbrath and Goel, 1977: 131). Although flagrant abuses of the registration system, such as the discriminatory use of poll taxes and literacy tests, have been abandoned, the need to register before voting remains a major impediment to Americans' political participation (Rosenstone and Hansen, 1993: 196–209; Timpone, 1998).

In an attempt to expand voter registration, a number of alternatives, usually focussing on making voter registration easier, have been advocated. For example, in 1992 Congress passed the National Voter Registration Act — more popularly known as the **motor-voter bill**. This Act eased voter registration requirements by allowing people to register to vote by mail or when renewing various types of government licenses (such as a driver's license). Highly favoured by Democrats, the motor-voter bill was vetoed by Republican President George Bush. After the 1992 election, the Democrats quickly passed the Act again, and this time it was signed by Democratic President Bill Clinton in early 1993 (Lowi and Ginsberg, 1994: 44). By the 1996 presidential election, an estimated 20 million new voters had been added to the electoral lists. Contrary to expectations, it appears that the impact of these new voters did not favour the Democratic party, nor did it lead to an increase in the rate of political participation in the 1996 presidential election among new voters (Ginsberg and Shefter, 1999: 22).

> The key disfranchising features of the Southern registration laws were the amount of discretion granted to the registrars, the specificity of the information required of the registrant, the times and places set for registration, and the requirement that a voter bring his registration certificate to the polling place (Kousser, 1974: 48).

A second important continuing legal restriction is the residency requirement, which has been quite lengthy in the American system. A **residency requirement** specifies that *a person must have resided within an electoral district for a given period of time before being entitled to vote*. The longer the residency requirement, the more people are disenfranchised. In addition, residency qualifications often apply to the state, local, and precinct levels, with a different time period for each level. The state residency qualification has typically been a year. Although there was a trend in the 1970s toward shorter residency requirements for national elections (i.e., six months), they continue to be a significant participation hurdle for many Americans at the beginning of the new century.

> Universal voting is so unquestioned a public good that in 1993 Congress enacted the long-debated "motor voter" bill to register people when they acquire drivers' licenses, on the theory that anyone's participation, even if ignorant and fleetingly motivated, enriches the collective judgment (Henry, 1994: 21).

In addition to the legal requirements, several political factors unique to the American system seem to discourage high levels of citizen involvement. For example, both frequent elections and complicated ballots appear to limit participation. Some voters may simply become weary of voting on an almost regular basis and so decide to participate differentially in various kinds of contests. Thus, we find voter turnout highest in presidential election years, lower in congressional election years, and lower still in state and local contests. In addition, American ballots are often long, with the voter being asked to decide on contests for national, state, and local offices, as well as various referendums and tax-related proposals. The ballot in some of the larger states may be several columns wide and several feet long, asking the voter to make numerous separate voting decisions. The result is that, as the voter goes through the ballot, more and more of the contests are not judged: faced by voter fatigue or lack of knowledge of the issues, the voter leaves the end of the ballot blank.

Frequent elections, numerous contests, lengthy ballots, registration requirements, and residency qualifications are some of the most distinctive legal and political factors that influence voter participation in the American system (Flanigan and Zingale, 1998). The bearing of the social and personal attributes on voting is basically similar to those already discussed for the Canadian and British systems (Rosenstone and Hansen, 1993: 211–227). For example, with respect to personal characteristics, those who feel a strong or intense psychological involvement in the political arena are more likely to participate, as are those with partisan attachments and feelings of political efficacy. In relation to social attributes, those characterized by more education, higher personal incomes, and middle age, as well as those who are white, male, non-Southern, and Jewish, usually have the highest rates of voting turnout (Hill and Luttberg, 1980: 91; Pomper, 1993: 135–140). The young, the poor, and minority groups have the lowest rates of political participation. In terms of voting turnout, there is no real difference between men and women. However, in terms of partisan support, the gender gap has emerged since 1960 to have a significant impact in American politics. For example, in 1996 the male vote divided equally between Bill Clinton and Bob Dole (44 percent each), but women favoured the Democratic candidate by 16 percentage points (54 percent to 38 percent).

Given such considerations, it is not surprising that voting turnout is low and, in fact, has been declining in recent decades. For example, turnout in presidential elections in the early 1960s was about 62 percent, but by 1984 it had dropped to 55 percent and to just over 50 percent in the 1988 presidential contest (Beinart, 1989). In 1992, a turnout rate of 55 percent in the presidential election temporarily reversed this longstanding trend in American politics; in 1996, turnout dropped again to just 49 percent, rising to 53 percent in 2000.

COMPARING ELECTORAL PROCESSES

Our analysis of the electoral process and the typical factors that influence political activity in Canada, Britain, and the United States demonstrates that in the last century all three countries have extended, with few exceptions, the right to participate to most adult citizens over the age of 18. Bitter political fights often occurred over the successive expansions of the electorate, while the right to vote remained a key domestic political issue well into the 20th century. Although voting rates are typically high in democratic systems, any optimistic conclusion about the impact of individual involvement must be tempered by the realization that for most citizens, most of the time, voting is their only mode of political activity.

If most individuals only participate through voting, what does this say about the role of the citizen in the political process? In democratic systems, voting is usually voluntary and occurs in a free election process characterized by competition between two or more parties fighting for control of governmental office. The individual's vote is thus a means of choosing between leaders or groups of leaders and only rarely indicates a specific choice of policy. It is through their role in selecting the leaders of the polity that most citizens have an indirect say in decision making. While such a function may be a far cry from the role perceived for the citizen among the writings of the classical democratic theorists (Pateman, 1970), it nevertheless remains a highly significant one, especially when we consider the alternatives.

Given the appeal of the democratic ideal in the modern age, even totalitarian systems seek to nominate candidates and to hold elections. Such elections may even achieve an almost 100 percent turnout of the electorate. However, the key point of comparison is the concept of choice. For example, participation in totalitarian countries is not voluntary, but expected: nonparticipation is usually interpreted by the state as evidence of dissent, if not downright disloyalty. Moreover, when citizens vote there is usually no choice presented on the ballot: they are merely ratifying choices already made by the sole party. Elections in such systems are a way of legitimating the regime and its leaders, not a means of citizen influence on, or control over, the polity: as a consequence, "those regimes often appear to be purer than Ivory Soap in voter turnout and approbation" (LaPalombara, 1974: 424). Almost perfect rates of turnout occur when such participation has no bearing on control of the polity: voting in a totalitarian system does not determine who governs. Voting does select who governs in a democratic system, even though such participation is intermittent and rarely controls policy in any direct fashion.

> In any political election . . . the voter is under an absolute moral obligation to consider the interest of the public, not his private advantage, and give his vote, to the best of his judgment, exactly as he would be bound to do if he were the sole voter and the election depended upon him alone (Mill, 1861: 232).

While democratic systems grant most citizens the right or opportunity to participate, individuals from the various social classes, regions, religions, and racial groups differentially involve themselves in the polity. Political activity, such as voting, is seen here as a political resource with which to increase an individual's or group's power and influence in the political process. The sectors of the electorate that vote often select as their leaders those who adopt policies that favour the very groups that elected them to office in the first place. Nonparticipation is not only a consequence, but also a cause, of the nature of political inequality found in democratic systems (Verba, Nie, and Kim, 1978).

One reason that the suffrage extensions produced such intense political controversies is a reflection of this conclusion: newly enfranchised groups would make use of their vote to ensure more responsive leaders and policies and thereby reduce the existing inequalities in the system. Those groups that benefited from the existing social and political arrangements were thus opposed to the enfranchisement process, while those who desired change argued for universal adult suffrage. The movement to universal adult suffrage has not, however, produced equality in the social, economic, or political spheres. While democratic systems have created the opportunities for extensive citizen participation, a major challenge in the years ahead is to translate more of the potential for involvement into actual participation.

> If those who take part and those who do not were similar on all politically relevant dimensions, then substantial inequalities in participation would pose no threat to the democratic principle of equal protection of interests. As our analysis has demonstrated, this is hardly the case (Verba et al., 1993: 314).

The nature, operation, and consequences of a polity's electoral process reflect the party and constitutional context within which it operates. In turn, elections condition and modify both the party and constitutional systems. As a result, the type of electoral process utilized by a particular country is often a good indicator of the nature of the overall political regime. Competitive elections characterize democratic systems, while noncompetitive ones are typically associated with autocratic and totalitarian political systems. Within the democratic variety, presidential and parliamentary systems differ with respect to both the political recruitment process and the mechanics of their election campaigns.

In making a comparative analysis of the recruitment and nomination of candidates for public office, the nature of the selectorate must be a critical concern. The group that has the effective power and influence to serve in this capacity has the ability to control the kinds of candidates from among which the public will choose their governors. While all systems reflect the law of increasing disproportion, the basis of that inequality may be education in one system, race in another, and religion in a third. The open or closed nature of the recruitment process will determine the size and composition of the selectorate, as well as the type of individual chosen for public service. As a result, a country's political stratification system is clearly revealed by the operation and consequences of the political recruitment process.

Comparing election campaigns in democratic polities focusses on such matters as their timing and length. While governments and oppositions typically seek mandates from the public for the content of policy during an election battle, rarely does the public clearly register its policy preferences. Elections are largely an unrefined tool of public control over the content of the political agenda. Instead, elections allow the governed to choose which members of the political elite will govern them.

SUMMARY

1. The most significant difference between electoral processes in democratic and totalitarian systems is the degree and effectiveness of the choice presented to the voter: in the former, the choice is real; in the latter, it is merely apparent.

2. In parliamentary systems the election call, within a five-year maximum, is at the prerogative of the political executive, except in rare circumstances. Elections are party-based and of relatively short duration, with either a temporary or permanent voters' list prepared by an enumeration of eligible participants. Presidential systems operate elections under fixed time constraints, put the burden of involvement on the citizen to register to vote, and are typically lengthy. A two-stage election process is utilized in the United States, with stage one selecting party candidates and stage two allowing the voter in a general election to choose between the party candidates so selected.

3. Political recruitment is the process of finding and nominating candidates for public office. Given the number of safe seats in democratic polities, nomination for office is often tantamount to election. The selectorate in any system is usually small, as the political elite attempts to control the holders of public office by determining which individuals are nominated to contest an election. Whether operating in a closed or open pattern, the political recruitment process produces candidates who are often unrepresentative of some of the major socio-economic interests of society. Generally, any person who is qualified as an elector is also legally entitled to run for, and serve in, public office.

4. Canadian elections are competitive and, traditionally, relatively lengthy. Voters' lists, until 1996, were temporary; a permanent voters' list was first prepared in April of 1997. Constituencies are allocated among the provinces primarily on a population basis. The selectorate in Canada is small, although more decentralized now than in the past. In most cases, effective control resides at the local level, although a national leader can, at times, challenge and overturn the decisions so made. The process of candidate recruitment can diverge rather sharply from the democratic ideal.

5. British campaigns are short, based on a permanent voters' list, called at the request of the prime minister, and are quiet, but usually decisive, in that they typically produce majority governments. Candidate selection is a secretive, internal party matter, under the control of the party's elite, involving the use of such practices as short listing. Centralization of national party control over candidate selection exists in theory but is rarely exercised in practice: local ridings have considerable autonomy to choose the candidate they desire.

6. American elections are noisy, lengthy, expensive, and nearly continuous. Popular sovereignty is imbedded in the two-stage election process through the use of the direct primary technique to nominate candidates for public office. Extensive avenues for political participation have not resulted, however, in high rates of actual involvement.

7. Citizen participation may take many forms, although the basic mode in modern systems is by voting in elections. Four major influences (legal, social, political, and personal) determine rates of participation in democratic systems. While legal restrictions are now minimal, the social, political, and personal factors keep many people from political involvement.

8. Rates of voting are greater in Canada and Britain than in the United States. In all three polities, participation is greater among the better off, among those with partisan attachments, and among those with feelings of political efficacy. The use of an enumeration process in parliamentary systems encourages participation, while the registration process in the United States disenfranchises an important segment of the electorate.

9. Participation in totalitarian systems is nearly 100 percent, but voting in such a polity is an act of legitimation rather than one of popular control. In democratic systems, voting is a choice between sets of leaders that determines who will govern, although it rarely involves a decision on specific policies or issues.

CONCEPT FILE

by-election
closed recruitment process
compulsory voting
direct primary
enumeration process
general election
graveyard vote
law of increasing disproportion
literacy tests
motor-voter bill
open recruitment process
parachuting
parliamentary elections

permanent voters' list
plural voting
political efficacy
political recruitment process
poll tax (Britain)
poll tax (United States)
residency requirement
safe seat
selection conference
selectorate
short listing
temporary voters' list

RECOMMENDED READINGS

The Electoral Process

BLAIS, ANDRÉ et al. (2001) "Deciding Who Has the Right to Vote: A Comparative Analysis of Election Laws," *Electoral Studies*, Volume 20, Number 1, pp. 41–62.

BLAIS, ANDRÉ (2000) *To Vote or Not to Vote? The Merits and Limits of Rational Choice Theory*. Pittsburgh: University of Pittsburgh Press.

BLAIS, ANDRÉ and AGNIESZKA DOBRZYNSKA (1998) "Turnout in Electoral Democracies," *European Journal of Political Research*, Volume 33, Number 2, pp. 239–261.

BRADY, HENRY E., SIDNEY VERBA and KAY LEHMAN SCHLOZMAN (1995) "Beyond SES: A Resource Model of Political Participation," *American Political Science Review*, Volume 89, Number 2, pp. 271–294.

—— (1999) "Prospecting for Participants: Rational Expectations and the Recruitment of Political Activists," *American Political Science Review*, Volume 93, Number 1, pp. 153–168.

D'AUGEROT-AREND, SYLVIE (1991) "Why So Late? Cultural and Institutional Factors in the Granting of Quebec and French Women's Political Rights," *Journal of Canadian Studies*, Volume 26, Number 1, pp. 138–165.

FRANKLIN, MARK N. (1999) "Electoral Engineering and Cross-National Turnout Differences: What Role for Compulsory Voting?" *British Journal of Political Science*, Volume 29, Number 1, pp. 205–216.

HART, RODERICK P. (2000) *Campaign Talk: Why Elections Are Good For Us*. Princeton, New Jersey: Princeton University Press.

HIGHTON, BENJAMIN and RAYMOND E. WOLFINGER (2001) "The Political Implications of Higher Turnout," *British Journal of Political Science*, Volume 31, Number 1, pp. 179–192.

KOCH, JEFFREY (1997) "Candidate Gender and Women's Psychological Engagement in Politics," *American Politics Quarterly*, Volume 25, Number 1, pp. 118–133.

LEDUC, LAWRENCE et al. (1996) *Comparing Democracies: Elections and Voting in Global Perspective*. Thousand Oaks, California: Sage.

MARSHALL, GEOFFREY (1997) "The Referendum: What, When and How?" *Parliamentary Affairs*, Volume 50, Number 2, pp. 307–313.

MORRIS, DICK (1999) *VOTE.com*. Los Angeles: Renaissance Books.

MUELLER, Carol M., ed. (1998) *The Politics of the Gender Gap: The Social Construction of Political Influence*. Beverly Hills, California: Sage.

PAMMETT, JON H. (1988) "A Framework for the Comparative Analysis of Elections Across Time and Space," *Electoral Studies*, Volume 7, Number 2, pp. 125–142.

PRATCHETT, LAWRENCE (1999) "New Fashions in Public Participation: Towards Greater Democracy?" *Parliamentary Affairs*, Volume 52, Number 4, pp. 616–633.

STUBBINGS, ROBERT G. and EDWARD G. CARMINES (1991) "Is It Irrational to Vote?" *Polity*, Volume 23, Number 4, pp. 629–640.

WELCH, SUSAN and DONLEY T. STUDLAR (1996) "The Opportunity Structure for Women's Candidacies and Electability in Britain and the United States," *Political Research Quarterly*, Volume 49, Number 4, pp. 861–874.

Canadian Election Process

BLAIS, ANDRÉ et al. (1999) "Campaign Dynamics in the 1997 General Election," *Canadian Public Policy*, Volume 25, Number 2, pp. 197–205.

BOYER, PATRICK (1992) *Direct Democracy in Canada: The History and Future of Referendums*. Toronto: Dundurn Press.

BRIANS, CRAIG LEONARD (1997) "Residential Mobility, Voter Registration, and Electoral Participation in Canada," *Political Research Quarterly*, Volume 50, Number 1, pp. 215–227.

CARTY, R.K. (1996) "The Electorate and the Evolution of Canadian Electoral Politics," *The American Review of Canadian Studies*, Volume 26, Number 1, pp. 7–29.

EVERITT, JOANNA (1998) "The Gender Gap in Canada: Now You See It, Now You Don't," *Canadian Review of Sociology and Anthropology*, Volume 35, Number 2, pp. 192–219.

GIDENGIL, ELISABETH et al. (1999) "Making Sense of Regional Voting in the 1997 Canadian Federal Election: Liberal and Reform Support Outside Quebec," *Canadian Journal of Political Science*, Volume 32, Number 2, pp. 247–272.

JOHNSTON, RICHARD et al. (1996) *The Challenge of Direct Democracy: The 1992 Canadian Referendum*. Montreal: McGill-Queen's University Press.

MACIVOR, HEATHER (1996) *Women and Politics in Canada*. Peterborough, Ontario: Broadview Press.

MENDELSOHN, MATTHEW (1996) "Introducing Deliberative Direct Democracy in Canada: Learning from the American Experience," *American Review of Canadian Studies*, Volume 26, Number 3, pp. 449–468.

NADEAU, RICHARD and ANDRÉ BLAIS (1993) "Explaining Election Outcomes in Canada," *Canadian Journal of Political Science*, Volume 26, Number 4, pp. 775–790.

NEVITTE, NEIL et al. (2000) *Unsteady State: The 1997 Canadian Federal Election*. Don Mills, Ontario: Oxford University Press.

O'NEILL, BRENDA (1998) "The Relevance of Leader Gender to Voting in the 1993 Canadian National Election," *International Journal of Canadian Studies*, Volume 17, Number 1, pp. 105–130.

PATTERSON, ROBERT (1998) "People Power: British Columbians Seek to Remove MLAs," *The Parliamentarian*, Volume 79, Number 4, pp. 376–378.

British Election Process

BUTLER, DAVID and DENNIS KAVAGNAH (1997) *The British General Election of 1997*. London: Macmillan.

DENVER, DAVID and GORDON HANDS (1997) "Turnout," *Parliamentary Affairs*, Volume 50, Number 4, pp. 720–732.

EVANS, GEOFFREY and PIPPA NORRIS, eds. (1999) *Critical Elections: British Parties and Voters in Long-term Perspective*. London: Sage.

HARROP, MARTIN (1997) "The Pendulum Swings: The British Election of 1997," *Government and Opposition*, Volume 32, Number 3, pp. 305–319.

HAYES, BERNADETTE (1997) "Gender, Feminism and Electoral Behaviour in Britain," *Electoral Studies*, Volume 16, Number 2, pp. 203–216.

JOHNSTON, R.J. and C.J. PATTIE (1997) "Towards an Understanding of Turnout at British General Elections: Voluntary and Involuntary Abstention in 1992," *Parliamentary Affairs*, Volume 50, Number 2, pp. 280–291.

KING, ANTHONY et al. (1993) *Britain At the Polls: 1992*. Chatham, New Jersey: Chatham House Publishers.

—— (1998) *New Labour Triumphs: Britain at the Polls*. Chatham, New Jersey: Chatham House Publishers.

LOVENDUSKI, JONI (1997) "Gender Politics: A Breakthrough for Women?" *Parliamentary Affairs*, Volume 50, Number 4, pp. 708–719.

MCALLISTER, IAN (1997) "Regional Voting," *Parliamentary Affairs*, Volume 50, Number 4, pp. 641–657.

NORRIS, PIPPA and JONI LOVENDUSKI (1991) "Gender Differences in Political Participation in Britain: Traditional, Radical and Revisionist Models," *Government and Opposition*, Volume 26, Number 1, pp. 56–74.

PATTIE, CHARLES and RON JOHNSTONE (2001) "Talk as a Political Context: Conversation and Electoral Change in British Elections, 1992–1997," *Electoral Studies*, Volume 20, Number 1, pp. 17–40.

SHAW, ERIC (2001) "New Labour: New Pathways to Parliament," *Parliamentary Affairs*, Volume 54, Number 1, pp. 35–53.

American Election Process

CARROLL, SUSAN J. (1994) *Women as Candidates in American Politics*. Bloomington, Indiana: Indiana University Press.

CONWAY, MARGARET M. et al. (1997) *Women and Political Participation*. Washington, D.C.: CQ Press.

CRONIN, THOMAS E. (1989) *Direct Democracy: The Politics of Initiative, Referendum, and Recall*. Cambridge, Mass.: Harvard University Press.

FLANIGAN, WILLIAM H. and NANCY H. ZINGALE (1998) *Political Behavior of the American Electorate*. 9th ed. Washington, D.C.: CQ Press.

FRANCIS, WAYNE L. and LAWRENCE W. KENNY (2000) *Up the Political Ladder: Career Paths in US Politics*. London: Sage.

GINSBERG, BENJAMIN and MARTIN SHEFTER (1999) *Politics by Other Means: Politicians, Prosecutors, and the Press from Watergate to Whitewater*. Rev. and updated ed. New York: W.W. Norton and Company.

GRANT, ALAN (1995) "The Term Limitation Movement in the United States," *Parliamentary Affairs*, Volume 48, Number 3, pp. 515–529.

IYENGAR, SHANTO and STEPHEN ANNSOLABEHERE (1996) *Going Negative: How Political Advertisements Shrink and Polarize the Electorate*. New York: Free Press.

KING, ANTHONY (1997) *Running Scared: Why America's Politicians Campaign Too Much and Govern Too Little*. New York: Free Press.

MARTINEZ, MICHAEL D. and DAVID HILL (1999) "Did Motor Voter Work?" *American Politics Quarterly*, Volume 27, Number 3, pp. 296–315.

MILLER, WARREN E. and J. MERRILL SHANKS (1997) *The New American Voter*. Cambridge, Mass.: Harvard University Press.

NORRIS, PIPPA (2001) "US Campaign 2000: Of Pregnant Chads, Butterfly Ballots and Partisan Vitriol," *Government and Opposition*, Volume 36, Number 1, pp. 3–26.

ORNSTEIN, NORMAN J. and THOMAS E. MANN (2001) *The Permanent Campaign and Its Future*. Washington, D.C.: American Enterprise Institute.

PIVEN, FRANCES FOX and RICHARD A. CLOWARD (1988) *Why Americans Don't Vote*. New York: Pantheon Books.

POLSBY, NELSON W. and AARON WILDAVSKY (1996) *Presidential Elections*. 9th ed. Chatham, New Jersey: Chatham House Publishers.

ROSENSTONE, STEVEN J. and JOHN MARK HANSEN (1993) *Mobilization, Participation, and Democracy in America*. New York: Macmillan.

THURBER, JAMES A. and CANDICE J. NELSON, eds. (1995) *Campaigns and Elections American Style*. Boulder, Colorado: Westview Press.

TIMPONE, RICHARD J. (1998) "Structure, Behavior and Voter Turnout in the United States," *American Political Science Review*, Volume 92, Number 1, pp. 145–158.

POLITICS ON THE NET

THE ELECTORAL PROCESS: For Canadian elections, see the website for **Elections Canada** at *www.elections.ca*; for American elections, see the site for the **U.S. Federal Election Commission** at *www.fec.gov*. For election results around the world, see *www.electionworld.org*. Data for the **American National Election Studies** can be accessed at *www.umich.edu/~nes*.

POLITICAL PARTICIPATION: Interesting information can be found on the website for the **Democracy Net** at *www.dnet.org*. Information on voting and registering to vote in the United States can be found at the site for **Rock the Vote** at *www.rockthevote.org*. The **Center for Responsive Politics** can be reached at *www.crp.org*.

Electoral Systems

Electoral systems do not arise from a vacuum but from political debate and struggle. They mirror the politics of the time of their creation and are altered when politics change to the point where the existing electoral system becomes too restrictive. While they last . . . electoral systems do shape politics. (Taagepera and Shugart, 1989: 234)

While it is probably the fate of man forever to pursue the better gadget, the power of man as an inventor seems to have found its real focus in the electoral system, where his passion for politics is wed to his passion for gadgetry. (Milnor, 1969: 71)

CHAPTER PREVIEW

- Electoral systems, by translating votes into seats, play an important role in the allocation of power in any political system.

- Electoral systems not only help to determine which party wins an election, but they also influence the number of parties and the competitive relationship between those parties.

- There are two basic types of electoral formulas: plurality systems and proportional representation systems. Plurality systems rarely equalize the distribution of votes with the distribution of seats; instead, they favour the larger parties and those parties with regional or sectional strongholds. Proportional representation systems seek to equalize the vote share with a party's seat share, but, as a result, they will often produce minority governments.

- The Canadian plurality system has helped Jean Chrétien win three successive majority governments on the basis of a minority of the popular vote. Proportional representation would help both the NDP and Tory parties win considerably more seats in the House of Commons.

- The plurality system in Britain has regularly produced strong majority governments for the House of Commons. Increasingly, various types of proportional representation are being introduced into the British system for elections to other political institutions such as the devolved legislatures in Scotland and Wales.

- The American electoral college is a special version of the plurality system used to elect the president and vice-president of the United States. Even the controversy surrounding the 2000 election is unlikely to produce changes in the American electoral college.

- Party and individual self-interest, rather than political principles, typically determine the attitudes toward, and fate of, various electoral reform proposals.

One of the most important consequences of election campaigns and the competitive party struggle in democratic political systems is the actual physical control of the political structure gained by the victorious political party. Control of the political structure provides the winning party with numerous political resources that it can use to maintain itself in office. These political resources include such items as the right to dispense patronage and government appointments, the ability to dominate media coverage, the right to determine the course of public policy and to focus the public's attention on certain priority areas, and the acquisition of the role of representative for the country in international affairs.

One important power is the ability of the victorious party to modify the rules of the political game before the next electoral contest. Such rules might include a wholesale change from one type of electoral system to another or a more modest reform of redesigning constituency boundaries in an electoral redistribution. Possible changes in the rules of the electoral process, however, are rarely neutral or even-handed in their effects on party competition. Nevertheless, this overt manipulation of the electoral system is often a common feature and tradition in the party battle in democratic political systems.

There are numerous Canadian instances, both historical and contemporary, of the manipulation of electoral boundaries. One of the most blatant historical examples is the famous gerrymander of 1882 by the Conservatives under John A. Macdonald (Beck, 1968: 40–41). The redrawing of electoral boundaries can often be utilized most effectively against individual opposition candidates. For example, when in 1945 the riding of Montreal Cartier elected a Communist Member of Parliament, its boundaries were extensively redrawn in 1947, resulting in a Liberal victory in that riding in the 1949 federal election (Winn and McMenemy, 1976: 119). However, if the party in power is too obvious and blatant in attempting to rid itself of a particular opposition member, it might find the voters returning that member anyway. For example, the federal Liberals tried on several occasions in the late 1940s and early 1950s to rid themselves of John Diefenbaker through the use of a gerrymander, but each time the voters sent Diefenbaker back to the Commons (Newman, 1973: 29–30). Such instances are not unique, of course, to the Canadian polity.

THE NATURE OF ELECTORAL SYSTEMS

Although blatant manipulation of the electoral process has declined in recent decades in most democratic political systems, the fact that so much effort has been invested in such exercises leads us to consider the strategic political importance of electoral systems. If the rules of the electoral process had little impact on the political and party systems, then there would be little, if any, incentive to make such changes.

THE SIGNIFICANCE OF ELECTORAL SYSTEMS

Probably the most significant consequence of electoral systems is their impact on the allocation of political power and influence within the political system. Since they transfer the percentage of popular vote won by the parties in the election into possible governmental control in terms of seats in the legislature, electoral systems help to determine which party actually wins an election campaign. As a result, electoral systems have important long-term effects on political parties' chances of gaining control of the political structure through the electoral mechanism. For example, some systems of electoral law prevent certain kinds of political parties from competing, thereby eliminating any chance for them to gain political power through normal democratic channels. In Germany, Article 21 of the Basic Law (the Constitution of the Federal Republic of Germany) prohibits political parties that seek "to impair or abolish the free and democratic basic order" of the state (Burkett, 1975: 17). Parties of both the left and right have been banned under this provision: the Communist Party, for example, was outlawed between 1956 and 1969 as a legitimate competitor in the then West German party system. Other systems, such as Canada's, are generous in allowing almost any type of party to compete in the electoral battle. For example, there were 11 officially registered parties in the 2000 federal election, including the Natural Law Party of Canada, the Canadian Action Party, the Green Party of Canada, the Marijuana Party, the Communist Party of Canada, and the Marxist-Leninist Party of Canada. Thus, by helping to determine which parties are officially eligible to compete and which parties will be rewarded with seats in the legislature, the first major consequence of electoral systems is their impact on the distribution of political power and influence in the polity.

A second effect of electoral systems is their important interface with the political party systems. The traditional view has been that specific kinds of electoral systems are a major factor in producing certain types of party systems. The most commonly held view is that the plurality electoral system tends to produce a two-party system, while proportional representation helps to generate a multi-party system (Duverger, 1964). While this hypothesis on the relationship between the electoral and party systems has generated considerable con-

Electoral systems intimately relate to questions of political power, and self-interest therefore dictates the reactions of most politicians (Jones and Kavanagh, 1991: 67).

troversy, most current interpretations admit that the nature of a country's electoral system does have an important bearing on the type of political party system that emerges (Rae, 1971; Duverger, 1986; Lijphart, 1990).

A third consequence of electoral systems is that all types tend to favour large parties over small parties in the allocation of legislative seats. Electoral systems appear to be cognizant of the Biblical injunction: "For whosoever hath, to him shall be given; but whosoever hath not, from him shall be taken away" (quoted in Rae, 1971: 134). As a result, electoral systems tend to favour the status quo parties, since new parties representing new ideas and ideologies are usually small to begin with. However, as a general rule plurality systems discriminate far more heavily against most small parties than do the proportional representation electoral systems.

A fourth consequence of electoral systems is their impact on individual parties in terms of their organization, campaign strategies, and leadership selections. For example, the failure of the Reform Party to gain seats outside of the West — and especially in Ontario — largely because of the plurality election system in the 1993 and 1997 federal elections, convinced its founder and leader, Preston Manning, to create a new political party, the Canadian Alliance, in 2000. The whole rationale for a new party was to create an organization that could win seats in Ontario — resulting in a new leader (Stockwell Day) as well. While not successful in breaking the Liberal stranglehold in Ontario (101 out of 103 seats in 2000), the Canadian Alliance party and its formation and electoral strategy clearly demonstrate the impact of electoral systems on party organizations.

A fifth result of electoral systems is a practical one, that is, the problems they present for using national opinion polls to predict the results of forthcoming elections. The percentage of national popular support for a party cannot necessarily be translated into the percentage of seats that party will win in the election, especially under a plurality electoral system. In other words, public opinion polls can give an accurate account of national views, but they are, at times, a very poor base for predicting election outcomes in terms of legislative seats. The reason for this is clear: it is the distribution of political preferences within the various electoral constituencies, not the national pattern, which will determine the election winner. Only if a poll were carried out within all or perhaps within a representative sample of constituencies could any serious attempt be made to predict the election results in terms of the number of seats that might be won by any political party.

The above five consequences of electoral systems have all focussed on the internal workings of a nation's political system. However, a sixth and often overlooked consequence of an electoral system is its impact on a polity's international behaviour. For example, the American presidential election system has a fixed term of office (four years) and a set election date (the month of November every four years). In the spring and summer of 1972, the continuing attempt to negotiate a peace settlement in Vietnam was delayed by the North Vietnamese and their allies because they hoped to wait and negotiate a better deal with the Democratic party's nominee, Senator George McGovern, were he to win the presidential contest. Only after it became clear to the North Vietnamese that President Richard Nixon seemed assured of a re-election victory did peace negotiations come to a successful conclusion before the actual presidential vote (Harris, 1973: 83–84).

TYPES OF ELECTORAL SYSTEMS

Up to this point in our analysis of electoral systems, we have dealt with their over-all importance, without getting into the specifics of the various types. As a starting point, we need to consider a few basic concepts. What do we mean when we talk of electoral law? The following definition will serve as our basic guide.

> **Electoral laws** are *those which govern the process by which electoral preferences are articulated as votes and by which these votes are translated into distributions of governmental authority (typically parliamentary seats) among the competing political parties* (Rae, 1971: 14; emphasis added).

In other words, electoral law is concerned with both the method of voting and the counting of those votes. As such, electoral law has to deal with two basic issues: first, how many candidates are to be elected in each constituency; and second, the method for translating the percentage of popular votes into the number of seats won by each party in the legislature. These two issues can be referred to as dealing with the magnitude of the electoral districts and with the selection of an appropriate electoral formula. Using these criteria, we will analyze the two basic types of electoral systems: the single-member district with a plurality electoral formula and the multi-member district with a proportional representation electoral formula.

In relation to our first criterion, the **magnitude of the electoral district**, our concern is with *the number of people elected in each constituency*, or, in other words, the number of seats to be filled within a given electoral district. In **single-member electoral districts**, only *one candidate is elected*, no matter how many candidates are running for office in that constituency. In contrast, in **multi-member constituencies**, *two or more members are elected*, with the number selected depending on the electoral law of the country. Countries that use the single-member district (i.e., a district magnitude of one) include Canada, Britain, and the United States. Political systems using multi-member electoral districts include the Scandinavian countries, Israel, and Austria. The magnitude of these electoral districts may range from a minimum of two up to the total number of seats in the legislature. For example, Israel considers the country as one large electoral district and thus ends up with a district magnitude of 120.

Our second criterion of electoral systems concerns the electoral formula for translating the popular vote into seats won in the legislature. There are two basic types of electoral formula: plurality and proportional representation.

Under a plurality electoral formula, the percentage of popular votes won by a party rarely equals the percentage of legislative seats obtained — in fact, there is often a rather large discrepancy between the two. The reason for this discrepancy is evident if we take a look at the mechanics of the plurality formula. A **plurality electoral formula** means that *the party and/or candidate with the largest number of votes wins the seat or constituency* (Table 8.1).

A plurality winner is not necessarily a majority winner. When only two candidates run for a specific office, the winner will have both a plurality and a majority.

For example, let us assume that a constituency has 60 000 voters and that two parties contest the election. If Party A wins 40 000 votes and Party B wins 20 000 votes, then Party A has received both a plurality (more votes than any competitor) and a majority victory (at least 50 percent plus 1). However, if three or more parties contest the election, then the winner often ends up with a plurality, but not a majority victory (Table 8.2). In our example, let us assume that three parties contest the election, with the following breakdown of the popular vote: Party A receives 25 000 votes; Party B, 20 000; and Party C, 15 000. Under these conditions, Party A still wins the constituency, but the outcome is a plurality, not a majority victory.

Table 8.1 Plurality Formula — Majority Victory

| *OKANAGAN-COQUIHALLA, BRITISH COLUMBIA — 2000** | |
Party	% of Vote
Canadian Alliance	59
Liberal	20
NDP	8
PC	6
Other	6

* Canadian Alliance leader Stockwell Day's riding

When this kind of distortion within a particular riding is multiplied throughout the entire number of constituencies, some rather strange results can occur: a party can win a respectable share of the popular vote on a national basis but end up with a small number of legislative seats. Such a result is especially true of a party whose support is spread rather evenly across the country (what is called a pattern of **diffuse** or **generalized electoral support**). In Canadian federal elections, the New Democratic Party traditionally feels the impact of this characteristic of the plurality electoral formula; in 1993, 1997, and 2000 the Progressive Conservatives suffered this result as well.

Moreover, because of such distortions a party can actually lose an election in terms of legislative seats obtained, even though it has received a greater percentage of the popular vote than its opponents. Such was the fate of the Liberals in the 1996 provincial election in British Columbia, when they received 42 percent of the popular vote and won 33 seats, while the NDP won 39 seats with 39 percent of the popular vote. Similarly, in the 1998 provincial election in Quebec the Liberals received 43.6 percent of the popular vote but won only 48 seats, while the Parti Québécois formed a majority government with 76 seats based on a popular vote of 42.9 percent. Because the electoral formula can sometimes turn winners into losers and vice versa, it is clear that the electoral system is an important factor in the obtaining of political power in any political system.

Table 8.2 Plurality Formula — Plurality Victory

| *HALIFAX, NOVA SCOTIA — 2000** | |
Party	% of Vote
NDP	40
Liberal	33
PC	18
Canadian Alliance	6
Other	3

* NDP leader Alexa McDonough's riding

The second major type of electoral formula, proportional representation, attempts to eliminate the distortion found in plurality systems. **Proportional representation**

electoral formulas seek *to have the percentage of popular votes received by a party equal the percentage of seats won by that party in the legislature.* The translation of popular support into legislative seats is determined by a specific type of proportional representation electoral formula: the two most common types are the **highest average** and the **greatest remainder** formulas. The actual calculations using these formulas can become very complex, so our examples will simply assume that proportional representation would equalize the percentage of votes and seats won by each party. It is also necessary to remember that proportional representation electoral formulas operate in multi-member constituencies.

Let us assume that a constituency with 100 000 voters selects 10 members to the legislature and that the breakdown of the party vote is as follows: Party A receives 60 000 votes; Party B, 30 000 votes; and Party C, 10 000 votes. The allocation of legislative seats under proportional representation would thus be distributed among the three parties in the resulting pattern: Party A would win six seats, Party B would obtain three seats, and Party C would elect one legislative member. In this example, each party's share of the popular vote equals its share of legislative seats, although in any real system this perfect equality is never reached.

> In a really equal democracy, every or any section would be represented, not disproportionately, but proportionately. A majority of the electors would always have a majority of the representatives; but a minority of electors would always have a minority of the representatives (Mill, 1861: 190).

Having calculated the number of seats won by each party, we must now determine which candidates have been selected. The most common type of candidate selection under proportional representation is the **list** or **party-list system**: in such a system, *citizens vote for parties rather than individual candidates and party candidates are selected in proportion to their party's vote share.* In our sample constituency, 10 members are to be elected. Each party contesting the election in this constituency would nominate up to 10 candidates before election day and list them on the party's nomination papers in order from 1 to 10. Once the number of seats won by each party is determined, then the specific members elected are chosen, in descending order, from that party's list of candidates. In our example, Party A elected six members; thus, those candidates in positions one through six on Party A's list of candidates would become Party A's elected members for this riding. A similar allocation procedure would occur for Party B and Party C. As this example demonstrates, the basic difference between plurality and proportional representation electoral formulas is in their effects on the allocation of legislative seats: plurality systems often show a great distortion between popular support and legislative representation, while proportional representation seeks to equalize a party's electoral support with the size of its parliamentary contingent.

In addition to the highest average and greatest remainder proportional representation formulas, there is also a widely advocated third type of proportional representation known as the single transferable vote (STV). The **single transferable vote** is *a type of proportional representation in which voters rank all candidates in terms of their preferences (first, second, third, etc.), and those preferences are counted until one candidate receives a majority.* The STV system is currently used in Ireland and Malta and for the Australian Senate. Moreover, the STV electoral system was one element of the 1992 Canadian constitutional proposals included in the Charlottetown Accord, in relation to an elected and reformed Canadian Senate. The STV has long been seen as the favoured alternative of electoral reform advocates in Britain. In fact, because it has only been used in countries (except for Denmark in the 1850s) which "have at some time been under British rule," the STV system has been called "the 'Anglo-Saxon' method of securing proportional representation" (Bogdanor, 1984: 76).

While the actual calculations involving an STV system of proportional representation can be very complex, its importance is as a possible alternative to the plurality system. The proponents of an STV system usually cite two major advantages: first, the results in terms of seats allocated to the parties is far more proportionate than under a plurality formula; and second, the personal connection between a voter and the elected representative is maintained. Based on the Irish experience (Mair, 1986: 292–307), the major disadvantage seems to be the extensive potential for partisan gerrymandering under an STV electoral system.

DRAWING ELECTORAL BOUNDARIES

No matter what type of district magnitude (single-member or multi-member) or electoral formula (plurality or proportional representation) is utilized, specific constituency boundaries must be drawn. Boundary decisions are needed in constructing an electoral system for a new polity, in changing from one type of electoral system to another, or in redrawing the existing boundaries to reflect emerging population trends. Who draws the boundaries, how often, and based on what criteria are crucial elements in determining future winners and losers in the electoral process.

Based on the notion of parliamentary sovereignty, the traditional pattern in liberal-democratic political systems has been for legislatures to dominate in the drawing of electoral boundaries. Given a majority government situation, what this has meant in fact is that the electoral boundaries have been decided upon by the government of the day, usually in a very partisan fashion. Such a practice is known as **gerrymandering**, that is, *the drawing of the constituency boundaries to maximize the political support of one's party and to minimize that of the other parties.* The name of this practice derives from American history: in 1812, Governor Elbridge Gerry of Massachusetts redistributed electoral boundaries in such a way that one of the districts of the electoral map looked like a salamander, hence the word gerrymander. The trend in the modern era is for legislatures to authorize independent boundary commissions to make the specific recommendations for electoral boundaries, hoping thereby to eliminate gerrymandering from the process.

How often boundaries are changed was initially a decision by the legislature as well. Typically, several decades might elapse (sometimes even longer) before a legislature would redraw its own constituency boundaries. Obviously a governing party that benefitted from the existing electoral redistribution would be hesitant to change it on a regular basis. The trend toward independent commissions has had a corresponding effect on the timing of redistributions. The emerging pattern is to have electoral boundaries reworked by independent commissions on a regular basis — for example, every ten years based on a national census.

In addition to the concerns of who draws the boundaries and how often they do so, a third feature of boundary selection is the criteria that guide the specific constituency decisions. Two broad factors have dominated the process: geography and population. Geography and its related factors (rural interests, community traditions, county and municipal units) have historically dominated the process, with the result that urban and then suburban areas have often been greatly underrepresented in the legislatures. In recent decades, the population criterion has increasingly emerged in many liberal-democratic polities as the dominant factor in electoral redistributions.

The conflict between the two criteria of geography and population has often produced a result known as **malapportionment**, that is, *constituencies of unequal population size.* The greater the emphasis on the criterion of geography, the greater will be the pattern of malapportionment. Those who favour population as a criterion seek to reduce the population discrepancy between constituencies through the battle cry of "one person, one vote; one vote, one value." Infrequent redistributions and population trends tend to increase the effects of malapportionment, while regular redistributions based on the principle of population equality produce opposite effects.

THE CANADIAN ELECTORAL SYSTEM

In both federal and provincial elections, the Canadian electoral system is an example of the single-member district and plurality electoral formula. The plurality or, as it is sometimes called, **first-past-the-post** system is the only type of electoral system ever used in federal elections, although several Western provinces (Manitoba, Alberta, and British Columbia) have in the past experimented with other forms in provincial elections. For example, between 1924 and 1956 a preferential voting system was used in provincial elections in Alberta. At the federal level "dual" constituencies (two members elected in a constituency) have been used, but this format is a variation on the plurality formula and not a type of proportional representation.

Like other political systems that use the single-member district and plurality electoral formula, the Canadian electoral system regularly distorts the relationship between a party's popular support and the size of its parliamentary representation (see Table 8.3). The most glaring recent example of this distortion occurred in New Brunswick in 1987, when the provincial Liberals under Frank McKenna captured all 58 seats in the legislature with 60 percent of the popular vote. The only other time a shutout happened was in the 1935 provincial election in Prince Edward Island, although history almost repeated itself in that province when the Tories won 26 out of 27 seats in 2000.

Table 8.3   Canadian Election Results — 1997, 2000

	# of seats	% of votes	% of seats won	electoral system bias %
1997 election				
Liberal	155	38	52	+14
PC	20	19	7	−12
NDP	21	11	7	− 4
Reform	60	19	20	+ 1
Bloc Québécois	44	11	15	+ 4
Other	1	2	0.3	− 2
2000 election				
Liberal	172	41	57	+16
PC	12	12	4	−8
NDP	13	9	4	−5
Alliance*	66	25	22	−3
Bloc Québécois	38	11	13	+2
Other	0	2	0	−2

* Formerly the Reform Party in 1997

The impact of the electoral system in the 1993 federal election produced patterns typical of the results of the plurality formula in Canada. The Liberals, the leading party in terms of votes with 42 percent, gained an advantage of 18 percent in terms of seats in the House of Commons. Thus, the electoral system produced what is known as a **manufactured majority**; that is, it took *a minority of the popular vote (42 percent) and transformed it into a majority of legislative seats (60 percent)*. Parties with support on a national basis (the Conservatives at 16 percent and the NDP at 7 percent), but whose support was generalized across too many ridings, were highly discriminated against. Thus, the Tories, while receiving 16 percent of the national vote, gained less than 1 percent of the seats in the Commons. Finally, regional or sectional parties did well, with the Reform Party only losing slightly from the electoral system and the Bloc Québécois receiving a gain of 4 percent in seats from the electoral system. An analogous pattern was evident in the results of the 1997 election.

Similar patterns, with some minor variations, were evident in the impact of the electoral system in 2000 as well. The Liberals, with 41 percent of the popular vote, formed a strong majority government, with 57 percent of the seats in the House of Commons — that is, a manufactured majority once again. The Tories received 12 percent of the national vote, but with a pattern of diffuse electoral support they were highly discriminated against, losing a possible 24 seats in the House of Commons. The NDP, with somewhat more concentrated voting support, gained one more seat than the Tories, even though the party had 3 percent less of the popular vote. The Bloc Québécois, because of its regional strength solely in the province of Quebec, gained an advantage of about a half-dozen seats from the electoral system.

On a national basis in Canada, therefore, the first-past-the-post system is usually biased in favour of the major parties, particularly the largest party in terms of votes, at the same time that it may discriminate against the major parties in particular regions of the country. In contrast, the present electoral system has disadvantages for the New Democratic Party on both a national and regional basis. While the NDP's traditional strength in terms of votes is fairly widespread (11 percent of the vote in the 1997 election and 9 percent in 2000), it is distributed in a pattern of generalized or diffuse support. The results of the 2000 federal election showed, once again, the deleterious effects of the plurality electoral system on the seat potential of the New Democratic Party, when the party gained only 4 percent of the legislative seats on the basis of 9 percent of the popular vote. For the Tories the pattern was even worse in 2000: 12 percent of the popular vote was reduced to just 4 percent of the seats in the House of Commons.

The plurality system, however, works to the advantage of minor parties that exhibit strong regional or sectional voting support. The Social Credit party over several decades (the 1960s and 1970s) benefitted the most from this pattern. The 1993 general election saw the re-emergence of regionally based minor parties in both the West (Reform Party) and Quebec (Bloc Québécois). The Reform Party, based in Western Canada, claimed 52 seats, while the new separatist party in Quebec, the Bloc Québécois, swept that province, winning 54 seats out of 75. In 1997, the Bloc Québécois received 8 percent less of the popular vote, dropping from 19 to 11 percent, but still won 44 seats (out of 75) in the province of Quebec. The Reform Party, with 19 percent of the vote, increased its seats from 52 to 60. In 2000, the Canadian Alliance (formerly the Reform Party) was hurt by the plurality system, while the Bloc Québécois benefitted, getting 13 percent of the seats with 11 percent of the vote.

In addition to these national and regional effects on the seat allocations for the political parties, the plurality electoral system in Canada also has a number of other important political consequences (Cairns, 1968). First, in contrast to other political systems that utilize the plurality formula, such as Britain, the present electoral system in Canada has not always produced majority governments on a regular basis. For example, between 1965 and 1980 federal elections witnessed a regular alternation between minority (1965, 1972, 1979) and majority governments (1968, 1974, 1980). In the last four decades, Canada has experienced 6 minority and 10 majority administrations. However, since 1980 the pattern of regular minority governments as a result of the plurality system appears to have ended, given six successive majority governments (1980, 1984, 1988, 1993, 1997, and 2000).

The electoral system also contributes to the public's misperception about the nature of the various political parties' status as national political organizations. The public perceives the parties in terms of their parliamentary representation, not in terms of their electoral or voting support. For example, in 1980 the Liberals were locked out of support in the three most western provinces in terms of seats, but not in terms of popular voting support, which was over 20 percent. Similarly, the Conservatives' lack of support in Quebec in 1980 and the NDP's failure to gain representation in six provinces in both 1980 and 1984 and in five provinces in 1988 is only true in terms of seats, not with respect to voting support. In 1993 and 1997, because of the regional support for the Reform Party and Bloc Québécois, the perception of the national status of the Conservatives and NDP was thrown into doubt, given their seat totals. In 2000, the Canadian Alliance won 64 of its 66 seats in the West (out of a possible 88 seats), thus enhancing its image as being only a regional protest party.

Third, the plurality electoral system reinforces the sectional and regional basis of the Canadian political system because it tends to reward those parties that have established regional strongholds. The most obvious example is the Liberal party's previous dominance of Quebec: in 1980, the Liberals won 74 of 75 seats (99 percent of the seats), but in terms of votes they won only 68 percent of popular support. Similarly, in 1980 the Tories won all 21 seats in Alberta on the basis of 66 percent support from the electorate. In 2000, the Bloc Québécois, which ran no candidates outside of Quebec, gained 38 of Quebec's 75 seats in the House of Commons by winning the support of 40 percent of the electorate in only one province.

Finally, the plurality system affects the process of governing. For example, the previously discussed nature of the regional composition of the cabinet is sometimes influenced by the workings of the plurality system. By preventing adequate regional Liberal representation from the West and Conservative representation from Quebec in the House of Commons, the plurality electoral system forced the 1979 Clark government and the 1980 Trudeau administration to use the Senate as a temporary base for cabinet selection. The large majority victories in 1984, 1988, and 1993 undercut this pattern considerably. In 1997, however, the Liberals, having won no seats in Nova Scotia, once again used the Senate to maintain the principle of regional representation in the cabinet. With the Liberals winning seats in all provinces in the 2000 election, such a practice will not need to be used again in the immediate future.

ELECTORAL REFORM PROPOSALS

The above effects of the plurality electoral system in the Canadian context have generated numerous proposals for electoral reform in relation to the House of Commons. Those reform proposals that have received the greatest attention can be broken down into two basic types: limited proportional representation and full proportional representation.

While varying on specifics, **limited proportional representation** proposals suggest *adding a given number of seats (ranging from 50 to 100) to the present number of seats in the House of Commons and then distributing these additional seats on a proportional basis among the various political party competitors* (Landes, 1980: 2–10; Smiley, 1978: 84–87; Irvine, 1979: 64–67). The allocation of these additional seats would generally correspond to the various parties' popular support and would be calculated under some system of proportional representation, either on a national, regional, or provincial basis (Table 8.4). As a result, and similar to the systems used in Germany and for the Scottish and Welsh Parliaments, the Canadian electoral system would become a **mixed electoral system**: *most constituencies would be selected under the present plurality formula, while the additional seats would be based on some kind of proportional representation.*

The primary effect of such a reform would be to increase the potential regional seat representativeness of all national federal parties: no such party would be entirely lacking in legislative representation from any region of the country. The impact of limited proportional representation (LPR for short) on the new regional protest parties (Canadian Alliance and Bloc Québécois) in the 2000 election would show a more mixed result. The Canadian Alliance would gain more seats (25) than the Bloc Québécois (11) and would remain the official opposition in the House of Commons. The national seat representativeness of the Canadian Alliance would be increased, but the Bloc Québécois would likely use all of its additional seats solely within Quebec. Such limited proportional representation proposals are a conservative way of achieving regional representation without greatly disturbing the overall election results in terms of seats won in the regular single-member plurality contests. One possible result would be that when a province (such as Nova Scotia in 1977) selects no MP in the governing caucus, a member of the House of Commons elected under LPR could be selected for a cabinet position rather than an unelected Senator.

All of the proposed limited proportional representation schemes, however, leave basically untouched the inequities produced by the plurality electoral formula in the initial single-member ridings. For those who believe that a party's vote share should equal its share of legislative seats, the obvious answer is to adopt

Table 8.4   Alternative Canadian Electoral Systems 2000

	Plurality	Limited PR*	Full PR**
Liberal	172	213	124
PC	12	24	36
NDP	13	22	27
Alliance	66	91	75
Bloc Québécois	38	49	33
Other	0	2	6
Total	301	401	301

* The limited proportional representation figures are based on the following calculations. An additional 100 seats in the House of Commons are allocated on the basis of the parties' national vote totals (percentage). In 2000, the results would be as follows: Liberals, 41 seats; Conservatives, 12 seats; NDP, 9 seats; Alliance, 25 seats; Bloc Québécois, 11 seats; other, 2 seats.

** The full proportional representation figures are obtained by multiplying the party's percentage of the popular vote in 2000 times 301 seats.

some form of **full proportional representation** (Irvine, 1979). Under such a plan, a party's legislative representation would approximately equal its share of the popular vote. Table 8.4 also includes an allocation of parliamentary seats for 2000 if a full proportional representation formula had been utilized.

The effects of full proportional representation on the parliamentary strength of the political parties would be dramatic. The smaller political parties (NDP and PC) in recent federal elections would be advantaged under any system of full proportional representation: in 2000, the NDP would have increased from 13 to 27 seats and the Tories from 12 to 36 (a 200 percent gain)! More importantly, not only would the NDP's parliamentary representation have greatly increased, in many elections it would also have held the balance of power within the House of Commons (i.e., 1988). Clearly, the primary beneficiaries of any system of full proportional representation in the past three elections would have been the New Democratic Party and the Tories. A full proportional representation scheme in 2000 would have greatly aided the Tory party, placing it third instead of fifth, with the Bloc Québécois dropping to fourth place.

The traditional impact of full proportional representation on the Liberal and Conservative parties, at least from their point of view, would usually be detrimental: the seat leader under the present plurality system would often face major losses. For example, in 2000 the Liberals would have lost 48 seats and would have formed a minority, rather than a majority, government. However, in contrast to most election results, proportional representation would actually have helped the Tories in 2000 (as well as in 1993 and 1997) to stave off their humbling at the polls.

> Had there been a proportional representation system in effect in 1988, there would have been no Free Trade Agreement, no GST, no North American Free Trade Agreement, and no second term for the Mulroney government (Hurtig, 1992: 30).

A further result of proportional representation would be a dramatic change in the internal regional composition of most of the parties. Most parties would become national parties in the sense of receiving seats throughout the regions, with the exception of the Bloc Québécois, which only received votes in Quebec. However, increased regional representation under proportional representation would have the effect of reducing a party's parliamentary seats. For the NDP and Tories, increased regional representation would result in a major increase in their legislative caucus. Such consequences would seem to make the adoption of any type of full proportional representation for the House of Commons by a Liberal administration very unlikely. Moreover, it is not in the political self-interest of the Bloc Québécois or the Canadian Alliance to support such a change either.

DRAWING ELECTORAL BOUNDARIES

Throughout much of Canadian history the practices of malapportionment and gerrymandering have been clearly evident. Since at the federal level only the plurality, single-member district system has ever been used, while at the provincial level it has rarely been replaced, the problem of drawing electoral boundaries arises most typically when an electoral redistribution takes place. An **electoral redistribution** can be defined as *the reallocation of legislative seats and the resulting redrawing of constituency boundaries.*

Since, traditionally, provincial redistributions are usually decided upon by the government of the day, the decision to reallocate constituency boundaries often carries important political consequences. If a party feels that it would benefit, then a redistribution will occur. For example, in 1993 the provincial NDP government in Saskatchewan announced plans to reduce the number of MLAs in the legislature from 66 to 58, thus creating the need to redraw the electoral boundaries only three years after the last redistribution was completed in 1990. In contrast, if the party in power perceives that a redistribution will undercut its base of support, then it will be postponed as long as possible.

Gerrymandering has been a regular feature of Canadian political life. However, since 1964 at the federal level such practices have been greatly minimized, with non-partisan boundary commissions now responsible for the redrawing of constituency boundaries. At the provincial level gerrymandering remains an accepted, if declining, practice. The very partisan electoral redistributions in Saskatchewan in 1989 and Alberta in 1990 demonstrate the prevalence of this practice. However, some provinces have begun to follow the federal practice of independent boundary commissions. Nova Scotia, for example, with all-party agreement in the House of Assembly, appointed the Provincial Electoral Boundaries Commission in July of 1991. This boundary commission (Landes Commission) was the first independent, nonpartisan boundaries commission in the province's history. However, as long as some provinces continue the practice of direct legislative involvement in the redistribution process, gerrymandering will remain as an ingredient of Canadian politics.

Because the timing of electoral redistributions has been a legislative prerogative, malapportionment has also been a characteristic of the electoral system.

> Independent electoral boundaries commissions have become a mainstay of representative democracy in Canada, relied upon to fulfil the task of delineating the electorate into constituencies necessary for the conduct of elections (Hyson, 1999: 175).

Historically, federal redistributions for the House of Commons take place after each census, although for the provincial legislatures several decades might pass before such a procedure is undertaken. Because of population shifts, some constituencies may end up with many more voters than others, thus undercutting the supposed equality of each citizen's vote. Until recent decades, malapportionment favoured those parties with a rural base, since urban ridings would usually be more densely populated. In the past 50 years, the major population trend has been to the suburbs, so that these areas have typically been underrepresented in the legislatures.

The Canadian view of malapportionment has always been to accept the general idea of population equality for constituencies, tempered by a strong dose of social and political reality; in other words, Canadians accept population equality as a goal, but at the same time recognize the need not to adopt a rigid pattern of population equality. Other factors, such as geography or community interest, can thereby be taken into account. The Canadian attitude is best reflected by the use of ± factors in the electoral redistribution process.

A **plus or minus factor** is *the percentage by which a constituency may be either over or under the ideal average of population equality.* For example, at the Canadian federal level a ± factor of 25 percent is utilized for most constituencies. This ± factor means that a constituency may be 25 percent above the average in population size or 25 percent below it. The pattern in Nova Scotia until 1992 allowed for a ± factor of 33 1/3 percent.

As a rule of thumb, we can say that the greater the ± factor that is allowed, the greater the resulting pattern of malapportionment. A ± factor produces inequalities far greater than one might expect from a first glance at the issue. For example, if the average-sized constituency is 12 000 voters and a ± factor of 33 1/3 percent is allowed, the largest constituency could contain 16 000 voters while the smallest constituency could have 8 000 voters. Thus, a ± factor of 33 1/3 percent in this example produces differences in actual constituency size of 100 percent (i.e., 16 000 voters versus 8 000 voters).

The history of electoral redistributions in Canada and other Western liberal-democracies demonstrates that the two practices of gerrymandering and malapportionment have often been politically linked. Gerrymandering is often most effective when it is used with an excessive pattern of malapportionment. The way the process works can be illustrated as follows. If the constituencies are not required to be of equal population size (i.e., malapportionment), then you put as many of the opposing party's areas of strength in as few ridings as possible (i.e., a gerrymander). Concurrently, spread your own political support over as many constituencies as possible, but in such a way as to ensure a majority position within each one. However, the two processes can be practiced separately: one can gerrymander without malapportioning and, conversely, one can malapportion without gerrymandering.

Charter politics

Given the principle of parliamentary sovereignty, both the federal and provincial legislatures have successfully maintained their control of the electoral redistribution process throughout most of Canadian history. Even the move to regular redistributions and independent commissions has not necessarily eliminated the practices of gerrymandering and malapportionment. For example, the principle of **representation by population** or "rep by pop" has usually been more honoured in its breach than in its observance.

The constitutional basis for challenging this traditional pattern was provided by the 1982 adoption of the Canadian Charter of Rights and Freedoms. Section 3 of the Charter states that "Every citizen of Canada has the right to vote in an election of members of the House of Commons or of a legislative assembly and to be qualified for membership therein." Interestingly, Section 33 — the override provision — cannot be used to bypass the right to vote granted in Section 3.

Within a decade of its adoption, Section 3 of the Charter would provide the constitutional basis for legal challenges to the traditional power of the legislatures to draw their own boundaries as they saw fit. Interestingly, in May of 1989 the British Columbia government was ordered by the Chief Justice of the B.C. Supreme Court, Madame Justice Beverley McLachlin, to redraw the province's electoral

The application of Charter rights and Supreme Court imperatives cannot be pre-determined by a precisely legislated political recipe (Smith and Landes, 1998:33).

boundaries because of obvious malapportionment among the constituencies (Ruff, 1990; 1992). Such an order, a result of an action by the B.C. Civil Liberties Association under Section 3 of the Charter, heralded the potential end of excessive malapportionment in the provincial legislatures.

Charter-based attacks on malapportionment quickly spread to other provinces. Based on Section 3 of the Charter, a challenge to an electoral redistribution produced by the Saskatchewan Legislature led to a decision by the Saskatchewan Court of Appeal (March 1991) which upheld the principle of population equality and thus rejected the proposed redistribution. The immediate implication of the ruling by the Saskatchewan Court of Appeal was that the existing electoral distributions in many provinces might be open to constitutional challenge, based on the principle of "one person, one vote." Several provinces, including Nova Scotia and New Brunswick, immediately embarked upon new processes of electoral redistribution.

The ruling by the Saskatchewan Court of Appeal was itself appealed to the Supreme Court of Canada. In a landmark ruling on June 6, 1991, the Supreme Court of Canada overturned the previous decision of the Saskatchewan Court of Appeal. The Supreme Court decision, popularly known as the *Carter* decision, rejected a strict population equality requirement and, instead, held that the goal was **effective representation**, to be achieved by **relative parity of voting power**.

Writing for the majority, Madame Justice McLachlin, by now a member of the Canadian Supreme Court, outlined clearly the differences between the competing conceptions of population equality versus effective representation based on relative parity of voting power. The following quotations are taken from pages 8–17 of Madame Justice McLachlin's decision; they summarize the opinion of the Supreme Court of Canada on this matter and, thus, they set the parameters for future political struggles and court challenges with respect to the federal and provincial electoral systems.

> The question for resolution on this appeal can be summed up in one sentence: to what extent, if at all, does the right to vote enshrined in the Charter permit deviation from the "one person — one vote" rule? The answer to this question turns on what one sees as the purpose of s. 3. Those who start from the premise that the purpose of the section is to guarantee equality of voting power support the view that only minimal deviation from that ideal is possible. Those who start from the premise that the purpose of s. 3 is to guarantee effective representation see the right to vote as comprising many factors, of which equality is but one. The contest, as I see it, is most fundamentally between these two views . . . .
>
> It is my conclusion that the purpose of the right to vote enshrined in s. 3 of the Charter is not equality of voting power per se, but the right to "effective representation." Ours is a representative democracy. Each citizen is entitled to be represented in government . . . .
>
> What are the conditions of effective representation? The first is relative parity of voting power. A system which dilutes one citizen's vote unduly as compared with another citizen's vote runs the risk of providing inadequate representation to the citizen whose vote is diluted. The legislative power of the citizen whose vote is diluted will be reduced, as may be access to and assistance from his or her representative. The result will be uneven and unfair representation . . . .

Notwithstanding the fact that the value of a citizen's vote should not be unduly diluted, it is a practical fact that effective representation often cannot be achieved without taking into account countervailing factors.

First, absolute parity is impossible. It is impossible to draw boundary lines which guarantee exactly the same number of voters in each district. Voters die, voters move. Even with the aid of frequent censuses, voter parity is impossible.

Secondly, such relative parity as may be possible of achievement may prove undesirable because it has the effect of detracting from the primary goal of effective representation. Factors like geography, community history, community interests and minority representation may need to be taken into account to ensure that our legislative assemblies effectively represent the diversity of our social mosaic. These are but examples of considerations which may justify departure from absolute voter parity in the pursuit of more effective representation; the list is not closed . . . .

In summary, I am satisfied that the precepts which govern the interpretation of *Charter* rights support the conclusion that the right to vote should be defined as guaranteeing the right to effective representation. The concept of absolute voter parity does not accord with the development of the right to vote in the Canadian context and does not permit of sufficient flexibility to meet the practical difficulties inherent in representative government in a country such as Canada. In the end, it is the broader concept of effective representation which best serves the interests of a free and democratic society.

Combined with the right to vote in Section 3 of the Charter, the 1991 Supreme Court decision in the *Carter* case has altered the process of electoral redistributions in Canada in several key ways. First, the idea of effective representation has become the overriding goal and it is premised on relative parity of voting power, as conditioned by factors such as geography and community interests. The American model of strict voter parity ("one person, one vote") has been rejected in the Canadian context. Second, electoral redistributions for provincial legislatures are subject to both the Charter and to possible judicial review by the Supreme Court of Canada. Third, the *Carter* case dealt with malapportionment; in fact, the word gerrymander was not contained in the Supreme Court decision. While malapportionment has been constrained, the potential for gerrymandering is alive and well. Finally, minority groups will increasingly claim the right to legislative representation in future electoral redistributions (Smith and Landes, 1998). Any electoral redistribution after the *Carter* case (June 6, 1991) is, therefore, constrained by this new context of electoral reform. For example, in March of 1999 the Supreme Court of the Northwest Territories ruled that the electoral law used in the Northwest Territories was unconstitutional because it "grossly underrepresented" the urban areas in Yellowknife.

THE BRITISH ELECTORAL SYSTEM

Like Canada, Britain uses the single-member district and plurality electoral formula for elections to the House of Commons (Butler and Kavanagh, 1992: 347–355). As might be expected, then, many of the consequences of the plurality electoral system are similar in Canada and Britain (see Table 8.5).

In Britain, the plurality system typically works to the advantage of the major parties and discriminates heavily against those parties with generalized or diffuse support (the Liberals and the Social Democrats in 1987 and the Liberal Democrats in 1992). In 1987, the Alliance (Liberal and Social Democratic Parties) won 23

Table 8.5   British Electoral System — 1987, 1992, 1997, 2001

	# of seats	% of vote	% of seats	effects of the electoral system %	# of seats under full PR
1987 election					
Labour	229	31	35	+ 4	202
Conservative	376	42	58	+16	273
Alliance (Liberal-SDP)	22	23	3	−20	149
Other	23	4	4	0	26
1992 election					
Labour	271	34	42	+8	221
Conservative	336	42	52	+10	273
Liberal Democrats	20	18	3	−15	117
Scottish National Party	3	2	0.5	− 2	13
Plaid Cymru	4	1	0.6	− 1	7
Northern Ireland Parties	17	2	3	+1	13
Other	0	1	0	− 1	7
1997 election					
Labour	418	43	63	+20	283
Conservative	165	32	25	− 7	211
Liberal Democrats	46	17	7	−10	112
Scottish National Party	6	2	1	− 1	13
Plaid Cymru	4	0.5	0.6	+0.1	3
Other	20	5.7	3.4	−2.3	37
2001 election					
Labour	413	41	63	+22	270
Conservative	166	32	25	−7	211
Liberal Democrats	52	18	8	−10	119
Scottish National Party	5	2	0.8	−1.2	13
Plaid Cymru	4	0.7	0.6	−0.1	5
Other	19	6.3	2.9	−3.4	42

percent of the popular vote but ended up with only 3 percent of the seats. In other words, the Alliance was denied 127 seats by the plurality system. In 1997, the Liberal Democrats (the revised Alliance of 1987) won 17 percent of the popular vote but only 7 percent of the seats in the House of Commons. The plurality electoral formula denied the Liberal Democrats 66 seats in the legislature, thereby keeping them in minor party status. In 1997, even the Conservative party (a major party) was heavily discriminated against by the plurality electoral system: it lost 46 seats. The 2001 election produced almost identical results to those in 1997!

In contrast, small parties with strong sectional or regional support (e.g., the Scottish Nationalist Party or the Welsh Nationalist Party) usually fare much better under the plurality formula than the Liberal Democrats. For example, in 1992 the Northern Ireland parties won 2 percent of the popular vote and 3 percent of the seats, while the Liberal Democrats won 18 percent of the vote but only 3 percent of the seats. The bias of the electoral system against the Liberal Democrats was again evident in the 1997 and 2001 elections, with that party losing 10 percent of their potential seat share in the House of Commons.

Thus, in both Canada and Britain the plurality system typically advantages the major parties (in Canada, the Liberals and, until 1993, the Conservatives; in Britain, the Labour and Conservative parties); discriminates against those parties with generalized or diffuse support (in Canada, the New Democratic Party and the Tories after 1993; in Britain, the Liberal Democrats in 1992, 1997, and 2001); and either aids parties with strong sectional or regional support or at least does not discriminate against them with the same intensity as it does against those parties with diffuse support (in Canada, the Reform Party in 1993 and 1997, the Canadian Alliance in 2000, and the Bloc Québécois in 1993, 1997, and 2000; in Britain, typically the various nationalist parties).

The differential effects of the plurality system in the British and Canadian contexts can be seen with respect to two areas: first, the creation of majority governments; and second, the regional composition of the major parties. Although similar to Canada in that the winning party rarely has a majority of the vote (the last election where a party won more than 50 percent of the vote took place in 1931), in contrast to Canada, the plurality formula in Britain regularly produces majority governments in terms of parliamentary seat allocations. In the postwar era (1945–2001), 16 elections have been contested, with majority governments resulting in 15 cases. The only exception was the February 1974 election, although the October 1974 Labour majority was so small that it became a minority government within a couple of years through defections, retirements, and deaths.

Majority governments have occurred in Britain because, until the 1974 elections and the rise of several nationalist parties, minor parties received a small number of legislative seats, while in Canada minor parties have consistently fared much better under the plurality system. In the 1960s and 1970s, Canada's four-party system (Liberal, Conservative, New Democratic Party, and Social Credit), combined with the effects of the plurality formula, helped to prevent the regular formation of majority governments. The success of several new regional protest parties after 1993 did not return Canada to the pattern of minority governments of the 1970s.

In fact, the 2000 election produced the third consecutive majority government for the Liberals under Jean Chrétien and the sixth majority government in a row.

A second difference between the plurality system in Britain and Canada concerns the regional nature of a political party's legislative representation. In the Canadian context, the combination of the plurality system with the regional bases of party support has often resulted in a party receiving no legislative seats from certain regions of the country (i.e., the Liberal party in Alberta obtained no seats in federal elections between 1972 and 1988). In Britain, parties have traditionally had regional strongholds, but a party has rarely been discriminated against to such an extent that it received no legislative representation from a region (Drucker, 1979: 216–217). For example, the Conservative party has traditionally received a block of seats in Scotland and Wales, although in 1997 it received no seats in those areas.

The trend of the 1980s and early 1990s was for a regionalization of party support in Britain between the North (increasingly Labour) and the South (increasingly Conservative) (Kendrick and McCrone, 1989). For example, in the 1987 election the Labour party won 42 percent of the vote in Scotland, but picked up 70 percent of the Scottish seats in the House of Commons. A similar regionalization of Conservative party support could be seen in the following results: in southeast England (outside of London), the Conservatives won 57 percent of the vote, which translated into 99 percent of the legislative seats. The 1992 election saw a modest attenuation of this pattern: the Tories gained some strength in northern England and Scotland, while the Labour party made similar gains in London and the Midlands (Curtice, 1992; Sanders, 1993: 173). However, Tony Blair's massive victories for the Labour party in the 1997 and 2001 elections were based, in part, on a resurgence of support in many areas throughout England, as well as strong popular support in Scotland and Wales.

ELECTORAL REFORM PROPOSALS

Proposals for electoral reform in Britain have centred, as in Canada, on alternatives that would increase the equality between a party's share of the popular vote and its share of legislative seats (Dunleavy, Margetts, and Weir, 1992). The most commonly advocated reform would call for the adoption of the single transferable vote or STV (Scammon, 1975: 165–176; Norton, 1982: 227–243). The STV system, or any specific proportional representation scheme, would greatly alter the electoral fortunes of the various political parties. Since the major parties are as unlikely to commit political hara-kiri in Britain as they are in Canada, prospects for the adoption of any system of proportional representation for elections to the House of Commons do not seem likely.

The reason that Labour and Conservative parties are opposed to any system of proportional representation can be clearly seen in Table 8.5. In most elections (i.e., 1987 and 1992, but not in 1997 and 2001) both major parties have often been advantaged by the plurality formula, while the centre party (i.e., Liberal Democrats in 1992, 1997, and 2001) has been highly discriminated against. Since "parties are not charitable organizations," neither the Labour nor Conservative party can see its self-interests served by electoral reform (Rasmussen, 1993: 158). For example, although some elements of the left wing of the Labour party favour proportional representation, the dominant view was expressed in the party's 1990 policy statement called *Looking to the Future*: "Labour is opposed to changing the electoral system for the House of Commons." However, in positioning itself for the 1997 election, the Labour party signed an agreement with the Liberal Democrats in which it promised to consider adopting proportional representation if the Labour party won the general election — a proposal the Labour party was still considering after its re-election victory in 2001.

As the party most discriminated against by the plurality system from the 1920s to the 1980s, the Liberal party and its successors have been the most vociferous proponents of proportional representation. Typically advocated is an STV system, although the precise details have varied over the years. One proposal called for 143 multi-member constituencies, with district magnitudes of up to eight. Other minor parties have often supported some form of proportional representation as well.

As long as one of the two major parties wins a majority of seats in the House of Commons, reform to a proportional representation scheme is unlikely. However, the possibility of a "hung Parliament," that is, a situation in which the largest party has obtained a minority of seats, might produce a scenario for electoral reform. As the Liberal Democrats maintained in the 1992 campaign, the price of their support for either a Labour or Conservative minority government would be adoption of proportional representation. Thus, proportional representation is possible in the future, even if it is not highly probable.

While changes in the plurality formula for the House of Commons seem unlikely, other institutions have moved beyond the plurality electoral system. For example, future changes to the House of Lords may make it an elected body, utilizing some form of proportional representation. Britain's membership in the European Union and the adoption of the 1998 European Elections Bill require British representatives in the European Parliament (who are selected after 1999) to be chosen using a regional party-list system of proportional representation. Elections for Northern Ireland members in the European Parliament have used an STV system since 1980. Since 1920, Northern Ireland has used some form of proportional representation in selecting members of the legislature, that is, when elections have been allowed. With devolution to Scotland and Wales in 1998, these new legislatures have been selected by using a form of proportional representation known as an **additional member system (AMS)**. In Scotland, for example, similar to the limited proportional representation alternative in Canada, 73 members are selected in the traditional constituencies based on a plurality formula, while an additional group of 56 are chosen from regional party-lists based on proportional representation (McLean, 1999). What all of these examples show is that, except for elections to the

> For the debate on electoral reform, seemingly part of an abstract constitutional argument, is in reality a debate about the distribution of political power in Britain. Its resolution therefore will depend not on the abstract merits of the arguments deployed, but upon the outcome of the party struggle (Bogdanor, 1987: 120).

House of Commons, electoral reform is moving Great Britain away from the long-dominant plurality system.

DRAWING ELECTORAL BOUNDARIES

Since the establishment of independent boundary commissions in 1944, explicit examples of gerrymandering have disappeared from the electoral reform process, even though many could be cited historically. Separate commissions have been established for England, Scotland, Wales, and Northern Ireland. The initial legislation called for boundary reviews every 3 to 7 years; however, by 1958 this frequent revision process was deemed to be too disruptive, so that the legislation was amended. Since 1958, a boundary revision must occur no less than 10 years and no later than 15 years from the previous redistributions. After the initial change in 1944 (implemented in 1949), electoral redistributions have occurred in 1954, 1969, 1983, and 1994.

Although blatant gerrymandering has been basically removed in the process of drawing specific constituency boundaries, politics has not been (McLean and Mortimore, 1992: 306). The major areas for political manipulation are deciding when a review will take place within the 10- to 15-year time period and when it will be implemented, that is, before or after the next election. For example, the 1969 redistribution was delayed from implementation by the Labour government because it was expected to benefit the Tories. Thus, the 1970 general election was fought on the constituency boundaries established in 1954. Moreover, the current redistribution (1994) was not initially expected to be ready before 1998 but, after their 1992 election victory, the Tories moved quickly to ensure that the new boundaries would be in place before the next election (McLean and Mortimore, 1992: 300). The 1994 redistribution was approved by Parliament in 1995 and served as the basis for the 1997 and 2001 contests. Eight seats were added to the House of Commons (651 to 659), with over 500 constituencies being redrawn.

The criteria to be used in the redistribution process are outlined in the 1986 Parliamentary Constituencies Act and are quite complicated. A minimum number of seats are guaranteed for Scotland (not less than 71) and Wales (not less than 35). The application of the other criteria, in fact, allocated 72 seats to Scotland and 40 seats to Wales for the 1997 and 2001 elections. On a population criterion Scotland and Wales are thus significantly overrepresented in the House of Commons.

While the average size of constituencies is approximately 70 000 in England, extensive malapportionment has always been an integral part of the redistribution process. The reason for this result is that the criteria that the commissions must use focus on municipal and county units as the primary bases of constituency boundaries. In contrast to the Canadian practice of using ± factors and the American obsession with mathematical population equality (the one person, one vote principle), the British practice sees little, if anything, wrong with malapportionment. Constituency boundaries focus on the *representation of places*, such as counties and boroughs, and not on the equal *representation of people* (Johnston, 1986: 280).

THE AMERICAN ELECTORAL SYSTEM

As in Canada and Britain, and with the same effects, the electoral system used in the United States is the single-member district, plurality electoral formula mechanism. For example, in selecting members for the House of Representatives, there are 435 congressional districts, with one member elected in each. For Senate elections, each district corresponds to a state's boundaries, with the person with the most votes (i.e., a plurality) winning a place in the national legislature. In electing a president, a special version of the single-member district, plurality formula is used — the electoral college.

DRAWING ELECTORAL BOUNDARIES

In American politics the need to **redistrict** (called a redistribution in Canada) by *redrawing constituency boundaries* affects the lower house of the national government (the House of Representatives) and the various state legislatures. At the national level, redistricting results from population shifts reflected in each census, as well as the reallocation of seats between states (Kromkowski and Kromkowski, 1991; Scarrow, 1989). For example, the 1990 census resulted in 19 House seats being reapportioned among 21 states (8 states gained seats — California alone gained 7, while 13 states lost representation). Even in states that neither gained nor lost seats, redistricting was necessary because of shifting population patterns within such states. The census completed in 2000 will be the basis for a new reallocation of seats in the U.S. House of Representatives among the states and will affect the number of electors states have in the electoral college, changes which will be in place for the 2004 congressional and presidential elections. Initial projections indicate further gains by Southern and Western states, with continued losses for Midwest and New England states. The Sunbelt states of Texas, Florida, and California will gain a total of five seats, giving those three states 116 electoral college votes — 43 percent of the 270 needed to win the presidency.

Although its worst effects have been minimized in the last four decades, the practice of malapportionment has long characterized the American electoral process. Because the constituency boundaries of the congressional districts in the United States House of Representatives are drawn by the respective state legislatures, which means, in fact, that they are drawn by the majority party in that state, manipulation of constituency size used to be a common political practice. However, in 1964 the Supreme Court ruled malapportionment among congressional districts unacceptable and ordered a redrawing of their boundaries on the principle of "one man, one vote."

The result of that Supreme Court decision has been a virtual elimination of malapportionment in the lower House and an increase in the number of seats from both the urban and suburban areas. However, malapportionment is guaranteed in the Senate, since each state receives two seats: a senator from Maine represents about 1 million constituents, but a senator from California 32 million.

> Redistricting always has been recognized as a fundamentally political activity: It is conducted by politicians (governors and legislators), it has implications for political representation of all levels, and it is subject to ratification and sometimes decision-making by the federal judiciary (Gronke and Wilson, 1999: 147).

An electoral redistribution for the House of Representatives takes place after each decennial census, with the Midwest and Northeast losing seats and the South and West gaining them in recent decades. Unlike in Canada, where seats are often added to the Commons during a redistribution, the size of the House of Representatives has remained constant since the Apportionment Act of 1929: if some states are to gain seats, others must lose them.

Although a reduction in malapportionment minimizes, somewhat, the leeway for gerrymandering the constituency boundaries, it has certainly not eliminated this finely honed practice from American politics. Gerrymandering, once described as "ingenious exercises in political geography" (Key, 1964: 302), has particularly characterized state legislatures, serving as one means, for example, of discrimination against minority groups, especially African-Americans. An almost sure sign that district boundaries have been gerrymandered is their misshapen outline: often districts were drawn right down to the individual block or house, instead of following more natural dividing lines, such as major streets, county boundaries, or geographical partitions such as rivers.

The American process of redistricting illustrates that malapportionment and gerrymandering do not necessarily rise or fall together as either political principles or practices. While malapportionment has disappeared, gerrymandering has been expanded into an American art form (one might suggest the phrase "theatre of the absurd" as the appropriate designation). With the aid of computers, modern political redistricting rivals and, indeed, surpasses the abuses of the past.

> They [congressional districts] might look like casual doodles, but there is nothing random about them. Far from it . . . . These sketches are the result of the intersection of idealism and opportunism. Each of these districts is drawn to make highly probable, if not to guarantee, a particular kind of winner (Will, 1992: 42).

Two basic factors account for this pattern: first, incumbents (i.e., legislatures) are in charge of redrawing the boundaries; and second, those incumbents are highly partisan. The first result is that incumbents rearrange electoral boundaries in order to protect their self-interest, that is, their re-election. A second result is that parties openly gerrymander the electoral districts. Such practices place a major blot on the nature of American representative democracy.

THE ELECTORAL COLLEGE

The election of the president and vice-president is accomplished through the electoral college, which is a special and complex version of the plurality electoral formula outlined in Article II (Section 1) of the Constitution. Interestingly, the Constitution does not use the term electoral college, but only refers to "Electors" and their role in choosing a president and vice-president. Coined through popular usage, the term **electoral college** is *the electoral process used in selecting the president and vice-president of the United States.*

The electoral college is only used in selecting the president and vice-president of the United States once every four years, but it is one of the unique aspects of American election practices. It was initially designed to provide an indirect method of electing the American president. The people would elect members of the state legislatures, who in turn would elect the individuals to serve in the electoral college. The members of the electoral college thus chosen would then select the president and vice-president. The ordinary citizen was, therefore, twice removed from direct involvement in the presidential election process.

As the idea of popular sovereignty became enshrined in the American political culture, the people were granted a somewhat greater role in the electoral college. The people now select the membership of the electoral college when they cast their ballot in the presidential election in November once every four years. However, from 1880 to 2000 the electoral college was largely a formality, with the real decision made by the people in the presidential election. The winner of the popular vote had always also won the electoral college vote throughout the 20th century (in fact from 1892 through 1996). The electoral college in the modern era merely ratified the outcome of the popular vote registered at the polls, until the presidential election of 2000 (see below).

The structure of the electoral college is roughly based on population, since each state receives presidential electors equal to its number of members in the national legislature. For example, since the 1990 census California has had two senators and 52 congressmen, so it has 54 votes in the electoral college. Because each state, whether large or small, receives two Senate seats and one member in the House of Representatives, a degree of malapportionment is built into the electoral college. The total number of votes in the electoral college is 538 (a figure equivalent to 100 senators, plus 435 representatives, plus three votes for the District of Columbia). To win, a candidate must receive a majority of votes, that is, a total of 270 (Table 8.6).

When American citizens cast their ballots in the presidential contest, they are really selecting their state's representatives in the electoral college. Each party or candidate in the presidential race draws up a list of people willing to serve as presidential electors. This slate of delegates is often listed after the name of the presidential candidate on the ballot. If a candidate wins the popular vote (i.e., a plurality) in that state, then his or her electors become the state's delegation to the electoral college.

The election in each state is based on the unit rule, a special version of the plurality formula. The **unit rule** means that *a candidate who wins the popular vote in a state wins all of the state's vote in the electoral college.* In other words, in each state a presidential election is based on a "winner take

Table 8.6 Electoral College — Minimal Winning Coalition

	2000*	2004**
1. California	54	55
2. New York	33	31
3. Texas	32	34
4. Florida	25	27
5. Pennsylvania	23	21
6. Illinois	22	21
7. Ohio	21	20
8. Michigan	18	17
9. New Jersey	15	15
10. North Carolina	14	15
11. Georgia	13	15
Total =	270	271

* Based on the 1990 census.
** Based on the 2000 census.

all" principle. For example, in the state of Georgia in 1996 the party vote was distributed as follows: Republicans (47 percent), Democrats (46 percent), Reform party (6 percent). However, the unit rule gave the Republican candidate Bob Dole all 13 electoral college votes (100 percent). The only exceptions to this application of the unit rule are in Maine and Nebraska, where electoral college votes are distributed according to the popular vote within the congressional districts. The use of the unit rule is not required by the Constitution but is a decision by the states, which are given the power to administer national (federal) elections.

The impact of the unit rule is particularly devastating against new parties in American politics, as Ross Perot learned in 1992. While receiving as much as 30 percent of the vote in Maine and 28 percent in Alaska, the best Ross Perot could do in the "winner take all" system was second place in Maine and Utah — and, thus, no votes in the electoral college. Similarly, in the 2000 presidential election Ralph Nader of the Green Party received about 3 percent of the national vote and no votes in the electoral college.

The unit rule means that a small shift in popular support in several states can make a significant difference in the election outcome. For example, in 1976 the presidential outcome would have been altered (i.e., Ford elected rather than Carter) if 5 559 voters in Ohio and 3 687 voters in Hawaii had voted for Ford. These changes, because of the unit rule, would have given Ford the 25 Ohio votes and the 4 Hawaii votes in the electoral college, producing a narrow Republican victory (270 votes for Ford versus 268 votes for Carter). Even more incredible were the 2000 results in the state of Florida. Out of about 6 000 000 million votes cast, George W. Bush was certified the winner of the state's electoral votes with only a 537 vote margin over Al Gore in the popular vote. The Republican candidate therefore won Florida's 25 votes in the electoral college (271 for Bush to 266 for Gore) and the American presidency. The total for Al Gore was expected to be 267, but one of his supporters, to protest the situation in the Florida recount battle, refused to cast a ballot. Thus, the presidential vote in November determines the composition of each state's slate of delegates in the electoral college.

The next step is for the presidential electors who have been selected to meet and cast their ballots for the president and vice-president. The electors meet in their respective state capitals in December and cast their secret ballots, which are then sent on to the president of the American Senate (i.e., the current vice-president of the United States). In early January a joint meeting of the House of Representatives and Senate is held to count the ballots and to officially declare a winner. Thus, the president and vice-president are not technically elected until the votes of the presidential electors are counted by Congress, although for all practical purposes they are usually assumed to be elected in November.

However, a further complicating factor might arise. If two candidates or parties are competing in a presidential election, then the electoral college will produce a majority winner as a result of the workings of the unit rule. (Since there are an even number of 538 votes in the electoral college, it is possible to produce a tie vote — something which almost happened in the 2000 election.) However, if more than two candidates compete and if the electoral college vote is splintered among three or more parties, then nobody may receive a majority of votes when Congress counts the ballots in January. The 1992 campaign success of independent candidate Ross Perot in winning 19 percent of the popular vote had no direct effect on the electoral college process because he won no votes under the unit rule. The decline in voting support for Ross Perot in 1996 to 8 percent meant that there was little likelihood that the electoral college would not produce a majority result. A slightly different scenario occurred in the 2000 election. Even though Ralph Nader's Green Party won 3 percent of the national vote but no electoral college votes, those votes, which largely came from normally Democratic party voters, cost Al Gore a plurality victory in at least a half a dozen states (including Florida). As a result, the electoral college vote from Florida (with 25 electors) would decide the outcome of the national election. However, if no majority is received in the electoral college, then the House of Representatives selects the president from among the three parties who received the most electoral college votes, with the Senate choosing the vice-president. This result has not happened since 1824, but it is a possibility when more than two parties gain a significant share of the popular vote and thus might gain a block of votes in the electoral college.

Even though its operation has largely become a formality in deciding who wins, the effects of the electoral college on presidential politics are many (Table 8.7). First, a party can win the presidency by winning the vote in the 11 largest states. Moreover, the presidential candidate with the largest national popular vote does not necessarily win a majority of presidential electors in the electoral college. For example, Democrat Grover Cleveland won 100 000 more votes than his opponent (Republican Benjamin Harrison) in the 1888 election, but he lost in the crucial arena of the electoral college. The next time this result occurred was in 2000, with Al Gore winning more of the popular vote than George

> To say that the electoral college introduces random distortions into the election of the President is, however, only a half-truth, for it also contains a variety of systematic biases conferring advantages on some voters and imposing disadvantages on others (Longley and Dana, 1992: 124).

W. Bush. Second, the Democrats and Republicans will most often select as their presidential and vice-presidential candidates individuals from these largest states. This custom, even though somewhat attenuated in recent decades, is based on the assumption that such candidates will win their home states in the presidential election. For example, in 1960 the Democrats chose John F. Kennedy from Massachusetts and Lyndon B. Johnson from Texas; this pattern was repeated in 1988 when Michael Dukakis from Massachusetts chose Senator Lloyd Bentsen of Texas as his running mate. Both Republican and Democratic tickets in the last three national elections have violated this traditional, informal rule of American presidential politics.

It used to be an assumption of American presidential politics that, to win the presidency, a candidate needed victories in the big-city states of the Northeast (i.e., New York, New Jersey). However, with the population shift of recent decades to the South and West, since 1980 it is possible to win the electoral college with votes from just those two areas. Such a shift in the voting strength of states in the electoral college was good news in the 1980s for the Republicans and conservatives in American politics. A key to the 1992 and 1996 Clinton victories was the ability of the Democratic party to break the Republican dominance in the Southern and

Table 8.7   Electoral College — Creating Majorities

	% of vote	Electoral College vote	% of Electoral College
1992 election			
Bill Clinton	43	370	69
George Bush	38	168	31
Ross Perot	19	0	0
1996 election			
Bill Clinton	49	379	70
Bob Dole	41	159	30
Ross Perot	8	0	0
2000 election*			
George W. Bush	47.5	271	50.4
Al Gore	47.6	266	49.4
Ralph Nader	3	0	0

* Electoral college votes do not total 538 because an Al Gore elector refused to cast a ballot.

Western states. Al Gore was unable to repeat this pattern in 2000, losing even his home state of Tennessee and, thus, the presidency.

A third impact of the electoral college is that election campaigns are centred around the largest states, since that is where most of the electoral college votes are determined (Longley and Dana, 1992). The importance of California in the electoral college clearly demonstrates this point: it has 10 percent of the American population, 10 percent of the total electoral college vote (54 out of 538), but 20 percent of the electoral votes needed to win the presidency (54 out of 270). California's power in the electoral college (54 votes) is equal to that of the 14 smallest states and the District of Columbia combined. Given California's political clout in the electoral college, it should be of no surprise to learn that Bill Clinton visited that state about 40 times during the 1996 campaign. In contrast, Bill Clinton's first and only trip to Nebraska came in December of 2000 — only a month before he finished his two terms and eight years as president. Thus, the electoral college not only helps to influence the kind of person nominated for president, but also the nature of American presidential campaigns.

The 2000 presidental election

The 19th century political satirist Ambrose Bierce described the American presidency as "the greased pig in the field game of American politics." If such a statement ever applied to a particular presidential contest, it would be the 2000 presidential race — especially with respect to the electoral college vote from Florida.

On election night, Al Gore was initially declared the victor in Florida. A re-assessment by all of the major American news organizations then declared a Bush presidential victory, which was followed by yet another reversal in the early morning hours of the next day. Although Al Gore won a plurality of the national popular vote, on election night the races in a number of states were too close to call with respect to the electoral college. Within hours, however, it became clear that whichever candidate won Florida and all of that state's 25 electoral college votes would win the presidency.

The issues in Florida centred on what was a legal vote, which affected who would win the state's electoral college votes and, thus, the presidency. Many critics blamed the electoral college for the Florida spectacle, but the critics were wrong. Once a vote total was decided, the electoral college worked fine — the problem was how to count the votes!

For 35 days, Democrats and Republicans launched lawsuit after lawsuit to try and control the vote counting process in the state of Florida, with issues going all the way to the Supreme Court twice. The legitimacy of absentee ballots, butterfly ballots, dimpled ballots, and hanging chads all became part of the political lexicon. Finally, on December 12, 2000 the American Supreme Court, in a 5–4 decision, ended further vote counting and recounts and, in effect, made George W. Bush president of the United States.

The battle for Florida's electoral college slate damaged all those involved, especially the American Supreme Court with its claim of "nonpartisanship." However, this debate spurred on political reform efforts not only in Florida, but also nationwide, so that hopefully such an occurrence will never be repeated in a future presidential contest. In addition to specific voting reforms, more general electoral reforms have been proposed for the American system.

ELECTORAL REFORM PROPOSALS

Because of the dominance of the plurality formula in American politics at the state and national levels, it would be an understatement indeed to say that proportional representation is viewed by many as a possible electoral alternative. Although it has been used at the municipal level (Weaver, 1986), proportional representation, even when it is suggested as a possible reform (Lind, 1992) is not taken seriously, except possibly in academia. In fact, proportional representation is so unlikely that it is not even on the periphery of the current American political agenda.

Reform of the electoral college, in contrast, has generated much debate and numerous alternative proposals. For example, a direct presidential vote which totally eliminates the electoral college is one possibility. In this situation, the winner would be the candidate with the most votes — period. Such a proposal was made by Senator-elect Hillary Clinton of New York in November 2000. An alternative would be to divide the electoral college vote within each state on a proportional basis. In other words, if the Republicans got 30 percent of the vote in California and the Democrats got 70 percent, then California's electoral college vote of 54 would be broken down on a similar basis.

The four-year cycle of presidential politics has produced a rhythm to proposals for reforming the electoral college. After a presidential contest concern wanes, since there is no immediate problem. As the presidential contest draws near, reform ideas resurface, particularly if there is a threat from a new party. Of course, by this time it is too late to amend the constitution before the next election, so possible reforms are once again set aside. As with possible reform to the plurality system in general, changes to the American electoral college are most unlikely, even after the debacle of 2000.

COMPARING ELECTORAL SYSTEMS

In comparing electoral systems, several basic criteria are significant: first, the kind of electoral system used; second, the effects of the electoral system on the party system; and third, how electoral reform is achieved. These three areas are interdependent, since the type of electoral system influences the type of party system created, both of which in turn condition the prospects for electoral reform.

Suggestions for electoral reform are evident in most democratic political systems. Yet most electoral reform proposals have died because of their expected political consequences, real or apprehended. Once a particular electoral system is adopted and used, a pattern of interests develops around its workings and effects; these interests then become opposed to further political change. Those political groups that benefit from the current system will obviously be opposed to, and suspicious of, political reform efforts, while those political interests disadvantaged by current practices will be the most vociferous champions of political change. In either case, self-interest, not abstract political principles of democracy or equality, determines a group's attitude toward reform proposals.

In the past decade, significant electoral system reforms have occurred in the following liberal-democratic systems: Italy, Japan, New Zealand, and Israel. Thus, alterations to electoral systems are not impossible, even if they are rare. In New Zealand (September 1992), voters overwhelmingly approved (85 percent) a change from the plurality system to some type of proportional representation. The voters were presented with four proportional representation options; 70 percent favoured what is known as a mixed-member system patterned after the one used in Germany. The mixed-member system was first used in the New Zealand general election of October 1996 and, as sometimes happens with a proportional representation system, a divided result produced a two-month delay in forming a new government (December 1996). In Italy in 1993, also in a referendum, voters rejected the existing proportional representation system by supporting reform — 83 percent favoured changing the electoral system to a version of the plurality system. In both cases, a discredited party system and its leaders were forced into reforming the electoral system because of public pressure; left to their own devices, they would not have done so.

Anytime an electoral system is changed, it is done because certain political consequences are expected to follow. However, all considerations of alternative electoral systems make one crucial assumption, namely, that voter preferences will remain the same under new election mechanisms as they were in previous elections. Such an assumption, of course, is false: as Duverger (1964) noted several decades ago, the first effect of any electoral reform is to modify not only the distribution of seats, but also the distribution of votes. It is probably fair to hypothesize that the greater the difference between the new electoral formula and the present system, the greater may be the change in the actual distribution of the vote.

The political context and consequences of electoral reform raise a number of significant considerations when comparing electoral reform efforts in democratic political systems. First, a change in the electoral system will modify not only the distribution of seats among the parties, but the distribution of votes as well. Second, a change in the electoral formula will have a bearing on the number of political parties that continue to exist or that are likely to develop in the future. In other words, the type of electoral system adopted by a political system has an important bearing on the type of political party system that emerges. Third, electoral systems not only help to determine the minority or majority status of governments, but their resulting stability as well. Finally, the electoral system influences a party's organizational structure and the internal power of the various party factions. Such conclusions support the view that "the electoral system affects the political life of a country mainly through the parties" (Duverger, 1951: 314).

SUMMARY

1. Electoral systems are significant elements of the political process because they help to determine the election winner, influence the number of parties that develop, and affect the internal composition of the political parties.

2. Two basic types of electoral systems can be identified: first, single-member districts with a plurality electoral formula; and second, multi-member districts with a proportional representation formula (highest average, greatest remainder, or STV). The plurality format usually distorts the relationship between a party's popular vote and its strength in the legislature, while proportional representation seeks to equalize a party's vote and seat share.

3. Drawing electoral boundaries is usually based on two competing criteria: geography and population. When constituencies of unequal population size are created it is known as malapportionment. Gerrymandering is the drawing of electoral boundaries for partisan advantage.

4. The Canadian electoral system is an example of the plurality type: it benefits both the larger parties and minor parties that have regional support, but is a disadvantage to minor parties that have diffuse or generalized support. Full proportional representation would greatly help the NDP (and in the past decade the Tories), but, for that very reason, it is a most unlikely occurrence.

Because of the trend toward independent boundary commissions, gerrymandering has been reduced. Malapportionment has also been reduced because of the impact of Section 3 of the Canadian Charter of Rights and Freedoms.

5. Britain's plurality formula has effects similar to those of its Canadian counterpart, greatly aiding the larger parties and sectional parties, but discriminating against those parties which have traditionally received generalized support. Because of the emphasis on geography rather than population as the criterion for electoral boundaries, malapportionment continues to be high. Independent commissions have largely eliminated gerrymandering from the electoral process. While the plurality electoral formula remains in place for elections to the House of Commons, proportional representation alternatives have been adopted for other political institutions.

6. Because of various American Supreme Court decisions, malapportionment has been virtually eliminated in the drawing of electoral boundaries. However, gerrymandering is more prevalent than ever. The plurality system appears to be immune to change in state and national politics.

7. The American electoral college, a special variation of a plurality system, is used to elect the president and vice-president. Although it has typically become a formality in American politics, with the real choice made by the people when they cast their presidential vote, it continues to influence the nomination of presidential candidates and the nature of presidential electoral strategies. The political conflict and controversy about the role of the electoral college in the 2000 presidential contest has, once again, raised the issue of electoral system reform in the American context.

8. Electoral reform often carries with it important political consequences for the existing parties. As a result, electoral reform is often blocked by the current successful parties in an attempt to protect their own political dominance in the polity.

CONCEPT FILE

additional member system (AMS)	gerrymandering
diffuse (generalized) support	greatest remainder formula
district magnitude	highest average formula
effective representation	limited proportional representation
electoral college	list (party-list) system
electoral law	malapportionment
electoral redistribution	manufactured majority
first-past-the-post system	mixed electoral system
full proportional representation	multi-member electoral district

one person, one vote
plurality electoral formula
plus-or-minus (±) factor
proportional representation
redistricting
relative parity of voting power
representation by population

representation of people
representation of places
single-member electoral district
single transferable vote (STV)
unit rule
winner-take-all system

RECOMMENDED READINGS

Electoral Systems

AMY, DOUGLAS J. (2000) *Behind The Ballot Box: A Citizen's Guide to Voting Systems.* Westport, Connecticut: GPG-Greenwood Publishing Group.

BOGDANOR, VERNON (1984) *What Is Proportional Representation? A Guide to the Issues.* London: Basil Blackwell.

BOIX, CHARLES (1999) "Setting the Rules of the Game: The Choice of Electoral Systems in Advanced Democracies," *American Political Science Review*, Volume 93, Number 3, pp. 609–624.

BOSTON, JONATHAN et al. (1997) "Experimenting with Coalition Government: Preparing to Manage under Proportional Representation in New Zealand," *Journal of Commonwealth and Comparative Politics*, Volume 35, Number 3, pp. 108–126.

DUMMETT, MICHAEL (1997) *Principles of Electoral Reform.* Oxford: Oxford University Press.

MONROE, BURT L. (1995) "Fully Proportional Representation," *American Political Science Review*, Volume 89, Number 4, pp. 925–940.

RAE, DOUGLAS W. (1971) *The Political Consequences of Electoral Laws.* Rev. ed. New Haven: Yale University Press.

REEVE, ANDREW and ALAN WARE (1992) *Electoral Systems: A Comparative and Theoretical Introduction.* London: Routledge.

REILLY, BEN (1997) "Preferential Voting and Political Engineering: A Comparative Study," *Journal of Commonwealth and Comparative Politics*, Volume 35, Number 1, pp. 1–19.

RULE, WILMA (1987) "Electoral Systems, Contextual Factors and Women's Opportunity for Election to Parliament in Twenty-Three Democracies," *The Western Political Quarterly*, Volume 40, Number 3, pp. 477–498.

Canadian Electoral System

ARCHER, KEITH (1993) "Conflict and Confusion in Drawing Constituency Boundaries: The Case of Alberta," *Canadian Public Policy*, Volume 19, Number 2, pp. 177–193.

BAKVIS, HERMAN and LAURA G. MACPHERSON (1995) "Quebec Block Voting and the Canadian Electoral System," *Canadian Journal of Political Science*, Volume 28, Number 4, pp. 659–692.

CAIRNS, ALAN C. (1968) "The Electoral System and the Party System in Canada, 1921–1965," *Canadian Journal of Political Science*, Volume 1, Number 1, pp. 55–80.

CARTY, R.K. (1985) "The Electoral Boundary Revolution in Canada," *The American Review of Canadian Studies,* Volume 15, Number 3, pp. 273–287.

GAINES, BRIAN J. (1999) "Duverger's Law and the Meaning of Canadian Exceptionalism," *Comparative Political Studies,* Volume 32, Number 7, pp. 835–861.

HYSON, STEWART (1999) "Electoral Boundary Redistribution by Independent Commission in New Brunswick, 1990–94," *Canadian Public Administration,* Volume 42, Number 3, pp. 174–197.

LANDES, RONALD G. (1992) *Effective Political Representation in Nova Scotia: The 1992 Report of the Provincial Electoral Boundaries Commission.* Halifax, Nova Scotia: Queen's Printer.

LOENEN, NICK (1997) *Citizenship and Democracy: A Case for Proportional Representation.* Toronto: Dundurn Press.

MILNER, HENRY, ed. (1999) *Making Every Vote Count: Reassessing Canada's Electoral System.* Peterborough, Ontario: Broadview Press.

RUFF, NORMAN J. (1990) "The Cat and Mouse Politics of Redistribution: Fair and Effective Representation in British Columbia," *BC Studies,* Number 87, pp. 48–84.

SMITH, JENNIFER and RONALD G. LANDES (1998) "Entitlement versus Variance Models in the Determination of Canadian Electoral Boundaries," *International Journal of Canadian Studies,* Volume 17, pp. 19–36.

YOUNG, LISA (1997) "Gender Equal Legislatures: Evaluating the Proposed Nunavut Electoral System," *Canadian Public Policy,* Volume 23, Number 3, pp. 306–315.

British Electoral System

BUTLER, DAVID (1992) "The Redrawing of Parliamentary Boundaries in Britain," pp. 5–12 in Pippa Norris et al., eds., *British Elections and Parties Yearbook 1992.* New York: Harvester Wheatsheaf.

CURTICE, JOHN (1992) "The Hidden Surprise: The British Electoral System in 1992," *Parliamentary Affairs,* Volume 45, Number 4, pp. 466–474.

DUNLEAVY, PATRICK et al. (1992) "How Britain Would Have Voted under Alternative Electoral Systems," *Parliamentary Affairs,* Volume 45, Number 4, pp. 640–655.

DUNLEAVY, PATRICK and HELEN MARGETTS (1997) "The Electoral System," *Parliamentary Affairs,* Volume 50, Number 4, pp. 733–749.

FINER, S.E. (1975) *Adversary Politics and Electoral Reform.* London: Wigram.

PUNNETT, R.M. (1991) "The Alternative Vote Re-visited," *Electoral Studies,* Volume 10, Number 4, pp. 281–298.

RALLINGS, COLIN and MICHAEL THRASHER (1994) "The Parliamentary Boundary Commissions: Rules, Interpretations and Politics," *Parliamentary Affairs,* Volume 47, Number 3, pp. 387–404.

ROSSITER, D.J. et al. (1997) "Redistricting and Electoral Bias in Great Britain," *British Journal of Political Science,* Volume 27, Number 3, pp. 466–472.

SQUIRES, JUDITH (1996) "Quotas for Women: Fair Representation?" *Parliamentary Affairs,* Volume 49, Number 1, pp. 71–88.

American Electoral System

AMY, DOUGLAS J. (1993) *Real Choices/New Voices: The Case for Proportional Representation Elections in the United States.* New York: Columbia University Press.

BEST, JUDITH A. (1996) *The Choice of the People? Debating the Electoral College.* New York: Rowman and Littlefield.

EPSTEIN, DAVID and SHARYN O'HALLORAN (1999) "A Social Science Approach to Race, Redistricting, and Representation," *American Political Science Review,* Volume 93, Number 2, pp. 187–191.

GROFMAN, BERNARD et al. (1992) *Minority Representation and the Quest for Voting Equality.* Cambridge: Cambridge University Press.

GRONKE, PAUL and J. MATTHEW WILSON (1999) "Competing Redistricting Plans as Evidence of Political Motives: The North Carolina Case," *American Politics Quarterly,* Volume 27, Number 2, pp. 147–176.

LIND, MICHAEL (1992) "A Radical Plan to Change American Politics," *The Atlantic Monthly,* Volume 270, Number 2, pp. 73–83.

POLSBY, NELSON W. and AARON WILDAVSKY (1996) *Presidential Elections: Strategies and Structures of American Politics.* 9th ed. Chatham, New Jersey: Chatham House.

RULE, WILMA and JOSEPH F. ZIMMERMAN, eds. (1992) *United States Electoral Systems: Their Impact on Women and Minorities.* New York: Praeger.

SAFFORD, JOHN L. (1995) "John C. Calhoun, Lani Guinier, and Minority Rights," *PS: Political Science and Politics,* Volume 28, Number 2, pp. 211–216.

WITCOVER, JULES (1999) *No Way to Pick a President: How Money and Hired Guns Have Debased American Elections.* New York: Farrar, Straus and Giroux.

POLITICS ON THE NET

GENERAL: For basic information on **different types of electoral systems,** see the following two websites: *www.psr.keele.ac.uk/election.htm* provides information on most types of election systems, as does *www.umich.edu* (on this site, do a search by "electoral systems"). General information on various proportional representation systems can be located at the **Proportional Representation Library** at *www.mtholyoke.edu/acad/polit/damy/prlib.htm* and at **World Policy Institute America's Project** on "Democracy: Electoral Systems" at *worldpolicy.org/americas/democracy/ democracy.html.* These sites all have good links to other relevant sites.

CANADA: The basic website for election information is **Elections Canada** at *www. elections.ca.* For proposed Canadian alternatives to the plurality system, see the following sites which advocate some form of proportional representation: (1) **Fair Vote Canada (FVC)** at *www.fairvotecanada.org,* (2) **Green Party's Campaign for PR in Ontario** at *www.votepr.org,* and (3) **Fair Vote B.C.** at *www.fairvotingbc.com.*

BRITAIN: Although aimed at a British audience, the website for the **Electoral Reform Society (ERS)** at *www.electoral-reform.org.uk* contains an excellent introduction to different types of voting systems and excellent links to other sites. As part of its overall package of constitutional reforms, **Charter 88** proposes proportional representation in Britain: *www.charter88.org.uk.*

UNITED STATES: Basic election information can be found at the **Federal Election Commission** at *www.fec.gov.* For information on the **Electoral College** see *www.nara.gov/fedreg/elctcoll/index.html#top.* For **Electoral College reform** see the site of "Citizens for True Democracy" at *www.truedemocracy.org.*

Political Parties

Our thesis is that parties are an essential part of democracy and, conversely, that the arguments for their irrelevancy are not simply neutral scientific statements but a combination of political advocacy and observation — an ideology. (Lipow and Seyd, 1996: 283)

So great are the political advantages of a party that in a representative democracy a politician without a party is a politician without power. (Dahl, 1970: 74)

Parties were created out of a blend of public and private interest. They are agencies for the acquisition of power, not selfless political versions of the Red Cross, to whom citizens may go crying in time of need. (Lawson, 1980: 23)

CHAPTER PREVIEW

- Political parties emerged in democratic political systems as a means for including the average citizen in the political process.
- Political parties serve a crucial role in providing leaders and leadership for the overall polity.
- Democratic political parties in Canada, Britain, and the United States perform three basic functions: an electoral function, a governing function, and an opposition function.
- Democratic polities have parties that are usually pragmatic in outlook and based on large coalitions of diverse elements. In addition, democratic polities have competitive party systems.
- Different mechanisms have developed to select party leaders in various polities. In Britain, parties traditionally selected leaders through the party caucus, while in the United States direct primaries are used. In Canada, national party leadership conventions are being replaced with universal membership votes.
- Party finance and fundraising remain key areas of political scandals and corruption in liberal-democratic systems.
- New forms of pubic participation are changing the ways political parties perform their functions.

Although it would be difficult to imagine how the Canadian political system could operate without political parties, it is also true that most political systems have only recently discovered their usefulness in organizing and operating the political process. On the whole, national political parties are predominantly products of the past century, with the first major theoretical analyses of parties written in the early decades of the 20th century. The recognition of their important role in modern politics was undefined in the works of the classical democratic theorists, so much so that parties have been referred to as "the orphans of political philosophy" (Schattschneider, 1942: 10). Born of circumstance rather than by design, political parties represent an organizational means for governing the political system.

THE NATURE OF POLITICAL PARTIES

Most definitions of **political parties** exhibit a common theme, namely, that parties are *organizations that seek to physically control the government by nominating candidates for office and winning power through the election process.* A typical view is that of Sartori (1976: 64), who defines a party as "any group that presents at elections, and is capable of placing through elections, candidates for public office." Thus, parties aim to acquire power and to retain such power once it has been won, organizing both the electorate and the government in the process.

THE ORIGIN OF PARTIES

The historical development crucial in the origin of political parties was the acceptance of the idea that the mass of people had to be taken into account in the organization of the polity. Throughout the 18th century and well into the 19th, a very small segment of the population was eligible for political participation. For example, in addition to such items as property qualifications, until the early decades of the 20th century over 50 percent of the population was prevented from participation by the disenfranchisement of women, a restriction which was not lifted until the 1940s in Quebec, France, and Italy. It is not merely coincidental that the expansion of the **suffrage** (i.e., *the right to vote and to participate in politics*) paralleled the development of political parties in countries such as Britain, the United States, and Canada. As the number of potential participants in the political process expanded, a mechanism was needed to organize the mass of people now legally qualified to vote. Such a structure was the political party.

While one can find historical antecedents that trace back many centuries, the origin of the modern political party dates from approximately the mid-19th century. The experience of Jacksonian democracy in the 1830s in the United States, the series of Reform Acts in the 19th century in Britain, and the achievement of representative and responsible government by the beginning of

Confederation in Canada all laid the basis and dictated the necessity for party organizations.

The historical development of a political party is a reflection, therefore, of the acceptance within a country's political culture of the legitimacy of mass participation: "the emergence of a political party clearly implies that the masses must be taken into account by the political elite" (LaPalombara and Weiner, 1966: 4). However, it is important to realize that being taken account of can mean either mass participation and control over the elite, as in democratic systems, or elite control over the masses, as in totalitarian systems. In either case, the political party serves in an intermediate position between the individual and the government. In carrying out such a role, political parties connect individual preferences with public policy, linking the governors with the governed in the process.

PARTY FUNCTIONS

Although the tasks, jobs, or functions that political parties carry out vary from one political system to the next (King, 1969), two basic functions of parties can be identified: organizing the electorate and organizing the government.

The **electoral function of parties** can be seen in *the way in which they recruit candidates to run for political office, dominate the election process, and serve as focal points for individual and group attachments.* In a Canadian federal election, literally hundreds of people must be found to compete in the election process (1 672 candidates in 1997; 1 807 in 2000). Most of these individuals are recruited to run for office through the political parties — there are few independent candidates in Canadian politics. While parties are crucial mechanisms in the recruitment of individuals for electoral competition, it should not be forgotten that parties are also key recruitment agencies for numerous nonelective positions. Electoral success provides the party with the opportunity to place party members within the bureaucracy and the various agencies, boards, and commissions of government. The surest route to a political sinecure is to be a defeated candidate of the winning political party.

Parties also serve an electoral function by organizing campaigns and simplifying the choices presented to the individual citizen. With a potential electorate of about 19 to 20 million people in recent Canadian federal elections, some way is needed to sort out, from among all the theoretically possible courses of action, a limited set of alternatives for public judgment. Moreover, the party campaigns help to stimulate public interest in the issues of the day, aid in the registration or enumeration of voters, and promote more widespread participation in the political process. Citizens may also *identify with a particular party by developing an emotional tie with it,* what is known as a **partisan identification**. While not the only factor, such partisan attachments help to influence how the citizen will vote in a specific election campaign.

The second major task of parties can be called the **governing function of parties**. As an electoral organization that seeks to gain control of the government, *the winning party serves as an integrating mechanism for getting the various branches* *and agencies to work together across institutional boundaries.* For example, in Canada a party with a majority mandate gains sole control of both the legislative and executive branches of government and thereby acquires the effective political power to implement its party's platform and policies.

As electoral organizations, parties are self-interested structures that seek power: "parties formulate policies in order to win elections, rather than win elections in order to formulate policies" (Downs, 1957: 28). Good examples of this assertion include the Liberals' stand against wage-and-price controls in the 1974 campaign, a program they later implemented in the fall of 1975, or their promise in the 1993 election, later forgotten, to repeal the GST. Similarly, in the 1988 federal election the Conservatives' support for free trade and the Liberals' opposition to it — contrary to each party's historical view — illustrate the Downsian proposition as well. In other words, parties propose policies in order to win votes, thereby linking their electoral and governing functions.

Parties serve a governing function not only by integrating the various institutions of government and providing policy direction but also by determining the leadership options presented to the voter. The Canadian citizen indirectly chooses the prime minister from among those individuals who lead a recognized political party by voting for that leader's party representative in their constituency. Parties put forth the pool of available talent from which the electorate picks its leaders: in the 2000 election, voters were presented with the following major party alternatives from which to choose: Joe Clark (Conservative), Jean Chrétien (Liberal), Alexa McDonough (NDP), Gilles Duceppe (Bloc Québécois), and Stockwell Day (Canadian Alliance). Thus, the process of national party leadership selection is significant because it sets the outer boundaries of electoral choice. By organizing the electorate and the government, parties provide a linkage mechanism between the citizen and the political structure.

PARTY TYPES

While innumerable classifications of party types have been developed, the most useful are those which relate party type to both the party's origin and the manner in which the electoral and governing functions are carried out. Three basic classifications will be considered: first, with respect to a party's origin, the difference between internally and externally created parties; second, in relation to party structure, the variation between cadre and mass parties; and third, in light of ideological concerns, the difference between programmatic and pragmatic parties.

Circumstances of party origin influence both a party's structure and ideology. The *parties that emerged from within the legislative branch* of government are referred to as **internally created** or **parliamentary parties**. Developing out of the various factions contending for control of the legislature, internally created parties were the first to appear historically. These parties have primarily been electorally oriented organizations intent on winning power rather than on implementing programs of reform. Loosely structured, except during elections, such parties have accepted the legitimacy of existing political arrangements, have rarely been ideologically inclined, and have dominated the party politics in most democratic political systems. Examples of internally created or parliamentary parties include the Liberal and Conservative parties in Canada, the Republican and Democratic parties in the United States, and the Conservatives and Liberal Democrats in Britain.

In contrast, **externally created** or **extra-parliamentary parties** are of more recent historical vintage, with *origins outside of the legislature*. These parties have usually challenged key aspects of the existing social, economic, and political structure, have been more intent on implementing programs than on winning power, and have usually been better organized and ideologically articulate than their internally created counterparts. However, they have generally been electorally frustrated (Duverger, 1964: xxiv–xxxvii; LaPalombara and Weiner, 1966: 7–14). Examples of externally created parties in the United States include the Communist, Socialist, and Reform parties, as well as Ralph Nader's Green Party in the 1996 and 2000 presidential elections; in Britain, the Labour party and nationalist parties (Scottish Nationalist Party and Plaid Cymru); and in Canada, the Parti Québécois, Social Credit, Reform, National, and New Democratic parties. Although the Bloc Québécois was started by parliamentary members resigning from the internally created Conservative and Liberal parties, in most ways this party represents an example of the externally created pattern.

A second classification of party types focusses on variations in party structure and membership. A basic structural distinction is that between cadre and mass parties. In a cadre party, the organization exists primarily for electoral purposes, with little formal activity undertaken between elections. A **cadre party** is a *"grouping of notables" whose primary goal is attaining office*. Membership is loosely defined, with no formal admission procedures or registration forms. The party's ideology is general rather than specific, if it is defined at all. Party finance is dependent on large individual and corporate donations. The major North American parties and most moderate European parties exemplify this type of party structure.

In contrast, the **mass party** is characterized by *permanent organization and effort even between election campaigns, by formal membership requirements, and by an emphasis on ideology and platform rather than simply electoral success*. Mass parties have based their party finances on individual membership dues, trade union support and, in recent years, the public financing of election campaigns. The closest examples to mass parties in Canada are the Parti Québécois, the Bloc Québécois, and the New Democrats, while in Britain the Labour party is a prime example.

Our final look at party types centres on the nature of a party's ideology. The *parties that have long-term goals and platforms* can be called **programmatic parties**, while *parties with little ideology and short-term goals (usually meaning winning the next election)* can be classified as **pragmatic parties** (Epstein, 1967: 261–272). A programmatic party would rather educate the public on the need for reform than win power, if electoral success meant giving up the party's reform ideals. In a pragmatic party, policy is a matter of electoral convenience, a tool for gaining power. In Canada, the Liberals and Conservatives are prime examples of the pragmatic type, while other party competitors have been programmatic in outlook (NDP, Reform, Bloc Québécois). In Western democratic systems, pragmatic parties have generally prevailed over programmatic ones.

As with any classification scheme, not all parties fit easily into discrete cate-gories. A good example of a hybrid party is the Canadian Alliance, which was cre-ated in 2000 to replace the Reform Party. While the Reform Party was externally created, its replacement was born out of the official opposition inside the Canadian Parliament. While the Canadian Alliance remains primarily a mass party, it is slightly less mass-based than its predecessor. On the question of party ideology, the Canadian Alliance was created to be more moderate and pragmatic than Reform, aiming to gain seats in electorally rich Ontario — in other words, to win power. Thus, the Canadian Alliance is a hybrid party which is beginning to look more like some of Canada's old-line political parties in its quest for power.

Although presented separately, these three classifications of party types based on origin, structure, and ideology are interdependent. Parliamentary parties are usu-ally cadre structures with pragmatic policies, while extra-parliamentary parties are typically mass structures with specifically delineated programs. These three typologies have for the most part dealt with the nature of individual parties. However, a party's origin, structure, and ideology also influence how it interacts with other parties, thus leading us to a discussion of the nature of party systems.

PARTY SYSTEMS

A **party system** refers to *the competitive relationship between two or more political parties* (Rae, 1971: 47). If only one party exists, then a party system is logically impossible. However, simply because a party exists does not mean that it is a rel-evant member of the party system. To say that a party is relevant implies that its presence more than marginally affects the behaviour of other parties; that is, it has an impact on the network of competitive relationships (Sartori, 1976: 121–125). For example, in January of 1997 Paul Hellyer, former Liberal cabinet minister and leadership candidate for both the Liberal and Conservative parties, announced the formation of a new political party, the Canadian Action Party. However, since its presence did not visibly affect the campaign strategies of the other parties in the 1997 and 2000 election campaigns, the Canadian Action Party is irrelevant in dis-cussions of the current Canadian party system.

On such criteria, the Canadian federal party system contained four relevant parties in the 1960s and 1970s — the Liberal, Conservative, New Democratic, and Social Credit parties. With the elimination of the Social Credit party after the 1980 federal election, the Canadian federal party system for the 1984 and 1988 elections was reduced to three relevant groups. With the rise of new political par-ties in the early 1990s (Reform, Bloc Québécois), the number of relevant com-petitors expanded to five for the 1993 and 1997 elections: Progressive Conservative, Liberal, NDP, Reform, and Bloc Québécois. The transformation of the Reform Party into the Canadian Alliance before the 2000 election left the number of rel-evant party competitors at five.

The United States usually has only two parties (Republicans and Democrats) that affect the competitive relationship, although once in a while a minor party must be included (e.g., John Anderson's effort in 1980; George Wallace's group in 1968;

and Ross Perot in 1992 and 1996). In the closely competitive 2000 presidential race, Ralph Nader's Green Party, even though it only won 3 percent of the national vote, clearly cost the Democratic party and Al Gore a victory by winning enough votes in states such as Florida to make George W. Bush the new president.

The growth of small parties in the 1970s greatly increased the number of significant parties in Britain; the relevant groups included the Conservative, Liberal, Labour, Scottish Nationalist, Plaid Cymru, and National Front parties, as well as the newly formed Social Democratic party in the mid-1980s. The demise of the Social Democratic party in the late 1980s and its transformation into the Alliance (Liberal-SDP) in 1987 and then into the Liberal Democrats for the 1993, 1997, and 2001 elections has left the British party system with two large parties (Labour; Conservative), one medium-sized party (Liberal Democrats), and several small nationalist parties — all of which has had an impact on the pattern of party competition.

If a party system concerns the interaction between two or more parties, then different types of party systems are possible. Two basic patterns are evident: competitive and noncompetitive party systems (LaPalombara and Weiner, 1966: 33–41; Sartori, 1976: 131–243). A **competitive party system** exists when the government of the day can be replaced through an election by an opposition party; in other words, *the government must compete with, and be challenged by, another party that is capable of forming a new government.* The struggle for power between two or more parties that have a chance of winning an election is the primary condition for calling a party system a competitive one. By such a criterion, the Canadian, British, and American party systems are competitive.

A **noncompetitive party system** exists *when one party dominates governmental office, is not effectively challenged for power through the electoral process, and, as a result, always forms the government of the day.* Opposition parties exist, but they pose no real threat to the governing party. What often happens is that the dominant governing party openly and aggressively discriminates against its political opposition. A classic example of a noncompetitive party system occurred in Mexico. The PRI (Partido Revolucionario Institucional) totally dominated the party battle for 71 years between the founding of the Mexican Republic in 1929 and the election of 2000, when it lost power for the first time to the National Action Party (PAN) led by Vicente Fox. As a result, Mexico has moved into the competitive party category. Many of the party systems in the developing countries are examples of the noncompetitive pattern.

Our typology of competitive and noncompetitive party systems does not, however, cover all of the possible configurations of party politics, because in some political systems only one political party is allowed to exist. However, we can classify these one-party polities as party-state systems, rather than simply party systems (Sartori, 1976: 42–47). In a **party-state system**, *a single party exists, no organized political opposition challenges it for power, and control of the party gives the party leaders control of the state* (Von Beyme, 1985). Party-state systems are usually associated with totalitarian political systems, such as those of Nazi Germany, the former Soviet Union (at least through the late 1980s), and China.

The essential assumption of a party-state system is the necessary congruence of interests between the sole political party and the governmental apparatus. As described by Yugoslav dissident Milovan Djilas (1957: 70), the party-state system "originates from the fact that one party alone . . . is the backbone of the entire political, economic, and ideological activity." Party-state systems are usually based on a comprehensive ideology or revolutionary doctrine, with the single party perceived as the mechanism for transforming society. In Marxism-Leninism, the single party is perceived as necessary so that the working class can overthrow the existing political arrangements. The single party is seen as the organizational weapon of the working class.

The competitive, noncompetitive, and party-state systems reflect the origins, structures, and ideologies of the individual parties. For example, the Communist Party of the Soviet Union, which originated under Czarist autocracy as a means of overthrowing the existing political system, adopted a cohesive structure and an all-encompassing ideology and thus rejected the need for, or the possibility of, establishing a competitive party framework. The result was a party-state system rather than a party system. Noncompetitive party systems that originated in the struggle to throw off colonial rule and to set up new nations have not always accepted the legitimacy of political opposition, arguing instead that nation-building is a higher priority than party competition. In democratic systems, the initial origin of parties within the legislature, the gradual extension of the suffrage, the pragmatic concerns of the major parties, and the acceptance of the legitimacy of political dissent and political opposition have created the conditions for competitive party politics.

THE CANADIAN PARTY SYSTEM

As with any particular aspect of a political system, the political analyst must be concerned not only with general patterns, as exemplified by the above classifications of party types and party functions, but also with how these patterns have developed within specific historical contexts. The interplay between general patterns and the specific Canadian milieu can be seen with respect to both the characteristics of the individual parties and the attributes of the party system.

CHARACTERISTICS OF CANADIAN PARTIES

While the emergence of political party organizations can be traced to pre-Confederation Canada, the birth process was an arduous one, consuming nearly half a century in an extended gestation period. As a consequence, modern political parties were not developed until the end of the 19th century (Thorburn, 1979: 2). In the initial decades of Confederation, the nascent parties were very loose coalitions of various factions within the legislature and thus poorly organized and lacking party discipline. For example, John A. Macdonald's "party" was composed of those interests favouring Confederation and his National Policy, while the opposition factions were, in the beginning, opposed to Confederation and its implications. Several characteristics of the election process helped to produce such a pattern.

Following Confederation, the federal electorate voted in a system of **nonsimultaneous elections** in which *the federal vote was taken on different days in different constituencies.* The government would call the election first in those constituencies that supported it and then work outward to the remaining areas, attempting to build up a bandwagon effect as it went. Such nonsimultaneous elections might occur over an extended period, as in the 1867 election, which stretched over six weeks. Combined with the lack of a secret ballot, which meant that the government knew how one voted, nonsimultaneous elections produced legislative factions of **ministerialists**, *members whose primary political aim was to be on the winning side in order to reap the rewards of office.*

As elected members of Parliament who were uncommitted to any particular coalition, these ministerialists would support the government of the day on the basis of what they or their constituency might receive from that government. Such ministerialists constituted a significant element in "all of the early parliaments: Macdonald called them 'loose fish,' George Brown, 'the shaky fellows,' and Cartwright, 'waiters on Providence'" (Reid, 1979: 13). While the elimination of nonsimultaneous elections and the introduction of the secret ballot for most electoral areas in 1878 gradually helped to solidify party organization and cohesion by the 1896 election, the effect of such initial election practices was to keep the emerging parties poorly organized, while at the same time emphasizing the rewards of a pragmatic style of party politics.

The historical success of the Liberal and Conservative parties is directly linked to their parliamentary origins and the attributes thus acquired. Born in the struggle for power in the legislature and for control of the new political structure after 1867, the Liberal and Conservative parties have been electorally focussed organizations whose primary goal has been winning power and the spoils of office. With such an aim, the traditional major parties have been "practical, flexible, and manipulative" (Winn and McMenemy, 1976: 11). As Pierre Trudeau said of the Liberal party in the 1960s, in a statement often true of the Conservatives as well, the party will say anything and do anything to win power.

This pragmatic style of the two traditionally dominant parties is clearly illustrated with respect to party platforms, principles, and policy positions. Rarely does either the Liberal or Conservative party take a stand that clearly differentiates it from the other. Specificity of purpose limits a party's electoral appeal. As a result, party platforms are general in nature or, at least, open to multiple interpretations, especially after the campaign is over. Revealing in this regard was the decision of the Liberal party to keep its total platform secret during the 1980 contest, a decision subsequently maintained even after victory had been achieved. One can assume, perhaps, that this approach to policy had the interest of the voters at heart — there is no point in confusing people with facts, especially in the midst of an electoral contest. Thus, the 1988 federal election stands out as a significant exception to the general pattern of Canadian party politics: not only did one issue dominate (free trade), but the parties took clearly defined positions on it.

The 1993 election both confirmed and also provided an important exception to this general pattern. For example, Prime Minister Kim Campbell's blunt assertion at the start of the Tory election campaign that the unemployment rate would remain high for several years, while possibly true, was a strategic electoral mistake, as a policy statement. In contrast, the Liberal party released its platform (the *Red Book*) early in the campaign and received widespread approval and support for this "nontraditional" approach to revealing its policies; this move was, at least, a contributing factor in the party's subsequent electoral victory.

In the 1997 election, campaign policy played a reduced role. In fact, the Liberal party's new *Red Book* was leaked by the Reform Party near the start of the campaign. Furthermore, while the economy seemed to be a priority at the beginning of the campaign, national unity emerged as the prominent issue as a result of the leaders' debate, displacing other issues. In the 2000 election, the Liberals again issued a *Red Book* outlining their policies, but again it seemed to be a minor factor in the overall election campaign.

The pragmatic nature of the Liberal and Conservative parties is clearly evident in relation to the question of party membership. At the mass level, a person is usually considered to be a party member simply by claiming such an affiliation. Offer your services at election time and you will, in all likelihood, be welcomed with open arms; background checks on previous partisan ties are not a precondition of current partisan loyalty. At the elite level, there are numerous examples of the flexible nature of party membership. An outstanding historical one would be that of Joseph Howe. Although initially opposed to Confederation, and elected to the House of Commons on that basis in 1867, Howe joined Macdonald's cabinet only two years later, after renegotiation of Nova Scotia's annual subsidy from the federal government (Winn and McMenemy, 1976: 11).

With respect to party organization, the Liberal and Conservative parties are traditionally weak. Since they are electoral organizations, the party structure is only fleshed out prior to and during an electoral engagement — between elections, the party organization remains a paper tiger. Most elements of the party structure, such as the constituency organizations or the provincial parties, hold an annual meeting of little consequence. Even when an election is expected or called, some party units are unprepared for the electoral battle.

A corresponding aspect of party organization concerns the component units of the federal Liberal and Conservative parties. While the federal Liberal and Conservative parties appear to be hierarchically organized, in fact, much of their real power traditionally lies in their provincial units; in other words, the party organizations are decentralized. As with constitutions in general, party constitutions are rarely accurate descriptions of the internal power relationships within either of the old-time parties.

The characteristics of Canada's traditional major parties, the Liberals and Conservatives, therefore include the following: their parliamentary origin; their pragmatic style of party politics with respect to platform, ideology, and membership; and their weak and essentially decentralized party structures. Electorally based organizations, the Liberal and Conservative parties are coalitions of individuals, groups, and regions intent on winning for themselves the spoils of office.

In addition to the two traditionally dominant parties of parliamentary origin, since the 1920s Canada has seen the rise and development of a series of minor parties. These newer parties typically illustrate opposite attributes from those identified for the Liberals and Conservatives, for the simple reason that their origins, structures, and functions are different. Parties such as the Progressives, the Cooperative Commonwealth Federation — which later became the New Democratic Party — and Social Credit are extra-parliamentary in origin and ideologically based. A more recent entrant into this category — the Western-based Reform Party — was founded in late 1987 and won its first seat in the House of Commons in March of 1989. The Bloc Québécois — a nationalist, Quebec-based separatist party that seeks the destruction of the current Canadian polity — was founded in the aftermath of the Meech Lake Accord negotiations and failure in the late 1980s. In 2000, the Reform Party changed both its name and party leader, becoming the Canadian Alliance led by Stockwell Day.

The success of the Reform (52 seats) and Bloc Québécois (54 seats) parties in the 1993 federal election meant that for the first time a party other than either the Liberals or Conservatives formed the official opposition in the House of Commons (i.e., the Bloc Québécois). More significant, perhaps, in the long run was the destruction of Brian Mulroney's Tory coalition built on Western protest and Quebec nationalism. These factors, combined with the significant losses of the NDP, meant the Canadian party system of the late 1990s operated very differently than in previous decades. Thus, even though the Bloc Québécois was the official opposition in Parliament after 1993, it could not possibly form a government if called upon to do so. With the Reform Party's limited regional base and the reduction of the NDP and Tory parties in 1993, no party, other than the governing Liberals, could be expected to form a government in the immediate future.

The 1997 election confirmed this prediction. With the Liberals forming a small majority government (155 seats or 52 percent of the seats in the House of Commons), four other parties gained enough seats to receive official party status. Thus, the House had a large government caucus facing a fractionalized political opposition, none of which could really expect to form a government in the near future. In the 2000 election this pattern repeated itself, with the Liberals gaining even more seats (172) and becoming a more dominant actor in the party system. Even the transformation of the Reform Party into the Canadian Alliance (with a new leader) did not alter this pattern.

These externally created parties have often been outgrowths of social movements that have sought extensive changes in the economic and political structures of Canada. Since they have a need to justify such proposed changes, these extra-parliamentary parties have usually propounded an ideology that both attacks the existing order and suggests the outlines of a new pattern of power relationships. Membership in such an organization entails acceptance of the party's ideology and platform, and the organization continues between election campaigns. These characteristics are exemplified by the New Democratic Party of Canada.

Although the NDP was officially formed in 1961, its predecessor, the Cooperative Commonwealth Federation (CCF), began in 1933, itself the outgrowth of some remnants of the Progressives of the 1920s. The CCF, as an externally created party, clearly attacked the existing economic and political structures of capitalism. The ideological commitment of the CCF was enunciated in the Regina Manifesto, the party's most famous declaration of principles. Membership obligated one to support the movement's principles and to help in party finance through annual membership fees.

The CCF was both a social movement and a party, with inevitable strains between these varying conceptions of its role in the political system (Young, 1969: 286–302). The evolution of the CCF from 1933 onward demonstrated this basic conflict between the demands of a political movement and those of a political party. Gradually the CCF became more electorally focussed, with an increasing concern for electoral results, symbolized by the role of David Lewis as national party secretary from 1936 to 1950.

The radical thrust of the Regina Manifesto became blunted and was eventually replaced in 1956 by a more moderate statement of party aims known as the Winnipeg Declaration. However, the attempt to refurbish the party's image failed, and combined with the Diefenbaker sweep of 1958, encouraged the CCF moderates to seek the establishment of a new party aimed at implementing social democracy in Canada. The result was the creation of the New Democratic Party in 1961, a party more power-oriented than the CCF, which sought to establish a union of farmer and labour groups within the party, and was predicated on a strategy of appealing more to urban than to rural voters. Thus, the formation of the New Democratic Party is itself a reflection of the pervasive nature of the pragmatic style of Canadian politics.

Many of the initial patterns of party structure, organization, and membership used by the CCF were continued by the NDP after 1961. As well, the inherent tension between reform and electoral victory persisted: "the NDP is both an electoral organization and a political movement, pledged to the eventual transformation of society" (Morton, 1974: 3). Within the NDP, the moderate wing, which focusses more on power than on principle, has carried the organization behind it in terms of leadership selection, party policy, campaign tactics, and parliamentary behaviour. However, the internal division in the NDP between pragmatists and idealists emerged into the public focus once again after the party's poor showing in the 2000 election, as the party debated its relationship with the labour movement and its policy directions for the years ahead. The pragmatic nature of the current NDP is perhaps best exemplified by its support of Pierre Trudeau's Liberal minority government between 1972 and 1974. Although more moderate than the CCF, the NDP still stands apart from the Liberal and Conservative parties with respect to its emphasis on platforms and ideology, internal party democracy, mass party membership, and reform of the social, economic, and political institutions of Canada.

Canadian parties, therefore, are not created from a uniform mold. The two major and, until 1993, long-dominant parties are parliamentary in origin, pragmatic in style, non-ideological in philosophy, and are electorally

> Here is the dilemma of the NDP in Canada: to remain true to its principles at the probable expense of permanently eschewing political power, or to move further to the centre where it risks losing its soul and becoming indistinguishable from other "liberal" opposition parties (Gerald Caplan, former NDP federal secretary, *The Globe and Mail*, September 3, 1983, p. 7).

centred coalitions whose primary goal is winning power. The series of minor parties since the 1920s have been, by contrast, extra-parliamentary in origin, programmatic in style, ideological in appeal, and are both political movements and partisan organizations. This combination of cadre and mass parties has helped to produce a unique party system in the Canadian context.

CHARACTERISTICS OF THE PARTY SYSTEM

The most important attribute of the Canadian party system is the fact that it is a **competitive** one, although it is not an equally balanced pattern of interaction. Historically, one party has tended to dominate national politics, with the Conservatives monopolizing that role from Confederation until 1896 and the Liberals bearing the mantle of power for most years between 1921 and 1984 (approximately 80 percent of the time). This pattern led one author (Thorburn, 1979: 45) to suggest that during this period the national party system contained the normal government party (the Liberals), the normal opposition party (the Conservatives), and the normal minor party (the Progressives, then the CCF, then the New Democratic Party). Such a system rarely produced party turnover in government; instead, the important alternation was "not between different parties in office but between majority and minority Liberal governments" (Meisel, 1979: 128). The destruction of the Tory party in the 1993 election, despite its two majority governments in 1984 and 1988, allowed the Liberal party to re-emerge as the normal governing party in Canadian politics — even as it was challenged in the 1990s by two new regional protest parties (the Reform Party and the Bloc Québécois).

Source: MOU (Theodore Moudakis), *The Daily News* (April 19, 1996). By permission.

The Liberal party victories in 1997 and 2000 mean that the Liberal party will end up being the government for an estimated 11 continuous years (to the next election in about 2004). Moreover, in terms of seats, at least, the Liberal party has become increasingly dominant, even as it faces four determined party competitors — Snow White versus the four dwarfs. While the Liberals face competition, they have not really feared party turnover in government, therefore making the party system less competitive than in the previous decades. With the political right in Canada divided between the Canadian Alliance and the remnants of the Tory party, with the NDP increasingly marginalized on the political left, and with the Bloc Québécois limited in its appeal to Quebec, the Liberals may remain as the normal governing party for many years.

The second characteristic of the party system is that it is federal in structure, paralleling the **federal** organization of government. While our main focus is on the national party system, the federalization of party politics has an important bearing on which party wins power in Ottawa. Federalism has created 11 main arenas for the party battle. Moreover, the parties have been differentially successful in these various political contests. For example, while the Liberal party may have been the normal governing party in Ottawa between 1921 and 1984, it had become either the major opposition party in provinces like Quebec and Ontario, or had been, for all practical purposes, eliminated from the partisan battle, as in Alberta and British Columbia. The 1984 Tory victory in national politics immediately helped to produce Liberal victories in the provincial arena. In Ontario, the Liberals won power in the 1985 election, after more than four decades in the political wilderness. In Quebec, a resurrected Robert Bourassa led the provincial Liberals into office in 1986 in a smashing victory over the Parti Québécois. In addition, there were Liberal provincial election successes in Prince Edward Island, New Brunswick, Nova Scotia, and Newfoundland (and almost in Manitoba), plus re-election victories in Ontario and Quebec. Thus, the Tory victories in national politics in 1984 and 1988 helped to rejuvenate the provincial Liberal party organizations. However, following the federal Liberal victory in 1993, Tory prospects again gained momentum in the provincial arena as voters reacted negatively to tax increases and cuts to major social programs such as health care. By the 2000 federal election, the only remaining Liberal provincial government was in Newfoundland.

The impact of federalism on the minor parties has been even greater than on the Liberals and Conservatives. Federalism has helped to promote minor parties, while at the same time it has limited their ultimate national success. By creating provincial units that are worth contesting for, given their powers in the Canadian system, federalism has encouraged new parties to emerge at the provincial level of government. However, even if a party wins control of a provincial government, it may find it difficult to expand successfully into the national party system. For example, it is difficult to conceive how the Parti Québécois might be extended either to other provinces or into control of the national government in Ottawa. In fact, René Lévesque, the party's founder, did not want the Parti Québécois to contest in the federal arena. Instead, after he was gone, the separatist movement founded a PQ analogue, the Bloc Québécois, to contest at the federal level. However, the development of the Bloc Québécois at the federal level illustrates this problem as well: how can a Quebec separatist party win seats outside of Quebec? The minor parties, such as the Progressives, the CCF, and Social Credit have primarily been provincial success stories which have failed in the national party arena. Thus, federalism promotes the emergence of new parties around the provincial units, while at the same time inhibiting their expansion into national politics.

The reverse pattern, that is, success in national politics followed by a temptation to enter provincial politics, can occur as well, even if less frequently. Thus, the success of the Reform Party in the 1993 federal election led to efforts by some party supporters to create a Reform Party in some of the provinces. Such efforts were strongly resisted by Reform Party leader Preston Manning because he felt that such a move might dissipate support for his federal party. Until its demise in 2000, the federal Reform Party did not compete in any of the provincial arenas. Its replacement, the Canadian Alliance, is, at least initially, following the same policy.

In addition to having an important effect on the success of the political parties in the various political arenas, federalism also influences a party's structure and ideology. The national parties are themselves federal organizations: for example, "it is an important part of Liberal mythology that the party, like the country itself, is a federation" (Wearing, 1981: 81). As federal structures, the party organizations have ended up granting considerable power to their provincial components. The result has been that Canada's national parties are decentralized around the provincial organizations; unity of effort, ideology, and personnel is rarely achieved.

A policy that is in the interest of the national party may be detrimental to provincial party success. For example, the Conservatives in the early 1990s provide a good example. The unpopularity of federal Tory leader Brian Mulroney and his policies such as free trade and the GST (the Goods and Services Tax) meant that provincial Tory party organizations sought to disassociate themselves from their federal counterparts in the public's mind. Federal Liberal policies (i.e., higher taxes, funding cutbacks) were a major factor in the demise of provincial Liberal governments in the Maritime provinces after 1993.

Such inconsistencies between provincial and federal party interests have sometimes led to the setting up of completely distinct party organizations for the national and provincial arenas. For example, the provincial Ontario wing of the Liberal party established its own structure in 1976, as had the Quebec component in the 1960s. In April 1989, as a way of handling the independence issue, the Quebec NDP decided to split from the national NDP structure, a move which was enforced by the federal council of the NDP in March of 1991. Because of the unpopular policies of the federal Tories, Alberta Conservatives severed their ties with the national party in April of 1991.

Even without a formal split between the national and provincial wings, federalism has an important bearing on party policy and platforms. There is no necessary agreement on policy or ideology between the party units that operate at each level of government. A Liberal provincial government or a Conservative one cannot assume ideological congruence from their federal counterparts, or vice versa. For example, while in the early 1980s Pierre Trudeau (national leader of the Liberal party) and Claude Ryan (leader of the provincial Liberal party in Quebec) were both Liberals, their positions on constitutional reform were diametrically opposed. Similarly, while national Liberal leader John Turner supported the Meech Lake Accord, several provincial Liberal premiers were strongly opposed to it in 1988 and 1989. In 1993, the NDP faced a highly visible split between the federal party in Ottawa and the NDP government of Bob Rae in Ontario over the province's budget and cutbacks to various social programs. After criticizing Ontario NDP Premier Bob Rae, federal NDP finance critic Steven Langdon was demoted by his leader, Audrey McLaughlin. Such disagreements are typical and widespread within all the party organizations.

One result is that, regardless of party label, provincial parties often campaign against Ottawa during provincial elections, rather than against the opposition provincial parties. In announcing an election, for example, existing provincial governments, in an effort to increase their bargaining power with Ottawa, often ask their electorate for a strong mandate. The result of such a system is a pattern of "federal-provincial schizophrenia" within the Canadian party organizations (Black, 1979: 90). In some instances it may turn into paranoia, as when "in the early part of the Second World War, Liberal Premier Hepburn of Ontario openly cooperated with the Conservatives in an attempt to oust the Liberal government of Prime Minister Mackenzie King" (Smiley, 1980: 146). In other instances, a federal party may welcome the defeat of its provincial counterpart: for example, the federal Liberal party, despite public protestations to the contrary, did not seem overly embittered by the defeat of the Quebec provincial Liberals by the Parti Québécois in the 1981 provincial election. The provincial Liberals returned the favour in 1984, when much of the party organization worked for the federal Conservatives during the September campaign. This pattern repeated itself in the 1988 election, with Robert Bourassa "openly" backing the free trade initiative of the federal Conservatives. Such examples show that important aspects of internal and external party relations in Canada are affected by the federal nature of the political system — a factor that is "so obvious as to be almost taken for granted, and yet so important that it can scarcely be overestimated" (Whitaker, 1977: 402).

The third characteristic of the Canadian national party system is its **regional** and **sectional** basis. Each of the national parties has regional strongholds and regional wastelands. For that reason it has often been suggested that "in reality, a Canadian national election is a series of regional contests, with the party competitors in each region varying in strength from coast to coast" (Landes, 1981: 105). The pattern of party competition, especially its regional nature, can be seen in the following analysis of the Canadian federal party system (Table 9.1).

Key to an understanding of the regional politics of the current Canadian party system is the nature of the Tory governing coalition of the 1980s. Fundamentally, Brian Mulroney forged a linkage between Western alienation and Quebec nationalism as a way of breaking the Liberal dominance in federal politics. However, the constitutional renewal failures of the Meech Lake and Charlottetown Accords alienated the nationalist/separatist aspirations of Quebec, while economic policy (GST, growth of the public debt) provided an impetus for renewed regional discontent in the West.

The onslaught of these two forms of sectional protest tore the Conservative coalition asunder in the 1993 federal election. In Quebec, nationalist aspirations were funnelled through the new party, the Bloc Québécois, while in Western Canada the Reform Party became the manifestation of regional alienation. The result was the destruction of Tory support in both regions, the success of both the Reform Party and the Bloc Québécois within their respective regions, and the return of the Liberal party to a majority government situation.

In those areas in which neither the Reform nor Bloc Québécois parties were of sufficient strength to win on their own, the Liberal party became the beneficiary of the plurality system, sweeping, for example, 98 out of the 99 seats in Ontario.

Table 9.1 Canadian Federal Election Results: 2000, 1997, 1993*

	SEATS WON BY EACH PARTY																
PROVINCE	*PC*			*Liberal*			*NDP*			*Alliance/Reform*			*BQ*			*Other*		
	[00]	97	(93)	(00)	97	(93)	[00]	97	(93)	[00]	97	(93)	(00)	97	(93)	(00)	97	(93)
Newfoundland	[2]	3	(0)	[5]	4	(0)	[0]	0	(0)	[0]	0	(0)	[0]	0	(0)	[0]	0	(0)
Nova Scotia	[4]	5	(0)	[4]	0	(0)	[3]	6	(0)	[0]	0	(0)	[0]	0	(0)	[0]	0	(0)
New Brunswick	[2]	5	(1)	[6]	3	(1)	[1]	2	(0)	[0]	0	(0)	[0]	0	(0)	[0]	0	(0)
Prince Edward Island	[0]	0	(0)	[4]	4	(0)	[0]	0	(0)	[0]	0	(0)	[0]	0	(0)	[0]	0	(0)
Quebec	[1]	5	(1)	[36]	26	(1)	[0]	0	(0)	[0]	0	(0)	[38]	44	(54)	[0]	0	(1)
Ontario	[0]	1	(0)	[100]	101	(0)	[1]	0	(0)	[2]	0	(1)	[0]	0	(0)	[0]	1	(0)
Manitoba	[1]	1	(0)	[5]	6	(0)	[4]	4	(0)	[4]	3	(1)	[0]	0	(0)	[0]	0	(0)
Saskatchewan	[0]	0	(0)	[2]	1	(0)	[2]	5	(5)	[10]	8	(4)	[0]	0	(0)	[0]	0	(0)
Alberta	[1]	0	(0)	[2]	2	(0)	[0]	0	(0)	[23]	24	(22)	[0]	0	(0)	[0]	0	(0)
British Columbia	[0]	0	(0)	[5]	6	(0)	[2]	3	(2)	[27]	25	(24)	[0]	0	(0)	[0]	0	(0)
NWT/Yukon/Nunavut	[0]	0	(0)	[3]	2	(0)	[0]	1	(1)	[0]	0	(0)	[0]	0	(0)	[0]	0	(0)
Total Seats **[301] 301 (295)**	[12]	20	(2)	[172]	155	(177)	[13]	21	(9)	[66]	60	(52)	[38]	44	(54)	[0]	1	(1)

* The Reform Party in 1993 and 1997 became the Canadian Alliance for the 2000 election.

In Atlantic Canada, the Liberals won 31 out of 32 seats; in Quebec, the Bloc Québécois gained 54 and the Liberals 19 out of that province's 75 seats; and in the provinces of Alberta and British Columbia, the Reform Party dominated.

What was unusual about the party system in 1993 was not its regional or sectional nature but the specific pattern in terms of seats: two new parties emerged in a single election with a significant bloc of seats, with one becoming the official opposition. Moreover, for the first time an avowedly separatist party formed the official opposition in the House of Commons. Challenged by two strong regional protest parties, the Liberal party had become, once again, the party of national unity, or, as it is sometimes called, "Canada's natural governing party."

The results of the 1997 election, due in part to the plurality electoral system, show an extreme pattern of regionalization (some might term it a balkanization) of the Canadian party system (Nevitte et al., 2000: 11–14; Bickerton, Gagnon, and Smith, 1999: 15–20). In Atlantic Canada, the election was a three-way race between the Tories, Liberals, and NDP. In Quebec, it was primarily a contest between the Bloc Québécois and the Liberals. Ontario emerged as its own region (a pattern begun in 1993), with the Liberal party totally dominant (with 98 of 99 seats in 1993 and 101 of 103 seats in 1997) and only challenged by the three "minor national" parties. A mixed battle was evident in Saskatchewan and Manitoba, with a three-way split in Manitoba and an NDP–Reform battle in Saskatchewan. In Alberta and British Columbia, the Reform Party totally dominated, winning 49 of 60 seats.

The 2000 election primarily reinforced the regional patterns of 1993 and 1997. Despite the Reform Party's rebirth as the Canadian Alliance for the 2000 contest, its base of support was almost identical to that of its predecessor in 1993 and 1997. In Quebec, the Bloc Québécois continued to lose ground, in terms of both seats and votes, to the Liberals. Vote-rich and seat-rich Ontario remained the key prize and the Liberals, because of the plurality electoral formula, won an unprecedented number of seats in that province for the third consecutive time. In Atlantic Canada, the Liberals either held their own or gained significantly (from 0 to 4 seats in Nova Scotia). The NDP declined below its 1997 level of 21 seats to just 13, while the Tories, with only 12 seats concentrated mostly in Eastern Canada, increased their status as a rump party.

The fourth characteristic of the national party system concerns the typical pattern of interaction among the parties. The party system from 1921 to 1984 was **centre-based**, with the Liberal party monopolizing the middle of the political spectrum (Alford, 1963; Horowitz, 1968). As a general ideological classification

Source: Malcolm Mayes, *The Edmonton Journal.* By permission.

of the federal parties, the following placement would seem to be an appropriate summary of party positions over the past several decades (1960–1990): as a social democratic party, the New Democratic Party is on the left; the Liberals are in the centre, usually on the left of centre but flexible enough to move to the right of centre if political conditions require it; the Progressive Conservatives are a centre-right party; and Social Credit is on the right of the political continuum. With the gradual demise of Social Credit, the party system in the 1960s and 1970s was composed of a large centre party challenged from both the left and the right.

Since the majority of voters are in the centre of the political spectrum, the major parties seek to occupy that position. However, once a party has gained control of the centre, it is difficult to dislodge, which is a key reason why a single party has dominated the federal government since the 1920s. In appealing to the centre, the winning party must find a theme that rallies people to its cause, while at the same time making it difficult for the opposition parties to disagree with it. The current Liberal party discovered such a theme in its emphasis on national unity, just as Macdonald's National Policy worked for the Conservatives in the 19th century. When the electorate does not feel that it is the key issue, as in 1979, the Liberal party fares badly. When the national unity theme is paramount, as in 1968, the Liberals win a majority victory. The opposition parties are put in the unenviable position either of arguing against a theme such as national unity, and thus appearing unpatriotic, or of trying to distinguish their policy from that of the Liberals in the minds of the electorate, a difficult undertaking.

Having established a key theme such as national unity as the basis of their political dominance, the centre-based party then utilizes several tactics: first, it ignores new policy options or issues, hoping that they will disappear so that no action is required; second, if a new issue is gaining public acceptance, the centre party seeks to undercut it by re-emphasizing their key theme; and third, if the first two tactics fail, the dominant party takes over or co-opts the issue, remaking it in its own image.

As a result, if the challenge to the centre party is from the left, the party moves left; if the challenge is from the right, the party moves right. The centre party thus establishes a moving equilibrium: its position on the left-right spectrum may change, but its placement between the other parties does not. Between 1921 and 1984, this technique was exemplified by the Liberal shuffle: three moves left, five right, three left, and another to the right produces a lot of action, but the party ends up in the same place as it started. Movement becomes mistaken for leadership, with the retention of power the ultimate party goal.

This pattern was first developed for the Liberals under Mackenzie King and has served as the party's most significant operating principle ever since. For example, in addressing the national Liberal meeting in the spring of 1978, Pierre Trudeau was asked by a reporter whether the party was moving to the right in preparation for the next federal election. Trudeau responded that the Liberal party was the party of the "radical centre" and would remain so.

Thus, after years of extensive federal government expansion, by the mid-1970s Trudeau had announced government cutbacks, promised a tightening up of welfare and unemployment benefits, increased military expenditures with the purchase of new tanks and planes, and even curtailed the federal government's bilingualism programs. In effect, the Liberal party in the 1979 campaign ran against its first 10 years in office in an attempt to move to the right of the political spectrum to undercut growing Conservative strength. By contrast, in the 1972–1974 period the Liberal party moved left, passing such legislation as the 1974 Federal Election Expenses Act and establishing Petro-Canada, in order to acquire NDP support in Parliament and to undercut NDP strength in the electorate. While the move to the right was not immediately successful in the 1979 election, it did lay the foundation for the Liberals' return to power within a year. The move to the left in the early 1970s had an even more immediate impact — NDP strength in the 1974 election was cut in half from its 1972 seat total. Such tactics allowed the Liberal party to dominate national politics between 1921 and 1984 by occupying the "triumphant centre" of the Canadian political spectrum (Horowitz, 1968: 29–44). As Mackenzie King (quoted in Morton, 1950: 22) said in 1921, the "Liberal party with its traditions and aspirations offers a means of escape from both extremes, neither of which is in the national interest."

This centre-based model of the Canadian party system provides a possible explanation for the Tory triumphs in 1984 and 1988. Although a series of factors obviously contributed to the Liberal downfall, an important component of that debacle was that the Tories replaced the Grits as the occupier of the centre position in the political spectrum. Failure on the part of the Liberals to deal adequately with economic problems alienated both working and middle class support. In addition, the Liberals' constitutional stand eroded support in Quebec (the federal Liberals' home province). Combined with John Turner's inept performance as leader, such factors allowed the Tories, under the Irish charm of Brian Mulroney, to move leftward to become the centre party, instead of a centre-right coalition. Thus, the Conservatives not only held their traditional areas of support in 1984 but added to it the key provinces of Ontario and Quebec. In 1988, although they lost support in Atlantic Canada, the Tories significantly increased their hold on Quebec. However, the rise of new regional parties (Reform and Bloc Québécois), the negative reaction to the "neoconservative" political agenda of Brian Mulroney, and the continuing effects of a severe economic recession all combined to destroy the Tory hold on the centre of the political spectrum, which was easily occupied by the Liberal party in the 1993 election.

Following their election victory, the federal Liberal party moved to the right of the political spectrum, specifically slashing social programs and transfer payments and generally cutting government spending. By early 1997, the Liberal government's targets for deficit reduction were well ahead of Finance Minister Paul Martin's projections. As a result, in anticipation of the next federal election, the party moved modestly to the left — improving support for a limited number of social programs and re-emphasizing traditional Liberal values.

The 1997 election showed that the Liberal government had badly misjudged the mood of the country. Even though the Liberals won a narrow majority, the first time they had gained two consecutive majorities in 40 years, they lost significant support in the Atlantic provinces and the Prairies. Entering the contest after only three-and-a-half years in office and with a comfortable lead in the polls (supported by about 50 percent of those polled), the Liberals lost some of that support during the 36-day campaign, dropping to 38 percent nationally. In effect, the Liberals, while retaining the centre of the political spectrum, were squeezed from the left by the NDP and from the right by the Tories and especially by Reform. In Quebec the Liberals did gain seats, primarily as a result of increasing Tory support, which split the vote among the other parties and allowed the Liberals victories in a half-dozen ridings.

A rejuvenated centre strategy was clearly used by the Liberals in the 2000 election. Challenged on the left by the NDP (and to some extent by the Tories on

> The election's [November 2000] unintended result is that we have invented a new and potentially lethal political phenomenon: an elected dictatorship. That's what the third Chrétien majority amounts to (Newman, 2000: B1).

social policy) and on the right by the Canadian Alliance, the Liberal party moved left on social policy and right on tax policy. For example, in September of 2000 the federal government signed a health deal with the provinces and then, in October, announced the largest round of tax cuts in Canadian history. The ghost of Mackenzie King appears to have inhabited the body of Jean Chrétien: govern to the right, campaign to the left, but always remain "the radical centre" in the moving equilibrium of the ongoing Canadian party system.

The Canadian party system is, therefore, best described by four key characteristics: it is competitive, federal, regional, and centre-based. However, underlying each of these attributes is the social, economic, and political diversity of the country. For example, federalism was adopted as a principle of government to help ensure the preservation of the two main cultural groups at the time of Confederation. Not surprising, then, is the finding that such diversity continues to exist and is channelled through the party system, exemplified by the regional basis of party support. Diversity also helps to explain the importance of the centre-oriented strategy of party politics, with a dominant party regularly challenged from both ends of the political spectrum. Finally, diversity makes it impossible for one party to represent all of the social, economic, and political interests of the nation, thereby promoting the development and maintenance of a competitive party system.

THE SELECTION OF NATIONAL PARTY LEADERS

The characteristics of the individual parties and the party system have had a significant impact on both the type of leader chosen and the process of selection (Courtney, 1995). Electorally oriented parties in a competitive party system, for the most part, prefer leaders who promise the chance of electoral success. Thus, after losing two national elections in 1993 and 1997, the Reform Party changed not only its name to the Canadian Alliance, but its leader as well (Stockwell Day replaced Preston Manning). Moreover, the significance of our national party leaders is enhanced because Canadian politics has always been leader-oriented (Perlin, 1980: 13–27). The history of Canadian politics is very much a history of its political leaders, such as John A. Macdonald, Wilfrid Laurier, Mackenzie King, Pierre Trudeau, Brian Mulroney, and Jean Chrétien.

The success of any political party in winning votes and elections is directly linked to the appeal of its leader, the leader's personality, and the policies enunciated by that leader. One reason Pierre Trudeau dominated national politics for a decade and a half was because of his personal appeal, his intellect, and his style. Moreover, political parties often make the question of leadership the focus of their election strategy, as the federal Liberals did with Trudeau on several occasions (e.g., the 1979 theme that "a leader must be a leader"). The 2000 election was no exception to this pattern, with much of the focus on whether Jean Chrétien had stayed on too long as Liberal leader and prime minister or whether the new leader of the Canadian Alliance (Stockwell Day) was ready yet to lead the country. If Canadian politics is indeed leader-oriented, then it is important to know how those leaders are selected.

National party leadership selection is also significant because, in a democratic political system, we expect our party leaders to be chosen according to certain political principles. For example, the traditional selection process has been representative (several thousand delegates are selected to attend from the various local, provincial, and national party organizations); open (public in nature and covered by the press and media); competitive (several candidates seek the leadership, thereby giving the delegates a choice between leaders); and based on the majority principle (the first candidate to receive a majority of votes is declared the new leader of the party), with votes cast using the individual secret ballot (a way of guaranteeing the political equality of each delegate). While the general public may not be directly involved in the selection of party leaders, the national party leadership selection process is used as a way of giving a small group of party members a direct voice in the choice of their particular leader. Interestingly, in contrast to their federal counterparts several provincial parties began selecting leaders through some form of direct democracy, such as **teledemocracy** (i.e., *a phone-in vote*).

For about 80 years, the major parties in Canada have selected their leaders through a **national party leadership convention**, which is *a gathering of party members from across the country who meet to choose the individual who will become their new leader*. In this way, the current practice of leadership conventions varies from the older Canadian tradition of having the party members in Parliament select the leader, a pattern that was used until 1919 in the Liberal party and until 1927 by the Conservatives.

Certain general rules of the selection process are typically employed by the various political parties, although specific details vary between parties or from one leadership convention to the next. The first thing a party must do is the obvious one of deciding to have a leadership convention. In some cases, the decision is straightforward, as when a leader resigns or announces the intention to do so as soon as a successor has been picked (e.g., Lester Pearson's decision to resign as Liberal party leader in 1967 and Brian Mulroney's decision to resign as Tory leader in 1993). However, a party leader who wants to retain the position may be forced to call a leadership convention against his or her will (e.g., John Diefenbaker's position in the mid-1960s).

Those not satisfied with their party leader may make use of the **leadership review process**. Under certain conditions, *the major party constitutions allow*

Source: Reprinted from *The Leader-Post* (Regina, Saskatchewan). By permission of the paper and Brian Gable.

delegates to the national meetings to propose and vote on a resolution that asks for a leadership review. If such a resolution passes with a majority vote, the party then calls a leadership convention. Thus, the party members who select their leader may have the final say over how long he or she remains at the head of the party.

Even if a leadership review resolution does not pass, a strong minority vote in favour of it is a clear indication to the party leader that the rank and file members are unhappy. Dissatisfaction was clearly evident in the Parti Québécois in November of 1996 when its members gave leader Lucien Bouchard only a 77 percent approval vote at the party's annual meeting — far below the expected vote of 95 percent. Premier Bouchard was certainly weakened by such a vote and only retained control of his party after threatening to resign. In 1981, 33 percent of the delegates to the national Progressive Conservative meeting voted in favour of a leadership review. Two years later a similar vote on the leadership question put Joe Clark in the position of calling a leadership convention. Technically, Clark did not have to do so, since the leadership review vote had not passed with a majority.

As the Clark example illustrates, a strong, but less than majority, vote may be enough to politically force a review process to be undertaken. In New Brunswick in 1985, a challenge to the continued leadership of Richard Hatfield in the Tory party ran into a new problem. The specific results of the vote on the leadership question were not made public. The convention was told only that the motion in favour of the review had not passed. Such a tactic, of course, prevented Hatfield from facing more pressure for a leadership review, as had happened earlier to Joe Clark. Similarly, while a 1995 challenge to Premier John Savage's continued leadership of the Nova Scotia Liberal Party was defeated, the specific results of the party's vote were never made public.

Once a decision to call a leadership convention has been made, the next order of business is to determine how the delegates to the national party leadership convention will be selected. The rules for delegate selection are important; if they are biased toward a particular candidate or region, for example, they may end up predetermining who has the best chance of winning. A party usually sends several delegates from each local constituency organization, a number of representatives from the provincial party organizations, and a group of delegates from the national party organization. Delegates are included from the party's youth and women's organizations, from the elected members of the party in both the provincial and national legislatures, and from the party's senators and privy councillors. On occasion, defeated candidates from the past election, as well as delegates-at-large appointed by the party leadership, have been given the right to participate. The delegate selection process produces a gathering of several thousand party members, who then choose the party's new leader.

The 1983 Conservative and the 1984 Liberal leadership conventions gave ample evidence of a very significant change in the delegate selection process within both parties — a trend that has become even more pronounced in recent conventions. At least in theory, and in practice through the 1960s, delegates from the constituency level were seen as "independent" electors who would attend the leadership convention and, after listening to the speeches and meeting the candidates, decide for whom they would vote. However, current practice suggests an opposite pattern, with delegates running as slates pledged to a particular candidate at the constituency level. Once selected, these delegates then attend the leadership convention as pledged backers of a particular candidate. Thus, the way to win national support is to pack the local delegate selection meetings so that your slate will win, even if that means having instant party members voting for your candidate (such as the 10-year-olds and winos who were recruited for the 1983 Tory leadership convention). **Instant party members** are *those individuals who have just joined the party for the sole purpose of voting for a specific candidate in the leadership race.* Sometimes instant party members are not even aware that they have joined the party for such a purpose, as happened for about 1 300 residents of British Columbia in the NDP leadership convention (February 2000) or thousands of people in the Gaspé in Quebec during the leadership race for the new Canadian Alliance party in 2000. In both of these cases, party workers added the names of residents to their party membership lists without the knowledge or agreement of the residents, thereby allowing other party members to cast ballots on their behalf — in other words, an example of electoral fraud!

The next stage is the nomination of candidates. In most cases, individuals seeking the position of party leader have announced their candidacy long before the convention begins, in order to have time to win the backing of delegates to the convention. Party leadership contests now last from several months up to a year before the convention, are widely covered by the news media, and can cost a candidate at least several hundred thousand dollars in expenses. For the 1990 Liberal leadership contest, a total of $1.7 million per candidate was set as the limit.

To be officially nominated a party usually requires the candidate to be a known party member and to have his or her nomination papers signed by a given number of party members (about 50 delegates attending the convention). Few restrictions are typically placed on who can run for the party leadership, although "frivolous" candidates (those with no party support or those unknown to the party) may be denied the right to enter the contest. One way to deny "frivolous" candidates is to require a financial deposit by leadership contenders, as the Tories did in their 1998 race. A requirement of nomination papers signed by 250 party members and a deposit of $30,000 prevented announced contenders, such as the "Reverend" Michael Baldasaro who favoured the legalization of marijuana, from officially contesting for the Tory leadership. Such restrictions have not prevented a large number of people from being nominated for their party's leadership: 9 candidates on the first ballot in the 1968 Liberal meeting and 12 candidates in the 1976 Progressive Conservative leadership convention. The Liberals in 1990 and the Conservatives in 1998 each saw five candidates compete on the first ballot.

Once the candidates have been nominated, they are given the opportunity to address the delegates. Following the speeches by the candidates, the voting procedure begins, according to the following rules. First, the voting is done by secret, individual ballot. Since no one else knows how they have voted, delegates are free from political intimidation by a leadership candidate. The secret ballot increases the importance of the individual delegate, since a vote from Newfoundland counts as much as a vote from an Ontario delegate. As well, since no candidate can win simply as a regional spokesman or "favourite son," each leadership hopeful must appeal to the delegates on a national or countrywide basis. For example, a candidate from the largest province, Ontario, cannot win solely as a favourite son candidate, even if all of the delegates from Ontario vote for him or her, because the Ontario delegation comprises only about one-third of the total number of participants.

A second operating rule is that each successive ballot (first ballot, second ballot, third ballot, etc.) is held almost immediately. As soon as the first ballot is finished, the second ballot begins, with only a short interval in between. Ballots are held until one nominee receives a majority of votes cast. The quick succession of ballots means that candidates have very little time to decide whether they will remain in the contest or make deals with the other candidates.

A third rule allows for the elimination of minor candidates after each ballot (e.g., those candidates not receiving a minimum number of votes, such as 50) and for the elimination of the least-placed candidate (e.g., the candidate with the fewest votes, once all minor candidates are no longer in the contest). This third operating rule helps to ensure a relatively quick decision by the convention. For example, in the 1968 Liberal convention the original nine candidates from the first ballot were reduced to three by the fourth ballot, while in the 1976 Progressive Conservative meeting 12 first-ballot nominees were cut to 2 by the fourth ballot. In 1993, five first-ballot Tory candidates were reduced to two nominees for the second and final ballot.

The victory of Joe Clark in the 1976 Conservative contest illustrates that the eventual winner need not be the most popular on the first ballot. Clark won because most of the candidates who were eliminated between ballots threw their support to him. An interesting anomaly regarding leadership selection occurred in the 1995 NDP leadership convention when front-runner Svend Robinson withdrew, allowing Alexa McDonough to win on the next ballot! However, more important than how many leadership candidates withdraw and give their support to a remaining candidate is the loyalty of their delegates.

Since delegates use the secret ballot, leadership candidates cannot guarantee how their supporters will vote after they have withdrawn or been eliminated from the contest. Because of the quick succession of ballots, all a leadership candidate can do is to ask supporters to cast their future ballots for a specific candidate, or to make some sort of symbolic gesture, such as sitting with a remaining candidate. However, many delegates simply ignore such a request and vote for their own choice anyway. The result of such voting rules is to make it possible for a relatively unknown and politically inexperienced candidate to win the leadership of a major Canadian political party.

Leadership selection in the New Democratic Party is based on a different philosophy than that of the two parliamentary parties. As an extra-parliamentary party that seeks to control its leader, the NDP requires that the party leader chosen be held accountable during his or her term as leader by the members of the party meeting in convention, and is expected to ensure that the party convention policy decisions are implemented once the NDP has gained power (Courtney, 1973: 174). As a result of this view, the party leader must automatically seek re-election at the NDP's biennial convention, thus eliminating the traditional need to push for a leadership review process, as in the Liberal and Conservative parties. However, in fact, no serious challenge to the party leader has ever developed within the NDP, thus resulting in a secure tenure of office. The decision (April 1994) by Audrey McLaughlin to step down as party leader following the party's massive defeat in the 1993 federal election circumvented the need for the NDP to implement a leadership review process. However, after the party's poor showing in the 2000 election, NDP leader Alexa McDonough, who announced that she would remain as party leader (January 2001), still faced an automatic leadership review vote scheduled for November 2001.

Although the major federal parties use the national party leadership convention to select their leaders, the type of leader chosen by the parties has differed historically between the Liberals and Conservatives (Smiley, 1968; Courtney, 1973; Perlin, 1980). In the Liberal party, candidates from Ontario and Quebec dominate. Conservatives are more likely to select nominees from either Western Canada (Joe Clark, Kim Campbell) or the Maritimes (Robert Stanfield). Thus, the regional nature of the party system and party support is reflected within the parties, as well as between them in election campaigns.

With the exceptions of Joe Clark (i.e., his first selection as Tory leader), Brian Mulroney, and Kim Campbell, Conservatives have relied on those who were veterans of elective office, especially on people who have served as provincial premiers. Liberals, in contrast, have rarely chosen a leader who has ever contested a provincial election and have been receptive to candidates who have had little political experience. In this sense, the Liberals have been more pragmatic than the Conservatives in the selection of their leaders, even accepting a candidate such as Trudeau, who had vehemently attacked the Liberal party shortly before joining it, or John Turner, who had left the cabinet for nearly a decade. Such pragmatism is also evident in the Liberal party's alternation between French and English leaders (King, St. Laurent, Pearson, Trudeau, Turner, Chrétien): the party of Ontario and Quebec rarely forgets where its power base lies. By contrast, Conservatives, until their selection of Brian Mulroney, failed to appeal to Quebec in terms of their leadership selection, as exemplified by Claude Wagner's defeat in their 1976 convention.

The type of leader selected varies not only between parties, but with other forms of leadership selection as well. For example, since the adoption of the national party leadership convention, the role of the party caucus has greatly diminished, thereby increasing the opportunity for the selection of outsiders. It is highly doubtful that Joe Clark, Pierre Trudeau, John Turner, Brian Mulroney, Kim Campbell, or Stockwell Day would have been chosen to lead their parties if the party caucus method had been used.

Moreover, being selected by a national party convention has enhanced the power of the leader over his or her party caucus, since leaders now argue that they can only be removed by such a convention (Courtney, 1995: 276). However, if a leader is removed, as Diefenbaker was in the 1967 Conservative convention, then the caucus is likely to become split between the supporters of the old and new leaders, as Robert Stanfield discovered. After his ouster, Diefenbaker remained a member of the Tory party caucus, "emitting all the baleful radiance of a whore at a family wedding" (Young, 1978: 290).

Finally, if the major parties are electoral coalitions, then the basic factor in leadership selection is whether the new leader can enhance the party's electoral prospects. As a result, the leaders so picked have typically been pragmatic politicians and non-ideological in outlook, with their primary goal that of electoral victory. Those leaders who cannot produce such results immediately come under attack, with internal party conflict over leadership replacement usually occurring after an electoral defeat. For example, Stockwell Day's leadership of the Canadian Alliance came under attack after the 2000 election because he was unable to increase by much the support for his party over that of Preston Manning and the Reform Party. Since Canadian politics is leader-oriented, the easiest way to change a party's image is to select a new leader.

In Canadian politics, issues have almost always been secondary to concerns about leadership. With the emergence of television as the dominant mechanism in the electoral process, campaigns have increasingly become, in the past three decades, leadership-based media contests. Therefore, to help change a party's electoral prospects, turnover or replacement of a party leader has become a common practice in the battle for power. A brief look at national party leadership conventions will illustrate some of these themes.

The 1990 Liberal leadership convention

Following his second massive electoral defeat in 1988, it was only a matter of time before John Turner would have to relinquish the mantle of Liberal party leadership. Finally ending months of speculation, Turner announced his intention to resign on May 3, 1989, having served five years as Liberal leader. The party's national executive decided in June to hold the leadership convention (Table 9.2) a year later in Calgary between June 19 and June 23, making it the longest convention race in Canadian political history. Each leadership candidate would be allowed to spend a maximum of $1.7 million, with the total cost of the convention estimated at $25 million. A total of about 5 200 delegates would be selected.

The clear frontrunner to replace John Turner was former Trudeau political ally and cabinet minister Jean Chrétien, who had finished second in the previous leadership race in

Table 9.2	1990 Liberal Leadership Convention
Candidates	First Ballot
Jean Chrétien	2652
Paul Martin	1176
Sheila Copps	499
Thomas Wappel	167
John Nunziata	64

1984. The only real challenge came from novice Quebec MP Paul Martin, Jr., son of long-time Liberal party stalwart, cabinet member, and twice-defeated Liberal leadership candidate Paul Martin, Sr. The key battle between these two candidates would be in Quebec. The three other official candidates were all junior members of the Liberal caucus: Sheila Copps, Thomas Wappel, and John Nunziata. Several potential leaders withdrew from the race early on: Lloyd Axworthy, MP from Manitoba, due to his inability to raise sufficient funds; and Clifford Lincoln, former Quebec environment minister, after his loss in the federal by-election in the Montreal riding of Chambly on February 12, 1990. Other possible candidates decided not to enter the fray: MP Dennis Mills and Ontario Premier David Peterson.

The leadership race consisted of a series of national debates held across the country and the battle for delegates at the constituency level, with the latter being, by far, the most important ingredient. The party again faced the problem of instant members at the delegate selection meetings, with the meetings often stacked by one or the other of the leader's supporters. On a national basis, particularly in Quebec, the Chrétien forces were far superior and won the delegate battle. While Sheila Copps gained considerable media coverage, she was not well organized at the grassroots level and was unable to turn public support into elected delegates. Both Thomas Wappel, mainly an anti-abortion candidate, and John Nunziata were minor players in the contest. Thus, the strong (57 percent) first ballot victory for Jean Chrétien was no surprise.

Overall, the leadership race was dull, given Chrétien's early and large lead, and overshadowed by the debates and conflict over the Meech Lake Accord, which died on June 22, 1990, one day before the leadership vote. As an anti-Meech candidate, Chrétien would face tough problems in the future in winning support in Quebec, where a strong majority had backed the Meech Lake Accord.

Following majority election victories in 1993 and 1997, many observers expected Prime Minister Jean Chrétien not to run for a third term, especially with his heir apparent, Paul Martin, Jr., waiting in the wings. The battle between Chrétien and Martin after 1997 became increasingly public by 2000, with the prime minister declaring his intention to run again at the Liberal party's annual meeting in March of 2000. Despite such statements, many expected the prime minister to retire before the next election call. Instead, and perhaps partly as a way of blunting Paul Martin's leadership aspirations, the prime minister decided to "call" an election on November 27, 2000. Winning a third mandate, however, did not quell

ELECTION 3000...

I'M RUNNING AGAIN.

DO NOT DROP

Source: MOU (Theodore Moudakis), *The Halifax Daily News* (March 26, 2000), p. 21. By permission.

speculation over the possibility of Chrétien retiring before completing his third term in office — nor did the prime minister's own suggestion that he might serve a fourth term.

Given the Liberal party's constitutional requirement that an automatic leadership review vote would have to be held at the next convention (March 2002), the Chrétien and Martin forces again publicly battled over the prime minister's wish to extend such a leadership review vote. A compromise was announced in April of 2001, with the next convention scheduled for February 2003. Many observers expect the prime minister to resign before that convention, so that a leadership review vote will not have to be held.

The future of leadership conventions

For the past 80 years, the major national parties have selected their leaders through the use of national party leadership conventions (Courtney, 1995). During that time their size, procedures, and impact have changed considerably. Recent conventions have been more open, more expensive, more relevant, and larger, that is, generally what we would call more democratic. Yet, such conventions have come under increasing criticism for many of the same reasons.

Two key factors account for the changing and declining legitimacy of national party leadership conventions: first, a growing public acceptance of and demand for participatory politics, especially direct democracy, inside the political parties; and second, new information technologies which expand the potential for such direct involvement by the mass public in party affairs (Alexander, 1996). Beginning with the Parti Québécois in 1985, many provincial parties now select their leaders through the use of some form of direct democracy.

The impact of such changes has also been felt at the national level. For example, the NDP, in replacing Audrey McLaughlin as leader in the fall of 1995, used an American-style series of nonbinding primaries, combined with a convention, to select Alexa McDonough as their new federal leader. Following their 2000 election loss, the executive of the federal NDP began considering other selection processes than just a convention, so that Alexa McDonough's successor will likely be chosen by a new leadership selection mechanism. The Tories, after confirming Jean Charest as their leader at a national party meeting in April 1995, then adopted a new procedure to be used in selecting future leaders (Courtney, 1995: 255–256). The Tories adopted a universal membership vote (UMV) to be weighted by constituencies, so that each riding will have equal voting power. A

universal membership vote (UMV) means that *all party members have a vote in the leadership selection process.*

A universal membership vote is a direct challenge to the legitimacy of national party leadership conventions. Instead of the representative democracy of political conventions, UMV systems institutionalize a pattern of direct democracy inside the political parties. Increasingly, both provincial and federal parties are moving toward some type of UMV system, even when it is combined with elements of the older convention model.

The first federal party to use a UMV system was the Bloc Québécois in 1997, when a mail ballot, which was to be returned by a specified deadline, was given to each party member. Over 50 000 party members voted for one of the six candidates, with Gilles Duceppe winning with 53 percent of the vote.

A version of a UMV procedure was used by the federal Tories in the fall of 1998. However, in this instance a winning candidate had to receive 50 percent of the votes cast; if the leading candidate did not get a majority, a further ballot would be required. Against five candidates, Joe Clark received 48.4 percent of the votes cast on the first ballot (October 25, 1998) and, since all other candidates then withdrew except for one, a second ballot was held on November 15. On the second ballot, Joe Clark received 77 percent of the votes cast and was declared elected leader. In this process, each of the country's 301 ridings were given equal status of 100 points each, with the breakdown in each constituency based on the actual vote for the leader in that riding.

The most dramatic use of a UMV process occurred in the leadership selection process for the new Canadian Alliance party. Preston Manning, founder and leader of the Reform Party, moved, after his second loss to the Liberals (1993 and 1997), to disband the party in order to create a United Alternative on the right to defeat the Liberals in the next election. At its founding convention (January 2000), the United Alternative delegates adopted the name Canadian Conservative Reform Alliance Party (CCRAP) — which was quickly changed to the Canadian Reform Conservative Alliance. More importantly, a UMV system was adopted to select the first leader of the Canadian Alliance party.

In this particular case, the UMV system worked as follows. Most party members would vote in their ridings with a traditional paper ballot and ballot box on Saturday, June 24, 2000. Those members who were overseas, lived in remote areas, or were unable to vote on June 24 could vote by telephone, beginning on June 22. The combined results would be tallied on June 24 and announced at the party's convention in Calgary later that day. If no candidate had a majority, a second ballot would be held on Saturday, July 8.

With five candidates in the race, the first ballot on June 24 showed three major candidates in contention: Stockwell Day (44 percent), Preston Manning (36 percent), and Tom Long (19 percent). Such a result was a clear defeat for Preston Manning, who had expected to, at the very least, lead on the first ballot. Even though third-place finisher Tom Long backed Preston Manning for the second ballot, it was not enough to stem the Day bandwagon. On July 8, out of about 114 000 votes cast, Stockwell Day won 63 percent and became the new leader of Canada's newest federal party.

Source: Gary Clement, *National Post* (February 1, 2000), p. A1. By permission.

CLEMENT, *The National Post*

Thus, by the start of the new century most of the federal parties had either adopted and/or used a UMV system or were moving in that direction. Even the Liberal party, after selecting Jean Chrétien as their leader by the convention method in 1990, adopted a direct vote method of selection. This proposed reform was modified in 1992 so as to combine primaries and a convention mechanism.

This brief review of how the various national parties have changed their leadership selection procedures for the future indicates that, while conventions have not totally disappeared from the scene, they are being replaced by newer mechanisms of leadership selection. Only time will tell whether such reforms will become permanent and whether a higher quality of candidate and party leadership will result. However, one fact should be kept in mind: every previous change in the method of leadership selection has changed the type of person selected!

> The Quebec Premier's [Lucien Bouchard's] impending departure has highlighted the realization that most levels of Canadian society suddenly seem to be populated by political midgets (Newman, 2001: B5).

PARTY FINANCE

As primarily electoral organizations, it is not surprising to find that the major expenses facing the parties are campaign expenditures. As a fundraiser who worked for both the Conservatives and Liberals, Israel Tarte's statement (quoted in Dawson, 1970: 478) that "elections are not won by prayers alone" points to the importance of financial considerations in the success of a political party. More recently (1990), Tory Senator Norm Atkins, who was chairman of the Conservative federal election campaigns in 1984 and 1988, put it rather succinctly: "You can't run national election campaigns by selling fudge." Changes in campaign techniques in recent decades, in particular the emphasis on costly mass media advertising, have greatly increased the necessity for party funds. Parties also need money to carry the organization through the inter-election period, an especially vulnerable situation for opposition parties.

The pattern of party finance differs between the cadre and mass party types. Traditionally, the cadre parties (Liberal and Conservative) have relied on contributions from the corporate sector, with large donations from relatively few sponsors. In contrast, mass parties have taken a grassroots funding approach, depending on small donations from numerous individuals or on union support.

In the initial years of Confederation, party leaders had to concern themselves directly with matters of party finance. The inevitable soon occurred: a party leader, John A. Macdonald, was involved in questions of party funding and corruption. The Pacific Scandal brought the downfall of the Conservative government and almost wrecked Macdonald's career. Consequently, party leaders have since sought to isolate themselves from matters of party finance by having specific party organizers for fundraising activities.

These **bagmen**, that is, *party members who solicit and collect money for their political party*, are often appointed to patronage positions such as the Senate and operate outside of the party leader's sight, so that when the political scandal eventually hits, the party leader is able to disassociate him- or herself from any involvement in political wrongdoing. Such was the case in the Patricia Starr scandal in Ontario: Liberal fundraiser Starr was accused in 1989 of making illegal political contributions to the provincial Liberal party and convicted in 1991 on four counts of violating that province's election finances act. However, Liberal leader and Premier David Peterson emerged from the scandal, at least initially, unscathed (although he was defeated unexpectedly in the next election). Seeing no evil allows the party leader to profess innocence, while the party's bagmen may be charged with criminal wrongdoing by the government controlled by their party; they may be left to defend themselves, as Liberal Senator Louis Giguère discovered in the Sky Shops Affair in the 1970s.

This pattern of fundraising by the Liberals and Conservatives, based on large corporate donations, has endured, in slightly modified form, to the present. The financial backing thus received helped to reinforce the dominance of the two major parties, since new parties were often hard pressed for cash. Moreover, because the extra-parliamentary parties represented a challenge to the existing social and economic interests of central Canada, they neither wanted, nor were they typically offered, corporate largesse. As a result, they sought a new means of party finance, attempting to use the mass-funding techniques of the European social democratic parties.

This grassroots approach centred on two sources of potential party income: annual dues from individual members and contributions from trade unions and interest groups. The initial attempts at mass funding through individual contributions were not particularly successful, usually leaving the party perpetually short of funds, as the experience of the CCF demonstrates. However, dues from paying members combined with labour union contributions have helped to give the NDP a more solid financial base than its predecessor. In the 1960s, trade union financial support for the NDP amounted to approximately 40 percent of party funds, allowing the party to challenge the financial dominance of the Liberals and Conservatives (Paltiel, 1970: 56–61).

The most successful mass-funding party in Canadian history (at least in its early years) is the Parti Québécois, which not only sent back corporate donations in the 1973 and 1976 provincial election campaigns but proceeded to make such contributions to all parties illegal after they became the government in 1976. Interestingly, outlawing corporate contributions had, from the PQ's perspective, the beneficial result of seriously harming their main party opponent, the provincial Liberals, in the ability to raise adequate party funds. When the Bloc Québécois was formed in 1990, it followed the PQ pattern and refused corporate donations and individual contributions over $3,000. However, because of its inability to raise adequate party funds under such restrictions, the Bloc Québécois reversed itself in January of 2000 and began accepting corporate donations of $5,000 or less.

The traditional pattern of party finance for the Liberals and Conservatives involved the use of several basic techniques, although these practices were regularly denied by the party bagmen. The essential first step in fundraising was to select bagmen who had access to the financial and corporate elite: as Mackenzie King (quoted in Wearing, 1981: 63) put it, "you need millionaires to get money from millionaires." These fundraisers would then visit wealthy individuals and corporate executives for their annual contributions. A long-time practice was for the donations to be split 60 percent for the government party and 40 percent for the opposition. Now that the record of party finance is public knowledge, a 50/50 split is often seen among the major corporate donors. Such contributions thus ensured that no matter which party won the next election, the individual or corporation, having donated to the party coffers, could count on access to the political leaders.

If such donations were not readily given, the governing party could institute the practices of toll-gating and kickbacks (Wearing, 1981: 58–64). In **toll-gating**, *government contracts or business would be allocated to those firms that had given to the party coffers*, while a **kickback** scheme meant that *once a firm had received government work, a certain percentage would be returned to the ruling party, usually by way of campaign contributions*. Advertising agencies and their lucrative contracts with government departments often provide suitable examples of this point. Finally, the party in power could also use patronage appointments to bolster party finances.

Problems and scandals relating to the area of party finance continue to occur in the Canadian polity on a regular basis. Many allegations of wrongdoing in the Mulroney government centred on the areas of patronage and party finance (Cameron, 1995). Because of a variation of a kickback scheme, Senator Eric Berntson, former deputy premier of Saskatchewan in the Conservative government of Grant Devine, was charged with fraud along with 20 other individuals in

January of 1997. This amounted to about half of Tory Premier Grant Devine's caucus being charged with fraud for allegedly stealing $1 million in a complicated kickback scheme between 1986 and 1991. Senator Berntson was consequently sentenced to one year in jail for fraud in March of 1999. In recent years, NDP governments in British Columbia seem to have been particularly prone to abuses in the party finance area. For example, in the "bingogate affair," a group closely linked to the New Democratic Party raised $18 million running charity bingos in Nanaimo between 1970 and 1993, but contributed only $400,000 to charities, with the remainder going to the provincial party. This scandal helped to force the resignation of NDP Premier Mike Harcourt in November of 1995, even though he was not personally involved in the affair. His replacement, NDP leader and Premier Glen Clark, resigned as premier in 1999 under allegations of a conflict of interest with respect to the granting of a casino license. In October of 2000, criminal charges were made against him alleging breach of trust and fraud.

These fundraising practices clearly favour the party in power, with electoral defeat often creating a crisis of party finance. For example, the defeated Liberals found themselves $3.5 million in debt after the 1984 contest, and an estimated $6.7 million in debt after their second consecutive election loss in 1988. However, as the next election approached with the Liberals leading in the polls and expecting victory, money became easier to raise, with the debt reduced to about $3 million before the 1993 campaign. After their 1993 electoral debacle, the Conservatives faced a debt of nearly $8 million. One of the significant factors in Kim Campbell's decision to resign was her expected inability to raise sufficient funds to pay off this debt and to raise additional contributions to help rebuild the party. Following their 1997 electoral loss, the Tories remained about $8 million in debt through the year 2000.

The major change in this traditional pattern of party finance came with the passage of the **Election Expenses Act (1974)**, which attempts both to regulate party fundraising activities and to provide public subsidies for election expenses. The adoption of such a measure has an interesting political lineage: the Liberal minority government between 1972 and 1974 needed the backing of the NDP caucus to stay in power and election finance reform was one payoff for the NDP's continuing support. Not surprisingly, the 1974 reforms greatly benefitted the NDP, putting the party on a more equal financial footing with the major parties. We would also suggest a further reason for the 1974 Election Expenses Act: campaign expenditures were increasing so rapidly that all of the parties feared their inability to raise adequate funds in future elections. As a result, the parties collectively turned to public funding and proceeded to raid the public treasury without greatly changing the existing practices of party finance.

One requirement of the Election Expenses Act is that the parties have to file an annual financial report with the chief electoral officer. The first reports, which covered the 1974–1975 fiscal year, indicated that it cost about $2 million to operate a national party in a nonelection year (*The Globe and Mail*, February 10, 1976 and February 11, 1976). By the beginning of the 1980s, the annual figure for party spending had reached $4 to $5 million; by the late 1980s, that figure stood somewhere between $6 and $10 million for each party to operate on a national level.

By the late 1990s, these figures had increased dramatically. Totals released by Elections Canada for the year 1999 showed the following pattern of party fundraising: Liberals, $15.4 million; Reform Party, $6.3 million; Tories, $5.6 million. Half of the donations to the Liberals came from corporations ($8.62 million), with $5.6 million contributed by 30 735 individuals. Most of the funds ($4.3 million) for the Reform Party came from 53 000 individuals. The Tories received $2.2 million from businesses and $2.8 million from 16 500 individual donors. In 1998, the Bloc Québécois raised $750 000, while the NDP raised over $5 million. Thus, in a nonelection year the five parties with representation in the House of Commons managed to raise about $33 million — a figure which would expand considerably during an election year.

In addition to requiring an annual report, the Election Expenses Act seeks to limit the amount of money that parties and candidates can spend, provides for the disclosure of the sources of party and candidate incomes, grants subsidies for candidate expenses and party media advertising, and establishes a tax credit for people contributing to party funds (Paltiel, 1975; see also Stanbury, 1996; 73–74). Although the Act was in effect as of August 1, 1974, the first election to which these provisions applied was the 1979 contest. The July 1974 election was conducted under the traditional pattern of party finance — an example of "once more for old times' sake" before the reform legislation became applicable.

While the 1974 Election Expenses Act represents a considerable improvement over past practices, its effectiveness is open to challenge (Paltiel, 1989; Stanbury, 1993; Jenson, 1995). For example, the limits on party and candidate expenditures were set relatively high, so that if the Act had applied to the 1974 election, no party would have exceeded them. Moreover, before the Act was applied the first time, these limits were raised in 1977 and the base year for indexing the spending ceilings was changed from 1974 to 1976, which added a possible $23 million to potential party and candidate costs. Since that change was made, an automatic escalator clause has also been inserted to handle the problem of inflation. In other words, limits which are set so high that no party approximates them in no way curtails party spending in campaigns. In fact, since the public now subsidizes these expenses, the costs of the campaigns have soared to unprecedented levels.

A second defect concerns the amount of individual contributions: any donation over $100 must be disclosed, but no limit is put on how much can be given. Thus, the financial dependence on small groups of financial backers has not been greatly undercut. Contrary to what might be expected, the largest single donations from an individual to a political party have, in recent years, gone to the NDP. Irene Dyck from Calgary contributed $216 000 in 1984 to the socialist cause, a decline from her 1983 largesse of $453 000. In 1992, her contribution was $502 200. However, in the summer of 1993, Bill Loewen of Winnipeg, a businessman and president of the National Party of Canada, made a financial contribution to his party that will likely be a record for many years to come: $4 million.

Third, the enforcement provisions for violations of this Act are weak — it is up to the public or the various parties to lay complaints with the chief electoral officer. With the "live and let live" attitude of the parties, few violations will be investigated. Given these limitations of the 1974 Election Expenses Act, the traditional pattern of party finance remains largely in place, with public funding grafted on. The parties successfully raided the public treasury without giving the public effective control over the area of party finance.

PARTY FUNCTIONS

Party finance is significant because it helps to determine whether a party will be successful in carrying out its electoral functions: money cannot buy electoral victory, but electoral victory is difficult to achieve without it, given the expensive nature of modern campaigns. Canadian parties are electoral organizations not only in the sense of aiming for victory, but also because they are important actors in organizing the electorate. For example, parties help to get the individual voters on the appropriate polling lists, provide the voters with information on the issues of the contest, and help to stimulate voter interest and participation. Parties are also the key structure in recruiting candidates for office, thus providing the electorate with someone to vote for or against, as the case may be.

Parties also help to structure the electorate by serving as political objects with which people can identify. These partisan attachments are some of the earliest linkages an individual develops with the political system. Although individual partisan attachments may vary, in the aggregate they help to structure the partisan coloration of the electorate; there is a reservoir of support for the parties, which they receive regardless of the issues or leaders in a particular campaign.

In addition to serving as objects of individual emotional ties, parties help to structure the electorate because the major socio-economic cleavages of society differentiate the group bases of partisan support in the Canadian polity. Historically, different regions, as well as religious, ethnic, and linguistic groups, have become linked with specific parties. The way these groups align themselves with the parties gives historical continuity to the party system. The most obvious example of this point was the usual preference, for most of the 20th century, of French Canadians for the Liberal party. Such group bases of party support reveal that the Canadian "party system is organized around the usual regional, religious, and social class oppositions to which is added a specific linguistic cleavage" (Laponce, 1972: 284). That basic pattern remains in place for the early years of the 21st century as well.

In addition to its electoral functions, the party that wins the election undertakes a number of what can be called governing functions. In the Canadian parliamentary system, the governing party is the key mechanism for achieving the fusion of the executive and legislative branches of government. Walter Bagehot's famous description of the mid-19th century British cabinet as "the hyphen which joins — the buckle which fastens — the executive to the legislative part of the state" is obsolete since the advent of parties. It is the party that lays the foundation for the fusion of executive and legislative powers, and only

Early Canadian political history includes a number of election riots, even some in which participants were killed. The 1988 election never reached that level of confrontation, but . . . enough noses were punched or heads gashed to push Canadian elections back into the category of a blood sport (Boyer, 1988: 72).

after the party does so can an institution such as the cabinet implement the fusion of powers on a day-to-day basis. In the modern era, cabinet government is predicated on party government; Walter Bagehot's buckle has a party label. Failure to recognize this relationship has often led to a denigration of the significant role parties play in the governing process.

Parties help to organize the government in several ways. It is the electoral success of a party, in terms of winning more seats than any other party in the legislature, which provides the group basis of government organization. Except in rare circumstances, the leader of the party with the largest block of legislative seats is asked by the formal executive to form a government. Thus, control of the legislature gives the party control of the executive.

While it is true that once a government has been formed the cabinet may dominate the party caucus and the legislature, the legislative base of the cabinet is often lost sight of. In a parliamentary system, the political executive retains office only as long as it has legislative support, and that support is provided by the party organization through the principle of party discipline. Only when a **free vote** is called (i.e., *when party discipline is relaxed and the legislative members decide on an individual basis how to vote*) does the group basis of legislative power momentarily recede.

An additional governing function of the successful party is that it directly provides the personnel to fill the cabinet portfolios. Except for the one experience of informal coalition government during the First World War (i.e., the formation of the Union Government in 1917), all subsequent federal cabinets have been formed by individuals from a single party. In this way, the party literally takes over physical control of the government by placing its members in positions of executive authority. Moreover, the cabinet, once formed, controls thousands of further job appointments to the various departments and agencies of government. Through the use of patronage appointments, the governing party oozes its way through the structure of government, linking unto itself the disparate realms of power and influence.

Patronage is the interstitial glue of politics, fusing together the otherwise inchoate elements of government. In 1994, for example, it was estimated that the new Chrétien government, through the Prime Minister's Office, would control about 2 700 appointments. Moreover, a longstanding practice in Canadian politics has been to appoint a political minister for each province who oversees and directs the filling of vacant federal governmental positions within his or her province. By such mechanisms, parties seek to organize the disparate structures of government into a working, if not necessarily a cohesive, organization.

> Patronage is the outward and visible sign of an inward and spiritual grace, and that is power (Benjamin Disraeli).

A final governing function of parties is to contribute to policy direction and leadership for the political system. In most cases the parties play only a small role in this process. Once a government is formed, the policy process is dominated by the cabinet and bureaucracy, with the party organizations relegated to a minor role. However, parties are an essential basis for the implementation of policy, because they provide the necessary support in the legislature for its passage. In addition, parties may play a policy-making role by providing the party platforms for election campaigns. Overall, however, the party organizations have a limited role in the policy process, serving instead as supporters of policy decided elsewhere.

While all parties have various electoral functions, it is only the winning party that directly participates in the several governing functions. However, the opposition parties are indirectly involved through their participation in the legislature, which can be used to attack, or to suggest changes in, government policy. Although no minor party has ever formed a government in Ottawa, they have often acquired limited governing functions because of the frequent occurrence of minority governments. As a result, minor parties have sometimes had a direct impact on government policy, which has enhanced their role as innovators in the Canadian party system.

BRITISH POLITICAL PARTIES

ORIGIN AND DEVELOPMENT

Historically, what were to become parties first emerged in the European context, with Britain leading in the development of these new political mechanisms. By the middle of the 17th century, factions, the forerunners of the modern party organizations, were present within the legislature. However, the importance of these new groups was not immediately appreciated, as evidenced by the labels Tories and Whigs, nicknames "given in a spirit of derision," since "Tories were bandits on the highways of Ireland" and the "Whigs a band of Scottish insurgents in 1648" (Duverger, 1972: 78).

By the middle of the 19th century, the Tories and Whigs had developed into the parties of the modern era. With the Reform Act of 1832, these parties expanded from their legislative birthplace to seek greater support among the electorate, in the process establishing party structures at the local level and cohesive groups within Parliament. Adopting the names Conservatives and Liberals, instead of Tories and Whigs, the two initial parties of parliamentary origin dominated the party system for three-quarters of a century.

However, parties of extra-parliamentary origin had a major impact on British politics in the 20th century. The most significant event was the formation of the Trade Union Congress in 1900, which aimed at establishing a mass-based, socialist, working-class party. Adopting the name Labour Party in 1906, this group gradually emerged as a challenger to the Liberals and Conservatives. By the 1920s, it had become the second largest party in Parliament, replacing the Liberals, with the first Labour government formed in 1923. With the long-term decline of the Liberal party from the 1930s to its demise in the 1980s, Britain has had primarily a two-party battle between the Conservatives and the Labourites.

In addition to the expansion of the Labour party in the early decades of the present century, Britain experienced the growth of a series of nationalist parties based on the regional and cultural concerns of Ireland, Scotland, and Wales. The most significant nationalist party was the Irish, which held 80 seats in the House of Commons from 1910 to 1918 and eventually succeeded in gaining Home Rule or independence for Ireland, although the Protestant areas remained within Britain as Northern Ireland. From the 1970s onward, nationalist parties in Scotland and Wales have continuously gained a small number of seats in the House of Commons. For example, in 1997 the Scottish Nationalist Party (SNP) won six seats, while the Welsh Nationalist Party (the Plaid Cymru) gained four. Because of devolution, such nationalist party representation may decline in future elections. In fact, in 2001 the Scottish Nationalist Party declined slightly to five seats, while the Welsh Nationalist Party retained its four seats in the House of Commons. In addition to these nationalist parties, other groups such as the Communist Party (in 1991 renamed the Democratic Left) and the National Front (a neofascist group) have competed in recent elections, but have had little electoral success and no great impact on the longstanding parties in British politics.

While the internally created parliamentary parties (Liberal and Conservative) and the externally created parties (especially the Labour party) show the characteristics of both the cadre and mass types of parties, British parties have some unique features as well, which reflect certain attributes of societal and governmental organization. Most important is the fact that Britain is both parliamentary and unitary, with the parties reflecting the resulting centralization of power. For example, while the Liberals and Conservatives may be traditional in organization, they are "rigid elitist parties" in operation (Duverger, 1972: 7). In comparison to Canadian parties, the British parties are more centralized in structure, recruitment, and leadership. British parties are also more ideological than their Canadian counterparts; they run on explicit platforms or party manifestoes that they are expected to implement if they acquire office.

The major parties in Britain (Labour and Conservative) can be classified as ideological in content and programmatic in function. One result of programmatic and centralized parties was the early development of unified groups within Parliament, with strict party discipline being seen historically as one of the hallmarks of British party organization. Although party discipline has been increasingly challenged in recent decades, the Labour and Conservative parties are still basically unified and cohesive organizations in Parliament (especially in the House of Commons), except on rare occasions — such as the vote on the Maastricht Bill in November 1993 (Baker, Gamble, and Ludlam, 1994; Kavanagh, 2000: 166–169).

In addition to their more ideological style and centralized structure, British parties are, historically, less regional than their Canadian analogues. Although there is a regional basis of party support even within England itself (Drucker, 1979: 217), the Labour and Conservative parties are more national in composition traditionally than either of the two major Canadian parties. However, up until the 1997 election there was an increasing North-South regionalization of the British party system, with Labour dominating Northern Britain and the Conservatives easily winning

> Party, not Parliament, determines the control of British government . . . . The slow pace of change and the very limited deviations from collective party discipline are a caution against the bark of dissent as evidence of a break in the bars of the iron cage of party government (Rose, 1983: 282, 298).

in Southern England and the Midlands (Bogdanor, 1992: 285; Coxall and Robins, 1994: 266). At least a temporary reversal of the party system's regionalization occurred in the 1997 and 2001 elections, given the Labour party's breakthrough in Southern England (Kavanagh, 2000: 122). The centralized nature of the political system has traditionally forced nationalist parties to compete for seats in the national legislature, although the impact of devolution may change that pattern in the years ahead. The result has been a greater impact of new parties in British politics in comparison to Canadian politics, although the appearance of such parties in Britain has been less frequent. In Canada, federalism has helped to contain nationalist sentiment, exemplified by the Parti Québécois and its power in provincial politics, while in Britain, nationalist emotion led to the granting of Home Rule for Ireland.

Although the characteristics of the major parties are reflective of the general origin and development of the cadre (Conservative) and mass (Labour) types, their evolution in the British milieu has produced these above unique features as well. The major British parties remain, however, electorally oriented parties: "the goal of the British political party is to win elections" (Finer, 1980: 167).

THE BRITISH PARTY SYSTEM

Since the Second World War, the party system in Britain can be described as competitive in nature; it is dominated by two major parties who are, however, challenged by both the growth of new parties and a corresponding decline in public support for themselves (Drucker, 1979; Coxall and Robins, 1994: 229–233; Dunleavy, 2000). The two major parties have controlled governmental office since 1945, with no other party participation and, unlike in Canada, election results have regularly produced majority governments (with the exception of the February 1974 contest). Moreover, during the 1960s and 1970s the two main parties alternated in office, although the Conservatives have more often been the government party since 1945. At the end of John Major's term in office (1992–1997), the Conservatives had governed for 35 years since 1945. Thus, the traditional turnover pattern ended in the 1980s, when Margaret Thatcher won three consecutive victories (1979, 1983, and 1987) with her successor, John Major, also winning in 1992. A party turnover pattern returned in 1997 with the Labour party's general election victory.

In addition to its competitive nature, the two-party battle is further characterized by the historical dominance of the Conservative party: from 1885 to 1945 the Conservatives "were in government for almost 75 percent of the time" (Gamble, 1979: 26). The normal governing party in British politics is the Conservative party, while in Canada in the modern era it has been the Liberals (1921–1984 and 1993 to about 2004). The continuing success of the Tory party has led one analyst to conclude that the British party system can no longer be classified as a competitive two-party system (King, 1993: 224). However, following their unexpected victory in 1992, the Tories faced a continuing series of scandals and policy failures which, combined with a new leader of the Labour party, left them badly trailing in the public opinion polls for four years. The 1997 election witnessed the return of the

Labour party to power, after 18 consecutive years in opposition. The Labour party's victory in the 2001 election was the first time that the party had ever won back-to-back majority election victories, raising the possibility of a period of Labour party dominance in the years ahead.

The cleavage basis of the British party system since the early 20th century has been the class division, which replaced the predominant religious cleavage of the 18th and 19th centuries. The transformation of the cleavage basis from religion to class had a significant influence on the party system: it destroyed the basis of Liberal party support and allowed for its replacement by the Labour party. In contrast, the continuing significance of the religious, ethnic, linguistic, and regional cleavages in Canada has been a key factor in the modern dominance of the Liberal party and has prevented the expansion of the federal NDP, which appeals to voters on the basis of class considerations.

PARTY LEADERSHIP SELECTION

The traditional British method of picking party leaders has been through selection by their respective party caucuses. If the leader of a British party resigned, members of the party caucus met and voted from among those candidates who had declared themselves for the office. Successive ballots were held until one candidate had achieved a majority. For example, in October 1980 James Callaghan resigned as leader of the Labour party. In November, British Labour MPs selected Michael Foot as their new leader after two ballots of the party caucus.

There are several advantages to choosing party leaders this way. First, only current members of Parliament have a chance of being selected, thus ensuring that the leader chosen will be well known, at least to the party. However, selection by the party caucus has a corresponding disadvantage of producing a closed process: it is practically impossible for an unknown to win, despite the example of Margaret Thatcher. The second advantage of the British practice is that a decision can be reached on a new leader in a matter of weeks (or days or hours, if necessary). For example, in 1975 the Conservatives announced their leadership call on January 24, with the first ballot held on February 4. Because no one had a majority on the first ballot, a second and final one was held a week later on February 11. Thus, the entire process of leadership selection took less than three weeks. In contrast, the Canadian pattern now takes at least several months to complete, and sometimes much longer. The third advantage of caucus selection is that the candidate so selected to lead the party in Parliament will have majority support in the caucus. By contrast, in Canada a leader selected by the convention method may find that he or she lacks the support of a significant section of the parliamentary caucus (and, in some cases, may not even have a seat in the legislature).

Although the caucus has traditionally been the key element in the party leadership selection process, there are some interesting historical differences between the British parties. Prior to 1965, the Conservatives did not take an explicit vote; instead, a leader "emerged" from the ranks of the party caucus. While this was a somewhat mysterious process even to party insiders, the system worked well until the 1960s, when an occasion arose where no clear-cut leader appeared from out of the ranks. As a result, reforms adopted in 1965 provided for an actual vote among Conservative members of Parliament.

The Conservative method of leadership selection, especially prior to the reforms of the 1960s, reinforced the leader's control: the "most striking feature of the Conservative party organization is the enormous power which appears to be concentrated in the hands of the leader" (McKenzie, 1967: 21). Initially, the British Conservative leader, once selected, was not required to face re-election by the party organization; however, beginning in 1975 re-election was required at the annual meeting. In December of 1989, Margaret Thatcher, for the first time in 14 years, faced an official challenge to her leadership. However, she easily defeated Sir Anthony Meyer by a vote of 314 to 33. By 1990, however, Thatcher did not fare so well: her ouster marked a major turning point in British politics — especially with respect to the power of leaders in the Tory party (Alderman and Carter, 1991; Wickham-Jones and Shell, 1991; Jesse, 1996).

Even though he retained office for the Tories in 1992, Prime Minister John Major was under attack from both within his party and within the electorate. Anticipating a leadership challenge, John Major announced on June 22, 1995 that he was resigning and then seeking re-election as Tory leader. Catching his opponents and leadership rivals off guard, Major won the ensuing first-ballot vote: Major, 218; John Redwood, 89; with 12 spoiled ballots and 10 abstentions (Alderman, 1996). Thus, John Major used a process designed to remove a leader (as had been done to Margaret Thatcher in 1990) as a weapon to force his continued leadership on a reluctant party. Following his 1997 election defeat, John Major resigned as party leader and was replaced by William Hague.

One month after their disastrous loss to the Labour party in the May 1997 general election, the Tory leadership selected William Hague in June of 1997 based on a vote of the party caucus in the House of Commons. To win, a candidate needed to have 83 votes (a simple majority) and a 15 percent lead over his or her nearest competitor on the first ballot. On later ballots, only a simple majority was required for victory. After the first-round vote on June 11, two of the five candidates withdrew. Since no candidate had a majority, a second round of voting was held on June 17 among the three remaining candidates — and again no majority was obtained. The third-place candidate withdrew before the third ballot, which was held on June 19. William Hague beat Kenneth Clarke by a vote of 92 to 70 on the final ballot.

Following the selection of William Hague as their new leader, the Tories then moved to change their method of leadership selection (Alderman, 1999). New rules adopted in 1998 include the following: (1) A vote of confidence on leadership can be held if 15 percent of Conservative MPs demand it; (2) If passed, the leader must resign and cannot re-offer; and (3) Depending on how many candidates run for the leadership, the caucus decides on the top two candidates who are then voted on in a national postal vote by all those who have been party members for at least six months. Thus, future Tory leaders will be selected, for the first time, by all members of the party organization (Webb, 2000: 163). Following his 2001 election defeat, Conservative leader William Hague announced on June 8, the day after the election, that he would step down as leader as soon as a successor had been chosen, thus necessitating the use of the new leadership process for the first time.

The selection and power of the Labour party leader reflects the extra-parliamentary origins of the party. In such a mass-based, ideological party, the party organization seeks to exert control not only over the party caucus, but over the party leader as well. At least in theory, both the leader and caucus are subject to the organization's directives and policy decisions: in fact, in most cases, the parliamentary leader and caucus have managed to retain a considerable measure of autonomy from the extra-parliamentary organization. One way of seeking to ensure control of the leaders has been the traditional practice of making them stand for annual re-election by the party organization, although in practice they are almost never opposed. The result has been to place Labour leaders in a less dominant position within the party hierarchy than their Conservative counterparts, particularly when the Labour party is in opposition. Although subject to outside advice and interference, if not control, by the extra-parliamentary organization, the party leader, prior to the 1980s, was always chosen by the caucus.

The longstanding battle between the parliamentary and extra-parliamentary wings of the Labour party finally became so intense in the fall of 1980 as to provoke a change in the party's leadership selection process (Punnett, 1990). The basic method of leadership selection, beginning in 1981, is based on a widening of the election process to include not only the party caucus but the trade unions and constituency parties as well. An electoral college type of mechanism was adopted in January 1981, which gave the party caucus 30 percent of the vote, the constituency associations 30 percent, and the trade unions 40 percent. This new pattern was designed to give the extra-parliamentary wing of the party, which was dominated by the trade unions and the more leftist elements, control of the leadership selection process in the Labour party. The first use of the new electoral college mechanism by the Labour party to choose a new leader occurred in 1983, when Neil Kinnock was selected to replace Michael Foot after the Labour party's disastrous electoral defeat in the general election (Drucker, 1984; Mitchell, 1984). Similarly, after Labour's bitter defeat in the 1992 election, Neil Kinnock resigned and was replaced by John Smith, using the electoral college mechanism once again (Alderman and Carter, 1993).

Unfortunately for the Labour party, John Smith died unexpectedly in 1994, necessitating another leadership battle (Alderman and Carter, 1995). The electoral college mechanism was utilized again, but with one slight modification, which had been adopted in 1993: the three key elements of the Labour party (caucus, constituencies, and trade unions) would all be given one-third of the total vote. Moderate Tony Blair won on the first ballot, gaining majority support in all three sections of the electoral college. The selection of Tony Blair as leader consolidated the position of the Labour party as a centrist party for the 1997 general election. Given Tony Blair's large consecutive majority election victories in 1997 and 2001, he is now in a more secure position with his party than any previous Labour party leader.

While party leadership mechanisms in Britain's other parties vary somewhat from those of the Labour and Tory parties, by the start of the new century the traditional pattern of leadership selection by a party's caucus had been replaced by a more democratized process in both the Labour and Tory parties.

PARTY SYSTEM DEVELOPMENTS

The 1981 change in the process of selecting the Labour party leader is the most important political development in the British party system since the formation of the Labour party in 1900, for it has had profound effects on the competitive party battle. First, the British Labour party splintered over this issue, with a number of key members and former ministers leaving the party to found a new, centre-based Social Democratic Party (SDP). Second, this new party, by aiming at the centre of the political spectrum, was seeking to capitalize on the increasing polarization of the old-line parties in the late 1970s and early 1980s, as the Labour party moved left and the Conservative party moved right. Third, the new party rekindled life into the Liberal party, which had had little influence in the party system for over 50 years.

The initial success of the SDP in 1981 was not continued in 1982 and 1983. Disputes within the Alliance (SDP and Liberals), as well as the war in the Falklands, undercut the party's popularity in 1982. In the 1983 election, although the Alliance won 26 percent of the vote and 23 seats, the SDP won only 6 seats and the party now ranked fifth in the House of Commons (at dissolution it was third in terms of seats). By 1985, the SDP was showing signs of renewed popularity in the public opinion polls, as the Conservative party's strength declined. However, the 1987 election was even more of a disaster than the 1983 contest for the SDP: while the Alliance won 23 percent of the vote and 22 seats, the SDP, as its share of these totals, gained only 5 seats (17 for the Liberals). Over the next few years, the Alliance faced leadership disputes, name changes, declining popular support, and internal policy disagreements.

By 1990, most of the Alliance members of the 1980s had merged to form a party first called the Social and Liberal Democrats (SLD), then just simply the Liberal Democrats (October 1989). A small rump group led by David Owen still retained the SDP name. Thus, the challenge mounted by the Alliance in the mid-1980s to the two dominant parties failed; by the early 1990s, the various remnants of the Alliance no longer appeared to be viable alternatives for most of the electorate. Moreover, the Labour party under Neil Kinnock had moved back toward the centre of the political spectrum by the early 1990s, thus positioning itself to be the main opposition party for the next general election. With the replacement of Margaret Thatcher by John Major, the Tories had also moved toward the political centre in anticipation of the next electoral battle.

These changes in the Labour and Conservative parties and their positioning in the political spectrum, as well as the continuing internal problems for the Liberal Democrats, resulted in a significant decline in the relevance of the "centre" in British politics in the 1990s. For example, while the Liberal Democrats won nearly 18 percent of the popular vote in the 1992 election, they only gained 20 seats (out of 651) in the House of Commons. Following the death of its leader, John Smith, in 1994, the Labour party continued to moderate its ideology and platform, exemplified by the choice of Tony Blair as its new leader (Kavanagh, 1996). Thus, in the 1997 election the popular vote for the Liberal Democrats continued to decline (to 17 percent), even though they gained more seats (46) than in 1992 (20).

The Labour party's return to power in the 1997 general election, combined with the future effects of devolution on the nationalist parties, appears to have ended the "centrist" challenge to the dominance of the Labour and Conservative parties. As long as both major parties continue to battle for the moderate centre of the political spectrum, it seems unlikely that new parties and new challengers will arise to confront them (Kavanagh, 2000: 169–171; Dunleavy, 2000: 146–150). As a result, in the 2001 election, while the Liberal Democrats gained 6 seats (going from 46 to 52), their popular support remained roughly what it had been in 1997 and 1992.

> In fact, the most striking feature of those who have broken away from the Liberal and Labour parties to form new parties is not their treachery but their failure. The overwhelming message of their experience is the strength of the adversarial two-party system (Bradley, 1981: 21).

Since the rise of the class alignment in the 20th century, the key factor in the social bases of party support in Britain is the class cleavage, with the middle and upper classes supporting the Conservatives and the working class backing the Labour party. However, both major parties appeal to members of all social classes. Moreover, in recent decades white-collar workers have given significant support to the Labour party. Labour's substantial victories in 1997 and 2001 were due, in part, to its increased support among the growing ranks of the middle class, while its appeal to working class voters was declining (Kavanagh, 2000: 127–129). The basic class patterns of party support in Britain are not evident, however, with respect to the nationalist parties, which appeal to cultural and regional loyalties instead.

PARTY FINANCE

Patterns of party finance show predictable characteristics in Britain. The Conservative party is dependent on the cadre type of party finance, with individual and business contributions from relatively few donors (Mitchell and Bretting, 1993; Fisher, 1994a). The party has opposed public subsidies, has been successful in constituency level finance and, as a result, clearly outspends the Labour party both between and during election contests (McKenzie, 1967: 653–659; Finer, 1980: 105–110). The Labour party was traditionally heavily dependent on trade union financial backing, which often accounted for 80 percent of party funds (Birch, 1983: 109; Fisher, 1992: 111–123), but such support declined to about 50 percent by the late 1990s (Coxall and Robins, 1994: 250) and to just 40 percent in the 1997 election (Webb, 2000: 164). With individual party membership declining and with the local constituency associations unable to raise adequate revenue, the Labour party favoured extension of the public financing of parties and election campaigns in recent decades, but has not done so since returning to power in 1997.

As in other liberal democracies, party fundraising has often been associated with party scandals and political corruption in Britain. For example, the Tories in the 1990s faced numerous allegations in this area, particularly in light of the "sleaze factor" in the 1997 election. Although out of power for 18 years and elected with a campaign promise to reform party finance (especially the use of large corporate donations for fundraising), the new Labour government under Tory Blair, within months of gaining power, faced a major scandal in this area. Abandoning a key election pledge, the Labour party, although at first denying it, admitted in November of 1997 that it had accepted a political donation of $2.4 million from Formula One racing, after it had exempted that group from a ban on tobacco advertising. Moreover, in 2000 the Labour party had to admit that it had accepted large donations from several wealthy individuals: $3 million each was received from Lord Sainsbury, Paul Hamlyn, and Christopher Ondaatje. The latter individual, a former Canadian billionaire businessman, brother of novelist Michael Ondaatje, and former Tory supporter was revealed to be a key Labour fundraiser in January 2001.

While local campaign costs have been limited since 1948, there is no limit on the amount spent by the national parties (Punnett, 1980: 57). A promise by the Labour party in 1999 to limit national campaign expenses to £20 million (based on 1998 prices) has not yet been implemented. Public subsidies cover such items as free TV party broadcasts, but the parties still need considerable additional funds to support the national party advertising campaign during an election. In a nonelection year in the early 1980s, total national party income and costs ran between £2 and £3 million. That figure had skyrocketed in the following two decades, so that in 1997, for example, the two major parties each spent between £26 and £28 million. In contrast to the Canadian pattern, the major donors to the Labour and Conservative causes do not contribute to both parties, a reflection, perhaps, of the more ideological and class-based party system in Britain (Fisher, 1994b).

While British parties have developed certain unique features of structure, style, and interaction, we should not lose sight of the fact that British parties, like their counterparts in other competitive polities, continue to be significant governing mechanisms.

AMERICAN POLITICAL PARTIES

ORIGIN AND DEVELOPMENT

Reflective of the political culture's suspicion of power and its concentration is the traditional American attitude toward political parties: at best, parties are viewed in an ambivalent manner; at worst, they are perceived as downright detrimental to democracy. In his famous Farewell Address, George Washington sought to alert the American public to "the baneful effects of the Spirit of Party," and even Thomas Jefferson (quoted in Hofstadter, 1972: 2, 123), who was later instrumental in the development of the longest-lasting political party in history — the Democratic party — remarked that "If I could not go to heaven but with a party, I would not go there at all." However, this aversion to parties was overcome, as in other countries, due to practical considerations, primarily the need to govern in a system of fragmented power.

The initial parties were of legislative origin, created in the early years of the 19th century. However, it was not until the era of Jacksonian democracy in the 1830s that the parties emerged as necessary ingredients of the governing process. The 19th century origin of the American parties is crucial in understanding their structure, organization, and attributes.

American parties are the pre-eminent examples of the cadre type of political party. The goal of electoral victory has produced a fundamental attribute of American parties — they are traditionally nonideological, especially in comparison with European parties. Ideological specificity repels rather than attracts voters, thereby typically leading to similar policy views for both the Republican and Democratic parties on most major issues and to the charge that the two parties are interchangeable in office. Below the level of rhetoric, not much distinguished Al Gore from George W. Bush in the 2000 presidential election on matters of public policy.

When a party becomes ideologically distinct from the main trends of public opinion, as the Republicans did with Barry Goldwater in 1964 and the Democrats achieved with George McGovern in 1972, a massive electoral defeat occurs. Although Ronald Reagan may have begun and sustained his political career by his image as a "man of the right," his years as governor of California and his 1980 and 1984 presidential election victories demonstrated his ability to moderate his views and to move to the centre of the political spectrum in the search for electoral victory. Paradoxically, then incumbent President George Bush, whose entire career was seen as one of a centrist and moderate politician, allowed himself to be portrayed as a "man of the right" at the 1992 Republican national convention. This image was a major factor in his defeat in the 1992 presidential election against the "moderate" Democratic ticket of Bill Clinton and Al Gore. Moreover, in 1996 the incumbent Democrats campaigned more against the right-wing policies of Speaker of the House Newt Gingrich than they did against the more moderate positions of their actual competitor, Republican nominee Bob Dole — with similar results. In the 2000 presidential race, the Republicans moved back toward the centre of the political spectrum when they nominated Texas Governor George W. Bush — a self-described "compassionate conservative" — as their presidential nominee. The centrist nature of American parties means that they appeal to a wide social and economic base; the parties are heterogeneous in makeup, not class-based. Party membership is not clearly defined; membership cards, annual dues, and agreement with a party's policy positions are basically unknown in the American context.

In terms of structure, the parties are extremely decentralized and power resides at the state and local levels. National party coalitions are created around the presidential contest every four years — between such events, the parties survive on a local base. The decentralization of power is evident in terms of party finance, membership, and recruitment. This dispersal of power is a reflection of several of the key principles of the American system of government, namely federalism and the separation of powers. The decentralized pattern was greatly strengthened in the 20th century by the adoption of the primary method of candidate selection, which countered the centralizing or nationalizing trends with respect to some aspects of American politics. If anything, the parties at the start of the 21st century are more decentralized now than they have ever been.

Within the parties, the decentralization of power is reflected in the lack of strong party cohesion both inside and outside of the legislature. While party members share a common label, they rarely share a common purpose. American parties are highly factionalized, with candidates forming their own organizations in their bids for elective office (Wattenberg, 1994). If successful, candidates thus owe little loyalty to the party organization but considerable loyalty to the group that helped them to win power. Candidate-centred groups have been strengthened by the use of the primary method of nomination for office, where the party can no longer even control who runs under its party label.

The effects of the decentralized pattern are clearly evident in the legislature, where party discipline is weak, particularly in any comparison with a parliamentary system. Party members, with almost total immunity from retribution from their party leaders, can vote as they wish, for the simple reason that the party leadership has few political resources to turn against them. Party unity is often dependent on the issue being considered.

> . . . parties are the custodians of our political standards. They bring coherence and continuity to our democratic practices. Strong rival parties watch each other, and the public interest is safer. Weak parties invite chaos (Theodore Sorenson, former aide to President John F. Kennedy, February 1987).

Each party contains both liberal and conservative factions, which may desert their party leadership on specific matters of public policy. Majorities are often forged across, rather than within, party lines. For example, Republican President Ronald Reagan, despite the fact that the House of Representatives had a solid Democratic majority, was able to win large cuts in government programs in his first few months in office in 1981 by aligning Republicans and conservative Democrats together in a working majority. This cross-party alliance was the key to Ronald Reagan's success with Congress during both terms of his presidency. Even though Bill Clinton had Democratic majorities in both Houses upon assuming the presidency in 1993, initial legislative successes depended on his ability to forge such cross-party legislative alliances on issues like NAFTA. Following the Republican legislative victories in both 1994 and 1996 (i.e., Republican majorities in both the House of Representatives and the Senate) and the bitter battle over the impeachment of President Clinton in 1999, such cross-party alliances were an endangered species during Clinton's second term of office (1997–2001). The result of the 2000 elections, which produced a narrow victory for the Republicans in the House of Representatives and an equal split of 50/50 for the two parties in the Senate (at least until Republican Senator James Jeffords' defection in May of 2001), means that the new president, George W. Bush, will have to seek cross-party alliances for most of his major legislative proposals.

THE AMERICAN PARTY SYSTEM

The two long-dominant major American parties can be described as cadre parties that are election-oriented, non-ideological, heterogeneous in social composition, and decentralized, with weak party unity. These attributes are reflected in, and conditioned by, the nature of the party system. The American party network is competitive, dominated by the two major parties, and highly discriminatory against new or minor parties.

The electoral battle between Democrats and Republicans, however, has not been, from an historical point of view, an equal battle. One party, as in Britain and Canada, has tended to dominate for long periods: the Republicans from the time of the Civil War to the 1920s and the Democrats from the 1930s to the 1960s, with the 1970s showing a more balanced competitive pattern, at least in presidential elections. If anything, however, the Republicans have emerged as the dominant party in presidential elections, given their victories in 1980, 1984, 1988, and 2000. The Democratic victories in the 1992 and 1996 presidential elections were the first consecutive wins by the Democratic party in half a century.

The two-party competition focusses on control of the centre of the political spectrum. However, unlike the Canadian system, where the centre is regularly occupied by one party, the centre of the political spectrum in American politics is up for grabs — either party may occupy it, and both usually try to do so. The battle for the political centre is a key reason why the Democrats and Republicans are non-ideological and socially diverse parties.

One of the most often described characteristics of the American party system is that it is a two-party system, dominated by the Republicans and Democrats since the middle of the 19th century. However, it is not true to say that only two parties exist — many parties officially compete, for example, in a presidential election. What is significant is that these other parties, unlike that of Ross Perot's Reform Party in 1992 and 1996, rarely affect the pattern of competition between the two major parties, a fact exemplified by the failure of John Anderson's National Unity Ticket in 1980, which received only 7 percent of the popular vote and no delegates in the electoral college. Despite receiving only 3 percent of the national vote and no electoral college votes, Ralph Nader's Green Party in 2000 did have a significant impact on the party system by taking away enough liberal votes from the Democratic ticket to give the Republican candidate a victory. New parties or minor parties are regularly formed, but their success is usually limited (Abramson et al., 1995).

Minor parties usually emerge around a specific issue or are based on a particular ideology, thereby limiting their appeal to the majority of the American electorate. If such a party begins to show signs of electoral success, its programs and leaders may be co-opted by one of the major parties, whose non-ideological stance allows for considerable flexibility and pragmatism in such matters. Moreover, the decentralized structure and weak cohesion of the major parties often entices new groups to work within one of the major parties, instead of forming a new party (e.g., Goldwater within the Republican party in 1964; McGovern within the Democratic party in 1972). The most successful new groups or movements in American politics have been those that have worked within the existing parties, a conclusion unlikely to be changed by the possible future success of Ralph Nader's Green Party.

In addition, the rules of the electoral system are designed to discourage minor parties (Lewis-Beck and Squire, 1995). New parties, for example, find it difficult to get their names on the ballot: in the 1968 presidential race, "George Wallace had a staff of twenty-five lawyers traveling from state to state researching election laws, filing suits, and getting petition signatures to meet local requirements" (Huckshorn, 1980: 70). Moreover, the plurality electoral formula used in the United States makes it difficult for a minor party to win legislative seats even when it wins a sizable share of the popular vote. For these reasons, since the Civil War minor parties have rarely disturbed the two-party battle between Republicans and Democrats. Even Ross Perot in 1992, with 19 percent of the popular vote, won no votes in the electoral college!

Why do minor parties develop in the first place and what accounts for their relative electoral success in a system such as the Canadian and their failure in others like the American? The reason for new parties in both systems is the same — social and economic diversity. The way these new groups operate varies because of the differing institutional contexts in Canada and the United States. It is wrong to assume that Canada has produced more minor parties than the United States — on a numerical basis it has not. However, Canada has produced more minor parties that have affected the pattern of competition in the party system. The basic explanation for this is that diversity, combined with federal and parliamentary principles and party discipline, encourages the formation of new parties. In contrast, the decentralized parties and the various election laws that discriminate against new groups in the American system make it likely that they will work within one of the existing party organizations. In Canada, a George McGovern or a Barry Goldwater would have formed a new political party; in the United States, they simply seized control of the existing party structures.

> There is . . . one other possible explanation for the chronic failure of the third-party argument: maybe there is something wrong with the idea itself. Maybe it never gets to first base, not because the American voter is a hopeless dullard, but simply because he rejects instinctively a notion which doesn't make sense in terms of his own experience (Fischer, 1948: 28).

SELECTING PARTY LEADERS

Given the characteristics of the major American parties and the party system, the essential aim in selecting party leaders is to win elections. The American parties have been in the forefront of developing new mechanisms of leadership selection, although it is open to question whether these new techniques have improved the quality of the nominees for political office. The current system of leadership selection is an amalgam of historical practice, containing elements of caucus, convention, and primary techniques. The most significant aspect of the change from one method to the next has been the desire to give the public, rather than the party bosses, control of the nomination and leadership selection process. In contrast to the Canadian system of party members meeting in a national party leadership convention, or the traditional British pattern of the parliamentary caucus casting a ballot, current American practice aims at providing an opportunity for involving the mass public in choosing party leaders.

American party leaders are selected through a two-stage process: first, delegates are chosen to attend a national party convention; and second, the national party convention selects the party leader. Unfortunately, what seems straightforward at first glance is exceedingly complex, since each of the 50 states sets its own rules for delegate selection, procedures which may change (and they usually do) from one election to the next.

The first stage of leadership selection uses two basic approaches: the primary and caucus techniques. The most important of the two methods of delegate selection is the presidential primary, which in 2000 picked about 90 percent of the delegates to the national conventions and was used by about 40 states. A **presidential primary** is an election *among party members to choose their delegates to the national convention*, which in turn selects the party's presidential candidate. Those candidates seeking their party's nomination enter a number of that party's presidential primaries. Generally, if a candidate wins 30 percent of the vote in a primary, he or she will receive approximately 30 percent of that state's delegates to the national convention. However, some states in their Republican primaries still used a version of the winner-take-all system during the 2000 nomination process. By winning significant strength in the primaries, a candidate can win the party's nomination for president.

Presidential primaries are held between February and June in an election year. These primaries have become the crucial component in the party leadership contest, since a candidate can win enough delegates to be guaranteed a first-ballot nomination victory at the leadership convention. Moreover, the delegate-selection process in the past several decades has become increasingly **frontloaded**; that is, *more and more states are holding their presidential primaries as early as possible (i.e., in February and March of an election year)*. Thus, in 2000 both the Democratic and Republican nominees had "won" their races by mid-March, even though their respective conventions were five months away. In recent decades, all party leaders have won first-ballot convention victories; in other words, the real decision-making power in winning party leadership is the delegate selection process, with the convention simply ratifying the choice already made.

The second method of delegate selection to the national convention is the caucus technique. The term caucus, as used in the American presidential system of delegate selection, is not the same as a caucus in a parliamentary system. In Britain and Canada, a party caucus means the group of party members in the legislature. In the American delegate selection process, **caucus** means *a meeting of party members from the mass public who decide on their delegates to the national convention*. These caucus meetings begin at the local or precinct level and work their way up through district, county, and statewide conventions. About 10 states used this procedure in the 2000 presidential race to pick about 10 percent of the total delegates. While it allows for public participation, the caucus method of delegate selection usually involves far fewer rank-and-file party members than does the primary technique.

Several aspects of the American delegate selection process need to be emphasized: first, at the mass level, party members are given the right to participate in the selection of the party leader in both the primary and caucus states; and second, at the elite level, anyone has the right to run for the leadership of the party. Both these characteristics emphasize the extent to which the political party, as an organization, has lost control of the nomination process: it controls neither who participates in the delegate selection mechanisms nor who can run for the leadership of the party. Such a pattern of selection might be characterized as "garage-sale politics": one never knows in advance who will show up to offer items for sale or to purchase the goods presented. The only thing that is definite is that few Van Gogh's will ever be found among the dusty artifacts of life, or, as one writer phrased it, "the primary-dominated system of nomination is an unqualified disaster" (McWilliams, 1981: 170).

Following the primaries and caucuses, each party usually holds its national convention during the summer months of July or August. The conventions previously held centre stage in the selection of party leaders; the satirist H.L. Mencken once said that there is "nothing quite as entertaining as a hanging or a good convention." In recent decades, there is nothing quite as boring as a national convention, because it has lost the effective power of choice — it merely ratifies the winner determined by the primaries and caucuses. Only if the primaries and caucuses fail to coalesce behind a single candidate would the national convention reacquire effective decision-making power.

The operating rules of an American national convention differ significantly from those utilized in the Canadian national party leadership conventions. First, balloting is open, not secret, and done by states, rather than by individuals. Until the reforms of the 1970s, this rule meant that large blocs of votes could be controlled by party leaders and that deals between leaders and state delegations could be arranged because *a state voted as a group in favour of one or the other candidates*, a procedure known as the **unit rule**. Although the unit rule no longer applies, voting is still done on a state-by-state basis, with delegates openly declaring their support for one of the nominees. Second, such a voting procedure is cumbersome, with the interval between ballots being at least several hours, if not longer. Third, there is no rule for the elimination of candidates between ballots, so that a nominee can stay in the race until someone receives a majority vote. The result, historically, has been long conventions, with the 1924 Democratic meeting holding 103 ballots. These rules of procedure make an American convention very different from a Canadian national party leadership convention.

Although we have assumed that a party's presidential nominee is the party's leader, in nonpresidential election years, especially for the party that loses the presidential race, there is no set way of deciding the question of leadership. For example, after the Republican defeat in the 1996 presidential contest, who was the leader of the national Republican party? Republicans would likely have agreed on only one thing — that it was not Bob Dole. Given the closeness of the 2000 election, defeated Democratic candidate Al Gore has at least a legitimate claim to be his party's leader. However, even in this current case, the decentralized structure and fragmented power of the American parties means that the party's legislative leaders in the Senate or House of Representatives, as well as the various leaders in state and national politics (i.e., Senator Hillary Clinton), also have a legitimate claim on that role.

The dominance of the Republican and Democratic parties has traditionally been reflected in the extent of partisan attachments: electors overwhelmingly identify with the two main parties. A chief characteristic of partisan loyalties in the United States is their public nature — most people are not reluctant to declare which party they support. Moreover, the strength of these partisan ties to the two main parties has often been cited as one important reason why minor parties have had little success at the polls; if people already have an emotional commitment to either the Republicans or Democrats, then it is difficult for a new party to gain adherents. The extent of partisan attachments gives each of the major parties a pool to draw on in any particular election. While appealing to the wider electorate, the Republicans and Democrats have traditional groups that support them (Burns et al., 2000: 184–198). Each party seeks to put together a large enough coalition of such groups to win power: the "supporters of the two American political parties have been distinguished from each other by economic, religious, and national-ethnic differences" (Nie, Uerba, and Petrocik, 1979: 213).

The social bases of party support in recent decades can be summarized as follows (Dye, 1997: 224–228; Hrebenar, Burbank, and Benedict, 1999: 93–122). First, the higher one's position in the social class hierarchy, the more likely one is to be a Republican. Second, with respect to religion, Jews are more Democratic than Catholics, who in turn are more Democratic than Protestants. Third, minority groups, particularly racial and the more recent immigrant groups, show a marked proclivity to support the Democratic party. Fourth, regional differences, noticeably the South as a bastion of Democratic strength, and Republican dominance in the Midwest and Northeast, have declined in recent years. Thus, the American parties, while socially diverse, do not appeal equally to all major groups in the polity. Although the majority Democratic coalition has been severely weakened during the past two decades, at the same time the Republican party has not been able to transform discontent with the Democrats into majority party status for itself, even when a Republican wins the presidency. Instead, more and more Americans are declaring themselves to be Independents. By the 2000 presidential election, partisanship of the electorate was composed as follows: Democrats, 38 percent; Republicans, 27 percent; and Independents, 35 percent (Edwards, Wattenburg, and Lineberry, 2000: 248).

PARTY FINANCE

As the pre-eminent cadre parties, the Republicans and Democrats have long depended on corporate backing and large individual contributions. As in other systems, the area of party finance has been regularly associated with major political scandals, with the Watergate scandal of the 1970s being only one major example from among many. Party finance is particularly important in American politics because of the large number of officials selected through the election process. With over 500 000 people chosen for government service in a presidential election year, the amount of money spent by the parties and candidates quickly accumulates into the hundreds of millions of dollars. For example, the initial estimate for all campaign spending in the 2000 election races totalled over $3 billion, with over half a billion dollars being spent on the presidential campaign alone.

Such expenditures have rapidly escalated, given the heavy emphasis on television advertising in both presidential and congressional elections. For example, to be considered a serious contender for the Republican presidential nomination in 1996 it was necessary to raise $20 million before the first presidential primary was even held in February (Dye, 1997: 261). In the 2000 presidential race, George W. Bush held the record for fundraising in one day (April 26, 2000) when he raised $21.3 million for the Republican National Committee. That record was soon broken by President Bill Clinton in the biggest fundraiser of all time: $26.5 million on May 24, 2000. The most expensive single contest for Congress in the 1990s took place in the California Senate race in 1994: the losing candidate, Republican Michael Huffington, spent $28 million, while the winner, Democrat Dianne Feinstein, spent $12 million. Even that outlandish total was surpassed in the 2000 Senate race in New Jersey, when an estimated $60 million was spent by the Democratic candidate ($55 million) and his Republican opponent ($5 million). Running for the House of Representatives now costs approximately half a million dollars per candidate in each constituency, and often much more in the larger states and in competitive races.

The cost of campaigns, along with the Watergate scandal, produced a climate of reform in the United States in the early 1970s. Although regulation of campaign donations had been on the books since the 1920s, such laws were regularly ignored or violated, given their very weak enforcement provisions. The reforms of the 1970s put more effective limits on contributions and spending for both individual candidates and parties. In a major departure from past practice, the United States in 1974 adopted provisions (the Federal Election Campaign Act) for the public financing of presidential election campaigns. A party's presidential nominee who accepts public money is prevented from obtaining private donations for general election expenses. However, allegations of improper and possibly illegal campaign fundraising by the Democratic party during the 1996 presidential election, including letting contributors sleep in the Lincoln bedroom in the White House, put campaign finance reform back onto the American political agenda in 1997. As a result, Republican Senator John McCain of Arizona and Democratic Senator Russell Feingold of Wisconsin co sponsored a campaign finance reform bill (the McCain-Feingold Bill), which was not passed before the 2000 presidential contest. However, Senator McCain's challenge to George W. Bush in the Republican primaries centred on this issue and consequently both the Republicans and Democrats, after the 2000 race was over, claimed that they would back campaign finance reform legislation in the new legislative session in 2001. A further impetus for such reform came to light after Bill Clinton left office. In the waning hours of his presidency, President Clinton pardoned Marc Rich, who was facing a possible 325 years in jail on charges of tax fraud, racketeering, and tax evasion. Rich's lawyer, a former White House counsel, had lobbied for the pardon and, interestingly, Rich's former wife had contributed over $1 million to the Democratic party in recent years.

A second major area for reform concerns the development of **political action committees**, or PACs for short. PACs may be formed by any group to support a particular cause, candidate, or party. By the 1980s, PACs had become the major source of political funding in the American system. Political contributions by PACs to congressional candidates mushroomed from about $8 million in 1971 to over $200 million in 1998. PAC money favours incumbents over challengers and increasingly gives corporate and business interests influence in the electoral process. Calls for limiting PAC contributions, such as President Clinton's 1995 State of the Union Address, have been ignored by the Republican-controlled Congress. Limits on PACs are unlikely to be adopted in the immediate future in the American system.

The above characteristics of the American parties and the American party system thus reflect certain unique patterns of origin, development, and operation. However, in broad comparisons with other political systems, the American parties show basic similarities with their counterparts in Canada and Britain, the most important attribute being the competitive nature of these three party systems.

PARTIES AND POLITICAL OPPOSITION

Political parties can perform any number of roles or functions in the political process (King, 1969; Meisel, 1996; Von Beyme, 1996). In our consideration of parties in Canada, Britain, and the United States, we have focussed on two basic tasks of the party organizations, which we designated as their electoral and governing functions. The origin, development, and characteristics of the individual parties and party systems in each country have resulted in different techniques in the performance of these functions. However, a third task of parties in democratic systems is to provide *the essential structural means to oppose the government of the day*, that is, an **opposition function**.

For those who have grown up in a democratic system, the acceptance of the idea of a political opposition institutionalized through the role of competitive parties appears normal. Historically, however, and even for the vast majority of current political systems, this is not the case. While political opposition functions may be carried out by various political mechanisms, such as an independent judiciary, interest groups, or a free press, the primary organizational agent of political opposition is the political party (Ionescu and de Madariaga, 1972: 52–62).

The distinguishing characteristic between competitive party systems (Canada, Britain, and the United States) and a party-state system (China, the former Soviet Union) turns on the role of parties: in the first instance, organized opposition challenges for power; in the second, it does not. While opposition exists in all systems, in a party-state pattern it is unorganized and takes place in private within or through the single party organization; in a competitive party system, opposition is organized and occurs in public, primarily through the battle for office. Elections by themselves do not make a system democratic, but elections with organized parties competing for power add immeasurably to such a result. Given the allure of the democratic ideal in the past century, party-states nominate candidates for office and

> The two-party system of modern parliaments uses the psychological structure of opposing armies (Canetti, 1966: 188).

hold elections — events which in no way change their classification as totalitarian systems.

Political opposition is not only significant in that it provides for a competitive struggle for power, but also because it is one way of handling the conflict that lies at the basis of politics: "political opposition . . . is the most advanced and institutionalized form of political conflict" (Ionescu and de Madariaga, 1972: 16). Allowing people and groups to contest for power through legitimate channels, such as the party system, decreases the likelihood that violence will be resorted to. Conversely, when the opposition feels that it cannot fairly contest for power through the party system, then violence and coercion may become the reciprocal tools of opposing and governing, as reflected in the events leading to the 1970 October Crisis in Canada. Providing organized political opposition continues to be an important current and future function of the political parties in the democratic systems of Canada, Britain, and the United States.

Predicting the future of political institutions, such as political parties, is very risky. However, the past can at least tell us that some events are more likely to occur in the future than others. An historical appreciation of the origins and functions of political parties can not only help us to understand their present status, but can keep us from denigrating the present because of our ignorance of the past. In recent years, a common criticism of parties in democratic systems is that they are failing to perform adequately (Landes, 1984: 4). Implicit in most such assessments is the view that previously parties were more effective and more efficient in carrying out their electoral and governing functions (Lipow and Seyd, 1996). Critics have gone so far as to suggest the possible demise of parties altogether (and they sometimes seem more than pleased by such a prospect)!

Such views do not give proper credit to either the historical or the contemporary contributions of political parties to the political process. Historically, parties, while not the sole creators, contributed strongly to the development of the democratic polity. Currently, the nomination of candidates, the selection of leaders, the organizing of election campaigns, the raising of party funds and, for the successful party, the burdens and rewards of office are no small feat. In fact, it would be difficult to conceive how other institutions might carry out these functions if the parties were to disappear (Dalton, 1996: 261–284). The disparagement of parties indicates, perhaps, that we expect too much of them, on the basis of a false analogy that in the past they somehow performed better. Reformers are perpetually upset with the nature of the democratic parties.

Concern with the supposedly declining role of parties in democratic systems is evident in Canada, Britain, and the United States. Concomitant with such negative views are a number of more specific party-related developments, including a decline in the trust and confidence the public has in political institutions in general and parties in particular, and an erosion of partisan attachments for the major parties and a growth in support for either new parties or for being independent from partisan ties. However, such developments need not herald the end of the significant role of political parties in democratic systems (Ware, 1995). What they do portend are some possible future changes in the way the parties perform their traditional electoral, governing, and opposition functions.

SUMMARY

1. Political parties are a way of giving the mass of people control over their lead-
    ers in democratic systems and a means of elite control over the masses in to-
    talitarian systems. Parties may be classified according to their origin (internally
    versus externally created parties), their structure (cadre versus mass parties),
    and their ideology (programmatic versus pragmatic parties). Party systems are
    either competitive or noncompetitive, while a one-party situation is classi-
    fied as a party-state system. All parties serve both electoral and governing
    functions; parties in democratic systems also provide a political opposition
    function.

2. The traditional major Canadian parties (Liberal and Conservative) are elec-
    torally oriented coalitions, pragmatic in style, parliamentary in origin, struc-
    turally decentralized around the provincial units, and cohesive in the legislature.
    The minor parties since the 1920s have been, by contrast, extra-parliamentary
    in origin, programmatic in style, ideological in appeal, and political move-
    ments as well as partisan organizations. The Canadian party system is com-
    petitive, federal, regional, and centre-based. Party leaders are chosen by national
    party leadership conventions, with party finance the key remaining area of
    political corruption.

3. British political parties are more centralized, ideological, class-based, and
    programmatic than their Canadian counterparts. The British party system
    is competitive between two major parties (Conservative and Labour), but
    challenged by nationalist parties (Scottish Nationalist Party and the Plaid
    Cymru) and by minor parties, such as the remnants of the once large Liberal
    party (i.e., the Social Democrats of the 1980s and the Liberal Democrats of the
    1990s). Party leaders have traditionally been selected by the party caucuses, al-
    though the Labour party broke with tradition and decided in 1981 to begin
    using an electoral college type of selection procedure.

4. The major American parties (Republicans and Democrats) are cadre parties that
    are election-oriented, non-ideological, heterogeneous in social composition, and
    decentralized, with weak party unity. The American party system is competitive,
    dominated by the two major parties, and highly discriminatory against new
    or minor parties. Party leaders are selected at national party conventions, but
    the key area of choice is the delegate selection process, which is now dominated
    by the presidential primaries. Unlike Canada or Britain, the mass public may
    be involved in the selection of party leaders in the United States.

5. Despite some obvious shortcomings, parties, especially the competitive parties
    in democratic systems, continue to be important political institutions. However,
    the way in which the existing parties carry out their traditional electoral,
    governing, and opposition functions may change in the future, as the parties
    adapt to a changing environment.

CONCEPT FILE

bagmen
cadre party
caucus (U.S.)
centre-based party system
competitive party system
Election Expenses Act (1974)
electoral function of parties
externally created parties
extra-parliamentary parties
free vote
frontloading
governing function of parties
instant party members
internally created parties
kickback
leadership review process
mass party
ministerialists
national party leadership convention

noncompetitive party system
nonsimultaneous elections
opposition function of parties
parliamentary parties
partisan identification
party-state system
party system
political action committees (PACs)
political parties
pragmatic parties
presidential primary
programmatic parties
regional/sectional party system
suffrage
teledemocracy
toll-gating
unit rule
universal membership vote (UMV)

RECOMMENDED READINGS

Political Parties

BLONDEL, JEAN (1997) "Political Opposition in the Contemporary World," *Government and Opposition*, Volume 32, Number 4, pp. 462–486.

FINEGOLD, KENNETH and ELAINE K. SWIFT (2001) "What Works? Competitive Strategies of Major Parties Out of Power," *British Journal of Political Science*, Volume 31, Number 1, pp. 95–120.

GAINES, BRIAN J. (1997) "Where to Count Parties," *Electoral Studies*, Volume 16, Number 1, pp. 49–58.

HAYES, BERNADETTE C. and IAN MCALLISTER (1997) "Gender, Party Leaders, and Election Outcomes in Australia, Britain, and the United States," *Comparative Political Studies*, Volume 30, Number 1, pp. 3–26.

HILL, RONALD J. and PETER FRANK (1986) *The Soviet Communist Party*. 3rd ed. Boston: Allen and Unwin.

IONESCU, GHITA and ISABEL DE MADARIAGA (1972) *Opposition: Past and Present of a Political Institution*. London: Penguin.

LIPOW, ARTHUR and PATRICK SEYD (1996) "The Politics of Anti-Partyism," *Parliamentary Affairs*, Volume 49, Number 2, pp. 273–284.

LOVENDUSKI, JONI (1997) "Women and Party Politics in Western Europe," *PS: Political Science and Politics*, Volume 30, Number 2, pp. 200–202.

PUNNETT, R.M. (1992) *Selecting the Party Leader: Britain in Comparative Perspective.* New York: Harvester Wheatsheaf.

VON BEYME, KLAUS (1985) "Karl Marx and Party Theory," *Government and Opposition*, Volume 20, Number 1, pp. 70–87.

WARE, ALAN (2000) "Anti-Partism and Party Control of Political Reform in the United States: The Case of the Australian Ballot," *British Journal of Political Science*, Volume 30, Number 1, pp. 1–29.

WELLER, PATRICK (1994) "Party Rules and the Dismissal of Prime Ministers: Comparative Perspectives from Britain, Canada and Australia," *Parliamentary Affairs*, Volume 47, Number 1, pp. 133–143.

Canadian Parties

ANGELL, HAROLD M. (1987) "Duverger, Epstein and the Problem of the Mass Party: The Case of the Parti Québécois," *Canadian Journal of Political Science*, Volume 20, Number 2, pp. 363–378.

ARCHER, KEITH and ALAN WHITEHORN (1997) *Political Activists: The NDP in Convention.* Toronto: Oxford University Press.

AZOULAY, DAN (1999) *Canadian Political Parties: Historical Readings.* Toronto: Irwin Publishing.

BASHEVKIN, SYLVIA V. (1985) *Toeing the Lines: Women and Party Politics in English Canada.* Toronto: University of Toronto Press.

BICKERTON, JAMES et al. (1999) *Ties That Bind: Parties and Voters in Canada.* Don Mills, Ontario: Oxford University Press Canada.

CAMPBELL, COLIN and WILLIAM CHRISTIAN (1996) *Parties, Leaders, and Ideologies in Canada.* Toronto: McGraw-Hill Ryerson.

CARTY, R.K. (1989) "Is There Political Life after Losing the Race?" *Journal of Canadian Studies*, Volume 24, Number 2, pp. 116–127.

COURTNEY, JOHN C. (1973) *The Selection of National Party Leaders in Canada.* Toronto: Macmillan of Canada.

—— (1995) *Do Conventions Matter? Choosing National Party Leaders in Canada.* Montreal: McGill-Queen's University Press.

FLANAGAN, TOM (1995) *Waiting for the Wave: The Reform Party and Preston Manning.* Toronto: Stoddart Publishing.

HIEBERT, JANET L. (1998) "Money and Elections: Can Citizens Participate on Fair Terms Amidst Unrestricted Spending?" *Canadian Journal of Political Science*, Volume 31, Number 1, pp. 91–111.

LANDES, RONALD G. (1994) "In Defence of Canadian Political Parties," in *Crosscurrents: Contemporary Political Issues*, 2nd ed., eds. Mark Charlton and Paul Barker, 247–255. Scarborough, Ontario: Nelson, Canada.

LIGHTBODY, JAMES (1999) "Finding the Trolls under Your Bridge: The New Case for Party Politics in Canadian Cities," *Journal of Canadian Studies*, Volume 34, Number 1, pp. 172–183.

MARTIN, GEOFFREY R. (1998) "We've Seen It All Before: The Rise and Fall of the COR Party in New Brunswick, 1988–1995," *Journal of Canadian Studies*, Volume 33, Number 1, pp. 22–38.

SMITH, DAVID E. (1981) *The Regional Decline of a National Party: Liberals on the Prairies.* Toronto: University of Toronto Press.

WHITAKER, REGINALD (1977) *The Government Party: Organizing and Financing the Liberal Party of Canada, 1930–1958.* Toronto: University of Toronto Press.

British Parties

ALDERMAN, R.K. and NEIL CARTER (1991) "A Very Tory Coup: The Ousting of Mrs. Thatcher," *Parliamentary Affairs*, Volume 44, Number 2, pp. 125–139.

—— (2000) "The Liberal Democrat Leadership Election of 1999," *Parliamentary Affairs*, Volume 53, Number 2, pp. 311–327.

ALDERMAN, KEITH (1998) "The Conservative Party Leadership Election of 1997," *Parliamentary Affairs*, Volume 51, Number 1, pp. 1–16.

—— (1999) "Revision of Leadership Election Procedures in the Conservative Party," *Parliamentary Affairs*, Volume 52, Number 2, pp. 260–274.

CREWE, IVOR and ANTHONY KING (1995) *The Birth, Life and Death of the Social Democratic Party.* Oxford: Oxford University Press.

DURHAM, MARTIN (1997) " 'God Wants Us to Be in Different Parties': Religion and Politics in Britain Today," *Parliamentary Affairs*, Volume 50, Number 2, pp. 212–222.

FISCHER, JUSTIN (1997) "Donations to Political Parties," *Parliamentary Affairs*, Volume 50, Number 2, pp. 235–245.

JOHNSON, NEVILL (1997) "Opposition in the British Political System," *Government and Opposition*, Volume 32, Number 4, pp. 487–510.

KELLNER, PETER (1997) "Why the Tories Were Trounced," *Parliamentary Affairs*, Volume 50, Number 4, pp. 616–630.

MCKENZIE, ROBERT (1967) *British Political Parties: The Distribution of Power within the Conservative and Labour Parties.* London: Heinemann Educational Books.

NORRIS, PIPPA (1997) "Anatomy of a Labour Landslide," *Parliamentary Affairs*, Volume 50, Number 4, pp. 509–532.

NORTON, PHILIP (1990) "Choosing a Leader: Margaret Thatcher and the Parliamentary Conservative Party, 1989–1990," *Parliamentary Affairs*, Volume 43, Number 3, pp. 249–259.

PELLING, HENRY (1985) *A Short History of the Labour Party.* 8th ed. London: Macmillan.

PUNNETT, R.M. (1993) "Selecting the Party Leader in Britain: A Limited Participatory Revolution," *European Journal of Political Research*, Volume 24, Number 3, pp. 257–276.

American Parties

ABRAMSON, PAUL et al. (1995) "Third-Party and Independent Candidates in American Politics: Wallace, Anderson and Perot," *Political Science Quarterly*, Volume 110, Number 3, pp. 349–367.

BECK, PAUL ALLEN (1997) *Party Politics in America.* 8th ed. New York: Longman.

HERRNSON, PAUL S. (1992) "Why the United States Does Not Have Responsible Parties?" *Perspectives on Political Science*, Volume 21, Number 2, pp. 91–99.

HREBENAR, RONALD J. et al. (1999) *Political Parties, Interest Groups, and Political Campaigns.* Boulder, Colorado: Westview Press.

LEWIS-BECK, MICHAEL S. and PEVERILL SQUIRE (1995) "The Politics of Institutional Choice: Presidential Ballot Access for Third Parties in the United States," *British Journal of Political Science*, Volume 25, Number 3, pp. 419–427.

LOWI, THEODORE J. (1983) "Toward a More Responsible Three-Party System: The Mythology of the Two-Party System and Prospects for Reform," *PS: Political Science and Politics*, Volume 16, Number 4, pp. 699–706.

POLSBY, NELSON W. (1997) "Opposition in the United States," *Government and Opposition*, Volume 32, Number 4, pp. 511–521.

POLSBY, NELSON W. and AARON WILDAVSKY (1996) *Presidential Elections: Strategies and Structures in American Politics*. 9th ed. Chatham, New Jersey: Chatham, House Publishers.

ROSENSTONE, STEVEN J. et al. (1996) *Third Parties in America: Citizen Response to Major Party Failure*. 2nd ed. Princeton, New Jersey: Princeton University Press.

ROYKO, MIKE (1971) *Boss: Richard J. Daley of Chicago*. New York: New American Library.

WATTENBERG, MARTIN P. (1998) *Decline of American Political Parties, 1952–1996*. Cambridge, Mass.: Harvard University Press.

POLITICS ON THE NET

CANADA: An essential website for information on parties, current and past elections, registration of political parties, and election financing is the **Elections Canada** website at *www.elections.ca*. This site also lists all of the registered political parties and their websites. The major **Canadian parties** can be located as follows:

Liberal party	*www.liberal.ca*
Canadian Alliance	*www.canadianalliance.ca*
Bloc Québécois	*www.blocquebecois.org*
New Democratic Party	*www.ndp.ca*
Progressive Conservative party	*www.pcparty.ca*

UNITED STATES: The **U.S. Federal Election Commission** can be found at *www.fec.gov*. Websites for the major **American parties** can be located as follows:

Democratic party	*www.democrats.org*
Republican party	*www.rnc.org*
Reform Party	*www.reformparty.org*
Libertarian Party	*www.libertarian.org*
Socialist Party	*sp-usa.org*

BRITAIN: The major **British parties** can be located at the following websites:

Conservative party	*www.conservatives.com*
Labour party	*www.labour.org.uk*

chapter 10

Interest Groups

Interest groups constitute the core and essence of civil society. Their very presence demonstrates the right of individuals to organize for the sake of influencing public authorities. (Yishai, 1998: 153)

Perhaps what characterizes political life is precisely the problem of continually creating unity, a public, in a context of diversity, rival claims, unequal power, and conflicting interests. (Hanna Pitkin, quoted in Stoker, 1992: 369)

. . . the first rule of politics: Every one, and every group, want more than they deserve, and demand more than they want. (White, 1982: 231)

CHAPTER PREVIEW

- In a modern, liberal-democratic polity, citizens can influence the political process by voting and by participating in the interest-group battle.

- Interest groups are now vital components of all democratic systems, although their impact varies because of differences in both political structure and political culture between polities.

- Interest groups are a plural, rather than a singular, phenomenon: they may be formed on the basis of material (economic) interests, on the basis of an ideological perspective, or on the basis of a more generalized public interest.

- The role of interest groups is the most significant in the American system, where they have come to dominate much of the political process. Constitutional guarantees of freedom of speech and association, combined with a fragmented and decentralized political structure and a litigious citizenry, have created a pattern of interest-group liberalism in the United States. Political action committees (PACs) are an American invention which now play a key role in political campaigns and the electoral process.

- In Canada, interest groups have always been important participants in the political process, a role which has increased in recent decades. Because of the 1982 Charter of Rights and Freedoms, interest groups are increasingly utilizing judicial rulings as a technique in the political battle.

- In Britain, interest groups, because of the traditional practice of corporatism or functional representation, have developed an intimate and powerful role in the political process.

- The interest-group process is one in which some segments of the polity receive dual representation (voting and interest groups), while other sectors of society are excluded from the process. "Madison's dilemma" pinpoints a conceptual and practical flaw in the theory of interest-group liberalism.

The individualistic outlook of Western society, symbolized by the role of the citizen in the electoral process (i.e., voting), has obscured, at times, the important place of groups in the polity. While the immediate impact of a single vote might be minimal, individuals in democratic systems soon discovered that, by combining forces with other like-minded citizens, they could enhance their influence in the political process. These **interest groups** or collectivities of individuals *"share a common set of goals and have joined together in an effort to persuade the government to adopt policies that will help them"* (Lowi and Ginsberg, 2000: 307).

Interest groups have traditionally played a significant role in the democratic electoral process by providing money for candidates and parties. However, such groups are probably even more important in the inter-election period as a means for connecting citizens with their government. In the modern era, interest groups have expanded their role in the political process, often at the expense of both political parties and the individual citizen. Interest groups have become crucial not only to the practice of democratic politics, but to the theory of liberal-democracy as well, best exemplified by the theory of pluralism or pluralist democracy. **Pluralism** might be defined as *the view that the competitive battle of group and individual self-interest somehow produces the public good.* Such a competitive battle is greatly influenced by both the political structure and the political culture of a particular polity.

THE NATURE OF INTEREST GROUPS

Several difficulties confront the political analyst in dealing with the role and impact of interest groups in the political process. First, political terminology has often been confusing and inconsistent, with interest groups variously referred to as pressure groups or lobbies. While some writers have tried to distinguish differences between these concepts, we will broadly use the term interest group to include all such related concepts. Second, we must distinguish between interest groups and political parties. The primary distinction is that parties are organizations that run candidates for public office, while interest groups are organizations that seek to influence those people selected to govern by the election process. Interest groups may be intimately involved in the electoral battle by providing money, by campaigning in favour of or against a particular policy, or by backing a specific candidate or party; however, they use such techniques to influence or control those in government rather than to become the government itself. Third, interest groups may cross national borders and lobby in other systems. For example, as part of an international lobbying effort, Greenpeace Canada, in the 1990s, was successful in focussing attention in Canada on an anti-logging campaign in British Columbia (1999) and on other areas of concern, such as the seal hunt. However, because of these lobbying activities, Revenue Canada in 1995 revoked Greenpeace's status as a charitable group for tax purposes, a ruling that was confirmed in June of 1999. In contrast to Greenpeace, most interest groups are domesticated organisms. Thus, our focus will be on the power and role of interest groups inside particular political systems.

A final problem for political analysis is the relationship between interest groups and liberal-democracy: can interest groups exist in nondemocratic systems? Our view is that interest groups, as previously defined, are democratic creatures, fundamentally dependent on the political and civil liberties of freedom of speech and freedom of association. Thus, we reject the view that interest groups exist in totalitarian systems such as the former Soviet Union (Skilling and Griffiths, 1971). While "interests" that are based on such factors as the economy, religion, region, class, ethnicity, or bureaucratic structures are endemic and universal, interest groups are not so ubiquitous. Interest groups are a democratic phenomenon.

TYPES AND FUNCTIONS OF INTEREST GROUPS

No social or political system is homogeneous in its makeup — diversity is a basic fact of life. As Aristotle (Barker, 1962: 151) observed, "the polis . . . is an aggregate of many members," and the size of the polis and its varying interests have expanded greatly since Aristotle's time. This diversity can be channelled into the political process by a number of mechanisms, including political parties, voting patterns, political culture, or interest groups. Thus, the potential bases for interest-group formation are coterminous with reality: almost any factor (religion, region, class, political idea) can spur a group's formation. Interest groups can range from the obvious (business, farm, labour, and consumer associations) to the sublime (the Flat Earth Research Society, which has

> The latent causes of faction are thus sown in the nature of man; and we see them everywhere brought into different circumstances of civil society . . . . But the most common and durable source of factions has been the various and unequal distribution of property (James Madison, *The Federalist Papers*, Number 10).

3 500 members worldwide). Interest-group creation and behaviour also reflect the problem of scarcity perceived through the filter of self-interest. Political conflict grows out of both diversity and scarcity and interest groups are one way of participating in that competitive battle, whether it concerns ideas (peace, abortion) or material interests (money, beneficial tax laws, direct government subsidies).

Under the general rubric of interest groups lies a series of different types of organizations. Most *traditional interest groups are economic in nature; that is, they represent particular sectors of the economy, especially producer groups.* Such associations include business, farm, labour, and professional organizations and they have long dominated the interest-group process. These groups are often designated as **special interest groups**.

A more recent phenomenon is *interest groups espousing the general interest or the public's interest,* such as that of consumers. These associations are typically fewer in number, poorer in their financial base, and not as well organized as the special interest groups. However, **public interest groups**, such as Greenpeace or Common Cause, can be successful in particular areas of concern.

A third type of interest group *focusses not on economic matters but on ideas.* In the past several decades, these groups have become particularly noticeable, with groups forming either in favour of or against particular policy positions. Classic examples of these **single-issue interest groups** would be those concerned with issues such as abortion, capital punishment, and disarmament. For example, even inside the American Republican party there is a single-issue interest group that

Source: *The Daily News* (August 24, 1999), p. 32. By permission of Dave Coverly and
           Creators Syndicate Inc.

focusses on the issue of sexual orientation: the party's gay rights lobbying group is called the Log Cabin Republicans.

The latest entrants into the pressure group arena, and ones still largely confined to the American polity, are the **political action committees (PACs)**. These political action groups *select particular candidates that they want either elected or defeated and, instead of channelling the money through a political party — the traditional pattern of special interest groups — they spend money on behalf of "their" candidate directly.* PACs have mushroomed in significance in the American system in the past two decades: for many candidates, they are now the most important source of campaign largesse. Until the 1988 federal election and the free trade debate, the impact of PACs on the Canadian election process had been slight. The emergence of PACs, as well as the rapid expansion of the more traditional groups, has created the paradox of Madison's dilemma for liberal-democracies.

In a democratic polity, with freedom of speech and freedom of association, interest groups will battle for their own self-interest. **Madison's dilemma** (Berry, 1984: 1–15), what he called "curing the mischiefs of faction," is thus created: *who looks after the public's interest or those segments of society not included in the interest-group contest?* The answer to that question tells us much about the nature of liberal or pluralist democracy in the modern era.

The political resources needed to compete fairly in the interest-group contest are, of course, not distributed evenly: the "flaw in the pluralist heaven is that the heavenly chorus sings with a strong upper-class accent" (Schattschneider, 1975: 35). Significant political resources such as time, money, and access are more available to some interests than to others. Thus, interest-group politics are not neutral in their effects: they help the advantaged over the disadvantaged, the rich over the poor, the organized over the unorganized. In the process, the public interest becomes distorted or ignored. Critics argue that the resulting pattern can be called **interest-group liberalism**:

> It is interest-group liberalism because it sees as both necessary and good a policy agenda that is accessible to all organized interests and makes no independent judgment of their claims. It is interest-group liberalism because it defines the public interest as a result of the amalgamation of various claims (Lowi, 1979: 51).

Although interest groups, like other political institutions, vary according to type and resource base, they can all perform a variety of functions. Our concern with why interest groups develop and with Madison's dilemma indicates that interest groups serve participation and representation roles. Interest groups provide a mechanism by which the citizen can participate in the polity both during and between election campaigns. In so doing, individuals seek to have their priorities represented in government, in order to protect their own or their group's self-interest. As an outgrowth of both participation and representation, a third consequence becomes apparent, namely, a policy-making function. Representation and participation are not ends in themselves, but are ultimately designed to affect the content of public policy. Finally, interest groups are involved in a bureaucratic function: once public policy has dealt with your concerns, does the government effectively implement and administer the legislative program? How a program

> If a central goal of participation in politics is to come to understand one's interests better, self-interest must have a legitimate role in the body politic (Mansbridge, 1990: 22).

works on a day-to-day basis is often of much greater consequence than the letter of the law. Successful groups monitor as well as propose program or policy changes. In carrying out the representation, participation, policy-making, and bureaucratic functions, interest groups utilize a variety of techniques.

INTEREST-GROUP BEHAVIOUR

The crucial problem for interest groups is access to those decision makers who are making public policy that affects the group and its members. The interest groups' methods of influence and behaviour, therefore, aim at guaranteeing access to key decision makers.

One way of ensuring potential governmental responsiveness is through the electoral pocketbook: money may not directly buy policy (except in cases of political corruption), but it is likely to guarantee an opportunity to make one's case to the policy makers. A typical example of this approach is through campaign finance. The electoral process in the modern era is incredibly expensive and politicians need money not only to run for office but to stay re-elected. Campaign contributions are, therefore, an important means of access to decision makers. Other related techniques based on money may be used as well: free travel, vacations, low-cost loans and, sometimes, outright bribery. Things which money can buy — such as meals, entertainment, and other services — have been known to make their way into the interest-group process as well.

An additional means of influence for interest groups is their control of information. Governments often depend on interest groups for the information on which government policy is based. Collecting and presenting data to the government, even if the government might suspect its accuracy, allows the interest group some impact in the decision-making process. Testimony before legislative committees, meetings with key bureaucrats, and annual reports or briefs to the government are all part of the information process.

Our emphasis on access and information leads to an often mistaken in perception of interest-group activity. Unlike in the electoral process, publicity and the mobilization of public opinion may not be very effective techniques for specific interest groups. As a general rule of thumb, the most successful interest groups are the least visible ones. Behind the scenes negotiations with key political and bureaucratic elites are a preferred and more effective strategy than public confrontations extensively covered by the mass media. While publicity may have beneficial results for some groups, the general pattern is the opposite: like resignations from the cabinet, appeals to the court of public opinion are usually admissions of political weakness, not political strength.

Explaining interest-group success

Before we can identify the factors that make for interest-group success, we must first decide on what success means in an interest-group context. Given our definition of interest groups, we assume that the primary criterion of success is favourable public policy, meaning policy compatible with an interest group's goals. A second measure of influence would be the ability of a group to get particular candidates elected to office or to be influential in the naming of individuals to the relevant bureaucratic positions. A third criterion of interest-group influence would be the group's ease of access to the key political and bureaucratic elites.

These three criteria of success all focus on the actual impact of an interest group on the political process. Thus, we consider the organizational survival of an interest group, in and of itself, to be a poor indicator of interest-group success. The ultimate goal of interest-group behaviour is to change the content and decisions of the political agenda; its secondary goal is to determine who the decision makers will be; its tertiary goal is to influence the relevant politicians and bureaucrats in the political decision-making process.

Interest-group success is determined by the interaction of three fundamental factors: the political structure, the political culture, and the internal characteristics of the interest group itself. The most influential groups are those that find means for meshing group concerns with larger movements of opinion (i.e., political culture) in such a way as to make effective use of existing political institutions (i.e., political structure).

Internal group characteristics would include such factors as the number of members, the number of active members, the political resources, such as time and money, which members are willing to commit to the cause, and the intensity of belief with which members adhere to the goals of the organization. Particularly important would be the skills of political leadership displayed by the organization's officers, including communication and fundraising abilities. What such internal characteristics point to is the fact that while it may be relatively easy to start an organization, it is an entirely different matter — and a complex one at that — for that organization to become an effective and influential participant in the political process. A myriad of groups exist; only a small proportion have much impact on the political agenda.

One basic way in which a polity's political culture influences interest-group behaviour is in terms of the legitimacy of such activity. Political attitudes define whether such behaviour should take place at all: for example, lobbying and lobbyists are political terms with negative connotations. A political culture based on the idea of popular sovereignty is more compatible with extensive interest-group activity than one based on parliamentary sovereignty. Key themes of a country's political culture, such as deference, elitism, or individualism, affect the formation, activity, and success of interest groups.

Intermingling with the political culture and the organization's internal characteristics is the political structure. Particularly crucial is the impact of the separation of powers or fusion of powers principles, that is, whether groups find themselves operating in a presidential or a parliamentary structure. A successful group has to know how the political structure works and where power resides before it can affect the content of public policy. For example, developing a good relationship with a powerful committee chair in the American legislature is often an important technique of interest group influence; in Canada, traditionally

Amongst the laws which rule human societies there is one which seems to be more precise and clear than all the others. If men are to remain civilized, or to become so, the art of associating together must grow and improve, in the same ratio in which the equality of condition is increased (de Tocqueville, 1835).

committee chairs are not key actors in the parliamentary process and, thus, such a relationship would be a sign of ineffective group tactics. In a parliamentary system, access to cabinet members or key bureaucratic positions is a surer route to power than intimate involvement in the legislative process.

An additional component of the political structure that affects the behaviour of interest groups is the federal or unitary structure of the polity. In a unitary system, such as Britain's, the number of sites at which interest groups contest is reduced, while in a federal system, such as Canada's, the number of points for interest-group activity is increased. If both levels of government in Canada are concerned with an interest group's policy area, then the organization may have to operate in 10 provincial capitals, as well as in Ottawa. The more sites at which interest groups have to participate in order to protect their concerns or achieve their goals, the harder it is for them to affect the decision-making process. Thus, the political structure largely defines the arena of the interest-group battle, as well as helping to determine matters of strategy and tactics.

AMERICAN INTEREST GROUPS

It is by no means coincidental that interest groups are more significant and widespread in the American polity than in any other comparable system (Skocpol, Ganz, and Munson, 2000). Several factors have produced such a pattern. First, key elements of the American political culture, such as individualism and popular sovereignty, encourage the formation of interest groups and serve to legitimate their behaviour and influence. Second, the constitutional system which explicitly protects, in the First Amendment, the rights of free speech, press, and assembly, as well as the right to "petition the Government for a redress of grievances," buttresses and protects interest-group activities. Third, a political structure that fragments and decentralizes political power has meant that a consequence unforeseen by the Framers of the Constitution "was to make it relatively easy for pressure groups to influence decisions on behalf of objectives that are often narrow and highly particularistic" (Dahl, 1982: 190). This confluence of political beliefs, constitutionally guaranteed rights, and a fragmented political structure has generated a literal explosion of interest-group formation and activity in the American polity.

Interest-group influence on the political process has often been seen, by both foreign observers (Singh, 1999) and internal critics (Lowi, 1979) alike, as a distinguishing feature of American government. An example of the significant role of interest groups in the policy process can be seen in the legislative demise of the Clinton administration's health-care reforms in 1993 (Johnson and Broder, 1996: 627–631) or in the continuing failure throughout the 1990s to pass meaningful gun control legislation (Singh, 1999). Moreover, particularly disconcerting has been the traditional linkage between interest groups and political corruption, such as in the Teapot Dome Scandal of the 1920s, the Watergate Scandal of the 1970s, or the campaign fundraising scandals of the 1990s. This connection between interest groups and political corruption has neither abated nor been adequately dealt with by reforming the political system.

Periodic demands for reforms to limit interest-group behaviour have often had, in fact, the opposite result, namely, an increase in interest-group activity and influence. For example, reform efforts in the early 20th century, such as the introduction of direct primaries to nominate candidates for public office, have not only weakened the political parties but, as an unintended consequence, have strengthened the importance of interest-group representation. In the American polity, the traditional strength of political parties and interest groups is inversely related (Chase, Holt, and Turner, 1980: 82–89). Moreover, reforms by Congress in the 1970s, which attempted to undercut the excesses of the seniority system and the power of committee chairs, resulted in a further decentralization of power and a corresponding increased role for lobbyists in the legislative process.

The expanding role of interest groups in American politics is indicated by the following figures: in the early 1960s there were less than 400 registered lobbyists in Washington, D.C., a number which had grown to over 25 000 in the 1990s. However, if unregistered lobbyists were counted, the total number might be as high as 80 000. Thus, lobbying has been a growth sector of the American economy: it has been estimated that, by the end of the 1990s, interest groups were spending as much as $100 million per month lobbying the executive and legislative branches of government. As a result, a new development has occurred: lobbyists now lobby other lobbyists. Lobbyists even have their own interest group (the American League of Lobbyists) to defend their profession.

The historically important and greatly expanding role of interest groups in the United States has affected not only the practice of politics, but the American theory of liberal-democracy as well. If any approach to political science is decidedly American in outlook, it must surely be the group theory of politics, as commonly incorporated into the theory of pluralist democracy (Dahl, 1982; Garson, 1978). In what is now considered a classic example of political analysis, Arthur F. Bentley (1908), in his book *The Process of Government*, defined that new meaning and approach to politics in group terms: "When the groups are adequately stated, everything is stated. When I say everything, I mean everything."

Pluralist theory, based on the interest-group perspective, made several significant changes to traditional or classical democratic theory. First, the public interest became defined as the end product of competitive self-interest, perhaps best exemplified by Harold Lasswell's (1958) definition of politics as "who gets what, when, and how." Second, the election process came to be conceived more in terms of means than of ends. Joseph Schumpeter's (1950: 269) famous definition of elections as "the competitive struggle for the people's vote" would illustrate such a change. Finally, group theory, by definition, reduces the importance of the individual's role in the political process: groups become the determining actors in the political arena (Perry, 1991).

The development and functions of interest groups have, therefore, changed not only the practice of democratic politics, but the conception of liberal-democracy as well (Jordan, 2000). Such modifications of both theory and practice may have advantages and disadvantages associated with them (Dahl, 1982; Lowi, 1979; Macpherson, 1977). A more detailed look at American interest groups will highlight several of these significant problem areas.

THE PATTERN OF AMERICAN INTEREST GROUPS

As one might expect in the pre-eminent capitalist society, the basis of most traditional interest groups has been economic, with an emphasis on producer groups. These special interest groups, formed around the business and farming sectors, dominated interest-group politics in the 19th century, although by the end of that period they were challenged by the growing labour movement. Corporate interests were particularly influential in the legislative process, receiving tax breaks and favourable policy in return for campaign contributions and, on occasion, political payoffs. Examples of such groups would include the American Farm Bureau Federation, the AFL-CIO, and the National Association of Manufacturers. These groups are the big-hitters of the interest-group battle because of their longevity, their large memberships, and their money, which has traditionally been channelled through the parties in electoral contests (Peterson, 1991).

Single-issue interest groups have appeared intermittently throughout American history. Historically, the abolitionists opposed to slavery in pre-Civil War days, the suffragettes who fought for women's right to vote, and the prohibitionists opposed to alcohol have all had considerable impact on American politics, as did the anti-Vietnam War groups in the late 1960s. In the 1980s, the anti-abortion or right-to-life groups gained considerable attention from the media and from some political leaders, such as Ronald Reagan and George Bush.

These single-issue groups have not been as significant as the special interest groups in the long run, however, because the public's interest in such issues ebbs and flows and because single-issue groups are frustrated by the bargaining and compromising required to be successful in the American polity. Moral issues and fervently held ideals tend to preclude conciliation, while the special interests concerned primarily with economic rewards can more easily gain access to, control over, and achieve compromise within the legislative and executive branches of government.

Public interest groups or people's lobbies really began to flourish in the 1960s, perhaps best exemplified by the various organizations created by Ralph Nader in the area of consumer protection and by Common Cause with respect to governmental reform. A public interest group is concerned with how government decisions affect the general welfare, as opposed to the narrower outlook of most groups centred on material self-interest (Bykerk and Maney, 1992). A public interest group, however, does not deal with all issues that might affect the public, but instead focusses on one or two particular areas of expertise. For example, Common Cause, started by John W. Gardner, previously head of the Carnegie Foundation and former American Secretary of Health, Education, and Welfare under Lyndon

Johnson, was founded in 1970. It had a membership of 200 000 people within two years, and concentrated on particular issues relating to the governmental process (McFarland, 1984: 6–10). Among its principal successes are support for changes in American campaign financing and a role in the elimination of the oil depletion allowance, a major tax loophole long held sacred by the oil industry. As a general rule, however, neither the single-issue groups nor the public interest groups can match, on a long-term basis, the money, access, and influence of the special interest groups.

The most important recent change in the pattern of interest representation in the American system has been the development of political action committees (PACs). Although PACs, such as the AFL-CIO's political education organization, COPE, have existed since the 1950s, these groups really mushroomed as a result of the reform legislation concerning party and campaign finance in the 1970s. From about 600 PACs in 1974, the number had increased to nearly 5 000 by the end of 2000.

Rather than simply giving money to a political party, PACs work directly in favour of or against a particular candidate, regardless of that candidate's party label. Because of a loophole in the reform legislation (the law limits how much candidates and parties can spend, but not what others may spend on their behalf), PACs became the most important source for interest-group campaign contributions and the largest single source of campaign fundraising for many seeking legislative office. Spending by PACs on the electoral process mushroomed from about $20 million in the mid-1970s to about $500 million during the late 1990s. In the 2000 presidential election year, an estimated $3 billion was spent on all election contests — much of it raised and spent by the PACs.

Lobbying techniques

Money, access, and lobbying techniques are all intimately related. The more traditional special interest groups still concentrate on campaign contributions, on gaining access to legislators in the key spots in the decision-making process (Hojnacki and Kimball, 1998), and on developing personal ties to the power brokers through lunches, gifts, and sometimes bribes. One rather ingenious way of giving money to officials, which is legal, is to pay them an "honorarium" for making a speech to your organization. If the fee or honorarium is excessively high, then it reflects a campaign contribution or a hold on the legislator out of all proportion to his or her effort — in other words, something very close to a good old-fashioned bribe.

While they may utilize these traditional and legal lobbying techniques as well, public interest groups and single-issue groups sometimes have a tendency to turn to the public through media campaigns, protest marches, or mass letter-writing projects. Threats of electoral retribution are also sometimes used, but as a general rule most groups are not large enough or organized sufficiently to make such a threat credible. Money and access remain the keys to interest-group success.

A specific technique, which has remained one largely utilized in the American system, is to use the courts to challenge government practices or legislation. Because the court system operates under the principle of full judicial review, litigation may be an effective tool for some interests. A notable historical success in this area was the use of the courts by the NAACP (National Association for the Advancement of Colored People) and various civil rights organizations to attack racial discrimination and its effects. However, litigation is often both a very lengthy as well as an expensive process for which most groups are not prepared (Epstein and Rowland, 1991).

In addition to the above techniques, major interest groups have sometimes used longer-term strategies to influence the policy process. One rather hidden but effective technique is the revolving door syndrome between governmental personnel, interest-group representatives, and government regulatory positions. The **revolving door syndrome** means that *individuals alternate between working for a government agency that regulates a particular special interest group or industry and working directly for that special interest group or industry.* Government agencies typically depend on industry or interest groups being regulated to provide personnel for the relevant government departments. However, individuals know that their government service is likely to last only a year or two, at the end of which they will again be seeking employment in the private sector, thus putting the public interest into potential jeopardy.

Such a career opportunity structure is likely to dull the reform instincts of all but the most ardent idealists. For example, former member of Congress, legislative assistants, or even White House aides typically become lobbyists as a kind of end-of-career promotion pattern. A rather unusual twist of the revolving door syndrome, since it involved a public interest group leader rather than the typical special interest group representative, came to light in January 1994. Candy Lightner, whose daughter had been killed by a drunk driver in 1980 and who had then founded and led MADD (Mothers Against Drunk Driving), became a paid lobbyist for the American liquor industry.

Of Madison's dilemma and iron triangles

The rapid expansion of interest-group formation and activity in the last three decades has created a paradox for American democracy: the more special interests are represented, the less well represented are the individual citizens and groups who are left out of the pressure group game (Duerst-Lahti, 1989). In particular, the traditional organizations used in the process of representation, namely the political parties, have been decimated, both organizationally and as representative institutions. Madison's dilemma in American politics has created a system of **dual representation**, that is, a process *whereby the ordinary citizen is represented through the election process by selecting legislative members, while interests and groups have developed their own representation process, that is, the pressure group game* (Wootton, 1985: 328–340). Moreover, this interest-group activity has overwhelmed and taken control of the traditional pattern of legislative representation.

Nowhere is this development more clearly demonstrated than in the **iron triangles** of American politics, that is, *the interaction and mutually supportive relationship between a government department or agency, the corresponding legislative committee of Congress, and the interest groups concerned with a particular policy area* (Figure 10.1). These three components bargain and work with each other to

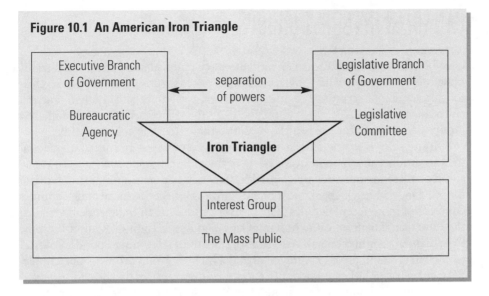

Figure 10.1 An American Iron Triangle

develop policy to deal with their priorities, thereby bypassing presidential control of the executive branch, the separation of powers principle and, often as well, the public interest. Power that is separated by constitutional prescription is united by iron triangle tactics based on complementary self-interests. As a result, the role of the individual citizen in, and the representative nature of, American democracy are further diminished.

EXPLAINING THE AMERICAN PATTERN

To understand the important and growing role of interest groups in the American polity, we must look to several interrelated factors. First, the American Constitution protects fundamental political and civil liberties that provide the bases for potential interest-group development and involvement in the political process. Second, the general fragmentation of political power in the United States, while it has often prevented government from acting in the public interest, has, at the same time, encouraged interest-group activity, particularly in the area of material self-interest. The separation of powers principle between branches of government, as well as the further fragmentation and decentralization of authority within each branch, has unwittingly enhanced interest-group access and provided a political structure amenable to manipulation. In particular, the legislative process, in terms of both the election of legislators and the passage of legislation, has expanded the opportunity structure for interest-group activity. Finally, the political culture of liberalism, with its emphasis on individualism, equality of opportunity, and popular sovereignty, intersects with the institutional structure to provide a congenial environment for the pattern of interest-group dominance of the American polity.

CANADIAN INTEREST GROUPS

Given elements of both Canada's parliamentary political structure and its traditionally elitist and deferential political culture, it is not surprising to find that the historical view of interest groups has centred on their non-importance, both in practical and academic contexts. It was not until the 1970s that a number of studies of interest groups began to appear (Kwavnick, 1972; Presthus, 1973). Even at that time, however, it was still necessary to make the argument that interest groups were essential to both the operation and understanding of the political process in Canada. While some of these groups predate Confederation (e.g., Société Saint-Jean-Baptiste founded in 1834 in Quebec), most interest groups reflect the social and economic concerns of more recent decades (e.g., the Committee for an Independent Canada; the Canadian Coalition on Acid Rain; Canadian Association of Retired Persons; Canadian Environmental Law Association; Friends of Clayoquot Sound). Political issues and divisions are also represented in the interest-group process. For example, the Conference of Defence Associations, a lobby group representing defence-oriented organizations, recommended (September 2000) a $2 billion increase in military spending. This action was subsequently criticized by the Canadian Peace Alliance, which represents 300 peace-related organizations in Canada.

Although often unperceived by the ordinary citizen, interest groups and lobbying activities make themselves felt on a daily basis in the political process. The following items are just a few of the many that could be cited to show the role of interest groups and lobbyists in the Canadian political process. In 1998–1999, the federally funded interest group for Quebec anglophones, called Alliance Quebec, continued its battle with the separatist provincial government in Quebec City over English-language health and social services. Two prominent women's lobby groups — the conservative group REAL Women (which stands for realistic, equal, active for life) and the left-wing feminist organization NAC (National Action Committee on the Status of Women) — continued to compete in their attempts to change government policy. As a further example, the government of the Northwest Territories (March 1999) hired a lobbyist to defend the northern caribou by lobbying the American legislature to protect the caribou herds' calving grounds. Lobbying has become so pervasive in Canada that in 1989 a biweekly publication entitled *The Lobby Monitor* was started to provide an overview of events and laws for those involved in the interest-group arena.

> And I concede your point too, that it's likely we heard more from the vested interests than we did from the little taxpayer who didn't have . . . the high-paid lawyers to speak for him . . . . I suppose in participatory democracy there will always be some whose voice is louder than others . . . (Trudeau, quoted in Lewis, 1972: iv).

THE PATTERN OF CANADIAN INTEREST GROUPS

The functions and types of interest groups in Canada are fairly typical of most liberal-democracies, as modified by the workings of a parliamentary system.

Business and corporate interests predominate with respect to influence, access, and money. By the late 1990s, for example, the Canadian Federation of Independent Business had a membership of 85 000, a budget of $14 million, and a staff of 230. Consumer groups have traditionally been poorly organized and relatively unsuccessful. For example, the 40-year-old Consumer Association of Canada faced a $1 million debt in 1988 and had to receive emergency aid of $300 000 from the federal government in order to survive. Unlike the American pattern (e.g., Common Cause), public interest groups have been neither very visible nor successful. Single-issue groups, such as the pro-life group Campaign Life, have become increasingly apparent in recent years but, as yet, have not achieved the successes of their American counterparts. Political action committees have been restricted in their impact because of the nature of the parliamentary party system, at least until the mid-1980s. Historically, interest groups have sought to work through the party system electorally and through the bureaucracy in the inter-election period. One distinguishing feature of Canadian interest-group formation has been the number and salience of groups dealing with nationalism and the bicultural cleavage. These groups range from the establishment of the Orange Order in Ontario in 1830 to the Committee for an Independent Canada nearly a century-and-a-half later.

Given the range and number of interest groups, almost every sector of society now has its own special representative body. Since the 1960s, the federal government, because it found it to be of help in the policy-making process, even went so far as to provide seed money with which to form new interest groups. For example, in 1998–1999 the federal government gave $180 000 to a group called the Southern Chiefs Organization, a political lobby group for Aboriginal bands in southern Manitoba. Government-sponsored groups proved to be quite influential in such areas of public policy debate as potential gas-and-oil development in the North (e.g., the Berger Commission Report). Another example of this practice occurred in April 1985, when the federal government announced a $25 000 grant to support a peace convention, even though the various peace groups had been strongly and vociferously opposed to the government's foreign and defence policies.

A further example of government funding of interest-group activity is the feminist movement in Canada. Funded through the Secretary of State's budget is the Women's Program, which by 1989 was giving $13 million a year to various groups "promoting the status of women." The largest women's lobby, the National Action Committee on the Status of Women (NAC), which was founded in 1972 with funds provided by the federal government, received half a million dollars a year from Ottawa in the late 1980s, an amount which had dropped to $270 000 in 1995. However, as part of overall government spending reductions, Finance Minister Paul Martin announced significant reductions in government subsidies for interest groups in his February 1995 budget. By 1997 1998, NAC's grant had been reduced to $234 000. Many interest groups, as a result, will likely not survive, at least in their current form. Any reduction in overall interest-group activity will likely be modest and probably temporary in the Canadian political process.

In many respects the connection between the government and interest groups in relation to funding is the Canadian version of the iron triangles of American politics. However, although we have a myriad of groups, no one would be likely to suggest that all interests are represented, equally or otherwise. Participation in most interest groups remains a pleasure and a prerogative of the middle and upper classes.

The participation of interest groups in policy-making usually centres on the executive branch, because interest groups have an acute sense of smell when tracking the scent of power. Interaction with the bureaucracy and not with MPs is the goal of most groups and one reason why interest-group activity is not highly visible to the untrained eye. Moreover, producer groups, such as the various farm associations, often aid in implementing government policy.

For the most part, Canadian interest groups have utilized the standard techniques of lobbying characteristic of such activity in liberal-democracies. However, in the American system the influence of parties and interest groups is inversely related; in Canada, we have had strong parties characterized by rigid party discipline and, at the same time, highly influential interest groups. The reason for this traditional pattern would seem to be that, for the most part, interest groups have worked within the parties and through the party system, not in opposition to it. The parliamentary structure, based on the fusion of powers principle, combined with broadly based brokerage parties, has provided a congenial atmosphere for interest-group activity, access, and influence.

In addition, the parliamentary structure has meant that emotional appeals to the court of public opinion have not been a particularly effective technique for most groups. However, some exceptions are worthy of mention. For example, women's and native rights groups were successful in pressuring the federal and provincial governments to reinsert constitutional guarantees of their rights during the patriation battle in the fall of 1981. Similarly, a group such as Greenpeace has been instrumental, despite government opposition, in undercutting the annual seal hunt in Canada. In both of these cases, however, one factor stands out: the appeal to public opinion worked because the interest groups were able to galvanize the public on the issue. In these cases, the public responded (in the Greenpeace situation — the international public), and only then did government policy respond. In other words, turning to public opinion is often a last-ditch effort and a high-risk strategy at the same time. If the public does not respond, then the interest group is, for all intents and purposes, dead in the water.

Because of the growing public recognition of the important role that interest groups play in the Canadian political process (lobbying is a business estimated to be worth about $250 million a year), in 1988 the federal Parliament passed the **Lobbyists Registration Act.** This law, which became effective on September 30, 1989, defines two types of lobbyists. The first category (Tier 1 lobbyists) is for those lobbyists who get paid by different clients for contacting and dealing with government officials. The second category (Tier 2 lobbyists) is for those lobbyists who work on behalf of a single organization or interest group. The number of individuals who initially registered as official lobbyists in either category is instructive. By early 1990, about 400 Tier 1 and about 2 200 Tier 2 lobbyists had registered;

by 1999, these figures had grown to 600 and 2 500 respectively. Such figures, however, greatly underestimate the number of lobbyists in Ottawa, which some people have estimated to be in the range of 15 000 (registered and unregistered).

Overall, the Lobbyists Registration Act has been quite ineffective. The requirement to register is poorly defined and the Act's enforcement provisions are weak. A review of the Act in 1993 by Parliament provided no real change in the original legislation. Many of the lobby groups argued that no changes were needed in the existing legislation, a sure sign of the ineffectiveness of the Lobbyists Registration Act. In 1995, some changes were finally made in the Act. These changes increased the amount of information which a lobbyist or interest group was required to make public and modestly increased the Act's enforcement provisions. The government also adopted a Conflict of Interest Code for government officials dealing with interest groups. However, such changes will do little to limit the growing influence of interest groups in the Canadian political process.

Interest groups and the Charter

Although the traditional method of Canadian interest-group activity has been to focus on the government rather than the public, the 1982 Canadian Charter of Rights and Freedoms has modified that pattern (Morton and Knopff, 2000). Groups, particularly public interest ones, that lack access or find that government policy has already gone against them, can now turn to the judiciary and litigation in an attempt both to stop government actions and to gain publicity for their cause. For example, in 1983 a coalition of 26 peace and disarmament interest groups, led by Operation Dismantle, challenged the federal government's decision to allow the testing of the American cruise missile in Canada. This court challenge was based on the Charter (especially Section 7), which proclaimed that "Everyone has the right to life, liberty and security of the person and the right not to be deprived thereof except in accordance with the principles of fundamental justice." The anti-cruise groups argued that a new weapon system and the resulting increased possibility of nuclear war might have something to do with the "security of the person." While a lower court judge initially agreed, the cruise challenge was later rejected by the Federal Court of Appeal. The cruise tests were begun in 1984. Although the tests were not stopped, this court challenge focussed significant attention on the nuclear question for many months and gave the disarmament movement a public forum that would have been denied to it in pre-Charter days.

Several recent studies that have analyzed the use of the Charter by interest groups show a significant increase in the use of the judiciary by interest groups to protect and promote their concerns. For example, a study by Gregory Hein (*National Post*, March 21, 2000) of both Supreme Court and Federal Court decisions in Canada between 1988 and 1998 found that 62 percent of challenges to government policies came from noncorporate interest groups, while the remaining 38 percent were corporate-based. A similar pattern was discovered by Osgoode Hall Law professor Patrick Monahan (*National Post*, April 5, 2000): in about half of its cases, the Supreme Court of Canada allowed interest groups that were not directly involved in the lawsuits to intervene in the litigation process.

The Charter of Rights also has had an impact on the development of political action committees in Canada (Hiebert, 1991: 12–29). The 1974 Election Expenses Act channelled money from the public purse through the political parties, candidates, or their official agents, thus preventing the growth of political action committees along American lines. Just to make sure that no PAC-like groups would develop, the parties amended the Canada Elections Act in the fall of 1983 (Bill C-169) to prevent groups other than parties from spending funds during an election campaign. The bill, which became effective on May 17, 1984, was supported by all three national parties and passed the House of Commons after only 40 minutes of debate.

However, a special interest lobby, the National Citizens' Coalition, challenged that law, because it felt the law violated at least several sections of the new Charter (including freedom of speech and association). An Alberta court agreed, prompting the chief electoral officer to announce that he would not prosecute such groups during the 1984 campaign until the law was clarified. The matter was still unresolved by the time of the 1988 federal election, so that for the first time special interest groups made a quantum leap forward in their participation in the electoral contest. For example, the free trade issue galvanized such groups, with the Pro-Canada Network spending about $1 million and the Canadian Alliance for Free Trade and Job Opportunities about $1.5 million.

Because of the fear that the loophole created by the court ruling would allow for American-style PACs to enormously increase their influence in the Canadian electoral process, the federal Parliament, in 1993, tried again to close the loophole, in anticipation of the next general election. A limit of $1,000 per person was placed on third party advertising that directly supported or opposed a specific candidate or party. Such a measure, if it had been in effect during the 1988 election, would have prevented the pro- and anti-free trade advertising battle. However, the National Citizens' Coalition again challenged the law and again won (June 1993), so that the law, even though the court decision was being appealed, could not be implemented during the 1993 federal election.

The saga of the "gag law" continued in June of 1996, when the Alberta Court of Appeal upheld the lower court's decision that portions of the law violated the Charter. In October of 1996, the federal government indicated that it would not immediately challenge that decision. Instead, a revised "gag law" was passed by Parliament (spring 2000), with an effective starting date of September 1. The "gag law" was again challenged by the National Citizens' Coalition and again struck down by the Alberta Court of Queen's Bench. Appealed by the federal government, the Supreme Court of Canada reversed the decision of the Alberta court and approved the "gag law" on November 10, 2000 — halfway through the 2000 election campaign.

Thus, after nearly two decades, it appears that the "gag law" controversy has been finally settled, and this law will have a major impact on future electoral battles. Third-party spending (mainly by interest groups) will not be allowed to follow the American pattern — PACs will not become a major Canadian problem.

EXPLAINING THE CANADIAN PATTERN

Both the basic political beliefs or themes of the political culture and the parliamentary political structure influence the pattern and tactics of Canadian interest groups. Each in turn affects the success of the organizations in the political process.

Political culture affects interest-group behaviour in a number of ways. Political beliefs help to define the legitimacy of such organizations. In Canada, while interest-group activity has, quite likely, always been important, the legitimacy of such activity, in the public's eye, has not always been benign. In a system of parliamentary sovereignty, group influence has been seen as undercutting that basic principle of government. Traditionally, a quasi-participative political culture has not enhanced nor legitimated such activity on the part of the ordinary citizen, acting either alone or in concert.

Interest-group activity is tainted by an aura of popular sovereignty, a belief which is still not particularly well accepted, especially by many in the political elite in Canada. Moreover, the elitist strain in Canada has helped to downplay interest-group growth as well, particularly single-issue and public interest groups. What has thus resulted, historically, has been a predominant pattern of special interest groups working outside of public view and interacting with the bureaucratic and political elites in the development of public policy.

Matters of strategy and organization are also greatly affected by the structure of the political system. The federal principle of organization has several consequences. For example, single-issue groups may be particularly affected by the distribution of powers between the levels of government. Since the federal level was given jurisdiction over criminal law, groups wishing to change the criminal law must deal with the national government and develop a national organization and movement or protest base. The issues of capital punishment and of prostitution control cannot be dealt with by the provincial governments. Getting the national government to act may be more difficult to do than dealing with the lesser units in the federal system. However, federalism is sometimes advantageous to certain groups, such as business groups, which have been quite successful in getting all of the federal and provincial governments to provide funding programs for businesses. If jurisdiction in a policy area is shared, as in agriculture, then the interest groups are forced to deal with 11 governments, rather than just one. Moreover, federalism affects an interest group's own organization, not just its tactics. Most groups in Canada's federal system are themselves organized as federations, so as to parallel the structure of government.

In addition to federalism, the parliamentary structure has an important bearing on interest groups. Most interest groups discovered long ago that parliamentary sovereignty was a myth. As a result, little time is spent lobbying backbenchers or opposition members. Instead, interest-group activity typically focusses on cabinet ministers and the bureaucracy in the relevant government departments. It should be kept in mind that the bureaucracy itself is structured to represent many of the major interests in Canadian society. Moreover, the cabinet, because of the representation principle, also reflects the major interests in Canadian affairs. Thus, interacting with the relevant minister and the key bureaucrats in the appropriate

Source: A billboard by PETA (People for the Ethical Treatment of Animals) which appeared in Canadian cities
           in July of 2000. By permission.

government departments or agencies is how successful interest groups operate. The reason interest-group activity has been difficult to spot is not that it does not take place, but that it occurs out of view of the ordinary citizen. If the political executive is the repository of power in the political structure, then it is also the key site which determines interest-group success.

Canada's parliamentary structure, disciplined parties, and powerful bureaucracy are the reasons why, unlike in the American system, iron triangles have not developed. Interest groups in Canada do not seek to bypass the political executive but to control it or influence it. Legislative committees have little power, reflecting Parliament's overall position. With the legislature and bureaucracy both under the control of the political executive, an interest group either deals with that reality or it does not deal at all. Wishful thinking has no bearing on interest-group reality. As C.E.S. Franks (1983: 205) has put it, "There is no Canadian counterpart to the powerful union in the United States of interest groups, Congressional committees and bureaucracy."

A key prerequisite to interest-group success is an understanding of the political structure and the skill to mesh interest-group concerns with movements of public opinion. Some interest groups have been very successful in Canada; others have not been. While interest groups will continue to influence the Canadian polity and while that influence will continue to grow as a result of the Charter, Canada's parliamentary democracy has not yet been completely taken over by interest-group expansion or dominance.

BRITISH INTEREST GROUPS

The basis for interest-group behaviour in Britain can be traced back nearly eight centuries to the Magna Carta in 1215, which guaranteed people the right to petition their government. Moreover, the term lobby itself is of British origin, in that the phrase was coined to describe the pressure put on members of Parliament in the lobby of the House of Commons before a vote was cast. However, interest groups began to make themselves particularly felt in the political process in the early decades of the 19th century.

Initially, interest-group activity was not seen as legitimate, because it was perceived as threatening the role of Parliament and the doctrine of parliamentary supremacy: as Gladstone put it in 1867, these groups were "agencies out of doors." In the 19th century, in a system in which few adults had the right to participate, it is not surprising to find that public pressure groups might not be well received either. However, this "pressure from without," that is, public pressure on Parliament, had achieved a number of successes by the end of the century, including some significant reforms in social and economic policy (Hollis, 1974: 5). Interest groups had become an accepted means of public influence and were increasingly incorporated into the party system (e.g., they operated through the major parties).

THE PATTERN OF BRITISH INTEREST GROUPS

A unique feature of the pattern of British interests, and one which reflects a historical tradition, is the interests of the realm (Verney, 1976: 191–196). Traditional interests of the realm would include the Royal Society, the City of London, and the Church of England, while more recent examples would be the British Broadcasting Corporation, the National Coal Board, and British Railways.

Current **interests of the realm** are *those groups brought into existence by an act of Parliament or by royal charter that are usually concerned with the public interest, are outside of direct government control by Parliament, and are used in particular in relation to key sectors of the economy.* In this regard, the closest Canadian analogue to these interests of the realm would be the semi-autonomous crown corporations, such as the CBC or Via Rail. The British interests of the realm are important actors in the political process, as demonstrated by the role of the National Coal Board in the bitter and lengthy miners' strike in 1984 and 1985. However, our main focus will be on more typical groups in the British polity.

As in most liberal-democracies, the major sectors of the economy are the bases for interest-group formation. These special interest groups would include the Confederation of British Industries (CBI), the National Federation of Building Trade Employers, the British Medical Association, and the Association of University Teachers. Particularly important in the pattern of British interest-group activity are the trade unions, which had a membership in 1999 of about 6.5 million and are organized as a national federation with 71 affiliated groups known as the Trades Union Congress (TUC).

Because of the class and ideological basis of 20th century British politics, the special interest groups have traditionally developed close partnerships with the major parties. For example, most business groups are associated with the Conservative party, while the labour movement, through the TUC, is formally linked to the Labour party. Unlike most Canadian and American interest groups, which seek to influence all the major parties because one never knows for sure which party will win the election, British interests traditionally make their electoral choice before the ballots are cast. Special interests in Britain do not act in opposition to the party system, but in conjunction with it.

Public interest groups, such as Friends of the Earth, have not had many victories in the British polity, although rare successes do occur, such as the achievements of the National Campaign for the Abolition of Capital Punishment. The lack of public-interest-group success reflects the strength of the more traditional special interests and the incorporation of those special interests in the policy-making process. As a result, governments tend to perceive the public interest through the eyes of the special interests.

What are categorized as single-issue groups in Canada and the United States are more typically called **promotional** or **cause** groups in Britain. A good example of a promotional group is the Royal Society for the Protection of Birds (RSPB), which has an estimated membership of 800 000, a staff of 600 full-time workers, and a budget of £30 million. Such groups have had a long history. For example, the Committee for the Abolition of the Slave Trade was begun in 1807. In more recent times, these groups have included both pro- and anti-abortion groups, both pro and con groups with respect to Britain's role in the Common Market, and the League Against Cruel Sports (an animal welfare association). In the late 1990s, groups both in favour of, or opposed to, fox hunting mobilized public protests for their cause. As in Canada and the United States, such groups are rarely any match for the special interest groups.

Political action committees are not a British phenomenon, because of the historically close relationship between interest groups and the party system. PACs are a means of doing an end run around the parties: however, in Britain there is no need to do so. For example, the Confederation of British Industries actually sponsors many Conservative party candidates and MPs and contributes financially to the party as well. This pattern of sponsoring MPs is particularly important for the Labour party, given the direct connection between it and the Trades Union Congress (Muller, 1977). In fact, pressure groups may not only work through the party system but actually control it, in the sense that the parties become subordinate to the pressure groups (Duverger, 1972: 119). In such a system, political action committees are not needed.

Corporatism and functional representation

The development and success of interest-group activity during the 19th and early 20th centuries led to a further enhancement and elaboration of their role in a number of European political systems, especially in Britain. In particular, interest groups became widely accepted as legitimate and were explicitly incorporated into the decision-making process (Panitch, 1977). This *co-optation of major social and economic interests directly within the policy-making machinery of government* is known as **corporatism** or **functional representation** (Leys, 1983: 275–279; Siaroff, 1999).

Although it is true that "governments have always struck bargains with barons" (Richardson and Jordan, 1979: 192), what corporatism does is to involve interest groups in the internal process of governing, both in terms of deciding policy and in implementing it as well. While interest groups in Canada and the United States, by and large, operate to bring pressure on or to influence the government, in corporatism or functional representation, the groups become part of the government. Interest groups have evolved in Britain from being "pressures from without" Parliament to being key actors within the executive decision-making process. However, the myth of parliamentary sovereignty remains.

The consequences of corporatism and, by implication, of the influence of interest groups in Britain are many. Moreover, such a pattern has developed in a traditional unitary political structure in which the civil service, known as Whitehall, had already acquired considerable power. Thus, corporatism is both a cause and consequence of the concentration of political power in the political executive.

Specifically, corporatism or functional representation has led ultimately to an undercutting of Parliament's role in the policy process, to a diminution of the functions of the political parties, and to an enhancement of the power of the political executive. As a result, interest groups focus their efforts on the political executive and bureaucracy. The average citizen, who is represented through the geographically based constituencies in the House of Commons, is shunted aside by the workings of corporatism (except, of course, for those people represented by the functional groups).

The "symbiotic relationship between groups and government" (Richardson and Jordan, 1979: vii) has clearly enhanced the power of interest groups in the British polity and made it difficult to successfully govern without, at least, their grudging co-operation. Former prime minister Edward Heath discovered this fact in his 1974 confrontation with the unions (i.e., he lost that struggle, his position as PM, and, ultimately, his role as leader of the Conservative party to Margaret Thatcher): "Probably the greatest limitation on a Prime Minister and his government comes from the various power blocs in the community, their power being largely negative; to refuse to cooperate, to strike, to fail to participate or to follow new rules" (Mackintosh, 1982: 89).

The political symbiosis of private interest and public policy in a pattern of corporatism that dominated British political life for a half-century (1930–1980) came under explicit attack with the emergence of Margaret Thatcher as Conservative prime minister in 1979 (Kavanagh, 1990: 159–164). Believing in market forces over government wisdom and opposed to labour unions on both theoretical and practical grounds, Margaret Thatcher directly challenged the long-dominant principle of collectivism. As a "conviction" politician, Margaret Thatcher "disliked the habits of mind and the institutions of corporatism. She believed that the freely elected government of the day had no business sharing its power and authority with unelected bodies . . . " (King, 1993: 234).

A result of the Thatcher era (1979–1990) and the years of her successor John Major (1990–1997) was a dismantling of significant aspects of corporatism and its replacement by a more American pattern of interest group activity. No longer enjoying automatic inclusion in the policy-making process, interest groups expanded and increasingly engaged in a competitive battle for access and power (Norton, 1994: 166–170). Moreover, such efforts became focussed on the political executive and the party in power, thus marginalizing many previously powerful groups, such as the trade unions (Coxall and Robins, 1994: 283–284). The return to power of the Labour party since the 1997 election has meant a rejection of some of the reforms of the Thatcher era and a move back toward a more corporatist approach to governance — although not to the extent of the pattern of the 1970s and 1980s.

COMPARING INTEREST GROUPS

Interest groups have developed as a means to fulfill or to carry out certain basic tasks in the political process. These functions include participation, representation, policy-making, and implementation. Therefore, the mix of functions performed by interest groups, and the way in which those functions are carried out, are important bases for comparing interest-group behaviour. In the modern era, interest groups have become particularly important mechanisms for involving people (or, at least, a segment of them) in the political process: "Interest and pressure groups are the living 'public' behind the parties" (Friedrich, 1968: 454).

A second basis for comparing group behaviour is the types of organizations prevalent in any system. We focussed on four different types of groups: special interest groups, public interest groups, single-issue groups, and political action committees. The presence and influence of these groups varies from one system to another.

> All polities are pressure cookers. They differ in all sorts of ways — and many of the differences between them reflect the differences in the pressures they contain, in the way the "cooker" has been designed or has found a durable shape, and in how they respond to the changing force and direction of the pressures (Gould, 1973: 242).

A third concern in any analysis of group patterns is the techniques of influence utilized. These methods of influence can range from contributing money during electoral contests, to providing information to government, to wining and dining key legislators and bureaucrats. In systems with constitutionally guaranteed rights, litigation may be used as well.

In seeking to account for the functions, types, and techniques of interest-group activity, several factors can be utilized as explanatory tools. First, organizational characteristics, such as the size of the group and the motivation of its membership, aid in accounting for interest-group success. Second, the nature of the political structure (e.g., federal or unitary, presidential or parliamentary) helps to determine interest-group strategies, tactics, and internal organization. Third, the political culture conditions the legitimacy of interest-group access and influence, as well as the responsiveness of the policy process to interest-group proposals. Thus, interest-group systems differ not only with respect to functions, types, and techniques, but also in relation to the factors responsible for such characteristics (e.g., organizational criteria, the political structure, and the political culture).

SUMMARY

1. Interest groups are representative creatures reflecting the struggle for competitive advantage, usually material in nature, in liberal-democratic polities. Such organizations involve citizens in the political process, both during and between election campaigns. However, as Madison's dilemma shows, not everyone benefits equally from a pattern of interest-group liberalism.

2. In democratic regimes, special interest groups based on producer segments of the economy have been the most successful in terms of access and favourable public policy. Public interest groups are less successful and less pragmatic, although they have achieved results in particular areas of public policy. Single-issue groups have proliferated in recent decades, but they are no match, on a long-term basis, for the special interests. Political action committees have been a particularly American phenomenon, although the Charter of Rights and Freedoms has allowed for their expansion in Canada during the past two decades.

3. Access to governmental decision makers is a key problem for interest groups, with the ultimate goal being favourable public policy from those decision makers. Interest-group success is dependent on three interrelated criteria: organizational composition, political structure, and political culture.

4. American interest groups have expanded greatly in the last few years and continue as significant elements in the struggle for power. As a result, many theories of liberal-democracy are now group-centred, with pluralism being the primary example. Special interest groups have long been associated with political corruption and scandals. Since the 1970s, the most important recent development has been the use of political action committees. Constitutionally guaranteed rights, a political culture based on popular sovereignty, and a fragmented political structure have all enhanced the role of interest groups in the American system.

5. Canadian interest groups have traditionally been less visible, but not necessarily less important, than their American counterparts. The parliamentary political structure and a party system with strong party discipline have resulted in interest groups focussing their attention on the political executive and the bureaucracy. Because of the 1982 Canadian Charter of Rights and Freedoms, interest groups have increasingly and successfully resorted to litigation as a technique in the political process.

6. The British system has been unique in the extent to which interest groups have been formally co-opted and incorporated into the decision-making process (i.e., corporatism or functional representation). The doctrine of parliamentary sovereignty remained in place, but the power of choice passed to the political executive and Whitehall (1930–1980). Britain developed a pattern

in which certain groups were explicitly and directly linked to particular parties. In this pattern of corporatism, the ability to govern was heavily dependent on the relationship between the prime minister and the interest-group system. The impact of the long reign of Margaret Thatcher was to dismantle much of the pattern of corporatism and replace it with a more American pattern of interest-group activity. With the return of the Labour party to power in 1997, a moderate pattern of corporatism is once again evident in the British polity.

CONCEPT FILE

corporatism
functional representation
dual representation
gag law (Canada)
interest-group liberalism
interest groups
interests of the realm (Britain)
iron triangles
Lobbyists Registration Act (Canada)

Madison's dilemma
pluralism
political action committees (PACs)
promotional or cause interest group
public interest group
revolving door syndrome
single-issue interest group
special interest group

RECOMMENDED READINGS

Comparing Interest Groups

BAUMGARTNER, FRANK R. and BETH L. LEECH (1998) *Basic Interests: The Importance of Groups in Politics and in Political Science.* Princeton: Princeton University Press.

BENTLEY, A.F. (1908) *The Process of Government.* Chicago: University of Chicago Press.

GREENWOOD, JUSTIN and CLIVE S. THOMAS (1998) "Regulating Lobbying in the Western World," *Parliamentary Affairs*, Volume 51, Number 4, pp. 487–499.

JORDON, GRANT (2000) " 'The Process of Government' and 'The Governmental Process'," *Political Studies*, Volume 48, Number 4, pp. 788–801.

MANSBRIDGE, JANE J., ed. (1990) *Beyond Self-Interest.* Chicago: The University of Chicago Press.

OLSON, MANCUR (1965) *The Logic of Collective Action.* Cambridge: Mass.: Harvard University Press.

SIAROFF, ALAN (1999) "Corporatism in 24 Industrial Democracies: Meaning and Measurement," *European Journal of Political Research*, Volume 36, Number 2, pp. 175–205.

TRUMAN, DAVID B. (1951) *The Governmental Process.* New York: Alfred A. Knopf.

WARREN, MARK E. (2001) *Democracy and Association.* Princeton, New Jersey: Princeton University Press.

WILSON, JAMES Q. (1995) *Political Organizations.* Rev. ed. New York: Basic Books.

YISHAI, YAEL (1998) "The Guardian State: A Comparative Analysis of Interest Group Regulation," *Governance,* Volume 11, Number 2, pp. 153–176.

American Interest Groups

BERRY, JEFFREY M. (1997) *The Interest Group Society.* 3rd ed. Boston: Little, Brown and Company.

CAMMISA, ANNE MARIE (1995) *Governments as Interest Groups: Intergovernmental Lobbying and the Federal System.* Westport, Conn.: Praeger Publishers.

CIGLER, ALLAN J. and BURDETT A. LOOMIS, eds. (1998) *Interest Group Politics.* 5th ed. Washington, D.C.: CQ Press.

GRAY, VIRGINIA (1998) "To Lobby Alone or in a Flock: Foraging Behaviour among Organized Interests," *American Politics Quarterly,* Volume 26, Number 1, pp. 5–34.

HERRNSON, PAUL S. et al., eds. (1998) *The Interest Group Connection.* Chatham, New Jersey: Chatham House.

HOJNACKI, MARIE and DAVID C. KIMBALL (1998) "Organized Interests and the Decision of Whom to Lobby in Congress," *American Political Science Review,* Volume 92, Number 4, pp. 775–790.

KOLLMAN, KEN (1998) *Outside Lobbying: Public Opinion and Interest Group Strategies.* Princeton: Princeton University Press.

LOWI, THEODORE J. (1979) *The End of Liberalism: The Second Republic of the United States.* 2nd ed. New York: W.W. Norton and Company.

RICHAN, WILLARD C. (1995) *Lobbying for Social Change.* 2nd ed. New York: Haworth Press.

ROZELL, MARC J. and CLYDE WILCOX (1999) *Interest Groups in American Campaigns.* Washington, D.C.: CQ Press.

SINGH, ROBERT (1999) "Gun Politics in America: Continuity and Change," *Parliamentary Affairs,* Volume 52, Number 1, pp. 1–18.

SKOCPOL, THEDA et al. (2000) "A Nation of Organizers: The Institutional Origins of Civic Voluntarism in the United States," *American Political Science Review,* Volume 94, Number 3, pp. 527–546.

THOMAS, CLIVE S. (1998) "Interest Group Regulation across the United States: Rationale, Development and Consequences," *Parliamentary Affairs,* Volume 51, Number 4, pp. 500–515.

Canadian Interest Groups

BURT, SANDRA (1990) "Canadian Women's Groups in the 1980s: Organizational Development and Policy Influence," *Canadian Public Policy,* Volume 16, Number 1, pp. 17–28.

COLEMAN, WILLIAM D. (1988) *Business and Politics: A Study of Collective Action.* Kingston, Ontario: McGill-Queen's University Press.

DOBROWOLSKY, ALEXANDRA (1998) "Of 'Special Interest': Interest, Identity and Feminist Constitutional Activism in Canada," *Canadian Journal of Political Science,* Volume 21, Number 4, pp. 707–742.

KAY, BARRY J. et al. (1991) "Single-Issue Interest Groups and the Canadian Electorate: The Case of Abortion in 1988," *Journal of Canadian Studies*, Volume 26, Number 2, pp. 142–154.

PROSS, A. PAUL (1992) *Group Politics and Public Policy*. 2nd ed. Toronto: Oxford University Press.

RUSH, MICHAEL (1998) "The Canadian Experience: The Lobbyists Registration Act," *Parliamentary Affairs*, Volume 51, Number 4, pp. 516–523.

STANBURY, W.T. (1993) "A Skeptic's Guide to the Claims of So-called Public Interest Groups," *Canadian Public Administration*, Volume 36, Number 4, pp. 580–605.

VICKERS, JILL et al. (1993) *Politics As If Women Mattered: A Political Analysis of the National Action Committee on the Status of Women*. Toronto: University of Toronto Press.

British Interest Groups

BAGGOTT, ROB (1995) "From Confrontation to Consultation? Pressure Group Relations from Thatcher to Major," *Parliamentary Affairs*, Volume 48, Number 3, pp. 484–502.

—— (1995) *Pressure Groups Today*. Manchester: Manchester University Press.

BERRY, SEBASTIAN (1992) "Lobbyists: Techniques of the Political 'Insiders'," *Parliamentary Affairs*, Volume 45, Number 2, pp. 220–232.

—— (1993) "The Rise of the Professional Lobbyist: A Cause for Concern?" *The Political Quarterly*, Volume 64, Number 3, pp. 344–351.

FISHMAN, NINA (1997) "Reinventing Corporatism," *The Political Quarterly*, Volume 68, Number 1, pp. 31–40.

GARNER, ROBERT (1991) "The Animal Lobby," *The Political Quarterly*, Volume 62, Number 2, pp. 285–291.

—— (1993) "Political Animals: A Survey of the Animal Protection Movement in Britain," *Parliamentary Affairs*, Volume 46, Number 3, pp. 333–352.

GRANT, WYN (1993) *Business and Politics in Britain*. 2nd ed. London: Macmillan.

JORDON, GRANT (1998) "Towards Regulation in the UK: From 'General Good Sense' to 'Formalised Rules'," *Parliamentary Affairs*, Volume 51, Number 4, pp. 524–537.

MARSH, DAVID (1992) *The New Politics of British Trade Unionism*. London: Macmillan.

MARTIN, ROSS M. (1980) *TUC: The Growth of a Pressure Group 1868–1976*. Oxford: Clarendon Press.

POLITICS ON THE NET

GENERAL: The website of the Internet Public Library Associations on the Net (AON) *(www.ipl.org/ref/AON/)* provides access to about 600 professional and trade associations. Information on interest groups can also be found at *www.yahoo.com/Government.*

CANADA: The following are the websites for some of the major interest groups in Canada.

Canadian Chamber of Commerce	*www.chamber.ca*
Canadian Ethnocultural Council	*www.ethnocultural.ca*
Canadian People for the Ethical Treatment of Animals	*www.goveg.com*

BRITAIN: Links to major interest groups can be found at *www.open.gov.uk.*

UNITED STATES: Some of the major American interest groups can be found at the following locations.

American Civil Liberties Union	*www.aclu.org*
Common Cause	*www.commoncause.org*
Christian Coalition	*www.cc.org*
AFL-CIO	*www.aflcio.org*
American Association of Retired Persons	*www.aarp.org*
National Education Association	*www.nea.org*
Sierra Club	*www.sierraclub.org*
National Rifle Association	*www.nra.org*
National Organization for Women	*www.now.org*
National Association for the Advancement of Colored People	*www.naacp.org*
Emily's List	*www.emilyslist.org*

Comparing Democratic Polities

A government may deserve to be credited not only with the positive successes it has achieved, but with the negative success of having escaped evils that have vexed other nations living under somewhat similar conditions. (Bryce, 1921: 42)

A political system is an accident. It is an accumulation of habits, customs, prejudices, and principles that have survived a long process of trial and error and of ceaseless response to changing circumstance. (Banfield, 1980: 148)

CHAPTER 11

Liberal-Democracy in the 21st Century

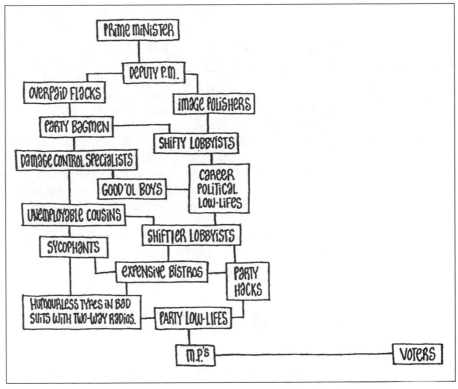

```
                    ┌──────────────────┐
                    │  PRIME MINISTER  │
                    └──────────────────┘
```

Source: Adrian Raeside, *The Victoria Times Colonist*. By permission.

To comprehend the interconnections of political life is, at once, both the most necessary and most difficult task of comparative political analysis. The various elements of a body politic represent a pattern, not of random discord, but of discordant harmony. The continuous interdependence of institutions and processes makes a polity complex and, therefore, difficult to understand, but it need not be either beyond reason or political analysis.

Studying the politics of one's own country from a comparative perspective should be an enjoyable experience. At the same time, it is a necessary prerequisite for effective participation in the polity. Knowledge and understanding are fundamental ingredients of a politically educated and a politically involved citizenry in liberal-democratic political regimes. Moreover, a comparative political analysis provides a basis for students to arrive at their own conclusions about the nature, advantages, and disadvantages of their political system. A comparative approach to the Canadian polity is particularly appropriate, given the historical impact of Britain and the contemporary impact of the United States on the origin and evolution of the institutions and processes of the political system. Moreover, a comparative perspective facilitates an appreciation of the Canadian polity by delineating the similarities and differences among the political structures and procedures of various liberal-democracies. For the most part, the comparative analysis in Chapters 2–10 focusses on the current patterns of politics in the three liberal-democracies of Canada, the United States, and Britain.

Two important questions, however, need to be asked: first, just how democratic are the Canadian, British, and American polities; and second, what is the future of liberal-democracy in the 21st century? In other words, what we will do in this chapter is to first make a "democratic audit" of the current political systems in our three countries of comparison and then make an assessment of the impact of future developments, what we call "POLITICS.com," on these same polities.

LIBERAL-DEMOCRACY: A DEMOCRATIC AUDIT

In political practice as well as in political theory, democracy — especially liberal-democracy — has been a normative ideal which has typically been in conflict with empirical reality. While few would disagree that Canada, Britain, and the United States are liberal-democracies, many would argue over the characteristics and criteria, as well as their assessment, in making such a conclusion. Democracy is a conveniently elastic concept, both in theory and practice (Foweraker and Krznaric, 2000).

As a result, in making an assessment of liberal-democracy in the 21st century, what we have labelled a "democratic audit," we need to be specific about the meaning and characteristics of a democratic system. Consistent with our previous discussion in chapter 1 of the meaning of liberal-democracy is the concept of polyarchal democracy advanced by Robert A. Dahl (1998). **Polyarchal democracy** is *rule by the many* and in terms of modern, large-scale representative democracies it has the following political institutions: elected officials; free, fair and frequent elections; freedom of expression; access to alternative sources of information; associational autonomy; and inclusive citizenship (Dahl, 1998: 83–99; see also Barber, 1995). Such a system of polyarchal democracy is still a far cry from the ideal democracy of the classical democratic theorists.

In the political world of the normative democratic theorists, the individual citizen was concerned, interested in, and knowledgeable about the polity, with active political participation a natural outgrowth of such characteristics. Political elites were responsive to the mass public; the electoral process was competitive and open; and political dissent, based on minority rights and the protection of civil and political liberties, was a fundamental ingredient of the political system. Certainly in comparison to the classical democratic ideal, current liberal-democratic polities remain tantalizingly suspect. Even the advanced liberal-democracies in Canada, Britain, and the United States are deficient in comparison. Perhaps it would be well to keep in mind what Winston Churchill is reputed to have said — that liberal-democracy is the worst form of government ever invented — except for all the others yet tried. In our view, it is in their participative aspects that modern liberal-democracies are at their weakest, perpetually frustrating even the most ardent political reformers. The structural organization of the polity is democratic in form, but often lacking in the substance of active and widespread political involvement. While the political institutions and processes of liberal-democracy have become democratized, the role of the individual citizen has been, at the same time, increasingly marginalized.

If, however, instead of comparing current liberal-democratic systems to the democratic ideal, we compare them to the concept of polyarchal democracy and consider how they have evolved in recent decades, we might come to very different conclusions. Thus, in making a democratic audit of the Canadian, British, and American systems, we will be comparing these polities to the characteristics of polyarchal democracy. Before doing so, we need to discuss the meaning and purposes of a democratic audit (Beetham, 1999: 567–570).

In general terms, an audit is an assessment or evaluation of practices and procedures to see that they meet certain criteria. Thus, if one is called for a tax audit, the government agent is reviewing your tax forms to see if you have done them properly. In a similar vein, we will define a **democratic audit** as *an assessment of political institutions and political processes to see how well a particular polity is implementing and developing democratic attributes.* We will perform our democratic audit by evaluating all three polities described in this

> Where is the Canadian who, comparing his country with even the freest countries, would not feel proud of the institutions which protect him (Sir Wilfrid Laurier)?

current edition (2002) with their democratic nature outlined in the first edition of *The Canadian Polity* published in 1983. This 20-year comparison of individual polities (Canada 1983 vs. Canada 2002; Britain 1983 vs. Britain 2002; United States 1983 vs. United States 2002) will then provide the basis for looking at the impact of technology on liberal-democracies in the 21st century.

CANADA 1983 VERSUS CANADA 2002

For a polity long-dominated by constitutional debates and political stalemates, Canada has witnessed a constitutional revolution during the past two decades. The Canadian constitution in 1983 had just been significantly altered with the adoption of the 1982 Constitution Act, which included the Canadian Charter of Rights and Freedoms. Prior to 1982, the judicial branch was a relatively minor player in the political process, operating under the principles of judicial restraint and limited judicial review. The 1960 Canadian Bill of Rights was very modest in its impact, applying only to the federal level and able to be bypassed through the use of the "notwithstanding clause," while the War Measures Act remained in place.

In the 20 years following the Constitution Act, constitutional debates and proposed reforms have run their course, so that Canada entered the new century in 2001 as a constitutionally quiescent polity. However, even with such a result, the last two decades have experienced serious constitutional disturbances, including the following: the defeat of the Meech Lake and Charlottetown Accords; the narrow rejection of the independence option in the 1995 Quebec referendum; the 1996 Regional Veto Act; the 1998 *Quebec Secession Reference*; the 2000 Clarity Act; and the resignation of Lucien Bouchard as Quebec premier and leader of the Parti Québécois. A period of constitutional quiescence may be, at least in part, a result of constitutional exhaustion.

The adoption in 1982 of the Canadian Charter of Rights and Freedoms is the most significant constitutional change since Confederation in 1867. Civil and political liberties at both the federal and provincial levels of government have been strengthened; the judiciary has moved from a pattern of judicial restraint to judicial activism; the Supreme Court of Canada has become a key actor, if not the key actor, in national politics; and the power of the judicial branch of government now rivals — and at times surpasses — the power of the executive branch of government. A further impact of the Charter has been the expansion of constitutional litigation by both individuals and, especially, interest groups. A judicial ruling is now not the last resort but often the first choice for those involved in the struggle for influence and power in the Canadian polity.

> It is commonly said that Canada produces more politics to the acre than any other country (Smith, 1891: 178).

The executive branch of government continues to dominate the legislative branch even more so than it did 20 years ago. Prime ministerial pre-eminence (i.e., *primus inter pares*) has clearly given way to simply the prime minister as *primus*. The prime minister basically has no equals in either the executive or legislative branches. In the executive branch, the prime minister totally dominates the cabinet and the various departments of government. Every recent prime minister who has served for any length of time (Trudeau, Mulroney, Chrétien) has expanded the power of the prime minister in Canadian politics. In the process the formal executive, the cabinet, and the bureaucracy have witnessed a diminution of their own powers.

With respect to its overall role, the legislative branch is clearly in third place behind the executive and the judiciary. Rigid party discipline has eviscerated the potential significance of the principle of parliamentary sovereignty. As evidenced by control of the legislative agenda, the increased use of the closure and time allocation procedures, the close supervision and control of parliamentary committees, and a pattern of increasingly short parliamentary and ministerial careers, the executive branch displays little toleration or appreciation of Canadian parliamentarians. Reforms such as the MPs selecting the Speaker of the House of Commons by secret ballot, a somewhat greater consideration of private members' bills, or the occasional free vote have really not done much to enhance the status or prestige of the Canadian Parliament. However, one important aspect of change has been the increased representation of women and minorities in both the House and the Senate.

The House of Commons dominates the Senate even more than it did two decades ago. While the Senate has never actually been equal to the House, it has become even less so over time. For example, the 1982 Constitution Act reduced the veto powers of the Senate in the constitutional amendment process from a potential full veto to one of six months, that is, a suspensive veto of half a year. In the 2000 Clarity Act, the Senate was completely bypassed in Parliament's decision regarding a potential move by Quebec toward separation and independence. In terms of normal legislative processes, the Senate rarely challenges the dominance of the House of Commons.

Senate membership remains patronage-based and, in the view of many, illegitimate. This problem was further exacerbated by Prime Minister Chrétien, especially in his second term of office, when he appointed a number of senators who had only a few months or years to serve. To be an effective legislator requires at least several years of training and learning. Attempts at broad-based reform of the Senate, such as that of the Triple-E plan, appear to be quite low on the current political agenda, if they happen to be on the agenda at all. Attempts to force change on the Senate, such as electing Senate nominees in Alberta, appear doomed to failure as long as the Liberal party dominates national politics.

In addition to the changes in the judiciary as a result of the Charter, the judicial branch has seen significant growth in terms of its numbers, its salaries, and its public perception. While unsuccessful to this point, there have been attempts to put judicial appointments to public scrutiny, instead of their remaining a prime ministerial prerogative. In the past two decades, the Canadian judiciary has become a significantly more representative institution of Canadian society, as women and minority groups receive judicial appointments and promotions.

In the area of political culture, concerns about the Canadian identity have decreased, as the Canadian polity has become even more integrated with the American one. Partly as a result of the various free trade agreements, continentalism and globalization have further eroded certain aspects of the Canadian identity, so much so that suggestions of Canada adopting the American dollar as its currency are now taken seriously. Although Canadian nationalism tends to ebb and flow, at the start of the 21st century it is no longer the concern it was two decades ago.

Quebec nationalism and the possibility of a third independence referendum remain as challenges to Canadian unity, although they appear to be descendent political options in the immediate future. Regionalism remains as strong, if not stronger, than it did in the 1980s, with the real possibility of a growing separatist movement in Alberta. Regional disparities remain high and, increasingly, the "have" provinces seem reluctant to support the "have not" provinces. A certain national crankiness has become evident in the political discourse of the Canadian polity.

Significant changes have occurred with respect to the Canadian electoral process. The political recruitment process has become more open and more diverse. While still a long way from a "mirror-image" of Canadian society, political leaders are increasingly representative of a diverse and multicultural polity. Restrictions on the right to vote have been reduced to minimal levels, although the rate of voter turnout has declined to historic lows. The length of national election campaigns has been reduced from two months to five weeks, largely as a result of the move from a temporary voters' list to a permanent voters' list.

The electoral system remains based on the plurality electoral formula, but a Charter-inspired change has occurred in the drawing of electoral boundaries. At both the federal and provincial levels, electoral constituencies must provide for effective representation based on a relative parity of voting power among Canadian voters. The result of this Supreme Court interpretation of the Charter has been a redrawing of electoral boundaries across the country.

Dramatic changes have occurred in the Canadian party system during the past two decades. Most important has been the revival and then the near-destruction of the Progressive Conservative Party of Canada. Following a period of Liberal-party dominance (1963–1984), the Tories under Brian Mulroney won two back-to-back majority victories in 1984 and 1988. It appeared that the Liberal party might cease to be a major player in the party system. Instead, the Conservatives, because of policies like free trade and the GST, failed constitutional reform efforts, and political scandals, managed to commit political hara-kiri. By the end of the 1980s, the Tory coalition had imploded, creating two new regional protest parties in its wake: the Reform Party in Western Canada and the Bloc Québécois in Quebec.

The Liberal party was the main beneficiary of these changes, greatly aided by the plurality electoral formula, which gave it strong majority governments in 1993, 1997, and 2000. In an attempt to "unite the right," Preston Manning disbanded the Reform Party and created the Canadian Alliance party in 2000. While it failed to unite the right, its popularity decimated the Tory party in the 1990s: the Tories barely maintained party status in the 2000 election, winning only 12 seats. The left, represented by the NDP, was also increasingly marginalized in the party system during the 1990s, winning only 13 seats in the 2000 election. As a result, for the past decade the Canadian party system has been dominated by one large party (the Liberals) and four minor and/or regional party challengers: Snow White versus the four dwarfs. Party leadership selection has become democratized at the national level, with parties now utilizing some form of a universal membership vote among party members.

Canadian interest groups have become more visible, more numerous, and more important — one result of the impact of the Charter on the political process. Charter Canadians and citizen interest groups have altered the political equation by their use of litigation and the courts to alter and expand civil and political liberties, in the process bypassing both the legislative and executive institutions of government. The two-decades-old battle over the "gag law" — which sought to restrict the role of interest groups in the election process — has come to an end, with the Supreme Court's decision in November of 2000 upholding this controversial law. While the Court's decision was a setback for interest groups in general, it is unlikely that the role and impact of interest groups will abate in the years ahead.

BRITAIN 1983 VERSUS BRITAIN 2002

Long viewed as a traditional and stable liberal-democratic polity with an unwritten constitution relatively immune to dramatic political reforms, Britain, following the Labour party's strong majority victory in 1997, began a process of constitutional change that is the most significant in at least several hundred years of British politics. Britain, with devolution to Northern Ireland, Scotland, and Wales, has moved from the pre-eminent example of a unitary state to an emerging pattern of "quasi-federalism." In addition, major and continuing reforms have altered the size and role of the House of Lords. Moreover, Britain has become subject to the European Convention on Human Rights, making the principle of parliamentary sovereignty a myth even in the nation of its birth. The constitutional revolution since 1998 has laid the basis for profound changes in the pattern of British politics in the years ahead.

On the one hand, the formal executive in Britain (the monarchy) has seen its public support decline dramatically and its constitutional position come under increasing scrutiny, especially by the Labour party. After the death of Lady Diana Spencer in 1997, the maturing of her sons, second and third in line to the throne, has managed to restore some public support for the monarchy but, quite likely, not to previous levels. Support for Prince Charles to succeed his mother is declining, with increased attention to the possibility of the new generation acceding to the throne. The political executive, on the other hand, has witnessed a strengthening of prime ministerial government, with the notion of cabinet government becoming an historical anachronism.

The 1980s and 1990s saw at least a temporary reassertion of the House of Lords in the legislative process, especially its willingness to vote against the government of the day on even major pieces of legislation. However, the dramatic reforms with respect to its size and composition seem to indicate that the House of Lords is more likely to be abolished than refurbished. The upper House is certainly not in a position to challenge the dominance of the House of Commons. The British Parliament may be bicameral in law, but it is quickly becoming unicameral in practice. The House of Commons, itself, has become even more subservient to the political executive than it was two decades ago.

The British system was long described as lacking in judicial review because Britain was a unitary state based on the principle of parliamentary sovereignty. However, recent constitutional changes have laid the basis for an evolving pattern of judicial review. Devolution ("quasi-federalism") may create the need for a limited judicial review process, while acceptance of the European Convention on Human Rights will provide the legal basis for a full judicial review process. Thus, it is no longer correct to describe the British polity as a system that lacks a process of judicial review.

With respect to the electoral process, Britain has become more open and diverse in relation to political recruitment, especially considering the Labour party's selection of female candidates in the 1997 election. The dominance of the "Oxbridge" connection is declining, as a multicultural Britain is reflected in the electoral process. Other than the introduction and then the elimination of the poll tax, few changes have taken place in the legal requirements for voting. However, as with other liberal-democracies, the rate of voter turnout has declined in recent national elections. Except for elections to the House of Commons, Britain is increasingly utilizing nonplurality electoral formulas.

The party system of the past two decades in Britain has seen continuing challenges from nationalist parties, the rise and fall of the Social Democratic Party and its evolution into the Liberal Democratic party of the 1990s, the ending of Tory party dominance (1979–1997), and the reform and rejuvenation of the Labour party under Tony Blair. As a result, "New Labour," after 18 years of trying, finally produced a majority government and party turnover in 1997. In terms of party leadership selection, the party caucus has been replaced by a democratized political recruitment process for the major parties.

Although trade union significance declined in the Thatcher years (1979–1990), interest groups, in general, have expanded their role and influence in the British polity. A pattern of corporatism has been supplanted by a more "American" approach to interest-group representation.

UNITED STATES 1983 VERSUS UNITED STATES 2002

While constitutional amendments are rare in the American system, the Twenty-Seventh Amendment was added in 1992 regarding salaries for members of Congress. During the 1980s and 1990s, with a Republican-dominated Supreme Court, the Constitution was generally interpreted in a pattern of judicial restraint, especially in the area of federalism. One significant exercise of judicial activism occurred in November and December of 2000 as the Supreme Court intervened in the disputed presidential election in Florida.

During these two decades, the presidency continued to be the key actor in the American political process, although the prestige and status of the office was greatly diminished. Concerns of an "imperial presidency" in the 1970s were supplanted by ones of an "imperilled presidency" in the 1990s. President Bill Clinton became only the second president in American history to be impeached (but not convicted). The role and significance of the vice-president continued to expand, which was especially true in light of Al Gore's relationship with Bill Clinton and Dick Cheney's initial political role for George W. Bush.

Executive-legislative deadlock reached near historic highs, as the federal government was actually shut down for lack of funds twice during the Clinton presidency. Legislative gridlock became the normal pattern, as an intense partisanship reinforced the principles of the separation of powers and checks and balances. A "politics of personal destruction" destroyed the prestige of public office, as well as the political careers, of both executive and legislative leaders.

Although somewhat restricted in its policy-making role, the Supreme Court continued as a centre of political controversy, in terms of both political issues, such as abortion, and its personnel. Supreme Court appointments became extremely politicized in the 1980s, a pattern that is likely to re-emerge in the presidency of George W. Bush.

With respect to political culture, two factors stand out. First, political morality seems to have been put to rest as a political issue as a result of the Clinton presidency, which managed to seduce the American public into believing that private morality has no bearing on public office. Second, race relations continued to dominate the domestic political agenda, combined with the growing multicultural nature of American society.

The electoral process faced new reforms, the most significant of which was the attempt to register as many voters as possible through such techniques as the motor-voter bill. However, in most elections the rate of voter participation and turnout continued to decline. Antiquated voting procedures were highlighted by the voting debacle in the state of Florida in the 2000 presidential election. Major changes are likely in the next few years in the techniques and technologies of voter registration and balloting.

The Republican and Democratic parties continued their dominance in the American party system, although a sizeable chunk of the electorate (about 35 percent) refuses to identify with either party. Third-party challenges had a significant impact on the competitive party system, as exemplified by Ross Perot's Reform Party in 1992 and 1996 and Ralph Nader's Green Party in 2000. However, these new parties do not appear to be possible replacements for either the Republican or Democratic parties in the years ahead.

Party finance remains a key area of political corruption and concern, with the amount of money needed to contest for a major elective office reaching astronomical levels. The ability to raise vast sums of money has allowed interest groups, especially PACs, to dominate both electoral and legislative politics in the American system.

A DEMOCRATIC AUDIT: CONCLUSIONS

In comparing our three key countries over a 20-year period, we have sought to make a democratic audit of the liberal-democratic nature and practices of these three political regimes. Certainly by comparison with existing political systems worldwide, few would deny that Canada, Britain, and the United States are liberal-democracies. Although the specifics differ from one country to the next, our 20-year survey reveals that all three polities are more democratic in 2002 than they were in 1983. The basic characteristics of polyarchal democracy are evident in all three political regimes, particularly with respect to democratic structures and practices.

If the comparison is not with utopias eternally waiting to be born but with real-world countries, the Canadian past will deserve a modestly honourable place in the annals of humanity's efforts to create civil polities. At a minimum, a "B+" would probably be awarded by impartial judges (Cairns, 1991: 33).

However, at the same time it is also clear that democratic content or substance is alarmingly low. Perhaps the best indication of this conclusion is the fact that in all three polities, voting in national elections — the pre-eminent democratic act for most citizens — is declining. While political structures and political processes have become democratized, the substance of democratic participation, especially the role of the individual citizen, has become increasingly marginalized. Opportunities for democratic participation have not been matched by actual citizen participation. The average citizen seems often to be characterized by political ignorance tempered by political apathy.

The future of liberal-democracy in the 21st century may largely depend on how this situation is changed in the decades ahead. Knowledgeable citizens who are politically active and involved are the key to the future success of liberal-democratic polities. Polities composed of Aristotles are unlikely; polities composed of citizens, in the best sense of that term, are at least a reasonable alternative. One possible way of achieving such a goal is through the use of technology in the democratic political process, what we have called POLITICS.com.

POLITICS.COM

New technologies have always had a profound, and sometimes revolutionary, impact on political processes and governmental institutions. Three great technological changes influenced the course of politics in the 20th century: radio, television, and the Internet. Each has changed, in its own way, the nature and practices of governance. For example, beginning in the 1950s, television revolutionized democratic practices, most notably in the area of campaign politics. The creation and rapid expansion of the Internet in the 1990s raises the question of not only how it will change the specific mechanisms of liberal-democracy, but also whether its impact will be beneficial or detrimental to the long-term success of liberal-democracy as a system of governance. The *impact of the Internet on the polity* is what we mean by the concept of **POLITICS.com.**

As with most new technologies, the long-term consequences of the Internet will likely be Janusian. In Roman mythology, Janus was a two-headed deity who symbolized new beginnings, looking forward and backward at the same time. In a similar vein, we could suggest that new technologies may have both advantages and disadvantages for the political arena. The impact of the Internet is unlikely to be neutral in terms of its political consequences. Moreover, it is important to remember that new technologies do not simply replace older ones, but work in combination with them. For example, all recent American presidents have continued to deliver a Saturday morning radio broadcast in the age of television and the Internet. Furthermore, new technologies are grafted onto existing political practices. Finally, new technologies are more likely to change the forms and techniques of politics before they change its substance and content. The Internet has the potential to both expand and restrict the art and practice of democratic governance.

The impact of the Internet can be seen by viewing democracy as an influence relationship between the government and the governed. The Internet has provided a new means for the government to inform citizens of their decisions. Major institutions and departments of government now have their own websites. For example, when the Supreme Court of Canada renders a decision, the full text of that decision can be immediately accessed on its website. Government information is more available now than it has even been in the past. The Internet has also allowed the governed to contact and influence the government more quickly. For example, members of Parliament in Canada now have their own websites which allow the average citizen to easily contact any MP. Views on public policy issues, requests for help with government agencies, or suggestions for political reform can be quickly and easily transmitted.

The Internet has also changed the internal workings of government itself. Bureaucrats do not need face-to-face meetings when e-mails will suffice. Documents can be easily transmitted electronically, with reports revised and finished in record time. Instead of "snail mail" and the use of hard-copy reports, much government work can be handled by way of the Internet. Government has become — dare we say it? — more efficient, allowing for the size and cost of government to be reduced as well.

The most dramatic impact of the new technologies has been on the electoral process. Over the Internet, an individual can now join a political party, contribute money to candidates or parties, register to vote in a general election, participate in a party leadership race, obtain political information, and create a new political party or interest group. In the near future, voting in an election may be done over the Internet, and it may also be utilized for the various forms of direct democracy. The Internet has already become a significant factor in organizing and running a modern election campaign.

Given these kinds of consequences, it would appear that the Internet has provided a means to enhance and support liberal-democratic polities. However, there is also a dark side to the politics of the Internet. First, while the Internet has democratized the techniques of democracy, it is open to question whether it will have the same impact on the substance of politics. Second, access to the Internet is not politically neutral, since it costs money to own a computer. Developed nations have a better chance to utilize "Internet democracy" than do poor nations. Moreover, economically and educationally disadvantaged groups in current liberal-democracies, are discriminated against by this new political technology. Third, instead of providing a means for citizens to influence and control their government, it is probably just as likely that government will use the Internet to control its citizens.

At the start of the 21st century, we are witnessing the implementation of a **total-surveillance society**, even in liberal-democratic systems (Whitaker, 1999). Almost everything that a citizen now does is recorded, ranging from phone calls, e-mails, and faxes, to use of the Internet. Surveillance in public spaces, such as shopping malls or downtown streets, is matched by increasing surveillance in private spaces, such as the workplace. Credit cards, debit cards, and health cards all track and potentially control citizen activity. Governments are now seeking to establish DNA banks, so that citizens can be tracked throughout their lifetimes. Video cameras are ever-present; everybody is now their own *Truman Show*.

> The remedy for these ills, however, does not lie in institutional reform but in political action, participation and commitment by more of the populace. Failing that, Canada is condemned like other countries to the most unhappy of fates: it has the government it deserves (Franks, 1983: 206).

How does liberal-democracy survive the emergence of a total-surveillance polity? It either survives with an educated citizenry that is actively involved in the political process or it does not survive at all. The threats to democracy can only be prevented by more democracy!

CONCEPT FILE

democratic audit
POLITICS.com

polyarchal democracy
total-surveillance society

RECOMMENDED READINGS

ALCOCK, REG and DONALD G. LENIHAN (2001) *Opening the E-government File: Governing in the 21st Century.* Ottawa: Centre for Collaborative Government.

BARBER, BENJAMIN R. (1999) "Three Scenarios for the Future of Technology and Strong Democracy," *Political Science Quarterly*, Volume 113, Number 4, pp. 573–589.

BARBER, JAMES DAVID (1995) *The Book of Democracy.* Englewood Cliffs, New Jersey: Prentice Hall.

BEETHAM, DAVID (1999) "The Idea of a Democratic Audit in Comparative Perspective," *Parliamentary Affairs*, Volume 52, Number 4, pp. 567–581.

BIMBER, BRUCE (1998) "The Internet and Political Transformation: Populism, Community, and Accelerated Pluralism," *Polity*, Volume 31, Number 1, pp. 133–160.

CANOVAN, MARGARET (1999) "Trust the People! Populism and the Two Faces of Democracy," *Political Studies*, Volume 47, Number 1, pp. 2–16.

DAHL, ROBERT A. (1998) *On Democracy.* New Haven: Yale University Press.

FOWERAKER, JOE and ROMAN KRZNARIC (2000) "Measuring Liberal Democratic Performance: An Empirical and Conceptual Critique," *Political Studies*, Volume 48, Number 4, pp. 759–787.

HUBER, EVELYNE et al. (1997) "The Paradoxes of Contemporary Democracy: Formal, Participatory, and Social Dimensions," *Comparative Politics*, Volume 29, Number 3, pp. 323–342.

KNOPFF, RAINER (1998) "Populism and the Politics of Rights: The Dual Attack on Representative Democracy," *Canadian Journal of Political Science*, Volume 31, Number 4, pp. 683–705.

MARQUAND, DAVID (2000) "Democracy in Britain," *The Political Quarterly*, Volume 71, Number 3, pp. 268–276.

MORRIS, DICK (1999) *VOTE.com*. Los Angeles: Renaissance Books, 1999.

NATIONAL AUDIT OFFICE, UK (1999) *Government on the Web*. London: HMSO.

PARKER, JOHN (2000) *Total Surveillance: Investigating the Big Brother World of E-Spies, Eavesdroppers and CCTV*. London: Piatkus.

PHARR, SUSAN J. and ROBERT D. PUTNAM, eds. (2000) *Disaffected Democracies: What's Troubling the Trilateral Countries?* Princeton, New Jersey: Princeton University Press.

PRATCHETT, LAWRENCE (1999) "New Fashions in Public Participation: Towards Greater Democracy?" *Parliamentary Affairs*, Volume 52, Number 4, pp. 616–633.

SCHLESINGER, ARTHUR, JR. (1997) "Has Democracy a Future?" *Foreign Affairs*, Volume 76, Number 5, pp. 2–12.

THOMPSON, DENNIS F. (1999) "Democratic Secrecy," *Political Science Quarterly*, Volume 114, Number 2, pp. 181–193.

TUCKER, AVIEZER et al. (2000) "From Republican Virtue to Technology of Political Power: Three Episodes of Czech Nonpolitical Politics," *Political Science Quarterly*, Volume 115, Number 3, pp. 421–445.

VIG, NORMAN J. and HERBERT PASCHEN, eds. (2000) *Parliaments and Technology: The Development of Technology Assessment in Europe*. Ithaca, New York: SUNY Press.

WEIR, STUART (1999) *Political Power and Democratic Control in Britain: The Democratic Audit of the United Kingdom*. London: Routledge.

WHITAKER, REG (1999) *The End of Privacy: How Total Surveillance Is Becoming a Reality*. New York: The New Press.

WRIGHT, STEVE (1998) *An Appraisal of Technologies for Political Control*. Luxembourg: European Parliament, Directorate General for Research.

APPENDIX: Constitution Act, 1982

PART 1

CANADIAN CHARTER OF RIGHTS AND FREEDOMS

Whereas Canada is founded upon principles that recognize the supremacy of God and the rule of law:

Guarantee of Rights and Freedoms

1. The *Canadian Charter of Rights and Freedoms* guarantees the rights and freedoms set out in it subject only to such reasonable limits prescribed by law as can be demonstrably justified in a free and democratic society.

Fundamental Freedoms

2. Everyone has the following fundamental freedoms:
    - (*a*) freedom of conscience and religion;
    - (*b*) freedom of thought, belief, opinion and expression, including freedom of the press and other media of communication;
    - (*c*) freedom of peaceful assembly; and
    - (*d*) freedom of association.

Democratic Rights

3. Every citizen of Canada has the right to vote in an election of members of the House of Commons or of a legislative assembly and to be qualified for membership therein.

4. (1) No House of Commons and no legislative assembly shall continue for longer than five years from the date fixed for the return of the writs of a general election of its members.
    (2) In time of real or apprehended war, invasion or insurrection, a House of Commons may be continued by Parliament and a legislative assembly may be continued by the legislature beyond five years if such continuation is not opposed by the votes of more than one-third of the members of the House of Commons or the legislative assembly, as the case may be.

5. There shall be a sitting of Parliament and of each legislature at least once every twelve months.

Mobility Rights

6. (1) Every citizen of Canada has the right to enter, remain in and leave Canada.
    (2) Every citizen of Canada and every person who has the status of a permanent resident of Canada has the right
    - (*a*) to move to and take up residence in any province; and
    - (*b*) to pursue the gaining of a livelihood in any province.
    (3) The rights specified in subsection (2) are subject to
    - (*a*) any laws or practices of general application in force in a province other than those that discriminate among persons primarily on the basis of province of present or previous residence; and
    - (*b*) any laws providing for reasonable residency requirements as a qualification for the receipt of publicly provided social services.
    (4) Subsections (2) and (3) do not preclude any law, program or activity that has as its object the amelioration in a province of conditions of individuals in that province who are socially or economically disadvantaged if the rate of employment in that province is below the rate of employment in Canada.

Legal Rights

7. Everyone has the right to life, liberty and security of the person and the right not to be deprived thereof except in accordance with the principles of fundamental justice.

8. Everyone has the right to be secure against unreasonable search or seizure.

9. Everyone has the right not to be arbitrarily detained or imprisoned.

10. Everyone has the right on arrest or detention
   (*a*) to be informed promptly of the reasons therefor;
   (*b*) to retain and instruct counsel without delay and to be informed of that right; and
   (*c*) to have the validity of the detention determined by way of *habeas corpus* and to be released if the detention is not lawful.

11. Any person charged with an offence has the right
   (*a*) to be informed without unreasonable delay of the specific offence;
   (*b*) to be tried within a reasonable time;
   (*c*) not to be compelled to be a witness in proceedings against that person in respect of the offence;
   (*d*) to be presumed innocent until proven guilty according to law in a fair and public hearing by an independent and impartial tribunal;
   (*e*) not to be denied reasonable bail without just cause;
   (*f*) except in the case of an offence under military law tried before a military tribunal, to the benefit of trial by jury where the maximum punishment for the offence is imprisonment for five years or a more severe punishment;
   (*g*) not to be found guilty on account of any act or omission unless, at the time of the act or omission, it con-

stituted an offence under Canadian or international law or was criminal according to the general principles of law recognized by the community of nations;
   (*h*) if finally acquitted of the offence, not to be tried for it again and, if finally found guilty and punished for the offence, not to be tried or punished for it again; and
   (*i*) if found guilty of the offence and if the punishment for the offence has been varied between the time of commission and the time of sentencing, to the benefit of the lesser punishment.

12. Everyone has the right not to be subjected to any cruel and unusual treatment or punishment.

13. A witness who testifies in any proceedings has the right not to have any incriminating evidence so given used to incriminate that witness in any other proceedings, except in a prosecution for perjury or for the giving of contradictory evidence.

14. A party or witness in any proceedings who does not understand or speak the language in which the proceedings are conducted or who is deaf has the right to the assistance of an interpreter.

Equality Rights

15. (1) Every individual is equal before and under the law and has the right to the equal protection and equal benefit of the law without discrimination and, in particular, without discrimination based on race, national or ethnic origin, colour, religion, sex, age or mental or physical disability.
   (2) Subsection (1) does not preclude any law, program or activity that has as its object the amelioration of conditions

of disadvantaged individuals or groups including those that are disadvantaged because of race, national or ethnic origin, colour, religion, sex, age or mental or physical disability.

Official Languages of Canada

16. (1) English and French are the official languages of Canada and have equality of status and equal rights and privileges as to their use in all institutions of the Parliament and government of Canada.
    (2) English and French are the official languages of New Brunswick and have equality of status and equal rights and privileges as to their use in all institutions of the legislature and government of New Brunswick.
    (3) Nothing in this Charter limits the authority of Parliament or a legislature to advance the equality of status or use of English and French.

17. (1) Everyone has the right to use English or French in any debates and other proceedings of Parliament.
    (2) Everyone has the right to use English or French in any debates and other proceedings of the legislature of New Brunswick.

18. (1) The statutes, records and journals of Parliament shall be printed and published in English and French and both language versions are equally authoritative.
    (2) The statutes, records and journals of the legislature of New Brunswick shall be printed and published in English and French and both language versions are equally authoritative.

19. (1) Either English or French may be used by any person in, or in any pleading in or process issuing from, any court established by Parliament.
    (2) Either English or French may be used by any person in, or in any pleading in or process issuing from, any court of New Brunswick.

20. (1) Any member of the public in Canada has the right to communicate with, and to receive available services from, any head or central office of an institution of the Parliament or government of Canada in English or French, and has the same right with respect to any other office of any such institution where
    (a) there is a significant demand for communications with and services from that office in such language; or
    (b) due to the nature of the office, it is reasonable that communications with and services from that office be available in both English and French.
    (2) Any member of the public in New Brunswick has the right to communicate with, and to receive available services from, any office of an institution of the legislature or government of New Brunswick in English or French.

21. Nothing in sections 16 to 20 abrogates or derogates from any right, privilege or obligation with respect to the English and French languages, or either of them, that exists or is continued by virtue of any other provision of the Constitution of Canada.

22. Nothing in sections 16 to 20 abrogates or derogates from any legal or customary right or privilege acquired or enjoyed either before or after the coming into force of this Charter with respect to any language that is not English or French.

Minority Language Educational Rights

23. (1) Citizens of Canada
    (a) whose first language learned and still understood is that of the

English or French linguistic minority population of the province in which they reside, or

(b) who have received their primary school instruction in Canada in English or French and reside in a province where the language in which they received that instruction is the language of the English or French linguistic minority population of the province, have the right to have their children receive primary and secondary school instruction in that language in that province.

(2) Citizens of Canada of whom any child has received or is receiving primary or secondary school instruction in English or French in Canada, have the right to have all their children receive primary and secondary school instruction in the same language.

(3) The right of citizens of Canada under subsections (1) and (2) to have their children receive primary and secondary school instruction in the language of the English or French linguistic minority population of a province

(a) applies wherever in the province the number of children of citizens who have such a right is sufficient to warrant the provision to them out of public funds of minority language instruction; and

(b) includes, where the number of those children so warrants, the right to have them receive that instruction in minority language educational facilities provided out of public funds.

Enforcement

24. (1) Anyone whose rights or freedoms, as guaranteed by this Charter, have been infringed or denied may apply to a court of competent jurisdiction to obtain such remedy as the court considers appropriate and just in the circumstances.

(2) Where, in proceedings under subsection (1), a court concludes that evidence was obtained in a manner that infringed or denied any rights or freedoms guaranteed by this Charter, the evidence shall be excluded if it is established that, having regard to all the circumstances, the admission of it in the proceedings would bring the administration of justice into disrepute.

General

25. The guarantee in this Charter of certain rights and freedoms shall not be construed so as to abrogate or derogate from any aboriginal, treaty or other rights or freedoms that pertain to the aboriginal peoples of Canada including

(a) any rights or freedoms that have been recognized by the royal proclamation of October 7, 1763; and

(b) any rights or freedoms that may be acquired by the aboriginal peoples of Canada by way of land claims settlement.

26. The guarantee in this Charter of certain rights and freedoms shall not be construed as denying the existence of any other rights or freedoms that exist in Canada.

27. This Charter shall be interpreted in a manner consistent with the preservation and enhancement of the multicultural heritage of Canadians.

28. Notwithstanding anything in this Charter, the rights and freedoms referred to in it are guaranteed equally to male and female persons.

29. Nothing in this Charter abrogates or derogates from any rights or privileges guaran-

teed by or under the Constitution of Canada in respect of denominational, separate or dissentient schools.

30. A reference in this Charter to a Province or to the legislative assembly or legislature of a province shall be deemed to include a reference to the Yukon Territory and the Northwest Territories, or to the appropriate legislative authority thereof, as the case may be.

31. Nothing in this Charter extends the legislative powers of any body or authority.

Application of Charter

32. (1) This Charter applies
     (*a*) to the Parliament and government of Canada in respect of all matters within the authority of Parliament including all matters relating to the Yukon Territory and Northwest Territories; and
     (*b*) to the legislature and government of each province in respect of all matters within the authority of the legislature of each province.
    (2) Notwithstanding subsection (1), section 15 shall not have effect until three years after this section comes into force.

33. (1) Parliament or the legislature of a province may expressly declare in an Act of Parliament or of the legislature, as the case may be, that the Act or a provision thereof shall operate notwithstanding a provision included in section 2 or sections 7 to 15 of this Charter.
    (2) An Act or a provision of an Act in respect of which a declaration made under this section is in effect shall have such operation as it would have but for the provision of this Charter referred to in the declaration.
    (3) A declaration made under subsection (1) shall cease to have effect five years after it comes into force or on such earlier date as may be specified in the declaration.
    (4) Parliament or the legislature of a province may re-enact a declaration made under subsection (1).
    (5) Subsection (3) applies in respect of a re-enactment made under subsection (4).

Citation

34. This Part may be cited as the *Canadian Charter of Rights and Freedoms.*

REFERENCES

ABRAMSON, PAUL R., JOHN H. ALDRICH, PHIL PAOLINO, and DAVID W. ROHDE (1995) "Third-Party and Independent Candidates in American Politics: Wallace, Anderson and Perot," *Political Science Quarterly*, Volume 110, Number 3, pp. 349–367.

ALDERMAN, KEITH (1996) "The Conservative Party Leadership Election of 1995," *Parliamentary Affairs*, Volume 49, Number 2, pp. 316–332.

—— (1999) "Revision of Leadership Election Procedures in the Conservative Party," *Parliamentary Affairs*, Volume 52, Number 2, pp. 260–274.

ALDERMAN, KEITH and NEIL CARTER (1991) "A Very Tory Coup: The Ousting of Mrs. Thatcher," *Parliamentary Affairs*, Volume 44, Number 2, pp. 125–139.

—— (1993) "The Labour Party Leadership and Deputy Leadership Elections of 1992," *Parliamentary Affairs*, Volume 46, Number 1, pp. 49–65.

—— (1995) "The Labour Party Leadership and Deputy Leadership Elections of 1994," *Parliamentary Affairs*, Volume 48, Number 3, pp. 438–455.

ALEXANDER, CYNTHIA J. (1996) "Plugging into New Currents: The Use of New Information and Communication Technologies in Party Politics," in *Party Politics in Canada*, 7th ed., ed. Hugh G. Thorburn, 594–610. Scarborough, Ontario: Prentice Hall Canada.

ALFORD, ROBERT R. (1963) *Party and Society: The Anglo-American Democracies*. Chicago: Rand McNally.

ALMOND, GABRIEL A. and SIDNEY VERBA (1965) *The Civic Culture: Political Attitudes and Democracy in Five Nations*. Boston: Little, Brown and Company.

BAGEHOT, WALTER (1867, 1963) *The English Constitution*. London: Collins, The Fontana Library.

BAKER, DAVID, ANDREW GAMBLE, and STEVE LUDLAM (1994) "The Parliamentary Siege of Maastricht 1993: Conservative Divisions and British Ratification," *Parliamentary Affairs*, Volume 47, Number 1, pp. 37–60.

BAKER, ROSS K. (1995) *House and Senate*. 2nd ed. New York: W.W. Norton.

BAKVIS, HERMAN (1989) "Regional Politics and Policy in the Mulroney Cabinet, 1984–88: Towards a Theory of the Regional Minister System in Canada," *Canadian Public Policy*, Volume 15, Number 2, pp. 121–134.

BANFIELD, EDWARD C. (1980) "In Defense of the American Party System," in *Political Parties in the Eighties*, ed. Robert A. Goldwin, 133–149. Washington, D.C.: American Enterprise Institute for Public Policy Research.

BARBER, BENJAMIN R. (2000) "Can Democracy Survive Globalization?" *Government and Opposition*, Volume 35, Number 3, pp. 275–301.

BARBER, JAMES DAVID (1985) *The Presidential Character: Predicting Performance in the White House*. 3rd ed. Englewood Cliffs, New Jersey: Prentice-Hall.

—— (1995) *The Book of Democracy*. Englewood Cliffs, New Jersey: Prentice Hall.

BARKER, ERNEST, ed. (1962) *The Politics of Aristotle*. New York: Oxford University Press.

BARRETT, JAMES R. (1992) "Americanization from the Bottom Up: Immigration and the Remaking of the Working Class in the United States, 1880–1930," *The Journal of American History*, Volume 79, Number 3, pp. 996–1020.

BASHEVKIN, SYLVIA B. (1991) *True Patriot Love: The Politics of Canadian Nationalism*. Toronto: Oxford University Press.

BECK, J. MURRAY (1968) *Pendulum of Power: Canada's Federal Elections*. Scarborough, Ontario: Prentice-Hall Canada.

BEER, SAMUEL H. (1973) "The British Political System," in *Patterns of Government: The Major Political Systems of Europe*, 3rd ed., eds. Samuel H. Beer et al., 119–329. New York: Random House.

BEETHAM, DAVID (1999) "The Idea of a Democratic Audit in Comparative Perspective," *Parliamentary Affairs*, Volume 52, Number 4, pp. 567–581.

BEINART, PETER A. (1989) "The Real American Voting Problem," *Polity*, Volume 22, Number 1, pp. 143–156.

BENN, TONY (1982) *Arguments for Democracy*. Middlesex, England: Penguin Books.

BENNETT, WILLIAM J. (1998) *The Death of Outrage: Bill Clinton and the Assault on American Ideals*. New York: The Free Press.

BENTLEY, A.F. (1908) *The Process of Government*. Chicago: University of Chicago Press.

BERCUSON, DAVID and BARRY COOPER (1997) "Should judges make the rules when lawmakers refuse to act?" *The Globe and Mail* (February 15), p. D2.

BERGER, THOMAS R. (1982) *Fragile Freedoms: Human Rights and Dissent in Canada*. Toronto: Clarke, Irwin and Company.

BERNSTEIN, EDUARD (1899, 1961) *Evolutionary Socialism: A Criticism and Affirmation*. New York: Schocken Books.

BERRINGTON, HUGH (1974) "Review Article: The Fiery Chariot: British Prime Ministers and the Search for

Love," *British Journal of Political Science*, Volume 4, Number 3, pp. 345–370.

BERRY, JEFFREY M. (1984) *The Interest Group Society.*Boston: Little, Brown and Company.BERRY, JEFFREY M. (1997) *The Interest Group Society.* 3rd ed. New York: Addison Wesley Longman.

BICKERTON, JAMES, ALAIN-G. GAGNON, and PATRICK J. SMITH (1999) *Ties That Bind: Parties and Voters in Canada.* Don Mills, Ontario: Oxford University Press.

BIERCE, AMBROSE (1911, 1958) *The Devil's Dictionary.* New York: Dover Publications.

BINDER, SARAH A. and STEVEN S. SMITH (1997) *Politics or Principle? Filibustering in the United States Senate.* Washington, D.C.: Brookings Institution Press.

BIRCH, ANTHONY H. (1983) *The British System of Government.* 6th ed. London: George Allen and Unwin.

BLACK, CHARLES (1963) *Perspectives in Constitutional Law.* Englewood Cliffs, New Jersey: Prentice-Hall.

BLACK, EDWIN R. (1979) "Federal Strains within a Canadian Party," in *Party Politics in Canada,* 4th ed., ed. Hugh Thorburn, 89–99. Scarborough, Ontario: Prentice-Hall Canada.

BLACK, JEROME H. (1991) "Reforming the Context of the Voting Process in Canada: Lessons from Other Democracies," in *Voter Turnout in Canada,* ed. Herman Bakvis, 61–176. Toronto: Dundurn Press, Volume 15 of the Research Studies of the Royal Commission on Electoral Reform and Party Financing.

—— (2000) "Entering the Political Elite in Canada: The Case of Minority Women as Parliamentary Candidates and MPs," *The Canadian Review of Sociology and Anthropology,* Volume 37, Number 2, pp. 143–166.

BLACKBURN, ROBERT and RAYMOND PLANT, eds. (1999) *Constitutional Reform: The Labour Government's Constitutional Reform Agenda.* London: Longman.

BLONDEL, JEAN (1973) *Comparative Legislatures.* Englewood Cliffs, New Jersey: Prentice-Hall.

—— (1987) *Political Leadership: Towards a General Analysis.* London: Sage.

BOGDANOR, VERNON (1984) *What Is Proportional Representation? A Guide to the Issues.* Oxford: Martin Robertson.

—— (1987) "Electoral Reform and British Politics," *Electoral Studies,* Volume 6, Number 2, pp. 115–121.

—— (1988) "Britain: The Political Constitution," in *Constitutions in Democratic Politics,* ed. Vernon Bogdanor, 53–72. Adlershot, England: Gower Publishing.

—— (1992) "The 1992 General Election and the British Party System," *Government and Opposition,* Volume 27, Number 3, pp. 283–298.

BORK, ROBERT H. (1986) "Judicial Review and Democracy," *Society,* Volume 24, Number 1, pp. 5–8.

—— (2000) "Courting disaster," *National Post* (February 18), p. A18.

BOYER, J. PATRICK (1985) *Equality for All: Report of the Parliamentary Committee on Equality Rights.* Ottawa: Supply and Services.

—— (1988) "Robust Democracy: The Canadian General Election of 1988," *The Parliamentarian,* Volume 70, Number 2, pp. 72–76

BRADLEY, IAN (1981) *Breaking the Mold? The Birth and Prospects of the Social Democratic Party.* Oxford: Martin Robertson.

BRADSHAW, KENNETH and DAVID PRING (1972) *Parliament and Congress.* London: Quartet Books.

BRADY, ALEXANDER (1947) *Democracy in the Dominions: A Comparative Study in Institutions.* Toronto: University of Toronto Press.

BRENNAN, WILLIAM J., Jr. (1987) "Interpreting the Constitution," *Social Policy,* Volume 18, Number 1, pp. 24–28.

BRODIE, JANINE and CELIA CHANDLER (1995) "More Women Wanted," in *Politics: Canada,* 8th ed., eds. Paul W. Fox and Graham White, 350–359. Toronto: McGraw-Hill.

BRODIE, JANINE and JILL VICKERS (1981) "The More Things Change . . . Women in the 1979 Federal Campaign," in *Canada at the Polls, 1979 and 1980: A Study of the General Elections,* ed. Howard R. Penniman, 322–336. Washington, D.C.: American Enterprise Institute for Public Policy Research.

BRYCE, JAMES (1921) *Canada: An Actual Democracy.* Toronto: Macmillan Company of Canada.

BUDGE, IAN, IVOR CREWE, DAVID MCKAY, and KEN-NETH NEWTON (1998) *The New British Politics.* Essex, England: Addison Wesley Longman.

BUNCE, VALERIE (1981) *Do New Leaders Make a Difference? Executive Succession and Public Policy under Capitalism and Socialism.* Princeton, New Jersey: Princeton University Press.

BURGESS, JOANNE HARRIS (1997) "René Levec? Low marks in history," *The Globe and Mail* (January 4), p. D3.

BURKETT, TONY (1975) *Parties and Elections in West Germany.* New York: St. Martin's Press.

BURNS, JAMES MACGREGOR, J.W. PELTASON, THOMAS E. CRONIN, and DAVID B. MAGLEBY (1997) *Government by the People, Brief Edition.* 2nd ed. Upper Saddle River, New Jersey: Prentice Hall.

—— (2000) *Government by the People, Basic Version* 18th ed. Upper Saddle River, New Jersey: Prentice Hall.

BUTLER, DAVID and BRUCE CAIN (1992) *Congressional Redistricting: Comparative and Theoretical Perspectives.* New York: Macmillan.

BUTLER, DAVID and DENNIS KAVANAGH (1992) *The British General Election of 1992.* London: Macmillan.

BYKERK, LOREE and ARDITH MANEY (1992) "Where Have All the Consumers Gone?" *Political Science Quarterly*, Volume 106, Number 4, pp. 677–693.

CAIRNS, ALAN C. (1968) "The Electoral System and Party System in Canada, 1921–1965," *Canadian Journal of Political Science*, Volume 1, Number 1, pp. 55–80.

—— (1981) "The Constitutional, Legal, and Historical Background," in *Canada at the Polls, 1979 and 1980: A Study of the General Elections*, ed. Howard R. Penniman, 1–23. Washington, D.C.: American Enterprise Institute for Public Policy Research.

—— (1991) *Disruptions: Constitutional Struggles, from the Charter to Meech Lake*, ed. Douglas E. Williams. Toronto: McClelland and Stewart.

CAMERON, STEVIE (1995) *On the Take*. Toronto: Seal-McClelland Bantam.

CAMP, DALTON (1984) "Reforming the Senate: a political game that never ends," *The Gazette* (March 8), p. B3.

CAMPBELL, COLIN (1978) *The Canadian Senate: A Lobby from Within*. Toronto: Macmillan of Canada.

CANETTI, ELIAS (1966) *Crowds and Power*. New York: Viking Press.

CASSIRER, ERNST (1946) *The Myth of the State*. New Haven, Conn.: Yale University Press.

CEASAR, JAMES W. (1979) *Presidential Selection: Theory and Development*. Princeton, New Jersey: Princeton University Press.

CERNEY, PHILIP G. (1999) "Globalization and the Erosion of Democracy," *European Journal of Political Research*, Volume 36, Number 1, pp. 1–26.

CHASE, HAROLD W., ROBERT T. HOLT, and JOHN E. TURNER (1980) *American Government in Comparative Perspective*. New York: Franklin Watts.

CHEFFINS, R.I. and R.N. TUCKER (1976) *The Constitutional Process in Canada*. 2nd ed. Toronto: McGraw-Hill Ryerson.

CHIROT, DANIEL (1994) *Modern Tyrants: The Power and Prevalence of Evil in Our Age*. Princeton, New Jersey: Princeton University Press.

CHRISMAN, ROBERT and ROBERT L. ALLEN, eds. (1992) *Court of Appeal: The Black Community Speaks Out on the Racial and Sexual Politics of Clarence Thomas v. Anita Hill*. New York: Ballantine Books.

CHRISTIAN, WILLIAM and COLIN CAMPBELL (1974) *Political Parties and Ideologies in Canada*. Toronto: McGraw-Hill Ryerson.

CHURCHILL, WINSTON (1949) *Their Finest Hour*. London: Cassell.

CLARK, IAN D. (1985) "Recent Changes in the Cabinet Decision-making System in Ottawa," *Canadian Public Administration*, Volume 28, Number 2, pp. 185–201.

CLARKE, HAROLD D., JANE JENSON, LAWRENCE LEDUC, and JON H. PAMMETT (1984) *Absent Mandate: The Politics of Discontent in Canada*. Toronto: Gage.

—— (1996) *Absent Mandate: Canadian Electoral Politics in an Era of Restructuring*. 3rd ed. Toronto: Gage.

COMMAGER, HENRY STEELE (1984) "Tocqueville's mistake," *Harper's Magazine*, Volume 269, No. 1611, pp. 70–74.

CONQUEST, ROBERT (1999) *Reflections on a Ravaged Century*. London: John Murray.

CONWAY, MARGARET M., MIKEL L. WYCKOFF, ELEANOR FELDBAUM, and DAVID AHERN (1981) "The News Media in Children's Political Socialization," *Public Opinion Quarterly*, Volume 45, Number 2, pp. 164–178.

COOMBER, DEREK (1992) "Britain's poll-tax protest: it gagged a million voters," *The Globe and Mail* (April 14), p. A7.

CORRY, J.A. (1947) *Democratic Government and Politics*. Toronto: University of Toronto Press.

COURTNEY, JOHN C. (1973) *The Selection of National Party Leaders in Canada*. Toronto: Macmillan of Canada.

—— (1995) *Do Conventions Matter? Choosing National Party Leaders in Canada*. Montreal: McGill-Queen's University Press.

COURTNEY, JOHN C., PETER MACKINNON, and DAVID E. SMITH, eds. (1992) *Drawing Boundaries: Legislatures, Courts and Electoral Values*. Saskatoon, Saskatchewan: Fifth House Publishers.

COURTOIS, STÉPHANE, MARK KRAMER (Translator), JONATHAN MURPHY (Translator), JEAN-LOUIS PANNE, ANDRZEJ PACZKOWSKI, KAREL BARTOSEK, and JEAN-LOUIS MARGOLIN (1999) *The Black Book of Communism: Crimes, Terror, Repression*. Cambridge, Mass.: Harvard University Press.

COXALL, BILL and LYNTON ROBINS (1994) *Contemporary British Politics*. 2nd ed. London: Macmillan.

CRICK, BERNARD (1964) *In Defence of Politics*. Baltimore, Maryland: Penguin Books.

—— (1973) *Basic Forms of Government: A Sketch and a Model*. London: Macmillan Press.

CROSSMAN, RICHARD H.S. (1972) *The Myths of Cabinet Government*. Cambridge, Mass.: Harvard University Press.

CURTICE, JOHN (1992) "The Hidden Surprise: The British Electoral System in 1992," *Parliamentary Affairs*, Volume 45, Number 4, pp. 466–474.

DAHL, ROBERT A. (1956) *A Preface to Democratic Theory*. Chicago: University of Chicago Press.

—— (1970) *After the Revolution?* New Haven, Conn.: Yale University Press.

—— (1982) *Dilemmas of Pluralist Democracy: Autonomy vs. Control*. New Haven, Conn.: Yale University Press.

—— (1984) *Modern Political Analysis.* 4th ed. Englewood Cliffs, New Jersey: Prentice-Hall.

—— (1990) "Myth of the Presidential Mandate," *Political Science Quarterly,* Volume 105, Number 3, pp. 355–372.

—— (1998) *On Democracy.* New Haven, Conn.: Yale University Press.

DALLEK, ROBERT (1996) *Hail to the Chief: The Making and Unmaking of American Presidents.* New York: Hyperion.

DALLIN, ALEXANDER and GEORGE W. BRESLAUER (1970) *Political Terror in Communist Systems.* Stanford, California: Stanford University Press.

DALTON, RUSSELL J. (1996) *Citizen Politics: Public Opinion and Political Parties in Advanced Western Democracies.* 2nd ed. Chatham, New Jersey: Chatham House Publishers.

DAWSON, R. MACGREGOR (1970) *The Government of Canada.* 5th ed. Rev. by Norman Ward. Toronto: University of Toronto Press.

DAWSON, RICHARD E., KENNETH PREWITT, and KAREN S. DAWSON (1977) *Political Socialization.* 2nd ed. Boston: Little, Brown and Co.

DELACOURT, SUSAN (1993) *United We Fall: The Crisis of Democracy in Canada.* Toronto: Viking.

DENVER, DAVID and GORDON HANDS (1997) "Turnout," *Parliamentary Affairs,* Volume 50, Number 4, pp. 720–732.

DE TOCQUEVILLE, ALEXIS (1835, 1945) *Democracy in America,* ed. Phillips Bradley. New York: Vintage Books.

DEUTSCH, KARL W. (1968) *The Analysis of International Relations.* Englewood Cliffs, New Jersey: Prentice-Hall.

DICKSON, MR. CHIEF JUSTICE BRIAN (1985) "The Judiciary — Law Interpreters or Law-makers?" in *Canadian Politics: A Comparative Reader,* ed. Ronald G. Landes, 213–218. Scarborough, Ontario: Prentice-Hall Canada.

DJILAS, MILOVAN (1957) *The New Class: An Analysis of the Communist System.* New York: Praeger Publishers.

DOBROWOLSKY, ALEXANDRA (2000) *The Politics of Pragmatism: Women, Representation, and Constitutionalism in Canada.* Don Mills, Ontario: Oxford University Press.

DOGAN, MATTEI and DOMINIQUE PELASSY (1984) *How to Compare Nations: Strategies in Comparative Politics.* Chatham, New Jersey: Chatham House Publishers.

DOWNS, ANTHONY (1957) *An Economic Theory of Democracy.* New York: Harper and Row.

DREWRY, GAVIN (1992) "Judicial Politics in Britain: Patrolling the Boundaries," *West European Politics,* Volume 15, Number 3, pp. 9–28.

DRUCKER, H.M., ed. (1979) *Multi-Party Britian.* London: Macmillan Press.

—— (1984) "Intra-Party Democracy in Action: The Election of Leader and Deputy Leader by the Labour Party in 1983," *Parliamentary Affairs,* Volume 37, Number 3, pp. 283–300.

DUCHACEK, IVO (1973) *Rights and Liberties in the World Today: Constitutional Promise and Reality.* Santa Barbara, California: ABC-CLIO Press.

DUERST-LAHTI, GEORGIA (1989) "The Government's Role in Building the Women's Movement," *Political Science Quarterly,* Volume 104, Number 2, pp. 249–268.

DUNCAN, GRAEME (1987) "Understanding Ideology," *Political Studies,* Volume 35, Number 4, pp. 649–659.

DUNLEAVY, PATRICK (2000) "Elections and Party Politics," in *Developments in British Politics 6,* eds. Dunleavy et al., 127–150. New York: St. Martin's Press.

DUNLEAVY, PATRICK, HELEN MARGETTS, and STUART WEIR (1992) "How Britain Would Have Voted under Alternative Electoral Systems in 1992," *Parliamentary Affairs,* Volume 45, Number 4, pp. 640–655.

DUNN, BRIAN A. (1989) "The Governor-General: The Changing of the Guard," *The New Federation,* Volume 1, Number 3, pp. 10–13.

DUVERGER, MAURICE (1951) "The Influence of the Electoral System on Political Life," *International Social Science Bulletin,* Volume 3, Number 2, pp. 314–365.

—— (1964) *Political Parties: Their Organization and Activity in the Modern State.* London: Methuen and Co.

—— (1972) *Party Politics and Pressure Groups: A Comparative Introduction.* New York: Thomas Y. Crowell.

—— (1974) *Modern Democracies: Economic Power versus Political Power.* Hinsdale, Illinois: The Dryden Press.

—— (1986) "Duverger's Law: Forty Years Later," in *Electoral Laws and Their Political Consequences,* eds. Bernard Grofman and Arend Lijphart, 69–84. New York: Agathon Press.

DYE, THOMAS R. (1997) *Politics in America.* 2nd ed. Upper Saddle River, New Jersey: Prentice Hall.

EAGLES, MUNROE (1991) "Voting and Non-voting in Canadian Federal Elections: An Ecological Analysis," in *Voter Turnout in Canada,* ed. Herman Bakvis, 3–32. Toronto: Dundurn Press.

Economist (1992) "The ascent of British man," reprinted in *The Globe and Mail* (December 29), p. A17

EDWARDS, GEORGE C., MARTIN P. WATTENBERG, and ROBERT L. LINEBERRY (2000) *Government in America: People, Politics and Policy.* 9th ed. New York; Longman.

ELSHTAIN, JEAN BETHKE (1993) *Democracy on Trial.* Concord, Ontario: House of Anansi Press.

EPSTEIN, LEE and C.K. ROWLAND (1991) "Debunking the Myth of Interest Group Invincibility in the Courts," *American Political Science Review,* Volume 85, Number 1, pp. 205–217.

EPSTEIN, LEON D. (1967) *Political Parties in Western Democracies.* New York: Praeger Publishers.

ERIKSON, ROBERT S. and KENT L. TEDIN (2001) *American Public Opinion: Its Origin, Content, and Impact.* 6th ed. New York: Longman.

FAGEN, RICHARD R. (1964) *Cuba: The Political Content of Adult Education.* Stanford, California: The Hoover Institution.

FINE, SEAN (1992) "Courts set seal on gay revolution," *The Globe and Mail* (November 24), p. A1.

FINER, S.E. (1980) *The Changing British Party System, 1945–1979.* Washington, D.C.: American Enterprise Institute for Public Policy Research.

FINER, S.E. and MICHAEL STEED (1978) "Politics of Great Britian," in *Modern Political Systems: Europe,* 4th ed., ed. Roy C. Macridis, 27–92. Englewood Cliffs, New Jersey: Prentice-Hall.

FISCHER, JOHN (1948) "Unwritten rules of American politics," *Harper's Magazine,* Volume 197.

FISHER, JUSTIN (1992) "Trade Union Political Funds and the Labour Party," in *British Elections and Parties Yearbook 1992,* eds. Pippa Norris et al., 111–123. New York: Harvester Wheatsheaf.

—— (1994a) "Political Donations to the Conservative Party," *Parliamentary Affairs,* Volume 47, Number 1, pp. 61–72.

—— (1994b) "Why Do Companies Make Donations to Political Parties?" *Political Studies,* Volume 42, Number 4, pp. 690–699.

FLANIGAN, WILLIAM H. and NANCY H. ZINGALE (1998) *Political Behavior of the American Electorate.* 9th ed. Washington, D.C.: CQ Press.

FLETCHER, MARTHA (1977) "Judicial Review and the Division of Powers in Canada," in *Canadian Federalism: Myth or Reality,* 3rd ed., ed. J. Peter Meekison, 100–123. Toronto: Methuen.

FORBES, H.D. (1976) "Conflicting National Identities among Canadian Youth," in *Foundations of Political Culture: Political Socialization in Canada,* eds. Jon H. Pammett and Michael S. Whittington, 288–315. Toronto: Macmillan.

FORCESE, DENNIS (1978) "Elites and Power in Canada," in *Approaches to Canadian Politics,* ed. John H. Redekop, 302–322. Scarborough, Ontario: Prentice-Hall Canada.

FORD, FRANKLIN L. (1985) *Political Murder: From Tyrannicide to Terrorism.* Cambridge, Mass.: Harvard University Press.

FORSEY, EUGENE (1974) *Freedom and Order: Collected Essays.* Toronto: McClelland and Stewart.

—— (1985) "The Role and Position of the Monarch in Canada," in *Canadian Politics: A Comparative Reader,* ed. Ronald G. Landes, 53–62. Scarborough, Ontario: Prentice-Hall Canada.

FOWERAKER, JOE and ROMAN KRZNARIC (2000) "Measuring Liberal Democratic Performance: An Empirical and Conceptual Critique," *Political Studies,* Volume 48, Number 4, pp. 759–787.

FRANKFORT, HENRI, H.A. FRANKFORT, JOHN A. WILSON, and THORKILD JACOBSEN (1949) *Before Philosophy.* Baltimore: Penguin Books.

FRANKLIN, MARK N. (1999) "Electoral Engineering and Cross-National Turnout Differences: What Role for Compulsory Voting?" *British Journal of Political Science,* Volume 29, Number 1, pp. 205–216.

FRANKS, C.E.S. (1983) "Borrowing from the United States: Is the Canadian Parliamentary System Moving toward the Congressional Model," *The American Review of Canadian Studies,* Volume 13, Number 3, pp. 201–214.

FRASER, ALISTAIR B. (1991) "A Canadian Flag for Canada," *Journal of Canadian Studies,* Volume 25, Number 4, pp. 64–80.

FRASER, GRAHAM (1992) "Schools blur the identity being sought at national unity conference," *The Globe and Mail* (February 6), p. A1.

FRAZER, ELIZABETH (2000) "Citizenship Education: Anti-political Culture and Political Education in Britain," *Political Studies,* Volume 48, Number 1, pp. 88–103.

FRIEDLAND, MARTIN L. (1995) *A Place Apart: Judicial Independence and Accountability in Canada.* Ottawa: Canadian Judicial Council, Canada Communication Group – Publishing.

FRIEDRICH, CARL J. (1968) *Constitutional Government and Democracy: Theory and Practice in Europe and America.* 4th ed. Waltham, Mass.: Blaisdell Publishing Co.

FUKUYAMA, FRANCIS (1999) "Women and the Evolution of World Politics," *Foreign Affairs,* Volume 77, Number 5, pp. 24–40.

GAMBLE, ANDREW (1979) "The Conservative Party," in *Multi-Party Britain,* ed. H.M. Drucker, 25–53. London: Macmillan Press.

GARSON, DAVID (1978) *Group Theories of Politics.* Beverly Hills, California: Sage Publications.

GEDDES, ANDREW and JOHNATHAN TONGE, eds. (1997) *Labour's Landslide: The British General Election 1997.* Manchester, England: Manchester University Press.

GERTH, H.H. and C. WRIGHT MILLS, eds. (1958) *From Max Weber: Essays in Sociology.* New York: Oxford University Press.

GIBBINS, ROGER (1982) *Regionalism: Territorial Politics in Canada and the United States.* Toronto: Butterworths.

GIBSON, GORDON (2000) "What does Ottawa do for B.C. anyway?" *National Post* (December 4), p. A14.

GIMPEL, JAMES G. and ROBIN M. WOLPERT (1995) "Rationalizing Support and Opposition to Supreme Court Nominations: The Role of Credentials," *Polity,* Volume 28, Number 1, pp. 67–82.

GINSBERG, BENJAMIN and MARTIN SHEFTER (1999) *Politics by Other Means: Politicians, Prosecutors, and the Press from Watergate to Whitewater.* Rev. ed. New York: W.W. Norton and Company.

GLASS, DAVID, PEVERILL SQUIRE, and RAYMOND E. WOLFINGER (1985) "Voter Turnout: An International Comparison," in *Canadian Politics: A Comparative Reader,* ed. Ronald G. Landes, 345–360. Scarborough, Ontario: Prentice-Hall Canada.

GOTLEIB, ALLAN (1989) "A welcome dose of discipline," *The Globe and Mail* (September 11), p. A6.

GOULD, JULIUS (1973) "Interests and Pressures," *Government and Opposition*, Volume 8, Number 2, pp. 242–258.

GRANATSTEIN, JACK (1996) *Yankee Go Home? Canadians and Anti-Americanism.* Toronto: HarperCollins.

—— (1998) *Who Killed Canadian History?* Toronto: HarperCollins.

GREEN, MARK J., JAMES M. FALLOWS, and DAVID R. ZWICK (1972) *Who Runs Congress?* Toronto: Bantam Books.

GREENHOUSE, LINDA (1999) "High court faces moment of truth in federalism cases," *The New York Times* (March 28), p. 23.

GREGG, ALLAN and MICHAEL S. WHITTINGTON (1976) "Regional Variation in Children's Political Attitudes," in *The Provincial Political Systems: Comparative Essays,* eds. David J. Bellamy et al., 76–85. Toronto: Methuen.

GRONKE, PAUL and J. MATTHEW WILSON (1999) "Competing Redistricting Plans as Evidence of Political Motives: The North Carolina Case," *American Politics Quarterly*, Volume 27, Number 2, pp. 147–176.

GWYN, RICHARD (1980) *The Northern Magus: Pierre Trudeau and Canadians.* Toronto: McClelland and Stewart.

HACKER, ANDREW (1992) *Two Nations: Black and White, Separate, Hostile, Unequal.* New York: Ballantine Books.

HALFACREE, KEITH (1992) "Whither the Universal Franchise? The Political Cost of Residential Migration," *Parliamentary Affairs*, Volume 45, Number 2, pp. 164–172.

HAMILTON, WILLIE (1975) *My Queen and I.* Don Mills, Ontario: Paperjacks.

HARPER, STEPHEN (2000) "Separation, Alberta-style," *National Post* (December 8), p. A18.

HARPER, STEPHEN, TOM FLANAGAN, TED MORTON, RAINER KNOPFF, ANDREW CROOKS, and KEN BOESSENKOOL (2001) "Open letter to Ralph Klein," *National Post* (January 26), p. A14.

HARRIGAN, JOHN J. (1993) *Empty Dreams, Empty Pockets: Class and Bias in American Politics.* New York: Macmillan.

HARRIS, LOUIS (1973) *The Anguish of Change.* New York: W.W. Norton and Company.

HAVEL, VÁCLAV (1992) "The honest politician," *Saturday Night*, Volume 107, Number 5, pp. 62–66.

HAZELL, ROBERT, MEG RUSSELL, BEN SEYD, and DAVID SINCLAIR (2000) "The British Constitution in 1998–99: The Continuing Revolution," *Parliamentary Affairs*, Volume 53, Number 2, pp. 242–261.

HAZELL, ROBERT and DAVID SINCLAIR (1999) "The British Constitution in 1997–98: Labour's Constitutional Revolution," *Parliamentary Affairs*, Volume 52, Number 2, pp. 161–178.

HEARD, ANDREW (1991) *Canadian Constitutional Conventions: The Marriage of Law and Politics.* Toronto: Oxford University Press.

HEATH, ANTHONY, BRIDGET TAYLOR, LINDSAY BROOK, and ALISON PARK (1999) "British National Sentiment," *British Journal of Political Science*, Volume 29, Number 1, pp. 155–175.

HENRY, WILLIAM A, III (1994) *In Defence of Elitism.* New York: Doubleday.

HERSH, SEYMOUR M. (1997) *The Dark Side of Camelot.* Boston: Little, Brown and Company.

HIEBERT, JANET (1991) "Interest Groups and Canadian Federal Elections," in *Interest Groups and Elections in Canada*, ed. Leslie Siedle, 3–76. Toronto: Dundurn.

HILL, ALFRED (2000) "Opinion: The Shutdown and the Constitution," *Political Science Quarterly*, Volume 115, Number 2, pp. 273–282.

HILL, DAVID B. and NORMAN R. LUTTBERG (1980) *Trends in American Electoral Behaviour.* Itasca, Illinois: Peacock Publishers.

HOCKIN, THOMAS A. (1973) "Adversary Politics and the Functions of Canada's House of Commons," in *The Canadian Political Process: A Reader,* Rev. ed, eds. Orest M. Kruhlak et al., 361–381. Toronto: Holt, Rinehart and Winston.

—— (1976) *Government in Canada.* Toronto: McGraw-Hill Ryerson Ltd.

HODGETTS, TED (1985) "The Deputy Ministers' Dilemma," in *Canadian Politics: A Comparative Reader*, ed. Ronald G. Landes, 139–145. Scarborough, Ontario: Prentice-Hall Canada.

HOFSTADTER, RICHARD (1948) *The American Political Tradition.* New York: Vintage Books.

—— (1972) *The Idea of a Party System: The Rise of Legitimate Opposition in the United States, 1780–1840.* Berkeley: University of California Press.

HOJNACKI, MARIE and DAVID C. KIMBALL (1998) "Organized Interests and the Decision of Whom to Lobby in Congress," *American Political Science Review*, Volume 92, Number 4, pp. 775–790.

HOLLIS, PATRICIA, ed. (1974) *Pressure from Without in Early Victorian England.* London: Edward Arnold.

HOROWITZ, GAD (1968) *Canadian Labour in Politics.* Toronto: University of Toronto Press.

HREBENAR, RONALD J., MATTHEW J. BURBANK, and ROBERT C. BENEDICT (1999) *Political Parties, Interest Groups, and Political Campaigns.* Boulder, Colorado: Westview Press.

HUCKSHORN, ROBERT J. (1980) *Political Parties in America.* North Scituate, Mass.: Duxbury Press.

HURTIG, MEL (1975) *Never Heard of Them . . . They Must Be Canadian.* Toronto: Canadabooks.

—— (1991) *The Betrayal of Canada.* Toronto: Stoddart.

—— (1992) *A New and Better Canada: Principles and Policies of a New Canadian Political Party.* Toronto: Stoddart.

HUTCHINSON, ALLAN C. (1987) "Veil of secrecy on top judges should be lifted," *The Globe and Mail* (March 6), p. A7.

HYSON, STEWART (1999) "Electoral Boundary Redistribution by Independent Commission in New Brunswick, 1990–94," *Canadian Public Administration,* Volume 42, Number 3, pp. 174–197.

IONESCU, GHITA and ISABEL DE MADARIAGA (1972) *Opposition: Past and Present of a Political Institution.* London: Penguin Books.

IRVINE, WILLIAM P. (1979) *Does Canada Need a New Electoral System?* Kingston, Ontario: Institute of Intergovernmental Relations, Queen's University.

JACKMAN, ROBERT W. and ROBERT A. MILLER (1996) "A Renaissance of Political Culture?" *American Journal of Political Science,* Volume 40, Number 4, pp. 632–659.

JAROS, DEAN (1973) *Socialization to Politics.* New York: Praeger Publishers.

JEFFREY, BROOKE (1993) *Strange Bedfellows, Trying Times: October 1992 and the Defeat of the Powerbrokers.* Toronto: Key Porter Books.

JENSON, JANE (1995) "A Critique of Election Financing," in *Politics: Canada,* 8th ed., eds. Paul W. Fox and Graham White, 372–374. Toronto: McGraw-Hill.

JESSE, NEAL G. (1996) "Thatcher's Rise and Fall: An Institutional Analysis of the Tory Leadership Selection Process," *Electoral Studies,* Volume 15, Number 2, pp. 183–202.

JOHNSON, CHALMERS (1983) *Revolutionary Change.* 2nd ed. London: Longman.

JOHNSON, HAYNES and DAVID S. BRODER (1996) *The System: The American Way of Politics at the Breaking Point.* Boston: Little, Brown and Company.

JOHNSTON, R.I. (1986) "Constituency Redistribution in Britain: Recent Issues," in *Electoral Laws and Their Political Consequences,* eds. Bernard Grofman and Arend Lijphart, 277–288. New York: Agathon Press.

JOHNSTON, RICHARD, ANDRE BLAIS, HENRY E. BRADY, and JEAN CRETE (1993) *Letting the People Decide: Dynamics of a Canadian Election.* Montreal: McGill-Queen's University Press.

JOHNSTONE, DAVID CAY (1999) "Gap between rich and poor found substantially wider," *The New York Times* (September 5), p. A14.

JOHNSTONE, JOHN C. (1969) *Young People's Images of Canadian Society.* Ottawa: Queen's Printer.

JONES, BILL and DENNIS KAVANAGH (1991) *British Politics Today.* 4th ed. Manchester, England: Manchester University Press.

JONES, CHARLES O. (1995) *Separate but Equal Branches: Congress and the Presidency.* Chatham, New Jersey: Chatham House Publishers.

—— ed. (2000) *Preparing To Be President: The Memos of Richard E. Neustadt.* Washington, D.C.: AEI Press.

JORDAN, GRANT (2000) "The 'Process of Government' and 'The Governmental Process,' " *Political Studies,* Volume 48, Number 4, pp. 788–801.

JOY, RICHARD J. (1972) *Languages in Conflict: The Canadian Experience.* Toronto: McClelland and Stewart.

—— (1985) "Canada's Official Language Populations, as Shown by the 1981 Census," *American Review of Canadian Studies,* Volume 15, Number 1, pp. 90–96.

—— (1992) *Canada's Official Languages: The Progress of Bilingualism.* Toronto: University of Toronto Press.

KAHAN, MICHAEL (1999) *Media as Politics: Theory, Behavior, and Change in America.* Upper Saddle River, New Jersey: Prentice Hall.

KAMINER, WENDY (1992) "Crashing the locker room," *The Atlantic Monthly,* Volume 270, Number 1, pp. 58–70.

KAVANAGH, DENNIS (1972) *Political Culture.* London: Macmillan.

—— (1980) "Political Culture in Great Britain: The Decline of the Civic Culture," in *The Civic Culture Revisited,* eds. Gabriel A. Almond and Sidney Verba, 124–176. Boston: Little, Brown and Company.

—— (1990) *British Politics: Continuities and Change.* 2nd ed. Oxford: Oxford University Press.

—— (1992) "Changes in the Political Class and Its Culture," *Parliamentary Affairs,* Volume 45, Number 1, pp. 18–32.

—— (1996) "British Party Conferences and the Political Rhetoric of the 1990s," *Government and Opposition,* Volume 31, Number 1, pp. 27–44.

(2000) *British Politics: Continuities and Change.* 4th ed. Oxford: Oxford University Press.

KEEBLE, EDNA and HEATHER A. SMITH (1999) *(Re)Defining Traditions: Gender and Canadian Foreign Policy.* Halifax, Nova Scotia: Fernwood Publishing.

KEEFE, WILLIAM J. and MORRIS S. OGUL (1985) *The American Legislative Process: Congress and the States*. 6th ed. Englewood Cliffs, New Jersey: Prentice-Hall.

KENDRICK, STEPHEN and DAVID MCCRONE (1989) "Politics in a Cold Climate: The Conservative Decline in Scotland," *Political Studies*, Volume 37, Number 4, pp. 589–603.

KEY, V.O., JR. (1956) *American State Politics: An Introduction*. New York: Alfred A. Knopf.

—— (1964) *Politics, Parties, and Pressure Groups*. 5th ed. New York: Thomas Y. Crowell.

KING, ANTHONY (1969) "Political Parties in Western Democracies," *Polity*, Volume 2, Number 2, pp. 111–141.

—— (1993) "The Implications of One-Party Government," in *Britain At The Polls 1992*, Anthony King et al., 223–248. Chatham, New Jersey: Chatham House Publishers.

KING, ANTHONY, DAVID DENVER, IAIN MCLEAN, PIPPA NORRIS, PHILIP NORTON, DAVID SANDERS, and PATRICK SEYD (1998) *New Labour Triumphs: Britain at the Polls*. Chatham, New Jersey: Chatham House Publishers.

KNIGHT, BARBARA B. (1989) *Separation of Powers in the American Political System*. Virginia: George Mason University Press.

KNOPFF, RAINER and F.L. MORTON (1992) *Charter Politics*. Toronto: Nelson Canada.

KORNBERG, ALLAN and WILLIAM MISHLER (1976) *Influence in Parliament: Canada*. Durham, North Carolina: Duke University Press.

KORNBERG, ALLAN, JOEL SMITH, and HAROLD D. CLARKE (1979) *Citizen Politicians — Canada: Party Officials in a Democratic Society*. Durham, North Carolina: Carolina Academic Press.

KOUSSER, J. MORGAN (1974) *The Shaping of Southern Politics: Suffrage Restriction and the Establishment of the One-Party South 1880–1910*. New Haven, Conn.: Yale University Press.

KROMKOWSKI, CHARLES A. and JOHN A. KROMKOWSKI (1991) "Why 435? A Question of Political Arithmetic," *Polity*, Volume 24, Number 1, pp. 129–145.

KWAVNICK, DAVID (1972) *Organized Labour and Pressure Politics: The Canadian Labour Congress 1956–1968*. Montreal: McGill-Queen's University Press.

LADD, EVERETT C. (1986) "The Foreign Policy Record: Reagan's Sphere of Influence," *Public Opinion*, Volume 9, Number 2, pp. 3–5.

—— (1993) "The 1992 Vote for President Clinton: Another Brittle Mandate?" *Political Science Quarterly*, Volume 108, Number 1, pp. 1–28.

LAFFIN, MARTIN (2000) "Constitutional Design: A Framework for Analysis," *Parliamentary Affairs*, Volume 53, Number 3, pp. 532–541.

LAMY, PAUL G. (1975) "Political Socialization of French and English Canadian Youth: Socialization into Discord," in *Socialization and Values in Canadian Society: Volume One – Political Socialization*, eds. Elia Zureik and Robert M. Pike, 263–280. Toronto: McClelland and Stewart.

LANDES, RONALD G. (1976) "The Use of Role Theory in Political Socialization Research: A Review, Critique, and Modest Proposal," *International Journal of Comparative Sociology*, Volume 17, Numbers 1–2, pp. 59–72.

—— (1977) "Political Socialization among Youth: A Comparative Study of English-Canadian and American School Children," *International Journal of Comparative Sociology*, Volume 18, Numbers 1–2, pp. 63–80.

—— (1979) "The Federal Political Culture in Canada." Paper presented to the annual meeting of the Canadian Political Science Association, Saskatoon, Saskatchewan.

—— (1980) "Alternative Electoral Systems for Canada." Paper presented to the annual meeting of the Canadian Political Science Association, Montreal, Quebec.

—— (1981) "The Canadian General Election of 1980," *Parliamentary Affairs*, Volume 34, Number 1, pp. 95–109.

—— (1984) "In Defence of Canadian Political Parties." Paper presented to the annual meeting of the Canadian Political Science Association, Guelph, Ontario.

LAPALOMBARA, JOSEPH (1974) *Politics within Nations*. Englewood Cliffs, New Jersey: Prentice-Hall.

LAPALOMBARA, JOSEPH and MYRON WEINER, eds. (1966) *Political Parties and Political Development*. Princeton, New Jersey: Princeton University Press.

LAPHAM, LEWIS H. (1992) "Who and what is American?" *Harper's*, Volume 284, Number 1700, pp. 43–49.

—— (1995) *Hotel America*. London: Verso.

LAPONCE, J.A. (1969) *People vs. Politics*. Toronto: University of Toronto Press.

—— (1972) "Post-dicting Electoral Cleavages in Canadian Federal Elections, 1949–68: Material for a Footnote," *Canadian Journal of Political Science*, Volume 5, Number 2, pp. 270–286.

—— (1985) "Protecting the French Language in Canada: From Neurophysiology to Geography to Politics: The Regional Imperative," *The Journal of Commonwealth and Comparative Politics*, Volume 23, Number 2, pp. 157–170.

LASKI, HAROLD J. (1940) *The American Presidency*. New York: Grosset and Dunlap.

LASKIN, BORA (1959) "An Inquiry into the Diefenbaker Bill of Rights," *Canadian Bar Review*, Volume 37, pp. 77–134.

LASSWELL, HAROLD (1958) *Politics: Who Gets What, When, How?* Cleveland: Meridian Books.

LASSWELL, HAROLD and ABRAHAM KAPLAN (1950) *Power and Society: A Framework for Political Inquiry*. New Haven, Conn.: Yale University Press.

LAWSON, KAY, ed. (1980) *Political Parties and Linkage: A Comparative Perspective.* New Haven, Conn.: Yale University Press.

LE LOHÉ, M.J. (1993) "Ethnic Minority Candidates in General Elections," *The Political Quarterly,* Volume 64, Number 1, pp. 107–117.

LE SUEUR, ANDREW (1996) "The Judicial Review Debate: From Partnership to Friction," *Government and Opposition,* Volume 31, Number 1, pp. 8–26.

LEVESQUE, RENE (1968) *An Option for Quebec.* Toronto: McClelland and Stewart.

LEWIS, DAVID (1972) *Louder Voices: The Corporate Welfare Bums.* Toronto: James Lewis and Samuel.

LEWIS-BECK, MICHAEL S. and PEVERILL SQUIRE (1995) "The Politics of Institutional Choice: Presidential Ballot Access for Third Parties in the United States," *British Journal of Political Science,* Volume 25, Number 3, pp. 419–427.

LEYS, COLIN (1983) *Politics in Britain.* Toronto: University of Toronto Press.

LIJPHART, AREND (1990) "The Political Consequences of Electoral Laws, 1945–85," *American Political Science Review,* Volume 84, Number 2, pp. 481–496.

—— ed. (1992) *Parliamentary versus Presidential Government.* Oxford: Oxford University Press.

LIND, MICHAEL (1992) "A radical plan to change American politics," *The Atlantic Monthly,* Volume 270, Number 2, pp. 73–83.

LIPOW, ARTHUR and PATRICK SEYD (1996) "The Politics of Anti-Partyism," *Parliamentary Affairs,* Volume 49, Number 2, pp. 273–284.

LIPSET, SEYMOUR MARTIN (1970) *Revolution and Counterrevolution: Change and Persistence in Social Structures.* New York: Anchor Books.

LONGLEY, LAWRENCE D. and JAMES D. DANA (1992) "The Biases of the Electoral College in the 1990s," *Polity,* Volume 25, Number 1, pp. 123–145.

LOOMIS, BURDETTE A. (1996) *The Contemporary Congress.* New York: St. Martin's Press.

LOVENDUSKI, JONI (1997) "Gender Politics: A Breakthrough for Women?" *Parliamentary Affairs,* Volume 50, Number 4, pp. 708–719.

LOWI, THEODORE J. (1979) *The End of Liberalism.* 2nd ed. New York: W.W. Norton and Company.

LOWI, THEODORE J. and BENJAMIN GINSBERG (1994) *Democrats Return to Power: Politics and Policy in the Clinton Era.* New York: W.W. Norton and Company.

—— (2000) *American Government: Freedom and Power.* Brief 6th ed. New York: W.W. Norton and Company.

MACIVER, R.M. (1965) *The Web of Government.* Rev. ed. New York: The Free Press.

MACKERRAS, M. and I. MCALLISTER (1999) "Compulsory Voting, Party Stability and Electoral Advantage in Australia," *Electoral Studies,* Volume 18, Number 2, pp. 217–233.

MACKINTOSH, GORDON H.A. (1985) "A Fateful Prorogation: The Death of Constitutional Proposals in Manitoba," *The Parliamentarian,* Volume 66, Number 2, pp. 60–66.

MACKINTOSH, JOHN P. (1982) *The Government and Politics of Britain.* 5th ed. Rev. by Peter Richards. London: Hutchinson.

MACKINNON, FRANK (1973) *Postures and Politics: Some Observations on Participatory Democracy.* Toronto: University of Toronto Press.

—— (1976) *The Crown in Canada.* Calgary, Alberta: McClelland and Stewart West, Glenbow-Alberta Institute.

MACPHERSON, C.B. (1977) *The Life and Times of Liberal Democracy.* Oxford: Oxford University Press.

MACRIDIS, ROY C. (1980) *Contemporary Political Ideologies: Movements and Regimes.* Cambridge, Mass: Winthrop Publishers.

MAIR, PETER (1986) "Districting Choices under the Single-Transferable Vote," in *Electoral Laws and Their Political Consequences,* eds. Bernard Grofman and Arend Lijphart, 289–307. New York: Agathon Press.

MALCOLM, ANDREW H. (1985) *The Canadians.* Toronto: Fitzhenry and Whiteside.

MALLORY, J.R. (1954) *Social Credit and the Federal Power in Canada.* Toronto: University of Toronto Press.

—— (1971) *The Structure of Canadian Government.* Toronto: Macmillan of Canada.

—— (1984) "The Charter of Rights and Freedoms and Canadian Democracy," *The Timlin Lecture,* University of Saskatchewan, Saskatoon.

MANFREDI, CHRISTOPHER P. (1993) *Judicial Power and the Charter: Canada and the Paradox of Liberal Constitutionalism.* Toronto: McClelland and Stewart.

MANSBRIDGE, JANE J. (1990) "The Rise and Fall of Self-Interest in the Explanation of Political Life," in *Beyond Self-Interest,* ed. Jane J. Mansbridge, 3–22. Chicago: University of Chicago Press.

MARSHALL, GEOFFREY (1988) "Canada's New Constitution (1982): Some Lessons in Constitutional Engineering," in *Constitutions in Democratic Politics,* ed. Vernon Bogdanor, 156–170. Aldershot, England: Gower Publishing.

MARTIN, LAWRENCE (1993) *Pledge of Allegiance: The Americanization of Canada in the Mulroney Years,* Toronto: McClelland and Stewart.

MATHESON, W.A. (1976) *The Prime Minister and the Cabinet.* Toronto: Methuen.

MAYO, HENRY B. (1960) *An Introduction to Democratic Theory.* New York: Oxford University Press.

MAZUR, AMY (1999) "Feminist Comparative Policy: A New Field of Study," *European Journal of Political Research*, Volume 35, Number 4, pp. 483–506.

MCCORMICK, PETER (1989) "Regionalism in Canada: Disentangling the Threads," *Journal of Canadian Studies*, Volume 24, Number 2, pp. 5–21.

—— (2000) *Supreme at Last: The Evolution of the Supreme Court in Canada.* Toronto: James Lorimer and Company.

MCFARLAND, ANDREW S. (1984) *Common Cause: Lobbying in the Public Interest.* Chatham, New Jersey: Chatham House Publishers.

MCILWAIN, CHARLES HOWARD (1947) *Constitutionalism: Ancient and Modern.* Rev. ed. Ithaca, New York: Great Seal Books, Cornell University Press.

MCINNES, CRAIG (1992) "Teens' preference for things American found in study," *The Globe and Mail* (September 11), p. A1.

MCKENZIE, ROBERT (1967) *British Political Parties: The Distribution of Power within the Conservative and Labour Parties.* London: Heinemann Educational Books.

MCLEAN, IAIN (1999) "The Jenkins Commission and the Implications of Electoral Reform for the UK Constitution," *Government and Opposition*, Volume 34, Number 2, pp. 143–160.

MCLEAN, IAIN and ROGER MORTIMORE (1992) "Apportionment and the Boundary Commission for England," *Electoral Studies*, Volume 11, Number 4, pp. 293–309.

MCMENEMY, JOHN (1980) *The Language of Canadian Politics: A Guide to Important Terms and Concepts.* Toronto: John Wiley and Sons Canada.

—— (1994) *The Language of Canadian Politics: A Guide to Important Terms and Concepts.* Rev. ed. Waterloo, Ontario: Wilfrid Laurier University Press.

—— (1999) *The Language of Canadian Politics: A Guide to Important Terms and Concepts.* Rev. ed. Waterloo, Ontario: Wilfrid Laurier University Press.

MCNAUGHT, KENNETH (1976) "Political Trials and the Canadian Political Tradition," in *Courts and Trials,* ed. Martin L. Friedland, 137–161. Toronto: University of Toronto Press.

—— (1983) "History and the Perception of Politics," in *Approaches to Canadian Politics,* 2nd ed., ed. John H. Redekop, 89–100. Scarborough, Ontario: Prentice-Hall Canada.

MCRAE, KENNETH, ed. (1974) *Consociational Democracy: Political Accommodation in Segmented Societies.* Toronto: McClelland and Stewart.

MCROBERTS, KENNETH and DALE POSGATE (1980) *Quebec: Social Change and Political Crisis.* Rev. ed. Toronto: McClelland and Stewart.

MCWHINNEY, EDWARD (1979) *Quebec and the Constitution 1960–1978.* Toronto: University of Toronto Press.

—— (1982) "Giving the governor-general a more active role to play," *The Globe and Mail* (February 6), p. 7.

—— (1987) "Judicial Review in a Federal and Plural Society: The Supreme Court of Canada," in *Comparative Judicial Systems: Challenging Frontiers in Conceptual and Empirical Analysis,* ed. John R. Schmidhauser, 63–74. London: Butterworths.

MCWILLIAMS, WILSON CAREY (1981) "The Meaning of the Election," in *The Election of 1980: Reports and Interpretations,* ed. Gerald M. Pomper, 170–188. Chatham, New Jersey: Chatham House Publishers.

MEISEL, JOHN (1979) "The Decline of Party in Canada," in *Party Politics in Canada,* 4th ed., ed. Hugh G. Thorburn. Scarborough, Ontario: Prentice-Hall Canada.

—— (1996) "The Dysfunctions of Canadian Parties: An Exploratory Mapping," in *Party Politics in Canada,* 7th ed., ed. Hugh G. Thorburn, 225–244. Scarborough, Ontario: Prentice Hall Canada.

MICHELMAN, HANS J. and JEFFREY S. STEEVES (1985) "The 1982 Transition in Power in Saskatchewan: The Progressive Conservatives and the Public Service," *Canadian Public Administration*, Volume 28, Number 1, pp. 1–23.

MILBRATH, LESTER W. and M.L. GOEL (1977) *Political Participation: How and Why Do People Get Involved in Politics?* 2nd ed. Chicago: Rand McNally.

MILL, J.S. (1861, 1948) *On Liberty and Considerations on Representative Government,* ed. R. B. McCallum. Oxford: Basil Blackwell.

MILNOR, A.J. (1969) *Elections and Political Stability.* Boston: Little, Brown and Co.

MISHLER, WILLIAM (1979) *Political Participation in Canada: Prospects for Democratic Citizenship.* Toronto: Macmillan of Canada.

MITCHELL, AUSTIN (1984) "A College Education: Electing Labour's Leader," *The Parliamentarian*, Volume 65, Number 2, pp. 104–116.

MITCHELL, NEIL J. and JOHN G. BRETTING (1993) "Business and Political Finance in the United Kingdom," *Comparative Political Studies*, Volume 26, Number 2, pp. 229–245.

MITCHELL, WILLIAM C. (1970) *The American Polity: A Social and Cultural Interpretation.* New York: The Free Press.

MONIERE, DENIS (1981) *Ideologies in Quebec: The Historical Development.* Toronto: University of Toronto Press.

MOORE, SUZANNE (1993) "Backlash: who's afraid of Anita Hill?" *The Globe and Mail* (May 22), p. D5.

MORTON, DESMOND (1974) *NDP: The Dream of Power.* Toronto: Hakkert.

MORTON, F.L. (2000) "Rulings for the many by the few," *National Post* (September 2), p. B3.

MORTON, F.L. and RAINER KNOPFF (2000) *The Charter Revolution and the Court Party.* Peterborough, Ontario: Broadview Press.

MORTON, W.L. (1950) *The Progressive Party in Canada.* Toronto: University of Toronto Press.

MULLER, WILLIAM D. (1977) *The 'Kept Men.'* Brighton: Harvester Press.

NEUSTADT, RICHARD E. (1980) *Presidential Power: The Politics of Leadership from FDR to Carter.* New York: John Wiley and Sons.

—— (2001) "The Weakening White House," *British Journal of Political Science,* Volume 31, Number 1, pp. 1–11.

NEVITTE, NEIL (1996) *The Decline of Deference.* Peterborough, Ontario: Broadview Press.

NEVITTE, NEIL, ANDRE BLAIS, ELISABETH GIDENGIL, and RICHARD NADEAU (2000) *Unsteady State: The 1997 Canadian Federal Election.* Don Mills, Ontario: Oxford University Press.

NEWMAN, PETER C. (1973) *Renegade in Power: The Diefenbaker Years.* Toronto: McClelland and Stewart.

—— (1979) *Bronfman Dynasty: The Rothchilds of the New World.* Toronto: Seal Books.

—— (1988) "A radical mandate: Canadians choose a new political order," *Maclean's* (December 5), Volume 101, Number 50, pp. 29–30.

—— (2000) "2000: the year the music died," *National Post* (December 30), p. B1.

—— (2001) "Bouchard the last of the political giants," *National Post* (January 20), p. B5.

NEWTON, KENNETH (1993) "Caring and Competence: The Long, Long Campaign," in *Britain At the Polls 1992,* Anthony King et al., 129–170. Chatham, New Jersey: Chatham House Publishers.

NIE, NORMAN H., SIDNEY VERBA, and JOHN R. PETROCIK (1979) *The Changing American Voter.* Enlarged ed. Cambridge, Mass.: Harvard University Press.

NIEMI, RICHARD G. (1973) "Political Socialization," in *Handbook of Political Psychology,* ed. Jeanne N. Knutson, 117–138. San Francisco: Jossey-Bass Publishers.

NIEMI, RICHARD G. and JANE JUNN (1998) *Civic Education: What Makes Students Learn.* New Haven, Conn.: Yale University Press.

NORRIS, PIPPA, ANDREW GEDDES, and JONI LOVEN-DUSKI (1992) "Race and Parliamentary Representation," in *British Elections and Parties Yearbook 1992,* eds. Norris et. al., 92–110. New York: Harvester Wheatsheaf.

NORRIS, PIPPA and JONI LOVENDUSKI (1993) "'If Only More Candidates Came Forward': Supply-Side Explanations of Candidate Selection in Britain," *British Journal of Political Science,* Volume 23, Number 3, pp. 373–408.

NORTON, PHILIP (1982) *The British Constitution in Flux.* Oxford: Martin Robertson.

—— (1994) *The British Polity.* 3rd ed. New York: Longman.

OAKESHOTT, MICHAEL (1962) *Rationalism in Politics and Other Essays.* London: Methuen and Co.

OBLER, JEFFREY (1981) "Legislatures and the Survival of Political Systems: A Review Article," *Political Science Quarterly,* Volume 96, Number 1, pp. 127–139.

O'CONNOR, KAREN and LARRY J. SABATO (1993) *American Government: Roots and Reform.* New York: Macmillan.

ODDO, GILBERT L. (1979) *Freedom and Equality: Civil Liberties and the Supreme Court.* Santa Monica, California: Goodyear Publishing.

OGMUNDSON, RICK (1976) "The Sociology of Power and Politics: An Introduction to the Canadian Polity," in *Introduction to Canadian Society: A Sociological Analysis,* eds. G.N. Ramn and Stuart D. Johnson, 157–211. Toronto: Macmillan.

OLESZEK, WALTER J. (1995) *Congressional Procedures and the Policy Process.* 4th ed. Washington, D.C.: Congressional Quarterly Press.

OLIVER, DAWN (1989) "The Judge over Your Shoulder, *Parliamentary Affairs,* Volume 42, Number 3, pp. 302–316.

ORNSTEIN, M.D. and H.M. STEVENSON (1984) "Ideology and Public Policy in Canada," *British Journal of Political Science,* Volume 14, Part 3, pp. 313–344.

OSTBERG, C.L. (2000) "Charting New Territory? Fifteen Years of Search and Seizure Decisions by the Supreme Court of Canada, 1982–1997," *The American Review of Canadian Studies,* Volume 30, Number 1, pp. 35–54.

OSTROGORSKI, MOISEI (1902, 1964) *Democracy and the Organization of Political Parties,* ed. Seymour Martin Lipset. New York: Anchor Books.

PALTIEL, K.Z. (1970) *Political Party Financing in Canada.* Toronto: McGraw-Hill.

—— (1975) "Campaign Financing in Canada and Its Reform," in *Canada at the Polls: The General Election of 1974,* ed. Howard R. Penniman, 181–208. Washington, D.C.: American Enterprise Institute for Public Policy Research.

—— (1989) "Canadian Election Expense Legislation, 1963–85: A Critical Appraisal or Was the Effort Worth It?" in *Comparative Political Finance in the 1980s,* ed. Herbert E. Alexander, 51–75. Cambridge: Cambridge University Press.

PAMMETT, JON H. (1991) "Voting Turnout in Canada," in *Voter Turnout in Canada,* ed. Herman Bakvis, 33–60. Toronto: Dundurn Press, Volume 15 of the Research Studies of the Royal Commission on Electoral Reform and Party Financing.

PANITCH, LEO (1977) "The Development of Corporatism in Liberal Democracies," *Comparative Political Studies,* Volume 10, Number 1, pp. 61–90.

—— (1981) "Elites, Classes and Power in Canada," in *Canadian Politics in the 1980's*, eds. Michael S. Whittington and Glen Williams, 167–188. Toronto: Methuen.

PARRY, GERAINT, GEORGE MOYSER, and NEIL DAY (1992) *Political Participation and Democracy in Britain*. New York: Cambridge University Press.

PATEMAN, CAROL (1970) *Participation and Democratic Theory*. London: Cambridge University Press.

PATTEN, STEVE (1999) "The Reform Party's Re-imagining of the Canadian Nation," *Journal of Canadian Studies*, Volume 34, Number 1, pp. 27–51.

PEAKE, LUCY (1997) "Women in the Campaign and in the Commons," in *Labour's Landslide: The British General Election 1997*, eds. Andrew Geddes and Jonathan Tonge, 165–178. Manchester, England: Manchester University Press.

PELTASON, J.W. (1979) *Corwin and Peltason's Understanding the Constitution*. 8th ed. New York: Holt, Rinehart and Winston.

—— (1997) *Corwin and Peltason's Understanding the Constitution*. 14th ed. Orlando, Florida: Harcourt Brace College Publishers.

PERLIN, GEORGE C. (1980) *The Tory Syndrome: Leadership Politics in the Progressive Conservative Party*. Montreal: McGill-Queen's University Press.

PERRY, HUEY L. (1991) "Pluralist Theory and National Black Politics in the United States," *Polity*, Volume 23, Number 4, pp. 549–565.

PETERSON, PAUL E. (1991) "The Rise and Fall of Special Interest Politics," *Political Science Quarterly*, Volume 105, Number 4, pp. 539–556.

PETERSON, THOMAS (1978) "Manitoba: Ethnic and Class Politics," in *Canadian Provincial Politics*, 2nd ed., ed. Martin Robin, 69–115. Scarborough, Ontario: Prentice-Hall Canada.

PHARR, SUSAN J., ROBERT D. PUTNAM, and RUSSELL J. DALTON (2000) "Trouble in Advanced Democracies? A Quarter-Century of Declining Confidence," *The Journal of Democracy*, Volume 11, Number 2, pp. 5–25.

PHELPS, TIMOTHY M. and HELEN WINTERNITZ (1992) *Capitol Games: Clarence Thomas, Anita Hill, and the Story of a Supreme Court Nomination*. New York: Hyperion.

PIANO, AILI and ARCH PUDDINGTON (2001) "The 2000 Freedom House Survey: Gains Offset Losses," *Journal of Democracy*, Volume 12, Number 1, pp. 87–92.

PICARD, ANDRÉ (1992) "Teenagers apathetic about Canadian unity, survey finds," *The Globe and Mail* (May 11), p. A6.

—— (1995) "Politics fodder for Leacock winner," *The Globe and Mail* (May 9), p. A2.

PINTO-DUSCHINSKY, MICHAEL (1985) "Trends in British Political Funding 1979–1983," *Parliamentary Affairs*, Volume 38, Number 3, pp. 328–347.

PIOUS, RICHARD M. (1979) *The American Presidency*. New York: Basic Books.

—— (1999) "The Paradox of Clinton Winning and the Presidency Losing," *Political Science Quarterly*, Volume 114, Number 4, pp. 569–593.

PIVEN, FRANCES FOX and RICHARD A. CLOWARD (1988) "National Voter Registration Reform: How It Might Be Won," *PS: Political Science and Politics*, Volume 21, Number 4, pp. 868–875.

POMPER, GERALD M. (1993) "The Presidential Election," in *The Election of 1992: Reports and Interpretations*, eds. Pomper et al., 132–156. Chatham, New Jersey: Chatham House.

PRESTHUS, ROBERT (1962) *The Organizational Society: An Analysis and a Theory*. New York: Vintage Books.

—— (1973) *Elite Accommodation in Canadian Politics*. Toronto: Macmillan of Canada.

PULZER, PETER G. (1972) *Political Representation and Elections in Britain*. 2nd ed. London: George Allen and Unwin.

PUNNETT, R.M. (1980) *British Government and Politics*. 4th ed. London: Heinemann.

—— (1990) "Selecting a Leader and Deputy Leader of the Labour Party: The Future of the Electoral College," *Parliamentary Affairs*, Volume 43, Number 2, pp. 179–195.

PUTNAM, ROBERT D. (1976) *The Comparative Study of Political Elites*. Englewood Cliffs, New Jersey: Prentice-Hall.

RAE, DOUGLAS W. (1971) *The Political Consequences of Electoral Laws*. Rev. ed. New Haven, Conn.: Yale University Press.

RANNEY, AUSTIN (1965) *Pathways to Parliament: Candidate Selection in Britain*. Madison, Wisconsin: University of Wisconsin Press.

—— (1975) "Selecting the Candidates," in *Britain at the Polls: The Parliamentary Elections of 1974*, ed. Howard R. Penniman, 33–60. Washington, D.C.: American Enterprise Institute for Public Policy Research.

RASMUSSEN, JORGEN S. (1993) *The British Political Process: Concentrated Power versus Accountability*. Belmont, California: Wadsworth.

REID, ESCOTT (1979) "The Rise of National Parties in Canada," in *Party Politics in Canada*, 4th ed., ed. Hugh G. Thorburn, 12–20. Scarborough, Ontario: Prentice-Hall Canada.

RENSHON, STANLEY A. (2000) "After the Fall: The Clinton Presidency in Psychological Perspective," *Political Science Quarterly*, Volume 115, Number 1, pp. 41–65.

RICHARDSON, J.J. and A.G. JORDAN (1979) *Governing under Pressure: The Policy Process in a Post-Parliamentary Democracy.* Oxford: Martin Robertson.

ROBERTS, PAULA (1986) "Bureaucracy: a ministerial portfolio," *The Atlantic Monthly,* Volume 257, Number 6, pp. 22, 24.

ROMANOW, ROY, JOHN WHYTE, and HOWARD LEESEN (1984) *Canada . . . Notwithstanding: The Making of the Constitution 1976–1982.* Toronto: Carswell/Methuen.

ROSE, DOUGLAS D., ed. (1992) *The Emergence of David Duke and the Politics of Race.* Chapel Hill, North Carolina: The University of North Carolina Press.

ROSE, RICHARD (1982) *The Territorial Dimension in Government: Understanding the United Kingdom.* Chatham, New Jersey: Chatham House Publishers.

—— (1983) "Still the Era of Party Government," *Parliamentary Affairs,* Volume 36, Number 3, pp. 181–299.

—— (1986) *Politics: England.* 4th ed. Boston: Little, Brown and Company.

—— (1991) "Comparing Forms of Comparative Analysis," *Political Studies,* Volume 39, Number 3, pp. 446–462.

—— (2001) "How People View Democracy: A Diverging Europe," *Journal of Democracy,* Volume 12, Number 1, pp. 93–106.

ROSE, RICHARD and EZRA N. SULIEMAN, eds. (1981) *Presidents and Prime Ministers.* Washington, D.C.: American Enterprise Institute for Public Policy Research.

ROSENBAUM, WALTER A. (1975) *Political Culture.* New York: Praeger Publishers.

ROSENSTONE, STEVEN J. and JOHN MARK HANSEN (1993) *Mobilization, Participation, and Democracy in America.* New York: Macmillan.

ROSSITER, CLINTON (1948) *Constitutional Dictatorship: Crisis Government in the Modern Democracies.* Princeton, New Jersey: Princeton University Press.

ROTH, DAVID F. and FRANK L. WILSON (1980) *The Comparative Study of Politics.* 2nd ed. Englewood Cliffs, New Jersey: Prentice-Hall.

RUFF, NORMAN J. (1990) "The Cat and Mouse Politics of Redistribution: Fair and Effective Representation in British Columbia," *BC Studies,* Number 87, pp. 48–84.

—— (1992) "The Right to Vote and Inequality of Voting Power in British Columbia: The Jurisprudence and Politics of the Dixon Case," in *Drawing Boundaries: Legislatures, Courts, and Electoral Values,* eds. John C. Courtney et al., 128–151. Saskatoon, Saskatchewan: Fifth House Publishers.

RUSSELL, PETER (1985) "The First Three Years of Charterland," *Canadian Public Administration,* Volume 28, Number 3, pp. 367–396.

—— (1993) *Constitutional Odyssey: Can Canadians Become a Sovereign People?* 2nd ed. Toronto: University of Toronto Press.

—— (1987) *The Judiciary in Canada: The Third Branch of Government.* Toronto: McGraw-Hill Ryerson.

RUSSELL, PETER, RAINER KNOPFF, and TED MORTON, eds. (1989) *Federalism and the Charter: Leading Constitutional Decisions, a New Edition.* Ottawa: Carleton University Press.

RYLE, MICHAEL (1994) "The Changing Commons," *Parliamentary Affairs,* Volume 47, Number 4, pp. 647–668.

SAGGAR, SHAMIT (1997) "The Dog That Didn't Bark? Immigration, Race and the General Election," in *Labour's Landslide: The British General Election 1997,* eds. Andrew Geddes and Jonathan Tonge, 147–164. Manchester, England: Manchester University Press.

SANDERS, DAVID (1993) "Why the Conservative Party Won – Again," in *Britain at the Polls 1992,* eds. Anthony King et al., 171–222. Chatham, New Jersey: Chatham House Publishers.

SARTORI, GIOVANNI (1976) *Parties and Party Systems: A Framework for Analysis.* London: Cambridge University Press.

SAUL, JOHN RALSTON (1995) *The Doubter's Companion: A Dictionary of Aggressive Common Sense.* Toronto: Penguin Books Canada.

SAVOIE, DONALD J. (1999a) *Governing from the Centre: The Concentration of Power in Canadian Politics.* Toronto: University of Toronto Press.

—— (1999b) "The Rise of Court Government in Canada," *Canadian Journal of Political Science,* Volume 32, Number 4, pp. 635–664.

—— (2000) "All Things Canadian Are Now Regional," *Journal of Canadian Studies,* Volume 35, Number 1, pp. 203–217.

SCAMMON, RICHARD N. (1975) "The Election and the Future of British Electoral Reform," in *Britian at the Polls: The Parliamentary Elections of 1974,* ed. Howard R. Penniman, 163–176. Washington, D.C.: American Enterprise Institute for Public Policy Research.

SCARROW, HOWARD A. (1969) *Comparative Political Analysis: An Introduction.* New York: Harper and Row.

—— (1989) "One Voter, One Vote: The Apportionment of Congressional Seats Reconsidered," *Polity,* Volume 22, Number 2, pp. 253–268.

SCHATTSCHNEIDER, E.E. (1942) *Party Government.* New York: Holt, Rinehart and Winston.

—— (1969) *Two Hundred Million Americans in Search of a Government.* New York: Holt, Rinehart and Winston.

—— (1975) *The Semisovereign People.* New York: Holt, Rinehart and Winston.

SCHLESINGER, ARTHUR M., JR. (1974) *The Imperial Presidency.* Toronto: Popular Library.

—— (1992) *The Disuniting of America.* New York: W.W. Norton and Company.

SCHUMAN, HOWARD, CHARLOTTE STEEH, LAWRENCE BOBO, and MARIA KRYSAN (1997) *Racial Attitudes in America.* Cambridge, Mass.: Harvard University Press.

SCHUMPETER, JOSEPH A. (1950) *Capitalism, Socialism and Democracy.* New York: Harper and Row.

SCHWARTZ, MILDRED A. (1974) *Politics and Territory: The Sociology of Regional Persistence in Canada.* Montreal: McGill-Queen's University Press.

SEARS, DAVID O. and NICOLAS A. VALENTINO (1997) "Politics Matters: Political Events as Catalysts for Preadult Socialization," *American Political Science Review,* Volume 91, Number 1, pp. 45–64.

SEDERBERG, PETER C. (1994) *Fires Within: Political Violence and Revolutionary Change.* New York: HarperCollins College Publishers.

SHAW, ERIC (2001) "New Labour: New Pathways to Parliament," *Parliamentary Affairs,* Volume 54, Number 1, pp. 35–53.

SHELL, DAVID (2000) "Labour and the House of Lords: A Case Study in Constitutional Reform," *Parliamentary Affairs,* Volume 53, Number 2, pp. 290–310.

SHELL, DONALD (1994) "The House of Lords: Time for a Change?" *Parliamentary Affairs,* Volume 47, Number 4, pp. 721–737.

SHENKER, ISRAEL (1988) "Lording it over England," *The New York Times Magazine* (May 8), pp. 34–36, 82–85.

SHERRILL, ROBERT (2000) *Why They Call It Politics: A Guide to America's Government.* 6th ed. Orlando, Florida: Harcourt College Publishers.

SHOGAN, ROBERT (1982) *None of the Above: Why Presidents Fail – and What Can Be Done About It.* New York: New American Library.

SIAROFF, ALAN (1999) "Corporation in 24 Industrial Democracies: Meaning and Measurement," *European Journal of Political Research,* Volume 36, Number 2, pp. 175–205.

SIMEON, RICHARD and DAVID J. ELKINS (1974) "Regional Political Cultures in Canada," *Canadian Journal of Political Science,* Volume 7, Number 3, pp. 397–437.

SIMPSON, JEFFREY (1980) *Discipline of Power: The Conservative Interlude and the Liberal Restoration.* Toronto: Personal Library.

—— (1993) *Faultlines: Struggling for a Canadian Vision.* Toronto: HarperCollins.

SINGH, ROBERT (1999) "Gun Politics in American: Continuity and Change," *Parliamentary Affairs,* Volume 52, Number 1, pp. 1–18.

SINOPOLI, RICHARD C. and TEENA GABRIELSON (1999) "Mirroring Modernity: America's Conflicting Identities," *Polity,* Volume 22, Number 1, pp. 67–92.

SKILLING, H. GORDAN and FRANKLYN GRIFFITHS, eds. (1971) *Interest Groups in Soviet Politics.* Princeton, New Jersey: Princeton University Press.

SKOCPOL, THEDA, MARSHALL GANZ, and ZIAD MUNSON (2000) "A Nation of Organizers: The Institutional Origins of Civic Volunteerism in the United States," *American Political Science Review,* Volume 94, Number 3, pp. 527–546.

SMALLWOOD, JOSEPH R. (1975) *I Chose Canada, Volume II: The Premiership.* Scarborough, Ontario: Signet Books.

SMILEY, DONALD V. (1968) "The National Party Leadership Convention in Canada: A Preliminary Analysis," *Canadian Journal of Political Science,* Volume 1, Number 4, pp. 379–397.

—— (1976) *Canada in Question: Federalism in the Seventies.* 2nd ed. Toronto: McGraw-Hill Ryerson.

—— (1978) "Federalism and the Legislative Process in Canada," in *The Legislative Process in Canada,* eds. W.A.W. Neilson and J.C. MacPherson, 73–87. Montreal: Institute for Research on Public Policy.

—— (1980) *Canada in Question: Federalism in the Eighties.* 3rd ed. Toronto: McGraw-Hill Ryerson.

—— (1983) "A Dangerous Deed: The Constitution Act, 1982," in *And No One Cheered,* eds. Keith Banting and Richard Simeon, 74–95. Toronto: Methuen.

SMITH, GOLDWIN (1891) *Canada and the Canadian Question.* Toronto: Hunter, Rose and Company.

SMITH, GORDON (1980) *Politics in Western Europe: A Comparative Analysis.* 3rd ed. London: Heinemann Educational Books.

SMITH, HEDRICK (1988) *The Power Game: How Washington Works.* New York: Random House.

SMITH, JENNIFER and RONALD G. LANDES (1998) "Entitlement versus Variance Models in the Determination of Canadian Electoral Boundaries," *International Journal of Canadian Studies,* Number 17, pp. 19–36.

SNIDERMAN, PAUL M., JOSEPH F. FLETCHER, PETER H. RUSSELL, and PHILIP E. TETLOCK (1996) *The Clash of Rights: Liberty, Equality and Legitimacy in Pluralist Democracy.* New Haven, Conn.: Yale University Press.

SOFSKY, WOLFGANG (1999) *The Order of Terror: The Concentration Camp.* Princeton, New Jersey: Princeton University Press.

STANBURY, WILLIAM T. (1993) "Financing Federal Politics in Canada in an Era of Reform," in *Campaign and Party Finance in North America and Western Europe,* ed. Arthur B. Gunlicks, 68–120. Boulder, Colorado: Westview Press.

—— (1996) "Getting and Spending: The Effect of Federal Regulations on Financing Political Parties and Candidates in Canada," in *Party Politics in Canada,* 7th ed., ed. Hugh G. Thorburn, 72–95. Scarborough, Ontario: Prentice Hall, Canada.

STARK, STEVEN (1993) "Too representative government," *The Atlantic Monthly*, Volume 275, Number 5, pp. 92–106.

STEVENSON, GARTH (1979) *Unfulfilled Union: Canadian Federalism and National Unity*. Toronto: Macmillan of Canada.

STEWART, WALTER (1971) *Shrug: Trudeau in Power*. Toronto: New Press.

STOKER, LAURA (1992) "Interests and Ethics in Politics," *American Political Science Review*, Volume 86, Number 2, pp. 369–380.

STONECASH, JEFFREY M. and MACK D. MARIANI (2000) "Republican Gains in the House in the 1994 Elections: Class Polarization in American Politics," *Political Science Quarterly*, Volume 115, Number 1, pp. 93–113.

SUTHERLAND, SHARON L. (1993) "The Public Service and Policy Development," in *Governing Canada: Institutions and Public Policy*, ed. Michael M. Atkinson, 81–113. Toronto: Harcourt Brace Jovanovich Canada.

SYMONS, THOMAS H.B. (1978) *The Symons Report*. Toronto: The Books and Periodical Development Council.

TAAGEPERA, REIN and MATTHEW S. SHUGART (1989) *Seats and Votes: The Effects and Determinants of Electoral Systems*. New Haven, Conn.: Yale University Press.

TEIXEIRA, RUY A. (1992) *The Disappearing American Voter*. Washington, D.C.: The Brookings Institution.

THORBURN, HUGH G. (1979) "The Development of Political Parties in Canada," and "Interpretations of the Canadian Party System," in *Party Politics in Canada*, 4th ed., ed. Hugh G. Thorburn, pp. 2–11 and 34–56. Scarborough, Ontario: Prentice-Hall Canada.

TIMPONE, RICHARD J. (1998) "Structure, Behavior and Voter Turnout in the United States," *American Political Science Review*, Volume 92, Number 1, pp. 145–158.

TRUDEAU, PIERRE ELLIOTT (1968) *Federalism and the French Canadians*. Toronto: Macmillan of Canada.

TRUDEL, MARCEL and GENEVIEVE JAIN (1970) *Canadian History Textbooks*. Ottawa: Queen's Printer.

TRUMAN, TOM (1971) "A Critique of Seymour M. Lipset's Article, 'Value Differences, Absolute or Relative: The English-Speaking Democracies,'" *Canadian Journal of Political Science*, Volume 4, Number 4, pp. 497–525.

UNDERHILL, FRANK H. (1960) *In Search of Canadian Liberalism*. Toronto: Macmillan of Canada.

VALPY, MICHAEL (1981) "Above and beyond the hurly burly," *The Globe and Mail* (December 12), p. 10.

VAN LOON, RICK (1970) "Political Participation in Canada: The 1965 Election," *Canadian Journal of Political Science*, Volume 3, Number 3, pp. 376–399.

VERBA, SIDNEY, KAY LEHMAN SCHLOZMAN, HENRY BRADY, and NORMAN H. NIE (1993) "Citizen Activity: Who Participates? What Do They Say?" *American Political Science Review*, Volume 87, Number 2, pp. 303–318.

VERBA, SIDNEY, NORMAN H. NIE, and JAE-ON KIM (1978) *Participation and Political Equality: A Seven-Nation Comparison*. London: Cambridge University Press.

VERNEY, DOUGLAS V. (1976) *British Government and Politics: Life without a Declaration of Independence*. 3rd ed. New York: Harper and Row.

—— (1979) *The Analysis of Political Systems*. London: Routledge and Kegan Paul.

VICKERS, JILL (1997) *Reinventing Political Science: A Feminist Approach*. Halifax: Fernwood Publishing.

VON BEYME, KLAUS (1985) "Karl Marx and Party Theory," *Government and Opposition*, Volume 20, Number 1, pp. 70–87.

—— (1996) "Party Leadership and Change in Party Systems: Towards a Postmodern Party State?" *Government and Opposition*, Volume 31, Number 2, pp. 135–159.

VON DER MEHDEN, FRED R. (1973) *Comparative Political Violence*. Englewood Cliffs, New Jersey: Prentice-Hall.

WALDMAN, STEVEN (1996) *The Bill*. Rev. ed. New York: Penguin.

WALTZ, KENNETH W. (1999) "Globalization and Governance," *PS: Political Science and Politics*, Volume 32, Number 4, pp. 693–700.

WARE, ALAN (1992) "Liberal Democracy: One Form or Many?" *Political Studies*, Volume 40, special issue, pp. 130–145.

—— (1995) "The Party Systems of the Established Liberal Democracies in the 1990s: Is This a Decade of Transformation?" *Government and Opposition*, Volume 30, Number 3, pp. 312–326.

WATTENBERG, MARTIN P. (1994) *Decline of American Political Parties, 1952–1992*. Cambridge, Mass.: Harvard University Press.

WEARING, JOSEPH (1981) *The L-Shaped Party: The Liberal Party of Canada 1958–1980*. Toronto: McGraw-Hill Ryerson.

WEAVER, LEON (1986) "The Rise, Decline, and Resurrection of Proportional Representation in Local Governments in the United States," in *Electoral Laws and Their Political Consequences*, eds. Bernard Grofman and Arend Lijphart, 139–153. New York: Agathon Press.

WEBB, PAUL (2000) "Political Parties: Adapting to the Electoral Market," in *Developments in British Politics 6*, eds. Patrick Dunleavy et al., 151–170. New York: St. Martin's Press.

WELCH, SUSAN (1975) "Dimensions of Political Participation in a Canadian Sample," *Canadian Journal of Political Science*, Volume 8, Number 4, pp. 553–559.

WHITAKER, REGINALD (1977) *The Government Party: Organizing and Financing the Liberal Party of Canada 1930-58.* Toronto: University of Toronto Press.

—— (1999) *The End of Privacy: How Total Surveillance Is Becoming a Reality.* New York: The New Press.

WHITE, GRAHAM (1998) "Shorter Measures: The Changing Ministerial Career in Canada," *Canadian Public Administration,* Volume 41, Number 3, pp. 369–394.

WHITE, THEODORE H. (1976) *Breach of Faith: The Fall of Richard Nixon.* New York: Dell Publishers.

—— (1978) *In Search of History.* New York: Warner Books.

—— (1982) *America in Search of Itself: The Making of the President 1956–1980.* New York: Harper and Row.

WHITE, WALTER L., RONALD H. WAGENBERG, and RALPH C. NELSON (1972) *Introduction to Canadian Politics and Government.* Toronto: Holt, Rinehart and Winston.

WHITTINGTON, MICHAEL S. and RICHARD J. VAN LOON (1996) *Canadian Government and Politics: Institutions and Processes.* Toronto: McGraw-Hill Ryerson.

WICKHAM-JONES, MARK and DONALD SHELL (1991) "What Went Wrong? The Fall of Mrs. Thatcher," *Contemporary Record,* Volume 5, Number 2, pp. 321–340.

WILL, GEORGE F. (1992) *Restoration: Congress, Term Limits and the Recovery of Deliberative Democracy.* New York: The Free Press.

WILLIAMS, ROBERT and ESTHER JUBB (1996) "Shutting Down Government: Budget Crisis in the American Political System," *Parliamentary Affairs,* Volume 49, Number 3, pp. 471–484.

WILSON, HAROLD (1977) *The Governance of Britain.* London: Sphere Books.

WILSON, JAMES Q. (1987) "Does the Separation of Powers Still Work?" *The Public Interest,* Number 86, pp. 36–52.

WILSON, JOHN (1974) "The Canadian Political Cultures: Towards a Redefinition of the Nature of the Canadian Political System," *Canadian Journal of Political Science,* Volume 7, Number 3, pp. 438–483.

WILSON, MADAME JUSTICE BERTHA (1990) "Will Women Judges Really Make a Difference?" *The Canadian Forum,* Volume 68, Number 787, pp. 7–10.

WILSON, WOODROW (1885, 1956) *Congressional Government: A Study in American Politics.* New York: Meridian.

WINETROBE, BARRY K. (1992) "A Tax By Any Other Name: The Poll Tax and the Community Charge," *Parliamentary Affairs,* Volume 45, Number 3, pp. 420–427.

WINN, C. and J. MCMENEMY, eds. (1976) *Political Parties in Canada.* Toronto: McGraw-Hill Ryerson.

WOLF, MARTIN (2000) "Government's golden age is over," *The Globe and Mail* (July 13), p. C15.

WOLIN, SHELDON S. (1960) *Politics and Vision: Continuity and Innovation in Western Political Thought.* Boston: Little, Brown and Co.

WOODHOUSE, DIANA (1995) "Politicians and the Judiciary: A Changing Relationship," *Parliamentary Affairs,* Volume 48, Number 3, pp. 401–417.

WOOTTON, GRAHAM (1985) *Interest Groups: Policy and Politics in America.* Englewood Cliffs, New Jersey: Prentice-Hall.

WRIGHT, F.J. (1973) *British Constitution and Government.* 2nd ed. London: MacDonald and Evans.

YISHAI, YAEL (1998) "The Guardian State: A Comparative Analysis of Interest Group Regulation," *Governance,* Volume 11, Number 2, pp. 153–176.

YOUNG, WALTER D. (1969) *The Anatomy of a Party: The National CCF 1932-1961.* Toronto: University of Toronto Press.

—— (1978) "Leadership and Canadian Politics," in *Approaches to Canadian Politics,* ed. John H. Redekop, 282–301. Scarborough, Ontario: Prentice-Hall Canada.

NAME INDEX

SUBJECT INDEX